Wilhelm II

Wilhelm and Hermine at Doorn

Lamar Cecil

WILHELM II

VOLUME 2

Emperor and Exile, 1900–1941

The University of North Carolina Press

Chapel Hill and London

The paper in this book meets the guidelines for permanence and
durability of the Committee on Production Guidelines for Book
Longevity of the Council on Library Resources.

This book was published with the assistance of the H. Eugene and
Lillian Youngs Lehman Fund of the University of North Carolina
Press. A complete list of books published with the assistance of the
Lehman Fund appears at the end of the book.

Library of Congress Cataloging-in-Publication Data
Cecil, Lamar.
Wilhelm II, emperor and exile, 1900–1941.

Bibliography: v. 2, p.
Includes index.
1. William II, German Emperor, 1859–1941.
2. Germany — Kings and rulers — Biography.   3. Germany —
History — William II, 1888–1918.   I. Title.
DD229.C4   1996   943.08'4'0924   [B]   88-27798
ISBN 0-8078-2283-3 (alk. paper)

00 99 98 97 96   5 4 3 2 1

For Grayson and for Geri

Contents

Preface

THIS VOLUME brings to a conclusion my biography of the last German Kaiser and covers the final half of his long life. It is the dispiriting narrative of a man and a nation brought to needless ruin, a barren portrait of a career that was without virtue or accomplishment. Wilhelm II was a man of strong likes and prejudices, tyrannically insistent on having his own way. I have tried to accommodate the Kaiser by stressing the affairs that most concerned him, particularly the obsession of his life — Great Britain and its relationship with Germany. Other matters that were vital to the history of his empire but that did not strongly interest him are therefore deliberately accorded little emphasis. This is the biography of a man whose vision was woefully constricted and is not the history of the broadly productive nation over which he so maladroitly ruled.

In the course of pursuing for almost three decades the life of the last Kaiser, I have accumulated more indebtedness than I am capable of recalling, and I regret being unable to remember each of the many persons and institutions who have helped further the completion of this work. Thomas Kohut, Peter Paret, Norman Rich, and Gerhard Weinberg all came to my assistance in various ways. Ron Maner and Lewis Bateman, once again, proved to be superlative editors, and Teddy Diggs reviewed the manuscript with a hawk-like eye. In Germany, the efficient staff of the Bundesarchiv in Koblenz and of the Bundesarchiv-Militärarchiv in Freiburg greatly facilitated my research, and I encountered an equally professional reception from Mr. D. T. Coen and his colleagues at the Rijksarchief in Utrecht. I am most indebted to Her Majesty the Queen of England for permission to examine and to quote from the priceless materials deposited in the Royal Archives at Windsor Castle and to the Right Honorable the Marquess of Salisbury for access to ancestral records at Hatfield House. I am also obliged to the late Prince Friedrich-Ferdinand of Schleswig-Holstein-Sonderburg-Glücksburg for his hospitality at Glücksburg while I examined family documents and to Freiherr Nicolai von Freytag-Loringhoven of Munich for permission to consult the papers of Admiral Paul von Hintze. On this side of the Atlantic, Jennifer Ashworth, word-processor wizard and secretary to the Department of History at Washington and Lee University, as well as Sue Olive, the equally skilled supervisor of the university's academic computer operations, often kindly abandoned more pressing matters to redeem my ineptitude with office machinery. I owe much to the John Graham Leyburn Library of the university, an exemplary institution in every respect, and especially to Betsy Brittigan, magisterial head of interlibrary loan, who cheerfully let herself be inundated with countless requests. The generous gift to the Murphy Fund of the Department of History by Dr. and Mrs. Robert James MacNaughton of Greenville, South Carolina, substantially helped to defray the cost of research in European archives. I am profoundly grateful to all who have helped me on my way.

My students at Washington and Lee, in welcoming me as their friend as well as their teacher, have been the greatest pleasure of a long and rich academic life, and I cannot adequately express my appreciation for the reception I have always found in their midst. Finally, I owe more than I can say to the two persons to whom this book is dedicated, but I believe, and hope, that they know the measure of my gratitude.

Lamar Cecil
Lexington, Virginia
13 December 1995

Wilhelm II

One

THE MAN AT MID-PASSAGE

A FEW WEEKS after the new century opened in 1900, Wilhelm II, King of Prussia and German Emperor, celebrated his forty-first birthday, an occasion that marked the halfway point in a long life that would finally come to an end in the summer of 1941. At forty-one, the Kaiser was not markedly different in personality or character from what he had been twenty years earlier, when, following his brief exposure to a university education at Bonn, he had begun his career in the Prussian army. Wilhelm proved immune to profiting from experience, and the strident, opinionated martinet of the 1880s would be easily detected in the octogenarian of 1940. As a superannuated graybeard in his twilight of exile and obscurity, he was just as dilettantish and mean, and entirely unrepentant, as he had been as a young man, one in whom parents, teachers, and friends had bemoaned an idle immaturity and a hardness of heart.[1]

Called early by destiny to a position of incomparable power, one that required wisdom and forbearance, the last Kaiser unfortunately stagnated into a sort of perpetual adolescence, confusing talk for thought, instantaneous opinion for genius, and remaining untouched by reflection, sentimentality, or hard work. Bluster, rhetoric, and martial swagger cloaked a profound emptiness, for ignorance and self-indulgence were his primary characteristics. These traits ensured that Wilhelm II would be a disaster as a monarch, leading his hapless subjects to a tragic end, one they could hardly have been able to foresee at the time he ascended the throne in 1888. The last Kaiser's egomaniacal personality also resulted in his inability, in the course of eight decades of life, to forge enduring and happy relationships with other men and women, even among those relatives, other rulers, or aristocrats who might ordinarily have been expected to be the mainstays of his existence. Wilhelm's cool alienation from his fellow human beings throughout his life was remarkable, and as a result he had only a handful of friends.[2] The few men who somehow managed to retain the Kaiser's favor over the years functioned more as loyal officials than as intimates to whom he revealed his innermost self. Almost no one — perhaps only the diplomat Count Philipp Eulenburg, and he for no more than fifteen or so years — managed to penetrate Wilhelm II's heart, and even Eulenburg was in the end abruptly cast aside, leaving the Kaiser bereft of anyone with whom he might have enjoyed a truly sustaining relationship.

In depicting the world in which Wilhelm II dwelled as he passed into the second half of his life, it would seem natural to begin with his family, ordinarily the closest attachment that life provides. But in fact, the other Hohenzollerns played for him a negative role, important only in that they uniformly failed to contribute anything positive to the development of his character. That is largely, but not entirely, because the last Kaiser never succeeded in establishing, and indeed never really tried to effect, an affectionate and nurturing bond with his parents, with either of his wives, with his many sons, or with his brother, sisters, aunts, or uncles. Only Wilhelm's daughter captured his love.

Wilhelm's mother and father, the unhappy Friedrich Wilhelm and his English consort, Victoria, eventually became the Kaiser's enemies. Neither made a conspicuous effort to understand their heir or to commend him on his accomplishments. Difficult though Wilhelm may have been as a young man, his parents, with the unattainable expectations they had for their eldest child, must bear much of the responsibility for his alienation from them and for his unfortunate character in manhood.[3] By the time the new century began, Friedrich III had long since been entombed at Potsdam, and the Kaiserin, fatally stricken by the same malignant disease that had killed her beloved husband in 1888, would die in 1901. After Friedrich III's death she lived in embittered seclusion in her castle in the Hessian countryside, far from Berlin. Victoria might as well have perished with her husband so far as Wilhelm was concerned, for he saw little of his mother in the long years of her inconsolable widowhood and rarely spoke of her after she died. The Kaiser's steeliness, which his mother had often deplored, pursued her even beyond the grave.

Wilhelm II's consort, the Kaiserin Augusta Victoria, or Dona as Wilhelm always called her, fared better, but her marriage was never easy, and the life she led as the wife of a notably self-centered man could have been gratifying only to a woman of meager expectations. It is a tribute to Dona's loyalty, though perhaps not to her intelligence, that she adhered blindly to Wilhelm for forty years, always defending, protecting, and comforting him in adversity and praising him no matter how foolishly he behaved. For these abundant efforts, Dona gained from her consort many formal, public tributes that attested to her maternal virtues, but in private Wilhelm treated her with indifference or neglect. Nevertheless, from their marriage in February 1881 until the Kaiserin's death in Holland four decades later, Dona and Wilhelm lived together in ostensible happiness, surrounded by an expanding progeny.

Dona had little besides virtue and faithfulness to promote her husband's attachment. She was never beautiful, although her amiable disposition and natural dignity imparted to her appearance an air more winning than mere good looks might have gained. She was once rather elliptically described — and perhaps it is as fair a characterization as can be found — as "neither pretty nor ugly but pretty rather than ugly."[4] In the swift course of her seven full-term pregnancies (in addition to at least two miscarriages), Dona subjected herself to drugs and rigorous dieting in order to stay svelte, for Wilhelm disdained plump women. She not only managed to overcome a tendency toward stoutness but gradually acquired a figure that was exceptional for a woman who had given birth seven times. "Who would believe," Wilhelm II once asked, with the exaggeration that was a lifelong failing, "that that woman had eight children?"[5] The Kaiser nevertheless found his wife somewhat frumpy and provincial in taste, and to atone for what he perceived to be Dona's shortcomings, he took it upon himself to choose and occasionally to design her clothes and jewelry.[6] Wilhelm especially liked for his wife to appear in elaborate hats and to be laden with ropes of diamonds, a couture that, regrettably, did not always produce the majestic effect he aspired to achieve. The Kaiser's interference in his consort's wardrobe eventually waned, and Dona thereafter succeeded in effecting a stately, although unexciting, appearance. With her matronly manner and prematurely white hair, Dona looked and acted older than her energetic husband. "Poor dear," her friend Princess Daisy of Pless noted sympathetically, "she looks more like the Emperor's mother than his wife." That did not dismay Wilhelm, who on Dona's fortieth birthday (a few months before his own) assured her that he preferred women who were mature.[7]

The dignified Kaiserin, no matter how tastefully turned out or how admirably slim, usually conveyed an impression of prosaic inconsequence. Dona's ponderous manner never managed to electrify or even to enthrall, which is why the aristocratic diarist Marie von Bunsen, in making an inventory of the Kaiserin's virtues and deficits, concluded, "She was everywhere respected, she commanded universal sympathy but no one panted after her."[8] By almost all accounts, including those of her admirers, the Kaiserin was very self-conscious of her high position and determined that everyone acknowledge it, undoubtedly a legacy of her being descended from a minor house scorned by Wilhelm's Hohenzollern and Hanoverian ancestors. Although the Kaiser was by no means devoid of regal hauteur, he was normally relaxed and jovial, whereas the Kaiserin always appeared reserved and queenly, insistent on formality and decorum and sometimes unable to conceal her boredom with ceremonial duties.[9]

Dona was not in the least clever but instead conventional, ordinary, and contrived in manner, endowed with none of Wilhelm's intelligence, which, if superficial, at least was quick. Her brother-in-law Bernhard, Duke of Saxe-Meiningen, deplored the Kaiserin's "stupidity, lack of education, and tactlessness," all of which led to embarrassments.[10] Whatever Wilhelm thought on any subject sufficed for Dona, who read sparingly, collected nothing, and left it to her consort to amass objects for the royal palaces. Travel did not interest Dona unless staying at home meant a separation from her husband, and in Berlin she played no role in society beyond the court, having no good friends other than the women in her retinue.[11] Dona's ideas were undeviatingly conservative. She protested that she understood "little about politics," which was probably true enough, and she never attempted, as had Wilhelm's mother, to play a central role in affairs of state. But that did not mean that Dona cut herself off from politics, for she believed ardently in the maintenance of Hohenzollern prerogative, German superiority, and conservative principles. Modernity, whether in the arts, in religion, or in social behavior, was beyond the pale, and Dona was swift to view with suspicion all that was not solidly old-fashioned and German. When the Kaiserin thought that any traditional values were threatened, she did not hesitate to intervene, urging Wilhelm to act decisively to ensure their preservation.

Although Wilhelm II and his consort were in some respects ill-matched, they were entirely in agreement about religion. Dona was devout, and no shadow of doubt disturbed her Protestant convictions. She abhorred any modern tendencies in the church, preferring to adhere to an absolutely literal interpretation of the Bible.[12] She was inalterably set against anything that smacked of Catholicism, a distaste that prevented Catholics from being included in her retinue or even among her personal body servants. Like their mistress, the members of Dona's entourage, the saintly "Hallelujah aunts," were ardently Protestant, inflamed with a bigotry that the Kaiser, who was himself by no means without prejudice against Catholics but who had a lively curiosity about religion, found excessive.[13]

Like Caesar's wife, Dona was morally beyond reproach, her rectitude as unassailable and as rigid as her religious beliefs. She disdained the English as immoral and the Russians as barbarians. She abhorred those men, such as Edward VII or Tsar Nicholas II, whose morality fell below her Olympian standard, and she once refused to be seated next to the French foreign minister, Jules Herbette, because she considered his conversation intolerably vulgar.[14] Anything that skirted even the outreaches of decorum was forbidden. Anecdotes that were only marginally suggestive aroused her ire, and a number of Wilhelm II's erstwhile confidants fell afoul of the Kaiserin because of their salacious banter. At a sign from the Kaiserin, the royal party would leave plays, ballets, or operas that contained offensive dialogue or indecent dress, and even for the great Anna Pavlova, in her skimpy tutu and décolletage, no exception was made. Dona's social prescriptions were absurdly inflexible, and she saw to it that royalty did not ride bicycles and that men kept their coats on when playing tennis on the imperial lawn.[15] Divorce was impermissible. Women who had left their mates were ostracized from the court, and Dona did what she could to make it difficult for their former husbands to hold on to positions in the government.[16] The Kaiserin was always on guard to ensure that neither Wilhelm nor her sons fell under the sway of fast women, especially the American socialites whom the Kaiser liked to invite to court and who were, from Dona's pinnacle of virtue, the epitome of meretriciousness.[17]

Throughout the forty years of her marriage to Wilhelm, Dona was always careful to treat her husband with a deference so conspicuous that it seemed to one friend to be positively abnormal.[18] In Wilhelm's presence, she was always eager instantly to provide whatever he required, sitting down only if he did so first, rarely arguing with him, and daring to take an independent line only very obliquely.[19] It was, her doctor declared with misgiving, a "fanaticism to duty," one that even her frequent migraines were not allowed to interrupt.[20] Queen Marie of Rumania, Wilhelm's first cousin, found Dona too stiffly regal; nonetheless, the queen admired "the patient courage with which this devoted woman carried out her husband's every order. There was a brave abnegation about it which is not given to every woman."[21] Dona's deference proceeded less from fear or timidity than from the real love and admiration she felt for her husband, who to her was truly a remarkable, but fragile, man. Although she recognized that Wilhelm was immature and overly excitable, she was proud of him and gloried when he met with success.[22] The Kaiserin did everything she could to integrate herself into her husband's life, memorizing the uniforms of his various regiments, forcing herself to read books on military subjects that she knew interested him, and accompanying him on his daily horseback rides, his early morning calls on his officials, and (when he would permit it) his trips. Dona's excessive wonder at what she perceived to be her husband's virtues, her constant attention to his every word and desire, undoubtedly intensified his already inflated self-esteem. She was the one person, other than his parents, whose lasting proximity might have instilled in Wilhelm prudence and restraint. But Dona lacked both the intelligence and the will to do so and was instead content to be the ever submissive, supportive wife, a role she played to perfection. The delight she took merely by being in Wilhelm's presence was transparent.[23]

The Kaiser made his distaste for Dona's attempt to cling to him equally clear, and he tried to establish as much freedom from her as conjugal obligations and the ceremonial demands of the crown allowed. She was discouraged from participating in his constant hunting and sailing excursions, for when Dona was present the tone became prudish and behavior more decorous. When she left, Wilhelm felt relief.[24] The Kaiser tried to fob his wife off by giving Dona her own yacht, but recognizing the motive that lay behind his generosity, she declined to have anything to do with her present.[25] Dona attempted to enlist Chancellor Otto von Bismarck's help to keep Wilhelm from traveling about so frequently, and when this failed, she resolved to accompany him. Wilhelm then took malicious pleasure in making his wife so uncomfortable that she would not want to come along again. On hunts, he required Dona to slog through the muck and rain, but in spite of his malign efforts, she refused to be deterred and doggedly followed her husband.[26] A clergyman friend noted with admiration: "No morning was too early; [and] if the Kaiser was going to a review or a hunt the Kaiserin was at his side in order to share breakfast with him and to read to him the precepts of the Moravian brethren. No horseback ride was too taxing for her to want to be along, no trip too far."[27]

Whether Wilhelm appreciated Dona's exertions is doubtful. He did laud her as a model of the true German mother who gladly produced sons who would be ready if necessary to sacrifice their lives for the Fatherland.[28] Although Wilhelm accepted his wife's ministrations in moments of crisis, he preferred for her to be reticent or, better, to stay to herself. He often treated Dona brusquely, gave her very little money, and made it clear that he placed no value on her opinions and that he generally disapproved of what she said and did. Friedrich von Holstein, observing the young couple from his vantage in the Foreign Office, declared that the Kaiser let the world know that his wife was "nothing but a broodhen."[29] In spite of Wilhelm's admiration for her maternal instincts, he found his wife unmistakably small-time. As he once declared with justification, Dona was hardly the woman his mother, however much he had disliked her, had been.[30] Once, at a house party in Silesia, the Kaiser complained that it was said that he wanted German women to confine themselves to *Kinder,*

Kirche, und Küche — children, church, and kitchen — an encomium rightly applied to the Kaiserin. "How," Wilhelm asked with annoyance, "could I, with the mother I had, envision women as such?"[31] Like so much else that the Kaiser said, this was mere rhetoric, for he insisted that a woman's place, much to the disappointment of German feminists, was at home under the rule of her spouse. Although Wilhelm believed that women might have interests outside the narrow confines of their household responsibilities, he was not prepared to allow them the domestic authority that his mother had possessed. He intended, as he informed a friend, to see to it that he, and he alone, ruled his "chicken house" (*Hühnerhof*).[32]

Dona was not inclined to challenge Wilhelm on this point, for she was very opposed to the feminist movement, which by the beginning of the century was slowly beginning to make headway in Germany. Yet she did, to her husband's irritation, vainly champion the right of women to vote. Wilhelm had no sympathy with that aspiration, in Germany or anywhere else, for women, being physically incapable of bearing arms, had no right to participate in the electoral process. The Kaiser regretted that the British did not deal more stringently with their bothersome suffragettes, who in his opinion needed to be flogged.[33] "The principal duty of German women," he once declared, in the presence of his consort, "lies not in the acquisition of alleged rights through which they might become equal to men, but rather in the quiet work of the household and the family. They should educate the younger generation, especially in obedience and respect for their elders."[34] If women (and specifically Dona) were to keep to the house, however, Wilhelm did not want to be there. He did not like to find himself in situations in which women dominated, for their society was too formal and restrictive. The Kaiser was always courtly, but sometimes rather oddly so, believing for example that he was paying a woman a compliment in telling her that she would make a "handsome grenadier."[35] Wilhelm could not talk easily in female company, leading his admirer Princess Daisy of Pless to declare, "In his secret heart he thought little of us women; he almost despised us." The princess was by no means the only woman, or man, to detect a misogynistic strain in the Kaiser.[36]

The relationship that developed over the years between Dona and Wilhelm was thus highly asymmetrical, for she uncomplainingly gave, and in return he unfeelingly took. She seems to have considered her wifely role to be that of a comforting mother to Wilhelm, and those who knew the Kaiserin saw a maternal aspect in her relations with him. When the Kaiser was depressed, she alone could restore his confidence; if excitement overwhelmed his nerves, she knew how to produce calm; when he was ill, she patiently nursed him back to health; when he seemed weak or indecisive, she could prod him to action. On the frequent occasions when Wilhelm behaved tactlessly, Dona tried to dispel the resentment that his behavior had produced.[37] She was Wilhelm's self-appointed protectress, guarding him from people — immoral relatives, ambitious courtiers, shameless women, or political schemers with dangerous ideas — whose influence she believed to be poisonous.

Although Dona had been healthy as a young woman, her repeated and closely spaced pregnancies, her fasting to enhance her figure, and her dutiful if unwelcome participation in Wilhelm's rigorous life exacted their toll.[38] When only in her mid-thirties, Dona's once-auburn hair suddenly turned white, and her complexion became very rubicund and blotched, leaving her looking puffy and aged. She frequently flew into rages over seemingly inconsequential matters, and Wilhelm ordered that his wife's schedule be strictly controlled to provide adequate rest and solitude.[39] Dona's mother had had mental difficulties, and Wilhelm feared that a hereditary disorder might lead to his wife's confinement in a hydropathic sanatorium, a step that had to be avoided at all costs.[40] Although the Kaiserin's nervous condition persisted for several years, by 1901 she had completely recovered.

As a mother, Dona was exemplary. She was the principal figure in the life of her family, for Wilhelm's relations with his six sons was formal, and he was only superficially concerned with their early education. The children were therefore drawn to their indulgent mother, who brooded ceaselessly over them and thereby further endangered her health.[41] In 1896, Wilhelm decided to send his two oldest sons, Wilhelm and Eitel Friedrich, to the cadet academy at Plön in Schleswig-Holstein in the hope that this would make Dona's life more tranquil. She vainly resisted this decision, and after they had departed she insisted on going to Plön no fewer than eight times in less than six months.[42] In 1900, Wilhelm ordered that Princes August Wilhelm ("Auwi") and Oskar, age thirteen and twelve, were also to matriculate as cadets. He believed that the boys needed to be liberated from their protective mother, whose nervous condition in any case required a further limitation of her maternal responsibilities. The Kaiserin was resolutely, even hysterically, opposed, insisting that the two boys remain in Berlin. A storm ensued, with Dona crying through the night and accusing Wilhelm of not loving her, but he remained firm, and Auwi and Oskar went to Plön.[43]

The Kaiser's relationship with his sons was remote, and he often elected to communicate with them through officials rather than in person. The sort of petty rancor that had marred Wilhelm's association with his own father was repeated in his behavior toward his sons. He refused to allow any of them to wear the resplendent uniform of the guard cuirassiers, his own favorite military dress, to grant them the army commands they desired, or to let them be indoctrinated into governmental or diplomatic affairs. Wilhelm, the eldest son and crown prince of Prussia, grew up to be a disappointment to his father, much in the way that the Kaiser, in his youth, had failed to measure up to his own parents' expectations. From the time that the crown prince went off to Bonn, destined like his sire to turn in an undistinguished performance, Wilhelm complained that his heir was lazy, foppish, and reactionary, charges that were quite true.[44] The crown prince, in contrast to his staid mother and father, led a racy life that centered on women and horses. He liked the newest fashions in dancing, in dress, and in the theater, all of which, as the prince realized to his annoyance, were anathema to his parents. Wilhelm could not understand his son, deploring the prince's sexual license and passion for steeplechasing and polo. For a long time, the Kaiser attempted to regulate his son's behavior, but eventually he abandoned the effort as fruitless.[45]

The crown prince was an enthusiastic soldier, brimming with visions of victorious campaigns against the Fatherland's enemies, and like his father, he was an enthusiastic designer of uniforms. His popularity in the army made Wilhelm II jealous; the Kaiser would occasionally explode, berating his son as his own father had belittled him in front of his fellow officers and giving his son a hussar's uniform precisely because the crown prince, even more fastidious about clothes than the Kaiser, disliked its cut.[46] It was left to the Kaiserin, no less disapproving than her husband of the crown prince's manner of life but, unlike Wilhelm, always forgiving of her children's transgressions, to redress the quarrels between her husband and his eldest son.[47] But Dona's efforts foundered when a number of courtiers, like the group who had years earlier worked successfully to spoil Wilhelm's relations with his parents, sensed that a cleft in the royal house might prove advantageous to their own positions. They therefore worked effectively to keep father and son apart.[48] As for the crown prince's younger brothers, they seldom saw the Kaiser, who was not much concerned with them and did not like to be alone in their company. Wilhelm's manner toward his younger sons was strict, more that of a sovereign than a father. He tended to be either ceremonial or martial, and when he disapproved of their behavior he usually sent an adjutant to set them straight.[49] Princess Victoria Louise ("Sissy"), the only daughter and the youngest of the Kaiser's seven children, had a happier relationship with the Kaiser.

Unlike her brothers, none of whom were in any way remarkable, Victoria Louise matured into an attractive and likable woman. Wilhelm adored her, a love that she fully reciprocated, and the crown prince noted with envy that of his siblings, she alone was close to their father.[50]

The Kaiser had little to do with most of his Hohenzollern relations. His only brother, the dutiful and commonplace Prince Heinrich, was devoted to Wilhelm. Heinrich uncomplainingly did as he was told, making his career in the navy, where he enjoyed a considerable following and for whose interests he had a sounder judgment than did his brother.[51] The Kaiser was often rude to Heinrich, whom he dismissed as a "political child," perhaps because he was jealous of Heinrich's popularity in the navy. The prince swallowed Wilhelm's rebuffs, but they wounded him, and he resented as well the constant and unproductive interference to which the Kaiser subjected the imperial navy. A disruptive element in the brothers' relationship was Heinrich's wife and first cousin, Irene of Hesse, whose sister Alix in 1894 had married Tsar Nicholas II. Wilhelm did not much care for any of his Hessian relatives, and his frequent barbs about them irritated not only Irene but also Heinrich, who was very attached to his wife's family.[52]

Wilhelm's four sisters never played a substantial role in his life. The eldest, Charlotte, to whom in boyhood he had been somewhat close, was a person, like her older brother, of strong and vividly expressed opinions, even in military affairs. Married to the Duke of Saxe-Meiningen, she liked to gossip and meddle in politics and, with her nephew the crown prince, moved in the fast set in Berlin. This did not endear her to Wilhelm or to Dona, both of whom eventually fell out with Charlotte and her husband.[53] The Kaiser pointedly refused to pay a visit to Meiningen, which offended the duke as well as Charlotte, who found her brother vain and entirely too susceptible to what others told him.[54] The Kaiser's three other sisters constituted what he scornfully referred to as the "English colony," young girls and later mature women conspicuously allied with their mother. Wilhelm never felt much attachment to them, and at times their relations were in a state of open conflict. The eldest of the three, Victoria, had been devastated by her failure in 1888 to wed Prince Alexander Battenberg, a match that Wilhelm had cruelly prevented.[55] She was a rather drab creature who eventually married a minor German princeling, and Wilhelm ignored her. Margaret, Wilhelm's youngest sister, became the wife of a Hessian duke and stayed as far away from her brother as possible, re-establishing contact with him only during his lonely years of exile in Holland.[56] The middle sister, Sophie, in 1889 married the crown prince of

Greece, who in 1913 became King Constantine I. She converted to orthodoxy, a step that enraged both Dona and Wilhelm, who refused to permit the apostate to return to Germany because of the "shame" she had committed against the house of Hohenzollern. For almost a decade she was banned from Berlin, and even after her reconciliation with Wilhelm in 1898 there was little love between them, for Sophie, like her sister Margaret, found her brother absurdly pompous and narrow-minded.[57]

The Hohenzollerns' tangled genealogy connected Wilhelm II with many of the other regnant houses of Germany, but he had close relations with very few of their sovereigns. Of all the federal princes, Wilhelm might have been expected to have been closest to Grand Duke Friedrich of Baden, who was his uncle by marriage. But both the grand duke and his consort, the sister of Wilhelm's father, were relentlessly pedagogical, a trait that Wilhelm could not tolerate in anyone. As a young man, Wilhelm had indeed been drawn to his aunt and uncle, who had actively supported him in Bismarck's overthrow in 1890; thus they anticipated that the advice they too gladly dispensed would now have more weight with their nephew. They were entirely mistaken and, stung by Wilhelm's increasing neglect and resentful that in the future they would clearly play no role in Berlin, lost no time finding fault with him.[58] Many other German rulers followed suit. There was a long princely catalog of objections to Wilhelm, whom these sovereigns found to be rude, boring, vain, philistine, too easily manipulated, and excessively moralistic. What was much worse — and this was the root of the federal princes' objection to Wilhelm — was that he treated them as though they were vassals, and in revenge they avoided his court in Berlin.[59] The Kaiser's tone toward the German princes, whom he expected to do his bidding unquestioningly, was indeed condescending, even to the rulers of Saxony, Bavaria, and Württemberg, the only German sovereigns who, like himself, held kingly titles.[60] Their crowns were tarnished, in Wilhelm's opinion, by having been the gift of Napoleon early in the nineteenth century, whereas Prussia's regal dignity, which the Hohenzollerns had unilaterally proclaimed in 1701, was proudly derived from military glory.[61]

Wilhelm's dismissive attitude, often publicly expressed, irked the federal princes, who considered his pride to be quite unwarranted. A leading critic was his first cousin, the liberal and cultivated Grand Duke Ernst Ludwig of Hesse, who detested the Kaiser's pretensions.[62] He feared that Wilhelm's imperious insistence on ruling alone and his contempt for the Reichstag might lead Germany into difficulties, especially because none of the Kaiser's sycophantic Prussian courtiers seemed inclined to try to deflate his unrealistic notions. "The Kaiser," King Wilhelm II of Württemberg once told Philipp Eulenburg, "wants even vinegar to taste sweet."[63] This arrogance seemed misplaced in a man who was a mere Hohenzollern. To many of these German princes, Prussia's dynasty was upstart, having risen gradually to prominence only since the fifteenth century. "They grew up overnight," the head of the very ancient and entirely unimportant house of Schwarzburg-Sondershausen declared in comparing Wilhelm's lineage to an excrescence of filthy mushrooms.[64] The Bavarian Wittelsbachs, whose antiquity far outdistanced that of the Hohenzollerns, were especially snobbish, and even as a young man, Wilhelm had bridled at what he castigated as their "envy, hate, scorn and contempt for the Hohenzollern parvenus."[65] Wilhelm, in retaliation, reminded Chancellor Chlodwig Hohenlohe that he had eighteen Prussian army corps that he could employ against these genealogically fastidious southern Germans.[66]

The German sovereigns, like Wilhelm II himself, were kin to many European royal houses, and the Kaiser's failure to get along with the German princes was repeated on a higher stage in the great capitals of Europe. Wilhelm, who had a high opinion of his personal diplomacy with his "colleagues" on other thrones, believed that diplomacy was best left to monarchs, who alone among mortals had the ability to predict the future. But then as Wilhelm put it, "The king proceeds from the grace of God, and therefore is responsible only to him."[67] This much-vaunted claim, when exercised by the Kaiser's own clumsy hand, was disastrous, especially in the two places where he was most determined to apply it, in London and St. Petersburg.

Wilhelm II's association with England up to 1900 had been almost uniformly troubled, and it did not improve in the new century. Queen Victoria's relations with her eldest grandson never entirely recovered from the strain occasioned by the Kruger telegram episode early in 1896.[68] Wilhelm II, perhaps aware of how he had offended the queen, was unusually solicitous during the remaining five years of her life. He assured his grandmother that her "queer and impetuous colleague," as he not inaccurately described himself, was always motivated by "goodwill, honesty or truthfulness" toward her.[69] But Wilhelm's conciliatory efforts did not have much effect on his grandmother, who believed that he was imprudent, coldhearted, and bent on trying to stir up trouble between Great Britain and Russia.[70] She therefore decreed that her grandson not be invited to the celebration of her diamond jubilee in 1897, a punishment for his delinquencies but also a relief, since Wilhelm, to her annoyance, always brought an enormous suite along when he visited England.[71] Although Queen Victoria could occasionally summon up some controlled enthusiasm for her "dear boy," as she sometimes referred to Wilhelm to his delight, her son and heir, who in January 1901 came to the throne as King Edward VII, had long felt nothing but distaste for his German nephew. Their unhappy relationship will be considered later, and it will here suffice to note that in Edward VII's opinion, Wilhelm possessed an irritating combination of pseudo-regal pretentiousness and pedestrian bourgeois morality. Besides, the Kaiser was a dangerous competitor in European diplomacy and was entirely too eager to propel Germany forward in every corner of the world. When the two rulers met, which was as seldom as Edward VII could manage, the king's reserve was evident; when apart, the British sovereign, according to his foreign secretary, Lord Lansdowne, talked about Wilhelm "in terms which make one's flesh creep."[72]

Edward VII was a superior diplomat, and one object of his attention was Tsar Nicholas II, his nephew by marriage. Wilhelm II had also made the young ruler an object of his highly personalized diplomacy. From the moment that Nicholas had ascended the Romanov throne in 1894, the Kaiser had bombarded St. Petersburg with advice, visited as frequently as he could wring invitations to Russia, and in general made himself an unwelcome pest.[73] Wilhelm believed that Nicholas badly needed the Kaiser's avuncular attention, for he was a "ninny," a "whimperer" who was dominated by women, certainly a charge that no one could level against the Kaiser. In a moment of exasperation Wilhelm incautiously told Lansdowne that the easily influenced tsar was "only fit to live in a country house and raise turnips."[74] If "Nicky" did not assert himself, his life might end as had that of Louis XVI of France, who had been martyred by revolutionary subjects, or he might share the fate of the demented Tsar Paul, Wilhelm's ancestor as well as Nicholas's, who was assassinated in 1801 in the course of a palace coup.[75] With the Kaiser as his mentor, however, a better state of affairs would prevail, and Wilhelm confidently assured Nicholas in 1902 that together the two sovereigns could "make history and guide the fates," especially by carefully maintaining an iron guard against anarchist France.[76]

Although Nicholas's talent for political judgment was minimal, he was rightly convinced that the Kaiser's exaggerated, unpredictable moods made Wilhelm a very unstable partner in diplomacy. The morose and reclusive Tsarina Alexandra Feodorovna, Wilhelm's Hessian first cousin, despised the Kaiser. "He thinks himself a superman," she sneered, "and he's really nothing but a clown."[77] Like many of his ministers, the tsar believed, certainly not without some justification, that the real purpose of

Wilhelm's constant blandishments was to involve Russia in difficulties with England or France, straits that would ultimately benefit Germany. Nicholas II, who was shy and laconic, resented Wilhelm's boisterous behavior, full of backslapping and pummeling in the ribs, and declared that the prospect of meeting the Kaiser was enough to make him vomit.[78] So deep was Nicholas II's dislike for Wilhelm that Count Sergei Witte, for many years the leading minister in St. Petersburg, discovered that the easiest way to win the tsar's consent to a matter was to inform him that the Kaiser was opposed to it.[79] Nicholas would eventually become not Wilhelm's ally but England's, and for this development Edward VII deserved considerable credit. The British monarch knew how to conceal his reservations about his immature and reactionary Russian nephew behind a screen of benign amiability, and he very clearly understood that the most effective way to deal with the reclusive tsar was not to badger Nicholas or gratuitously intrude in Russia's affairs. So Edward VII, quite unlike the Kaiser, did not invite himself to St. Petersburg and wisely declared that he had "no desire to play the part of the German Emperor, who always meddles in other people's business."[80] Where Wilhelm II failed entirely, his wiser uncle achieved a significant success.[81]

The Kaiser had better results when he attempted to promote brotherly ties with Franz Joseph in Vienna. The Habsburg sovereign, like the tsar, wished that Wilhelm would not insist on visiting him so frequently and with such a massive retinue, and he found Wilhelm's antic behavior and graphic jokes undignified in a monarch. Nevertheless, he believed the German Kaiser to be a true and loyal ally and an earnest man of Christian principle, and Wilhelm in return declared that the old Austrian sovereign epitomized the institution of monarchy, in spite of the emperor's deplorable liaison with the well-known Viennese actress Frau Kathi Schratt.[82] One gesture of Wilhelm's that endeared him to Franz Joseph was his unfailing remembrance, on every 30 January, of the anniversary of the death at Mayerling in 1889 of the Habsburg Crown Prince Rudolf, who had died in an unseemly suicide with his lover. This was one of the Kaiser's theatrical contrivances, for he had never liked Rudolf.

The crown prince's sudden death promoted Franz Joseph's nephew, the Archduke Franz Ferdinand, to the position of heir apparent. Franz Ferdinand, who in his youth had had no prospect of such a brilliant future, was a solitary, prideful man with a passion for medieval armor, roses, and butterflies. He and Wilhelm did not get on well until 1900, when Franz Ferdinand married Countess Sophie Chotek. The Habsburgs, like most other European royalty, spurned Sophie as a commoner, but the Kaiser, who agreed that it was an unfortunate mésalliance, for once had the tact not to say so. On acquaintance, Wilhelm came to like Sophie and paid her marked courtesy.[83] The archduke was grateful for the Kaiser's attentions; he and his wife visited Berlin frequently, and when the two men were apart they wrote to one another about political and diplomatic issues. They found that they had considerable agreement on these matters, but even so, no close personal relationship ever developed. Although grateful to Wilhelm and not unsusceptible to his charm, the archduke, like so many others, was not entirely comfortable when in the presence of the always volatile Kaiser.[84]

Wilhelm II's conception of monarchical allegiance rarely embraced the other German sovereigns or the lesser European crowned heads, for whom he had a low regard and with many of whom he had hardly any contact. He made an exception for Wilhelmina of the Netherlands, who ascended the throne in 1890 at the age of nine. The Kaiser was very protective of the young queen, and Wilhelmina once expressed her enduring gratitude by sending Wilhelm thirty thousand tulip bulbs.[85] In neighboring Belgium, the vast wealth of the avaricious Leopold II impressed Wilhelm greatly, and he respected the crafty Belgian ruler even though he thought Leopold to be the greatest intriguer in Europe.[86] Wilhelm later became disenchanted with the king, who surrendered the Congo, once virtually his personal fiefdom, to the Belgian parliament.[87] In any case, Belgium was a weak, "feminine" nation lacking the robustness of the Teutons. The Italians were worse, and the house of Savoy was unworthy of its regal position in Rome. Wilhelm did nothing to ingratiate himself with his diminutive colleague Victor Emmanuel III, deliberately having the king photographed alongside the Kaiser's gigantic bodyguards and dismissing Victor Emmanuel as a "dwarf" and the queen, Elena of minuscule Montenegro, as the daughter of a Balkan cattle thief. Victor Emmanuel, not surprisingly, despised Wilhelm, for both his rudeness and his incessant theatricality.[88]

The family from which the Italian queen was descended was admittedly of brigand origin, but elsewhere in the Balkans there were other states, especially Greece, Rumania, and Bulgaria, that were more important than Montenegro and on whose thrones sat men who were distant relatives of the Kaiser. In the Balkans, destined to play such a fatal role in the European catastrophe of 1914, Wilhelm had succeeded in alienating all of his fellow monarchs. King Carol of Rumania, a dour, eremitic descendant of the southern German Catholic branch of the Hohenzollern family, did not at all like the Kaiser's frenetic personality, nor did the crown princess, who was Wilhelm's first cousin.[89] Across the Rumanian border in Bulgaria ruled "tsar" Ferdinand, a clever and ambitious man, whose enormous nose Wilhelm ridiculed by calling him "Fernando Naso" and whom the Kaiser treated with unbecoming familiarity, clasping Ferdinand on the back, pinching his rear, and proclaiming in public that the Balkan ruler was a hermaphrodite.[90] Wilhelm nevertheless had a grudging regard for the "fox" Ferdinand, whom he declared to be the cleverest and most unscrupulous of Europe's rulers. The Kaiser detected in the Bulgarian sovereign, and not without reason, an "arch-plotter" with heady ambitions for the expansion of his little kingdom. It is hardly surprising that Ferdinand did not have a high opinion of his remote Prussian cousin.[91]

Scandinavian royalty were hardly more enthusiastic about the Kaiser than were their Balkan counterparts. Wilhelm believed that King Christian IX of Denmark, a kindly and intelligent man, had a sort of "fatherly inclination" for him; Wilhelm thus treated the Danish sovereign with a winning deference, hoping thereby to secure an alliance.[92] But Wilhelm's success with the king never produced the pact for which he aspired and did not extend to the rest of the Danish royal house, especially not to Christian IX's consort, Louise of Hesse, whose family had been dispossessed by Prussia in a war in the 1860s. The queen refused ever to set foot in Germany, and until her death in 1898 she did all she could to poison her many children against the Kaiser. Wilhelm hated the "old spider" and blamed her for many of the problems he encountered with other European sovereigns. In fact, Wilhelm himself was responsible for his failure to get on in Copenhagen, where his ill-natured strictures concerning King George I of the Hellenes, Christian's son and a decent if somewhat bedraggled man whom the Kaiser ridiculed as a bourgeois nonentity, created much resentment.[93] It would be wise, a Danish prime minister once observed, for the tactless Kaiser to stay in Germany.[94] Wilhelm had a number of relatives elsewhere in Scandinavia, where Queen Maud of Norway and the crown princess of Sweden were cousins, but he did not succeed in capitalizing on these relationships. He sniffed that King Haakon, elected to the throne when Norway was separated from Sweden in 1906, was a "king by the 'peoples' [*sic*] will" and therefore no better than the president of some republic.[95] The Kaiser frequently cruised along the Atlantic coast of Scandinavia, but the Norwegian majesties resented these uninvited incursions into their waters—the queen undoubtedly because she was Edward VII's daughter, and the king very probably because Wilhelm II had opposed his election.[96] If ever there was a monarch whose presence among his peers was undesired, it was the last German Kaiser.

Like his royal colleagues on Europe's thrones, the Kaiser was viewed with considerable alarm by his own noble subjects, some of whom were his relatives. The German aristocracy, a diverse class whose members might have been expected to provide the crown with its most devoted allies, had generally supported Kaiser Wilhelm I, but it kept his grandson at a distance and often openly opposed him. The apogee of the nobility were the mediatized princes and counts, who had possessed sovereign rights before the French Revolution but thereafter had only ceremonial privileges and equal status with royalty in respect to matrimony. This group, an army of intricately related Hohenlohes, Schönburgs, Schönborns, Stolbergs, and others, was richly connected with the Hohenzollerns in spite of the fact that few lived in Prussia. Wilhelm was a descendant of the Leiningens, his wife of the Hohenlohe-Langenburgs, and there were various more distant kinships with other lines. The mediatized nobles were insistent on being accorded all the privileges that were their right as once royal houses. The Kaiser addressed all those whom he knew well with the familiar "*du*" used by sovereigns among themselves, but otherwise he ignored the old mediatized nobles in favor of newer, lower-ranking peers, some of whom he raised to princely rank.[97] In retaliation, the mediatized had little to do with Wilhelm II unless they required a favor that only the crown could bestow, preferring Munich and the Wittelsbachs' engaging court to Hohenzollern Berlin.[98]

The mediatized peers were very intermarried with the high aristocracy (*Hochadel*), who did not share their privileges but who were in many cases also of illustrious lineage and substantial wealth. Many of these great nobles, such as the snobbish Dohnas, whose line stretched back to the eighth century, were not prepared to tolerate the Kaiser's autocratic disposition, for to them the Hohenzollerns were parvenus, still tarnished by vulgar, arriviste tastes. The *Hochadel* were in many instances not remarkable people — the contemporary epithet that ran "proud as a Dohna, dumb as a Dönhoff, gross as a Groeben, and false as an Eulenburg" was not entirely undeserved — but they could trace their descent to ancestors who had been prominent when the Hohenzollerns were only inconsequential knights, and they therefore considered Wilhelm II, for all his imperial trappings, not an overlord but, at most, an equal.[99] The Kaiser had only a few friends among these nobles, who avoided his court and in fact in many cases left Berlin altogether, not even returning for the great social season between New Year's Day and the beginning of Lent.[100] An entirely different group were the Junkers, small-scale noble proprietors of the East Elbian provinces of Prussia — families, like the Bismarcks, of intense pride in their genealogy (including a perceived superiority to the Hohenzollerns) and fierce resentment of any changes that would diminish their agricultural incomes or the superior position their forefathers had established in both the army and the Prussian bureaucracy. Wilhelm had alienated the Junkers in the 1890s by supporting a downward revision of the grain tariff and by showing a preference, quite unnatural in a Hohenzollern, for the navy rather than the army. In the following decade, his pretensions to autocracy upset these doughty and rigidly conservative aristocrats, and they resented the contempt Wilhelm openly expressed for such "stupid" reactionary aristocrats and the Conservative Party that constituted their political arm.[101]

There were many nobles who were blind to the Kaiser's failings or who, if more perceptive, nevertheless felt such a measure of devotion to the institution of the Hohenzollern monarchy that they were able to set aside their reservations about the monarch. Others sought salaried positions at court, but whatever the cause or motive among candidates for office it was the Kaiser who chose the members of his entourage. Most of these had made their careers exclusively in the army, which imbued them with a strangulated view of humanity. General Friedrich von Scholl, one of the Kaiser's adjutants, typified this view in his ipse dixit that a Prussian captain knew more than all German professors and intellectuals.[102] With too few exceptions Wilhelm, in assembling his retinue, looked less for men of talent or intelligence than for old acquaintances who were expected to fulfill his wishes unfalteringly. Indeed, to Wilhelm II, loyalty was the primal virtue, and he did not at all like to find himself eclipsed by men of strong intelligence.[103]

The deference shown to the Kaiser had no counterpart elsewhere in Germany, not even at the Habsburg court, where no one would have thought of kissing the emperor's hand. In Berlin, however, what Philipp Eulenburg, himself a great sycophant, called "the ever silent corona of the court establishment" ensured that no one would challenge or question, much less rebuke, the Kaiser.[104] The men who surrounded the throne, especially the military adjutants and the various court chaplains, learned to handle the Kaiser by entertaining him so that he could revert to the carefree life of a Potsdam lieutenant.[105] They catered to his many prejudices, assured him that his views were correct, and saw to it that he was the object around which all else revolved. Wilhelm therefore could spout ideas without penalty, bolstered by the approbation of his retinue, and of his dutiful wife, and by their assurances that he was always right. The Kaiser believed, as he had once declared to his outraged Bavarian subjects, that "the desire of the prince" had "the force of law" (*regis voluntas suprema lex*), and he was most comfortable with those who submitted to the truth of that maxim. "The Kaiser demands creatures whom he doesn't respect," an adjutant wrote, "but who are agreeable to him."[106] Even in his youth, he had not liked to be lectured to, by Bismarck or anyone else, and with maturity this tendency only increased.[107] His officials were anxious to keep their places, and the surest way to fall into oblivion was to cross Wilhelm. "I would rather go to the devil than tell the Kaiser something unpleasant," Colonel Count Dietrich von Hülsen-Haeseler, one of Wilhelm's favorite adjutants and General Hahnke's successor in 1901 as chief of the Military Cabinet, confessed in 1897. "My fate would soon be sealed, and I would make way for someone else who would be even more careful than I and therefore even less useful than I am."[108] Even if opposition to the Kaiser did not result in dismissal, Wilhelm's cold eyes, a feared harbinger of displeasure, could reduce a seasoned general to tears. Courtiers in Berlin therefore reserved their opinions, fatalistically resigning themselves, as Chancellor Bernhard von Bülow described the prevailing attitude, to accepting the Kaiser as he was, faults and all, and putting their trust in God.[109]

There were, to be sure, a few members of the entourage who found the servility of Wilhelm II's other courtiers repellent and who were eager to speak frankly to the sovereign. To intercede effectively with the Kaiser required first that an interview be a private affair between only two men, a privilege Wilhelm did not often grant because he liked to be accompanied at all times by his military adjutants, who were always on guard to protect their master from any unpleasantness.[110] When closeted with the Kaiser, one had to be careful. Evasiveness would yield nothing, for he demanded a concrete tone in discussions. As Philipp Eulenburg noted, Wilhelm's sense of argumentation was so pronounced that sometimes the best avenue for obtaining a desire was to come close to asking for its opposite.[111] An audience with Wilhelm II exposed a courtier to a flood of verbal exaggeration that had to be discounted in order to fathom the Kaiser's true feelings. A powerful conversationalist, Wilhelm could dazzle by his memory, by his command of detail, and by his ability swiftly to grasp the larger dimensions of a problem. "Oh that he could reign so well as he can speak," Eulenburg once lamented.[112] Except in naval matters, on which he refused to entertain any views counter to his own, the Kaiser sometimes graciously admitted the force of arguments that challenged him.[113] But even when accepted, advice tendered to the Kaiser had a brief life. A prominent diplomat, Count Anton Monts, recalled that what Wilhelm heard unfortunately "went in one ear only immediately to exit from the other. The last person [to see him] was always in the right, especially if he knew how to peddle something pleasant."[114]

The result was a bewildering inconstancy in the Kaiser's opinions, a "zick-zack course" that left his officials and foreign statesmen dismayed or perplexed. This was the situation that Bernhard von Bülow inherited when he succeeded Prince Chlodwig zu Hohenlohe-Schillingsfürst as chancellor and minister-president of Prussia in the fall of 1900. The problem was one Bülow already clearly recognized, since for the preceding three years he had served Hohenlohe as state secretary of the Foreign Office. On assuming that position in 1897, the perceptive Hermann von Lucanus, chief of the Civil Cabinet, had informed Bülow, "Everyone has influence on our allhighest ruler but actually no one does."[115] That was true, and Wilhelm himself declared that there was not a man who could sway him.[116] Bülow, who owed his position not to wisdom but to connections and even more to his unparalleled gift for ingratiating himself with those in authority, would as chancellor devote almost a decade in an attempt to assert his own mastery over Wilhelm II. Like all before and all after him, Bülow too would fail.

Only a few men, who were very careful or very lucky, managed to survive to stand by Wilhelm II's side decade after decade. None, curiously, were men of the Kaiser's age but rather were from his father's generation. Count August zu Eulenburg (1838–1921), who served as the high marshal of the court (*Oberhof- und Hausmarschall*) from 1890 to 1914, Generals Hans von Plessen (1841–1929), Gustav von Kessel (1846–1918), and Wilhelm von Hahnke (1833–1912), all three of whom served as adjutants for decades, and Hermann von Lucanus (1831–1908), who was chief of the Civil Cabinet from 1888 until his death, were the principal fixtures of the Kaiser's entourage. These men had in common an unperturbable loyalty to the monarch, one that survived many crises and in the case of Plessen lasted until Wilhelm's flight to Holland in November 1918.

The most impressive man in this group was Eulenburg, a cousin of Wilhelm's confidant, Philipp Eulenburg, and the only figure at the Kaiser's court who seems to have enjoyed virtually unanimous respect.[117] Eulenburg, who by virtue of his office controlled access to the sovereign, was a man of great equanimity and grace; popular with everyone, he was therefore able to smooth over problems caused by the Kaiser's tactlessness. Although closely identified with the conservative, agrarian element, he did not mix in politics and did not press his views on Wilhelm, who highly valued this admirable servant. Just as August Eulenburg was first among the civilians, Plessen, the Kaiser liked to say, was his most important military courtier.[118] For over a quarter of a century (1892–1918), Plessen served as Wilhelm's adjutant and as the commander of military headquarters, a task he handled very adroitly by catering to the Kaiser's dislike of seeing any new faces in his entourage. Descended from an old Mecklenburg family, Plessen was very opinionated and ignorant of both politics and diplomacy, into both of which he nevertheless often intruded. He was unusual only in that he was quite fearless in telling the Kaiser his views, which were essentially that the guards regiments of the Prussian army should have exclusive right of entrée with the monarch. Plessen's solutions to Wilhelm II's many problems were unfailingly martial, an example being his notion that newspaper editors who had dared to criticize the Kaiser should be shot. "That will stop their attacks," he crowed. As Philipp Eulenburg once observed, Plessen was responsible for the Kaiser's unfortunate submersion in an *"Adjutanten-Politik"*, but Wilhelm II did not in fact pay a great deal of attention to the general's bellicose opinions.[119] General Hahnke had been Wilhelm's commanding officer in the First Infantry Guards brigade, and on becoming Kaiser, Wilhelm at once made him an adjutant and chief of the Military Cabinet, a position for which he was not intellectually suitable.[120] As chief, Hahnke was a stickler for orderliness; always respectful of Wilhelm's desires, he strengthened the crown's authority by undermining the position of the generals who successively served as ministers of war.[121] Hahnke surrendered his position at the Military Cabinet in 1901, but he remained an adjutant until his death in 1912.

General Kessel, who became an adjutant of Wilhelm's while he was still a Prussian prince, was the least admirable figure in the entourage. The scion of an old but impoverished Silesian family, he was a cousin of the Eulenburgs and Bismarcks and a ferocious Anglophobe. For that reason Wilhelm's mother had loathed Kessel, who reciprocated by working successfully to alienate Wilhelm from his parents.[122] Once Wilhelm became Kaiser, Kessel was constantly at Wilhelm's side and remained in service until his death in 1918. Not long after his ascension, Wilhelm informed his horrified mother, "*All* that my *excellent Kessel* says I believe implicitly." Kessel himself boasted that under the right circumstances he could easily influence Wilhelm.[123] Kessel was a consummate companion, always at the ready with an endless supply of crude stories that delighted the Kaiser. The general had, or pretended to have, a weakness for being tickled and would laugh uproarishly as Wilhelm groped about at his ribs. Kessel's sycophancy was notorious, but the general was not above criticizing the Kaiser behind his back. Kessel was altogether a false and odious man. On the other hand Lucanus, the son of a pharmacist, came from an entirely different background. Having been ennobled as recently as 1888, he did not fit in comfortably at court. Philipp Eulenburg, like others of the Kaiser's officials, was contemptuous of the plebeian cabinet chief, deriding him as "Look-anus." Lucanus, however, was an astute courtier and an able administrator who never questioned Wilhelm's opinions. He was much feared because it was well-known that, next only to August Eulenburg, he possessed the Kaiser's confidence completely and that, by virtue of the prerogative of his office, he could recommend how vacant posts were to be filled. Lucanus the "minister killer," it was believed, could make or break any Prussian bureaucrat.[124]

The court over which Count Eulenburg as high marshal presided followed an elaborate and highly circumscribed code, which in minute detail governed precedence, dress, and conduct.[125] Prussian custom prescribed that eligibility to appear (*Hoffähigkeit*) was limited to military officers, nobles, and bureaucrats of high rank, together with their wives. Once in the palace, however, the elect were segregated into complex gradations as to who might sit and when and next to whom, who was to be addressed by this or that courtesy title, or whose train (and of what length) was to be affixed to the shoulders or merely to the waist. Such arcana, and many others, were hawkishly watched by Count Eulenburg and his staff, and by the Kaiserin and her "Hallelujah aunts," who always insisted on the most intractable standards of deportment. Between them, they succeeded in imparting a marmoreal rigidity to all royal functions, and this slavish adherence to ritual and tradition ensured that the Berlin court was tedious.

Wilhelm was determined to create a royal establishment quite different from that presided over by his father and grandfather. Anxious about his own stature as one of Europe's youngest sovereigns, as well as the fact that Germany was the most recently founded empire on the Continent, he was eager to impress not only his own subjects but all the world. The Kaiser intended that his court, like his navy or his army in respect to power, was to become the acknowledged cynosure of elegance and splendor. Unfortunately, he confused grandeur with size and pomposity, and his alienation from much of the old nobility resulted in his court's being stocked with figures who, if not demimonde, were not entirely in their element in the highest reaches of society.

The Hohenzollern court under Wilhelm I had been select and traditional, hostile to ostentation of any sort but rigorous in maintaining an exclusive society, precisely ranked in sixty-two degrees of precedence, from the high chamberlain down to the most freshly commissioned second lieutenant. Although the Kaiser greatly admired his grandfather, he felt that during Wilhelm I's rule the Berlin court, too dominated by Bismarck, had unfortunately been relegated to the background. The Hohenzollern monarchy therefore needed to be restored to its proper station.[126] Under Wilhelm II the Prussian court swelled enormously, with all sorts of people admitted whom his grandfather would have rejected. Wilhelm II's penchant for creating nobles led to a vast inflation of honors during his reign, with the crown heaping titles and decorations on some who deserved recognition but also on others who were driven by a lust for honors that was castigated as "ermine fever."[127] What once had been a distinguished rendezvous of ancient titles now became a vast throng of less fulsomely pedigreed aristocrats, and the traditional formal ritual was gradually transformed into a histrionic spectacle. Wilhelm wanted to impress, for he was worried that Berlin was regarded, as he put it, as a "parvenu court."[128]

The Prussian capital did not offer the magnificence or fashionability to be found at Vienna, St. Petersburg, London, and the Bavarian court in Munich. The Kaiser was therefore jealous of all these competitors, and he acutely resented the fact that European socialites and statesmen preferred other cities.[129] Wilhelm admitted that Berlin was a dowdy wasteland when compared with London and was badly in need of a British antidote for its frumpiness. "Ask your smart London friends to come here," he implored the wife of one of Queen Victoria's diplomats. "Let them teach my court ladies how to do their hair and put on their clothes."[130] Wilhelm did not realize that he and Dona were themselves responsible for some of the tedium of the relentlessly moral Hohenzollern court, for according to Wilhelm's prescription, the palace was a place to cultivate manners and a sense of duty rather than to have a good time.[131] In the Kaiser's opinion, only soldiers knew how to dance properly, and his guardsmen were trained in the precise execution of historic quadrilles that he believed would serve to improve the behavior of his younger courtiers. To the horror of the Austro-Hungarian envoy, the minuet became the "permanent rubric" of dancing at court balls, and Dona and Wilhelm would not permit unseemly foxtrots or, for a long time, even waltzes on their glistening parquet.[132] And though he yearned for Queen Victoria to appoint him colonel of a Highlander regiment, the Kaiser found kilts, as well as sacklike dresses, indecent, and he forbade them at his palace.[133]

Wilhelm worked energetically to infuse both his court and his capital with the majestic pomp that he believed appropriate. He ordered his courtiers to dress more impressively, and he loaded Dona with brilliants so that she might not look, as he uncharitably put it, "like the parson's wife" (*comme l'as de pique*).[134] In spite of his efforts, the Kaiser was rarely successful. His own affected gestures, a curious mixture of bombast and affability, disturbed rather than impressed his guests, and although the Hohenzollern court functioned with impressive clockwork, visitors could find little to entice them to return. The Kaiser's ceremonies, no more than the man himself, did not survive the pitiless scrutiny of the nobility, which found Berlin stiff, boring, and vulgar, a poor substitute for the authentic aristocratic tone that prevailed in London and Vienna or for the stupefying Oriental sumptuousness of St. Petersburg. In Berlin, there were too many American heiresses who were overdressed, too many Prussian countesses in plain gowns and inadequate jewelry, and too little food and drink; as hosts, the imperial couple were unable to promote the grandeur they so avidly sought.[135] Count Hugo Lerchenfeld-Koefering, the supremely elegant Bavarian envoy in Berlin, who lived in style and despised Wilhelm, dismissed the Kaiser's contrivance and declared, "One must put such a Hohenzollern parvenu in his place."[136] Wilhelm was aware that his social ambitions for Berlin were not entirely successful, but he illogically blamed this failure, so often due to his own pomposity, on the Jewish press.[137] Although the Kaiser remained dissatisfied that his court had failed to secure a reputation as the glass of fashion, he was determined to make Berlin the unquestioned cultural capital of Europe, a Hohenzollern Athens or Florence reborn along the banks of the Spree.

Two

A MEDICI ON THE SPREE

WILHELM II, king and kaiser, was also the first citizen of his realm, a private man with a variety of interests that sometimes threatened to eclipse the responsibilities that weighed on him as a sovereign. He spent much of every year away from Berlin, as much in pursuit of pleasure as in his role as Germany's ruler, and even when in the capital, he often applied his energy to matters that had little to do with affairs of state. Wilhelm was a lifelong dilettante, rushing from place to place, from friend to friend, from enthusiasm to enthusiasm, all the while failing to develop a real expertise in anything he touched. He liked to complain that the titanic efforts necessary to execute his royal responsibilities left him breathless, and he even claimed that his life might serve, for the benefit of his subjects, as an example of indefatigable industry.[1] The Kaiser, who for two decades had left Berlin for weeks on end, could with complete imperturbability declare in 1907 that he had finally taken his first vacation after nineteen years of wearing his heavy crown.[2] But his friend and admirer Philipp Eulenburg, himself no paragon of energy, declared: "[Wilhelm] never worked as I and thousands of Prussian officials labored. He has no idea what work is."[3] Some things that Wilhelm *appeared* to do, including most of the books that he allegedly wrote as well as a portion of his personal correspondence, were in fact executed by others, and the innumerable, feverish marginal comments that he *did* scribble on documents were not taken seriously by his officials or even, in fact, by the Kaiser himself.[4]

Wilhelm's greatest love was travel, a passion that led his subjects to complain that imperial Germany had had three kaisers: *der Greise, der Weise, und der Reise* — the old graybeard (Wilhelm I), the wise one (Friedrich III), and the last, the traveling Kaiser. Should not the royal anthem, "Hail Be to Thee in Thy Laurelled Crown of Victory" (*Heil Dir im Siegerkranz*), be amended to "Hail Be to Thee in Thy Private Railroad Car" (*Heil Dir im Sonderzug*)? Wilhelm II, I.R. (for *immer reisefähig* and *ich reise* as well as Imperator Rex), was aware of these aspersions. He found them amusing and defended his incessant "student" journeys (as contemporaries called them) by declaring that in addition to facilitating the exercise of what he falsely believed to be his diplomatic finesse with other sovereigns, they enabled him to make new friends and to become better acquainted with his empire.[5] That was an idle boast, since he preferred surrounding himself with familiar faces in customary haunts in Prussia, cleaving to a schedule that changed very little over the years. Wilhelm found Berlin tedious, for its court, thanks to his own prescriptions, was dull, and his wife and her ladies were tiresomely old-fashioned.[6] He was by all accounts happiest when, far from the capital and surrounded by his miscellaneous assortment of male friends, he could indulge in his passion for sailing and hunting, the one occupying much of his summer and the other entertaining him through the fall.

The company that Wilhelm II kept while enjoying himself consisted of his official entourage, exclusively aristocratic and largely military in composition, and an eclectic circle of civilian friends, some of whom were of nonnoble birth. Neither group had much appreciation for the other, even though they were frequently thrown together in close quarters aboard the Kaiser's yachts or in his hunting lodges. Wilhelm's varied acquaintances rarely met in Berlin or Potsdam, for the Hohenzollern court was closed almost without exception to all but those whose noble ancestry or rank in the military or bureaucracy automatically provided them with the privilege of waiting on the sovereign. Even men to whom Wilhelm II was close, such as Albert Ballin, the head of the Hamburg-American Steamship Company, or Robert von Mendelssohn, one of his bankers, came to court only once or twice and then over the objections of the aristocratic court marshals.[7] What is remarkable about the Kaiser's circle, apart from its transitory character, is not its membership but rather the people who were conspicuously absent. The retinue included a plenitude of generals and admirals and great appointive servants of state in the official retinue, but there were few outsiders. No members of Parliament (except for a handful of aristocratic conservatives), only a smattering of talented artists or intellectuals, and not many businessmen, Catholics, or Jews were to be found at court. Other than diplomats, the only foreigners whom the Kaiser saw were the conspicuously rich, with whom he liked to cruise.

In his youth Wilhelm had complained that he had no good friends, and as he matured he made few. Kings do not necessarily have to be lonely, as the relentlessly social life of Wilhelm's uncle, the Prince of Wales and later King Edward VII, amply confirmed, and the Kaiser might have developed close attachments had he possessed any gift for friendship. It rarely occurred to him that his companions were to be treated as men, not subjects, and he was merciless in putting lesser mortals in their places. The colonial secretary Bernhard Dernburg, a man of considerable ability but rather grisly manners, dined at the palace with the Kaiser one day and stuck his napkin in his collar. For that impropriety Dernburg, whom Wilhelm indeed liked, received an ill-humored and offensive rebuke: "This is not a barbershop." Later, the Kaiser consented to the appointment of Wilhelm Solf as colonial secretary but only after being assured that he was "a Dernburg transposed into a gentleman."[8] When Wilhelm was in a better mood there was much conviviality, a good deal of it noisy and vulgar, but even at play, the Kaiser ordered the drift of conversation, the amusements, and the daily program that his guests were to follow — in all of which he arranged to take the most prominent place. In his long life, there were few men, and except for his daughter no women, to whom he was really close, and he eventually dropped almost all of these, sometimes with brutal finality, often not so much for cause as for the fact that no person, and no thing, ever commanded Wilhelm's attention or loyalty for very long. It is not surprising that those who knew the Kaiser well believed that he had no friends.[9]

By 1900, most of the men attached to Wilhelm in his youth or early manhood, such as Herbert von Bismarck, Alfred von Kiderlen-Wächter, and General Alfred von Waldersee, had fallen from grace. Even Count Philipp zu Eulenburg, the closest friend Wilhelm II ever had, did not retain his singular position forever. Eulenburg, who was made a prince on the first day of 1900, saw Wilhelm with great frequency, for the Kaiser arranged his friend's diplomatic career so that Eulenburg would never be too far from Berlin, and when the men were apart, Eulenburg wrote regularly not only to Wilhelm but to Dona as well. By the end of the century, however, the relationship between the two men had begun to cool, probably because of the implication of Eulenburg's brother in a homosexual scandal.[10] Eulenburg resigned from the diplomatic service in 1902 and thereafter saw the Kaiser infrequently. The final rupture between the two men occurred in 1906 when, to Wilhelm's horror, Eulenburg himself was charged with homosexuality. The Kaiser abruptly broke with his old friend and never saw him again.

By the time that Eulenburg's star had begun to set, another person emerged who would become Wilhelm's close friend, although not one so inseparable as Eulenburg once had been. This was Prince Max Egon von Fürstenberg, an Austro-German bon vivant of great wealth, superficial charm, and limited intelligence. For several years, the Kaiser visited Fürstenberg at his castle at Donaueschingen in Baden, which he had encouraged the prince to renovate in an ornate Louis Quinze style. Fürstenberg, unlike Eulenburg, was unassertive and had no political ambitions, but he was Eulenburg's equal in devising ways in which to please the Kaiser. Wilhelm delighted in the prince's crude badinage and his propensity for gossip, and he attributed to Fürstenberg an intellectual prowess that was in fact completely absent. The friendship, ardent at first, eventually waned, perhaps because Dona disapproved of Fürstenberg, and Wilhelm thereafter saw his friend only occasionally.[11] In a similar fashion, Bernhard von Bülow, once a member of the Kaiser's innermost circle, lost Wilhelm's confidence, and their old familiarity vanished.[12] By the time the first decade of the new century had come to an end, Wilhelm II no longer had any intimate friends, and he did not make any in the remaining thirty years of his life.

Even though the Kaiser had a propensity to seasickness, he had been an enthusiastic sailor from youth. One of his first acts as sovereign was to commission the construction of a steam oceangoing yacht, the *Hohenzollern*. According to one of its captains, the ship was a "monstrosity," unbearably rough in heavy seas and primitive in technology. Whatever its nautical failings, the *Hohenzollern*, with its three broad gold stripes circling the hull, was a glamorous vessel.[13] Wilhelm also owned several sailing ships in which he competed or cruised for pleasure. Besides his own vessels, he had the entire Germany navy to commandeer, and the Kaiser happily traveled on vacations by warships. "A whole navy is put into service in order to kill two days' time," the high court marshal complained.[14] At the beginning of his reign, Wilhelm informed Bismarck that he intended to spend six weeks every summer in Norway. The chancellor, who thought the young Kaiser's place was in Berlin, complained that with Wilhelm's love of moving about, keeping up with him was "rather like a man trying to catch hold of the skirt of a star as it travelled through the air."[15] Wilhelm meant what he had told Bismarck, and in 1889 he began what became an annual custom of sailing for about a month in Scandinavian waters in the company of some fifteen or twenty male friends.[16]

The trips were elaborately organized along the lines of Wilhelm's Borussia student fraternity at the university in Bonn, with the sailing party enlisted in a so-called Northland Travel Society (*Nordlandsfahrtgesellschaft*), the Kaiser being the "most serene travel master" (*allerdurchlauchtigster Fahrtmeister*), and the other guests cast as pledges or fully initiated brothers. All the travelers dressed in the uniform of the Imperial Yacht Club and were subject to the club statutes that prescribed everyone's duty. Rule sixteen, for example, noted, "The most renown punsters of the firm Hülsen, Kessel, Kiderlen & Co. are responsible that all stale jokes shall be replaced monthly."[17] For years, General Count Dietrich von Hülsen-Haeseler, an adjutant and later chief of the Military Cabinet, and Adjutant-General Gustav von Kessel were regular members of the Kaiser's party, but only two guests had perfect records. They were Dr. Paul Güssfeldt, a well-known African explorer, and the vice-marshal of the court, Baron Maximilian von Lyncker, both of whom accompanied Wilhelm on all twenty-six cruises between 1889 and 1914. Other regular guests had varied backgrounds: Philipp Eulenburg; Admiral Baron Gustav von Senden und Bibran, the chief of the Naval Cabinet; Wilhelm's favorite marine artist, Karl Saltzmann; his body physician, Dr. Rudolf von Leuthold; Hülsen's brother George, the director of the Imperial Theater; Count Emil Schlitz genannt von Görtz, a childhood friend of Wilhelm's; and a number of junior officers, such as Count Kuno von Moltke and his cousin Helmuth, both of whom were adjutants.

The purpose of Wilhelm's trips was pleasure, and he was reluctant to interrupt his juvenile routine to deal with business.[18] The mood was to be joyous, with all these middle-aged, overweight men expected to behave like fraternity boys or young lieutenants. The company was awakened to the strains of the imperial anthem, rendered by the band that was always on board, after which there were calisthenics led by the Kaiser. Shipboard life was given over to talking, telling jokes, and listening to Wilhelm read from books that had caught his momentary fancy or from endless tables of naval statistics that left his guests stupefied. When the Kaiser was not reading, he talked on and on, often in an alarmingly inane manner, and even though the cruise was supposed to promote relaxation, the Kaiser was often nervous or petulant, so much so that Dr. Leuthold became concerned. Wilhelm might on occasion denounce his subjects as the "dirty, obstinate, stupid, poor, ill-bred Germans, who should let the English or the Americans be their example."[19] Or he might thunder: "The British are all sheep. Mr. Balfour is a sheep; Chamberlain is one, Sir Edward Grey is the greatest of all." One observer marveled that anyone in the entourage could last long in the face of such a "pathological disposition," and a young naval officer who overheard this last piece of royal bombast told his superior that he would resign rather than serve a sovereign who clearly was demented.[20] Meals on the *Hohenzollern* were solid German fare with mediocre wine, an affront to the gourmets in the entourage, and Wilhelm's shipmates insisted that the seating be rotated, so that no one would have to endure being placed permanently next to the host. If the ship was in port, a hike on shore might be in order. On Sundays, the Kaiser led the prayers and preached the sermon, but otherwise the Sabbath, like the other days of the week, was devoted to relaxation and horseplay. The day sometimes ended with the Kaiser chasing his companions to the doors of their staterooms. It might have been an honor to travel with royalty, but whatever pleasure a trip aboard the *Hohenzollern* had afforded usually vanished well before the return to home port, leaving both the Kaiser and his traveling companions (who had to pay a portion of their expenses) out of sorts.[21]

Except for the royal yachts, there were few other private vessels flying the German ensign, for the aristocracy had little interest in water sports and in any case could rarely afford the prodigious expense involved. The haute bourgeoisie, which had the money and which was usually eager to imitate the nobility, for the most part shared this disdain. Since Germans were so unfamiliar with sailing, Wilhelm and millionaire German yachtsmen such as Alfried Krupp von Bohlen und Halbach, Baron von Scheller-Steinwartz, and an occasional Jewish financier for many years had to recruit their crews in England.[22] The Kaiser's cruises and appearances at regattas therefore took him into the orbit of international yachting society, which was composed for the most part of British and American plutocrats. Wilhelm hoped sailing would make him popular in England, but most yachtsmen there seem to have given him a wide berth, perhaps because they did not consider him to be a good sport. They offended the Kaiser by not appearing more frequently at the regattas he patronized at Kiel, and he complained that at sailing events at Cowes on the Isle of Wight his splendid *Meteor* could find no worthy opponent.[23] Wilhelm's small number of acquaintances in the British Isles included the earl of Lonsdale, an international sportsman of whom he was very fond, Earl Brassey, a peerless yachtsman who had inherited a large railroad fortune, Viscount Pirrie, who controlled the great Harland and Wolff shipyards in Belfast, and the Marquess of Ormonde, whose only distinction seems to have been that he was the commander of the Royal Irish Yacht Club.

Americans were more to Wilhelm's taste, and he to theirs. He delighted in the company of rich Yankees, and these titans of commerce or industry were flattered to receive the marked attentions of a European ruler. There was an active exchange of visits between the *Hohenzollern* and the ships of his transatlantic sailing acquaintances, and the sumptuousness of their yachts put him in a childish rapture. Philipp Eulenburg regretted that "possession of a yacht renders one eligible for court" (*Jacht-Besitz macht hoffähig*). He added that with Wilhelm, "money and wealth were 'the thing' " and that nothing worked quite so effectively as a floating palace.[24] The Kaiser met J. P. Morgan and an assortment of Vanderbilts, Wanamakers, Armours, Drexels, and Goelets, company that his prim consort entirely disapproved. There was more than a trace of jealousy in the Kaiser, who resented the ability of American magnates to buy anything they wanted, from British steamship lines to European art and divas for New York's Metropolitan Opera.[25] Wilhelm liked to think that his frequent encounters with America's leading capitalists worked to improve relations between the two great powers, but there is no evidence of this beyond an occasional stray observation, such as Morgan's laconic comment, "[The Kaiser] pleases me." The American financier's opinion of the Kaiser may have been due to the high decoration he received from Wilhelm in appreciation for his gift to the Reformation museum at Wittenberg of a letter by Martin Luther.[26]

The Scandinavian cruises, for which Wilhelm occasionally substituted an excursion to the Mediterranean, and his frequent appearances at regattas in North Germany and England all took place in the summer months, and once fall came he had to find diversion on land. Like his grandfather, Wilhelm I, the Kaiser was an enthusiastic huntsman, and in spite of his withered left arm, he was an excellent shot. His Hohenzollern ancestors had led the chase on their own extensive properties, but their appearances in the field, if frequent, were brief. Wilhelm II changed all that, adding various sporting holdings to the royal domain and greatly increasing the time devoted to the pursuit of game. Sometimes he would hunt for two or three days at a time, twice a week, leaving almost no opportunity for work. "Le roi s'amuse" became the complaint shortly after Wilhelm assumed his crown, and it did not abate with time. The Kaiser's passion for sport, according to the shrewd and disillusioned retired diplomat Count Anton Monts, had after twenty-odd years become almost grotesque.[27]

The Kaiser sometimes took guests to his shooting box at Hubertusstock, which lay about twenty-five miles northeast of Berlin and which, for a few pfennigs, tourists could visit when he was not in residence. Wilhelm also had property at Cadinen, situated on the Baltic in East Prussia not far from Elbing, which he acquired in 1898 and where he manufactured majolica tiles that decorated the subway stations in Berlin and Hamburg. His favorite estate was at Rominten, located in the same province and near the Russian border. He bought the land in 1889 and a few years later built a wooden house that imitated the medieval dwellings he had seen on his cruises to Norway. Rominten was located in the middle of an immense coniferous forest that offered excellent deer hunting for the

Kaiser and, long after his abdication, for Hermann Göring, to whom Wilhelm's heirs sold the estate in 1942.

Frequently, however, the Kaiser invited himself to the seats of his friends among the great landowners of Brandenburg, East Prussia, and Silesia. The prospect of an imperial visit was a source of considerable trepidation for these proprietors, since Wilhelm was not an easy guest. What he called "a cozy little visit" required guest quarters for as many as eighty persons, each courtier taking along anywhere from six to thirteen suitcases to ensure being properly attired.[28] The Kaiser prescribed when he would arrive and depart, who the other guests were to be (including people his hosts might not know), and what provision was to be made for his entertainment. On the appointed day, Wilhelm descended with his enormous suite of adjutants, friends, and miscellaneous retainers, clearly without the least awareness of the difficulties, both physical and financial, that his visit entailed. Except for the wives or daughters of the house, women were never invited, since the Kaiser felt that this would impose an unwelcome formality on what was supposed to be a free and easy gathering. Wilhelm was at his best in the company of his fellow hunters, provided that his bag was greater than anyone else's, and a landlord anxious to please would spend vast amounts of money importing exotic animals for annihilation by the imperial rifle.[29] Eulenburg, who was Wilhelm's constant companion in the field, declared that even someone who despised the Kaiser would be favorably disposed if he encountered Wilhelm while hunting, for the Kaiser would then invariably be in a good humor. That is why Admiral Alfred von Tirpitz, whose relations with his master were never easy, preferred to discuss naval affairs at Rominten, where Wilhelm was less nervous and more inclined to pay attention.[30]

Two of the Kaiser's favorite hunting preserves were Eulenburg's estate at Liebenberg in Brandenburg and Prince Richard von Dohna-Schlobitten's more imposing property at Prökelwitz in East Prussia. Eulenburg was astute in knowing how to please Wilhelm, and the hunts at Liebenberg, which sometimes lasted two weeks and which were a regular feature of the Kaiser's winter schedule from 1888 to 1901, always achieved the proper mixture of sport, music, and banter. This was hard work for Eulenburg, who, after entertaining his sovereign, took to his bed for days.[31] Prökelwitz, where Wilhelm shot regularly from 1885 until shortly before the First World War, was not quite so pleasant, for the prince entirely lacked Eulenburg's grace. Dohna was kin to the Eulenburgs, but unlike that family of facile courtiers, he had a rough manner and was a stupendous drinker. An excellent horseman, Dohna was also an avid collector of titles and decorations, and he was fond of delivering to the Kaiser addresses of such abject sycophancy that the hunting party, including Wilhelm, found their host's slavish behavior more appropriate in a mere "shoemaker" (*Schuster*), the nickname they gave their host. Dohna acknowledged that he groveled and pleaded with his friends to leave him alone. "I know I'm a shoemaker," he said, "but it gives me such pleasure."[32] Rich, mindless, crude, but indefatigably hospitable, Dohna encouraged Wilhelm to acquire Cadinen so that the crown would be more securely attached to East Prussia.[33] Although Wilhelm rewarded Dohna in 1900 by promoting him to the rank of prince, the Kaiser eventually tired of him and also of Prökelwitz, finding the shooting better at nearby Rominten.

It was in the Prussian province of Silesia that Wilhelm hunted in a style that put Liebenberg, which was plain because Eulenburg had only modest wealth, or even Prökelwitz in the shade. The Kaiser had three Silesian friends who were, next only to the Krupps in the Rhineland on the opposite side of Germany, probably the richest of his subjects and who lived in a splendor so regal that Wilhelm was reduced to envy. All three — the princes of Pless and Hatzfeldt-Trachenberg and Count Guido Henckel von Donnersmarck — were astute courtiers eager to cater to the Kaiser's every whim.

Pless was a nonentity, lazy and pompous, and except for his enormous wealth and his beautiful English wife, whom Wilhelm greatly admired, was of little interest or consequence to the Kaiser.[34] He possessed, however, a stupendous and very luxurious castle high on a hill overlooking the small town of Pless in southernmost Silesia and a vast spread of game-filled forest. Wilhelm was enthralled by the elegance of the prince's establishment, where he would make his eastern headquarters during the First World War. Hatzfeldt, a Catholic whom Wilhelm in 1900 raised to the ultimate dignity of duke (*Herzog*), the only such honor of his entire reign, was a more substantial figure who at one point was seriously considered as a suitable candidate for chancellor. Although somewhat heavy in manner and too lethargic for the frenetic Kaiser's taste, Hatzfeldt was a generous host, and Wilhelm enjoyed being a guest at his immense castle at Trachenberg not far north of Breslau, especially because the duchess was very winning.[35]

Henckel, who was born in 1830 and thus slightly older than Wilhelm's father, was the most important and the most interesting of the Kaiser's Silesian friends. He had a grandiose palace on the Russian border at Neudeck just north of Beuthen, where he lived in Oriental luxury. Henckel had been a partisan of Bismarck's and supported him after his fall from office in 1890, earning Wilhelm's enmity as well as that of court society. Henckel thereby acquired the opprobrious sobriquet of "rebel," but after the Iron Chancellor's death in 1898 he returned to favor. The count was stupefyingly rich and was prepared to use his money to ingratiate himself with the Kaiser. Henckel's fortune had been built on a series of industrial amalgamations, and Wilhelm hoped that this entrepreneurial zeal would become a model for other Silesian magnates.[36]

Henckel was ostentatious and a little vulgar, but thanks to the Kaiser's patronage he and his second wife in time became established figures at court. On the first day of the new century, Wilhelm made him Prince Henckel von Donnersmarck, an elevation, it was said in Berlin, that created a prince among the merchants and a merchant among the princes. The Kaiser began to hunt once more at Neudeck, the party sometimes exterminating as many as forty-two hundred pheasants in a single day, and dined with Henckel several times a year in Berlin.[37] Henckel was a well-informed man and, like Pless and Hatzfeldt, sat in the Prussian House of Lords (*Herrenhaus*), the upper house of the state legislature, where he, along with Hatzfeldt, was regarded as liberal. The Kaiser was not interested in Henckel's ideas, or Hatzfeldt's, but only in the sumptuousness of their estates, and if either of these two magnates (or Pless, who had no ideas at all but bottomless reaches of money) introduced some lavish domestic arrangement, Wilhelm would insist that the same feature be installed in the palace in Berlin.

Wilhelm II's life was not entirely given over to sport, and even while sailing or hunting he would occasionally turn the conversation to artistic or intellectual matters, which were mysteries to almost all of the military members of the entourage but not to Eulenburg, who encouraged the Kaiser in these interests.[38] Throughout his reign the Kaiser was concerned with the arts, but only as a dilettante. His skittish enthusiasms, which ranged widely but never deeply, were initially intense but soon forgotten. Wilhelm had no comprehension for the artistic and literary innovations of his time, for his tastes were conventionally bourgeois, without a trace of the discrimination that had distinguished some earlier Hohenzollerns.[39] In the Berlin palace, the Kaiser often gave the prominent places on his walls to indifferent ancestral portraits, relegating the family's fine collection of Velázquezes to dark corners. In the dining room, good pictures alternated with prize antlers. When Count Harry Kessler, a fastidious collector, toured the deserted palace in December 1918 after the revolutionaries had ransacked the building, he declared that what remained of the royal possession was so commonplace and tasteless that it was hard to be angry at the plunderers.[40] The only areas of the arts that Wilhelm II vitalized were marine painting, in which he himself indulged, the use of mosaic decoration in churches, and the manufacture of majolica ceramics.[41]

To the Kaiser, German art was to be German and it was to be didactic. Foreign influences were unhealthy, if not degenerate, and should be purged. Wilhelm regretted that the Jews, whom he tended to hold responsible for modernism, had acquired so much influence in cultural affairs, as in everything else. He was hostile to a number of leading Jewish artists, even though he implausibly claimed that since the army and the loftier bureaucratic posts in Prussia were closed to Jews, he had tried to steer them in the direction of academic and artistic careers.[42] All forms of art — whether canvases hung in museums, plays performed in the numerous state theaters, or the Kaiser's statuary displayed in the Tiergarten allée in the heart of Berlin — were to proclaim German virtues and Hohenzollern accomplishments, thereby inculcating an appropriate sense of nationalism in Wilhelm's subjects and raising them above crass mammonism.[43]

Wilhelm considered himself to be the general supervisor of German artistic life and believed that his taste, like his flair for politics and diplomacy, was exceptional and therefore not to be challenged. He treated his views on art, one critic declared, as "gospel," a fact that Wilhelm's cousin, the Grand Duke of Hesse, attributed to the Kaiser's satisfaction in his accomplishments, admittedly not negligible, as a seascape painter.[44] When a museum official informed the Kaiser that in Munich a committee of artists and patrons advised the Bavarian minister of culture on acquisitions for the royal gallery, he was silenced with the imperial retort that such collective judgment was "entirely superfluous." Wilhelm noted, "The ruler does that better acting alone."[45] He was confident that superior art proceeded not from competitions but rather from a discriminating ruler's association with people of artistic talent. That had been the glory of the Italian Renaissance, whose greatest geniuses he believed to have been of German descent, and Wilhelm did not blanch at comparing himself to the Medicis or at equating his artistic commissions with those of the Florentine Quattrocento.[46] The Kaiser spent sometimes as much as two million marks every year on works of art and furnishings for his seventy-six royal residences; he was often quite helpful to museum directors in the acquisition of works of art, and he exercised considerable influence over painting through his active role in the Royal Academy of Arts.[47] He reviewed the appointment of members, determining who might or might not sit on juries that considered pictures for inclusion in shows, and he scrutinized the annual nominations for prizes, for which he paid and which he personally awarded.

Wilhelm II's frequent intervention in the arts caused much resentment, for Germany was notable for the active challenge that modernists were mounting against the sort of traditional, established forms of art that the Kaiser championed. Artists had grown used to enjoying considerable license under his grandfather, who had seldom intruded into such matters.[48] The Kaiser's obtuse regressivism, which a friend noted was not merely "biased but almost fanatical," in insisting that art be either fantasy or historical parade placed not only artists but also the educated classes at large against the crown and produced exactly the result Wilhelm had hoped to prevent.[49] At the same time, Wilhelm II's repeated visits to ateliers, to the theater, and to the opera, although always with a marked favor for conventional efforts, and his awards, somewhat grudgingly agreed to, of titles and decorations to approved painters, sculptors, or playwrights helped to raise the status of *all* artists, including those whom he despised. Works that Wilhelm condemned thereby won special attention by virtue of being objects of imperial malediction.[50] The Kaiser's concern, and his patronage, would have been welcome had his taste been more discriminating and his judgment about the political utility of art more informed. To those who were patrons, collectors, or admirers of art, Wilhelm's artistic judgment was regarded as parvenu, bourgeois, and uninformed. They expressed their criticism openly, as did a number of deputies in the Reichstag, and even the conservative newspaper, the *Kreuzzeitung*, complained in 1904 that the Kaiser was trying to impose a personal regime in cultural affairs. German artists, whose opinion of their ruler's discrimination was usually very low, made no attempt to hide their contempt.[51] Wilhelm knew that he enjoyed little popularity with most artists and intellectuals, but it did not greatly trouble him. "If I do things right people complain," he told his friend the traditionalist sculptor Walther Schott, "and if I do them wrong they complain. Good or bad, all I get is criticism."[52]

The Kaiser believed that in painting, he was entitled to a special role because he was himself an amateur artist, but he considered his expertise to be formidable in many other art forms as well. Wilhelm could lecture at some length on choreography, about which he knew nothing at all, and had no hesitation in altering architects' plans for public buildings, even though his ability in this respect was minimal.[53] In the theater, Wilhelm considered himself an authority on stage scenery and costuming, for which he had a consuming passion, but also on how characters should be portrayed. He insisted, for example, that the great Napoleon, however inimical he might have been to the Germans, had to be made to rise majestically above his lowly French courtiers.[54] Wilhelm composed a play entitled *Sardanapal*, portraying an Assyrian king who, trapped in an unsuccessful war, nobly immolated himself and his family rather than be captured by the enemy. The Kaiser had his play performed at a gala honoring his uncle, King Edward VII, on the king's last visit to Berlin in 1908. The portly British sovereign slept through most of the play, awakening only at the fire scene. His muddled reaction was that the theater was ablaze, and in alarm he asked the Kaiserin why the fire department had not been called. *Sardanapal*, which Berlin wits said was in fact the name of a sleeping potion, was never performed again.[55]

It was in painting that Wilhelm's involvement in the arts was most marked. He made pronouncements about pictures with the same foolishness that so often characterized his political and diplomatic obiter dicta, declaring, for example, that Rembrandt was inferior to a minor German painter with whose works he was enamored.[56] The principal objection that many contemporary artists had to the Kaiser was that he was so resolutely opposed to anything that was modern. His preference was for the traditional seascapes of Karl Saltzmann, who had taught him painting in the early 1880s while Wilhelm was a young officer at Potsdam and whom he called "Uncle August." He also favored Willy Stöwer's equally prosaic marine paintings and the inflated portraits of Max Koner, who executed several pompous likenesses of Wilhelm.[57]

What Wilhelm admired most were historical canvases extolling the house of Hohenzollern, himself included. He treasured, as had his father and his grandfather, the endless representations of Frederick the Great by Adolph von Menzel, an artist of real ability. In 1898 Wilhelm awarded Menzel the order of the Black Eagle, Prussia's highest civilian order, the only artist ever so honored. To express his appreciation for Menzel's most celebrated picture, a representation of Frederick performing on the flute at a concert at Sans Souci, the Kaiser staged a *tableau vivante* of the scene and at the conclusion knelt before the artist.[58] On Menzel's death at the age of ninety in 1905, Wilhelm violated precedent by marching in the funeral procession. The Kaiser had the Prussian government buy the pictures in Menzel's estate and then ordered them hung in a commemorative exhibition in the National Gallery, the only occasion in the history of imperial Germany that a painter received such an honor. After the artist's death, Wilhelm continued to patronize other artists, such as Georg Schöbel and Richard Friese, who also specialized in studies of Frederick the Great. Almost equally high in the Kaiser's estimation was Anton von Werner, for many years the director of the Royal Academy of the Arts as well as president of the traditionalist League of Berlin Artists. Werner painted glossy, almost photographic, historical pictures of considerable dramatic impact and helped Wilhelm stage great state occasions, such as the memorial service following Bismarck's death in 1898. As a young man, Wilhelm had studied drawing under Werner, a shameless flatterer who worked effectively to turn his patron against modern art.[59]

The Kaiser's favorite artist, however, was neither Menzel nor Werner but Hermann Knackfuss, a mediocre painter who had limned many scenes of Hohenzollern glory, including several that featured Wilhelm II himself. Wilhelm had become familiar with Knackfuss in 1886, when he saw a series of pictures the artist had executed for the Berlin city hall. He thereupon hired the artist to paint several frescoes for the casino of the Guards Hussar regiment that he commanded. In 1895, the Kaiser, in a state of acute agitation because of Japan's victory in the Sino-Japanese War, concluded that this event heralded an invasion of Europe by a gigantic Asian horde under the mikado's leadership. In response to this danger, Wilhelm provided Knackfuss with a sketch and ordered him to convert it into a painting. What emerged from the artist's palette was the notorious canvas, said to be even inferior to Wilhelm's sketch, entitled *People of Europe, Protect Your Most Sacred Possessions!* (*Völker Europas, wahrt eure heiligsten Güter!*), a stupendous iconographic mélange depicting the Christian powers of Europe threatened by the pagan East. The archangel Michael, patron saint of the Germans, leads the defense, with the other powers, notably Marianne, Britannia, and the Russian bear, portrayed as cowards deficient in Germanic heroism. To the Kaiser, Knackfuss's picture was a masterpiece, and whenever a crisis arose in the Far East he would crow that his predictions about the predatory Orientals were coming true.[60] German steamship lines were commanded to hang copies of the picture on their ships, a gesture sure to give offense when calling at Eastern ports, and Wilhelm's diplomats, to their dismay, were entrusted with presentation copies of the picture for delivery to rulers and other dignitaries. A military adjutant who had been designated to take one to Nicholas II recommended that to avoid unpleasantness, he might tell the tsar that Germania in fact represented Russia.[61] For most of the rest of Wilhelm II's life, *People of Europe* was his favorite picture, and well into the 1920s he carried out much of his fitful correspondence on postcards featuring Knackfuss's handiwork. Wilhelm's patronage of a hackneyed artist and his insistence on such parochial subject matter did nothing to enhance his reputation as a connoisseur. Bismarck, to whom the Kaiser sent a copy of *People of Europe*, did not know what to make of it, and Count Leo Tolstoy, who considered the Kaiser to be ridiculously pretentious and ignorant, cited Wilhelm's enthusiasm for Knackfuss's picture as proof of his intellectual bankruptcy.[62]

In the Kaiser's opinion, aspiring artists would do well to study the giants of the past, especially those of the German Renaissance, for no painter could escape such a powerful tradition.[63] The Kaiser's hostility toward modernity, and his boundless distaste for most things French, isolated him from the promising developments in German art during his reign. He despised the great Jewish artist Max Liebermann, perhaps the most distinguished of Berlin's many painters, because the artist's pictures depicted the misery of the working class. That, Wilhelm declared, was impermissible. Painting was to elevate rather than depress, and artists should not remind those who toiled relentlessly of their dismal lot in life but instead should raise their consciousness to a more sublime level. "If art . . . does nothing more than to make misery even more hideous than it already is," the Kaiser declared, "then it sins against the German people. The fostering of the ideal is the greatest work of culture. . . . That it can do only if art lends a hand, if it raises up instead of drawing down into the gutter."[64] Wilhelm would not allow Liebermann's pictures to be hung in official exhibitions and denounced him as a revolutionary whose degenerate art was poisoning the German soul.[65] Only in 1912 did he consent to the acquisition by the National Gallery of a picture by Max Slevogt, one of the most prominent German impressionists, whose works were represented among all of Germany's leading collections of modern art.[66] Nevertheless, when the Kaiser visited the gallery a year after the acquisition, Slevogt's picture had to be temporarily removed to a corner that was not to be inspected. After Wilhelm's departure, the painting was returned to its proper place.

The Kaiser especially despised anything that smacked of the Secession, the avant-garde movement founded in Munich in 1892 and that had many disciples throughout Germany. The Bavarian Wittelsbach rulers had often been more artistically adventurous than the Hohenzollerns in Berlin, and the Secession had a powerful patron in the prince regent, "Ludwig the viewer" (*der Besichtiger*), as he was called because although he visited showrooms with regularity, he rarely bought anything. Wilhelm's attitude toward the art world of Munich was somewhat ambivalent; he found the Secession decadent but admired some of the pictures in its annual show. Such art might do in Bavaria, but he did not intend to have this sort of thing prosper in Berlin.[67] In 1898, a group of Berlin artists seceded from the annual exhibition patronized by the Kaiser and formed their own Secession. The occasion of the revolt was Wilhelm II's veto of the award of a gold medal to Käthe Kollwitz, a promising young realist, for her disturbing etchings of the impoverished Silesian cottagers whose plight had been dramatized in Gerhart Hauptmann's celebrated play of 1892, *The Weavers*.[68] The Berlin Secession was dedicated less to a specific style than to an effort to promote both artistic excellence and an appreciation for modern French and British art. To Wilhelm, it featured nothing but dreary subject matter painted in a manner that was unrealistic and therefore indigestible. Art, he declared shortly after the turn of the century, was not to stray beyond "the feelings in mankind for beauty and harmony," and pictures should be immediately intelligible and not require (as a museum official once dared to advise him) being viewed at a distance of ten feet in order to grasp what the artist was attempting to convey.[69] Wilhelm treated the Secession as a sort of general artistic scapegoat, thundering at people who sympathized with the avant-garde, "You modern, you Secessionst you!"[70]

Berlin had in Wilhelm's reign, as it does today, a number of splendid museums, and although the Kaiser often gave the directors free rein on some matters, he frequently insisted on imposing his will. Because of his interest in art, prosaic though it may have been, Wilhelm actively intervened in museum affairs, often to the consternation of his officials. He had a taste for impressive, but often useless, exhibition halls, he decreed what pictures could be hung, and he supervised the purchase of new acquisitions. The rationale behind the Kaiser's interference was made clear in a letter he wrote in 1899 to the artistically conservative minister of culture, Robert Bosse.

> I have noticed on the occasion of a visit this spring to the National Gallery that certain pictures that might, thanks to the subjects they depict, be particularly suitable to have an educative influence on the visitor and in their artistic merit to represent national art in a superior way have been removed from their prominent places and replaced by pictures of modern taste, some of them of foreign origin. I do not approve of these changes, and I want the indicated works to be returned to their old sites and the new pictures demoted to a less prominent place. I also order that in the future that all acquisitions for the National Gallery, whether by purchase or donation, first receive my approval.[71]

Wilhelm Bode, who in 1905 was named to head all of the royal Prussian museums, was the crown's principal adviser about painting, and he was by temperament well suited to deal with the Kaiser. Bode had first met Wilhelm in the 1870s and found that the young prince, still in his teens, was already knowledgeable about museums and art.[72] The magisterial Bode, known as the "Bismarck of the museum world," had tastes not quite so conservative as the Kaiser's, but he was a graceful courtier and knew how to deal with Wilhelm. Museum officials who lacked Bode's suavity and who too ardently sponsored modern, and especially French, paintings quickly fell from favor. The director of Berlin's National Gallery from 1896 to 1909, Hugo von Tschudi, admired modern French and German painters and did not share Wilhelm's tendency to judge art in terms of its patriotic content. Tschudi suffered from a form of lupus that caused a growth in the bridge of his nose, a malady so disfiguring that the once elegant man frequently contemplated suicide. Wilhelm and the Kaiserin found the unfortunate Tschudi repulsive to look at and therefore did not like to be around him.[73] The temperamental director spoke fearlessly to the Kaiser, who was not pleased to find such frankness in an official, but he could make little headway in persuading Wilhelm to purchase modern paintings, especially if they were French. The Kaiser liked Antoine Watteau, Jean Honoré Fragonard, and the other rococo geniuses of the eighteenth century, but among more modern painters he loathed Édouard Manet, Gustave Courbet, and Honoré Daumier, exempting only the military artist Jean Meissonier and a few members of the Barbizon school from his tirades. The Kaiser would, however, permit French impressionist canvases to be accepted as gifts, since this did not convey official recognition of their quality, but he decreed that all offensive paintings that were already in the gallery were to be relegated to out-of-the-way rooms.[74]

In 1908 Tschudi quarreled with the Kaiser over the purchase of a number of French paintings and soon thereafter left Berlin to become director of the Bavarian state museums in Munich, where the government and the prince regent both had a more accommodating attitude toward artistic modernity.[75] Wilhelm wanted his obsequious favorite, Anton von Werner, to take over Tschudi's post, but Bode managed to convince him that Ludwig Justi, the nephew of Wilhelm's art history teacher at Bonn, Karl Justi, was more suitable. Justi proved an enlightened choice, for he had both discrimination and courage. By threatening periodically to resign, Justi persuaded the Kaiser to add contemporary works to the gallery's collection and to make room for them not only by adding to the building but also by removing scores of mediocre Hohenzollern portraits to the royal armory on the Unter den Linden.

The Kaiser once declared that had he been an artist, he would have been a sculptor, the reason for the preference being that in his opinion sculpture, unlike painting, appealed to the intelligence rather than to the senses.[76] Wilhelm never tried his hand at this art form, but his designs for trophies and monuments involving human figures are quite ordinary.[77] The most distinguished sculptor of the Wilhelmine era was Louis Tuaillon, a French-born Jew who was a member of the Berlin Secession and whose monument in Bremen to Kaiser Friedrich III Wilhelm admired. Tuaillon received several minor honors from the crown but only one royal commission, for some enlarged copies of Amazons that he had earlier sculpted.[78] The Kaiser's old friend Count Emil Görtz, a sculptor of some talent, executed several statues that adorned Wilhelm's palaces. A special favorite of Wilhelm's was Walther Schott, a man whose artistry, like his political views, was profoundly traditional. Schott was a notorious sycophant, and the Kaiser often had him carve the elaborate ornamentation that was a standard feature on the bowsprits of all German warships.[79]

It was through Schott that Wilhelm became acquainted with Reinhold Begas, who would gain his favor more completely than any other sculptor. Begas was an admirer of Schott's work, and his own sculpture never transcended a sort of pretentious and sterile neoclassicism. Begas excelled Schott in deference, declaring that in his creations he followed the Kaiser's devotion to Greek ideals. He denounced Secession art and expressed the hope that some doctor might develop a "serum against this disease."[80] Begas specialized in colossal representations of Hohenzollern triumphs, royal busts, and sarcophagi, and for this loyalty he was rewarded by being named head of the sculpture section of the Prussian Academy of Learning, a post he held from 1876 to 1903. Another sculptor in favor was Cuno von Uechtritz, who also fashioned likenesses of various Prussian kings and their victorious generals. Both Begas and Uechtritz made several contributions to the "Avenue of Victory" (*Siegesallée*), the parade of marble monuments to German heroes spaced along the main thoroughfare that bisected the Berlin Tiergarten. This pedestrian forest of statuary, erected under the general supervision of Schott, was the gift of the Kaiser to the city, and on its inauguration in 1901 he proclaimed that Begas might now be compared to Michelangelo.[81] The poses and period costumes of these figures were executed from drawings provided by the Kaiser, who ordered that some of the faces resemble not his long-dead ancestors but rather his contemporary friends. The features of the founder of the Hohenzollern dynasty, the elector Frederick I, thus looked more or less like Philipp Eulenburg. Other likenesses were supplied by male models, for whom Schott advertised in the Berlin newspapers.[82]

Although the purpose of these large pieces was not only to decorate the Tiergarten but also to arouse patriotic feelings, the *Siegesallée* became an object of ridicule. The Baedeker guidebooks withheld the double star that would have signified that the project was a great work of art worthy to be viewed. Art students indicated their opinion of the Kaiser's taste by breaking off the noses of his heroes, and a foreign diplomat declared that until he had seen a statue-encrusted fountain commemorating the legendary Hohenzollern hero Roland, adorning the park, he had not realized that "even flowing water could be made to be ugly."[83] Wilhelm II, however, regarded his creation as an artistic triumph, and he saw to it that both Begas and Uechtritz were chosen to decorate various public buildings in Berlin. One notably inflated contribution was Uechtritz's massive stone group *The Crown as Guarantor of Peace*, which stood at the entrance to the building housing the Prussian House of Lords. It was eclipsed by Begas's even more enormous bronze *Germania*, which crowned the portico of the Reichstag building.

Hohenzollern rulers, most notably Frederick the Great, had taken an active role in patronizing architecture, and their informed taste (or that of their advisers) had resulted in the erection in Berlin and Potsdam of a procession of elegant buildings. This tradition had come to an end with King Friedrich Wilhelm IV, who died in 1861, because his successor, Wilhelm II's grandfather, the King-Emperor Wilhelm I, had no interest in architecture and did not interfere with real estate speculators who defaced much of the city with shoddy, tasteless structures. Wilhelm II, however, was determined to revive the Hohenzollern role in architecture, and throughout his reign he intervened constantly in the design of public buildings erected or renovated by the Prussian government. He corrected drawings of post offices, churches, and other edifices, insisting that they be designed in various traditional styles, preferring a sort of modified Romanesque. Wilhelm also took great delight in restoration projects involving ancient Roman forts and medieval bastions.[84]

The last Kaiser's favorite architect was Ernst von Ihne, who in 1886 had designed the casino in Berlin for his Guards Hussar regiment and the Empress Friedrich's castle, Friedrichskron, in the Taunus Mountains, where she wiled away her last unhappy years. Ihne, whom Wilhelm ennobled in 1906, was an ambitious courtier who had some talent in designing houses for the Berlin plutocracy. Prince Fürstenberg, at Wilhelm's urging, hired him to renovate the castle at Donaueschingen. Ihne remodeled the Berlin palace, built the royal library and the Kaiser Friedrich museum of Renaissance art, and advised the Kaiser on many architectural projects. Next to

Ihne in royal favor came Ludwig Hoffmann, also a conventional drafts-man without much imagination but full of extravagant conceptions.[85] In architecture, as in painting, Wilhelm II had no comprehension that a fixed adherence to the canons of the past would petrify creativity. The younger generation of German architects, like their artistic colleagues in painting and sculpture, found such regressive ideas dispiriting.[86]

Sometimes even the traditionalists fell afoul of the Kaiser, especially if their handling of domes struck him as unfortunate, and Ihne himself had to watch his drawings suffer revisions by the imperial hand. This was also the fate of Paul Wallot, whose 1894 neoclassical Reichstag building failed to earn Wilhelm's approbation. The Kaiser declared, not entirely without justification, that Wallot's immense glass dome was the "pinnacle of taste-lessness."[87] Wilhelm did not like anything about buildings designed by the imaginative architects of the Secession, and the more stolid, brutalist mod-ernism of Alfred Messel, Berlin's leading architect, failed to excite him. The Kaiser agreed to let Messel, a Jew who was the favored architect of other Jews, design an enormous building on the "museum island" in the heart of Berlin, but this commission was awarded only at Bode's insis-tence.[88] When Messel died in the midst of this building program, the anodyne Hoffmann was brought in to complete the work, which was executed without much fidelity to the original plans. Wilhelm preferred, especially for churches, the Gothic or Romanesque styles served up by a number of traditionalist architects. The most prominent of these was Franz Schechter, who with some help from Wilhelm II designed Berlin's Kaiser Wilhelm Memorial Church at the head of the Kurfürstendamm.

One of Wilhelm II's major buildings, a straightforward and ordinary neoclassical pile, was the Berlin opera house, which — by the Kaiser's order — Hoffmann designed. This was to be the scene of much of the musical life of Berlin, which Wilhelm avidly followed. His tastes here were conventional, and as in painting and sculpture, he scorned almost every-thing that was modern. On ceremonial occasions the Kaiser liked to enter-tain his guests by devising a program that featured snippets from various operas. The preferred composers were, among others, Daniel Auber, Al-bert Lortzing (who got a commemorative statue in the Tiergarten), and Giacomo Meyerbeer, but Wilhelm also liked Georges Bizet's *Carmen*. Among living composers, the Kaiser admired Ruggiero Leoncavallo, from whom in 1904 he commissioned an opera, *The Roland of Berlin*.

Wilhelm wanted a stylish celebration for the inauguration of the Ro-land fountain in the midst of the Tiergarten, the hideous hydraulic night-mare the British envoy had condemned for its ugliness. By Wilhelm's instructions, *Roland* was freighted with contemporary political and social messages. The libretto dealt with a legendary ancestor of the Hohenzollerns who, as elector of Brandenburg, suppressed a revolution led by the citizens of Berlin. Wilhelm was generally pleased with the opera, but he required that the libretto be amended to eliminate the sovereign's mistress. "A courtesan," Wilhelm II declared, "has no place in a Hohenzollern drama."[89] Leoncavallo attended the premier, with his copious mustache waxed and upturned in imitation of his imperial patron, but the opera quickly vanished from the repertory and led to popular ridicule of both the Kaiser and the composer.

In a rare departure from his abhorrence of most things French, Wilhelm once received Camille Saint-Saëns and Jules Massenet in Berlin, both of whose operas he admired.[90] But for Richard Strauss, Germany's preeminent composer during his reign, Wilhelm had the greatest dislike. Although the Kaiser defended his patronage of the Italian Leoncavallo by declaring "the fact" that Germany did not have "any impressive composers," he had sanctioned Strauss's appointment in 1898 as the conductor of Berlin's new opera house. Wilhelm II liked the bombastic marches for huge orchestras that Strauss composed and dedicated to the Kaiser, but he viewed with dismay the composer's increasingly modernist dramas. "I raised a snake in the grass to bite me," he complained, leading to the composer's thereafter being called the "court viper" (*Hofbusenschlange*).[91] Wilhelm rudely told Strauss that "all modern music," because of its lack of discernible melody, was "worthless" and that among its lamentable practitioners, Strauss himself was the worst.[92] Except for one performance of *Der Rosenkavalier* — in which Hugo von Hofmannsthal's libretto had been altered to make Baron Ochs, the court chamberlain to the Empress Maria Theresa, less boorish — Wilhelm never attended a performance of any of Strauss's operas. About *Der Rosenkavalier* he could say only, "That's no music for me!"[93] In 1901, the Kaiserin graced a performance of *Feuersnot*, a peasant drama with erotic overtones. Midway through the opera, the scandalized empress, whose cultural discernment was minimal and even more antimodernist than that of her consort, rose in disapproval from her place in the royal loge and ostentatiously swept from the house. In spite of this mark of imperial disfavor, Strauss managed to keep his position at the opera throughout the remainder of Wilhelm's reign, but the Kaiser ordered that *Feuersnot* be forever banned from the repertory of the royal opera.[94]

Even Richard Wagner, who in Wilhelm's youth had been a favorite, gradually lost the Kaiser's allegiance. As a young man in the 1870s, Wilhelm had had a number of older friends who were passionate Wagnerians, and he soon developed a taste for Wagner's musical dramas. The Kaiser composed at least one musical composition in a Wagnerian style, and the piece, with the adornment of Philipp Eulenburg's libretto, was performed at court.[95] Having no knowledge of music, Wilhelm was incapable of fathoming Wagner's musical dramas, although he valued very highly the patriotic sentiments they evoked.[96] Eulenburg, who became Wilhelm's good friend in the mid-1880s, was close to Cosima Wagner, who after her husband's death in 1883 presided over the Wagner shrine at Bayreuth. In Eulenburg's company Wilhelm often visited Bayreuth, and Cosima asked him to assume its patronage. On Chancellor Bismarck's advice, the Kaiser declined the request in order not to offend the prince regent of Bavaria, in whose kingdom Bayreuth lay.

The Kaiser's enthusiasm for people was usually shallow and inconstant, and his infatuation with Wagner began to decline soon after he ascended the throne. "Gluck is the man for me; Wagner is too noisy," he declared.[97] This disenchantment was perhaps because Wilhelm's musical taste had become increasingly attached to strictly ordered martial music, with its steady beat and predictable rhythms. Except for *Die Meistersinger* (which remained an imperial favorite), there was not much of this in Wagner, for whose music, both Cosima and Eulenburg admitted, Wilhelm had little understanding. "The Kaiser is a very likable man," the master's widow declared, "but in order to clarify for him the basic principles of art I would have to spend three years alone with him on a deserted island."[98] It may be, as Bernhard von Bülow suggested, that Wilhelm II's abandonment of Wagner in about 1888 had to do with his mother. The Empress Frederick found the composer's anti-Semitism disgusting, and although she liked his music, she preferred Felix Mendelssohn. Wilhelm, always ready to challenge his mother and untroubled by the composer's racism, thereupon adopted Wagner with enthusiasm. Once her son became Kaiser, however, the widowed empress retreated from the scene, leaving Wilhelm free to drop Wagner.[99] Although there were several Wagnerians at the Berlin court, one notable anti-Wagnerian was Count Georg von Hülsen-Haeseler, who, as the intendant at the royal theater and opera, had considerable influence with the Kaiser.[100] By the turn of the century Wilhelm had developed a strong dislike for fare from Bayreuth, asking: "What do people see in this Wagner anyway? The chap [*Kerl*] is simply a conductor [*Kappelmeister*], nothing other than a conductor, an entirely commonplace conductor."[101] Although the Kaiser designed a monument commemorating Wagner and had it erected in the Tiergarten, eventually little survived of his once great admiration for the master besides the horn of his automobile, which sounded the thunder motif from *Das Rheingold*.[102]

Wilhelm had meanwhile migrated from operas to more popular forms of music. He liked to conduct military bands, to play the zither, and to listen to accordion music. The Kaiser took great pleasure in singing, and he occasionally composed songs and collected old army ballads. He encouraged folk chorals by establishing prizes and ordering the publication of songbooks that contained male choruses, based on German folk lieder, that Wilhelm had commanded Strauss to compose. He vainly imagined himself an expert in folksinging, insisting that traditional German songs — "*Ich hatt' einen Kamaraden*" was a favorite — be included in the repertory.[103]

Wilhelm II's taste for the theater, like his notions about other art forms, was both historic and moral, praising the Hohenzollerns and inculcating idealism in his subjects. Plays celebrating the past, he informed the great Russian dramaturge Konstantin Stanislavsky, were the only kind he enjoyed.[104] The royal theaters, the Kaiser declared, were to serve this purpose as "an instrument comparable to the schools and the universities."[105] Like painting or opera, the theater was to avoid the depressing routine of everyday life and instead transport the observer by depicting the heroic accomplishments of historic figures. "We should leave the theater not discouraged at the recollection of mournful scenes, of bitter disappointments," the Kaiser declared in 1902, "but purified, elevated, and with renewed strength to fight for the ideals which every man strives to realize. . . . Actual life makes it its duty to bring before our eyes day by day the most miserable realities. Our modern authors, who have ever more and more inclined to set this before our eyes on the stage, are setting themselves an unwholesome task, and producing work which cannot but have a depressing influence upon us."[106] For moral elevation the Kaiser liked Shakespeare's historical dramas; otherwise, few foreign playwrights appealed to him, although he did like Edmond Rostand's *Cyrano de Bergerac* and Victorien Sardou's *Madame Sans-Gêne*, a racy play that he was able to attend only when the sanctimonious Kaiserin was otherwise engaged.[107]

Among contemporary Germans, one dramatist who had a secure place at court was Joseph von Lauff, a major in the Prussian artillery who owed his patent of nobility to Wilhelm. He specialized in depictions, both dramatic and poetic, of historic events and had written the libretto for Leoncavallo's dreary *Roland of Berlin*.[108] Lauff rarely failed to extol the virtues of the Hohenzollerns, and Wilhelm was especially fond of *Der Burggraf*, which apostrophized a medieval Prussian ancestor, Rudolf, Duke of Swabia, and which, by the Kaiser's order, had a scenic backdrop executed by Professor Knackfuss. Although Lauff was sometimes referred to as Wilhelm's poet laureate, this title, at least in drama, belonged to Ernst von Wildenbruch, who more than any other writer enjoyed imperial favor.[109] Wildenbruch, the illegitimate descendant of a Hohenzollern prince and, like Wilhelm, an officer in the First Guards regiment in Potsdam in the 1880s, wrote patriotic poems on the Franco-Prussian War as well as historical plays that the Kaiser admired. Wildenbruch had considerable dramaturgical talent, but it was not always revealed in these pieces, few of which rose above mediocrity and some of which were embarrassingly banal. It was rumored that Wilhelm had cooperated with Wildenbruch in writing *Willehalm*, an allegory with a medieval setting intended to celebrate the rebirth of Germany as a result of Prussia's victory over France in 1870. The Kaiser ordered the play to premiere in 1897 as part of the ceremony marking the centenary of Kaiser Wilhelm I's birth. It proved to be a dramatic farrago that put his uncle, the Grand Duke of Saxe-Weimar, to sleep and that drove the head of the Foreign Office, Baron Marschall von Bieberstein, to vacate this "acme of nonsense" after the third act.[110] This was not only the first performance of *Willehalm* but also the last. Wildenbruch did not escape royal criticism, and several of his plays, which in the Kaiser's judgment contained undesirable situations, such as a prince being dominated by his wife, were kept off the stage altogether or were altered to Wilhelm's satisfaction. These revisions, however, did not always placate the sanctimonious Kaiserin, who on one occasion left the theater midway through one of Wildenbruch's dramas.[111]

The Kaiser's intendant at Berlin's Royal Theater beginning in 1903 was Count Hülsen-Haeseler, an anti-Wagnerian, amateur magician and a notorious groveler. Hülsen, who had known Wilhelm in childhood, for many years had presided over the Wiesbaden Royal Theater — the *Zirkus-Hülsen*, as one critic lampooned it — and specialized in staging productions of great pomp that delighted the Kaiser.[112] Like his brother Dietrich, the chief of the Military Cabinet, Georg was a surefooted courtier, and he suppressed his desire to produce plays that ran against Wilhelm II's antimodernist tastes. The Kaiser declared of his intendant: "I have in him a splendid man who understands my ideas and who has found means to translate them into reality. He is an indefatigable, creative, great, very great, artist."[113] This was an opinion not widely shared in Berlin, and the Royal Theater under Hülsen's management did not equal the reputation of a number of other stages in the capital.

The plays by Lauff and Wildenbruch that Wilhelm liked were often greeted with derision, and works that were genuinely popular encountered only opposition from the throne. The playwright Ferdinand Bonn, to whom the Kaiser referred to as a *Schweinehund*, was criticized by Wilhelm for having princesses fall in love with tradesmen or for including other violations of propriety.[114] The Kaiser's special bête noire was Germany's most talented dramatist, Gerhart Hauptmann, whom German Socialists regarded as their voice on the stage and who won a Nobel prize in 1912. Hauptmann's searing plays, which graphically depicted working-class deprivation and bureaucratic injustice, electrified Germany, but to Wilhelm they were not only personally disrespectful of his majesty but also depressingly rooted in the dreariness of the life of the poor, the very sort of subject matter he condemned to be as inappropriate for the stage as for works of art.[115] The Kaiser was powerless to stem Hauptmann's popularity and was reduced to malicious gestures such as setting aside the award of the prestigious Schiller prize and giving it to Wildenbruch, thereby provoking a national scandal.[116]

Wilhelm II's fusty, conventional tastes in the arts could hardly substantiate his claim that he was a Florentine Medici moved north to the banks of the Spree. To his subjects, he was clearly a man who neither understood nor approved of anything that was novel or progressive and who imposed the thralldom of tradition on all forms of artistic expression, insofar as they were subject to state supervision. Yet the Kaiser tirelessly proclaimed that in all matters related to the arts, he was a genius whom his subjects should faithfully follow. Few Germans believed that, and indeed the longer Wilhelm II ruled, the more suspicions abounded that this was a man deficient not only in taste but, much more troubling, in intellect as well.

Three

REASON AND RELIGION

WILHELM II, although never a distinguished student and without any professional training except in military affairs, was a man who, even his most stringent critics admitted, possessed considerable intelligence. The two qualities that were most frequently commented on, often with considerable amazement, were the swiftness with which he could grasp a problem and his truly astounding memory.[1] The Kaiser could recite extended passages from favorite books verbatim and toss about complicated numbers with ease, and on a staggering number of issues Wilhelm could buttress his opinions with facts and figures. Unfortunately, those who were impressed also had reservations as to how deep and consequential this babble of information was, for all too often Wilhelm's knowledge, like his enthusiasms, proved to be superficial and flimsy. The Kaiser tended to confuse the possession of facts with the mastery of a subject.[2] He was therefore dismissive of experts who labored in a field in which he falsely believed that he possessed uncommon ability. No one suffered from this hubris more than the Kaiser's ambassadors, for Wilhelm II believed that he was Germany's quintessential representative abroad. "You diplomats are full of shit," he magisterially informed one of his envoys. In a reference to the location of the German Foreign Office, he added, "The whole Wilhelmstrasse stinks."[3]

Wilhelm's intelligence did nothing to endow him with discernment in intellectual affairs, where he displayed the same dilettantism, the same delusions of genius, and the same essential vacuity that characterized his knowledge about the arts. Talk, enthusiastic but uninformed, was what he liked and was the means through which he both absorbed and disseminated his opinions. Although he intruded himself into many areas of learning, he had no real understanding of any of them. The Kaiser might have been more adept in such matters had he liked books more, but reading was something he could do only fitfully. Wilhelm's librarian testified that he rarely appeared in the palace book room, where in any case there were few volumes to be consulted.[4] The books that Wilhelm himself wrote hardly promote his reputation as an intellect, for they were all replete with errors and trusted ghostwriters were often the true authors.[5]

What the Kaiser did read changed very little in the course of his life. His claim to familiarity with Georg Hegel and Johann Fichte as "bedside reading" and to a similar grounding in Johann Goethe seems highly improbable. Wilhelm did know *Faust*, but he did not care for the doctor's character or for the piece in general.[6] What he preferred were adventure novels and stories by British and American writers, particularly Rudyard Kipling, Mark Twain, Bret Harte, Charles Dickens, Sir Walter Scott, and especially Frederick Marryat. There were also some German novels on the Kaiser's shelf and a number in French, but nothing by Émile Zola, whom he greatly disliked, undoubtedly because the author dealt sympathetically with the misery of working-class life. Georges Ohnet, who wrote an immensely popular "Les Batailles de la Vie" series of romantic novels, and Jules Verne were more to his taste.[7] History held considerable interest for the Kaiser, especially accounts of the military glories of Frederick the Great and his other illustrious kinsmen. In youth, the fiery historian Heinrich von Treitschke had influenced Wilhelm, but in later years Treitschke, like the great Heinrich von Sybel, failed — in the Kaiser's opinion — to adopt a properly reverential tone toward the Hohenzollerns, and the historian fell from grace. Thereafter, his two preferred chroniclers were Heinrich Schiemann and Reinhold Koser, both lesser talents. Schiemann, who strenuously courted the Kaiser and whose reward was to be taken on many sailing trips, was more polemical journalist than historian and was a dedicated Russophobe.[8] Koser wrote a properly adulatory biography of Frederick the Great and assisted Wilhelm in the historical details of the *Siegesallée* statuary groups. Wilhelm eventually appointed him to be general director of the Prussian State Archives and historiographer of the Prussian state.[9]

As an adult, Wilhelm concentrated his intellectual activity on two fields, archaeology and religion. His interest in the former began at boarding school in Cassel in 1874 and continued steadfastly until his death almost seventy years later. Like Wilhelm's concern with religion (and with warships), it was one of the few constant enthusiasms of his long life. In Germany, the Kaiser took a special interest in the excavation and rebuilding of the Roman frontier post on the Saalburg near Homburg vor der Höhe, a favorite resort in the Hessian countryside. The fort was in ruins when, in 1897, Wilhelm funded its reconstruction and secured the service of Theodor Mommsen, the famous historian of ancient Rome.[10] Wilhelm's frequent travels abroad provided him an opportunity to deepen this interest, and German archaeological museums were the richer for his gifts to their collections. He knew Rome, Pompeii, and Baalbek firsthand and avidly followed the expeditions of excavators in many parts of the world, especially in the Near East. He was often kept up-to-date by the great classicist Ulrich von Wilamowitz-Möllendorff and the distinguished archaeologist Wilhelm Dörpfeld.[11] Wilhelm's most beloved dig was on the Greek island of Corfu, where in 1907 he purchased the Achilleion, a hillside villa that had been the property of the Habsburg Empress Elisabeth, who had been murdered by an Italian anarchist nine years earlier. He made a number of alterations, including removing a statue of the great German-Jewish lyricist Heinrich Heine. Almost every summer the Kaiser spent several weeks on the island, supervising the diggings with more relish than discrimination and unrealistically expecting everyone else to share his passion.[12] He found particularly entrancing the remnants of a bas-relief that he believed to be a likeness of one of the Gorgons, the three women of Greek mythology whose very glance could turn men to stone. After Wilhelm sailed away, the excavation sites would be closed and then — according to Alfred von Kiderlen-Wächter, a sardonic diplomat who was in the royal party traveling to Greece and whose malice would make the story somewhat improbable were it not corroborated elsewhere — restocked with fragments garnered elsewhere so that the Kaiser could make further "discoveries" on his next visit to Corfu.[13]

Much of the Kaiser's interest in archaeology was connected to his fascination with religion, especially with the origins of Christianity. Although Wilhelm, under Philipp Eulenburg's influence, toyed briefly with spiritualism in the 1880s, his religious inclinations somewhat uneasily combined his father's unquestioning allegiance to Protestant Christianity and his mother's inclination toward theological speculation.[14] All his life Wilhelm had a great interest in dogmatic debate, but the Kaiserin Augusta Victoria, a true fanatic, was dead set against any sort of innovation in religious belief, an attitude that annoyed her husband. Unlike his wife, Wilhelm believed that religious thought could not be permitted to become ossified but rather had to move forward, even in the face of the "dogmatic trash" peddled by clerics, so that faith and reason could be reconciled.[15] Although husband and wife differed in their religious views, they shared a conviction that Christianity was a revealed truth that churchgoing and devotional reading should nurture. Night after night, Dona and Wilhelm's courtiers had to listen to his reading from biblical passages or sermons, and no Sunday passed without the court being summoned to worship. The royal couple were united in imposing on their children a rigid Christian upbringing, one that seemed, at least to their eldest son, excessive and that apparently ensured that he, like his siblings, would never share the intense religious convictions, however differently expressed, of his parents.[16]

To Wilhelm II, Christianity was more than a belief that led to the redemption of sin and the promise of eternal life. It also served in this world as an antidote to materialism and political radicalism. He was convinced that religion, if properly marshaled, could combat Socialist propaganda and liberalism, inculcate youth in the proper values, and imbue German soldiers with an invincible spirit.[17] "Only a good Christian," the Kaiser often proclaimed, "can be a good soldier." He was dismayed that writers and artists too often portrayed Jesus as a pallidly feminine figure, when in fact Christ's real nature was manly. So too was the character of the devil, and Wilhelm preferred John Milton's heroic Satan in *Paradise Lost* to the weaker figure in Goethe's *Faust*.[18] For the Kaiser, there was a martial quality about Christianity that led him to refer to God as Prussia's "ancient ally" in its many victories and to compare the confirmation ceremony for his sons to a soldier's taking the oath of loyalty to his king.[19]

This viewpoint was a reflection of the Kaiser's belief in the simple and natural connection between Christianity and the throne. Wilhelm unhesitatingly believed that God had entrusted to the house of Hohenzollern a mission that set it above all other Germans. In the late summer of 1897 he went to Koblenz to unveil the monumental statue of his beloved grandfather Wilhelm I, high on a pedestal overlooking the "German corner" (*deutsches Eck*) at the confluence of the Mosel and the Rhine. The Kaiser declared that his grandfather had been entrusted with a "mighty treasure, kingship by the grace of God" (*ein herrliches Kleinod . . . das Königthum von Gottes Gnaden*), one that he himself was now struggling to uphold. Wilhelm was convinced that God had conveyed this responsibility to him and that therefore he was beholden to no man, or people, or parliament. He declared that he must go his way, regarding himself "as the instrument of God, without concern for the notions or views of the moment."[20] Wilhelm believed that, being delivered from error by grace, he was a rock of virtue and righteousness. "I have myself been trying all my life," he wrote in English to an Anglican bishop in 1906, "to adapt, nay, to reconcile modern life with its numerous intricacies and sometimes superhuman tasks to the words and exhortations of the Savior and His apostles. It is by no means easy, but yet most fascinating and interesting. Often moments came when in a dilemma of choice I was at a loss how to act, and fell back on His admonitions. I chose His side. . . . The conviction of having done right, of having *a good conscience* and thereby feeling Him on your side, also in distress, what a staff to lean upon!"[21] Wilhelm informed Tsar Nicholas II in 1895 that Christian rulers shared in a duty "to uphold the principle of divine right" and that he had only contempt for sovereigns who would not subscribe to this godly command. "I cannot respect a monarch," he told Leopold II of the Belgians, no slouch with respect to despotism but not a claimant to royal divinity, "who feels responsible to deputies and ministers rather than exclusively to our father in heaven."[22] Although the British sovereign was a constitutional monarch, this unfortunate state, according to Wilhelm's inscrutable logic, was nullified by the ruler's being a Protestant Teuton, and Queen Victoria and her descendants were therefore qualified for enlistment into the great work of saving the world from error.[23]

The Kaiser's personal piety and theological inquisitiveness brought him into contact with many of the religious leaders of his day, with some of whom he had brief but close relationships. Ernst von Dryander, whom Wilhelm had known since his university days and who became chief court preacher (*Oberhofprediger*) in 1897, was for the rest of Wilhelm's reign the leading religious figure at court. Although the Kaiser praised Dryander as a wise and informed cleric, one who emphasized the human qualities of Jesus rather than dry dogmatics, the pastor was in fact theologically quite conventional. Dryander, however, excelled in both conversation and preaching, careful in both to make himself agreeable to the Kaiser. Under Dryander's long tenure, the royal pulpit was not a place from which Wilhelm heard anything that would disturb his religious views.[24]

Equally conventional was another clerical friend, William Boyd Carpenter, the Anglican bishop of Ripon in Yorkshire, who found favor with Wilhelm because he urged Christians to look at Jesus in a more human, psychological light. Boyd Carpenter, who was a good friend of Wilhelm's mother and who delivered her funeral oration in 1901, became acquainted with the Kaiser in the course of Wilhelm's frequent trips to England. The bishop had an eloquent homiletic style and wrote many popular religious books of an intellectually undemanding content. To Wilhelm, Boyd Carpenter's merit was that, in contrast to most German theologians, he was a practical man who could write about Christ in terms that avoided both gooey devotionalism and rigid dogmatism.[25] The Kaiser saw to it that Boyd Carpenter's books, with introductions by Dryander, were translated into German and distributed to university theological faculties and to Wilhelm's friends and family. The Kaiser liked to read the bishop's sermons to his wife and their entourage and recommended Boyd Carpenter's books to those who shared his interest in religion.[26] The bishop and the emperor had in common a conviction that the destiny of the world rested properly in the hands of the Teutonic races, for the other tribes of humankind were either pagan or, if Christian, pitiably degenerate.[27]

A rival of Dryander and Boyd Carpenter in their solicitude for the Kaiser but theologically an entirely different man was the famous biblical scholar Adolf von Harnack, whom Wilhelm, with the encouragement of his childhood tutor Georg Hinzpeter but over objections from church authorities, had appointed professor of ecclesiastical history at Berlin in 1888. In a series of powerful books, Harnack had developed the view that Christ was properly to be understood as a figure in history and that most ecclesiastical dogmas, including the belief that the Bible was infallible, must be rejected. Christianity needed to return to its historical roots and jettison the centuries of ceremonial and doctrinal glosses that had obscured the true and eternal Savior. Harnack's ideas produced consternation in orthodox circles, where there were whispers that he had denied the divinity of Christ. The Kaiserin, always a foe of any sort of religious novelty, did not at first care for Harnack, though she approved of his support for the education of women. Wilhelm, however, delighted in his new professor. "What a personality Harnack is," he proclaimed, "what usefulness and how much knowledge has come to me through my contact with this dynamic mind."[28] The Kaiser's only reservation was that Harnack, who thrived on controversy and publicity, was inclined to take extreme theological positions, such as his tendency to consider Christianity as only one of many "myths" that had emerged from man's psychological need for forgiveness and salvation, instead of acknowledging the unique revelation vouchsafed to man in Jesus Christ.[29] Harnack, who found the Kaiser intelligent but also too narrowly dogmatic, was replete with courtly gestures and easily ingratiated himself with Wilhelm, who in 1905 made him director of the Royal Library and nine years later raised him into the hereditary nobility.[30]

The historical dimension in Harnack's religious ideas and his assault on conventional wisdom appealed to Wilhelm, who liked theological speculation especially if it touched on early Christianity. For this reason, the Kaiser felt a strong attraction to Houston Stewart Chamberlain's cyclopean work *The Foundations of the Nineteenth Century* (1899), which argued, with inelegant prolixity, that Western culture had developed from the competition of distinct races, with each historical era being the creation of the dominant tribe. Nineteenth-century Europe owed its form to Hellenic culture, the universal dominion of the Roman Empire, and the "chaos of peoples" (*Völkerchaos*) that had resulted from its fall.

Through all of this, the Jewish race had exercised a negative influence, introducing its own alien ideas and corrupting not only Greco-Roman civilization but also, with its legalistic aridity, the conception of Christ. The hour was at hand, Chamberlain prophesied in his jumble of pseudo-intellectual pretension, for the Teutonic race, under the Germans and their king-emperor, to restore the Roman Empire and to purge Christianity of the baleful influence of the Jews.[31]

Infused by Chamberlain's "great hymn to the Germans" with an even greater sense of Christian duty, the Kaiser declared with typical exaggeration that *Foundations* was "the greatest and most meaningful work" ever written and was "so valuable that every word should be stamped in gold."[32] Chamberlain's view that race constituted the dominant force in history was, so the Kaiser in 1911 assured the British prime minister, Herbert H. Asquith, "a new Gospel."[33] Not long after devouring Chamberlain's work and memorizing long passages from it, Wilhelm began to read excerpts to his wife and courtiers, some of whom did not share his enthusiasm and drifted off to sleep. The Kaiser's friend Eulenburg, who knew Chamberlain and also admired his works, arranged in October 1901 for him to come to Eulenburg's estate at Liebenberg, where Wilhelm would be hunting.[34] Although the military entourage was not pleased that a civilian writer (who was an Englishman to boot) had been invited, the Kaiser effusively greeted the guest by saying, "I thank you especially for what you have done for Germany."[35]

Harnack, who joined the party at Liebenberg, could not endorse Chamberlain's adulation for the Aryan race or his pronounced distaste for the Jews, even though Harnack agreed with Chamberlain that the Old Testament had to be cleansed of harmful rabbinical influences. Wilhelm's sympathies were clearly with Chamberlain, and he forced the reluctant but ever courtly Harnack to acknowledge that *Foundations* contained a number of compelling arguments.[36] When the hunt was over, the Kaiser insisted that Chamberlain accompany him to Potsdam, where he was presented to the Kaiserin, who was suitably impressed. For the next decade, Wilhelm saw Chamberlain only once, but he corresponded with him frequently, valuing their intellectual companionship and their mutual disdain for the worship of mammon that characterized Anglo-Saxon culture. After a rash of impassioned letters, however, the Kaiser's communications became brief and ceremonial.[37] He praised Chamberlain for illuminating with "magic blows" (*Zauberschläge*) how the destiny of the Aryan Germans would be to captain the "moral world order" that the Kaiser had spoken of at their meeting at Liebenberg. Wilhelm quickly put his friendship with Chamberlain to use, incorporating passages from *Foundations* into his speeches and expressing a hope that the author's fervent German nationalism might promote a higher level of patriotism in German Catholics, who unhappily had succumbed to the "deathly power of 'ubiquitous' Rome."[38]

Chamberlain's diatribes against the Jews were welcome to Wilhelm, for they confirmed his own curious but well-developed anti-Semitism, one the aristocratic-military environment in which he lived did much to encourage.[39] Not long after Wilhelm came to the throne in 1888, his friend General Count Alfred von Waldersee, an ardent foe of the Jews, declared that the young Kaiser's dislike of his Hebrew subjects, one rooted in a perception that they possessed an overweening influence in Germany, was so strong that it could not be overcome.[40] Wilhelm never changed, and throughout his life he believed that Jews were perversely responsible, largely through their prominence in the Berlin press and in leftist political movements, for encouraging opposition to his rule.[41] For individual Jews, ranging from rich businessmen and major art collectors to purveyors of elegant goods in Berlin stores, he had considerable esteem, but he prevented Jewish citizens from having careers in the army and the diplomatic corps and frequently used abusive language against them.[42] The Kaiser's diatribes against the Jews, even if they were only flights of loose rhetoric, are unsettling to read. "The Jews are the curse of my country," he declared in a typical peroration. "They keep my people poor and in their clutches. In every small village in Germany sits a dirty Jew, like a spider drawing the people into the web of usury . . . [and] gradually gains control of everything. The Jews are the parasites of my Empire."[43] Although the Hebrews numbered only about 1 percent of the German population, the Kaiser felt they were entirely too numerous. He informed the British Foreign Secretary Sir Edward Grey in 1907, "They want stamping out."[44]

In January 1903, Wilhelm, Augusta Victoria, Dryander, and various members of the retinue heard two addresses, "Bible and Babel," by Friedrich Delitzsch, Germany's most distinguished Assyriologist. In his remarks, which produced an uproar among European theologians, Delitzsch passionately argued that Assyrian religious literature antedated the Bible, which was in many respects linked to this earlier writing and which was also a cultural document illustrative of humankind's search for God.[45] To hold, as Christian dogma did, that Jesus Christ was a singular figure of divine revelation was, to Delitzsch, a view that was parochial and narrow, the vain invention of the Jews. Delitzsch implied, although he denied that he had said so outright, that the belief that Christ was the Son of God was incapable of being rationally sustained. The Kaiserin's pious court ladies immediately cornered the professor and berated him for his heretical notions.[46]

Wilhelm was also annoyed. Christians were Jews, but according to the Kaiser, the Jewish religion did not come from the Babylonians but from Abraham, whom he considered to be neither a Jew nor an Israelite but a "monotheistic Semite." The concept of grace and redemption was neither Jewish nor, as Delitzsch argued, Babylonian but instead was Indian in origin.[47] A few weeks after hearing Delitzsch's lectures, the Kaiser, determined to refute the professor, wrote an unusually long letter, soon thereafter published, to his old acquaintance Admiral Friedrich Hollmann, president of the German Oriental Society, to which Wilhelm awarded a handsome annual subvention.[48] In a mélange of historical and theological obfuscation, Wilhelm informed Hollmann that there were two sorts of revelation that God had vouchsafed his people. One consisted of the prophets, the psalmists (the very figures whose preaching Delitzsch had tried to reduce to mere mythology), and Christ Himself. The other revelation, a view already expounded by Harnack, proceeded through sages, priests, and kings — pagan, Jewish, and Christian. To Wilhelm, this stream included, among others, Abraham, Homer, Charlemagne, Luther, Shakespeare, and Goethe, to whose august company he added his grandfather, Kaiser Wilhelm I, all elected by God's grace to lead their peoples. The divinity of kings, which Wilhelm believed in so ardently, was thus part of a wider revelation that God had provided to humankind. Religion, like German art, was to support the Hohenzollern monarchy and, again like art, was not to stray into dangerous modern currents, such as those proposed by Delitzsch. "Religion," he assured Admiral Hollmann, "was never the fruit of scholarship but rather an emanation of the heart and being of humankind through its communion with God." So it was for the Kaiser, whose own attachment to religion was essentially emotional and not, in spite of all his superficial concern for theology, intellectual. Harnack, with untypical frankness, made the mistake of agreeing with Delitzsch, and thereafter Wilhelm no longer consulted him on theological matters.[49]

The arts, archaeology, and religion were the Kaiser's principal interests, but he had other numerous, if undeveloped, enthusiasms that brought him into contact with various members of the German intelligentsia — university professors, museum directors, and writers, to some of whom he awarded orders and decorations.[50] He succeeded in establishing close relations only with very few of these men, a failure his good friend Eulenburg thought was due to the Kaiser's uncomfortable recognition that they were wiser than he. This was a difficult realization for Wilhelm to accept, since he liked to imagine himself the smartest man in any group of which he was a part.[51] One of the Kaiser's favorites was the stately Konrad von Studt, Prussian minister of culture from 1899 to 1907. Studt was a decorous cipher, ridiculed as the "minister of good appearances," but Wilhelm declared that Studt was in fact his best cabinet official. Since Studt was a nullity, his assistant, the dictatorial *Ministerialdirektor* professor Dr. Friedrich Althoff, became the guiding force in university matters.[52] The jovial and energetic Althoff soon won Wilhelm's consent to the extraordinary expansion of the Prussian system of higher education, as well as to the institution of professorial exchanges with Harvard and Columbia Universities.

Although Althoff was conservative in his political views and Caesarean in manner, he believed that freedom of expression was a prerequisite for academic distinction. On this point he often ran up against Wilhelm's detestation of socialism or indeed of opposition from any quarter. "I will tolerate no socialist among my officials," the Kaiser warned Althoff in 1897, "and certainly not among the teachers of our youth in the royal universities."[53] Wilhelm would not allow Althoff's friend, the distinguished economist Gustav von Schmoller, to become head of the Prussian State Archives because of his Socialist sympathies; even professors who were not bona fide Socialists or sympathizers with the movement but who simply dared to challenge the Kaiser's policies might find themselves summoned before a court of law.[54] Hans Delbrück, a Reichstag deputy, professor of history at Berlin, and editor of the *Preussisches Jahrbuch*, a periodical that was both scholarly and polemical, was brought to trial at the Kaiser's order, convicted, and fined for printing articles critical of the policy of Germanization being carried out in Polish areas of eastern Prussia and among the Danes in Schleswig.[55] What Wilhelm II preferred were docile, compliant teachers, such as the distinguished physiologist and rector of the University of Berlin, Emil Du Bois-Reymond, who proudly declared that his faculty members were "the spiritual bodyguard of the Hohenzollerns."[56]

The applied sciences appealed greatly to Wilhelm, who in 1902 declared, "The new century will be ruled by science, including technology, and not by philosophy as was its predecessor."[57] Eulenburg once observed that the Kaiser valued no one higher than an inventor whose discovery led to the laying down of a fortune, but those whom he singled out for attention — for example, the inventor of the X-ray, Wilhelm Roentgen, or the aircraft pioneer Count Ferdinand von Zeppelin — made no money from their inventions.[58] The Kaiser often referred to himself as a "modern man," a reference to his interest in discovery and invention. This enthusiasm was quite real, but it was paradoxical to contemporaries, since in Wilhelm II it was allied with a determination to impose an antediluvian autocracy on Germany.[59] The Kaiser never mastered the theoretical knowledge on which science and technology depended but rather was obsessed with the size and power of machines. He imagined himself to be a sound marine architect, and he did possess a facile hand for drawing warships. These romantic exercises abounded in artistry but were so bereft of technical expertise that had they been built, the Kaiser's majestic vessels would have capsized and sunk.[60]

Wilhelm paid marked attention to technical education and in 1892 decreed that professors in *Technische Hochschulen* were to have the same rank as those in universities. Althoff was active in encouraging the Kaiser's interest in science and worked out a plan at the turn of the century whereby a number of scientific research institutes, as envisioned when the university had been established in Berlin in 1810, would be created under crown patronage but paid for by private contributions. These would be located on the vacant royal domain at Dahlem, a suburb to the west of Berlin, which would thereby become "a German Oxford."[61] Althoff, who was nearly seventy, resigned in 1907, but Professor Harnack and Friedrich Schmidt-Ott, the latter a friend of Wilhelm's since their school days together at Cassel in the 1870s, continued the work of organizing the venture and raising the necessary funds. Late in 1909, Harnack presented to the Kaiser the final plan, one that stressed the danger of Germany's falling behind the other powers in technology. Scientific progress, the polished professor argued in a vein sure to appeal to Wilhelm II, was, like military preparedness, an aspect of national self-esteem.[62] The Kaiser enthusiastically agreed and set aside forty acres of the Hohenzollern forests to accommodate the buildings that would be required. On 11 October 1910, a date that marked the centenary of the founding of the University of Berlin, Wilhelm ceremoniously announced the establishment of the Kaiser Wilhelm Society for the Promotion of the Sciences (*Kaiser Wilhelm Gesellschaft zur Förderung der Wissenschaften*). Wilhelm's sponsorship of the society was a vital factor in its establishment, but once the society had been formed, his role was confined to insignificant details, such as the design of the ceremonial chain that Harnack, whom he appointed president, was to wear and of the insignia for other dignitaries. The Kaiser rarely came to meetings or took any part in deliberations.[63] The society, whose research institute for chemistry was the first to open in 1912 in a building designed at Wilhelm's order by Ernst von Ihne, steadily expanded to cover many branches of science.

The Kaiser's artistic and intellectual enthusiasms, swiftly formed and often changing, rested not on deep study but on his momentary impressions and prejudices. He would not gladly read documents or even newspapers, both of which had to be fed to him in excerpts. Inconstant, impatient, contradictory, and instantaneous in judgment, Wilhelm displayed intellectual abilities that were, for practical purposes, barren. His profligate mind was sometimes described as a Hohenzollern trait or was put down to Dr. Hinzpeter's unfortunate direction of his early schooling, but as the Kaiser grew older there was increasing speculation that his peculiarities were due to some form of mental abnormality.[64] From his early childhood, Wilhelm had been temperamental, but his mother, usually swift to criticize her eldest child, did not detect any disturbing traits in the boy. As he matured, however, it gradually became apparent that the prince had a difficult temper. If Wilhelm lost at tennis, he would fling his racket, and he spoke nastily to or about people (or countries, notably England) who had annoyed him, sometimes so recklessly that his courtiers nearly came to blows with him. Servants in the palace on occasion refused to wait on the Kaiser because of his rages, and on a higher plane, his fury could reduce military stalwarts to tears.[65] While these excesses were known to only a few men and women at court, there were other, more publicly recognized indications that Wilhelm had an exceptionally nervous constitution. His relentless traveling, his occasional facial tics, the bombastic utterances that his officials had to denature for publication to avoid giving offense, his utter inability to concentrate on affairs of state, and the constant contradictions and vacillations of the imperial mood were all signs that the Kaiser, as his tutor Hinzpeter had long ago observed, had a soul like that of no other mortal.[66]

By the time Wilhelm succeeded to the throne in 1888, the first murmurs were beginning to surface among his subjects as well as foreigners that he was mentally unstable and perhaps even insane.[67] The Kaiser's eccentric behavior provided copious material for speculation on this theme, including the dark prospect that his unbalanced mental state was congenital, a fatal inheritance from both his maternal and his paternal lines. The Hohenzollerns had produced, among a number of curiosities, King Friedrich Wilhelm IV, who had ruled Prussia ineffectively from 1840 to 1861. The king was a discriminating patron of the arts, and the face of Berlin in Wilhelm II's day owed much to his predecessor's sound architectural taste. This was, unhappily, almost the only intellectual virtue that Friedrich

Wilhelm possessed. He believed unquestioningly in the divine right of kings and consequently treated his ministers with autocratic disdain. Although the king thought himself to be a person of genius, he was in fact notoriously inconstant in his views and preferred military parades, court ceremonial, and traveling to the hard work of ruling. These traits produced resentment in the king's ministers and consternation in his subjects, but Friedrich Wilhelm did as he pleased until the late 1850s, when apoplexy deprived him of his reason. A regency was created under his brother, Prince Wilhelm, who succeeded as Wilhelm I in January 1861, when the king, now completely insane, finally died.

Wilhelm II was only a collateral kinsman of the demented sovereign, the cause of whose insanity was vascular rather than psychotic, but the fact that both were Hohenzollerns and had quite similar dispositions produced a spate of comparisons. It is significant that some of these proceeded from people, such as Chancellor Otto von Bismarck and General Waldersee, who knew Wilhelm intimately and who also had been acquainted with the deceased ruler.[68] The unhappy strain in the Hohenzollern tree received a telling confirmation in 1894 with the publication of the fifth volume of Heinrich von Treitschke's *German History*, which contained a devastating indictment of King Friedrich Wilhelm IV's pretensions and incompetence. Treitschke's portrait of the long-dead king immediately struck contemporaries as an unmistakable and deliberate caricature of Wilhelm II. Treitschke apparently intended to give just that impression, for he thought little of the young Kaiser's political or diplomatic talents and considered him to be in fact intellectually inferior to his insane predecessor.[69] Equally negative was another work that also appeared in 1894, a pamphlet by Ludwig Quidde entitled *Caligula: A Study in Caesarian Neurosis*, in which Wilhelm, although not by name, was compared to the lunatic Roman emperor.[70] No rebuttal of either of these very popular works was attempted.

Although Friedrich Wilhelm IV was not Wilhelm's forefather, the Kaiser's descent through his grandmother, the Empress Augusta, consort of Wilhelm I, contained an ancestral figure who was cause for alarm. The Empress, a granddaughter of Tsar Paul of Russia, had a notoriously inflammable temper, a trait some of her friends thought was due of her Romanov blood.[71] The disturbed tsar had been a megalomaniac whose visions of world empire and whose insistence on a degree of tyranny excessive even in Russia had so alarmed his courtiers that in 1801 they murdered him. Although Wilhelm II never displayed the cruelty that disfigured his ancestor, he shared some of the tsar's wayward autocratic manner, and the unfortunate similarity between the two rulers was not lost on the Kaiser's contemporaries, including Wilhelm's own mother and Otto von Bismarck.[72] Another great-great-grandfather, George III of England, was the victim of a blood disorder and died insane in 1820. Some of Wilhelm's acquaintances drew a comparison to the sadly demented British ruler.[73]

By the 1890s, the concern in Germany that the empire was in the hands of a ruler who was perhaps not mentally normal acquired a certain immediacy because of a contemporary psychotic to whom comparisons to the Kaiser were ominously drawn. This was Ludwig II, king of Bavaria from 1864 to 1886, whose Prussian mother was a first cousin of Wilhelm's grandfather, Kaiser Wilhelm I. Ludwig II suffered from fantastic delusions, which were vividly manifested in the many romantic palaces he built. Exceedingly restless in disposition and imbued with an obsessive adulation of the autocratic "Sun King," Louis XIV of France, Ludwig was eventually declared insane and, after dying by his own hand in 1886, was succeeded by his even madder brother Otto. The luckless Bavarians, many of whom disliked the Hohenzollerns and had a particular distaste for Wilhelm II, were swift to point out how similar the Kaiser's regal pretensions were to the Francophile absolutism of their late sovereign.[74] These comparisons could also be heard in Berlin, where the Kaiser's imperious airs and ambitious building projects seemed to have unfortunate Wittelsbachian overtones. So widespread were the parallels being drawn that Friedrich von Holstein, the éminence grise of the Foreign Office in Berlin, in 1894 warned Wilhelm's friend Philipp Eulenburg that the unfavorable commentary could not "go on like this much longer."[75]

By the early 1890s, the discussion of the Kaiser's mental incapacity had become widespread, and even in Wilhelm's family there were those who questioned whether he was right in his head.[76] The Empress Frederick noted that her son resembled not only the mad Tsar Paul but also Friedrich Wilhelm IV, whom she had known. Wilhelm's sister Charlotte, unlike her mother, did not specify the source of her sibling's malady but indicated a similar conclusion by tapping her head when her brother's mental state was mentioned.[77] Among the Kaiser's English relatives, the two who knew him best, Queen Victoria and the Prince of Wales, were both sure that he was not quite lucid. The queen wrote as early as 1888 about her grandson's "very unhealthy and unnatural state of mind," while the prince adopted his niece Charlotte's gesture of a rap to the forehead to indicate his view on the subject.[78] Among the royal cousinage of Europe, there were many whisperings that something was amiss in the throne in Berlin. The Grand Duke of Baden, Wilhelm's uncle by marriage who usually took an indulgent view of his nephew, expressed concern that the Kaiser's excessive nervousness was likely the prelude to a serious debility, and a brother-in-law, the Duke of Saxe-Meiningen, also had misgivings about Wilhelm's mental state.[79] To Nicholas II of Russia, distant in kinship but often thrown with the Kaiser, "Willie" was "raving mad."[80]

In Berlin there were many prominent figures — among them Chancellor Chlodwig Hohenlohe, Holstein, Admiral Alfred von Tirpitz, Eulenburg, and Ambassador Adolf Marschall von Bieberstein, all of whom except Holstein knew Wilhelm quite well, along with various parliamentary deputies and diplomatic officials — who expressed varying degrees of concern about the Kaiser's emotional condition.[81] Nor was Wilhelm's peculiar manner lost on foreign observers, especially the British. The British ambassador, Sir Frank Lascelles, writing from Berlin in 1901, advised London that the Kaiser's overstrung nerves should be regarded as a "very serious factor in all our calculations," and a few years later the perceptive British minister at Munich, Sir Fairfax Cartwright, tendered the same advice.[82] Lord Salisbury, prime minister during most of the first half of Wilhelm II's reign, believed the Kaiser to be very odd, and like Wilhelm's relatives, Salisbury put a finger to his head to signify this conviction. One of Salisbury's successors, Herbert H. Asquith, as well as Asquith's foreign secretary, Sir Edward Grey, shared this concern. Various continental statesmen or diplomats who knew Wilhelm II reasonably well were also troubled. President William Howard Taft never met the Kaiser but believed that he was a megalomaniac, an opinion shared by Taft's predecessor, Theodore Roosevelt, who had been accorded an audience in Berlin.[83]

These declarations that Wilhelm II was of unsound mind came from men who were not versed in the medical analysis of abnormal behavior, and some had grudges or differences with the Kaiser that may have colored their judgment. But the frequency of comments on Wilhelm's bizarre behavior and putative insanity and the similarity of the descriptions of his extreme nervousness indicate that these observers, whatever their animus against the Kaiser, were not off the mark. It is, moreover, instructive to note that the portrait of Wilhelm's psychosis given by those whose dealings with him were social or political corresponds quite closely with the judgment of men who did not know the Kaiser at all but who analyzed his public behavior in light of their professional expertise in disorders of the mind.

As a child, Wilhelm had frequently suffered from colds, earaches, and lack of appetite. These problems were eventually overcome, with the exception of his ear complaint, a condition known as otitis, which afflicted him until he was well into his forties. Any prolonged illness involving the ear created anxiety about the spread of disease to the brain, and in the mid-1870s, when Wilhelm was in his teens, an unknown German physician declared that the ailing prince would always be susceptible to "sudden accesses of anger" that would prevent his "forming a reasonable or temperate judgment." The doctor's prognosis was that "while it was not probable that he would actually become insane, some of his actions would probably be those of a man not wholly sane." If, however, the ear condition became more aggravated, he might lose not only his mind but his life as well.[84] Wilhelm's ear problem did not worsen over the years, but it was persistent, and by the time of his ascension in 1888, questions were beginning to be raised as to whether the infection might have penetrated his brain.[85] Not long after he became Kaiser, Wilhelm's excessive nervousness disturbed his principal physician, Dr. Rudolf von Leuthold, who attributed it to an overburdened schedule of hunts, ceremonial affairs, and continuous traveling. The doctor entreated Eulenburg to try to persuade Wilhelm to take more rest, but Eulenburg, who considered Leuthold unwarrantedly pessimistic, did not act on this advice.[86]

In the spring of 1892 Wilhelm's otitis recurred; he experienced episodes of narcolepsy that led to a loss of some physical and mental acuity, and he occasionally became afflicted with a sort of violent nervousness. The Kaiser's bad ear was not affected, but there was, as Leuthold described it, a "not entirely equalized psychic disposition," "a certain nervous tension" due, the doctor believed, to Wilhelm's frenetic activity. Once again Leuthold prescribed rest away from Berlin, and the Kaiser did go to his hunting lodge at Hubertusstock for a few days' vacation.[87] The situation was sufficiently grave for rumors to spread that a regency under Prince Henry was impending.[88] Wilhelm himself admitted to Queen Victoria that he had been ill, though he assured his grandmother, "I am slowly recovering, but am not yet allowed to go out or to work much, as I was too much overworked and the doctor wishes some rest for me."[89] The British envoy in Berlin described the situation as a "nervous breakdown," and Lord Salisbury found that the descriptions of Wilhelm's behavior depicted a man who seemed to be "strangely excited."[90]

It was during this illness that the first medical opinions of the Kaiser as perhaps mentally ill were recorded. In 1892 Felix Semon, a German-born British specialist in disorders of the larynx, was consulted either by Leuthold or by Salisbury about the Kaiser's condition. Semon, to whom Wilhelm had earlier granted a decoration as well as a professorial title because of his pioneering research on throat cancer, declared that the Kaiser's restlessness was the initial stage of a psychiatric disorder, one, however, that should be dealt with as a physiological rather than a psychological disturbance.[91] Semon did not know Wilhelm II at all, but at about the time he was developing his misgivings about the Kaiser's mental state another doctor, who had had some contact with Wilhelm, arrived at a similar conclusion, less specific in its details but perhaps more ominous. This was Ernst Schweninger, an internist who numbered among his distinguished patients former Chancellor Bismarck and the great Rhineland industrialist Friedrich Alfried Krupp. In 1893, Schweninger expressed concern that the Kaiser was alarmingly like the late mad King Ludwig of Bavaria. The physician did not elaborate on what aspects of Wilhelm's behavior led him to this conclusion, but undoubtedly he meant the extreme perturbation that was so prominent a characteristic of both rulers.[92]

During the next few years, Wilhelm's agitated nerves grew worse. In the summer of 1893, following the receipt of news indicating that France and Britain were about to go to war because of their rivalry in Siam (a conflict that might extend to involve Germany), he suffered an emotional collapse. Eulenburg, who was with the Kaiser at the time, described how Wilhelm "completely lost his nerves" and, in spite of his friend's reassurances, remained pale and nervous for some time.[93] Wilhelm's aural infections meanwhile did not abate, and in 1896 his ear problem reoccurred with nervous complications. In the next year, the Kaiser suffered two recurrences, the second in July as he was cruising along the Norwegian coast. Dr. Leuthold, elevated to the hereditary nobility earlier that year, ordered an immediate return to Germany because brain complications were feared. These did not in fact develop, but the Kaiser's medical situation was slow to improve and in October was still not in order, a fact that depressed the patient. These repeated episodes disturbed Leuthold, but he insisted that although Wilhelm's behavior was occasionally puzzling, the Kaiser was in no way maniacal.[94] The opinion in some other quarters in the capital was less salutary. The Prussian minister to Weimar, Ludwig Raschdau, who had wide connections in Berlin officialdom, wrote in his diary in March 1897: "The belief that the Kaiser is to be regarded psychopathically is steadily growing. Matters have gone so far that such things are unabashedly said not only *in front of* officials and even officers but in fact are being expressed *by* them."[95]

By 1900, Eulenburg, who for long had dismissed any talk of mental problems, had become quite worried, but Leuthold continued to insist that although the Kaiser's nerves were clearly undermined, Wilhelm was not in danger of mental collapse.[96] The cause of Wilhelm's state was undoubtedly related to Dona's far more serious mental deterioration, one that was characterized by hysteric outbursts often directed against her husband.[97] In 1903, by which time Dona's condition had improved, Wilhelm's own psychic state had become so serious that even Leuthold, always inclined to be optimistic, told Eulenburg that it might soon be necessary for the Kaiser to be placed in a sanatorium so that the requisite tranquility could be imposed.[98] Leuthold was not a forceful personality, and he did not succeed, nor did Eulenburg, in persuading Wilhelm to alter his frenetic manner of life. The Kaiser's condition nevertheless seems gradually to have improved — though it is more difficult to trace his medical history after 1903 because Eulenburg vanished from the entourage, and no one continued Eulenburg's frequent notations about Wilhelm's mental condition — and the Kaiser's ear problems did not recur. Still there were further episodes of extreme nervousness, of prostration from depression, and of talk and gestures that were alarming to witness. Medical diagnoses of psychological instability continued to be noted, such as the opinion advanced in 1909 by Dr. Rudolf von Renvers, the director of the celebrated hospital for nervous disorders in Moabit in suburban Berlin. Renvers stated that Wilhelm suffered from pseudollogia phantastica, a condition that only rest and serious reading, two pastimes in which the Kaiser had no interest whatsoever, might cure.[99]

To those who knew him well, the Kaiser seemed to teeter on the edge of mental collapse. His constant oscillation between exaltation and depression, his insistence on construing innocent developments as personal affronts, the violence of his language, his gestures and sometimes even his appearance, and his obsessively febrile activity were all signs that Wilhelm was a man not completely in control of himself. To professional experts in the field of mental disorders, the Kaiser was at best a candidate for a breakdown, at worst someone in possession of a mind that had already passed into the shadows of psychiatric disorder. On the brink of mental dissolution, he stopped just short of realizing the worst fears of his courtiers and doctors, managing to fulfill his imperial role in a way that often caused alarm or embarrassment to his servants but that did not warrant interference or restraint. As Dr. Renvers observed, according to the often untruthful Bernhard von Bülow, a psychotic fantasist might live a long life — as indeed Wilhelm II did — and accomplish much, but it was a most undesirable trait in a man to whom destiny had awarded a crown.[100]

Bülow himself would in time learn, to his chagrin, that no sovereign could be more difficult to serve than Wilhelm II. A man as manifestly perturbed as the Kaiser required courtiers of consummate sensitivity, able to deal with his ever-changing moods and enthusiasms and to play up to his vanity and to his exaggerated sense of theater. Of Wilhelm's many servants of state, no other proved so virtuosic in this respect as Bülow, who served Wilhelm II as imperial chancellor from October 1900 until his fall from grace almost nine years later. A friend of the Kaiser's once declared that Bülow could play on the sovereign as though he were a musical instrument, coaxing from him whatever tone was desired.[101] Although Bülow was not without professional ability, his focus was narrow, and relentless ambition alone determined his behavior. He made no effort to master subjects that did not interest him. A diplomat by profession, the chancellor always put foreign affairs first, and his knowledge of and concern for domestic matters were always secondary. In this respect, as in others, he resembled Wilhelm II, for both men delighted in the glamour and pageantry of diplomatic encounters and in the Olympian conduct of *grosse Politik*.[102] What Bülow lacked was character. Unlike the Kaiser's earlier chancellors, all men of principle, he was an utter careerist, devoid of any concern except personal advancement. Once Bülow had come to the pinnacle of power as chancellor, his sole objective was to retain his position, and he was prepared to sacrifice anyone, including the Kaiser himself, to succeed. The chancellor's own brother Adolf, in Wilhelm's youth his adjutant and close adviser, bemoaned the fact that Bernhard's character in no way measured up to his vibrant personality, an opinion shared by an erstwhile colleague, the diplomat Count Anton Monts. The two men had been close friends, but Monts summed up Bülow as "a man of rare gifts, but — unhappily! — without character, more courtier than diplomat, and still more diplomat than statesman."[103]

Bülow was indolent to a fault. On the very day of his arrival in Berlin as chancellor, he issued an order that he was not to be disturbed — except in emergencies — before 9 A.M., during lunch, or after 7:15 in the evening. In discussing the chancellorship with a friend, he once candidly declared: "You don't think that I'm going to kill myself. I'm an independent man and intend to enjoy life!"[104] Bülow had much social charm, but it was often squandered in too many meaningless compliments and false intimacies. Truth was to him no special virtue, for as he unabashedly observed, "One can accomplish a great deal by lying."[105] The chancellor's conversation, like his posthumously published memoirs, abounded in a pretentious rash of literary allusions that gave him an unfounded reputation for learning. Bülow was notorious for his vacant effusions and shallow confidences. His mother-in-law, the Roman socialite Donna Laura

Minghetti, once observed that Bernhard made "a secret of everything." She added, "He'll take you by the arm, lead you to the window and say: don't tell anyone but there's a little dog pissing down there."[106] Bülow could orate brilliantly, he purveyed diplomatic gossip with wit, and his panache bedazzled society, but he relished these talents too much and therefore ultimately made an impression that was theatrical and false. The chancellor amused and fascinated many people, not the least the Kaiser, but he could not win or sustain their trust. In the end he was quite alone, almost entirely without either friends or admirers.

Bülow did not make his career by himself. At his side almost from the beginning was Philipp Eulenburg, who, like Bülow, was an army officer turned diplomat through Bismarck's intervention. Eulenburg was the elder by two years and always played an avuncular role with the appropriately deferential Bülow, whom he identified as a man marked someday to be chancellor.[107] As a junior diplomat in various posts in continental Europe, Bülow had forwarded to the Wilhelmstrasse dispatches that brimmed with scandal. Bismarck had no taste for this sort of reportage, but Wilhelm II delighted in learning of the peccadilloes of his fellow sovereigns. So industrious was Bülow in fluttering about for scintillating material that he was known to his colleagues in the St. Petersburg embassy in the 1880s as "the moth." In later life, by which time Bülow's excessively ingratiating manner had made him notorious, he was condemned as the "eel."[108] Eulenburg, however, was an admirer and had no cause to be jealous of Bülow, who was junior to him in the diplomatic service, who lacked wealth, and who did not yet enjoy Eulenburg's intimate connection with Wilhelm II. According to Eulenburg's vision, Bülow would be the public instrument of a personal regime, under Wilhelm II, that Eulenburg would covertly direct in his preferred role as the royal favorite. The point for Bülow, no less than for his protector, was that his advancement to the chancellorship, for which Eulenburg would enlist the Kaiser, should come only when the time was exactly right.[109] In 1897, the preparatory appointment as state secretary of the Foreign Office was secured when Baron Marschall, of whom Wilhelm had become thoroughly tired, was sent off to Constantinople as ambassador. For the next three years Eulenburg schemed, with insincere protests of unsuitability or untimeliness from Bülow, to maneuver his friend into the chancellorship when the aged Hohenlohe became too feeble to fulfill its responsibilities. The watched-for moment came late in 1900, and from then on, having now ascended to the position to which he had always aspired, the new chancellor began to act more and more independently of his former patron. A generous sense of loyalty did not figure among Bülow's virtues. Although the chancellor took every advantage of Eulenburg's help and was generous in his declarations of affection and loyalty, he was not blind to his colleague's limitations.

The two men still had in common a strong attachment to Wilhelm II. Both Bülow and Eulenburg were genuinely fond of the Kaiser as a person and were tireless advocates of a powerful, assertive monarchy. Both were aware that Wilhelm's friendship was not without advantages, and neither had any hesitation about using their positions of royal intimacy to advance their own interests. To Bülow, as to Eulenburg, Wilhelm II was a truly remarkable personality, although admittedly not perfect. As Bülow observed after his career was over, there had been three stages in his relationship with Wilhelm: admiration, then disappointment, and finally sympathy.[110] Traits to admire were Wilhelm's effervescent manner, his swift comprehension of issues, and his resoluteness in action. "I must often struggle with myself not to give into him too much," Bülow confided to Eulenburg. "He is such a charmer! One capitulates to him even when it's not in his [the Kaiser's] interest."[111] But Bülow noted that even these positive features had negative corollaries. Wilhelm's quick judgment was at times merely pure impetuosity. The Kaiser said and did too many things without reflection, spewing off his opinions in a tactless or exaggerated fashion. In addition, he was extraordinarily sensitive to criticism or to what he perceived as a lack of appreciation or respect. As a result, Wilhelm offended people, such as his "colleagues" on other thrones, who might otherwise have sympathized with him. Being the Kaiser's chancellor was not an easy task, and Bülow frequently complained how arduous serving such a royal master could be.[112] To Bülow, a figure as redoubtable as Wilhelm II was not to be challenged either openly, as Bismarck and Leo von Caprivi had done, or subtly, with the evasive tactics that had successfully characterized Hohenlohe's chancellorship. He remembered the fate of his predecessors, all of whom Wilhelm had hustled out of office, and he was prudently apprehensive about the Kaiser's ever-changing moods.[113] As far as Bülow was concerned, the most efficacious method of dealing with his sovereign was an unctuous combination of flattery and supinity. "I stand always at the command of my dear ruler," Bülow assured Eulenburg in 1896, "wherever, whenever and however he wants. Every personal impulse or personal consideration is far from my mind, I wish to be only a card in play for the Kaiser."[114] No one else, not even Eulenburg, knew how to handle Wilhelm so adroitly, but many of Bülow's friends and all of his enemies correctly regarded this talent not as a virtue but as a danger to the throne and ultimately to Germany.

Bülow's flattery succeeded in perpetuating him in office, but it severely damaged the Kaiser. Wilhelm II, lulled by the chancellor's sycophancy, was strengthened in his conviction of personal infallibility. Bülow, if reproached that his inclination to yield to the Kaiser was excessive, would reply that his accommodating manner had worked to prevent even more disastrous eruptions of Wilhelm's willfulness. "You do not suspect," he bragged with satisfaction to a courtier, "what all I have prevented and what a major part of my time I must dedicate to bringing back into order all that our Most High Ruler has thrown off the rails."[115] Bülow spent an enormous amount of time closeted with Wilhelm, so much so that, as chancellor, he ceased to grant diplomats accredited to Berlin the audiences that had been part of his routine from 1897 to 1900, when he had served as state secretary of the Foreign Office.[116] Bülow's audiences were time well spent, for the chancellor succeeded in making Wilhelm believe that he was indispensable. Eulenburg wrote to Bülow in 1903 that Wilhelm II had a "mixture of respect and anxiety" for the chancellor. Eulenburg added, "He realizes, sometimes clearly, sometimes weakly, that he cannot get along without you."[117]

From the beginning of Bülow's chancellorship, two men who knew him very well — his predecessor Prince Hohenlohe and Holstein at the Foreign Office — were confident that in the end the chancellor's flattering manipulation of the Kaiser would, for all its virtuosity, prove incapable of controlling Wilhelm's unpredictable disposition.[118] But in fact during much of his service in Berlin (from 1897 to 1900 as state secretary and for the first half of his nine years thereafter as chancellor), Bülow's prescription worked well. At first Wilhelm II was positively rapturous, especially when he contrasted his newly appointed servant with the man Bülow had replaced, Baron Marschall, a Badener whom the Kaiser had never liked. "I adore him," the Kaiser declared to Eulenburg in 1897 shortly after Bülow had taken up his new post in the Foreign Office. "My God, what a difference between him and the south German high traitor!"[119] Over the ensuing years, however, there were occasional outbursts against Bülow; these seem to have proceeded from the Kaiser's irritation, one he had also harbored against Bismarck, that the chancellor wanted to be the architect of German diplomacy in spite of the fact that Wilhelm II had made it clear that this was his province.[120] Moreover, as the years wore on, Bülow became inclined to adopt too preceptorial a tone with the Kaiser, a failing that had created difficulties for earlier chancellors.[121]

Bülow, unlike any of his predecessors, had a considerable diplomatic asset in his Italian-born wife. Johanna von Bismarck had been difficult and reclusive, Caprivi had been unmarried, and Princess Hohenlohe had preferred hunting bears on her Russian estates to Berlin society. Marie von Bülow, on the other hand, lived only to further her husband's career. She had useful connections in Italy and Russia, Holstein was her admirer, and many of her husband's diplomatic colleagues were her good friends. Although Marie did not mix directly in her husband's business, her influence was considerable. She was, as their friend Count Monts noted, an extension of Bülow's ego.[122] Her charm was more genuine that Bülow's, and her use of flattery, which was not insignificant, was more restrained; her talent for entertaining constituted a useful device for fortifying her husband's position, even though her diaphanous gowns and coquettish manner scandalized the reactionary element at court. Although Wilhelm and Dona had initially disapproved of Marie because she had been a divorcée when she had married Bülow in 1885, they soon became enraptured with the diminutive countess.[123]

Figuring in society, keeping the Berlin press at bay, and "managing" the Kaiser rather than the earnest conduct of affairs of state were in fact Bülow's forte. Like the Kaiser, Bülow was both histrionic and indolent and also alarmingly ignorant of many important matters. It was revealing that the chancellor called his office in the Wilhelmstrasse the "studio," for he was as much concerned with the artistic effect of what he did and said as he was with the substance of state affairs. A Bülow oration before the Reichstag was an event that excited all of Berlin, and beforehand the chancellor would call on his staff to help him perfect the synchrony of words and gestures.[124] These discourses were masterpieces of ingratiation, full of sonorous vacuities and false climaxes, and Bülow treated the Reichstag with the same mixture of flattery and unctuousness that he used to cajole Wilhelm.

The chancellor was very jealous of competitors and kept a tight rein on his subordinates in the Foreign Office. Bülow's policy, he often declared, had as its foundation the 1879 defensive alliance with Austria-Hungary. At the same time, the chancellor was insistent that among all the remaining European powers, Russia should be Germany's closest partner. This was to be achieved through what he called his "free hand" policy, a stratagem through which German diplomacy would appear to cultivate the friendship of both Russia and Great Britain but in actuality would always be tilted in favor of St. Petersburg. To the chancellor, as to Bismarck in his day, imperial Germany and Romanov Russia shared a natural, conservative identity. As the great European colossus, Russia was a diplomatic, economic, and military asset incomparably more valuable than any other nation.

Bülow's Russophilia, however, did not coincide with Wilhelm II's views about Germany's position among the powers, for at the beginning of the twentieth century the Kaiser believed that the Fatherland's diplomatic future lay not in an association with Russia but rather in one with Great Britain. In Wilhelm's opinion, he had labored manfully to achieve this goal ever since coming to the throne in 1888, but British indifference had frustrated all his efforts. Even so, the Kaiser had not abandoned hope of an accommodation with London, and he would fitfully attempt to bring his dream to fulfillment. Chancellor Bülow, who had no sympathy with the Kaiser's ambitions, consequently had to turn his attention, more often than he might have liked, to the troubling relationship that prevailed at the turn of the century between Berlin and London.

Four

L'ALLEMAGNE, C'EST L'ENNEMI

IN 1900, when Bernhard von Bülow succeeded Prince Chlodwig zu Hohenlohe as chancellor, the relationship between London and Berlin was not at all cordial. Since the 1870s, Germany had begun to confront Britain with growing economic competition in European as well as in world markets, and the British regarded the construction of a massive German navy, begun in 1898, as a threat to their security. Wilhelm II's congratulatory telegram in 1896 to President Paul Kruger of the Transvaal Republic, the enemy of the British in what would soon become the Boer War, had led to a serious diplomatic crisis that left a residual hostility between London and Berlin. Moreover, there was an unhealthy friction between Wilhelm II and his Hanoverian relations in England, especially his grandmother Queen Victoria and her eldest son, the Prince of Wales. In spite of all these contretemps, both powers recognized that in Russia and France, they had potential enemies of formidable strength, and therefore, since the end of the nineteenth century, statesmen in both London and Berlin had been engaged in trying to determine if there was a possibility of some sort of diplomatic association between Britain and Germany.

Bülow was uninterested in these aspirations for accommodation. He could speak English well, but he was virtually ignorant of the country, visiting it only once.[1] Like Wilhelm II, Bülow had nursed a prejudice against the British, in the chancellor's case since his teenage years in the 1860s, when his ancestors had lost their property in Denmark as a result of an unsuccessful war by King Christian IX against Prussia. Bülow was always convinced that the defeat had been due to Britain's treacherous failure to come to Denmark's aid. The chancellor's frequent protestations about the desirability of Anglo-German accord ill concealed his antipathy for England, and those German diplomats who believed in the need for, and worked to promote, good relations between the two nations therefore rightly regarded him with suspicion.[2] Bülow's well-known distaste for England, together with his facile manner, meant that he was also looked upon askance in London. Sir Frank Lascelles, the popular British ambassador in Berlin from 1896 to 1908, earnestly desired an improvement in relations and was a remarkably open-minded and conciliatory envoy. But he soon learned to place little trust in what Bülow told him, a reservation that a number of influential figures in British diplomatic circles shared entirely. With Bülow in command of the government in Berlin, the task of drawing the two nations more closely together seemed to the British to be highly problematical.[3] These statesmen had good reason to be wary of the chancellor's diplomacy, for his bonhomie was only a cover for an essentially deceptive nature, and he could indeed not be trusted. Bülow was swift to blame the British for the problems that had arisen between Berlin and London and once informed a skeptical Lascelles that he therefore had been forced to turn to Russia.[4] This was characteristically false, for Bülow had never been drawn to England, preferring instead Russia and Germany's old ally Austria-Hungary. "Were we to ally with England," the chancellor often told one of his favored assistants in the Wilhelmstrasse, "we would definitely lose Russia's friendship, and Russia is worth more to us than England."[5] Furthermore, Bülow recognized that a policy that held London at a distance constituted an asset in appeasing the Anglophobe sentiments that were widespread in Germany.[6]

When dealing with Wilhelm II, Bülow registered his dislike of England very craftily, for the Kaiser himself intended to direct German policy toward England. Only a few months after Bülow had replaced Hohenlohe at the end of 1900, Wilhelm imperiously informed Ambassador Lascelles: "Understand that all you have to do is to keep me in a good humor. The rest does not signify, but you must not annoy me."[7] The chancellor nevertheless succeeded, to the exasperation of Friedrich von Holstein and the British party in the Wilhelmstrasse, in nurturing in the sovereign a suspicion and envy of England that would coexist with the real love that Wilhelm felt for his mother's native land.[8] As far as the Kaiser was concerned, the same reasons that had, since his accession in 1888, argued for close ties between Germany and Great Britain continued to apply in the early twentieth century. A common Protestant heritage as well as a mutual ethnic root in Teutonic blood bound the two nations together, and a dynastic relationship that made Wilhelm first the grandson and then, after Queen Victoria's death early in 1901, successively the nephew and the first cousin of the British sovereign reinforced this union.[9] The British, in his opinion, needed to subordinate their imperial ambitions to the greater task of upholding these sacred bonds of kinship and common interests. As usual, the Kaiser took a romantic and highly personalized view of the situation, blaming everyone except himself for the fact that the association between

London and Berlin had become so frayed. Wilhelm was quick to lambast the errant liberality in the political and social ideas that the British worshipped at home and eagerly tried to export to Germany.[10] Furthermore, the British Empire's great wealth, now under challenge from both Germans and Yankees, had made them overweeningly materialistic, bossy, contemptuous, and snobbish. As a result, London treated the Germans, Wilhelm once complained, as though they were no more consequential than Venezuelans.[11]

The Kaiser sometimes thought about the irritations caused by the British in abstract terms, but more frequently, and with considerably more passion, he regarded anything unpleasant emanating from London as an affront to his august majesty. Philipp Eulenburg and Bernhard von Bülow, the two men who knew Wilhelm most intimately at the turn of the century, recognized his irrepressible propensity for judging every event in terms of his own person.[12] At the time Wilhelm ascended the throne in 1888, the British envoy had perceptively warned London that nothing would be more decisive in forming the young Kaiser's behavior toward Britain than a feeling that the British were spurning his efforts at friendship.[13] The Kaiser tended to regard the refusal of the British government to enter into an alliance with Germany, the subject of protracted negotiations from 1898 to 1901, as a rejection of his untiring, Sisyphus-like efforts to improve relations. The British, he informed Queen Victoria in 1898, regarded his friendly gestures as "something between a joke and a snub." This mistreatment, he reminded his grandmother, was not only demeaning to Germany but personally humiliating as well.[14] How indeed, Wilhelm asked her, could he even think of paying a visit to England under such grievous circumstances?

A source of British criticism that the Kaiser regarded with special malevolence was the London press. Although he claimed never to read newspapers, he in fact throughout his life paid very close attention to opinions about him expressed in their columns, and with the exception of Germany, nowhere else did he peruse newspapers as closely as he did those published in England.[15] Wilhelm was acutely resentful of articles in major London papers that were critical of Germany or of himself — to the Kaiser it was one and the same thing — and that therefore frustrated his attempts to bring the two nations together. He threatened to expel from Germany any British correspondents who had the temerity to write carping articles.[16] These onslaughts, he declared, made his personal conduct of Anglo-German diplomacy impossible, destroying his reputation among the British and weakening his authority in Germany as well.[17] The Kaiser was convinced that the hostile British press, which in his opinion was largely under the control of Jews, was part of an international conspiracy in which the British, French, Russians, Belgians, and Americans were all actively suborning European newspapers.[18] He found it intolerable that 10 Downing Street did nothing to prevent the treatment the British press meted out to Germany, for Wilhelm II believed, inaccurately to be sure, that Queen Victoria's statesmen were quite capable of curbing the London papers. Indeed, Wilhelm II suspected that the British government was not only behind these attacks but had bribed foreign papers to join in the anti-German fronde.[19]

What stung Wilhelm II even more than criticism of himself in notices in the London papers was his realization that his English relations were also hostile to him. Lascelles once assured Lord Salisbury that the Kaiser was extraordinarily sensitive to anything unkind that was said or done in England affecting him, especially if such offensive behavior could be traced to a member of the royal family.[20] As the old century closed, Queen Victoria — arbitrary, authoritarian, and very conscious of her great position — was, after more than sixty years as sovereign, still actively involved in affairs of state. The sovereign's diamond jubilee in 1897 testified to the veneration with which she was held and was the occasion of much celebration. Wilhelm II, although her eldest grandchild, was conspicuously absent, for the queen had refused to invite him because of what she considered his unwarranted interference in a number of diplomatic problems. Wilhelm expressed his displeasure in a curious equine idiom. "I feel," he told the queen, "like a charger chained in the stables who hears the bugle sounding, stomps and chomps his bit, because he cannot follow his regiment."[21] Two years later, the queen declined his request to be present at her eightieth birthday celebration in May 1899, suggesting that instead he come later in the year. So in November, Wilhelm was her guest for several days at Windsor, accompanied on this occasion by Bülow. Both the Kaiser and his chancellor were on their best behavior, and the visit went very smoothly, "a really great success," as the queen described it.[22] This welcome improvement in the Kaiser's relations with England did not last long, however, and by the spring of 1900 his grandmother was once again complaining that Wilhelm was too impulsive and ill-behaved. It was regrettable that he could not manage to be more like Tsar Nicholas II, who had married one of the queen's Hessian granddaughters. To Queen Victoria, the "dear young emperor" in St. Petersburg, whom she found quite sensible, was eager to promote good relations with Britain.[23] The Kaiser, on the other hand, she held responsible for a number of "insults heaped on

England and the family," notably his gratuitous offer of military advice on how Britain's embarrassingly futile campaign against the Boers might be more successfully conducted.[24] There were also what the queen characterized as Wilhelm's "threats" regarding the succession to the ducal throne of Coburg, in question since the death in 1899 of the only son of the Kaiser's uncle Alfred, Duke of Edinburgh. Over the Kaiser's opposition, Queen Victoria, who was tyrannical on dynastic questions, decreed that her choice, rather than Wilhelm's, would eventually assume the crown.[25]

Although Queen Victoria was well enough to make her only trip to Ireland in the spring of 1900 and continued to keep up with affairs of state until the first week of the new year, her health quickly failed in the middle of January 1901. On receiving word that his grandmother was dying, Wilhelm immediately prepared to leave for England, informing the Prince of Wales that he would come not as a fellow sovereign but as a grandson.[26] According to the Kaiser's account, one of the attending physicians asked the dying sovereign if she was pleased that Wilhelm had sped to England. The queen's reply was, "Yes, very glad, for I love him very much."[27] Wilhelm was at his grandmother's bedside, propping up her pillows, when she died early in the evening of 22 January, and three days later he assisted his uncles, the new King Edward VII and the Duke of Connaught, in placing the queen — "so little and so light" — in her coffin.[28] Although the royal family probably would have preferred for the Kaiser to have stayed in Germany, his behavior during the death throes and at the state funeral was exemplary, if uncharacteristic, in its modesty and deference. According to the Duchess of Cornwall and York: "Wilhelm has been too dear and nice and so full of feeling. We were all quite glad that he was here and dear Grandmama knew him and spoke to him."[29] The Kaiser returned to Berlin feeling "riveted," as he put it later, to his English relatives.[30]

Queen Victoria's successor, King Edward VII, who would rule until his death in 1910, was Wilhelm's maternal uncle. The Kaiser's deportment at the funeral greatly pleased the new king, who proposed that his nephew write to him to deal with problems that might arise between the two nations.[31] This was a chivalrous gesture, but except for the duty imposed by kinship, there was little reason to expect any closeness to develop between the English king and his German nephew. Almost the only quality they had in common was an insistence on the punctilious execution of court etiquette and a delight in the company of plutocrats. Otherwise Edward VII was both different from and superior to the Kaiser. The British monarch, all Europe acknowledged, was a figure of assured majesty, dignified, gracious, and imposing, the arbiter of the taste of his times.

Wilhelm II, in comparison, for all his flamboyant poses and costumes, was counterfeit and lacked the aplomb and suavity that the British king possessed in such notable abundance.[32] The Kaiser recognized that his uncle was a major factor in international affairs, and he was wary of being entrapped by the king's diplomatic maneuvering.[33] He was convinced that Edward VII, resentful of Germany's economic challenge to Britain, was responsible for the decline of Anglo-German relations at the turn of the century. From that pique proceeded his uncle's diplomatic intrigues all over Europe and the British king's underhanded dealings with the London press directed against Germany. "He is a Satan," Wilhelm informed his courtiers in 1907. "You can't believe what a Satan he is."[34] There was also the king's intolerable condescension, which never failed to ignite Wilhelm II. "My uncle never seems to realize that I am a sovereign," he fumed, "but treats me as if I were a little boy."[35] Wilhelm also disapproved of the amorous liaisons that Edward VII handled discreetly but hardly with secrecy. In 1905, the German ambassador in London, Count Paul von Wolff Metternich zur Gracht, reported to Bülow that at a regatta at Kiel the Kaiser had made uncomplimentary remarks about the king's relationship with the elegant Mrs. George Keppel, censure that eventually made its way back to Buckingham Palace. Wilhelm's criticism was undoubtedly fueled by the Kaiserin's distaste for the ruler's mistress, whom she refused to receive at Kiel, where Mrs. Keppel was a guest aboard the king's yacht.[36] The Kaiser's disapproval of Mrs. Keppel probably won him little credit with Queen Alexandra, who treated the king's inamorata with great forbearance. The queen despised both Wilhelm and his wife and declared that the "awful Emperor" was "a mad and a conceited ass."[37]

Queen Alexandra was not the only person in British society or at Edward VII's court who mistrusted or disliked the Kaiser; he had few friends among those who were influential or powerful in London at the opening of the century.[38] The haute monde of London and the country-house circuit, of which the king was a popular fixture, were uninterested in Berlin and the Hohenzollern court, finding them dreary and pretentious. The Kaiser took this as a personal snub, and it irritated him greatly.[39] Edward VII's favorites were by and large Germanophobes who had a particular aversion for Wilhelm. Among these intimates was Sir Charles Hardinge, whom Wilhelm criticized for his preachy manner and his meddling in diplomatic matters, an involvement that the Kaiser felt was entirely gratuitous.[40] Hardinge did in fact imagine that he possessed considerable political prowess, and he was on occasion unreasonably hostile to the Kaiser, whom he disliked and unfairly held to be personally responsible for *any* unfriendly act on Germany's part. He was convinced that with Wilhelm on the German throne, kinship could count for little in Anglo-German relations. "The feelings of the German Emperor," Hardinge wrote in 1910, "may at any time be swept aside by a wave of chauvinism arising from some more or less trifling incident. In such cases one cannot count on blood relationships."[41]

Equally prominent at Edward VII's court were Viscount Esher, the king's archivist and confidant, who did not hold political office but who knew everyone, and Baron Knollys, for forty years the king's trusted private secretary. In Esher's opinion, the Kaiser was feckless, imagining himself to be "immortal and omnipotent." Esher believed that a nation ruled by such a man had to be watched with care. "L'Allemagne, c'est l'ennemi," he declared in 1906.[42] To Knollys, Wilhelm was an intolerably "vain, theatrical and ridiculous creature."[43] In addition to these aristocrats there was Edward VII's favorite in the diplomatic corps, the darkly hirsute Marquess of Soveral, ambassador of Portugal to the Court of St. James. Wilhelm did not like the envoy and called him to his face the "blue ape," rudeness that ensured that Soveral, who had originally been well-disposed to Germany, became a diplomatic opponent.[44] The king was also much attached to the German-Jewish banking elite in London, many of whom had left Germany not so much to make their fortunes as to escape the prejudice that was notable in Germany and at the Kaiser's court. None of these magnates seem to have cared anything for Wilhelm II, who could muster no philo-Semitic credentials.[45]

Edward VII's annoyance at his nephew had been long maturing. In the king's opinion Wilhelm was a deliberate troublemaker, always trying to stir up resentment against his uncle and England. When German statesmen or policies were unfriendly to Germany, the king, like his friend Hardinge, was convinced that his nephew was personally responsible.[46] This was unfair, but it reflected the king's dislike of his nephew. Edward VII resented the fact that a much younger relative had become a sovereign long before he succeeded to his own throne; in addition, his nephew had tirelessly advertised satisfaction at being a monarch rather than merely an heir apparent.[47] Wilhelm was inclined to adopt toward his uncle a gushing, palavering tone, "his heartsblood" he called it, expecting in return a reciprocal show of enthusiasm. To the Kaiser's irritation, this was never forthcoming, for the king, who found Wilhelm's manner annoying, spoke and wrote in a much more measured tone than his nephew.[48] A little of Wilhelm, he once observed, went a long way.[49] An additional problem was the fact that the Englishman whom Wilhelm seems to have liked above all others was persona non grata to the king. This was Hugh Lowther, Earl of Lonsdale, a soldier, passionate sportsman, and dandified bon vivant who was mentally quite unremarkable. The king loathed Lonsdale, who, he believed, exercised a deleterious influence on his nephew. The Kaiser, for reasons that puzzled contemporaries but that were perhaps due to a perverse desire to challenge his uncle, had taken a great liking to the wealthy peer.[50] To Wilhelm, Lonsdale was the best sort of plain-talking English army officer, and according to Bülow, the Kaiser believed every word that the earl uttered to be true. Lonsdale, in return, proclaimed of Wilhelm II, "There is no greater soldier, no greater mind."[51] It was a case of undeserved mutual admiration.

No one seems to have been surprised that Edward VII disliked having anything to do with his nephew. That included corresponding with the Kaiser, for Wilhelm's letters contained passages critical of England, observations that the king found quite outrageous.[52] Face-to-face meetings were sometimes much worse. Outward cordiality masked what had always been, and what would always be, a mutual dislike. Sir Frederick Ponsonby, Queen Victoria's private secretary, described the atmosphere that prevailed at their encounters as either "thunder" or "dangerous electricity."[53] To Wilhelm's credit, he sometimes made a real effort to be agreeable, but the king often deliberately provoked his nephew by treating the Kaiser with avuncular condescension.[54] Edward VII, who was as suave as Wilhelm was blustering, knew how to put Wilhelm in his place, and Bülow described with dismay how the king's parrying with the Kaiser reminded the chancellor of a wily cat at play with a shrew.[55] A German courtier noted that on a trip to Berlin in 1908 the king was "distinctly unresponsive to the shafts of conversation the Kaiser launched at him across the table." The courtier continued: "The Kaiser was in great spirits . . . and was rather like a schoolboy showing off in his effervescence, which the King received with chilly politeness. It is not difficult, seeing them together at close quarters like this, to realize the total absence of understanding between them which, detached from all questions of international politics, is temperamental."[56] These frequent spats between the two sovereigns were more than unpleasant social contretemps. They did nothing to make diplomacy easier, and statesmen in both Britain and Germany recognized that these personal difficulties could seriously endanger the relationship between the two countries.[57]

Although Wilhelm II spent most of life belittling England, he had in fact a strong affinity for the land of his mother's birth and particularly for the elegance and opulence that characterized the set that his uncle, as Prince of

Wales and later as king, established. The Kaiser admired the wealth and ostentatious display of English society, and he delighted in thinking of himself as being by inheritance one of its authentic members. "A Hohenzollern king is a gentleman," he once declared, and throughout his life he used the word "gentleman" frequently, always with approbation.[58] But even as Wilhelm enviously observed the splendor of the British court and the lavish houses in which the upper class pursued its glittering pleasures, his jealousy was alloyed with disapproval. The Kaiser was especially censorious of the loose sexual morals, the bibulousness, and the enthusiasm for gambling (to all of which he was immune) in belle époque England. Quite as bad was what Wilhelm deplored as the British mania for money, a sort of depraved mammonism that contrasted so poorly, in his opinion, with the sturdy values exemplified in aristocratic Prussian life.[59] In the Kaiser's opinion his uncle was identified much too closely with many of these lapses. Edward VII cavorted openly with his mistress, Mrs. Keppel, and he took a vast delight in plutocrats, some of them Jews, shamelessly plundering their fortunes for his own enjoyment.[60] It is true that the king liked rich men, but Wilhelm II took an equally great delight in their company. This love of wealth, as Bülow observed, was a characteristic that uncle and nephew shared.[61]

The Kaiserin Augusta Victoria was of much the same mind as her consort, and at every opportunity she expressed her suspicion and mistrust of anything that emanated from London. The xenophobic Kaiserin did not like foreigners in general, the English in particular, and Edward VII most of all. "The old fat king," as she referred to him, was guilty of gross impropriety, and she became alarmed if her husband or her sons tarried too long when they went to England, where loose women abounded.[62] Edward's consort, the exquisite Queen Alexandra, was related to the royal house in Copenhagen; her branch of the Danish dynasty was a rival to that of Augusta Victoria, and the Kaiserin did not at all like her. "My wife, " Wilhelm II declared with truth in 1908, "has a fanatical hatred for the [British] majesties."[63] Edward VII and his queen reciprocated these sentiments in full, for both shared the general opinion that Augusta Victoria was a tedious and lackluster woman.[64] The Kaiserin's dislike of England and the British king and queen was reflected in her entourage. Dona's ladies-in-waiting, the "hallelujah aunts" whom Wilhelm's English mother had contemptuously dismissed as "donkeys," were offended by almost anything or anyone English. The most vacuous of the "aunts," Countess Mathilde von Keller, complained that England was impressively rich, but she noted that if German courtiers had newer and less impressive jewelry, it was because their fearless ancestors, years before in the long wars against Napoleon, had unstintingly sacrificed their wealth.[65]

The Kaiser's retinue was no less hostile to England. From the beginning of Edward VII's reign, the prescient British ambassador in Berlin, Sir Frank Lascelles, noted that Wilhelm II's courtiers, notable for their dislike of the British, feared that if the Kaiser became too amicable with his uncle, it would imperil Germany's traditional friendship with Russia.[66] At the turn of the century, the Kaiser's closest friend was Count Philipp zu Eulenburg, whom Wilhelm raised to princely dignity in 1900. Like Bülow and many other aristocrats, Eulenburg believed that Germany's future lay with Russia and not Great Britain, and he disliked everything about England, a country he visited only once.[67] Nor did Eulenburg approve of Edward VII, and he warned Wilhelm that the Kaiser's uncle was smarter and more of an intriguer than anyone suspected.[68] Eulenburg had once been a soldier, and his anti-English feelings may well have been drawn from his experience in the Prussian army, in which there was a marked distaste for Britain. The Kaiser's two favorite general-adjutants, Gustav von Kessel and Hans von Plessen, were particularly ill-disposed to England. Wilhelm's mother had hated Kessel, who she declared was "false, dangerous and a direct mischief-maker."[69] Plessen was reckless in expressing hatred for England, and during the Boer War, he tried to persuade the Kaiser to capitalize on Britain's embarrassment in South Africa by declaring war. Not surprisingly, Count Metternich, the German ambassador in London who was anxiously attempting to improve Anglo-German relations, described Plessen as "an enemy of the English and a committed pro-Russian."[70] What was true for Kessel and Plessen applied also to many other highly placed generals, naval officers, and bureaucrats with whom Wilhelm was frequently in contact.[71]

From the beginning of the Boer War with South Africa in 1899, German public opinion had supported the Dutch settlers against their British opponents, and there had been allegations in the press about the savagery and brutality with which Queen Victoria's armies had pursued their foes. In late October 1901, Joseph Chamberlain, the colonial secretary, in the course of a speech in Edinburgh, declared that if the British had in fact acted forcefully against the enemy, there were many precedents in the military annals of various continental powers, one of which was the punitive behavior of the German army in the Franco-Prussian War of 1870–71. Chamberlain's remarks created great resentment in Berlin, but Ambassador Metternich, as well as Holstein and other Foreign Office dignitaries, advised the chancellor to keep quiet and let the furor die down. Bülow, however, saw in the crisis a means of strengthening his popularity among the pan-German Anglophobes as well as of deflating any move in Berlin toward an accommodation with London.[72] And so, in January 1902, the chancellor mounted the Reichstag tribune to put Chamberlain in his place. Bülow reminded the parliamentary audience of what Frederick the Great had been accustomed to saying of anyone who tried to abuse him or his soldiers: "He is biting on granite." The chancellor went on to declare that the historic record of Germany's arms had been blameless and that Berlin would hold true to its diplomatic partners Russia and Austria. He concluded his speech by declaring, "We must continue to keep Germany strong enough so that, as is the case today, our friendship is worthwhile to everyone, and no one can be indifferent to our enmity."[73] The result of Bülow's speech was a furious outbreak of mutual enmity in both the British and the German press. Chamberlain and Bülow, either the hero or the villain depending on the nationality of the commentator, rose to new heights of popularity among their respective peoples.

Wilhelm was full of indignation at Chamberlain, whose imperialist views he had never approved, and he excitedly told his British friend Colonel Wallscourt H.-H. Waters, the British military attaché in Berlin from 1900 to 1903, that the colonial secretary should be "taken to South Africa, marched across the continent and then shot." Wilhelm added, "A firing party is what he wants."[74] If Anglo-German relations were now worse than ever, it was because of Chamberlain's foolish oratory, for Wilhelm II declared that *he* was full of goodwill toward England in spite of all the obstructions and "idiocies" (*Sotissen*) that London had continuously put in his path. Germany had a right to continue its policy of *Weltpolitik*, but this ought to be carried out with England's cooperation.[75] The British must be made to recognize that Germany could not be abused with impunity. Moreover, those who ruled in London needed to be reminded that Wilhelm II, emperor and king, was no *quantité négligeable*, for, as he reminded Ambassador Lascelles, *he* alone was the architect of German diplomacy.[76]

Wilhelm did not hesitate to let his uncle, King Edward VII, know how profound his irritation was. On 6 January 1902, the Kaiser wrote to complain about Chamberlain's speech, which he denounced as "a conglomeration of bluff, overbearing and secret insult." Wilhelm added, "It was a most unlucky thing to do, and if he does not stop these elucubrations . . . one fine day he will wake up to see his country in the greatest of muddles ever yet seen."[77] Wilhelm reminded the king that in spite of the way the British newspapers had reviled him, he had personally prevented this insulting behavior from provoking a crisis in Germany. "The press is awful on both sides, but here it has nothing to say," the Kaiser wrote to his uncle on 30 December 1901, "for I am the sole arbiter and master of German foreign policy, and the government and country *must* follow me even if I have to face the music. May your government never forget this and never place me in the jeopardy to have to choose a course which could be a misfortune to both them and us."[78]

The Chamberlain affair eventually died down, and by the end of 1902, relations between Germany and Great Britain had become sufficiently calm to allow the two powers to cooperate in forcing the revolution-torn republic of Venezuela to pay claims to their citizens for injuries suffered. Nevertheless, the colonial secretary's inflammatory speech at Edinburgh, like the Kruger telegram imbroglio several years earlier, left an enduring scar in Anglo-German relations. The Kaiser now considered Chamberlain, once the proponent of alliance with Berlin, to be a dangerous and implacable foe of Germany.[79] Wilhelm was not wrong, for Chamberlain, whose vanity was pronounced, reacted to the attacks made on him in the press by turning swiftly into an opponent of Germany. With his defection, Berlin lost one of its few influential sympathizers in the British government.

The troublesome exchange between Chamberlain and Bülow was not the cause but rather the reflection of the tension between Germany and Great Britain in the first decade of the twentieth century, tension that had been growing since the 1880s. It was derived from three causes: the hostility between the two royal families after Wilhelm II came to the throne in 1888, the increasing economic rivalry that dated from the last quarter of the nineteenth century, and the naval competition initiated by the passage by the Reichstag of the First Naval Law in 1898. The Kaiser, as the contentious and impolitic head of the house of Hohenzollern, as the enthusiastic proponent of Germany's industrial development and expansion in Europe and in the world, and as the avid promoter of a great German battle fleet, was prominently identified with all three areas of discord.

Wilhelm's attitude toward Britain's surpassing wealth alternated between jealousy and amazement, and he was proud of Germany's industrial and commercial achievements that were seriously challenging Britain's long ascendancy in the world marketplace.[80] He recognized that in trade, Britain for the moment had the upper hand, since it possessed the naval strength to dominate the international commerce of all nations. Britain could force opponents to yield to its might on the water or to threats of closing its markets to their imports, a prospect that the Kaiser took very seriously indeed.[81] At the same time, this economic rivalry could not be permitted to jeopardize the bond that ought to exist between the two nations because of their common Teutonic, Protestant heritage. Great Britain, the Kaiser was certain, would someday have to abandon its isolationism toward the other European powers and seek an ally on the Continent. Of all the possibilities, Germany, together with the two other signatories of the Triple Alliance, Austria-Hungary and Italy, was to him clearly a far more worthy partner for Great Britain than the Franco-Russian entente. Conveniently overlooking the Italian contribution to this diplomatic coalition, Wilhelm declared that the Latin races were "dropping down the ladder." The Teutons therefore needed to take "no account" of such degenerates but instead should join forces to prevent the rising Slavs from destroying the European order.[82]

If Britain's high-handedness in commerce and diplomacy was due to the majestic strength of the Royal Navy, Germany, as Wilhelm II recognized quite clearly, was in no position to challenge it. The Kaiser was firmly convinced, thanks to having earlier read Captain Alfred Thayer Mahan's *The Influence of Sea Power upon History* (1890), that a navy was the decisive force in war, one against which no fortifications could prevail.[83] Germany's allies unfortunately could offer Wilhelm very little naval protection as he pursued a policy of *Weltpolitik*, and he therefore believed that he had to construct, singlehandedly, a navy in order to be, as he put it, desired as a friend and feared as an enemy.[84] There was also the fact that Germany was a grain importer, and in time of war, battleships and cruisers would be necessary to ensure an adequate supply of food stores, whereas in peace, naval might was an advantageous diplomatic tool. "A strong navy," he advised a journalist friend, "is a mighty factor in compelling arbitration." Without one, a nation could not participate in international diplomacy.[85] As usual, however, the fundamental reason for Wilhelm II's interest in acquiring a powerful fleet was his identification of the German navy with himself, for it was to be *his* contribution to the Fatherland, just as the great Prussian army had been that of his Hohenzollern ancestors.[86] Though it might take decades to construct a vast armada, Germany would then at long last be immune to threats and ensured of an international standing equal to that of England, the object of both Wilhelm's affection and his jealousy.[87] It did not occur to the Kaiser that building his gigantic fleet, initiated in the naval laws of 1898 and 1900, would only increase British suspicions. This was the case since most of this German argosy, rather than being dispersed around the globe, would be stationed in the North Sea opposite England.[88]

Although the British found the inauguration of a German fleet through the passage of the First Naval Law of 1898 vaguely perturbing, Wilhelm II's fleet was not initially regarded as a serious threat. What worked against Germany at this time was less Admiral Alfred von Tirpitz's new battleships than the British perception that both the Kaiser and Bülow were unreliable and that the diplomacy they both pursued worked counter to British interests. This seemed especially true in the Far East, the area that at the turn of the century was most troublesome to the British. By 1900, Russia had expanded into Manchuria, much to the resentment of the Japanese, who wanted to have Korea and part of Manchuria for themselves. This Russian advance also disturbed Britain, which had preponderant interests in central China and which was contending in Afghanistan and Persia with Russian advances that seemed intended to threaten India. Lord Salisbury and his government were alarmed that the rivalry between Japan and Russia might lead to a war, one that would complicate Britain's interests in the Far East and thus constituted a problem to be avoided as long as London was involved in the Boer War in South Africa. The British could not afford to take a decisive role in China without an ally, and of the choices available, Germany, which had developed its own commercial interests in China in the late 1890s, seemed to be the most useful.

Bülow, whose determination to maintain his ties to St. Petersburg had been made plain in his Reichstag speech defying Chamberlain, deflated British overtures to devise a mutual policy in China. This in turn meant that the British, rebuffed by Berlin and at odds with Russia in Asia and with France in Africa, had to find, faute de mieux, an accommodation with Japan. In January 1902 an Anglo-Japanese alliance was concluded that recognized Tokyo's interests in Korea, prevented either party from entering into separate agreements with other powers about China, and prescribed either neutrality or intervention, depending on the number of belligerents involved, in the event of war. The Kaiser assured Edward VII that he considered the Anglo-Japanese pact a guarantee of peace in the Far East.[89] But Wilhelm could not repress his distaste for its architect, Lord Lansdowne, who had succeeded Salisbury as foreign secretary in 1900. Concerning the British cabinet's negotiation of the treaty, the Kaiser undiplomatically remarked to Ambassador Lascelles, "The noodles seem to have had a lucid interval."[90] Wilhelm's spiteful comment, however graceless it may have been, nonetheless revealed that he had grasped how significant the treaty would be for European diplomacy. The effect of the Anglo-Japanese alliance was to strengthen Britain's position in the Far East so effectively that London no longer felt constrained to entertain any notion of a continental European alliance. Although both Chamberlain and Lansdowne had considered, and indeed favored, an Anglo-German consortium before 1902, their interest now dwindled. They felt it would be sufficient in the future to try to arrange piecemeal settlements with Germany on colonial differences, but when Lansdowne approached Ambassador Metternich, he was informed that Germany would have either an alliance or nothing at all.[91] With that chill reply, the prospect of an Anglo-German alliance vanished, not to be revived for a decade.

Lansdowne and Arthur James Balfour, who in 1902 replaced his uncle Lord Salisbury as prime minister, both continued to advocate a conciliatory policy toward Germany, but it seemed increasingly clear to both statesmen that a détente with France, an imperial power with African and Asian interests far more extensive and strategically valuable than those held by Germany, would establish a community of interests on both continents. A revolution in Morocco at the very end of 1902 illustrated the wisdom of this viewpoint, for France and Britain quickly saw that they both wanted to shore up the tottering regime of the sultan and prevent Germany, which had only marginal interests in the Mediterranean, from intruding into the area. A number of Balfour's advisers were Francophile, but unlike Lansdowne, they were also very hostile to Germany. These included Lord Salisbury's son-in-law Lord Selborne, the first lord of the admiralty from 1900 to 1905, Francis Bertie, an important figure in the Foreign Office who in 1903 became ambassador successively at Rome and Paris, and Edward VII's intimate, Sir Charles Hardinge, envoy in St. Petersburg from 1904 to 1906. By late 1902, all of these men were working not only against Germany but in favor of an accommodation with France that would both settle colonial differences and reorient Britain's diplomatic policy on the European continent.[92] This would involve not only entering into a diplomatic agreement with Paris but also making a reassessment of the strength of the Royal Navy calculated not in terms of the combined number of Russian and French ships of the line, the basis of England's traditional two-power standard, but rather in terms of the vast increases in the Kaiser's fleet provided at the turn of the century by the two naval laws, which Selborne viewed with enormous suspicion.

Neither Bülow nor the Kaiser recognized the growing sentiment in London for an accommodation with France, for both men were entirely confident that no matter what diplomatic maneuvers London undertook, Britain would remain isolated. The chancellor, like Wilhelm II, was sure that the British would never be able to overcome their antagonism to both

Russia and France, a distaste born of a vast number of colonial difficulties ranging across the world from North Africa to the Chinese coast. So the chancellor, with Wilhelm II's approval, continued with his "free hand" policy, simultaneously courting both the British and the Russians but always covertly preferring the latter. If anything, the Kaiser by early 1904 seemed to be more interested than Bülow in entering an alliance with Russia.[93] France, meanwhile, under the enterprising and conspicuously anti-German minister of foreign affairs, Théophile Delcassé, had inaugurated a more forward colonial policy in Africa. Between 1900 and 1902 Delcassé had bargained successfully with Italy for its cooperation in Africa and then turned to arrange an agreement with Great Britain. He proposed that in return for acknowledging Britain's suzerainty in Egypt, London would uphold a claim exerted by France to be paramount in the sultanate of Morocco, which since an international treaty dating to 1880 had been open to the commerce of all European nations. To the British, Delcassé's overture might not only lead to a productive settlement of old colonial rivalries but also serve as a welcome deterrent to German arrogance. The Anglo-French Entente Cordiale was signed, with considerable public fanfare, on 8 April 1904. This treaty accorded France the right to "preserve order" in Morocco, and a secret annex that was simultaneously ratified formally anticipated the eventual partition by France and Spain of the sultanate.

Although the Entente Cordiale was a profound, indeed revolutionary, development in European diplomacy and one that should have embarrassed Bülow, who had repeatedly maintained that there was no possibility of a Franco-British colonial accommodation, the chancellor made light of the pact. He mistakenly believed that the ultimate result of France's joining with Britain would be a rupture of the 1894 Franco-Russian military alliance.[94] Wilhelm II took a more sober view of the treaty, acknowledging that the British, with Paris in tow, would now feel more able to act energetically in world affairs.[95] At the same time, the Kaiser believed he could use the Entente Cordiale to raise suspicions of France among the Russians, convincing them that its purpose was in fact to thwart Nicholas II's ambitions in Asia. He therefore wrote to the tsar to warn Nicholas that the Anglo-French combination had but one purpose — "to stop the French from helping" Russia.[96] Nicholas, however, badly needed to be able to count on France, with whom his father had signed a defensive alliance in 1894, because at the very beginning of 1904 he had gone to war with Japan over Manchuria. From the beginning, the conflict was a disaster for the Russians. Wilhelm was sure that Russia's reverses were due to the incompetent tsar, who, the Kaiser had frequently argued, was incapable of ruling his empire.[97] The Kaiser had a very low opinion of the military capacity of the Russian military leaders, who were, he told his own generals, a passel of corrupt, befuddled alcoholics. The antiquated Russian navy, he declared, was no match for Japanese Admiral Heihachiro Togo's more modern fleet, a fact on which Germany would do well to reflect in contemplating its future as a maritime power.[98]

The Kaiser believed that Russia's desperation, which was financial and material as well as military, might enable Berlin to replace Paris as the tsar's ally. The result would be Great Britain's retreat from the Continent, France's diplomatic isolation, and the emergence of a countervailing Russo-German bloc powerful enough to neutralize the Anglo-Japanese alliance of 1902. All this could come about only if Nicholas II could be enticed into signing an alliance with Germany, a development that Wilhelm believed could be his own contribution to this great diplomatic triumph. He therefore went to work, bombarding the tsar with letters that were effusive with goodwill and with sympathetic advice on how to deal with unruly subjects. Nicholas, although never predisposed in Wilhelm's favor, was in despair at the dismal course the war with Japan had taken, and he gradually succumbed to Wilhelm's blandishments, to the alarm of both his mother and his wife, both Anglophiles who detested the Kaiser.[99] The foreign minister in St. Petersburg, Count Vladimir Lambsdorff, shared this dismay, for he realized that the purpose of the Kaiser's overtures to Nicholas was to remove Russia from its alliance with France and make it solely dependent on Germany, a development to which Lambsdorff was firmly opposed.[100]

In spite of all these reservations about Wilhelm and his design to ensnare Russia for Germany's diplomatic purpose, the tsar and his ministers found themselves embarrassingly in need of securing loans and matériel in their war with Japan. Russia's particular exigency was coal, for the Japanese army and navy had laid siege by land and sea to Port Arthur, the principal anchorage in southern Manchuria, bottling up the Russian Asiatic fleet as well as a large garrison of troops. Nicholas II had come to the conclusion that the war with Japan could be won only by sending his Baltic squadron halfway around the world to relieve the beleaguered fortress. Russia was ill-prepared for such an extraordinary undertaking, since its navy had few colliers and no colonial ports in which to take on coal. Fuel would therefore have to be delivered by foreign ships in harbors belonging to friendly powers. To get the Baltic squadron under way, Russia contracted with the Hamburg-American Line (HAPAG), Germany's largest steamship company, to coal the fleet as it moved from Kronstadt, the harbor for St. Petersburg, to Vladivostok, Russia's principal port on the Pacific, from which point the relief of Port Arthur would be undertaken.[101] Wilhelm had given formal approval to the HAPAG contract, and from the beginning he was determined to use Nicholas's naval plight to extract an alliance from Russia. By the end of 1904, the Russian armada lay at anchor off German South West Africa, where it took on coal. The fleet's progress had been beset with difficulties with the British, Japan's treaty partner. Wilhelm claimed, with some truth, that the HAPAG coaling contract was a risky business exposing Germany to the danger of war with Great Britain. This required that further provisioning of the Russian fleet had to be contingent on guarantees that Russia would come to Germany's aid in such an eventuality. Wilhelm knew that he had Nicholas in a corner, and he wrote smugly to Bülow, "But as the Chinaman says in pigeon English: 'if no have got coal, how can do?'"[102] Only when Russia had indicated its willingness to enter into negotiations with Germany was enough coal provided to Admiral Zinovi Rozhdestvensky to enable him to make for his next coaling point, Nossi-bé in Madagascar.

The tsar's war was by now completely in shambles. On 22 January 1905 a rebellion broke out in St. Petersburg and soon spread throughout Russia; by late spring, the tsar had a full-fledged revolution at home with which to contend as well as a disastrous war in distant Asia. At the very beginning of 1905, Port Arthur had fallen to the Japanese, leaving Admiral Togo now free to go out in search of the Russian fleet. At Bülow's urging, the Kaiser, increasingly fearful of British intervention, reluctantly permitted the Russian fleet to take on coal at Nossi-bé, but he was now more than ever determined to wring a pact from Nicholas II, thereby leaving France without a continental ally. Delcassé would then have an opportunity to discover the meager value of his Entente Cordiale with his newfound friends in London. Bringing about France's isolation was critical to Wilhelm II because in the spring of 1905 he found himself involved in a confrontation with Delcassé over the sultanate of Morocco, a collision that raised the prospect that Germany might soon find itself at war.

On 12 April 1904, four days after France and England entered into the Entente Cordiale, Chancellor Bülow addressed the Reichstag, some of whose members sensed that the agreement concluded in London presaged a profound redirection in European diplomacy, a tack that would prove disadvantageous for Germany. Bülow noted that the sultanate of Morocco, which the Entente Cordiale treated with special attention, was an area in which Germany had economic interests that it "must and would protect."[103] The chancellor assured the deputies that Germany welcomed the resolution of Anglo-French colonial differences that the pact had effected. But the truth was that the Entente Cordiale, like so many other developments in European diplomacy since Bismarck's fall from office in 1890, was a defeat for Germany, another sign of Berlin's alienation from the other powers. "We need a success in our foreign policy," Prince Lichnowsky, one of Bülow's trusted advisers in the Foreign Office, complained a few days after the signing of the treaty.[104] The chancellor agreed, and Morocco, it seemed, might be the place for a restorative diplomatic victory.

Germany was not unique among the powers in its concern about Morocco. The French and the Spanish had been active there for many years, followed by the merchants of most of the other European powers as well as by American traders, but the native government at Fez had thereafter proved incapable of preserving order and protecting the lives and property of European residents. In 1901 the Sultan Abdul Aziz had signed a treaty yielding to the French patrol rights along his border with Algeria, and three years later the British acknowledged, in the Entente Cordiale, France's superior position in Morocco. The sultan and other Moroccans who resented French rapacity were on the lookout for a protector who would guard the sultanate against despoliation by France. Bülow regarded the fact that Paris had not consulted Germany before acting in Morocco to be a deliberate provocation by the anti-German foreign minister, Delcassé, the architect of France's aggressive Moroccan policy, and he wanted Germany to react with vigor.[105] He made no headway in enlisting the Kaiser. Some years earlier Wilhelm II had toyed with the notion of having Germany take Morocco as compensation if, as rumor early in 1896 had it, France succeeded in buying the Canaries from Spain.[106] He subsequently abandoned this idea and five years later informed both Edward VII and King Alfonso XIII of Spain that Germany, although commercially active in the sultanate, had no territorial ambitions there.[107] The French were in fact welcome to such a wasteland. Possession of the desert would take their minds off the loss of Alsace-Lorraine and would weaken France's military power, and after the French had spent a fortune and countless lives pacifying the unruly country, German traders could reap the advantage.[108]

Bülow's underlings in the Foreign Office, unperturbed by the Kaiser's lack of interest, were virtually unanimous in encouraging the chancellor to press vigorously for a naval demonstration in Tangiers, Morocco's principal port and the sultan's capital, since both economic interests and diplomatic prestige were at stake.[109] Especially influential with the chancellor at this juncture was the senior counselor in the Foreign Office, Friedrich von Holstein, who agreed with Bülow that Germany needed forcefully to remind France that it could not act unilaterally in matters affecting Germany's interests. This was especially necessary in light of the Entente Cordiale, for Paris would now be bolder than ever.[110] A German challenge to France would of course increase the danger of war between two powers that had for decades been at dagger's point, but Holstein's expectation was that the Moroccan issue would eventually be settled not by taking up arms but rather by convening an international conference, one that Holstein was sure would result in a rejection of French designs in Morocco.[111] If Britain then jettisoned France in such a moment of crisis, the Entente Cordiale would be a dead letter, with the French wondering what use the pact had been to them, militarily or diplomatically. To Holstein, German policy in Morocco was thus a means of dealing simultaneously with both France and Great Britain, frustrating one ally and discrediting the other. It was a stratagem that Bülow wholeheartedly embraced.

In January 1905, the French government sent a special diplomatic mission to Fez, presumably to arrange France's takeover of the Moroccan government, and this development finally convinced the Kaiser that Germany must act. After receiving assurances from the war minister, General Karl von Einem, that the army was in a state of readiness in the event of hostilities with France, Wilhelm agreed that the light cruiser *Stein* should be sent to Tangiers as a sign of Germany's intention to participate in Morocco's future. The ship dropped anchor briefly and without incident in mid-February 1905.[112] Wilhelm, meanwhile, decided to go to Morocco. His travel plans for the spring of 1905 called for a state visit to King Carlos in Lisbon, followed by a Mediterranean cruise on board the Hamburg-American Line steamer *Hamburg* that would include stops at Tangiers and Gibraltar en route to Italy. Wilhelm's notion of anchoring at Tangiers had a cultural rather than a political aim. In 1898, he had made a trip to the Holy Land and from that experience had developed an interest in Moslem civilization. This had whetted his desire to see North Africa, and having the *Hamburg* at his disposal would mean that the Kaiser could take along a large number of guests.

Wilhelm ordered that the *Hamburg* was to call at Tangiers for only several hours, which he believed would suffice to acquaint the German party with the exotic culture of the area.[113] By his command, the layover was to be devoted exclusively to sightseeing, and there were to be no official receptions or audiences. It might be, the Kaiser informed Bülow, that he himself would remain on the *Hamburg* and only the entourage would disembark for a tour of the port. Although there was not a trace of cowardice in Wilhelm, his reluctance to land stemmed from concern about the physical dangers, ranging from assassination to accident, attendant on landing at Tangiers. The port was unprotected and notoriously beset by winds, and once in the city, Wilhelm would have either to walk or to ride an unfamiliar Berber horse through narrow, crowded streets that might harbor Moslem fanatics or Spanish anarchists. Bülow dismissed these reservations, for he had decided, quite contrary to the Kaiser's view of the stop at Tangiers, not only that Wilhelm should disembark at Tangiers but that his excursion on land should have a manifest, diplomatic purpose. To convey this, Wilhelm's visit should be invested with as much official pomp as possible, in order to drive home to the French that Germany expected to play a role in Morocco. Bülow, who remained in Berlin after the Kaiser's departure in mid-March, knew how to get what he wanted. The chancellor repeatedly telegraphed the *Hamburg*, appealing to Wilhelm's vanity by reminding him that if he failed to land or even if he did so incognito, Delcassé would claim that the Kaiser had retreated before French pressure. If, on the other hand, a triumphal entry was made into Tangiers, Delcassé would be embarrassed, and Wilhelm's forthright action would frustrate France's adventurous attempt to appropriate Morocco.[114]

After steaming south from Lisbon on 28 March, the Kaiser still had not resolved whether to land at Tangiers. The *Hamburg*, delayed by high winds, was late arriving off the port, and he remained in a state of uncertainty.[115] An adjutant was sent ashore to determine whether the ship's launch could safely make the passage. He returned with a favorable report, whereupon Richard von Kühlmann, the German chargé d'affaires at Tangiers, implored Wilhelm not to forget that "all Africa" was watching him. The Kaiser thereupon suddenly announced, "We'll land."[116] Clambering into the launch, he made the trip through drenching seas—one of his adjutants dramatically characterized the stormy passage as a "murderous business" (*Mordgeschichte*)—and arrived safely on shore.[117] Wilhelm then rode on horseback to the German legation, where he was received by the diplomatic colony and by the Sultan's uncle, Mulay Abdul.[118] From Berlin, Bülow had provided precise, even literal, directions as to what the Kaiser should say to the various persons to whom he would be presented in Tangiers, urging him to restrict his greeting to the French secretary of legation in Tangiers, Count de Chérisy, to a silent handshake. That would serve as a tacit sign of German determination and would avoid the complications that might ensue if Wilhelm were to indulge in his notorious verbosity.[119] The Kaiser disregarded Bülow's directions entirely, speaking at some length with the count and warning Chérisy that he was determined to uphold Germany's commercial interests in the sultanate. He may also have declared that Germany would insist on equal rights in Morocco and that he would not tolerate the sultanate's becoming a second Tunis, where in 1881 the bey had been forced to acknowledge a French protectorate.[120] After receiving the German colony at the legation, Wilhelm retraced his steps to the harbor, reboarded the *Hamburg* without incident, and made for Gibraltar, very satisfied with his performance.[121]

The Kaiser then continued his voyage and on 5 April reached Naples, where he learned that the landing at Tangiers had created international consternation.[122] The press in London and Paris declared that his visit to Morocco was a premeditated provocation designed not only to challenge France in Africa but also to break up the newly formed Entente Cordiale, thus attributing to Wilhelm what Bülow and Holstein had in fact conceived. Diplomats who knew the Kaiser supposed that he had provoked the crisis because of his pique at having been disregarded by France in resolving the future of Morocco.[123] In St. Petersburg, the Germanophobe foreign minister, Count Lambsdorff, regarded Wilhelm's act as characteristically gratuitous, but at the same time he noted that eventually the Kaiser's inconstant attention would move on to some object other than Morocco.[124] President Theodore Roosevelt noted a pointed and unflattering contrast between Wilhelm and his uncle, Edward VII, the one a "jumpy" troublemaker, the other an effective agent in European diplomacy. "I get exasperated with the Kaiser because of his sudden vagaries like this Moroccan policy," the president wrote to his friend, the British diplomat Cecil Spring-Rice.[125] The entire expedition was, in Foreign Minister Lord Lansdowne's opinion, "an extraordinarily clumsy bit of diplomacy," and it added to Edward VII's already great mistrust of both Bülow and Wilhelm.[126]

Although Wilhelm airily characterized his visit to Tangiers as a "minor incident" (*Nebenaktion*), he was probably not unpleased to be at the center of European attention. If at first reluctant to land, the Kaiser had come wholeheartedly to support the policy of his government. As far as Wilhelm II was concerned, it was Delcassé, abetted by Edward VII, who was responsible for having precipitated the crisis in Morocco. The French arrogantly assumed that France, acting with London's connivance, could seize the sultanate.[127] The Kaiser declared that he was willing to assent to France's having a predominant role in Morocco, but he had been offended — treated, in his favorite expression, as a *"quantité négligeable"* — by not having been consulted. In the face of such deliberate provocation, he had had no choice but to maintain the sultan's sovereignty, the integrity of the Moroccan state, and the free economic access there by all the powers.[128] The open door could not be secured if France received disproportionate financial privileges in the sultanate, and its military forces were to be restricted to policing the Algerian frontier but no more. "I will not have a second Tunis," he declared, reiterating what he claimed he had told Count de Chérisey during his stop at Tangiers.[129] The Kaiser assured Bülow that he did not intend to back down, but that did not mean that he was prepared to draw the sword for the sake of Morocco. Only a day after speaking to the chancellor, Wilhelm told a deputation of disappointed commanding generals that he would "never go to war over Morocco."[130]

The French also wanted a peaceful solution, for neither Delcassé nor the government of Premier Maurice Rouvier, nor French public opinion, was prepared to allow Morocco to precipitate war with Germany. Almost from the moment that he had heard that Wilhelm II intended to call at Tangiers, Delcassé had indicated that he was prepared to enter into bilateral negotiations with Germany.[131] The chancellor and Holstein, however, believed that Germany must fixedly insist on an international conference of all the powers. This conclave would bind Delcassé to the treaty of 1881, which recognized Morocco as an area that was to be dealt with by international agreement, thereby scuttling his attempt to take Morocco with Britain's cooperation. Germany could proclaim that in invoking the treaty, it was not advancing its own interests but rather was insisting on the maintenance of an existing diplomatic arrangement. Bülow was confident that Britain would inevitably support his view, leaving France isolated. Premier Rouvier would then be aware that the much vaunted Entente Cordiale was in fact worth little and that the retention of Delcassé, Rouvier's political rival for years, was imprudent. Wilhelm II's trip to Tangiers could therefore be used not only to nip in the bud the Anglo-French pact of 1904 but also to eliminate a man whom Holstein called Germany's "most dangerous enemy" and who to the Kaiser was an "Anglophile enragé." The chancellor and Wilhelm agreed that as long as Delcassé served as foreign minister in Paris, no solution to the Moroccan problem would be possible.[132]

Rouvier was newly installed in office and a novice in diplomacy, making him increasingly apprehensive about retaining the controversial Delcassé. On 11 June 1905 he decided to act, dismissing the foreign minister and assuming his portfolio. Rouvier hoped that Bülow might now be willing to negotiate with *him*, but the chancellor, emboldened by Delcassé's fall, spurned all overtures, and Rouvier therefore was compelled to agree to an international conference. Wilhelm II was jubilant, as were Holstein and the chancellor, for the French surrender was, as President Roosevelt described it, a "diplomatic triumph of the first magnitude."[133] Having got the conference that he believed would decide in Germany's favor, the Kaiser informed a French general, then in Berlin for the crown prince's wedding, that he would "make no further difficulties about Morocco."[134] Wilhelm's reward to Bülow for having inflicted this humiliation on France was to raise him to the dignity of prince. The chancellor did not know it, but this moment of glory was the peak of his career.

Five

THE EULENBURG ROUNDTABLE

C HANCELLOR BERNHARD von Bülow, refulgent in his new princely dignity, had obtained what he and Friedrich von Holstein, counselor in the Foreign Office, had planned in Morocco. Théophile Delcassé, the French minister of foreign affairs, had been felled, and Premier Maurice Rouvier had soon thereafter agreed to a conference of all the powers, to be convened in January 1906 at Algeciras, a port city in southern Spain. This was an illusory victory, however, for if Rouvier lacked Delcassé's combativeness, he did not flinch from energetically defending France's interests. Furthermore, Germany could not count on much goodwill to be forthcoming at Algeciras, for many diplomats feared that the conference would raise issues already believed to be settled, provoke new differences, and in general create difficulties that could have been avoided had Germany not insisted on a conference but instead accepted Delcassé's, and then Rouvier's, invitation to enter into bilateral negotiations.[1]

From the moment the conference opened, Germany's delegates found themselves isolated, and they were unable to overcome this disadvantage. Bülow's two plenipotentiaries, Joseph von Radowitz and Count Christian von Tattenbach, envoys respectively to Spain and Morocco, were particularly unsuitable for the work at hand. Radowitz was old and frail, and the brusque Tattenbach, long a strenuous advocate of an aggressive German policy in Morocco, was soon thoroughly at odds with his conference colleagues. Wilhelm II's unpopularity in almost every capital significantly increased Germany's diplomatic liability. Nowhere was he more mistrusted than in London, for the British, and particularly King Edward VII, were very annoyed at both the Kaiser and Bülow for what they saw as an attempt to sabotage the Entente Cordiale and to promote Germany's power in Europe. As the German ambassador, Count Paul von Wolff Metternich zur Gracht, warned, this attempt was grounds for war.[2] Wilhelm II was not unaware of this feeling in London, but he insisted that his uncle and the British government, rather than himself or Berlin, were responsible for the recent decline in Anglo-German relations, never very warm in any case.[3]

Elsewhere in Europe the story was much the same, for in spite of the diplomatic talent that Wilhelm II alleged he possessed, the Kaiser had long since managed to alienate almost everyone. The French blamed the Kaiser for having precipitated the entire crisis, while the Italians held him responsible for trying to browbeat them into supporting the German position. Both President Theodore Roosevelt and his secretary of state, John Hay, believed that what was at play was the Kaiser's inflated vanity.[4] The Spanish royal family, acutely interested in the fate of neighboring Morocco, was quite hostile to Wilhelm, and the obtuse dowager Queen María Cristina, born an Austrian archduchess, feared that from *folie des grandeurs* Wilhelm might try to annex Austria after the aged Emperor Franz Joseph died. Her son Alfonso XIII, who was unmarried, resented Wilhelm's attempts to have him wed a German princess and to have him outfit the Spanish army with guns from the German industrial firm of Krupp. Alfonso was also afraid that the Kaiser hungered to replicate his forefathers' exploits on the battlefield, perhaps in the Moroccan desert.[5]

The Russian attitude toward Germany at the time of the Moroccan crisis was also profoundly suspicious, and the object of St. Petersburg's concern was not so much Bülow as it was the Kaiser, who in 1905 was attempting to use Russia's desperate straits in the war with Japan to force Nicholas II to sign an alliance with Berlin in return for German help in coaling the Russian fleet being sent around the world to raise the siege of Port Arthur.[6] The British, determined to do nothing to undermine their ally Japan, interfered with Germany's coaling operations, refusing to permit the sale of Welsh coal or to allow the Russian fleet the use of their colonies in Africa and Asia as coaling stations. An unfortunate incident in October 1904 off Dogger Bank in the North Sea, during which the Russians had opened fire on a British fishing fleet in the mistaken belief that it was the Japanese navy sent to Europe to head off the Russians, had raised the possibility of an Anglo-Russian war. Nicholas II believed that Britain's intransigence was an unhappy by-product of the Entente Cordiale of 1904, which had made the British confident that France would not honor its 1894 alliance with Russia but would instead stick by the Entente Cordiale.[7] If that were true, then on whom other than Germany could Russia depend? The war with Japan therefore forced Nicholas II reluctantly to consider the notion of a Russo-German combination, and he authorized negotiations with Berlin in the hope that France could eventually be induced to join in, although given its long hatred of Germany because of the

Franco-Prussian War of 1870–71, this would not be easy to accomplish. Nicholas II insisted that his ally France be kept abreast of the Russo-German pourparlers, for the Rouvier government might well resent being confronted with a fait accompli. Wilhelm, who agreed to the eventual inclusion of France in a pact between Berlin and St. Petersburg, nonetheless feared that drawing Paris into the initial negotiations might spoil the chances of the swift conclusion of a Russo-German alliance.[8]

At the end of October 1904, Wilhelm supplied the tsar with a draft alliance, and this led to a flurry of exchanges between the two sovereigns. What emerged from these negotiations was a treaty in which both powers promised to provide the other with military aid in the event either was attacked in Europe *or elsewhere*.[9] Nicholas, however, was unwilling to commit himself without first consulting his French ally, and Wilhelm's insistence that confidences were properly to be shared only between princes or rulers made no impression on the tsar.[10] The matter therefore lay in abeyance as 1904 turned to 1905. The new year, however, brought a series of grave reverses for Nicholas II: the loss of Port Arthur on 2 January 1905; the colossal defeat of the tsar's Manchurian army at Mukden early in March; and finally, on 27 May, the annihilation in the Sea of Japan of the Russian fleet, which was laboriously making for Port Arthur. In addition, at the end of January 1905, Russia had exploded in what the Kaiser called the "Jew revolution."[11] Nicholas II's ability to resist Wilhelm's importuning to enter into an alliance was therefore considerably weaker than it had been during their negotiations in the fall of 1904, and he agreed to meet the Kaiser off the island of Björkö in the Gulf of Finland. After the *Hohenzollern* and the tsar's *Polar Star* dropped anchor at Björkö on 23 July 1905, Nicholas boarded the German yacht for dinner and, in an unusual show of affability, stayed until 3 o'clock in the morning. He assured Wilhelm II that with the Moroccan crisis defused by Delcassé's fall, there were no further barriers to Franco-German accord. Moreover, the tsar declared that he would never enter into an entente with England, most especially not one directed against Germany.[12] At nine the next morning, Wilhelm boarded the *Polar Star*, and he and the tsar retired to Nicholas II's cabin to affix their signatures to the so-called Björkö treaty. Wilhelm had brought along a copy, written in his own hand and in French, of a proposed treaty, a "little agreement" as he called it, that he assured Nicholas would serve as an answer to the Entente Cordiale.[13]

The treaty, to be effective only after Russia had concluded peace with Japan, provided, in the first of its four short paragraphs, that "in the event that one of the two empires were attacked by a European power, its ally would aid it in Europe by land and by sea with all of its forces." The final clause obligated Nicholas II to inform Paris of the pact and to enlist France as a signatory.[14] The Kaiser told Nicholas that the document was a copy of the draft agreement considered in 1904, but in fact Wilhelm had added an important alteration to the handwritten document that he now presented to the tsar. This was the restrictive inclusion of the words *"en Europe"* limiting the area in which the signatories promised one another aid, and it was based on the Kaiser's reasoning that this would relieve the German fleet of the obligation to protect Russia's highly exposed position in Asia.[15] Nicholas II signed the document, which Wilhelm proclaimed to be a "cornerstone in European Politics," one that turned "over a new leaf in the history of the world," all due to the benevolent mercy of God. No sooner had the Kaiser left Björkö than he rapturously assured Nicholas that their pact was only the beginning of a gigantic constellation of nations, embracing not only Germany with its Austro-Hungarian and Italian allies and Russia together with France, but Holland, Belgium, Denmark, Sweden, and Norway as well. The exclusion of Great Britain was pointed.[16]

Whether the Björkö treaty would in fact have brought about the diplomatic revolution Wilhelm claimed is moot because the pact never came into effect and was therefore only another of the Kaiser's unsuccessful diplomatic escapades. The treaty was rejected both in Berlin and in St. Petersburg, for neither Bülow nor the tsar's government wanted to see it implemented. In the Russian capital, Foreign Minister Count Vladimir Lambsdorff, who was neither present at Björkö nor consulted beforehand about what was going on, was anti-German even though he was of Teuton extraction. The treaty, Lambsdorff argued, was an attempt by Germany to tear apart the Entente Cordiale (as indeed it was) and was incompatible with the alliance that Nicholas's father, Alexander III, had signed with France in 1894.[17] Meanwhile, Premier Rouvier informed the Russian ambassador that he had no intention of permitting France to join the league. To ally with Germany would deprive France of revanchism for Alsace-Lorraine, one of the few forces in the fragile Third Republic that provided a sense of national unity. A charismatic leader might be able to carry off such a diplomatic revolution, but Rouvier realized that he could not, for he was a novice in diplomacy and in any case not a particularly forceful personality.[18]

Although Bülow had for years tirelessly advocated a close relationship between Berlin and St. Petersburg, he did not like the Björkö pact any better than did Lambsdorff. The chancellor believed that he could use it to fortify his position by submitting his resignation, since he was confident that Wilhelm would hardly dismiss someone who had only days before claimed a major diplomatic victory over France in bringing about Delcassé's fall. On 3 August 1905 Bülow wrote to the Kaiser, pointing out that Wilhelm's insertion of the limiting phrase "*en Europe*" in defining the spheres in which the treaty would require Germany and Russia to help one another had deprived the document of most of its value.[19] In the chancellor's opinion, Russia, with most of its Asiatic fleet destroyed and in possession of a gigantic but very antiquated army, was not in a position to assist the Fatherland militarily in Europe, although its presence in the Far East and along the Indian frontier could be used to intimidate England. Germany, on the other hand, had the military and naval strength to provide the tsar with substantial aid in Europe. Such a lopsided partnership could not be to Germany's advantage, and rather than agree to it, Bülow was prepared to vacate his office. Wilhelm's reaction to the chancellor's "few cool lines" was hysterical.[20] How could Bülow, his "best and most intimate friend," betray him in this way, especially after the sacrifice the Kaiser had made in carrying out the dangerous landing at Tangiers? Resignation was simply out of the question, for if the chancellor departed, Wilhelm himself would have to bear the responsibility for the international crisis occasioned by his unwilling descent at Morocco. This would kill him, Wilhelm declared, and he implored Bülow to consider the plight of the Kaiserin and his children.

The Kaiser's language was extravagant, his prediction of death absurd, but the urgent froth of his language reveals the depth of his outrage at the chancellor. In the face of Wilhelm's annoyance, Bülow eventually backed down.[21] The Kaiser's problem was now to hold the tsar to the treaty and to combat the influence of Count Lambsdorff, who believed that the Björkö treaty had placed the Franco-Russian alliance in jeopardy. Lambsdorff was a sort of red flag in Berlin, for he was regarded there, as he himself put it, as the "Delcassé russe."[22] Wilhelm insisted that the Björkö agreement did not conflict with Russia's 1894 treaty with France and reminded the tsar that in the recent war between Russia and Japan, it had been Germany, not France, who had been Nicholas's steadfast friend. "This puts Russia morally also under obligation to us," he insisted. "We joined hands and signed *before God*, who heard our vows! . . . What is signed, is signed! and God is our testator!"[23] His entreaties were unavailing, for Nicholas declared in response that the treaty would not go into force until and unless France signed it, for which there was not the least inclination in Paris, or until Wilhelm agreed that the treaty would not apply in the case of a Franco-German war, which the Kaiser correctly noted was the same thing as saying the treaty had never been entered into.[24] By the end of the year, the Björkö treaty was worthless, the Franco-Russian alliance against Germany was still intact, and Nicholas II was more than ever mistrustful of the Kaiser. The real significance of the aborted pact was not diplomatic but internal, for the contention between Bülow and Wilhelm II over the language of the agreement proved to be the beginning of a fatal erosion in the chancellor's once impregnable position at court.

The Kaiser's inability to entice Nicholas into an alliance also meant that, except for Austria-Hungary, Germany was virtually without supporters at the Algeciras conference that convened in January 1906 to settle the Moroccan situation. The German position, Wilhelm declared, was exactly what it had been on the occasion of his trip to Tangiers: Berlin had no territorial interest in Morocco, which was an independent land, but it expected the rights of all nations to be respected. France could not reduce Morocco to the enslaved fiefdom that Tunis had become, but as Wilhelm assured Edward VII, the French might enjoy "exceptional position and rights" along the border with Algeria.[25] Bülow was appalled. For years, the chancellor had been concerned about Wilhelm's careless and sometimes insincere volubility, his touchiness, his lack of tact and tendency to exaggerate, and his love of negotiating singlehandedly with his royal "colleagues." All of this had been regrettably prominent in the Björkö affair. Bülow took the position that although Wilhelm might discuss with the tsar the idea in principle of a treaty, the formulation of the articles should have been left to professional diplomats.[26] The Moroccan crisis, however, presented Bülow with a new problem, for the Kaiser, in spite of all his accustomed bravado, had failed to show the fearlessness needed to execute the diplomatic maneuver in Morocco that the chancellor and Holstein had concocted. Wilhelm had for a long time resisted the landing at Tangiers and then had undermined the chancellor's Moroccan policy by being too fainthearted and by indiscreetly assuring French military figures that he had no intention of becoming involved in a war over Africa with France.[27]

The Kaiser's irresolution aggravated Bülow's already tenuous position at Algeciras. The chancellor instructed the German delegates that France's special position in Morocco might be recognized but that it could not be allowed totally to control the sultanate. Germany would therefore have to take a firm position on the limits of French authority but do so in such a way as not to alienate the other powers. The primary goal of German policy at Algeciras was therefore to avoid becoming isolated.[28] Bülow hoped that the German representatives at Algeciras might succeed in securing a "worthy" peace for Germany and its neighbors, but he complained that his ambitions were being undermined by Wilhelm II, whose quite obvious aversion to going to war over Morocco was confining the chancellor's diplomatic maneuvers.[29] The fear Bülow had of being excluded at the conference table proved in fact to be the reality. One after another, the powers represented at Algeciras adhered to the Anglo-French combination; they were willing to give Germany only enough in the way of concessions to enable Wilhelm and Bülow to save face. The chancellor recognized this quite clearly, and he told a French senator midway through the conference that if France would uphold the Kaiser's dignity by not insisting on absolute authority in Morocco, afterward France could have almost anything in the sultanate it desired.[30] This was a far cry from the assurance with which Bülow had launched the entire crisis a year earlier, when he had been certain that Wilhelm's landing in Tangiers would result in a major coup for Germany.

Throughout the spring of 1906 the delegates had to contend with one German demand after another, all having the Kaiser's backing. The powers, firmly entrenched against Germany, stood united in support of compromises more advantageous to France. Wilhelm II bemoaned the fact that Germany found itself alone, confronted by a Latin alliance of France, Spain, and Italy that clung tenaciously to England.[31] "All the wretched, degenerate Latin peoples have become instruments in England's hands in order to combat German trade in the Mediterranean. Not only do we no longer have any friends," he complained a month before the conference closed, "but this race of eunuchs descended from the farrago of peoples assembled by Rome hates us with all its heart! . . . A struggle between the Germans and the Latins all across the board!"[32] Wilhelm consequently had no alternative but to agree in early April 1906 to the conference terms, which conceded to the French very wide powers in Morocco. At work in the Kaiser's decision to accept the Algeciras treaty was his fear that further wrangling between the European powers might tempt the Moors to take advantage of the fray between the white European powers. Europe could not allow this, for as monotheists, the Moslems were potential allies in the sacred battle that must someday be fought against the yellow race.[33]

Before the Reichstag, Bülow defended the treaty signed at Algeciras as "equally satisfactory to Germany and France and useful to all nations," even though it was in fact a diplomatic defeat of the first order.[34] The Algeciras settlement did indeed maintain the open door in Morocco for foreign commerce, although this right would now be largely supervised by France. King Edward VII correctly observed that the upholding of international rights in Morocco was a Pyrrhic victory, for if Germany's position in the sultanate had been acknowledged, its reputation for diplomacy was now reduced to tatters.[35] The entire crisis had never basically been about Morocco but about Germany's relationship to the other European powers, and the most important diplomatic consequences of the question lay not in northern Africa, which was relatively insignificant, but rather in Paris, London, St. Petersburg, Madrid, and Rome (as well as in Washington). For Germany, it was in these capitals that the real disaster of the Moroccan crisis of 1905–6 was to be found, for virtually everywhere, the reputation of both the chancellor and the Kaiser declined headlong, a descent from which there would be no recovery.

As was always the case with the Kaiser, it was in England that the diplomatic ramifications of the Moroccan crisis were most important. To Wilhelm, the British not only had destroyed the Björkö treaty but also had plotted with France against Germany's role in Morocco and had done everything in their power to ensure that France got what it wanted at Algeciras. The Kaiser believed that Edward VII had even been ready to provoke war, retreating from such a step only when he sensed that his subjects were opposed.[36] The king in fact thought the crisis that Germany had provoked in Morocco was mere bluff, for he was certain his nephew would not draw his sword over such a distant land.[37] To Wilhelm, Edward VII's victory at Algeciras came about because France had been willing to serve as his accomplice and therefore had, with British encouragement, derailed the Kaiser's attempt at Björkö to enlist St. Petersburg and then Paris to enter into an alliance with Germany. France consequently would have to forfeit his goodwill, never very demonstrable, and the Kaiser concluded that it would not be possible in his lifetime to establish truly good relations across the Rhine.[38] Paris had become England's "docile slave"; that being the case, he had no intention of letting France get away with its policy of "offering the Russians her arm, the British her hand, and the Germans [merely] a greeting."[39]

The Moroccan situation also strained Germany's relations with the United States. President Roosevelt considered that the "incommensurable vanity" and "intense egoism" of the ever "jumpy" Kaiser were largely responsible for the problems bedeviling the relationship of the powers. Roosevelt believed that Wilhelm's inflated ego had to be punctured, and he therefore had cooperated with the French at Algeciras.[40] A much more serious consequence of the Kaiser's landing at Tangiers and the later negotiations at Algeciras was the strain they introduced into Germany's relations with Russia. To the tsar, Wilhelm II was responsible for the protraction of the discussions at Algeciras and indeed for the entire crisis over Morocco. At Björkö and in the voluminous correspondence with which Wilhelm II bombarded Nicholas II, the Kaiser had been full of assurances of his friendship for France and his desire to attract the French to the Russo-German alliance, and yet it seemed to Nicholas that Wilhelm was being intransigent about the terms to which Paris would have to agree in order to effect a settlement of the Moroccan issue.[41] The tsar's attitude in turn enraged the Kaiser, who denounced his "colleague" for being weak, indecisive, entirely incapable of dealing with Russia's grave problems, and outrageously ungrateful for all the support Germany had supplied in Nicholas II's disastrous war with Japan. Russia's position at Algeciras, where the tsar's diplomats had steadily supported France, plainly revealed that its value for Germany was "absolutely nil."[42] As a result, Wilhelm came to the conclusion that the forbearance and friendship he had for years shown to Nicholas II had been obviously to no avail and would have to give way to a more brutal policy. Being Slavs, the Russians understood only force, and that was what, in the future, they would get from Berlin.[43]

It would be difficult to overestimate the unhappy inheritance for Germany of the Moroccan crisis that Bülow and Holstein provoked in 1905. Although the two had invented Germany's diplomatic strategy, Wilhelm II received most of the blame, for it was his personality that seemed to mirror Germany's ambitious policy and its lack of sensitivity for the position of France and the other powers. Bülow's Moroccan stratagem wrecked his "free hand" policy with Russia. Nicholas II, alarmed by what Wilhelm had importuned him to sign at Björkö and confused by the Kaiser's contradictory attitude toward France, no longer wanted to have anything to do with Berlin, and one can detect, as Wilhelm himself did, a falling off after 1906 not only in the volume but also in the cordial tone of the correspondence between the two sovereigns.[44] With the tsar disaffected, Bülow's "free hand" had no future, and at the same time, Germany's behavior in the Moroccan crisis had worked quite effectively to bring France and Russia closer together. Thus in 1906 Russia, for the last time, wrote off Germany in favor of France. The Moroccan crisis was instructive to the French and determined the future diplomatic policy of the Quai d'Orsay. It reminded diplomats in Paris once again of the German propensity for challenging France's position as a great power as well as of the intention clearly present in Berlin to destroy the Entente Cordiale. In that, Germany had been foiled, for the British had been resolute in their support of France at Algeciras. Because of the diplomatic assistance not only of London but also of Washington, together with that of Russia and Spain,

Rouvier had succeeded not only in maintaining but even in improving France's preeminence in Morocco as well as its diplomatic position among the powers.

Even among Germany's allies, the picture was almost equally dismal. Italy, although bound to Germany in the Triple Alliance organized by Chancellor Otto von Bismarck in 1882, had done nothing to give Berlin any comfort during the Moroccan crisis. The French ambassador described to Premier Rouvier in June 1905 the "instinctive hatred" of the vast majority of Italians for the haughty attitude of both the Kaiser and his people. The Italian government and King Victor Emmanuel III were equally annoyed.[45] None of this was lost on Wilhelm, who denounced the Italians for trying deceitfully to be all things to all men, serving France and Britain while attempting to retain the advantage of being a partner in the Triple Alliance. The Moroccan crisis had shown that at its core, Italy was in the Anglo-French camp, and the Kaiser advised Bülow that Germany would do well to recognize this fact in planning for the future. Italy was treacherous, and Wilhelm predicted that the moment Germany and Great Britain fell out with one another, Italy would abandon the Triple Alliance, which was exactly what Italy in fact did in 1915.[46] The Italians were profoundly annoyed at Wilhelm II's attempt to poison their relations with France by drawing them into the matter, and even Bülow, whose Italian wife provided him with a vast network of connections in Rome, could not succeed in repairing the damage that both he and the Kaiser had done.

The support that Germany received at Algeciras from the Habsburg Empire was also lukewarm and ineffective. It seemed to the Austrians that the entire Moroccan situation was "one of the numerous fantasies of a brain in a state of ebullition," as the Habsburg envoy in Paris described Wilhelm's contribution to the affair. The Emperor Franz Joseph, one of the few European sovereigns who was able over the years to maintain a good relationship with Wilhelm II, found the Kaiser's behavior during the Moroccan crisis contradictory. The elderly ruler was "baffled" that Wilhelm would on the one hand proclaim that his ambition was a peaceful relationship with his neighbors and then on the other hand insist at Algeciras on terms to which the French could not agree.[47] As the conference entered its final month, the French envoy at Vienna reported to Rouvier that the emperor, his government, and public opinion at large in the Habsburg Empire attributed the difficulties at Algeciras to "the bad faith, the incoherence, and the Caesarean intransigence" of the Germans.[48] The alienation of Germany at Algeciras from the rest of Europe had a major impact on Austro-German relations. Aware after 1906 of the diplomatic encirclement of Germany, Berlin had little choice but to become more tightly entwined with the one power that during the treaty negotiations had not openly assailed the German position. The Moroccan crisis of 1905–6 consequently had the ominous effect of making Berlin in the future more dependent on Vienna, a prospect that for good reason alarmed Bülow.[49] The Algeciras conference had shown how negligible Austria's diplomatic support was, for the allegiance of Franz Joseph's envoys had been tepid and they commanded almost no influence with the other plenipotentiaries. It could hardly be in Germany's interest to attach itself more closely to an ally that was a diplomatic mediocrity, was militarily and financially weak, and was internally divided among Germans, Magyars, and Slavs. And yet, since Austria was the sole great power that Berlin could enlist as a loyal ally, this would prove to be precisely what happened. Even in Vienna, the one place where he still had friends, Wilhelm II managed to blunder. The Kaiser sent Foreign Minister Count Agenor von Goluchowski a telegram thanking him for serving as a "brilliant second" in furthering Germany's interests at the Algeciras conference, a remark that, if well-intended, seemed insulting to the Austrians.[50]

The domestic repercussions of the Moroccan incident in Germany were also telling. Although Bülow claimed that his policy had been successful, the results at Algeciras hardly offered much confirmation of such an argument, and Wilhelm II had few illusions on the subject. The Kaiser believed that Holstein was the person responsible for the Moroccan situation and Germany's resulting diplomatic isolation and that Bülow had been too susceptible to his friend's erroneous plans.[51] Even before the unfortunate landing at Tangiers, Wilhelm had warned the chancellor that it would all end in Germany's standing alone in Europe, and now it was painfully clear that he had been right.[52] The Kaiser complained that after Tangiers, Bülow had used him as a "puppet," a charge that he was still making when he was in exile in Holland over thirty years later.[53] In the wake of Algeciras, Wilhelm tended to believe that diplomatic affairs would be better served by avoiding the chancellor and the Foreign Office, and rumors consequently arose that Bülow might soon be replaced.[54] Wilhelm assured Philipp Eulenburg in September 1905 that he and the chancellor had everything "in order." Eulenburg was not convinced that this was so, however, for the Kaiser continued to complain about Bülow's aborted resignation over the Björkö treaty and declared that the chancellor was jealous that it had not been *he* who had made the treaty with Nicholas II. By September 1906, five months after the conference at Algeciras had concluded, Wilhelm II was in fact contemplating replacing Bülow with someone more to his satisfaction.[55] The chancellor was certainly aware of his problematical position, and he believed, if his memoirs are to be trusted, that although he had succeeded in surviving this first trial of wills with the Kaiser, it was not at all certain that he would emerge the victor from a second encounter.[56] Enmeshed in a failure that might well prove fatal to his future, Bülow was determined in 1906 to find a scapegoat for the Moroccan fiasco and to ensure that the efforts of his enemies and rivals did not further diminish Wilhelm's confidence in him.

Bülow's first casualty was Holstein, for many years the senior counselor at the Foreign Office in the Wilhelmstrasse. The two men had been intimates for years, but there were liabilities in a friendship with Holstein, who was pathologically suspicious and an intriguer without parallel. A fellow diplomat, Arthur von Brauer, who claimed to be one of only four men who had remained Holstein's friend throughout his life, declared that the counselor was "difficult to his superiors, distasteful (*unsympathisch*) to his colleagues, and sinister (*unheimlich*) to diplomats in the field."[57] By the spring of 1906, the chancellor had no desire to retain Holstein, one reason being that after the Moroccan incident, Wilhelm II had turned against Holstein. The Kaiser met the reclusive counselor only once, and then only because Holstein, fearful even before Morocco that he was falling from grace, asked for an audience. The meeting took place at a dinner given by Bülow on 12 November 1904, but Wilhelm curiously, and perhaps deliberately, ignored Holstein and had only a perfunctory conversation with him.[58] Not long after the Algeciras conference had come to its unsatisfactory conclusion, the Kaiser declared that Holstein had become "completely crazy" and that his eccentric behavior had utterly demoralized the Foreign Office.[59]

Holstein determined that if he was doomed to fall, he would take his principal enemy, Count Philipp Eulenburg, with him. Until about 1900, Eulenburg had enjoyed a particularly intimate relationship with Wilhelm II, who in that year had called Eulenburg his "best friend."[60] The two men shared an enthusiasm for hunting and music, and the Kaiser, with his delight in always appearing to be the autocrat, undoubtedly found the count's ardent monarchism congenial. Eulenburg was a Prussian conservative, a foe of any sort of parliamentary authority, and unlike the Kaiser, he was fixedly hostile to England. Liberals consequently were opposed to Eulenburg, but even among the conservative aristocrats who dominated the government, he was not popular, especially not in the military circles to which the Kaiser was particularly close.[61] He was considered an opportunist, a man of ambition rather than talent, a dilettantish aesthete with exotic mannerisms who surrounded himself with a small circle of like-minded friends. They constituted the membership of the "roundtable" that, sometimes in the company of the Kaiser, frequently joined Eulenburg at his country seat at Liebenberg in Brandenburg not far from Berlin. It appeared that Eulenburg's entire career could be attributed to his assiduous cultivation of the Kaiser, who had promoted Eulenburg from one diplomatic post to another, keeping him always close to Berlin.

Like Eulenburg, Holstein was a Prussian, a conservative, and a monarchist, and for years Eulenburg had been one of his protégés in the Foreign Office, the recipient of frequent and voluminous letters. Holstein, however, differed with Eulenburg over the question of the extent to which the crown should rule Germany. To Eulenburg, royal autocracy was Prussia's governing principle, and although not blind to Wilhelm's faults, he applauded and encouraged the sovereign's energetic intrusion into diplomatic and domestic policy. Eulenburg also acted out of self-interest, for as long as he was the all-powerful ruler's closest friend, his influence in affairs of state would be enormous. Holstein, on the other hand, had a very meager estimation of the Kaiser's ability, one that shrank with experience, and he therefore found it intolerable that Eulenburg should encourage Wilhelm's delusions of majesty. From the mid-1890s, after half a decade of the young ruler's vagaries, Holstein had warned Eulenburg of the dangers of inflating Wilhelm's ego, and Eulenburg's unwillingness to heed Holstein's advice, a trait that Holstein could not tolerate in anyone, brought an end to their friendship.[62]

Holstein made no move to attack Eulenburg publicly, a reticence that was not due to any spirit of generosity, of which he seems to have been devoid, but to the fact that by early in the new century, Eulenburg's friendship with Wilhelm II had declined to the point that Eulenburg no longer seemed to Holstein to be worth pursuing. Even Eulenburg himself admitted in 1902 that the Kaiser seemed to be unhappy with him.[63] A few years earlier, Eulenburg's brother Friedrich had been charged with homosexuality during a divorce proceeding, and rather than attempting a defense, Friedrich had resigned his commission as an officer in the guards. Friedrich's failure to defend himself affected his relations with Eulenburg, who had tried in vain to persuade Wilhelm to help Friedrich.[64] At the end of August 1902, Eulenburg resigned from his ambassadorial post and returned to Liebenberg, where for several years he led a rather reclusive life. The Kaiser did not hunt there in the fall of 1902, as had been his custom for some years, and it seemed that Eulenburg's once great influence at court had come to an end, a development that gave Holstein great satisfaction.

Holstein's confidence that Eulenburg had been eliminated was premature, however, for by 1904 there were conspicuous signs that the old attachment that Wilhelm II had felt for his friend was beginning to revive.[65] In April 1906, while hunting with Eulenburg in Silesia, Wilhelm awarded his friend Prussia's highest decoration, the Black Eagle. He simultaneously made the same award to Joseph von Radowitz, the ambassador to Spain who had limply represented Germany at the recently concluded Algeciras conference. Radowitz's eagle could be explained as a means of proclaiming, however unpersuasively, that Germany had secured its objectives at Algeciras. There was no specific accomplishment that could account for Eulenburg's award, however, and therefore it seemed reasonable to interpret the decoration as a sign by the Kaiser of the return of his friend to an intimate place in the retinue. That in any case was precisely the interpretation that Holstein put on the matter, and if Eulenburg was now in Wilhelm II's good graces, it meant that he would once again be active in encouraging the Kaiser's Caesarean inclinations. As a more troubling consideration to Holstein, Eulenburg's return to grace could be construed as the repudiation of the policy of the Bülow government in Morocco and the crown's assumption of the direction of foreign affairs.[66] It was Eulenburg, Holstein was sure, who had convinced the Kaiser that Holstein wanted to foment a European war over Morocco and who had persuaded Wilhelm not to press France too hard at Algeciras.[67] That being the case, there was nothing left for Holstein to do but submit his resignation, and on 3 April 1906 Holstein sent Bülow such a letter, his fourteenth in recent years. The chancellor replied that he wanted to discuss the matter with the Kaiser before acting, but he had no opportunity to do so because two days after receiving Holstein's resignation, Bülow fainted on the floor of the Reichstag.

From early April until mid-November 1906 the ailing chancellor was either away from Berlin or out of public view. This worked to his advantage, for he could now proceed to have the Kaiser accept Holstein's resignation without himself being personally involved in the affair.[68] The chancellor's duplicity succeeded, for Holstein believed that it was Eulenburg who had brought about his fall. On 1 May, he therefore wrote an extraordinarily insulting letter to Eulenburg: "Your aim of many years, my removal, has now at last been achieved. The filthy attacks against me are also supposed to be in accord with your wishes. . . . I am now free, I need exercise no restraint, and can treat you as one treats a contemptible person with your characteristics. I do so herewith and expect to do more."[69] In early November 1906 Wilhelm went to Liebenberg for an extended hunt.

The visit attracted attention because the chancellor was still recovering from his fainting episode seven months earlier, and the question remained as to whether or not he would be able to return to his post when the Reichstag reconvened later in the month. In such an unresolved situation, Wilhelm's actions were closely watched.[70] There is no doubt that the Kaiser wanted to ease Bülow out of office in 1906, probably in part because of the chancellor's uncertain physical condition and in part because of his irritation over Bülow's opposition to the Björkö treaty and his failure in Morocco. Eulenburg encouraged him to do so.[71] In August, Wilhelm asked the ambassador to Italy, Count Anton Monts, to assume the chancellorship. Monts, who championed an Anglo-German rapprochement, was convinced that he would find himself in perpetual conflict with Admiral Alfred von Tirpitz and other Anglophobes. He therefore declined the offer, forcing the Kaiser to continue the search for a replacement.[72] Before a successor could be determined, however, Bülow recovered and returned to Berlin.

Holstein was happy to see the chancellor back in office, but he was determined that Eulenburg, whose return to the Kaiser's fold he believed represented a threat to Germany's future, be brought to ruin. His agent would be Maximilian Harden, editor of the irreverent *Die Zukunft* ("The Future"). This journal for years had attacked, although not by name, Eulenburg and other members of the Kaiser's entourage, as well as the sovereign himself, for their attempt to create a "personal regime" (*persönliches Regiment*), and Harden's diatribes had contributed to Eulenburg's decision in 1902 to resign as ambassador in Vienna.[73] Harden had been fined and jailed more than once on charges of lèse-majesté, but this did not deter him in the least from continuing his campaign. Holstein proceeded to give the vitriolic journalist advice and information to promote suspicion that Eulenburg and his circle had for years carried on a policy designed to magnify the Kaiser's importance. Hearing of Holstein and Harden's maneuvers against him, Eulenburg was alarmed. "What will *these two* brew?" he wrote in his diary.[74] Harden needed neither Holstein's information nor his encouragement to move against Eulenburg, for Harden had been observing, over twenty years and with increasing disapproval, the thralldom that the prince exercised on Wilhelm II. The revival of the Kaiser's friendship in 1906 revealed by his presence at Liebenberg and the award of the Black Eagle drove Harden to act, not only because these were unmistakable signs of Eulenburg's restored position but also because one of the other guests at Liebenberg was Eulenburg's old friend, Raymond Lecomte, the second secretary of the French embassy in Berlin.

It seemed diplomatically indiscreet that so soon after the Moroccan crisis a French officer should be asked to join the Kaiser and a small group of his friends. Harden would have been yet more alarmed had he known that Wilhelm, on meeting Lecomte at Liebenberg, was very taken by the officer, whom he described as one of the most charming men he had ever encountered.[75]

Thus on 17 November 1906, Harden published in the *Zukunft* his first open attack on Eulenburg, calling him by name the evil genius behind Wilhelm II's pretensions to absolute rule. In a second article, which appeared a week later, Harden threatened to continue the attack, whereupon Eulenburg, who was now nervous, as Harden had anticipated he would be, about what might next appear in the pages of the *Zukunft*, left for an extended sojourn in Switzerland. When, however, Eulenburg returned after a month and was again, in mid-January 1907, seen in Berlin with the Kaiser, Harden attacked him again, this time for enabling the French to insert their agent Lecomte in the "roundtable" of the Kaiser's intimate friends. Bülow, resentful at what he believed to have been Eulenburg's attempt in April 1906 to persuade Wilhelm II to replace the ailing chancellor, assembled an incriminating dossier on Eulenburg and quietly passed it on to Harden. The chancellor had secretly brought about Holstein's removal, and he would now do the same for Eulenburg.

In two articles, published on 13 and 27 April 1907, Harden implied that several members of the "roundtable" were secret homosexuals: Eulenburg; Count Kuno von Moltke, an adjutant-general to the Kaiser and commandant of the garrison in Berlin; the French diplomat Lecomte; and General Count Wilhelm von Hohenau, one of Wilhelm's aides-de-camp. Naming no names, Harden implied that the Kaiser ("*Liebchen,*" in the terminology of the homosexual coterie) was involved. Harden's articles occasioned the widest interest in Berlin, where there had already been considerable speculation about the homoerotic tendencies of the Liebenberg set. Everyone knew, it seemed, except the Kaiser. Wilhelm was aware that for years Harden had published articles that were obliquely critical of his court and himself, but he had not read them. In his opinion, Harden was a "poisonous monster from some bottomless pit, a blemish on our people."[76] Wilhelm was notorious for liking all news to be good, and none of his entourage were prepared to tell him that his "best friend" Eulenburg, as well as Moltke, who was also a close companion, were both widely believed to be homosexual. It was imperative that the Kaiser be informed, for not only was Berlin afire with gossip based on the *Zukunft* insinuations, but there were rumors that Chancellor Bülow and the general-intendant of the royal theater, Count Georg von Hülsen-Haeseler, were also suspected of perversity. This was a matter that had clearly got entirely out of hand, for if the Kaiser's closest friends were implicated, might not the scandal ultimately extend to the throne itself? There had been rumors for years that the Kaiser and Eulenburg were lovers.[77] If pushed to the wall, what might Eulenburg or other members of the "roundtable" allege about Wilhelm's sexuality? What use had Wilhelm and his friend made of the arrangements that permitted private access between their bedrooms at Rominten and Liebenberg or between their cabins on the royal yacht?[78] Someone had to inform the Kaiser, but who would be the bearer of bad news?

Two of Wilhelm's adjutant-generals on whom he relied without question, Generals Hans von Plessen and Count Dietrich von Hülsen-Haeseler (the brother of the general-intendant), decided that the Kaiser would believe the incriminating information only if it came from a person whose only motive in telling him was to save the Prussian crown from the scandal that seemed about to overwhelm it. That person was the crown prince, and the two generals persuaded him to confront his father with the unsavory revelations. On 2 May 1907 the prince showed Wilhelm the two *Zukunft* articles, informing his father that "as future bearer of the throne and as the first subject of His Majesty," he had "the right and the duty to explain relationships to the Kaiser that could no longer be tolerated."[79] The Kaiser's reaction was one of stupefied astonishment; he could at first believe only that the charges leveled against his friend were gross calumnies. He understood, however, that the dignity of the Hohenzollern crown was at stake, and he therefore decreed that Eulenburg would have to be either "cleared or stoned" (*gereinigt oder gesteinigt*).[80] Apart from his alarm at the *Zukunft* allegations of homosexuality in his entourage, Wilhelm had an additional reason to be concerned. Harden's aim was to discredit the attempts made by Eulenburg's coterie to create a royal despotism, and his articles consequently argued that Wilhelm II had allowed himself to become the willing puppet of this group of sexual perverts. Harden's revelation of the Kaiser as a pliable weakling in the hands of such an unsavory crew might destroy Wilhelm's dignity, which was already imperiled through his close connections to these alleged homosexuals.[81]

The Kaiser ordered General Gustav von Kessel to write to Eulenburg, curtly telling him that his sovereign expected to be informed as to what he intended to do about the *Zukunft* allegations and asking whether he felt that he was "guiltless of these insinuations (*Anspielungen*)."[82] Eulenburg at once replied, in a letter to the Kaiser, that Harden's charges were false and that Wilhelm should have known from their friendship over two decades that this was so. The prince explained that he had not moved against the *Zukunft* because he had no desire to involve Wilhelm in Harden's claim that the Eulenburg "roundtable" existed to advance the monarch's "autocratic appetites."[83] Meanwhile Bülow and his friends among the royal adjutants were busy stirring up the Kaiser to take a more punitive position against Eulenburg and Moltke. Bülow may well have recognized that the mounting Eulenburg scandal, with its focus on *other* minions of the Kaiser's, might somehow help him salvage his own position.[84] On 31 May, Wilhelm instructed Eulenburg that he was either to introduce legal proceedings against Harden at once or to return his Black Eagle insignia and immediately leave Germany. In any case, he was to take his pension and retire formally from the diplomatic service.[85] Eulenburg took no steps to sue Harden, nor did he return his decoration. Moltke, however, elected to try to clear himself. His suit against Harden for slander, heard in October 1907, found for the defendant, and the sordid evidence spread before the court suggested that a group of deviants surrounded the Kaiser. The Moltke trial proceedings were the subject of tempestuous debate on the floor of the Reichstag, where the chancellor lamely attempted to turn aside the criticism of Wilhelm's retinue. The Kaiser was enraged that this parliamentary "band of rascals" (*Lumpenpack*) had had the temerity to involve itself in the affair, and he was annoyed with the chancellor for having let the matter come to such public attention.[86] Meanwhile, in early November 1907, Bülow himself was at the center of another homosexual trial. Adolf Brand, the publisher of the journal *Gemeinschaft der Eigenen* ("Brotherhood of One's Own"), a journal directed at a homosexual readership, had accused the chancellor of perverse sexual acts. Eulenburg, who had been excused for reasons of health from testifying in the Moltke case, appeared in court on behalf of Bülow and testified under oath that he, Eulenburg, had never had homosexual relations as defined under article 175 of the Prussian civil code, nor had he known Bülow to have done so.

A month later, in mid-December 1907, Eulenburg was again called as a witness, this time in a second action for slander that Moltke had filed against Harden. Eulenburg repeated his earlier testimony that he had done nothing actionable under article 175, but when asked whether he had ever indulged in any homosexual relations that were *not* included under its rubric, he became evasive. This trial reversed the earlier decision and decided in favor of Moltke, with Harden being given a four-month term in jail. Eulenburg and Moltke, it seemed, were safe, and Wilhelm declared that both were once again to be restored to favor.[87] That might have happened except that Harden learned, through detectives in his employ, that there were two working-class Bavarian men who had declared that many years earlier, in the 1880s, they had had homosexual relations with Eulenburg.[88] If the two could be led to provide convincing testimony under oath in court, Eulenburg would be guilty of perjury. Harden therefore set about to have a Munich newspaper print, on 25 March 1908, an article alleging that the *Zukunft* had called off its attack on Eulenburg either because Harden in fact had no incriminating evidence or because Eulenburg had paid Harden a million marks not to reveal further evidence about his homosexuality.[89] Harden then brought suit for libel against the newspaper, arguing that he did in fact have ample evidence, notably the testimony that could be given by the two humble Bavarians. At the ensuing trial, the testimony of these two witnesses could not be controverted, and as a result Harden won the case and collected a one-hundred-mark fine, with costs levied against the defendant. The crucial outcome of the case, and the one for which Harden had engineered it, was that it revealed that Eulenburg had perjured himself not once but twice when he had declared that he had not violated article 175. On 1 May, Eulenburg, whose health had seriously deteriorated, was charged in a Prussian court with perjury and shortly thereafter was transported to the Charité hospital in Berlin to await trial. What might be revealed in this proceeding alarmed Bülow, and he ordered that all letters or other documents directed to himself, to Wilhelm II, or to any other high officials were to be secreted.[90]

The Eulenburg trial began in late June 1908, but three weeks later it was broken off because, in the court's opinion, the defendant's health would not allow further proceedings. The Kaiser was exceedingly annoyed, and he notified Bülow that the action must be recommenced.[91] But neither the chancellor nor the Kaiser had the authority to intervene in judicial matters, and the trial was not resumed. In September 1908, Eulenburg was allowed to post bond and return to Liebenberg, where he lived in embittered seclusion until his death in 1921. Not a word or a line ever again passed between him and Wilhelm II, although Eulenburg believed, almost certainly without warrant, that the Kaiser had written an undelivered (or unsent) letter to him and had also wanted to see him, but that Generals Plessen, Kessel, and Hülsen had persuaded the Kaiser not to do so.[92]

Eulenburg's fall was gratifying to the chancellor, for it eliminated the only person whose intimacy with the Kaiser exceeded his own. Bülow had, however, no real cause for confidence. The Eulenburg affair had done nothing to improve his already frayed relationship with Wilhelm II. Bülow was certainly aware of the decline in his status with the Kaiser, and since he was always closely attuned to, and in part responsible for, the rumor mills of Berlin, he must have known of the speculation, widely entertained, that he was no longer secure in his position. Bülow realized that Wilhelm, always so resistant to advice, found him too often preceptorial in manner, but none of this seems to have caused much worry, for the chancellor was airily confident that these little irritations could be soothed.[93] As for Germany's diplomatic isolation, Bülow's extraordinary vanity immunized him from the thought that *he* might be responsible for this unenviable situation. If the Fatherland had problems, he was certain that they were of Wilhelm's making. In Bülow's opinion, the Kaiser all too frequently acted, as he had at Björkö, without proper consultation; he refused to entertain reports that contained unfavorable information, and he was alarmingly indiscreet in what he said to foreign statesmen and rulers, was overindulgent in showering awards, titles, and decorations, and in general was a liability rather than an asset for his government.[94]

The Kaiser amply reciprocated the chancellor's criticism. Although during Bülow's illness in the spring of 1906 following his collapse in the Reichstag, Wilhelm had brought flowers to Princess Bülow every day and inquired sympathetically about the chancellor's condition, had Count Monts been willing to take the post, he would have installed him in office at once. Wilhelm was not happy about Germany's diplomatic situation, and in his opinion the chancellor was responsible for what had gone wrong, first in the failed aftermath to Björkö, then in Morocco, and finally at Algeciras, as a result of all of which Germany had become cut off from almost all of the other great powers. It was not only in diplomacy that Wilhelm II found Bülow disappointing: the chancellor's handling of domestic affairs also struck the Kaiser as maladroit. From the beginning of his chancellorship, Bülow had established a favorable relationship both with the Catholic Center Party, the largest faction in the Reichstag, and with the Conservatives—a tour de force in that the chancellor united behind himself two parties with very different aims. The Conservatives were generally Prussian, militaristic, opposed to social legislation, and in favor of an aggressive diplomatic and colonial policy, to all of which the Catholic Center, an essentially confessional party, was either opposed or, at best, only tepidly interested.

The chancellor, in forging a "saints and knights" league of Catholics and Conservatives, exposed himself to Wilhelm II's ire, for the Kaiser had no enthusiasm for the Conservative Party and was an implacable foe of the Catholic Center as well as the Roman Catholic Church. Almost from the beginning of his reign, Wilhelm had encountered difficulties at the hands of the agrarian and aristocratic Conservatives, who were suspicious of his early, and fleeting, interest in accommodating the Socialist movement and were hostile to the reductions in the grain tariff that Chancellor Leo von Caprivi had engineered with the Kaiser's support. Wilhelm insisted that the noble Conservatives, whose families supplied his army and bureaucracy with many of their leaders, had an obligation to support the government appointed by the crown.[95] The party, under its resourceful chieftain, Ernst von Heydebrand und der Lasa, had no intention of following Wilhelm's lead. The Conservatives believed that the Kaiser had wrongly sacked Bismarck, sold out agriculture, appeased liberalism, embarrassed Germany by his incessant blabbering, and attempted to impose his rule not only on their party but on Germany itself.[96] As the years went by, Wilhelm became increasingly exasperated with the Conservatives, with their oppositional party newspaper, the *Kreuzzeitung*, and with the protectionist Agrarian League (*Bund der Landwirte*) they sponsored, and the Kaiser disliked Heydebrand for his opposition and for his having won the popular sobriquet "Uncrowned King of Prussia."[97] By 1900, Wilhelm's enmity was so great that it seemed to Eulenburg that he would rather embrace the liberals than traffic with the Right. The Kaiser declared a year later that the party "had outlived itself and no longer understood modern times. It had ceased, once and for all, to be capable of governing." But, as usual, Wilhelm did not mean what he said. He soon admitted to Bülow that he had his disagreements with the Conservatives, but he added: "They are after all the only ones with whom one can govern. The Liberals just aren't gentlemen."[98]

The Catholic Centrists were worse. In his youth Wilhelm had believed that the Roman Catholic Church was useful in combating socialism and democracy, and he was suspected of being sympathetic with the authoritarian character of its hierarchy, its magnificent liturgy, and its learned prelates.[99] The Kaiser, to be sure, never shared the raving anti-Catholicism of his wife and her court ladies, who were incapable of finding anything whatsoever about Catholicism that was not in direct conflict with their orthodox Evangelical faith. Wilhelm was, however, highly suspicious of the Catholic clergy, believing that "ubiquitous" Rome had led his subjects astray and had even seeped into his beloved army, in which therefore the loyalty of Catholic officers was not to be trusted.[100] Although Wilhelm admired a few leading Roman Catholic prelates, he particularly detested the Catholic Center Party. The Kaiser was a foe of *all* parliamentary factions, for the body to which they belonged represented, in his opinion, an illegitimate rival of the crown. The Germans, he declared, were sick of their legislature and would prefer to be ruled by a military junta, a view for which there was in fact almost no evidence.[101] Wilhelm knew few deputies or party leaders, and on the ceremonial occasions on which they met he was not notably cordial. They were, he liked to say, a "band of apes" — black, red, and yellow in hue and unfit to govern.[102] It was the Catholic Center that took the brunt of Wilhelm II's outrage, for to him that "pack of dogs" was too beholden to the papacy, too Bavarian in composition, and too stingy in military appropriations.

In March 1906, a serious division arose between Bülow and the Catholic Center when the party turned against the chancellor's colonial policy, a move that would decisively end the cooperation Bülow had had with the Catholic deputies ever since becoming chancellor in 1900.[103] Until 1906, the Catholic Center had favored Germany's expansion in Africa, largely because of the opportunities provided for Christian proselytization. In March of that year, Bülow, under considerable pressure from the Kaiser, requested the Reichstag to dissolve the colonial section of the Foreign Office and establish a separate imperial Colonial Office with its own state secretary. This administrative rearrangement would not have offended the Catholic Center but for the fact that it was known that Prince Ernst zu Hohenlohe-Langenburg, head of the colonial section in the Foreign Office, was slated to become the first colonial state secretary. That was too much for the Catholic Center, for Hohenlohe not only was considered a man of meager ability but also was a favorite of the Kaiser's and, like his master, was a fervent Protestant. In May 1906, as Bülow lay recovering from his fainting spell, the Catholic Center was a prominent part of a parliamentary constellation that defeated the bill providing for the creation of a Colonial Office.

Wilhelm II was furious at this clerical-Socialist conspiracy, and he demanded that Bülow punish these Catholic traitors. "The Center has become too powerful," Wilhelm declared at the end of 1906. "I must knock it down (*je dois l'abbatre*) even if it costs me dearly."[104] Bülow, aware that his opposition to the Björkö treaty and the failure of his Moroccan policy had diminished the Kaiser's goodwill, believed that he had to act forcefully to avoid losing Wilhelm's favor altogether. The Reichstag would have to be dissolved and an attack mounted in the press against the Catholic Center and its Socialist allies in the hope that the elections for the new chamber would bring about a defeat for both opposition parties. The chancellor might then once again be securely in favor. On 13 December 1906 Bülow, piqued by the rejection of the budget for German South West

Africa, read the Kaiser's dissolution order to the chamber. He then proceeded to involve the government on an unprecedented scale in a campaign against the Catholic and Socialist factions.[105]

The elections occurred on 25 January 1907, with the Socialists losing half of their representation in the Reichstag, falling from 81 to 43 seats. The Catholic Center, however, increased by 5 seats to 105 and was still far and away the largest faction in the chamber, but its position was no longer critical. The elections of 1907, perceived as a battle for or against Germany's international position as a colonial and naval power, resulted in the creation of a nationalist-imperial coalition of conservative and liberal parties that, contrary to the Catholic Center, favored aggressive imperial expansion. This new parliamentary grouping, one that came to be known as the "Bülow bloc," profited by the shrunken number of Socialist deputies, and Bülow could now reign with his "bloc" composed of Conservatives, Free Conservatives, National Liberals, and Progressives, to the exclusion of both the Catholic Center and the Social Democrat Parties. The votes of the Catholic Center, unlike the situation in the Reichstag in the early years of the chancellor's regime, ceased to be numerically decisive. "No longer Catholic, but German [are] trumps," the conservative *Vossische Zeitung* proclaimed with satisfaction two weeks after the election.[106] Wilhelm II, although disappointed that the Catholic Center had done so well, was otherwise exultant at the election results, which he believed might open a new era in parliamentary politics.[107] For the first time since the early years of his reign, a large number of well-wishers assembled in front of the palace in Berlin, and the Kaiser not only appeared on the balcony but addressed the crowd, enjoining them not to "let this festive hour go up in smoke as a temporary wave of patriotic enthusiasm."[108] Wilhelm made it clear to Bülow that the "bloc," welcome as it might be, was to be kept subservient to the government and to the crown. He would tolerate no impertinence from this new parliamentary constellation even though it supported his colonial and naval ambitions.[109]

Bülow's electoral victory in January 1907 and the resulting establishment of a conservative-liberal bloc isolating the Catholic Center formed only the first step in his attempt to regain his position. He now resolved to cull both the Prussian and the imperial cabinets of those who had failed to support the formation of his parliamentary coalition or who otherwise were suspect. In June, Konrad von Studt, the aging Prussian minister for culture who had ties to the Catholics, was pressed into retirement, as was — on the same day and for the same reason — Count Arthur von Posadowsky-Wehner, the industrious but schoolmasterish state secretary of the interior, who had been openly critical of both the chancellor and the Kaiser.[110] *Exzellenz* Studt was a thorough conservative, impervious to criticism from the Left and therefore much admired by the Kaiser. "Of all my ministers," Wilhelm II declared in a remark that recorded his notion of bureaucratic virtue, "Minister Studt is the best. He concerns himself neither with attacks in the press nor with attacks in the parliament. He is content reliably to fulfill my orders, and nothing else concerns him."[111]

The elimination of Studt and Posadowsky, although convenient for Bülow, left him with one unresolved personnel problem. This was the state secretary of the Foreign Office, Heinrich von Tschirschky und Bögendorff, who had assumed the position early in 1906. Tschirschky's appointment had taken Berlin by surprise, for he was neither distinguished nor especially able but instead vain, an awkward speaker, and notably complaisant. Wilhelm II was clearly behind the nomination, for he had taken a great liking to the dutiful young diplomat when, shortly after 1900, Bülow had assigned Tschirschky to accompany the Kaiser when he traveled abroad.[112] The nomination of the ever accommodating Tschirschky, handpicked by Wilhelm II, to the Wilhelmstrasse was an ominous warning that the Kaiser intended to manage foreign affairs for himself.[113] Bülow did not like Tschirschky, who rivaled the chancellor in ingratiating himself with Wilhelm II. This was an area in which Bülow did not tolerate competition, and when he noticed that a warm friendship seemed to be growing between Tschirschky and the Kaiser, he had Tschirschky removed from the entourage.[114] Wilhelm II's revenge, an indication that he did not place much store in Bülow's wishes, was to appoint Tschirschky state secretary, in which position Tschirschky not only had frequent contact with the Kaiser in Berlin but also was once again able to travel with him. Tschirschky had not sought the position, but once in office, he was determined not to be Bülow's minion, and after the chancellor's fainting spell in the Reichstag in April 1906 he, like Eulenburg, attempted to convince the Kaiser that Bülow should be replaced. The chancellor, slowly recuperating at Norderney, was no less determined to get rid of this "mere echo" of his imperial master.[115] Bülow knew that given Wilhelm's enthusiasm for his friend, the chancellor would be able to do this only if Tschirschky could be inserted at a major European embassy.

The opportunity arose in the fall of 1907, when the envoyship in Vienna fell vacant. Wilhelm insisted that Tschirschky's replacement as state secretary would have to be someone he found agreeable. Bülow therefore, with some distaste, served up Baron Wilhelm von Schoen, ambassador in St. Petersburg, who yearned to return to Berlin and whom the Kaiser gladly accepted. Like Tschirschky's appointment in 1906, Schoen's in the following year was interpreted as an indication that Wilhelm II intended to take foreign affairs into his own hands.[116] Schoen would serve for four years, sustained in office over Bülow's objections because, like Tschirschky, he was the Kaiser's favorite. He was, if anything, even more eager than Tschirschky to defer to Wilhelm. The chief of the Naval Cabinet, Admiral Georg von Müller, recorded in his diary that if the always unctuous Schoen was asked in Wilhelm's presence what day it was, he would reply, "The ninth, provided that [the Kaiser] does not order it to be something else."[117] Schoen had not even a trace of the mettle that, on rare occasions, had surfaced in Tschirschky's handling of diplomatic affairs. Schoen's desire always to please applied not only to the Kaiser but to everyone. Not for nothing was he known as "safe Schoen." As ambassador to France, when asked the identity of an enigmatic statue in the embassy garden, he had responded with typical equivocation, *"Peut-être c'est la guerre ou peut-être c'est la paix."*[118]

The appointment in swift succession in 1906–7, against Bülow's own preference, of two state secretaries of the Foreign Office who had little claim to the post other than their sycophancy toward the Kaiser showed how sharply the chancellor's standing had deteriorated. The entrusting of the diplomatic machinery in Berlin to such nonentities was also disturbing evidence of Wilhelm II's insouciant failure to realize how steeply Germany's position had declined under Bülow's long administration, for the difficulties that Germany faced might have suggested to him that talent, not favoritism, should now be the primary qualification for office. The situation could hardly have been more problematical. The treaty at Björkö had been a diplomatic stillbirth, leaving the tsar offended and Russia more closely than ever tied to France. The Algeciras conference, which had brought the Moroccan crisis to a doleful conclusion, had been a triumph not for Germany but for France and Great Britain, historic enemies who now had become loyal friends, and the Kaiser was perceived as having needlessly provoked between the powers in Africa a confrontation that had stopped just short of war. Wilhelm's erratic, bellicose diplomacy, moreover, was accompanied by a determination to build a colossal navy and to enlarge what was already the Continent's most splendidly trained army. This unsettling combination of bravado and firepower in Berlin was an omen that did nothing to allay fears that the preservation of the European balance of power would someday very likely require a reckoning with Kaiser Wilhelm II.

Six

THE *DAILY TELEGRAPH*

DYNAMITE BOMB

NO ONE, in Chancellor Bernhard von Bülow's opinion, was less suitable for diplomacy than Wilhelm II, and the Kaiser's unfailing indiscretion, Bülow declared not long after his fall from office in 1909, had characterized the Kaiser's entire reign.[1] Wilhelm's insuperable vanity had added greatly to the chancellor's problems, and ideally Bülow would have liked to have seen him retire altogether from diplomacy.[2] That, however, was impossible, for the Kaiser considered himself a master diplomat, and as chancellor, Bülow could do little more than point out to Wilhelm that he needed to be more careful. Advice, no matter how deftly proffered, only annoyed the Kaiser, who complained that the chancellor was treating him like a junior diplomat (*Legationsrat*) or a gossip (*Kaffeeschwester*).[3] Bülow was thus virtually defenseless, and so he could only resign himself, as had all chancellors before and after him, to adjusting as well as possible to Wilhelm's constant and singularly unfortunate interference in affairs of state.

This interference occurred most frequently in the case of England. The Kaiser never tired of noting that for years he had labored to win England's friendship, only to be cruelly rebuffed.[4] In promoting good relations with England, Wilhelm II had one essential difficulty, other than his own antic personality: there were few others in Berlin who shared his interest in doing so. Most of the Kaiser's subjects, including the military, the press, the professoriat, and the middle class, tended to share the chancellor's marked hostility to Britain. Only in the ranks of German diplomats were partisans of England to be found, among whom the most prominent was the envoy in London, Count Paul von Wolff Metternich zur Gracht.[5] The chancellor had also to deal with a sizable contingent of the business world who believed that an understanding with Britain was imperative. But for the most part, Germans held little esteem for England, and the Kaiser was, for once, not exaggerating greatly when he declared that he was the *only* person in Berlin who really loved Britain. Metternich had some sympathy with this view, for he believed that Wilhelm II, for all his quirks of personality, was the only force that kept the two powers from sinking into a deadly enmity with one another.[6] Whatever ties the Kaiser had forged in London were quite tenuous, however, for in spite of his frequent trips to England, his innumerable protestations of affection for the land of his mother's birth, and his identification of kinship between British and German civilization, Wilhelm in fact had few friends or admirers in Britain, and they were of little consequence or influence.

The unsettled nature of Anglo-German relations at the beginning of the twentieth century made Ambassador Metternich's position very onerous. The envoy got on well with British officials, although his position at court was somewhat shaky because Edward VII found him a "dull dog." The king's volatile confidant, Sir Charles Hardinge, declared that he could not tell whether Metternich was a "fool or a humbug."[7] Metternich was indeed cryptic and peculiarly antisocial in manner, reproaches that could not be made of the king or of Hardinge, but he was also fearless in saying what he believed, specifically that the root of Anglo-German difficulties was Admiral Alfred von Tirpitz's extravagantly large navy. Metternich's frankness won him Tirpitz's enmity, as well as the dislike of the influential naval attaché in his own embassy, Captain Wilhelm Widenmann, a malicious and ill-tempered devotee of his chief.[8] Metternich disliked Bülow because he did nothing to curtail Tirpitz, whereas the chancellor resented the ambassador's independent streak, a characteristic that Bülow, himself a diplomat by career, did not like to encounter in his plenipotentiaries. The chancellor nevertheless admitted a grudging admiration for Metternich's forthrightness. He was a man, Bülow rightly declared, who valued his ideas above his position.[9]

The chancellor's dislike of Metternich, as well as Tirpitz's, would have been troubling, although not decisive, had the ambassador received Wilhelm II's support. The Kaiser liked Metternich, whom he described to Edward VII as "a trusted and true friend," but his enthusiasm began to wane when he discovered, to his dismay, that his envoy in London opposed the building of a great German navy because of the consternation that Tirpitz's battleships created in England. "He is incapable of understanding the fleet or of defending it," Wilhelm concluded.[10] Metternich's ambassadorial counterpart in Berlin from 1896 to 1908 was Sir Frank Lascelles, who also ardently favored an accommodation between Germany and England. Lascelles, however, had a very low opinion of Bülow because of his manner and his dislike of Britain. The chancellor, Lascelles observed, "talked much but said little."[11] The Kaiser liked the British envoy, *persona gratissima* the Austro-Hungarian envoy declared, and Lascelles found Wilhelm quite agreeable much of the time.[12] On many occasions, however, Wilhelm stupefied the diplomat by making appallingly tactless remarks about the British sovereign or London officialdom, such as the imperial obiter dictum that the cabinet was composed of "noodles" or his strikingly undiplomatic observation in 1905 when he said to Lascelles, "You are, and will always be, my personal friend, but since you are the representative of the King of England I can regard you in your official capacity only as my enemy."[13] Not surprisingly, the ambassador once noted that if he reported to London all that he heard from Wilhelm, Germany and Britain would have long since been at war.[14] The Kaiser believed that Lascelles's goodwill toward his country, and to him personally, was of limited effectiveness because, in his quite mistaken opinion, the ambassador had little influence in London. Besides, Lascelles came to Berlin as the representative of King Edward VII, a fact that diminished the Kaiser's regard. The ambassador in fact worked hard, and occasionally with temporary success, to convince Edward VII that his German nephew was a better person than he believed. When regulations governing age required that Lascelles retire in 1908, the Kaiser denied that this could be the case and believed his removal was due to the conviction shared by Edward VII and Prime Minister Henry Campbell-Bannerman that the envoy had been too friendly to Germany, a suspicion that in the case of the king may have been well founded. His replacement was Sir Edward Goschen, a rather lackluster diplomat who had served for the last three years as ambassador in Vienna. Wilhelm considered the appointment of such a nonentity unflattering to his dignity, and he never established any rapport with the rather fusty diplomat, who never achieved the position Lascelles had enjoyed in Berlin.[15]

Both Lascelles and Goschen reported to a Foreign Office that was markedly mistrustful of Germany, and many of the leaders of the diplomatic service and of the government after Lord Salisbury's departure from Downing Street in 1902 were profoundly critical of the Kaiser. The prime minister, however, was not one of them. Arthur James Balfour, who succeeded his uncle Lord Salisbury, said that Wilhelm II was one of the few royalties with whom he felt he could speak "with perfect freedom, through perfect respect, as *man to man*," and indeed the Kaiser was the only one, Balfour declared on another occasion, who was at all interesting to talk to.[16] If the prime minister was favorably disposed to Wilhelm, his foreign secretary, Lord Lansdowne, was certainly not. He believed that Wilhelm was an impulsive mischief-maker, vain, bombastic, irresponsible, and probably mentally unstable. "The Emperor's speeches are certainly rather alarming," the foreign secretary wrote to Ambassador Lascelles in 1901, "and give me the idea that his *nerves* are as you suppose overstrung. . . . This is a very serious factor in all our calculations."[17] At the end of 1905, Balfour and Lansdowne gave way to a Liberal government in which Sir Henry Campbell-Bannerman served as prime minister, with Sir Edward Grey at the Foreign Office. Campbell-Bannerman desired to foster better relations with Germany, but he was very suspicious of the Kaiser's often repeated assurances of friendship, apropos of which the prime minister quoted an Italian adage: "He who is kinder to you than he is wont has either injured you or wishes to do so."[18] Grey was thoroughly attached to the Entente Cordiale that Lansdowne and Balfour had concluded with France in 1904, and he mistrusted any alliance overtures by Germany, including those of the Kaiser, as disingenuous attempts to establish Berlin's hegemony on the Continent. Like his predecessor Lansdowne, Grey believed that Wilhelm II was mentally disturbed as well as very superficial, and he was therefore probably disposed to agree with Metternich's successor in 1912 as ambassador, Prince Lichnowsky, who felt that the Kaiser was not to be taken seriously.[19]

The suspicion that characterized the British government's view of Wilhelm II and his empire was reflected, possibly even more intently, in the military. After the turn of the century the Kaiser had little to do with the British military and naval attachés posted to London and had few friends elsewhere in the service.[20] He and the most formidable naval personality of the era, Admiral Sir John Fisher, who was created Baron Fisher of Kilverstone while serving as first sea lord from 1904 to 1910, thoroughly disliked one another. Wilhelm correctly believed that the admiral, in imitation of the Royal Navy's celebrated attack in 1807 on the Danish fleet, would gladly have "Copenhagened" the Kaiser's fleet by sinking it as it lay in harbor before it could undertake the attack that Fisher was certain Berlin was plotting against Britain.[21] "The German Empire," the sea lord warned King Edward VII in 1906, "is the one Power in political organization and in fighting strength and in fighting efficiency, where one man (the Kaiser) can press the button and be confident of hurling the whole force of the Empire instantly, irresistibly, and without warning on its enemy."[22] One of Fisher's admirers was King Edward VII, who wholeheartedly shared the admiral's suspicion of the Kaiser. No real cordiality ever existed between the two sovereigns, and they both blamed one another for the troubles that afflicted Anglo-German relations. Edward VII took the Kaiser at his word that it was *he* who made German policy, and attempts by the king's courtiers to persuade Edward otherwise were of little avail.[23] Wilhelm for his part believed that Europe could dwell in peace were it not for the diabolical machinations of the "arch plotter" and "satan," his uncle in London. "It's the king alone," the Kaiser in 1907 told his friend the French diplomat Raymond Lecomte, "the king and his evil genius, Admiral Fisher, who direct everything and aim to stir up the continental powers at the risk of setting Europe on fire."[24] There was, in a way, some truth in the Kaiser's accusations against his uncle, for although it was the government in London that actually determined British policy, King Edward VII exemplified it, and his diplomatic expertise helped facilitate it. Ambassador Lascelles, who knew both Wilhelm II and his English uncle very well, once declared, "King Edward is his own Foreign Minister — and a jolly good one too!"[25]

The Kaiser's tattered reputation in London did not unduly disturb Bülow, whose insidious manner enabled him to pretend to favor good relations with Britain while in fact working to prevent any alignment of German diplomacy in that direction. Bülow recognized, from the moment he became state secretary of the Foreign Office in 1897, that a pact with Britain was not compatible with the construction of a German navy and in any case was not so desirable as one with Russia, Berlin's natural diplomatic partner. To Bülow, a powerful fleet was a matter of life or death (*Lebensfrage, Existenzfrage*) for a nation deeply involved in worldwide commerce. Naval affairs were nevertheless not a primary interest to the chancellor, and Bülow was therefore ill-prepared to deal with the dictatorial Tirpitz, who was incapable of appreciating any viewpoint other than his own.[26] From the moment that Wilhelm II had appointed Tirpitz state secretary of the Imperial Naval Office in 1897, the admiral had systematically developed the "risk theory" that would be the heart of his naval policy.[27] The Royal Navy was Germany's future enemy, and this would require achieving, within approximately twenty years, a German-British capital ship ratio of 2:3. This would provide Berlin with a navy strong enough to deter Britain from action or to inflict significant damage on the British fleet in the event of war. Bülow had consistently endorsed Tirpitz's plans, which were enshrined in the two naval laws that the Reichstag passed in 1898 and 1900.

The construction program contained in the Second Naval Law was completed in 1907, and the Kaiser was now in possession of an impressive rank of battleships and heavy cruisers. Tirpitz had always considered the naval laws no more than initial steps toward what would ultimately become an even larger navy, and having completed what now was called the High Seas Fleet (*Hochseeflotte*), he was ready to ask for more. By this time, however, the rationale behind his "risk theory" had begun to fall apart. Britain now had Japan (1902) and France (1904) as either allies or diplomatic partners, enabling a greater concentration of the Royal Navy in the North Sea. The British government and Parliament both showed no signs of relaxing their determination to maintain a 2:1 naval ratio with the rival Germans. It was, unhappily for Tirpitz, at almost precisely this juncture that the London admiralty embarked on a revolutionary alteration in ship construction. On 3 December 1906 King Edward VII commissioned the H.M.S. *Dreadnought*, namesake of one of the ships with which Sir Francis Drake had defeated the Spanish Armada over three hundred years earlier. This leviathan — the largest, most powerfully armed, and most expensive battleship the world had ever seen — was to be the British answer to Tirpitz. By this time, the naval situation had finally begun to cause Bülow considerable alarm, for Germany's finances would not permit the continued building of battleships, especially gargantuan vessels such as the *Dreadnought*, unless new or more punitive taxes were introduced, a demand that would lead to a parliamentary crisis. Yet to back down in armament expenditures without exacting corresponding concessions from the British would be an admission of defeat or, at the least, of weakness, a loss of face that Bülow, whose vanity was boundless, was not prepared to suffer. The chancellor therefore came to the conclusion that although Germany would persist in its naval building program, the rate (*Bautempo*) at which ships were being constructed under legislation already approved by the Reichstag might be slowed down and the total number of ships spread over more years, thereby easing the financial burden and avoiding friction with London.[28] The navy would continue to be strong in spite of this alteration, and the savings would ensure that the German army would continue to get the money it needed. "We cannot have both the largest army and the biggest navy," Bülow declared. "We cannot weaken the army, for our destiny will be decided on land."[29]

Wilhelm did not share Bülow's doubts about Tirpitz's naval mania. From the moment that the Kaiser had appointed Tirpitz state secretary in 1897, Wilhelm had enthusiastically supported all his proposals for naval increases, for a fleet not only was a suitable insignia for both Germany's standing and his own but also was a powerful adjunct of diplomacy. "A strong navy," the Kaiser in 1907 reminded his friend the journalist Theodor Schiemann, is a "mighty factor in compelling arbitration. Battleships, after all, cost less than wars."[30] Russia, Great Britain, and France, the three other great European naval powers, might be allied, but with a fleet, Wilhelm felt confident that Germany would be "desired as a friend and feared as an enemy," and for that reason he never understood that building a great navy and maintaining good relations with Britain were incompatible aims. In his opinion, British concern about German navalism was nonsensical, as absurd as it would be for Germany to worry that it might someday be ravaged by the Swiss.[31]

Tirpitz knew quite well that it paid to stay on the good side of the Kaiser, to whom he owed his position and whose support had been the decisive factor in winning public opinion for the idea of constructing a battle fleet.[32] The admiral was masterful in playing up to Wilhelm's vanity. This was not an easy business, for Tirpitz admitted that he and Wilhelm were very unlike. Tirpitz's disposition was as autocratic as that of the Kaiser, who imagined himself to be an expert in maritime affairs and gave the admiral much unsolicited advice.[33] Furthermore, Tirpitz was a model of deliberate, bureaucratic calculation, a man who wanted to proceed only when all the pieces were in order and who would countenance no trifling with his plans. Wilhelm II, on the other hand, lived — to the admiral's regret — "outside the world of reality," preferring appearances to substance, and was desperately anxious to make sure that he was regarded as *the* naval leader.[34]

In February 1908, just before the Reichstag voted to approve Tirpitz's naval estimates, a crisis developed that created considerable dismay in both Berlin and London. On 6 February, the *Times* (London) published a letter by Lord Esher, the intimate of King Edward VII, to the Imperial Maritime League in which he pilloried the league for criticizing Admiral Fisher. Esher argued that the first sea lord's militant insistence on building *Dreadnought*-class ships would make his fall from office very welcome to Wilhelm II and the Germans.[35] Without consulting Chancellor Bülow or anyone else except the chief of the Naval Cabinet, Admiral Georg von Müller, the Kaiser sent a letter to Lord Tweedmouth, first lord of the admiralty. He did so, Wilhelm declared, in his capacity as an admiral of the fleet in the Royal Navy and out of a desire to dampen the naval armament race that had seized both countries.[36] In language that was entirely cordial, the Kaiser informed Tweedmouth that his fleet was being built openly and programmatically in order to protect German commerce and *not* to challenge Britain, who might, as far as he was concerned, build as many ships as it felt necessary.

Tweedmouth was astounded to receive the Kaiser's letter, for communication between one sovereign and another's ministers was virtually without precedent. Tweedmouth at once informed Grey, and with his consent replied in a brief and innocuous letter, enclosing the naval budget, which the cabinet had just approved but which had not yet been laid before Parliament.[37] Notifying Grey was the proper course, but Tweedmouth was also quite indiscreet and proceeded to inform various friends of the letter he had received from Berlin.[38] The Germanophobe military correspondent of the *Times*, Colonel Charles à Court Repington, soon heard of the exchange, and on 6 March the paper published a letter by Repington to the editor, hinting at the contents of Wilhelm's communication and declaring that its malign purpose was to pressure the first lord into lowering the British naval estimates.[39]

The reaction in England was instantaneous and almost uniformly negative. King Edward, to whom Wilhelm had sent a copy of his letter to Tweedmouth, was enraged at all concerned: at Esher for having ignited the controversy, at Wilhelm for communicating with one of his ministers, at Fisher (who was in no way involved), and at the *Times* for Repington's "vicious" letter. He wrote in a rather brusque tone to the Kaiser, noting that he found Wilhelm's missive a "new departure," a regrettable one sure to lead to difficulties in European diplomacy.[40] The king was not alone in his consternation, and his heir, the Prince of Wales, declared that the Kaiser's letter to Tweedmouth meant that Britain now had "no alternative but to build as many battleships" as it could "as fast as possible."[41] Grey, always inclined to regard Wilhelm II as a troublemaker, described the unfortunate episode as a "sudden inpouring of strong Rhine wine."[42] In Berlin, Wilhelm's blundering effusion, sent off in the heat of the moment without consulting his government, was seen as further evidence of his tendency toward personal rule as well as an additional manifestation of his diplomatic ineptitude.[43] Bülow, who learned of the Kaiser's communication to Tweedmouth only after it had been sent, was most embarrassed, and like Ambassador Metternich, he was eager for the British to know that he was in no way party to the unfortunate matter.[44]

Both the British and the German governments had every interest in burying the matter as quickly as possible. The Kaiser should not have written without Bülow's consent, and Tweedmouth was foolish to have communicated the content of the naval budget to Wilhelm before Parliament had been given knowledge of it. The solution adopted in both capitals was to represent the gaffes as personal exchanges and therefore without political significance, and although this was true on the first count and false on the second, it succeeded in defusing the crisis. Wilhelm II was, as usual, unrepentant and took a cavalier attitude toward the Tweedmouth affair, dismissing the negative reaction of British public opinion in general and of Edward VII in particular and insisting that his letter had in fact put "everything in order."[45] The Kaiser was equally indifferent to the disapproval expressed in Germany, and his curious reaction was to order that a list be drawn up of all the other lies that had been told about him. It was his intention that this digest would then be printed as an indictment of the press for its gross calumnies.[46]

Although the Tweedmouth imbroglio was hushed up before becoming a major crisis, Bülow as well as other observers in Berlin believed that it would be only a matter of time before the Kaiser involved Germany in another predicament. Baroness von Spitzemberg, a shrewd and well-connected diarist, summed up the feeling when she wrote, "Unfortunately the Kaiser, that incorrigible 'vibrateur,' as usual will not at all profit by his errors and will neither hold his tongue nor let his pen rest."[47] Her reservations would be fully confirmed when, in October 1908 in an interview in the *Daily Telegraph* (London), Wilhelm provoked a mammoth eruption in Anglo-German relations, one that dwarfed the Tweedmouth affair in significance. The *Daily Telegraph* crisis would lead to an irreversible decline in Wilhelm's reputation in both England and Germany, and it would eventually cost Bülow the chancellorship, in which for almost a decade he had taken such unwarranted satisfaction.

A few months after the Tweedmouth affair had been smoothed over, King Edward VII made a trip to Germany to visit his niece, Princess Margaret of Hesse, the Kaiser's youngest sister, who lived in her mother's castle at Cronberg in the Taunus Mountains. The king scrupulously avoided discussing naval affairs with Wilhelm, knowing that this was the most incendiary topic that could be broached. He left the task to Sir Charles Hardinge, the permanent undersecretary of the Foreign Office, who was a member of the British entourage. This was a mistake, for Hardinge was somewhat overbearing, and Wilhelm did not like him, nor Hardinge the Kaiser. Their exchange at Cronberg on naval estimates was somewhat frosty, with Wilhelm berating the British for their gratuitously hostile attitude toward his navy and refusing the demand, made by Hardinge with a frankness inconceivable in a courtier in Berlin, that the Kaiser show his pacific intentions by reducing Tirpitz's shipbuilding program.[48] Wilhelm later announced to Tsar Nicholas that "Uncle Bertie was all sunshine at Cronberg and in very good humour," but in fact the king was annoyed at the truculent manner in which Wilhelm had spoken to Hardinge.[49]

What passed at Cronberg between Wilhelm and the British party remained private, but many of the Kaiser's rhetorical effusions often made their way into the press in spite of his entourage's efforts to suppress them, and they frequently caused much embarrassment. No one deplored Wilhelm's verbal indiscretions more than Bülow, who declared that they were a sickness the Italians called *"parlantina."* The chancellor therefore might have been expected to be vigilant in watching out for the Kaiser's oratorical lapses. After the Tweedmouth affair Bülow indeed declared that he intended to do so, but in fact he continued to manage affairs in a lax and careless manner.[50] This was easier to do when Wilhelm was off on one of his incessant jaunts, and the chancellor therefore encouraged the Kaiser to travel about as often as he pleased. Wilhelm was only too happy to oblige.

The Kaiser fancied himself an English gentleman, and he enjoyed hunting on the great estates of the British aristocracy. Here he found an "undefinable something," a relaxation from kingship in favor of the life of a milord, fitted out in British haberdashery. It was comfortable but also ludicrous, for the Kaiser, with his defective command of English idiom and his garish mufti bespoke in London, looked, as one amused British spectator put it, "more of an incongruous cad than most Bank Holiday trippers to Margate."[51] In 1907, after completing a state visit to King Edward VII, Wilhelm made an extended stay at Highcliffe Castle, a rambling mock-Tudor pile on the Hampshire coast near Bournemouth. This was the property of Colonel the Honorable Edward Montagu-Stuart-Wortley, a General Staff officer attached to the British War Office and an ardent exponent of cordial Anglo-German relations. Wilhelm did not know Stuart-Wortley and had proposed renting Highcliffe, but the owner insisted instead that the Kaiser come as his guest. Wilhelm stayed for three and a half weeks, taking long motor drives and hunting with the local gentry. As usual, he also spent a great deal of time talking to his host and other English sportsmen on all manner of subjects, but especially on the unsatisfactory state of Anglo-German relations.[52]

In conversing with his English friends, the Kaiser was eager to present himself as the leading German proponent of goodwill toward the British, a role he believed he had played handsomely, although with insufficient appreciation from the British, ever since coming to the throne in 1888. Wilhelm later would claim, apparently truthfully, that he had periodically informed Bülow of the gist of his conversations with his English comrades at Highcliffe and in turn had received the chancellor's approval.[53] Eight months after leaving Highcliffe, in August 1908, Wilhelm II invited Colonel Stuart-Wortley to come to Alsace for the fall maneuver of the German army, and on that occasion he continued their earlier talks.[54] Wilhelm conceived the idea of composing an article outlining the views he had expressed at both Highcliffe and the maneuvers, with a view to having the piece published in an English newspaper as a gesture aimed at improving Anglo-German relations. It might, Wilhelm believed, cause the Germanophobe British press to take a more positive view of Germany.[55] Stuart-Wortley secured the cooperation of Lord Burnham, the owner of the *Daily Telegraph*, a paper that had a history of being reasonably favorable to the Kaiser. Burnham sent a reporter to Highcliffe, where he got from Stuart-Wortley an account of the things Wilhelm had told him. At the end of September 1908, Wilhelm, on vacation at his hunting lodge at Rominten, received a typed version of his remarks, together with an appeal from Lord Burnham that publication would reduce the friction between the two countries.[56]

Wilhelm II read the document and showed it to his guest, Admiral Tirpitz, who expressed the opinion that printing the Kaiser's remarks might have an unfortunate effect in England. The Kaiser nevertheless persisted in thinking that his observations ought to be published, but perhaps because of the questions that Tirpitz had raised, he decided first to consult Bülow. Since July, the chancellor, as was his custom, had been on his annual summer vacation on the island of Norderney in the North Sea. From his villa, he supervised state affairs, having as his assistant Felix von Müller, the Prussian minister to Holland who was temporarily assigned to accompany the chancellor. Bülow's holiday had been disturbed by an unusually great number of problems, which primarily concerned unrest in the Balkans and financial difficulties in Germany and which would have to be dealt with in the fall Reichstag session.[57] On 2 October, the chancellor received a letter from Martin Rücker-Jenisch, Prussian minister to Hamburg who was for the moment at Rominten assigned as Foreign Office adviser to the Kaiser. Attaching a clearly typewritten article that the Kaiser proposed to have printed in a London newspaper, Jenisch requested, in Wilhelm II's name, that Bülow, who was instructed to act alone and without consultation with the Foreign Office, give it close scrutiny and correct any errors of fact. Jenisch noted that in his opinion the article would be better left unpublished.[58]

Bülow felt that the article was not the sort of thing that should claim his personal attention. "A minister," he later wrote defensively of his role, "and especially a leading minister, cannot himself become involved in mechanical functions but must concentrate his time and efforts on great matters. No prime minister would have found the time himself to go over the Wortley document; any such figure would have given it to his underlings to be proofed."[59] Bülow, however, did in fact read the draft and pointed out to Jenisch that there were several passages that seemed to him undesirable.[60] Jenisch then advised the Kaiser of the omissions recommended by Bülow, incorporating them into a revised draft that he returned to Wilhelm and that he believed was now suitable for transmission to Colonel Stuart-Wortley.[61] Meanwhile, the chancellor, in violation of Wilhelm's order, sent the original document, containing the Kaiser's infelicitous observations, to the Foreign Office in Berlin, but since his covering letter has not survived, it is not certain precisely what he expected his staff to do with Wilhelm's interview. According to Bülow's notoriously unreliable posthumous memoirs, he asked his assistants to examine the document "with care" (*sorgsam*) and advise him what should be corrected, added, or omitted.[62] Wilhelm Stemrich, the state undersecretary in the Foreign Office who was in charge in the absence of his chief, State Secretary Baron Wilhelm von Schoen, interpreted this command to mean that his responsibility consisted solely of ascertaining the veracity of Wilhelm II's statements in the article. Stemrich was a careful and experienced diplomat, one utterly loyal to the chancellor, and therefore did what he believed Bülow wanted him to do. Stemrich, about to leave on vacation, entrusted the matter to Reinhold Klehmet, a bureaucrat of considerable maturity, who dug through the files, corrected a few facts, and, convinced that he had fulfilled the chancellor's orders, returned the amended article to Bülow without comment.

The chancellor adopted Klehmet's corrections and noted a few places where he thought omissions might be made.[63] Unfortunately, Bülow made no attempt to ensure that the document was not returned to Stuart-Wortley until and unless the indicated changes had been made. What he did instead was to give the article to Müller, asking him to check the article carefully. Müller interpreted this not as a command to make editorial corrections but instead to pass on the suitability of printing the interview as it stood. According to Bülow, Müller declared there were no grounds for preventing publication and, armed with that advice, the chancellor had Müller so inform Wilhelm II. The result, Bülow would sadly note many years later, was a "dynamite bomb."[64] The Kaiser in turn told Colonel Stuart-Wortley on 15 October that he had had only minor changes to make and declared of the article: "[It] embodies correctly all the principal items of our conversation during the recent maneuver and deals in a most reasonable and straightforward manner with the justified complaints that I have to make against certain organs of the English press. . . . I authorize you to make a discreet use of the article in the manner you think best. I firmly hope that it may have the effect of bringing about a change in the tone of some of the English newspapers."[65]

So it was that on 28 October 1908 the *Daily Telegraph* printed the Kaiser's article.[66] The article took the form of an interview that Wilhelm II had granted to an anonymous Englishman and that had been granted in the hope of creating a more favorable image of the Kaiser in Great Britain. Wilhelm was reported as maintaining that his intentions toward the British were entirely peaceful and amicable, even though he noted, "The prevailing sentiment among large sections of the middle and lower classes of my own people is not friendly to England." This was one of the several passages that Bülow had wanted omitted. The Kaiser reminded his interlocutor that in the Boer War, he and his government had conspicuously befriended Britain, even providing Queen Victoria a plan of battle, one that "ran very much on the same lines as that which was actually adopted by Lord Roberts." As for the German navy, it was not directed against England but in fact had been constructed to support Germany's commercial ambitions, specifically in the Orient. The Kaiser, his partner in the conversation concluded, needed to be seen in England for what he was: a man of true goodwill toward England but one who was growing weary of having his overtures of friendship spurned.

The representation in the article of Wilhelm's ideas was, by his own admission, entirely accurate.[67] It contained the Kaiser's usual foolish and exuberant language (the English were "mad, mad, mad as March hares" to be so suspicious of him), exaggerations (his statement that Lord Roberts had followed his plan), and dark reminders (Wilhelm noted that his Anglophilia put him in a minority among his subjects) that could, and ultimately did, easily offend. But the general tenor of the article was to present a ruler who, although clearly annoyed at the criticism leveled at him by the British, genuinely wanted to be their friend. The *Daily Telegraph* interview did not create a public sensation in Great Britain, for the press was uncharacteristically restrained and the government avoided making any official comment. Beneath the surface in England, however, consternation was sufficiently widespread for Colonel Stuart-Wortley to feel compelled to write to the Kaiser to express his regret at all the hubbub that the interview had unleashed.[68] Even among the shrinking band of British Germanophiles, the Kaiser's remarks raised questions about his sanity.[69]

In Germany, however, the reaction to the *Daily Telegraph* interview was a frenzy of outrage against Wilhelm II among the population and in the press, even in papers that were ordinarily inclined to treat him with favor.[70] Among the Kaiser's subjects, the prevailing note was anger mixed with stupefied dismay. In Dresden, capital of the liberal kingdom of Saxony, everyone, according to the British envoy, was "purple in the face" because of Wilhelm's indiscretions.[71] The aristocratic diarist Baroness von Spitzemberg summed up the feeling with her usual asperity. It was, she declared, "the most disgraceful, deplorable, the most indiscreet and most serious thing the Kaiser" had yet done. "[He] ruins our political position and makes us the laughing stock of the world. It makes one wonder whether one is in a madhouse!"[72] Bülow, never one to accept blame or even to suffer criticism, now had to disassociate himself from the *Daily Telegraph* disaster by shifting the blame to someone else. On sensing the negative reaction to the article in Germany, the chancellor had immediately written to Wilhelm, offering to resign if the Kaiser's confidence in him had been destroyed. That Wilhelm refused, but he did agree to Bülow's request that the chancellor be allowed to issue a statement to the semi-official *Norddeutsche Allgemeine Zeitung*.[73] Bülow's text falsely declared that Wilhelm had sent the article to him for approval but that, burdened with more pressing matters, he had forwarded it instead to his diplomatic staff for examination. The Foreign Office had recommended only minor changes and had raised no objections to publication, so that the odium lay with the other Berlin officials and not with either him or the Kaiser. The outcry in Germany produced by the *Daily Telegraph* interview paled in comparison with the storm of indignation that followed Bülow's statement, for not only the Kaiser but also now Bülow was shown to have acted thoughtlessly. Bülow had been negligent, for if he had (as he untruthfully claimed) *not* read the article, his past experience with the voluble Kaiser should have compelled him to do so. Some critics speculated, and Wilhelm himself seems to have believed, that Bülow had in fact read the draft of the interview but had agreed to its publication, perversely hoping that the resulting scandal would — as it did — destroy the Kaiser's reputation but would also — as it did not — leave the chancellor an open field of power.[74] Bülow's failure lay in the fact that he *had* read the document and recognized its potential for harming both relations with Britain and the Kaiser's reputation but had then done nothing effective to ensure that the unfortunate text was altered before being sent forward for publication.

Condemnations of the sovereign suddenly appeared in the press, opinions that earlier would have been considered affronts of lèse-majesté but that now were greeted with approval. Jenisch of the Foreign Office and General Count Dietrich von Hülsen-Haeseler, the chief of the Military Cabinet, took it on themselves to warn the Kaiser that he, not Bülow, was the primary object of the outrage that was sweeping through Germany.[75] This became unmistakable when, on 10 November before a packed house, Parliament began to discuss the *Daily Telegraph* affair. One after another, members of the five leading parties, ranging from the Conservatives to the Social Democrats, with a causticity that was unprecedented in German parliamentary history, assaulted both Bülow and the Kaiser for their irresponsibility. After listening to three hours of abuse, Bülow had his chance to reply. Uncharacteristically haggard in appearance, the chancellor responded without his usual rhetorical flourishes but instead stated, in plain language, nothing more critical of Wilhelm than that he had used exaggerated language in the interview. This failing, Bülow reminded the deputies, should not be allowed to obscure the Kaiser's many efforts to improve Anglo-German relations. The umbrage that the *Daily Telegraph* interview had produced would, Bülow assured the house, in the future persuade Wilhelm II to exercise more discretion in what he said, and the chancellor would see to it that German diplomats read documents with a more discriminating eye.[76]

Meanwhile Wilhelm was visiting the Archduke Franz Ferdinand in Austria, and Bülow insisted that the Kaiser continue on as planned to Donaueschingen in Württemberg, the palatial seat of his close friend Prince Max Egon von Fürstenberg, the banal but indefatigably hospitable host for a male-only hunting party.[77] This was bad advice, perhaps deliberately tendered, for it hardly seemed appropriate that in a moment of crisis the sovereign should be entertaining himself in the company of his aristocratic friends. Wilhelm was denounced throughout Germany, and it was said that the outrage expressed against him in the Reichstag was reminiscent of the revolutionary convention in France in 1792.[78] The Kaiser was in the midst of this ill-considered frolic when, on 11 November, Adjutant-General Hans von Plessen brought him the account of Bülow's speech before the Reichstag on the tenth in which the chancellor had conspicuously failed to defend his sovereign. Wilhelm fell apart completely and, with welling tears, asked his courtiers how Bülow could have betrayed the Kaiser by denying that he knew the contents of the interview when Wilhelm, in proper constitutional fashion, had provided him with the text in advance. This was, the Kaiser declared, a case of judicial murder, with the man who was innocent becoming the victim.[79] Wilhelm raised the question of firing Bülow, but the chief of the Civil Cabinet, Rudolf von Valentini, a man of perfect calm, convinced him that this would be a mistake because it would imperil the financial reform proposals that the chancellor was soon to lay before the Reichstag. The Kaiser agreed that in the future he would be more circumspect in what he said, that he would, as he put it, "swallow the bitter pill." He had, however, no intention of playing before the chancellor the role of an "abject sinner" (*pater peccavi*).[80]

Valentini and other of Wilhelm's courtiers, although not Bülow, urged him to return to Berlin, but the Kaiser, who spent most of his time closeted with Fürstenberg, remained in Donaueschingen. Even though he went out hunting during the remaining two days of his stay, he would burst into tears while in the field or on his return to the castle.[81] The Kaiser was thus in a very agitated state when, on 14 November, further catastrophe unexpectedly struck. That evening Prince Fürstenberg, following a tradition in Wilhelm's court entertainments, planned for various members of the entourage to participate in a ballet spectacular for which they would don female costumes.[82] On this occasion the chief of the Military Cabinet, Field Marshal Count Dietrich von Hülsen-Haeseler, to whom Wilhelm for years had shown marked favor, was cast in the starring role. After dinner, the house party filed into the salon, where a military band was playing. Suddenly the field marshal, fifty-six, portly, and suffering from heart disease, pirouetted through a door; he was fitted out in one of Princess Fürstenberg's ball gowns, complete with a feathered hat and fan.[83] This was by no means the first time Hülsen had dressed as a woman to perform before the Kaiser, and he gyrated to the music with great aplomb, blowing kisses and completing his routine by exiting through a doorway into a loggia. A loud crash was heard, and on investigation Hülsen was found stretched out lifeless on the floor, the victim of a stroke. Wilhelm was not exaggerating when he declared that his dead comrade was his truest friend, one he had promoted to high office and who had accompanied him on many a trip on land and sea.[84]

On 16 November, the Kaiser left Donaueschingen for Potsdam, ordering Bülow to appear at ten on the following morning. This was their first meeting since the *Daily Telegraph* crisis, and on this meeting Bülow's future might well depend. All Germany, it was said, held its breath with anticipation.[85] The audience, to which there were no witnesses, lasted two hours and was unusual in that Bülow talked and Wilhelm said almost nothing.[86] The chancellor itemized the Kaiser's many foreign and domestic indiscretions that had created difficulties over the years and expressed his hope that Wilhelm might thereby realize that the *Daily Telegraph* was not an isolated event but part of an unfortunate pattern. Wilhelm's response was to give his reluctant consent to the chancellor's issuing of a statement in the official *Reichsanzeiger*. This would declare that although the Kaiser dismissed the outcry in public opinion against him as unwarranted, he did acknowledge his obligation to behave with constitutional responsibility. The communiqué was to conclude with Wilhelm's declaration of his continuing confidence in his chancellor.[87] The talk was a standoff, leaving both men dissatisfied about the future and in doubt as to how long their association could be expected to last. Bülow arrived back in Berlin in a troubled state of mind, as well he might have, for Wilhelm was profoundly angry. The Kaiser looked pale and shaken when he emerged from the palace later in the day to go to Hülsen's funeral, and as he and the Kaiserin drove through the streets of Berlin to the Invalides Church they were greeted by a hostile silence as icy as the weather.[88]

Wilhelm was barely able to perform his part as chief mourner. The effect of the crisis on the Kaiser's physical appearance and on his nerves, an effect that had begun with his crying fits at Donaueschingen, became worse in Berlin. On the day of the Kaiser's talk with Bülow, Prince Fürstenberg, who had come to the capital for the field marshal's funeral, warned the Austrian envoy that he would not be able to recognize the Kaiser if he saw Wilhelm: "His entire appearance is that of a broken man."[89] On 21 November Wilhelm managed to make a ceremonial appearance together with his family at the Berlin City Hall, mechanically reading a speech that Bülow had written and that the chancellor handed to him page by page. When the ordeal was over, the crown prince, in considerable distress because of his father's deteriorating condition, fixed the blame on the chancellor, who he declared had betrayed the Kaiser.[90] On the next day, 22 November, Wilhelm suffered a complete nervous breakdown, taking to his bed and declaring that he must abdicate.[91] In the middle of the night the Kaiserin summoned the crown prince, who had a long talk with his distraught father. They agreed that Wilhelm would not give up the throne but would grant his son "a sort of proxy" to be used until he recovered.[92]

For several days the Kaiser was completely bedfast, and his court physician, Dr. Friedrich von Ilberg, prescribed doses of bicarbonate of soda, baths saturated with pine needles, massages, and valerian, assuring his imperial patient that excessive traveling had brought on the collapse. The acute period of Wilhelm's illness, complicated by an attack of flu, lasted only three or four days, and by 25 November some improvement in his condition could be noted. Even so, the Kaiser's behavior was alarming. He sat "in a kind of stony stupor, eating and drinking in a vacant way, as though he did not heed what he was doing," a courtier reported.[93] Although Wilhelm's neurotic symptoms gradually abated, he refused for a full month to take any interest in affairs of state, declining to see Bülow, other government officials, or foreign diplomats. It was very difficult for him, he told his friend "Franzi," the Habsburg Archduke Franz Ferdinand, to act as though all were in order and to continue to have anything to do with Bülow and the others who had betrayed him in the *Daily Telegraph* affair.[94] By mid-December, three weeks after his collapse, Wilhelm felt up to corresponding with his fellow royals, writing to his aunt Queen Alexandra of England, who had inquired about his "cold." "I am not suffering from cold," he confessed to her, "but from complete collapse."[95] Wilhelm described what he had been through as a "severe shock of nerves" (*Nervenchoc*). He was confident that he would eventually be vindicated, for he had had many letters from English people of all classes attesting to their outrage at the demeaning way the Reichstag and the press had treated him. And the German people, long deluded by the "Jewish press-carnival," were beginning to see how their sovereign had been mistreated.[96]

Throughout his illness, the Kaiser made his bitterness at Bülow very plain, clearly confident that he would eventually have his revenge.[97] The Kaiser told the Austro-Hungarian envoy, Count Ladislaus von Szögyényi-Marich, that he had been scrupulous in behaving in a constitutional manner and that it was Bülow who had been irresponsible, all of which was entirely true. He assured his friend Fürstenberg that in the future, he intended to practice the greatest reserve in becoming involved in diplomatic or internal affairs. That was what Bülow, in their talk on 17 November, had insisted he do, and therefore if the chancellor wanted to see him, Bülow could apply for an audience. Wilhelm had no intention of seeking Bülow out.[98] He was prepared eventually to overlook his own feelings and keep Bülow in office for the moment, since the presence of the chancellor at the helm was critical for the financial reforms soon to be laid before the Reichstag.[99] Without the strong support of the Kaiserin, Bülow might have fallen from office in the immediate aftermath of the *Daily Telegraph* crisis. Augusta Victoria had pleaded with Bülow to stay at his post, and she went out of her way to show him her support. The Kaiserin's influence with her consort was greatest in times of emergency, and as the scandal receded and Wilhelm's confidence returned, her opinions counted for less, and Bülow's position consequently became weaker.[100] Meanwhile, Wilhelm found consolation in never ceasing to believe that his subjects would eventually come to realize, as he certainly did, that Bülow had duped them and acted in a way that was both stupid and unwarranted.[101] The Kaiser's confidence was not, for once, unjustified. By the time of Wilhelm's fiftieth birthday celebrations at the end of January 1909, public opinion, although by no means showing any favor to the crown, had begun to turn against the chancellor. Cries of "*à bas Bülow*" were heard in the streets of Berlin, and it was now the chancellor, rather than the Kaiser, who looked worn and dispirited.[102]

The only positive effect of the *Daily Telegraph* affair was that it created sufficient alarm about the Kaiser's tactless volubility to make officials in both Berlin and London anxious to avoid any similar embarrassments. Because of this concern, another interview based on Wilhelm II's frothy and ill-considered comments was fortunately suppressed. In the summer of 1908, in the course of his annual Scandinavian cruise, the Kaiser had granted an audience to William Bayard Hale, a correspondent of the *New York Times*, to whom he talked expansively and bitterly about a number of subjects.[103] His intemperate remarks against Britain far eclipsed the comments that he had made to Colonel Stuart-Wortley in England and that had served as the basis of the *Daily Telegraph* article. Wilhelm informed Hale that Germany was ready for war with Britain, the sooner the better. London would be humbled since its allies, France and Russia, were militarily worthless, and India, riddled with Japanese provocateurs, would soon rise in revolution against the Raj. Germany and the United States would emerge triumphantly from this bloodbath as the world's leading powers.

What purpose the Kaiser imagined his foolish concoction would serve is murky, but he probably hoped that his identification of America and Germany as a white bulwark against Japan would find a welcome reception with President Theodore Roosevelt.[104] There is no evidence that the Kaiser envisioned publication of his remarks, for he was under the mistaken impression that Hale was a not a journalist but a clergyman, which Hale had in fact once been.[105] Meanwhile Hale, without further contact with the Kaiser, wrote an account of the interview for the *New York Times*. The editors found the Kaiser's remarks too "strong," and so Hale in August 1908 persuaded the *New York Century Magazine* to buy his article with a view to publication the following December.[106] In the interim, the *Daily Telegraph* interview, in which the Kaiser had tried to pose as Britain's friend, had caused a furor. Publication of Wilhelm's tirade to Hale, remarks so full of hatred against England, would lead to an immeasurably more bitter conflagration both in Germany and in England. Hale meanwhile had given a copy of his article to Lord Northcliffe, the anti-German proprietor of the *Times* (London) and the *Daily Mail*, and Northcliffe in turn passed it on to the equally Germanophobe Sir William Tyrrell, private secretary to Sir Edward Grey, the foreign minister. From Tyrrell the article proceeded to Sir Charles Hardinge, the permanent undersecretary of state for Foreign Affairs, and from Hardinge to King Edward VII.[107] Bülow arranged for both Hale and the *Century* to be bought off, and the full text of the article never appeared.[108] Hardinge persuaded Northcliffe to keep the interview out of the *Daily Mail*. As he told the British ambassador in Berlin, "If it were to appear in print now, I really think it would be the end of the Emperor."[109] The *New York World*, however, had obtained parts of Hale's interview and published them on 22 November. The semi-official *Norddeutsche Allgemeine Zeitung* at once denied that the interview was authentic, and within a week the *World* repudiated the article.[110]

The Kaiser does not seem to have been grateful to Bülow for minimizing the damage Hale's interview might have caused. Wilhelm's irritation at the chancellor continued into the new year, and he assured courtiers that as soon as the financial reforms had safely passed through the Reichstag, he would dismiss Bülow.[111] He was delighted when Edward VII, on a state visit to Berlin in early February 1909, snubbed the chancellor, telling Wilhelm afterward that monarchical principle, quite apart from kinship, would not allow the king to forgive the chancellor's behavior in the *Daily Telegraph* scandal.[112] The trip to Germany by the British majesties was an unparalleled success, with both the king and the Kaiser in excellent humor. Edward VII and Queen Alexandra charmed all Berliners, and the king was most accommodating in his views on diplomacy and naval construction. There were a few minor problems, such as the perception of the British entourage, a view entirely justified, that Wilhelm's courtiers were not favorably disposed to England, and the Kaiser was annoyed that his guests seemed to be amazed that his palace had bathrooms and that his capital had paved streets and luxury hotels.[113] Wilhelm II's English guests recognized that Bülow's position, in spite of outward cordiality with the Kaiser, was not at all secure.[114] The very success of the visit had inflated the Kaiser's self-esteem and therefore increased his bitterness that the chancellor had treated him so shabbily. Moreover, Bülow's close relationship with Friedrich von Holstein, who had served in the Foreign Office until 1906, further discredited him with the Kaiser, who blamed Holstein for the Moroccan debacle of 1905. It was Holstein, Wilhelm declared, who had Bülow under his influence and who, working with the Reichstag and the Jewish press, had been responsible for the Kaiser's humiliation in the *Daily Telegraph* matter.[115]

Bülow's fall from grace with the Kaiser barred him from the palace for months, and it was only on 11 March 1909 that Rudolf von Valentini, the chief of the Civil Cabinet, finally persuaded Wilhelm to receive the chancellor.[116] The accounts provided by Bülow and the Kaiser, both notorious for exaggeration, are in reasonable agreement about the course of the conversation but not about its tone.[117] The chancellor began by declaring that since he no longer enjoyed Wilhelm's confidence, he wanted to resign, an offer Wilhelm at once rejected. It seems likely that Bülow expressed just enough regret about the *Daily Telegraph* affair for the Kaiser to construe his words as apology sufficient to permit him to retain his office. Bülow may indeed not have been awash with tears as he pled for forgiveness, a tableau the Kaiser depicted after the event, but he said what was necessary to save himself at least for the time being. Wilhelm, however, offered small comfort to the chancellor that his future in office would be long, all but promising that once the Reichstag passed the financial reforms in the coming summer, the moment of Bülow's departure would be at hand. "That is important business," Wilhelm told his chancellor, "and if it succeeds you will then have a decent departure. To go now would hurt me and the empire and would besides do nothing for your honor."[118]

Wilhelm clearly believed that he had set the chancellor straight, for after Bülow's audience on 11 March, the Kaiser was described as being positively buoyant. The Kaiser now once again began to make daily calls on the chancellor, and Bülow was momentarily confident that, forgiven of his sins, he was once again in control.[119] No one else shared the chancellor's optimism, however, and within a month even Bülow had come to realize that the so-called reconciliation had little value, for Wilhelm once again became distant and mistrustful. The Kaiser had no need to ingratiate himself with a man whom he had taken, as he told his entourage, "completely in . . . hand."[120] Satisfied that he was in charge, Wilhelm left Potsdam in mid-April to spend several weeks on Corfu, making his way back slowly via Vienna and returning to Potsdam on 23 May. Three weeks later he was off again, this time to the Baltic, where he lingered for a month, returning to Berlin on 14 July.

In the course of his career, one governed by ambition rather than principle, Bülow had made many enemies, and they now came forward to settle their scores with the discredited chancellor. He found himself marooned without help at court, in the bureaucracy, among the Kaiser's generals and admirals, and in Berlin society.[121] He was also embroiled with a hostile Reichstag over the finance reforms, and the deputies' perception that Bülow no longer enjoyed the Kaiser's favor did not improve a position that the *Daily Telegraph* crisis had already seriously weakened.[122] The finance reform, which the chancellor introduced on 19 November 1908, called for almost 500 million marks in new property, inheritance, and consumption taxes, an increase unprecedented in the history of the empire and one that heralded a fundamental overhaul of Germany's tax structure.[123] Because of the opposition of the Conservatives and the Catholic Center, the inheritance tax provisions were defeated by a narrow vote on 24 June 1909. Bülow had been repudiated, and although after several weeks of further negotiation a majority in the Reichstag was found for an alternate financial reform that depended on increased or new consumption taxes and various imposts on financial transactions, his position as chancellor was no longer tenable.

Wilhelm II was not prepared to dismiss Bülow until the tax bill had been passed. That objective had been met, but the question of who was to succeed him as chancellor had to be dealt with. The Kaiser once again, as he had in 1905 when Bülow fainted in the Reichstag, wanted to appoint Count Anton Monts, who had only recently retired as ambassador to Italy. Under way to Corfu, the Kaiser ordered that Monts, who was notorious for his acerbity, was to meet Wilhelm in Venice, and there the Kaiser informed him that he would succeed Bülow.[124] Bülow, who had a reciprocated distaste for Monts, immediately went to work to prevent this, and his friend Valentini eventually convinced the Kaiser that Monts, who in any case again spurned the Kaiser's overtures, was too abrasive to make an effective chancellor.[125] Bülow and Valentini both supported the candidacy of the vice-president of the Prussian ministry and minister of interior, Theobald von Bethmann Hollweg, but when his name was submitted, Wilhelm at once objected. The Kaiser told Valentini: "I know him well. He is always lecturing me and always knows best. I can't work with him."[126]

The Kaiser instead instructed Valentini to offer the chancellorship to the Prussian house minister, Count August zu Eulenburg, a Prussian bureaucrat who had been politically inconspicuous for many years, and after his refusal, to the count's brother Botho, who also declined. Wilhelm now mulled appointing General Baron Colmar von der Goltz, who had just become military adviser to the Ottoman sultan, but on reflection he decided that the general was of more use in Turkey than in Berlin.[127] The preferred candidate, faute de mieux, now seemed to be Bethmann. Bülow, who by his own account was working "zealously" (*eifrig*) for Bethmann's candidacy, succeeded first in overcoming Bethmann's objection that he was not suitable for the office and then in persuading the Kaiser to agree to the appointment.[128] On 14 July, the day of his return from his long Baltic cruise, Wilhelm accepted Bülow's resignation and invested a reluctant Bethmann with the office. The Kaiser invoked God's blessing on his choice, but the new chancellor's wife was appalled, for she believed that her husband was not really suitable for the position. "He can't do it!" Frau Bethmann declared in anguish.[129] On the fifteenth, Wilhelm II and the Kaiserin went to dinner with Prince and Princess Bülow, who, like Bismarck twenty years earlier, were now prepared to leave Berlin. To Wilhelm it was good riddance, and he was heard to say, immediately after Bülow's resignation, that the former chancellor was a "criminal character" who had been responsible not only for the *Daily Telegraph* nightmare but also for many other errors.[130] It would take the fallen chancellor twenty years to exact his revenge on the Kaiser. Bülow would achieve this in his posthumously published memoirs, a notorious travesty of exaggeration and misrepresentation in which Wilhelm was made the object of Bülow's malevolent ridicule.

Seven

BETHMANN AND THE BRITISH

A S SUCCESSOR to the fallen Bernhard von Bülow, Theobald von Bethmann Hollweg was not Wilhelm II's preferred choice, and there was no ardent honeymoon of goodwill such as Bülow had enjoyed at the outset of his chancellorship. Nevertheless, for a while the Kaiser and his new chief servant, so dissimilar to one another in personality, managed to get on reasonably well, and Bethmann admitted that Wilhelm acceded to all his requests, although not always as quickly as he might have wanted.[1] The Kaiser had known Bethmann for almost thirty years, for he had hunted with the future chancellor at Hohenfinow, the Bethmanns' large estate east of Berlin, when they were both young men.[2] Entering the service of the Prussian crown, Bethmann had made his way up the bureaucratic ladder unusually quickly, leading to speculation that he was one of the Kaiser's favorites.[3] Wilhelm in fact liked him but no more than (and in fact not as much as) a number of other officials. What worked in favor of Bethmann's appointment were his experience and his proven competence as an administrator. Furthermore, like the Kaiser, the chancellor was anti-Socialist, antidemocratic, and anti-Polish — in a word, thoroughly Prussian. Bethmann accepted office solely out of a sense of duty, for he had worked with Wilhelm for years and was fearful of the Kaiser, probably because he knew what a difficult master Wilhelm would be. "Only a genius or a man driven by ambition and lust for power can covet this position," Bethmann declared, "and I am neither."[4]

An identity of political views contrasted with a distinct disparity in the personalities of Wilhelm and his newly appointed chancellor. Unlike the effervescent and garrulous Kaiser, Bethmann had a ponderous air, a tendency to didacticism, and no humor whatsoever. From the outset of his administration, those who knew the new chancellor predicted that he would sooner or later bore his master.[5] Bethmann had none of the love of pomp that so excited Wilhelm; the acclaim of crowds left him unmoved (nor did he equate cheers with popularity), and he deplored the frivolity and parvenu ostentation with which Wilhelm often behaved.[6] A serious problem for Bethmann was Wilhelm's autocratic streak, which led the Kaiser to believe that Prussian ministers and imperial state secretaries did not belong to the chancellor or to the Reichstag but to the crown.[7] The *Daily Telegraph* episode had tended to still Wilhelm's tongue, and there were thereafter no spectacular diplomatic faux pas, but this by no means meant that the Kaiser intended to retreat entirely from affairs of state. Indeed, the appointment of Bethmann, whose career had been made in internal administration, was interpreted as a sign that Wilhelm himself would continue in the future to try to direct German diplomacy.[8] The new chancellor openly admitted that he knew very little of the Foreign Office and that it would not be easy to master its intricacies. He therefore at once began to involve himself as much as possible in diplomatic affairs.[9]

The state secretary of the Foreign Office was a charming mediocrity, Baron Wilhelm von Schoen, by nature incapable of standing up to the Kaiser's desire to control diplomacy, but Wilhelm II liked him greatly, perhaps for that reason.[10] On leaving office, Bülow had urged Wilhelm to appoint a stronger figure to the post as a counterbalance to Bethmann's inexperience in foreign affairs. If we may believe Bülow, the Kaiser airily responded: "Just leave foreign policy to *me*! I've learned something from you. It will work out fine."[11] Bülow had in mind Alfred von Kiderlen-Wächter, the German envoy in Bucharest who, without any enthusiasm on Wilhelm's part, had recently been on temporary assignment in Berlin to supervise Germany's policy toward Britain. Kiderlen was exactly the man whom Bethmann preferred, for the new chancellor considered his first diplomatic responsibility to be the improvement of Anglo-German relations. To accomplish this aim, he would need an expert on Great Britain effectively to parry Admiral Alfred von Tirpitz's strong dislike of England. There seemed to be no question that Kiderlen could hold his own with the admiral, and indeed a diplomatic colleague in Rumania described him as a man who delighted in confrontation much in the manner of the great Otto von Bismarck.[12] It took a year before Bethmann could hustle Schoen off to Paris as ambassador and have Wilhelm II appoint Kiderlen in his place. Only by warning that the indigent Kiderlen might give up his diplomatic career to assume a lucrative business post was Bethmann able to move Wilhelm to consent. In the 1890s the Kaiser had relished having Kiderlen, whose Swabian anecdotes he found very amusing, as a member of his summer cruise parties. The prim Kaiserin, however, thought his salaciousness revolting. Kiderlen had a very acerbic tongue, which on occasion he could not resist directing against Wilhelm himself, and this had led the resentful sovereign to exile the "bull in a china shop" to the German legation in Bucharest.[13] Here Kiderlen had languished for a decade, until finally, at the end of June 1910, his ambition was realized with his appointment as state secretary. Wilhelm elevated Kiderlen to this post with exceeding reluctance, for the Kaiser cared neither for his rough manner nor his belligerent style in diplomacy. Wilhelm therefore warned Bethmann: "Be careful. You're planting a louse in your pelt."[14]

Bethmann was happy to have Kiderlen in Berlin, and even Schoen admitted that he would contribute to diplomacy a forcefulness that neither he nor Bethmann possessed.[15] Kiderlen, moreover, shared what would be the new chancellor's overriding diplomatic interest in the first years of his administration: the formulation of a naval and political agreement with Great Britain, a subject that had figured in Bethmann's correspondence with Kiderlen in Bucharest during 1909 and early 1910.[16] At the same time, Kiderlen's summons to Berlin was not to mean that authority over German diplomacy would belong to the state secretary, for Bethmann had every intention of being his own foreign minister, inexperienced though he might be in international relations. From the beginning, the chancellor made it clear that he was determined, as Bülow had been, to take a leading role in diplomacy. On the occasion of Kiderlen's appointment, Bethmann assured the British ambassador, Sir Edward Goschen, that it was the chancellor, not his newly appointed official, who would be in charge of foreign affairs.[17] Bethmann must have known that to impose his authority on Kiderlen would not be easy, for the state secretary, although admittedly Germany's most capable diplomat, was also, as the chancellor put it, "a very unpleasant colleague but nonetheless quite a man."[18] Kiderlen did in fact jealously guard his office, and he did not always keep the chancellor fully informed, nor did Bethmann render the same courtesy to Kiderlen.[19] For the most part, however, the chancellor and his new state secretary got along quite well, and Kiderlen's relations with Wilhelm II were equally cordial, somewhat to the state secretary's surprise. The Kaiser, Kiderlen noted, acted as if the long years of exile in Rumania to which Wilhelm had consigned him had never happened. Kiderlen was under no illusions about what he had to deal with in the Kaiser, who was careless in speech and too excitable. He was also aware that the somewhat graceless Bethmann, whom Kiderlen described as an "earthworm" forever undulating between being forceful and being weak, did not possess a personality that was ideal for coping with Wilhelm II.[20]

As far as Bethmann was concerned, only an approach to Great Britain would serve to relieve Germany's encircled position in Europe. This predicament had resulted because of the firm entrenchment of both Russia and France in their opposition to Berlin and also because of the general disenchantment with Germany that had resulted from the Moroccan crisis and the Algeciras conference. The chancellor was prepared to take the initiative in working out a settlement of Anglo-German differences.[21] In his opinion this would require the simultaneous conclusion of an agreement on naval armaments as well as a diplomatic and colonial settlement, such as the Entente Cordiale that Britain had signed with France in 1904 and the similar pact that Britain had entered into three years later with Russia through which the two powers had resolved their rival ambitions in Persia. If the differences with Britain could be reconciled, Germany would be delivered from isolation, and the ability of the French and the Russians, both financially dependent on London, to conduct anti-German policies would also be diminished.[22] In this view of Germany's diplomatic future, Bethmann had the Kaiser's enthusiastic concurrence, but the chancellor heard with misgivings Wilhelm's insistence that personal interaction between the sovereigns of the two nations was the best means of improving Anglo-German relations.[23]

The initial good relationship that Bethmann enjoyed with Wilhelm II soon dissipated, exactly as it had, sooner or later, with all of his predecessors. The longer he stayed in office, Bethmann declared, the harder it became to exercise his influence with the Kaiser.[24] The chancellor found much in Wilhelm II about which to complain. The problem was not limited to the Kaiser's troublesome personality, which Bethmann, like so many others, deplored for its volubility and general lack of dignity, tact, and seriousness of purpose.[25] He also had to worry about another tendency of Wilhelm's, one that every chancellor including Bismarck had deplored: the Kaiser's habit of shutting himself off with his trusted courtiers and avoiding the chancellor for long stretches of time.[26] Bethmann had good reason to be concerned, for neither Wilhelm II's wife nor the Kaiser's eldest son and heir, nor many of the favorites among the various generals and admirals at court, liked him, and they were eager to undermine his standing with the Kaiser. The crown prince, a man whose interests were largely confined to horses, uniforms, and women, would prove to be a particularly persistent enemy. Both the prince and his mother, the Kaiserin Augusta Victoria, had regretted Bülow's fall from office and viewed the successor with suspicion. Bethmann, who dismissed the prince as a fop, had little to do with him or with the empress.[27]

The longer Bethmann remained in office, the more Wilhelm II discovered that his new chancellor was a man with whom it was not easy to work. The Kaiser did not at all like to be lectured to, and the preceptorial quality he encountered in Bismarck, in Leo von Caprivi, and in Chlodwig Hohenlohe had contributed to the fall from office of each one of them. It was something he gradually found very tiresome in his new chancellor as well. One of Bethmann's virtues, admirable in a man but dangerous in a person dealing with the Kaiser, was his inability to be anything but straightforward; he was "a fanatic for frankness and openness," a friend declared.[28] Moreover, Bethmann shared with the Kaiser a trait that was also likely to produce difficulties. Even the chancellor's admirers regretted that he, like Wilhelm, was quite touchy, tending too often to treat opposition as a personal affront.[29] Bethmann was unnaturally resistant to quick decisions, so in contrast to the Kaiser's penchant for instantaneous orders. Adolf Wermuth, who served Bethmann as imperial secretary of the treasury, declared: "He weighed things incessantly but acted unwillingly. His main concern was not what he should do but what he might *not* be permitted to do. The words 'I can't do it' were so much his favorite expression that they became a sort of nickname."[30] The chancellor's ponderous manner, his "minuscule scruple," at least had the virtue of giving him a European reputation — one that was useful after all the diplomatic commotion that had attended Bülow's last years in office — of being no hotspur but rather a sober, responsible statesman.[31] But Wilhelm did not regard deliberation as a virtue in handling domestic affairs, and he feared that at home Bethmann was regarded as a weakling.[32] On occasion Wilhelm was inclined to interpret the chancellor's indecisiveness as a means of trying to defy the imperial will. When, for example, Bethmann showed what the Kaiser felt was undue delay in agreeing to his nominee for the vacant envoyship to the Court of St. James, Wilhelm wrote in exasperation and reminded the chancellor, "I send only *my* ambassador to London, who has *my* confidence, obeys *my* will, fulfills *my* orders with *my* instructions."[33]

Wilhelm often treated Bethmann shabbily, criticizing his errors and deprecating his successes.[34] The chancellor therefore could not always rely on the crown's help in coping with the many problems Germany faced at home and abroad. He enjoyed a slight advantage in domestic matters, for this had been the specialty of his long career in the Prussian and imperial bureaucracy and was besides an area of considerably less interest to Wilhelm II than were foreign affairs. Bethmann recognized that he had inherited from Bülow an unenviable legacy, for the collapse of Bülow's "bloc" of Conservatives, National Liberals, and Progressives during the bitter struggle over the introduction of an inheritance tax in 1908–9 had left these factions isolated and vindictive. This meant that Bethmann could not hope to build a permanent coalition but instead would have to assemble ad hoc majorities for every Reichstag bill. For such a policy to succeed, he considered it imperative for his administration to rise above the parties. It was fruitless to try to suppress the Socialists, who were in virtually permanent opposition to the government, and instead Bethmann favored trying to bring them gradually within the group of parties from which majorities might be assembled. The empire, he declared, could be run neither from the extreme Right nor the extreme Left, for to attempt either policy would automatically alienate half the nation. The only course was the diagonal, crossing over the parties in the hope of assembling a majority much in the way that Bismarck in his day had been forced to do.[35] That would not be easy for Bethmann to accomplish, for he had little appreciation of the psychology of the Reichstag as a whole. He lectured the deputies in a schoolmasterish tone, and he admitted that his inability to serve up the sort of flattery that Bülow had used in the chamber.[36] The chancellor consequently had a very limited following in any of the parties. The Conservatives loathed Bethmann, whom they saw as too inclined to capitulate to the Left; the National Liberals disliked him, seeing Bethmann as a Prussian agrarian aristocrat; and the Socialists were dogmatically opposed to his regime. Only with the Catholic Center and the Progressives did he enjoy a relationship that was tolerable, though hardly harmonious.

The domestic situation with which the chancellor would have to deal early in his administration was a minefield, certain to lead to further exacerbation with the parties. His first act was to introduce legislation providing for a reform of the Prussian constitution, an alteration so cautious that he succeeded in obtaining Wilhelm II's agreement. This reform aimed at reducing the hold that landed wealth enjoyed on the election process by altering the existing franchise, one that gave disproportionate representation to those owning large amounts of property. Bethmann's proposal was anathema to the Conservative landlords but too modest to please the liberal factions, with the result that the bill failed.[37] The Conservatives also opposed Bethmann's attempt to relax somewhat the Germanization policy in the formerly Polish areas of Prussia, as well as his proposal to grant Alsace-Lorraine representation in the *Bundesrat*, the upper house of the imperial legislature. The Right blocked the Polish reform, but Bethmann did succeed in Alsace, to the lasting hostility of the Conservatives.

The chancellor also had to deal with the empire's acute financial situation. The taxation scheme that Bethmann, as vice-president of the Prussian ministry and imperial secretary of the treasury, had got through the Reichstag and *Bundesrat* in the last week of Bülow's chancellorship raised an additional 500 million marks of income annually, but this was barely enough to cover expenses. Bethmann's successor at the treasury, Adolf Wermuth, was determined to authorize "no expenditures that [were] not covered," a policy that the chancellor endorsed. Most of the government's outlay went for military purposes, with the result that from the beginning, Bethmann's fiscal conservatism put him at odds with the army. The minister of war, General Karl von Einem, bluntly declared that the chancellor had "absolutely no relationship with the army," and he resigned, shortly after Bethmann took office, in disgust at the government's determination to pare army expenditures to the bone.[38] Bethmann was aware that the size and the historic aggressiveness of the Prussian army were factors in diplomatic calculations in many European capitals, especially Paris and St. Petersburg. Money was short in Berlin, and suspicions were growing abroad, and for both reasons, any increases in Germany's armed strength needed to be carefully weighed.[39] Although Bethmann had served in the guards, he had few army friends and negligible appreciation for the military mind. He wore his uniform, but only because it was expected in the Reichstag and was commanded at court, and it gave him little pleasure. "Would the day finally come," he told one of his sons, "that a German chancellor might go to court in mufti."[40] To the officer corps, Bethmann was only a civilian, one entirely too blind to the dangers facing Germany from the Left. Nor was he a genuine Prussian, for although he had been born near Berlin, his forebears had come from Frankfort on the Main, now part of the kingdom but earlier an independent city-state.[41] It was therefore incumbent on the Prussian army, allied with its commander-in-chief, Wilhelm II, to guard Germany against the democratizing, federal tendencies of the chancellor and the Reichstag. "The King of Prussia and the German Kaiser," declared Elard von Oldenburg-Januschau, a former officer and Conservative deputy, "must at every moment be able to say to a lieutenant: take ten men and shoot the Reichstag!"[42]

The German fleet steadily being constructed after 1898 under Admiral Tirpitz's supervision was an even more difficult matter, for naval construction annually consumed millions of marks, and this German armada was correctly perceived in Britain as the arm of an eventual confrontation with the Royal Navy. Bethmann's principal diplomatic dilemma from 1909 to 1914 was how, or whether, the growth of the German navy could be reconciled with an improvement in relations between Berlin and London, a course that the chancellor was determined to pursue. He recognized that the Kaiser's fleet would inevitably be at the heart of any attempt at diplomatic reconciliation.[43] The matter was acutely important to Bethmann, not only because he was aware of the financial consequences for

Germany but also because he believed that an arrangement with the British had to be accomplished while the Liberal government of Herbert Asquith was still in power, since this government, whose future seemed questionable, was more friendly to Germany than were the Conservatives.[44]

Bethmann was certainly aware that the two personalities most likely to frustrate his desire to improve Anglo-German relations were Tirpitz and Wilhelm II. The admiral was a serious threat, for he disliked England intensely and was certain that conflict with it was inevitable. This was an attitude that permeated the ranks of German naval officers, who drank to "the day" when Tirpitz's fleet would have its reckoning with the British.[45] Germany had no choice but to engage in massive armament on the sea, a development that would either cripple the Royal Navy in the event of war or, if peace could be maintained, make Britain diplomatically amenable to Germany's interests. Tirpitz was a formidable personality and a resourceful enemy, one with friends in high places. He did not like Bethmann, claiming that a talk with the chancellor never yielded any results, and he regarded as utterly mistaken the chancellor's belief that a diplomatic accommodation could be obtained by naval reductions. Like the Kaiserin and the crown prince, Tirpitz remained attached to Bülow long after his fall from office; the admiral declared that Bülow's chancellorship, in which the government had secured huge naval budgets, had been "the best years of the post-Bismarck era."[46]

Wilhelm II agreed with Tirpitz's vision to the extent that he believed that a powerful naval force in Germany's hands would either decisively wound the Royal Navy in battle or deter Britain from any thought of going to war.[47] The chancellor acknowledged that Wilhelm fervently desired to get along with England, but the Kaiser's unfortunate manner, even when proclaiming his friendship, worked in London in a countervailing direction. Had it not been for Wilhelm's constant intrusions, Germany and Britain would have, in Bethmann's opinion, long since reconciled their differences.[48] Wilhelm's maladroitly phrased declarations of his affection for England, as in the *Daily Telegraph* affair, in addition to his occasional less-public rattlings about an inevitable war with England, were constant problems for the chancellor. The Kaiser, however, persisted in believing that if relations with Britain were in decline, it was not his fault. As he told the British naval attaché to Berlin in 1910, he had tried to be friendly, but no one in England had believed him, displaying the sort of ingratitude that reminded him of the question in a popular London music-hall song "Julia, Why Are You So Peculiar?"[49] Instead of responding to his offers of friendship, the British had behaved arrogantly in bossing Germany about in diplomacy, had conspired with Wilhelm's enemies in St. Petersburg and Paris, and had tried to intimidate the growth of Tirpitz's magnificent fleet.[50] Even so, Wilhelm insisted that harmony between the two peoples from whom he was descended was both worth striving for and indeed realizable. Great Britain must recognize that it was Germany, a nation that was Protestant, Teutonic, industrially dynamic, and powerfully armed, who was its natural ally, not Russia or France.[51]

With the appointment of a new chancellor in the summer of 1909, it was Wilhelm II's intention that the first task of the new government would be the improvement of relations with England, and with Bethmann ensconced in office, the signs soon seemed propitious for the revival of Anglo-German amity.[52] Edward VII died in May 1910, an event that a friend said left the Kaiser "extremely relieved." As he departed Berlin for the funeral of the man he had castigated as the greatest of intriguers, the Kaiser declared that the king's demise would clear the way for an improvement in Anglo-German relations. Wilhelm's mournful performance at the obsequies at Windsor therefore seemed somewhat contrived.[53] The Kaiser was entirely confident that the new sovereign, his first cousin George V, would prove much more satisfactory, since the king was an apolitical homebody who spoke no foreign tongues and who would therefore not be inclined, as his father had been, to run off to Paris to conspire with the French and their Russian allies.[54] Although as a young man the king had found his cousin an obnoxious busybody, he had gradually come to tolerate Wilhelm fairly well.[55] George V was delighted that the Kaiser had appointed Bethmann in place of Bülow, a man whom the king believed to have been responsible for the misunderstandings that had arisen between Germany and England.[56] Wilhelm was satisfied that on Henry Campbell-Bannerman's resignation Asquith had succeeded, but he was unaware that the new prime minister thought that the Kaiser's mind was unsettled.[57] Wilhelm found the foreign secretary, Sir Edward Grey, to be an honorable man, although Grey was difficult to talk to and too susceptible to French influence. By and large, Wilhelm believed that British statesmen were reasonable men with whom he could work.[58]

In the Kaiser's opinion, the economic rivalry between England and Germany, although admittedly an unwelcome complication, was not the sort of competition that could lead to war. Wilhelm declared that as far as he was concerned, the British could colonize the world, so long as German traders were allowed to do business in their ports.[59] Except for some continuing problems in Morocco, over which England and Germany had clashed in 1905–6, there were now no serious conflicts in colonial areas.

The only impediment to good relations between London and Berlin, one about which Wilhelm had intensely strong feelings, was the naval race that had existed since Germany's passage of the First Naval Law in 1898. If relations between Great Britain and Germany were to be improved, something would have to be done about their two fleets.

This would require dealing with Tirpitz, who considered the German navy sacrosanct, above interference within the Fatherland and immune to threats from foreign powers. Arrogant in personality, Tirpitz would brook no opposition from his fellow officers, and he was positively contemptuous of civilian authorities, such as the German ambassador in London, Count Paul von Wolff-Metternich zur Gracht, who tried to mix in maritime affairs. The admiral felt an instinctive dislike for Bethmann, whom he chastised for being afraid to "provoke the bulldog" England. The chancellor, he declared, was unduly touchy and suspicions, which was true enough, though these were traits that others had observed in Tirpitz himself.[60] Both Kiderlen and Bethmann deplored Tirpitz's naval policy as an "unending screw," counter to their own efforts to create better relations with Britain.[61] But to oppose Tirpitz too forcefully was unwise, for Bethmann realized that given a choice between himself and the admiral, Wilhelm would certainly side with Tirpitz.[62] The Kaiser's preference was not due to any affection he felt for the admiral. Although in the 1890s Wilhelm had heaped praise on Tirpitz and regularly advanced him in rank and office, the Kaiser had eventually grown resentful of his overbearing, Bismarckian manner and his tendency, when the Kaiser had the temerity to question him, instantly to submit his resignation.[63] The admiral was very skillful at appealing to Wilhelm's vanity as the creator of the navy, pointing out that unless Germany continued to build enough ships to withstand or prevent a British attack, the Kaiser's entire naval policy would become a "historical fiasco," with the Fatherland dependent on England for whatever position it might enjoy in the world. Wilhelm was very susceptible to this sort of argument but also was not above being jealous that his subjects seemed to revere Tirpitz more than their ruler.[64] Although Wilhelm considered Tirpitz suitable to be state secretary at the Foreign Office or even chancellor, he sometimes showed his irritation by delaying or protesting the award of honors to which the admiral was entitled. The Kaiser could also be obnoxious, dealing with disagreements by telling Tirpitz that he did not know what the admiral was talking about. But Wilhelm recognized that Tirpitz had a vast following among his fellow officers and many adherents in the Reichstag, and the Kaiser therefore never let their disputes get out of hand.[65]

It was obvious to Wilhelm that the British would not welcome Germany's naval ambitions and therefore would threaten to prevent their fulfillment. The Kaiser warned that he would not be intimidated. "I cannot and will not allow John Bull to dictate to me the pace at which I build my warships," he informed Bülow at the end of June 1909.[66] Wilhelm was sure that Admiral Sir John Fisher, the "arch-rascal" (*Erzhalunke*), dreamed of undertaking a sudden attack on the German fleet at Heligoland so that he could end his career, in imitation of Lord Nelson's title commemorating his victory over the French at Trafalgar, as "Lord Fisher of Heligoland."[67] Tirpitz's fleet in the making since 1898, however, had deterred Fisher from doing so, and once the admiral's 2:3 ratio of German capital ships to their British counterparts was reached in about 1919, Germany would have an enhanced freedom of diplomatic and military action as well as a fully realized degree of national honor.[68] The cost of such an armada could not be allowed to stand in the way of its completion, for Wilhelm was certain that Germany could better afford the huge costs involved and, besides, had a sufficient supply of able-bodied seamen, natives rather than the sort of immigrant riffraff who peopled the Royal Navy.[69] Admiral Fisher had made a serious error in assuming that Germany could not match the British in the construction of battleships, for a nation whose passenger liners rivaled those of the Cunard and the White Star Lines could also compete in ships of the line.[70]

The naval competition between Germany and Great Britain had entered an acute phase with the Moroccan crisis of 1905 and the decision made by London in the same year to proceed with the construction of *Dreadnought*-class battleships. Germany retaliated in 1907 when the Reichstag passed a new naval law providing for the annual construction of four comparable leviathans, one more than the British had expected. The Liberal cabinet under Prime Minister Campbell-Bannerman, who viewed with alarm the high financial and diplomatic cost of a maritime armament race, made several semiofficial overtures to Berlin in 1908, but Bülow showed little interest in pursuing them. As a result, in 1909 the new Liberal government under Asquith initiated a naval building program that further exacerbated relations between the two nations. This was the unfortunate situation that Bethmann inherited when he assumed the chancellorship in July of that year.

A month after taking office, Bethmann approached the British, proposing that Germany and Britain enter into negotiations to conclude a combined naval and diplomatic agreement. His reasoning was twofold. First, a joint approach, unlike a purely naval negotiation, would give the civil government in Berlin the upper hand over Tirpitz in the talks. Second, he believed that German public opinion would not be willing formally to acknowledge the superiority of the Royal Navy unless it got, in return, a clear indication of Britain's diplomatic goodwill toward the Fatherland in the form of a diplomatic treaty. This was moreover a concession that the Kaiser was determined to secure.[71] Bethmann reminded Ambassador Goschen that Germany's shipbuilding program was set by law and could not be altered, so that the only negotiable point would have to be the tempo of construction and the retirement of vessels. This argument impressed neither Goschen nor Edward VII, who tartly remarked that whoever had made a law could also retract it.[72] In spite of this skepticism, the king declared, "This subject is one of grave importance — but it is satisfactory that the first move comes fr[om] Germany — through the new Chancellor!"[73] The Asquith cabinet made it clear to Berlin that although prepared to negotiate, it could enter into no arrangement that would undermine the ententes already in existence with France and Russia, a point to which Bethmann subsequently raised no protest.[74]

In any consideration of naval armaments, the Kaiser believed that his reputation was at stake. A powerful navy, he often declared, was necessary for strategic purposes and for the protection of German commerce, but Wilhelm also believed that once his majestic navy had been built, other sovereigns would accord *him* more attention than they had in the past.[75] Until Tirpitz had completed his construction program, Wilhelm believed that he would have to rely on a certain bluntness of expression as his arm of defense, but with a battle fleet he would have a physical weapon at hand. Only naked power impressed the British, he told the Archduke Franz Ferdinand, for in London, "politeness" was "regarded as weakness."[76] Great Britain had no legitimate reason to fear his navy, he had assured Kind Edward VII's intimate, Sir Charles Hardinge, in 1908, for the Royal Navy was far superior numerically. Germany had no intention of attacking England and indeed had done what it could to allay British suspicions by minimizing the activity of German warships in the English Channel. The British, however, would do well to realize that the German fleet was being built according to parliamentary legislation; the provisions were public knowledge, and once introduced, they could not be withdrawn.[77] Hardinge's unequivocal response on that occasion had been that the British expected a reduction in German naval armaments, an answer that annoyed Wilhelm for months on end. On 3 April 1909 the Kaiser wrote at length and in considerable exasperation to Bülow, complaining of "the whole English fleet — and Dreadnought-*Schweinerei*."[78] British arrogance was intolerable but also unwarranted, according to the Kaiser, for London had no allies on whom it could depend.[79] If talks began, Asquith and Grey would have to understand that Germany would negotiate only as an equal. Wilhelm was prepared to offer concessions in naval armaments, specifically the elimination of a supplementary law scheduled for 1912 to provide for additional ship construction, but only if Britain reduced the Royal Navy's building program to establish a 3:4 ratio of German to British warships.[80]

The Kaiser was determined not to have the British dictate to him, and he was equally resistant to any and all attempts at an international mediation regarding armaments. He looked with disfavor on disarmament projects and for that reason had been very hostile to the two international peace conferences convened at The Hague in 1900 and 1907. The first, initiated by Tsar Nicholas II, was in his opinion nothing but an attempt to limit the strength of Germany's army. He endorsed the view of one of his diplomats who stated, "Preparation for eternal peace is a childish illusion." Wilhelm refused to have anything to do with such "humanitarian dizziness" (*Humanitätsdusel*) and contemptuously told Bülow, "I shit on the whole affair."[81] For once Wilhelm was in agreement with his uncle, the Prince of Wales, who described the tsar's maneuver as "the greatest nonsense and rubbish" he had "ever heard of."[82] The second Hague conference, for which Theodore Roosevelt was the inspirator, was to the Kaiser a similar ruse, this time one by the British to constrain the growth of the German navy. Wilhelm argued, not without justice, that the development of his fleet was a matter of public record, enshrined in legislation passed by the Reichstag and therefore quite unlike the secretiveness with which the Royal Navy was building its *Dreadnought*-class ships.[83]

Wilhelm was insistent that if an Anglo-German accord in armaments was to be reached, it would have to be forged through mutual compromises. According to the Kaiser's analysis of the situation, no progress had been made in realizing a settlement because of the ineptitude of the German ambassador in London, Count Metternich. The envoy argued, in opposition to Tirpitz, that the deterioration of Anglo-German relations was due squarely to naval rivalry and not to economic competition. Although Metternich was notoriously reticent in society, he was fearless in telling Wilhelm II what he felt the Kaiser needed to hear. "I cannot sell my convictions for the favor of my sovereign," he declared.[84] That made little headway with the Kaiser, however, for Wilhelm had his own notion of reality and thought that his plenipotentiary was entirely too conciliatory toward the British, was ignorant of the critical necessity of the German fleet, and was at every turn prepared to negotiate away the naval power that had been steadily built up by Admiral Tirpitz since the passage of the First Naval Law in 1898. "Merely cease building [ships] in Germany and then England will be in a good humor," was how he characterized the ambassador's advice.[85] Tirpitz shared Wilhelm's meager estimation of Metternich, and the admiral told the envoy to his face that he would be sure to botch the German position in any negotiations with England.[86] Both the Kaiser and Tirpitz considered the naval attaché in London, Metternich's foe and rival Captain Wilhelm Widenmann, a far more reliable source of information on British naval policy. Widenmann had no enthusiasm for making an armament agreement with the British, for he resented what he perceived to be London's disdainful treatment of Germany.[87]

The British reaction to Bethmann's overtures made in the fall of 1909 was tepid, for it seemed a case of Britain's being asked to tie its hands in naval construction in return for Germany's being permitted free play on the Continent. From the outset of the ensuing negotiations, a difference of emphasis as well as of opinion was perceptible in the two parties. To the British, the naval question was paramount, to the Germans the diplomatic, and both insisted that their agendas take precedence. In armaments Tirpitz insisted on a 2:3 ratio of German to British capital ships in the face of an equally resolute determination on London's part to fix the relationship at 1:2. The chancellor acknowledged that with respect to a political treaty committing the signatories to mutual aid in specified eventualities, the terms that Berlin envisioned would constitute a diplomatic departure for Great Britain, whose ententes with France and Russia contained not binding provisions but only expressions of amity and agreements for mutual consultation.[88] In any case, the prospect of negotiations with Germany, thus not off to a promising start, had to be deferred until after the general election already announced for January 1910. It was just as well, for much of the electioneering rhetoric was strenuously anti-German, a fact that annoyed both the Kaiser and Bethmann. It was as though, Wilhelm declared, the British believed him to be "standing here with [a] battle axe" behind his back "ready to fall upon them at any moment."[89]

The elections diminished the majority in the Commons of the Liberals, who were better disposed to Germany than were the Conservatives. In spite of appeals from both Ambassador Metternich and the chancellor, Prime Minister Asquith made no move to proceed with negotiations. Finally, in the fall of 1910, the British cabinet put out feelers to Berlin, and Bethmann's response, once again, was that no naval reductions could be made until Britain pursued a diplomatic policy more friendly to Germany.

In October, Wilhelm II received Ambassador Goschen in an audience that he began by declaring that a political understanding "*must* be made."[90] He defended the construction of a great German navy by making reference to the aggressive enmity of France and Russia and the need to protect himself against England in the event London should decide to aid either or both of his foes. England's association with the Franco-Russian entente and its support for France in Morocco were clear evidence of hostility. Germany was prepared to acknowledge England's supremacy on the seas, but the margin of British superiority would have to be calculated so as to maintain a German strength sufficient to implement Tirpitz's "risk theory," and any agreement would have to take into account the naval strength of Britain's friends, Russia and France.

In 1911, the Anglo-German negotiations, so meager in expectation, had to be momentarily relegated to second place because of a diplomatic crisis, once again one involving Morocco. The Algeciras Treaty signed by the major powers in 1906 had decreed that Morocco was to be open to the trade of all nations, with France awarded a preponderant role in the supervision of police and banking there. Three years later in a separate agreement, France and Germany confirmed these terms, with Germany recognizing France's "special political interests" in return for an acknowledgment of Germany's economic presence in the sultanate. Should any changes in the sultanate prove necessary in the future, Germany and France alone were to determine what was to be done. With his accustomed vanity, Wilhelm II declared that this treaty had been possible only because of his efforts and in spite of the obstructionism of the Foreign Office, although he in fact had little to do with its conclusion.[91] By 1910, the Kaiser was convinced that France, with the support of the British, was bent on interpreting the Franco-German accord as giving it license to reduce Morocco to the status of a protectorate.[92] The most striking sign of this was the French occupation of Fez on 6 April 1911, a move Paris declared to be necessary to protect Europeans in the capital from marauding Berber tribesmen. Wilhelm did not find this intensification of French involvement in Morocco necessarily undesirable, for it would indeed preserve order. Moreover, for France to sustain its presence in the sultanate, vast sums of money would have to be spent to maintain troops there, to Germany's strategic advantage in Europe. For that reason he did not want to make any dramatic gestures of protest against French ambitions such as ordering a warship to proceed to a Moroccan port.[93] He was insistent only that German trading rights, guaranteed both by the Algeciras Treaty of 1906 and by the Franco-German accord of 1909, be respected. Hostilities were out of the question.

Wilhelm explained to King George V, whom he visited in London in May 1911, that Germany had no intention of going to war over Morocco but that it expected that its economic position there be upheld. The Kaiser also suggested that in the event France appropriated Morocco, Germany might expect territorial compensations elsewhere in Africa.[94]

Kiderlen, however, believed that it would be necessary to deal stringently with France, for he was certain that because of Alsace-Lorraine, there was no possibility whatsoever of Germany's ever forging a satisfactory diplomatic relationship with Paris.[95] A neighboring power so infected with abiding hostility had to be kept aware that Germany would not tolerate any aggressive behavior. That was precisely what France, according to Kiderlen, was up to, arrogating to itself more and more authority in Morocco and now marching into Fez. Kiderlen therefore adopted a "high and blustering" tone toward the French ambassador, Jules Cambon, pointing out that the French seizure of Fez had violated the Algeciras Treaty and that Germany would have to receive compensation. Kiderlen indicated that the award of extensive portions of the French Congo to Germany would be suitable, a demand that had originated with Wilhelm II.[96]

Although Bethmann thought Kiderlen much too bellicose, the chancellor left the handling of the matter to him, and the state secretary devised a scheme whereby German warships, in a maneuver he likened to a "blare of trumpets" (*Trompetenstoss*), would be sent to Agadir, which was a "closed" port under the terms of the Algeciras Treaty and was adjacent to Mogador, the "open" harbor favored by British commercial interests in Morocco. The justification would be to protect German business interests in western Morocco, but the effect would be to preclude ships of other nations from occupying Agadir. Kiderlen did not want, nor did he expect, the Moroccan situation to lead to war, but the possibility was plainly envisioned.[97] The appearance of German gunboats off Agadir would be a sort of "trick," as Chancellor Bethmann later described it, whereby should France or England dare to move against the German vessels, the treaties that Germany had long ago signed with Austria and Italy would require them to come to Berlin's defense against such an aggressive act.[98]

At the time of the French occupation of Fez, Wilhelm II was annoyed by what seemed to him to be a conspiracy by the Entente Cordiale to seize not only Morocco but most of northern Africa. His own ally Italy was known to have ambitions in Tripoli and would, in a move that the Kaiser was sure had originated with his late uncle Edward VII, in the fall of 1911 invade and seize it.[99] Britain's diplomatic partner France obviously intended to have Morocco. Wilhelm had initially approved the French move on Fez, believing that it would restore order for the benefit of all European traders in Morocco, but on reflection he decided that this audacious move by France should, as Kiderlen proposed, be used to extract concessions favorable to Germany. Negotiations had in fact begun between Kiderlen and Ambassador Cambon in mid-June, but they had come to nothing, much to Wilhelm's irritation. The Kaiser was annoyed that Bethmann was not pressing France aggressively, which he believed was the only way to force Paris to offer suitable recompense. He informed the chancellor that a warship should be sent to Agadir for the purpose, as he described it after the fact, of obtaining a "suitable compensation" by a "calm but forceful presence" in Morocco, though he acknowledged that the British would very likely be upset.[100] Admiral Tirpitz and the navy were not consulted, and when they expressed concern that the gesture was potentially dangerous, the Kaiser haughtily replied to the chief of the Naval Cabinet, "It is better not to ask the army and navy for their opinion in political questions."[101]

With the Kaiser's consent obtained, Bethmann gave the necessary orders, and on 1 July 1911 the gunboat *Panther* steamed into Agadir and dropped anchor.[102] Bethmann's official justification was that native tribes had endangered German business interests in that part of Morocco and that Germany was required to protest the violation of the Algeciras Treaty represented by the French occupation of Fez.[103] The French did not for a moment believe this and were convinced that Germany was trying to take advantage of the fact that a new government with an inexperienced foreign minister had just taken office in Paris. To the premier, Joseph Caillaux, the German sally at Agadir was a deliberate provocation, the "aggravating counterpart of the voyage of the Kaiser to Tangiers."[104] Although Kiderlen was prepared, as a last resort, to press the French to the point of war over Morocco, he preferred a diplomatic solution, and so did Caillaux. He proposed that in return for permitting France carte blanche in Morocco, Paris might cede to Germany its entire Congolese territory. If the French agreed, Germany would be worthily compensated, but if Caillaux balked, Berlin would then insist on the strict maintenance of the Algeciras Treaty of 1906, which would mean that France would have to surrender the predominant position it had gained since then in Morocco. Thus the German position was fraudulent: the *Panther* had been sent to Agadir allegedly to protect German interests in Morocco, but Kiderlen nevertheless was prepared to surrender Morocco to France provided that Germany could find sufficient compensation elsewhere in Africa.

From the beginning Wilhelm was dissatisfied with the way the affair proceeded. Germany's remonstrances to France should have been made *immediately* after the French occupation of Fez, but Kiderlen had allowed three months to elapse before the *Panther* had been dispatched to Agadir. The Kaiser believed that had Germany moved at once, Britain would have been sympathetic to Berlin's protests, but now there was the danger that Britain would support France, just as it had in the first Moroccan crisis in 1905–6.[105] Wilhelm, no less than the chancellor, mistrusted Kiderlen's intentions, believing, quite correctly, that the state secretary was prepared to act much more aggressively toward France than proposed by the "calm but forceful" formula the Kaiser had laid down in authorizing the dispatch of the *Panther*.[106] Crises tended to inflate the Kaiser's vanity. Two weeks after the *Panther* dropped anchor at Agadir, Wilhelm declared that he must terminate the cruise he was then enjoying in Norwegian waters and return at once to Berlin in order to take charge of the dangerous situation, a move that Bethmann succeeded in discouraging.[107] Kiderlen meanwhile threatened to resign if he was not granted permission to proceed with his plan for forcing France's hand, and the Kaiser reluctantly agreed, but he was insistent that the German demands were to be such as to avoid any possibility of hostilities with France.[108] The British, who had steadfastly sided with France, had no intention of standing aside if Germany tried to force France to the wall. In a speech at the Mansion House in London on 21 July 1911 before a group of bankers and merchants, David Lloyd George, the chancellor of the exchequer and until now a moderate in the naval armament issue, issued an admonition that was unmistakably meant to apply to the situation in Africa. If Britain was "treated where her interests were vitally affected as if she were of no account in the Cabinet of nations," Lloyd George warned, "Then I say emphatically that peace at that price would be a humiliation intolerable for a great country like ours to endure."[109]

The Kaiser, who was already alarmed that the Moroccan entanglement created by the *Panther* had become dangerous, interpreted the speech as an unnecessary and "illoyal" provocation and an attack on his person not only by Lloyd George but also by Sir Edward Grey, the foreign minister, who he rightly believed had been involved in its composition.[110] Why, he asked Ambassador Lascelles, did the British always rush to condemn the one person intent on good Anglo-German relations, the one who was their "only real friend in Europe"?[111] All he had done was to send a "little ship with only two or three little pop guns" in response to the pleas of German firms that felt endangered by natives. The French did not want to go to war, and they would not unless encouraged to do so by the British government and the Germanophobe press, in particular the *Daily Mail* and the *Times*. It was appalling, the Kaiser declared, that the British were always at work trying to spoil Germany's development as a world power and its relations with other European nations. William informed Lascelles that either the French could offer Germany appropriate compensation or he would see to it that, "by fair means or foul," they would be cleared out of Morocco in compliance with the Algeciras Treaty.[112]

Lloyd George's speech, like the international consternation that greeted the anchoring of the *Panther* in Agadir, once again convinced Wilhelm that he had to return to Germany. This time he proceeded to do so. Fear ran high among some of the entourage aboard (though not with the Kaiser himself) the *Hohenzollern* as it made its way home from Norway, and there was even talk that the Royal Navy might try to intercept Wilhelm's yacht. In Berlin the rumors of war seemed so credible that the stock market crashed, but eventually all the parties involved intensified their efforts to find a diplomatic solution.[113] In spite of Wilhelm's conviction that he was needed in Berlin, he did not play an active role in the long negotiations between Kiderlen and Ambassador Cambon, talks that stretched through the summer and into the fall of 1911. The Kaiser supported the state secretary's position that if Germany granted France a free hand in Morocco, it would be entitled to substantially all of the French Congo, but he was eager not to give the British any cause to be hostile because the German fleet was not ready for war. He became annoyed when Ambassador Cambon, supported by Britain, refused to cede the entire Congo. Wilhelm, who was very concerned that his subjects might believe that he had "folded under" to the French, threatened to break off negotiations altogether and fulminated about naval and military mobilization until he was assured that Cambon was trying to arrange a compromise.[114] After much wrangling, the terms were finally worked out, and a pair of treaties, one on Morocco and the other on the Congo, were signed between France and Germany and concluded the crisis. The French were acknowledged to have predominance in Morocco, and Germany took substantial but commercially worthless portions of the French Congo.

Wilhelm II, who had earlier complained about Bethmann's conduct of the affair, wired the chancellor congratulating him on having brought "this delicate matter" to an end.[115] That was putting a good face on what was, like the first Moroccan crisis in 1905–6, a diplomatic defeat for Germany. The rightist factions in the Reichstag branded the treaties a surrender to France. In the royal loge, the reactionary crown prince, the darling of German Conservatives, ostentatiously applauded the protest against his father's government, a gesture that at once produced a paternal reprimand.[116] In the officer corps of the army, there were murmurings of dismay that Wilhelm II, derisively referred to as the "peace Kaiser" (*Friedenskaiser*), had not upheld the fatherland's honor vis-à-vis France.[117] And even the Kaiser recognized that Germany, not once but twice checked in Morocco, found itself now at the crossroads. The British and the French had again stood firm against Germany, and this solidarity, Wilhelm speculated, was a preparation for the great war that must one day inevitably descend on Europe.[118]

The Algeciras Treaty of 1906, which Wilhelm II claimed to be a diplomatic accomplishment for Germany, seemed to the Kaiser's subjects to be in fact a capitulation to France and its British ally. All the brouhaha over trading rights in Morocco, the incantations of national honor, and the showing of the flag at Agadir five years later had done nothing but deliver to France a valuable economic protectorate in Morocco, with Germany being awarded, in alleged compensation, several hundred thousand acres of France's Congolese swamplands. The Kaiser was branded a coward, but his heir, who had publicly denounced Germany's accommodation with France, became the idol of the Right. "Have we become a generation of women?" the *Berlin Post* asked. "What is the matter with the *Hohenzollerns?*"[119] The Kaiser, however, believed that it had been his vigor in prodding German diplomats to be firm that had resulted in bringing the French to the bargaining table and in securing the award to Germany of a vast portion of equatorial Africa. What was less satisfactory to Wilhelm II was Britain's unflinching support of France during the crisis, especially since there was widespread feeling in Berlin that at Algeciras, Austria-Hungary, under the leadership of the foreign minister Count Alois Lexa von Aehrenthal, had not given Germany the unstinting support that an ally ought to render.[120] Wilhelm was convinced that it had been England, not France, who had been the leading architect of the opposition to Germany in Morocco and that it was therefore Great Britain who had to be put on notice. He was especially mistrustful of Grey, attributing to the foreign secretary an overbearing streak that was in fact entirely lacking. Grey genuinely wanted better relations with Germany within the context of protecting Britain's naval supremacy, an attitude that Wilhelm wrote off as a Caesarean arrogance that would make any political understanding with Britain impossible as long as Grey held office. "He dictates and we are supposed to accept," he declared of a conciliatory position Grey had expressed at the end of 1911 regarding Anglo-German colonial affairs. "There can be no question of that. We must be approached and taken *at our own worth.*"[121] Wilhelm believed that he stood up to this sort of browbeating by calling for substantial increases to be made in 1912 in the military and naval budgets.[122]

Bethmann admitted that the Moroccan affair had worked out in a less than satisfactory way, for he shared none of Wilhelm's illusions that it had been, if not a triumph, at least a respectable showing. The chancellor maintained, as did the Kaiser, that the British had lurked behind France during the crisis in Africa. But the Moroccan situation was over, for better or worse, and he could now attempt to pursue what he considered his foremost diplomatic aim, the improvement of Anglo-German relations. Although the difficulties over Morocco in both 1905 and 1911 had shown that German diplomacy could not detach Britain from its Entente Cordiale of 1904 with the French, there remained a possibility that Germany might someday strike its own agreement with the British, not nullifying but at least neutralizing the Entente Cordiale. The critical ingredient in any rapprochement between Berlin and London would be a resolution of naval armaments, an issue often raised after 1898 between the two powers but never brought even close to settlement. Bethmann was determined now to try again, but in doing so he would have to deal with the Kaiser, whose proprietary interest in the German navy, the one area in which it was almost impossible to influence him, inclined him to regard any British criticism of his battle fleet as a personal affront. Any demand for naval reductions was, he declared, a "heavy insult" for Germany and for himself. He would prefer war, Wilhelm told Hardinge in the course of King Edward VII's visit to Germany in 1908.[123] The Kaiser wanted to have a diplomatic treaty that affected the European continent and that would serve as a mortgage for friendly Anglo-German relations in the future. Once *that* was in place, but only then, a naval agreement as well as a mutually advantageous dismemberment of Africa could be arranged. Meanwhile Germany would continue to build the ships provided for in legislation already passed by the Reichstag.[124]

In this view, the Kaiser had the full support of Admiral Tirpitz, who was eager to capitalize on the Anglophobia that emerged in Germany in the course of the Moroccan crisis of 1911. Tirpitz, midway in the work begun in 1898 of creating a German battle fleet that could inflict severe damage on the Royal Navy in the event of war, feared that Germany's chances of doing so were as yet "thoroughly inadequate." To gain the necessary time, which Tirpitz reckoned at nine or ten years, he proposed that Wilhelm II make an agreement with Britain acknowledging the 2:3 ratio of German to British ships, in return for which Germany would declare that it had no intention of using its fleet against Great Britain.[125] Wilhelm gave Tirpitz's proposal his "enthusiastic" support, declaring fulsomely that the British, eager to avoid the financial strain of building a vast number of battleships, would agree and that thus "a decisive turning point in the history of [the] Fatherland would be reached."[126] The 2:3 ratio, no matter what the financial cost, would make Britain more respectful of Germany. "At the present moment," Wilhelm noted in a letter to Tirpitz of 27 September 1911, "our friendship seems to mean nothing to [Britain], for we are not yet strong enough. It is impressed only by power and strength represented in unmistakable evidence."[127]

Bethmann, consumed with bringing the Moroccan crisis to a conclusion without resort to war and eager then to get on with the task of improving Anglo-German relations, feared that increases in the German navy might fatally jeopardize any chance of bringing Berlin and London closer together and indeed might even lead to war. A raft of new ships would also cost a vast amount of money, and like Bülow before him, the chancellor would have to petition a hostile Reichstag for the introduction of an inheritance tax. Naval armaments, rather than being expanded, should become the subject of negotiation. A continental power needed a great army, and Britain, for similar geographical considerations, was entitled to possess a superior navy. But Tirpitz, to the chancellor's exasperation, kept insisting on ever more ships, demands that, when granted, only increased British hostility. "The entire naval policy of Grand Admiral von Tirpitz," Bethmann once declared, was a business without end, one that was "hopeless," the very adjective Tirpitz used to describe what he saw as the chancellor's inability to sympathize with Germany's naval aspirations.[128]

Bethmann managed in October 1911, as the Algeciras Treaty was being readied for signature, to deter Wilhelm from the introduction of a supplementary naval law (*Novelle*) until the spring of 1912. Wilhelm would not countenance a delay beyond that point, however, for German public opinion, in a flush of rage against both Britain and Bethmann because of the unsatisfactory outcome of the Moroccan crisis, supported a fleet increase. The Kaiser was so insistent that Bethmann was convinced that if he resisted the Kaiser, he would be asked to resign.[129] And indeed in mid-October 1911, Wilhelm II informed Tirpitz that he was prepared to dismiss Bethmann if the chancellor did not agree to the immediate introduction of a supplemental naval law. In December he declared, "I must be my own Bismarck." He followed this by again threatening to dismiss Bethmann, on this occasion in talks with the chief of the Naval Cabinet, Admiral Georg von Müller.[130] The chancellor, fearful that a *Novelle* might conceivably lead Britain to launch a preventive war against Germany, was determined to engage the British in negotiations leading not only to a settlement of naval armaments but to a diplomatic agreement as well.[131] Conveniently enough, at the beginning of 1912 a welcome opportunity presented itself that would enable Bethmann to enter into negotiations with the British.

Eight

OLD ALLIES AND FUTURE OPPONENTS

WILHELM II'S closest advisers were almost exclusively aristocrats, usually professional army officers, but from time to time exceptions emerged. One of the most prominent of these outsiders was Albert Ballin, the managing director of the Hamburg-American Line, the largest steamship company in the world. The friendship was remarkable, for Ballin was not only bourgeois but also a Jew. He was a person of inordinate charm, deferential but forthright, and his worldwide maritime operations provided him with uniquely rich sources of information. The Kaiser delighted in Ballin's company, his opulent passenger liners, and his fund of news from many quarters. Ballin was an ardent champion of good Anglo-German relations, a desire that he shared with his friend in London, Sir Edward Cassel, an immensely wealthy Jewish financier who was a companion of King Edward VII's and who was also acquainted with the Kaiser.[1] In 1909, Ballin had, with Wilhelm's authorization, sounded out Cassel about the possibility of an Anglo-German negotiation treating armaments, but the Foreign Office in Berlin had objected to the use of such unofficial intermediaries, and the matter had come to nothing.[2] In early 1912, Ballin and Cassel together conceived the idea of having a member of the British cabinet go to Berlin to discuss the naval situation with the Kaiser, Admiral Alfred von Tirpitz, and other members of Chancellor Theobald von Bethmann Hollweg's government. Wilhelm II was receptive when Ballin approached him, and by the beginning of 1912 an active exchange was in progress between Berlin and London for the purpose of establishing the agenda for such a meeting.

On 29 January 1912 Cassel arrived in Berlin to prepare the way for negotiations. The basic point on which the British would insist was Germany's recognition that the Royal Navy must remain superior. This meant that Tirpitz's existing naval program would have to be "retarded and reduced." In return, Britain was prepared to endorse an expansion of Germany's African empire and to conclude a diplomatic agreement that would prevent either signatory from joining a combination directed aggressively against the other.[3] Bethmann agreed, and Wilhelm II's response was to welcome this overture ecstatically, with Cassel describing him as "enchanted, almost childishly so," at the British overtures.[4] As for a diplomatic convention, the Kaiser desired either an alliance with London or, failing that, at the least a pledge of neutrality in the event of war with a third power. To effect this aim, Wilhelm declared that he would personally negotiate with the foreign secretary, Sir Edward Grey.[5]

The British government, reluctant to invest the negotiations with an official air or indeed to make any public announcement that talks were in progress, wanted to send neither Grey nor Winston Churchill, the first civil lord of the admiralty, who would have been the logical participants in negotiations over either diplomatic arrangements or naval armaments. Instead, Prime Minister Herbert H. Asquith selected Viscount Haldane, the secretary of state for war, to be his representative. Ballin made it clear to the Kaiser that Haldane's mission was purely for purposes of orientation. If there seemed to be a genuine spirit of compromise in Berlin, Haldane could be replaced at a later time by Grey and Churchill, who could then proceed to draw up the agreement.[6] The British planned that Haldane, an intellectual of considerable ballast, would go incognito to Berlin under the pretext of being engaged in investigating German scientific education; in fact the reason for his choice was that he was a Germanophile with a fluent command of the language. Haldane was virtually ignorant of the technicalities of naval affairs, but he believed that the size and strength of Germany's fleet was the foremost consideration for Britain's diplomatic strategy. Consequently, in his opinion, there could be no question of abandoning the ententes with France and Russia until and unless the Kaiser introduced limitations of some sort in the German navy.[7]

Haldane arrived in Berlin on 7 February 1912 and at once plunged into negotiations on a terrain that Sir Edward Grey admitted was "very vague."[8] On the next day, he saw Bethmann and argued for the inclusion of language in a political agreement that would require "mutual undertakings" against all aggressive attacks. Bethmann, however, countered by insisting on a quite different formula, namely a pledge of neutrality in the event of war, whether aggressive or not.[9] The two powers seemed equally far apart when the negotiations turned to ships. Haldane declared that Germany's expanded naval armaments were incompatible with a political agreement and would inevitably dictate corresponding increases in the Royal Navy. Even so, he left open the possibility that if Germany would extend the number of years in which the battleships were to be built, as provided for in legislation (the *Novelle*) soon to be laid before the Reichstag, some accommodation might be found. The chancellor's reply held firmly to the view that it would be necessary for Germany to make the fleet increases that the Reichstag had already authorized and insisted that an arid debate on naval numerology could not be allowed to jeopardize the peace of Europe.[10]

The Kaiser's attitude toward England on the eve of Haldane's visit was, as usual, ambivalent. On the one hand, he was quite excited at the prospect of forging a diplomatic arrangement with Britain, one that might create, as he described it, a United States of Europe and a German empire in central Africa.[11] At the same time Wilhelm was still resentful of what he considered British troublemaking in Morocco and was still annoyed at the way the British trumpeted their naval superiority. On the day that Haldane arrived in Berlin, the Kaiser had wired Ambassador Paul von Wolff-Metternich zur Gracht that he would mobilize the German navy if the British tried to strengthen their North Sea fleet by bringing in ships from the Mediterranean, but he knew in fact that such braggadocio was, for the moment, futile.[12] "Until my fleet is developed I [must] put up with every slap in the face from the English," Wilhelm admitted. "But then I can say: you want trouble, you can have it."[13] He was convinced, although not for good reason, that the British would try to involve Germany in difficulties with other colonial powers in Africa, difficulties that would then make Britain free to preside, together with Japan and the United States, over the dismemberment of the Chinese Empire. The British had to be made to understand that Germany expected to participate in whatever partitions were made in Asia (or anywhere else) and that the path to good Anglo-German relations lay not in British gifts of other people's property in Africa but in a political understanding that acknowledged a parity between the two great Teutonic peoples. Both empires would have to maintain fleets that were appropriate to their responsibilities around the world.[14]

In spite of Wilhelm's reservations about Britain's objectives, he was delighted to see Haldane, whom he had met on earlier occasions and whom he liked. Neither Tirpitz nor Bethmann nor State Secretary Alfred von Kiderlen-Wächter wanted the Kaiser to be involved in the negotiations, for he was prone to introduce unexpected arguments in windy language, and besides he had little appreciation for the connection between the political and the naval aspects of the discussions.[15] They saw to it that Wilhelm played only a nominal role in the so-called Haldane Mission, which concluded with an informal agreement that a political formula would first be concluded, whereupon Wilhelm II, basking in public approbation, would then declare that Germany's naval construction schedule, the *Tempo*, was to be drawn out over more years than originally provided for in the *Novelle*, even though the number of ships would remain the same.[16]

Haldane returned to London on 9 February, carrying with him a bronze bust of the Kaiser and, at Wilhelm's insistence, a copy of the forthcoming *Novelle*, which was to be shown to British naval officials. The Kaiser now awaited London's reaction. He was concerned that the Anglophobic Tirpitz might spoil any future talks by being secretive and intransigent, but if the negotiations succeeded, he would generously see to it that the admiral was acknowledged as "the greatest German since Bismarck."[17] If the admiral was dangerous because he might prove to be too unyielding toward the British, Wilhelm worried that his diplomats might take the opposite tack, falling over themselves to offer London unsuitable compromises. Bethmann was particularly to be watched, for his spinelessness, Wilhelm fumed, had become so pathological that he was a fit candidate for admission to a sanatorium.[18] The Kaiser therefore informed Kiderlen that he himself would conduct any future negotiations with the British regarding naval matters lest they be spoiled by "too much diplomacy."[19]

Wilhelm need not have worried, for at the end of February the British government informed Berlin that a political agreement could not be entered into because of the additions to the German navy projected in the *Novelle*. Churchill and his colleagues found the naval increases projected in the bill, which Haldane had brought for their examination, to be alarming, with respect both to ships and to manpower. This was to Wilhelm II "absolutely unacceptable" — yet another instance of Britain's "grandiose impudence." "What all this comes to," the Kaiser complained, "is that England wants . . . to force us to *buy* from her a quite doubtful declaration of neutrality, the honesty of which is very contestable (*anfechtbar*), in return for our giving up our defensive chances against England! I must as Kaiser in the name of the German empire and as commander-in-chief in the name of my armed forces absolutely *reject* such a view as incompatible *with our* honor."[20] To the Kaiser the whole business was insulting, a revelation not only of "characteristic English bluff" but also of the stupidity of his own diplomats, who, as he put it, were "full of shit."[21] That "shylock," Grey, and the government in London had tricked Germany into taking Haldane's proposals seriously, only then to repudiate them. The result was that Germany had been made a laughingstock and Wilhelm personally insulted. He had no intention of abandoning the *Novelle*, for that would lead to Tirpitz's resignation. Besides, being resolute was the only behavior that the British understood, and they would learn that in trifling with the Kaiser, they would encounter an implacable enemy.[22] Much influenced by Tirpitz, by Captain Wilhelm Widenmann in London, and by the Kaiserin (an avid admirer of both naval figures), he ordered that the *Novelle* as well as a bill for increases in the army be laid before the Reichstag without delay. With that the Haldane Mission collapsed.

In commanding that the *Novelle*, together with a bill increasing the Prussian army, be brought in at once, Wilhelm had not consulted the chancellor. On discovering what the Kaiser had done, Bethmann submitted his resignation, for this was a violation of procedure and also a step that the chancellor feared would destroy any hope of further negotiations with England. Wilhelm, whose nervous state was at the time causing concern, flew into a rage, denouncing Bethmann for having no understanding of naval affairs and for being entirely too cowardly toward the British.[23] The Kaiser eventually calmed down, and Bethmann agreed that the *Novelle* should be presented to the Reichstag. This placated Wilhelm as far as the chancellor was concerned, but he remained thoroughly enraged at the British for having renounced the agreement that he believed he and Haldane had reached in good faith. He worked himself up to the point that by May he was fulminating about the possibility of war with England. "I don't want war," he told King George of the Hellenes in May, "but apparently England does and if they do we are quite ready."[24] This was the sort of verbal pyrotechnics that disillusioned Bethmann and led him to declare, just after Wilhelm had made this denunciation of England, that Germany could have forged an alliance with England had it not been for the perpetual intervention in Anglo-German affairs by the Kaiser, either in love or in hate.[25]

Great Britain was always the principal calculation in Wilhelm II's mind, sometimes providing him with pride or pleasure but more often, as in the question of naval armaments, reducing him to outrage. What made matters yet more aggravating to the Kaiser was the fact that the British were omnipresent. Not only was the Royal Navy the commanding naval force virtually around the world, but British diplomats, intriguers, and spies were at work to undermine German interests all over Europe, Asia, and Africa. A particular area of concern to Wilhelm was the Balkans, the tinderbox of fervent nationalism and of rival diplomatic ambitions by the great powers, an area that as early as 1903 the Kaiser had declared would someday be the scene of a great war.[26] In this primitive corner of continental Europe, like everywhere else, Wilhelm was certain that London was exercising a pernicious influence. On the last day of 1908 he warned the Austrian archduke Franz Ferdinand, heir to the Habsburg throne, that the British were "conducting a premeditated campaign against both . . . nations everywhere in the world. In Paris, Madrid, Rome, and especially in Petersburg and Constantinople." He continued, "Their aim is a great continental war of all against all so that they may then fish in troubled waters and weaken everyone else."[27]

The only protection that Wilhelm had against these British machinations, other than his fine army and his burgeoning navy, was the Habsburg Empire, tied to Germany in a defensive alliance designed by Otto von Bismarck in 1879. Alone among the great powers, Austria-Hungary had maintained an untroubled relationship with the Kaiser for years. He considered himself to be a loyal ally and was so regarded in Vienna, where the critical importance of Germany in shoring up the tenuous position of the Habsburgs in the Balkans was clearly recognized. The old emperor, Franz Joseph, who at the end of 1910 had celebrated his eightieth birthday and his sixty-second anniversary as ruler, had not enough energy to preside effectively over the complexities that beset his empire. His Hungarian partners were eager to have a greater role in the Dual Monarchy, the economy was lagging, and the finances of the state were in perpetual arrears. The most profound difficulty faced by the Habsburgs, however, was the Slavic agitation inside and beyond the empire, calling for the separation of all Slavs from their German and Hungarian rulers. Within the monarchy, the Czechs in the North and the Bosnians and the Herzegovinians along the Adriatic were especially vociferous in their demands for independence, or at least for autonomy within the empire. Beyond Franz Joseph's frontiers, these unruly subjects had powerful supporters in the neighboring Slav kingdom of Serbia, which in turn was supported by Russia, the greatest of all the Slav powers. At every turn the Habsburg Empire was threatened with crisis or perhaps even with dissolution, an eventuality that would leave Germany bereft of allies. For that reason, Wilhelm II was determined that Austria-Hungary must be preserved and that its enemies, at home or abroad, must be dealt with firmly.[28] In this he had Bernhard von Bülow's support until the chancellor's fall in 1909, for in the words of a friend, Bülow believed that Germany's attachment to the Habsburgs was "an article of political religion." This was hardly less true for the chancellor's successor, Bethmann, and his state secretary at the Foreign Office, Kiderlen.[29]

The association of Vienna and Berlin was facilitated by the fact that the two foreign ministers in Vienna from 1906 to 1915, Baron (and later Count) Alois Lexa von Aehrenthal and Count Leopold von Berchtold, were men who were equally devoted to the Hohenzollern-Habsburg alliance and who got on well with Wilhelm II and his chancellors. Aehrenthal, in office from 1906 until his death early in 1912, valued the alliance with Germany, but he had no intention of being led by Berlin and was relentless in asserting Habsburg interests in the Balkans in the face of Russian opposition. This had embroiled Austria-Hungary in a bitter quarrel with St. Petersburg and Belgrade in 1908, when Aehrenthal had arranged with Russia that the former Ottoman provinces of Bosnia and Herzegovina, occupied by the Habsburgs since 1878, would be formally annexed in return for Austrian support for Russia's gaining the right to send its warships through the straits at Constantinople. Although the powers ultimately refused to accede to Russia's desire in the Bosporus, Austria nevertheless insisted on retaining Bosnia-Herzegovina, an act that enraged not only Russia but also Serbia, which believed that the two Slavic provinces were properly Serbian.

The Kaiser, who liked Aehrenthal very much and who approved of this limitation of Slavic power in the Mediterranean, strongly supported the Austrian position, and when the crisis passed, he assured Aehrenthal that he had been pleased to serve as the minister's "good second" (*gutes Sekundant*).[30] Indeed, Wilhelm informed the Austrians that they would have done well to have gone ahead and invaded Serbia in the wake of the Bosnian crisis.[31] Russia's ally France was to be made aware that if, in the event that the Bosnian imbroglio of 1908 led to war, France did anything other than observe a strict neutrality, Wilhelm would mobilize his entire army.[32] These fulminations about Germany's going to war to protect Austria's position vis-à-vis Slavdom were probably only rhetorical, but the Kaiser's conspicuous attachment to Aehrenthal and the Austrians made some German diplomats and Reichstag deputies anxious that it was more and more Vienna, specifically the wily Aehrenthal, and not Berlin, that was the leading partner in their diplomatic combination.[33] That fear did not vanish when, in February 1912, Aehrenthal died and was succeeded by Count Berchtold, a cool, methodical grand seigneur who shared his predecessor's view that the aim of Habsburg policy was to guard against Serbia and maintain the traditional close connection with Germany.[34]

The annexation of Bosnia-Herzegovina by the Habsburgs in 1908, which led to a lasting enmity between the Habsburg Empire on the one hand and Russia and Serbia on the other, was another step in the ongoing dismemberment of European territory once held by the Ottoman sultan in Istanbul. Any further erosion of Ottoman authority was likely to result in the complete dissolution of the empire, leaving the great powers and the smaller Balkan states to compete for possession of its fragments in both Europe and Asia. For Russia the coveted prize would be gaining the warm-water port of Istanbul, and for the Serbs it would be liberating Franz Joseph's millions of Slav subjects and claiming them for Belgrade. To Wilhelm, the Slavs were not only the potential destroyer of the Habsburg Empire but also, as a degenerate unworthy race, a danger to all of western Europe. There was a "Slavic danger" no less than a "Yellow Peril," both ready to destroy western Europe. "I hate the Slavs," he informed the Austro-Hungarian military attaché. "I know it's a sin but I cannot help myself. I hate the Slavs."[35] There could be no doubt, the Kaiser warned an Austrian official at the end of 1909, that within five or six years the Slavs would rise up in war against the German and Habsburg Empires. Russia would be heavily involved in this assault, but the kingdom of Serbia, the "pig monarchy" as the Kaiser referred to it, was the tsar's satellite, constantly at work stirring up the Slavs against their Habsburg rulers.[36] Austria should therefore adopt a firm attitude toward the Serbs but at the same time try to attract them through economic concessions and financial grants and by bringing young Serbs to Vienna to be educated. Furthermore, Belgrade must be required to sign a military alliance that would place the Serbian army at Austria's disposal. If the Serbs declined, as they would surely have done, Wilhelm declared that Habsburg Emperor Franz Joseph must bombard and occupy Belgrade.[37]

In the five years leading up to the outbreak of the Great War in 1914, Wilhelm regularly let Vienna know that in the event of hostilities between Austria and the Slav powers, Germany stood ready to help. There was nothing ambiguous in the Kaiser's assurances. Austria, he informed the Austro-Hungarian envoy Count Ladislaus von Szögyényi-Marich in August 1913, could in the event of war "depend in the most positive way on Germany's sword." This promise reiterated similar assurances Wilhelm had given the envoy ever since 1909, but even before the Kaiser had provided this welcome pledge, Szögyényi was convinced that Wilhelm II would not shrink from upholding the Habsburg monarchy, even in the event of a world war.[38] Wilhelm did in fact believe that the Balkan problem would eventually have to be settled by "blood and iron," and therefore it would be better, since both Russia and France were unprepared to fight, if Austria dealt once and for all with Serbia.[39] Although Wilhelm expected to stay out of an Austro-Serbian conflict, the dangerous situation required that Germany and the Habsburg Empire draw more closely together, especially since England was "full of poison and hate and jealousy at the untroubled development of our nations and their alliance with one another."[40] A pact between Austria-Hungary and Germany represented a military combination that, in the Kaiser's opinion, was the best in the world, a "granite-like foundation" that would ensure "obedience and respect" from all of Europe.[41] The Kaiser's calculation of Austria's military competence, an assessment that in 1914 proved to be very overestimated, rested largely on his high opinion of Field Marshal Count Franz Conrad von Hötzendorf, Franz Joseph's chief of staff from 1906 to 1917. Wilhelm found the marshal to be a "wonderful character," one whom he had come to *"value highly."*[42] Hötzendorf and Franz Joseph's government would nevertheless bear close watching, for the Kaiser found that there was too much excitability in Vienna. He boasted in 1912 that he had been a moderating influence: "If I had not held the Austrians back, the fellows (*Kerls*) would have got us involved in a war."[43]

Wilhelm preferred for the Ottoman sultan to be strengthened and maintained as long as possible, thus containing Russia and keeping the Balkan powers in line.[44] Given the Turks' enmity for Russia, the Sublime Porte was a prospective ally in the event that Germany and Austria ever went to war with Russia.[45] The Kaiser believed that the British were, as usual, at the heart of the problem. They were suborning the Young Turk movement that was plotting to overthrow the sultan.[46] Moreover, in his opinion, the ringleader among the Balkan Slavs hard at work to decimate the Ottoman Empire was Tsar Ferdinand of Bulgaria, a sovereign of whom the Kaiser was profoundly suspicious and whom he found personally distasteful. Wilhelm admitted that Ferdinand's shrewdness had raised Bulgaria to a leading position among the Balkan states, and he predicted that the remote kingdom, which yearned to plant its flag at Istanbul, would one day be a power to be reckoned with.[47] The duplicitous Ferdinand seemed, unfortunately, to be a tool of King Edward VII, and the Kaiser referred to them respectively as the "arch-plotter" and the "arch-intriguer" of Europe.[48] He therefore urged his friend Archduke Franz Ferdinand to keep a watchful eye on Sofia and to do everything he could to entice the Bulgarian ruler to desert his Slav brothers and instead place himself under Austria's benevolent protection. The Kaiser believed that he had both Turkey and Greece on his side, and if the Austro-German Dual Alliance could enlist Bulgaria and Rumania, the two most formidable military powers in the Balkans, a broad "street" would thereby be cut through the Balkans, separating Russia and its remaining Slav allies from the rest of Europe.[49]

Wilhelm's hopes were utopian, for Ferdinand of Bulgaria despised him and was drifting ever more in the direction of Russia. In Rumania, King Carol, although of Hohenzollern ancestry, was constantly being importuned by Russia to place Rumania's future not with the Dual Alliance but rather with St. Petersburg. In that manner, the three most important Balkan states — Bulgaria, Serbia, and Rumania — were either, like Serbia, in Russia's camp or, at the least, in danger of passing into its orbit. It was Russia, even more than Austria-Hungary and Turkey, who dominated the Balkans, and therefore all crises that erupted along the Danube eventually called into question the role that St. Petersburg would play in their solution. The Kaiser might claim that Great Britain meddled gratuitously in the area, but he knew that the ultimate challenge he faced in the Balkans was Tsar Nicholas II and his millions of Slav subjects. Wilhelm's notion of how Russia was to be dealt with changed from month to month, alternating quickly between hopes for a Russo-German alliance directed against England and visions of a great Anglo-German coalition that would vanquish the tsar.[50] In the end, however, he concluded that the Russians, as Slavs abetted by their Serbian satellites, had to be regarded as a permanent menace to both Germany and the Habsburg Empire.

Wilhelm believed that Russia's hostility was due not to Nicholas II, whom he considered to be his friend, but instead to Alexander Izvolski, the tsar's foreign minister from 1906 to 1910. Izvolski was certainly anti-German, and it was through his diplomacy that Russia in 1907 had secured with Britain a diplomatic convention settling many of their colonial rivalries.[51] Nicholas II placed great confidence in his minister, and by the time Izvolski came to power, Wilhelm's influence on the tsar had become quite negligible, with Nicholas much preferring his British relatives to the antic German sovereign. Count Sergei Witte, the leading minister in St. Petersburg, declared in 1906 that the Kaiser no longer had any influence over Nicholas, an unfortunate fact that Wilhelm himself was compelled to acknowledge.[52] The Kaiser was not unduly alarmed, however, for he was certain that Russia, though hostile to Germany, posed no immediate danger since its armies, although already immense and increasing in size, were incapable of action following the tsar's disastrous defeat in the Russo-Japanese War of 1904–5.[53]

By 1912, both Britain and Russia, the two powers that Wilhelm II had pursued most ardently, were not only joined to one another but distinctly suspicious of Germany. The Kaiser, who did not easily abandon his certainty that he could exercise a salutary effect in diplomacy, was nevertheless optimistic that Britain would come to its senses and realize that Russia, being Slavic and therefore barbarian, was not fit to be an ally. With equally dim vision, he believed that Nicholas II, whose dislike of the Kaiser was indelible to everyone but Wilhelm himself, might still be delivered into the German camp.[54] All of the Kaiser's activity, and all of his aspirations, were in vain. After the collapse of the Haldane Mission negotiations in the middle of 1912, the British no longer seriously entertained the possibility of a rapprochement with Germany, and London thereafter concentrated its attention on preparing for the eventuality of war against the Kaiser. In Russia, Nicholas had no intention of being beguiled by Wilhelm and was prepared if necessary to draw the sword against Germany in order to preserve Russia's interests.[55]

The Kaiser's optimism, largely based on an inflated estimation of his own talent, was as broad as it was ill-founded. In Vienna, Foreign Minister Count Berchtold, who, like many others, perceived in the Kaiser a disquieting streak of fantasy, declared in 1909 that Wilhelm acted "as though he felt himself omnipotent to do as he pleased, as though all other leaders would willingly embrace his wishes and commands."[56] The Kaiser created the same sort of uneasiness in many of his servants in Berlin, who saw much more clearly that Germany was not in fact all-powerful but instead was encircled with enemies, beholden to the dilapidated but belligerent Austro-Hungarian Empire and outnumbered in battleships and regiments. Even more alarming was the fact that the German Empire was ruled by a man who had no clear understanding of the volatile situation that prevailed in Europe and who would be manifestly incapable of leading the Fatherland to victory should one or more of the many diplomatic difficulties that beset Germany result in war.

There were also by 1912 serious difficulties on the domestic front, problems that seemed equally incapable of solution. In the last years of his chancellorship, Bülow's attempts to introduce an inheritance tax and a liberalization of the Prussian constitution had alienated the Conservatives, and many deputies of all political sympathies found the administrative carelessness revealed in the *Daily Telegraph* crisis in 1908 very troubling. Bethmann, coming to office in 1909, inherited all of Bülow's problems. The question of finance had become inextricably bound up with the issue of constitutional reform. The imperial constitution of 1871 had granted to the German people (except the Kaiser's newly conquered subjects in Alsace-Lorraine) a remarkably generous franchise for elections to the lower house, or the Reichstag, enabling virtually all males of the age of twenty-five or over to vote. The result was a parliament that had a significant oppositional element, and Bismarck, the architect of the constitution, had anticipated that a safeguard might be necessary. He therefore had prescribed that although the Reichstag alone could initiate legislation, no bill could become law unless it was ratified by the upper house, the *Bundesrat*, in which population determined representation and in which

Prussia and its allies among the German states therefore enjoyed an unchallenged domination. Furthermore, even a law passed by both houses of the imperial legislature could not take effect unless the Kaiser, who was simultaneously king of Prussia, gave his assent. Prussia's control of the imperial legislative process, as well as of the crown, was unpalatable to non-Prussians and liberals, who made increasingly strident demands for constitutional reform both in the kingdom and in the empire.

Wilhelm II was entirely uninterested in such appeals, for in his opinion the existing structure was if anything too liberal rather than excessively conservative. He deplored the generous Reichstag franchise that had resulted in the election of so many Socialists and other enemies of the state, and he was exceedingly reluctant to agree to any changes in the constitution except those that were essentially superficial.[57] The Kaiser frequently, and unconvincingly, declared that he was a constitutional sovereign, but he in fact gloried in appearing to be Caesar. When Lady Gwendolen Cecil, the daughter of his old nemesis Lord Salisbury, tried to convince him of the virtues of the British constitution, Wilhelm exclaimed, "Thank God, I am a tyrant!"[58] The Kaiser admired Edward Dicey, an English journalist and author who believed that a monarchy was preferable to a parliamentary regime. He regretted being unable to find similar opinions in the German press, but making the best of the situation, he had an article by Dicey sent to all his ministers. Part of the Kaiser's marginal comment on Dicey's effusion noted, "In a word, old Homer was right in holding that only one is the leader, only one is the king."[59]

Wilhelm II was considerably closer to being an autocrat in Prussia than in the empire, and for that reason he had no problem with the Prussian lower house (*Landtag*) and the appointive and hereditary upper chamber (*Herrenhaus*), both of which were by and large in the hands of noble landowners. It was the Reichstag that bedeviled the Kaiser, and he publicly reviled it as a disgrace to the Fatherland. Wilhelm declared that this "band of apes" (*Affenband*), convened in their "chatter chamber" (*Schwatzbude*), ought to have their skulls strung up in the manner of certain African tribes or given as a present to the constitution-besotted British.[60] He had a long memory of voting records, and he was known to bear grudges dating to when his grandfather had been on the throne.[61] The behavior of the members was entirely too insolent (*frech*) and therefore created the impression, as false as it was dangerous, that the Reichstag had the power to force his hand. What he would prefer was a dutiful, powerless body such as the imperial duma convened in 1906 by Tsar Nicholas II.[62] In Wilhelm's opinion the only thing worse than a legislator was a Frenchman, and he airily informed King Umberto of Italy, "When we see a black coat at a social gathering and when in answer to our question 'Who is that?' we are told he is a deputy, we turn our back on him."[63] On the few occasions on which Wilhelm saw parliamentary deputies, he treated them with an unsettling combination of indifference and rudeness that did nothing to make him popular with the body.

The Conservatives, concentrated in Prussia and captained by landed aristocrats, were the faction that had traditionally supported Bismarck and Kaiser Wilhelm I, and indeed it was de rigueur for the East Elbian nobility to be members of the party.[64] The Conservatives were fierce monarchists, but to Wilhelm's dismay they had no intention of being vassals of a sovereign whose behavior and whose policies often seemed to them to be unsuitable.[65] There was considerable concern within the party at Wilhelm's role in the *Daily Telegraph* scandal, at his tempestuous political diatribes, which could serve only to drive the working class more firmly into the Socialist camp, and at his Caesarean notions of personal rule.[66] Even more alarming to the Conservatives was the Kaiser's steady endorsement of a number of measures, some going back to the beginning of his reign, that seemed to endanger the foundations of Prussian agrarianism. The trade treaties that had been designed by Chancellor Leo von Caprivi in the early 1890s and that gave Russian grain a preferential status in the German market had been anathema to the Conservatives, as had been the successful attempt by Caprivi's successor, Bülow, to construct a canal linking the North and Baltic Seas, an excavation that the Prussian aristocracy feared would undermine their position in the domestic grain market. Under Bethmann, who enjoyed little following among the Conservatives even though he was a substantial landowner, the Kaiser had erred in favoring the extension of costly social welfare benefits to farm workers.[67] Wilhelm II's reaction when the Conservatives refused to support the crown was predictably explosive. He believed that all aristocrats owed him a personal allegiance, and he therefore expected the Conservative Party unquestioningly to support the crown at every turn. Even in matters of foreign policy, which all parliamentary factions were reluctant to debate, the Conservatives sometimes dared to criticize Wilhelm.[68] This he regarded not only as political treachery but also as social betrayal.[69] The Kaiser gradually conceived an enormous dislike for the party, declaring that some Conservatives were even more dangerous than Socialists.[70] His enmity eventually became so great that his friend Philipp Eulenburg informed Bülow that Wilhelm was so full of "hate and bitterness" that "*nothing*" could overcome it.[71]

If to Wilhelm II the entire apelike Reichstag was a menagerie, the deputies of the Catholic Center Party were an especially despised "pack of dogs" (*Hundebande*).[72] The Kaiser, to the distress of his ministers, never hesitated to conceal his hatred of the Catholic Center and declared that because of the party's inordinate power, it would have to be crushed.[73] It was not so much that they were Catholic, for the Kaiser admired the Roman church's sense of pomp, the mysticism of saints and believers, and papal authoritarianism.[74] The problem for Wilhelm lay in the threat to his own authority, a threat that he saw manifested in various Catholic figures. The Italian pope exercised entirely too much sway over his German subjects, and if these wayward ultramontanes vassals of Rome did not repent, they would have to be hung.[75] Although some of the princes of the German church enjoyed Wilhelm's goodwill, he found the lower clergy to be too democratic, and the Jesuits, whom he referred to as "villains" or "scum" (*Teufelsbraten, Höllensöhne*), were conniving — with the consistent support of the Catholic Center — to diminish the power of the Hohenzollern throne.[76]

For the other parties, Wilhelm had only disdain because there were no gentlemen in their ranks.[77] Of all deputies, the Social Democrats were the least palatable. Wilhelm could accept Catholics who were neither ultramontanes nor figures prominently identified with the Catholic Center Party, and an occasional National Liberal or Progressive deputy who voted for naval increases might win his favor, but *all* Socialists were anathema to him and to the Prussian nobility. The Kaiser would not receive Socialist deputies, who were increasingly open in expressing their contempt for him. They had no recourse other than to vacate the chamber before the obligatory *Hoch* was raised to the monarch at the conclusion of every session.[78] In Wilhelm's opinion the Jews and their Jesuit allies were behind the Socialist movement, wanting to curry favor with what they believed to be the wave of the future.[79] The triumph of the Social Democratic Party at the polls, success that the party leader, August Bebel, said advanced by 100,000 votes every time the Kaiser made a speech, was something Wilhelm could not ignore. He might declare that it did not matter how many "red apes" there were in the Reichstag "cage" (*Käfig*), but in fact the increasing popularity of socialism alarmed him greatly. One must handle Socialists the way one dealt with the British, he thought. Only firmness was effective, and Socialists, like the despised ultramontanes, ought to be hung or, at the least, banished to the Caroline Islands in the mid-Pacific.[80] It was "dumb," he declared in 1904, to believe that "these unpatriotic dogs" could be "won over by pretty phrases and concessions.

All discipline and order would then go to the devil and the nation would lose millions forever."[81]

A particular source of great irritation for the Kaiser was the party-sponsored newspapers. Although Wilhelm frequently declared that he never read the press — "I am indifferent to what these blockheads (*Schafs-köpfe*) think of me" — he was in fact an avid follower not so much of the news as of his own appearance in the columns.[82] He was, however, highly selective in what he read. What was the point, he asked his friend Princess Radziwill, in reading items that only irritated him because they were contrary to his own views?[83] Wilhelm liked a few journalists, but he was generally very hostile not only to the German press but to that of the rest of Europe, in particular the London papers, and he was convinced that his uncle, King Edward VII, was behind these attacks.[84] Journalists who had the temerity to attack the crown thereafter found that the Foreign Office refused to give them any information, and the Kaiser recommended that such "scoundrels" (*Schufte*) be thrown down the stairs of the Wilhelm-strasse 76.[85] Throughout Wilhelm's reign, no other organs of the press enraged him quite so much as those owned by Jews. Even before becoming Kaiser, he had declared that he would make it legally impossible for Hebrews to be active in the press. Jews owned some of the most important and respectable dailies in the capital and other major cities, and Wilhelm seems to have been convinced that they also dictated the policy of the official newspaper of the Social Democratic Party, *Vorwärts*.[86]

The five-year term of the Reichstag elected in 1907 expired at the beginning of 1912, and Wilhelm II was determined that the new chamber would do his bidding, no matter what its composition might be. The Socialists were equally intransigent, and one of the party leaders, Gustav Noske, had declared at a party meeting in 1910, "Against the avowals of the Kaiser in favor of divine right and absolutism in the forthcoming election we on the other hand [will] call for a republic."[87] The result at the polls was an electrifying victory for the Social Democrats, whose Reichstag strength of 110 seats (up from 43 in the 1907 elections) made it, by a wide margin over the 91 Catholic Center deputies, the largest faction in the house. The socialist gains came at the expense of the conservative parties and were the more alarming to the Kaiser because of the close cooperation between the Socialists and the 42 newly elected deputies of the Progressive Party. Furthermore, most of the leaders of all but the Conservative faction were now non-Prussians, men whose allegiance would be to the empire rather than to the Hohenzollerns.

Bethmann acknowledged that he had little support among the newly elected deputies, men whom he described as being guided only by their own selfish interests.[88] Poised between crown and Parliament, the chancellor had somehow to make his way between rival points of view over armaments, constitutional reform, and fiscal policy. In this dilemma, Bethmann received little help from the Kaiser and his court. From the moment of Bethmann's appointment, Wilhelm II had been impatient about the chancellor's tendency toward procrastination and obstinacy. Bethmann had his own complaints, especially (and justifiably) that Wilhelm did not consult him on important decisions, and he told his confidants early in 1912 that after almost three years in office, he had no desire to keep on.[89] There was no one at court who was prepared to help Bethmann, and the Kaiserin and the crown prince both thought he was not resolute enough in standing up for Germany's interests, particularly vis-à-vis Britain.[90]

National defense was another area of difficulty for Bethmann. Admiral Tirpitz insisted on ever-larger expenditures for ships and naval personnel, while the chief of the General Staff, General Helmuth von Moltke, argued just as adamantly that the army should receive the lion's share of any future expenditures. Bethmann feared that increases in Germany's military strength, especially an augmentation in the German navy, would lead to apprehension abroad.[91] The Kaiser, unlike his chancellor, rejoiced in his vast navy and his large and well-disciplined army, and he had no qualms about increases for both arms of the service being presented simultaneously to the Reichstag. No sacrifices were to be made for Germany's security, and Wilhelm was prepared to insist that both the army and the navy should get virtually all of the ships, arms, and manpower they considered necessary, even if it meant an increase in taxes. There was pride at work, for Wilhelm believed his military machine on land was superior to any other in the world, and the Kaiser proclaimed that he alone was its commander.[92] If anything, Wilhelm II took an even more proprietary interest in the navy, but he did not know that his admirals, although eager for his support, sneered at his yachting expeditions here and there, at his insistence on daily battles at maneuvers, and especially at his grandiose ambition to make the annual regatta at Kiel equal in magnificence to the similar British event at Cowes.[93]

Wilhelm often vowed that Germany's military and naval machine must be kept inviolate from foreign interference. Anyone who tried to dictate armament policy to Berlin would regret having done so. "He who proposes such a step," the Kaiser imperiously informed his friend Albert Ballin of the Hamburg-American Line, "if he is a minister will be dismissed, and if he is a foreign potentate he'll have to reckon with an immediate declaration of war."[94] Wilhelm recognized that this independent attitude would make a rapprochement with Great Britain difficult, for the British insisted always on having their way. "What England doesn't want just doesn't happen," he declared with exasperation in 1910.[95] Nonetheless, at least down to late 1912, the Kaiser believed in the possibility of an accommodation with Britain, one that would guarantee European peace.[96] As he reminded Admiral Prince Louis Battenberg, a cousin and aide-de-camp to King George V in 1911, the French were useless. "We have beaten them once and we will beat them again. We know the road from Berlin to Paris. You know you can't mount your Dreadnoughts on wheels and come to your dear friends' assistance."[97] To the Kaiser, war across the Rhine seemed less likely than a conflict in the Balkans, to him an "eternal storm-center" (*Wetterwinkel*).[98] Although Germany was absolutely committed to the preservation of the Habsburg Empire, Wilhelm was careful to emphasize that he would not see Germany go to war over some *minor* cause in this remote and backward area.[99]

The likelihood of a collision of the powers along the Danube increased greatly when, in October 1912, Bulgaria, Serbia, and Greece, anticipating victory and the award of Ottoman territory, declared war on Turkey. Wilhelm followed the Balkan War, the first of two that would occur back to back, with frenzied interest, bombarding Bethmann and his diplomats with telegrams and covering documents with brief but apoplectic marginalia. Wilhelm was inalterably opposed to any German intervention in behalf of Turkey, which suffered defeat after defeat, for the price of military ineptitude would be the forfeiture of the sultan's European holdings. The smaller Balkan powers could hardly be blamed for wanting to dismantle a structure as rickety as the Ottoman Empire, and such a division would not create any broader consequences, since in the Kaiser's opinion France, Russia, and Great Britain were at the moment ill-prepared to fight.[100] If Austria and Serbia should go to war over the Balkans, Russia might enter, in which case the 1879 alliance with the Habsburgs would require Germany to come to Austria's aid. To Wilhelm the Balkans were not worth that risk, and Vienna must therefore be instructed not to provoke Serbia, for if it did so, Germany would be under no obligation to bail Austria out in the event that Russia became involved.[101]

In mid-November 1912 the Balkan situation took an ominous turn when the Austrians began to amass an army on the Russian frontier in response to reports that the tsar was moving troops into the area. Fearing that this could be the prelude to a Russian attack on the Habsburg Empire, an attack that would require German intervention, Wilhelm declared that he must at once plan an increase in the reserve strength of the imperial army. He assured State Secretary Kiderlen at the Foreign Office that he was prepared to come to Austria's aid "to the fullest extent and with whatever consequences." Kiderlen publicly agreed, as did also Bethmann, who said so in a speech before the Reichstag on 2 December 1912.[102] With peace hanging in the balance in what was, according to the Kaiser, the most critical moment that Germany had faced since the war of 1866 between Prussia and Austria, it was imperative for Berlin to know what position France and Britain would take in the event of a Balkan war.[103]

Ambassador Lichnowsky believed that the British would, if at all possible, stay out of a conflict involving the Balkans. This was also Wilhelm's view, and on 3 December he approved a naval plan that should war break out with France and Russia, the activity of the German fleet against the French was to be limited in such a way that Britain might elect to remain neutral.[104] On 3 December 1912 Haldane, who had recently become lord chancellor in Britain, responded to Bethmann's Reichstag speech the previous day by seeking out Lichnowsky and informing him that Britain would in all likelihood *not* remain idle if, on Austria's invasion of Serbia, a "general" European war erupted; he added that Britain would certainly intervene if Germany tried to destroy France. Three days later, King George V indicated to the Kaiser's brother, Prince Henry of Prussia, that Britain would "very certainly under certain circumstances" join with France and Russia in the event of a continental war, circumstances that the king did not prescribe. Wilhelm did not learn of George V's remarks until 12 December.[105]

It was only on 8 December that Wilhelm II read Lichnowsky's dispatch describing his talk with Haldane. Bethmann and Kiderlen, as well as other officials, did not attach particular importance to the lord chancellor's statement, for he had merely reiterated, as Berlin had always known, Britain's attachment to the concept of a continental balance of power, one that could not permit France to be destroyed. The Kaiser, however, was deeply resentful of what he characterized as an abrupt and unprovoked gesture of hostility to Germany. As far as Wilhelm was concerned, this settled once and for all the nature of Anglo-German relations. Haldane's pronouncement, the Kaiser told his brother Henry a few days later, was a "moral declaration of war" (*moralische Kriegserklärung*).[106] Haldane had thrown down the gauntlet, leaving him with no alternative other than preparing for war. This should be done by forming military alliances with Bulgaria, Rumania, Turkey, and Japan — "Any power that is available is good enough to help us" — and by readying Germany's army and navy for the approach of a European conflict.[107]

The Kaiser's talk about alliances was largely bluster, and none were in fact signed until after the World War of 1914 had begun, and then only with Bulgaria and Turkey. The readying of Germany's military forces, however, began at once, for on the day he received Lichnowsky's dispatch, Wilhelm summoned the chief of the General Staff, General Moltke, and his three leading admirals — Tirpitz, August von Heeringen, and Georg von Müller, respectively state secretary of the Imperial Naval Office, chief of the Naval Staff, and chief of the Naval Cabinet — to meet with him at the Berlin palace. Chancellor Bethmann was not invited, nor was Kiderlen present, doubtless because Wilhelm felt that Haldane's remarks had proved that both men, who had long entertained at least the possibility that Britain would remain neutral in the event of a continental war, had erred and would now be nervous about the situation.[108] At this "war council" or *Kriegsrat*, as Bethmann later christened it, Wilhelm declared that Germany must urge Austria-Hungary to take firm action against Serbia. Moltke took a more radical position, declaring that Germany should initiate a preventive war against France and Russia, "the sooner the better."[109] Tirpitz succeeded in dampening any thought of immediate war by informing those present that the German fleet would not be ready to fight until the summer of 1914, when the canal under construction connecting the Baltic and North Seas would be completed. The others present acknowledged this fact but argued that in the interim there was much to be done, including the promotion of closer cooperation with Vienna, budgetary increases for the army and navy, and the indoctrination of public opinion for the battle to come. Wilhelm believed that he stood at the crossroads. For over two decades he had worked for an accommodation, even an alliance, with England, but now the British had forced him instead to plan for what was clearly an inevitable war between Germany and Great Britain. It all came, he told the Archduke Franz Ferdinand in Vienna, as a "desirable clarification," and as far as the Kaiser was concerned, planning for the future was now made much easier.[110]

Bethmann, to his annoyance, did not learn of the *Kriegsrat* until 16 December, eight days after it had occurred. He refused to take Haldane's observations to Lichnowsky as a serious threat to peace, and he continued to believe that Britain might possibly stay out of a continental war and limit its role to diplomatic rather than military action provided that France and Russia could be made to appear to be the powers that had provoked the conflict. Germany must therefore present a pacific face to the world, and that in turn meant keeping any increases in the military budget a secret until their submission to the Reichstag and avoiding the naval increase that would serve only to bind Britain and France more tightly together.[111] Wilhelm took an entirely different view. The British, according to the Kaiser's mistaken logic, were responsible for the naval race; the German fleet had been brought into being only because London, in forming ententes with both France and Russia, had upset the European balance. This argument made no sense, since Tirpitz's navy, begun in 1898, long antedated both the Entente Cordiale of 1904 and Britain's pact with Russia signed three years later.[112] Wilhelm was convinced that only the awesome prospect of having to do battle against a powerful German fleet would deter the British from becoming involved in a continental war and would force London to the negotiation table.[113] That being the case, the Kaiser, quite contrary to Bethmann, believed that the government should immediately place before the Reichstag a bill providing for substantial increases in naval strength. This difference of opinion occasioned considerable debate between Wilhelm and the chancellor, who finally, early in January 1913, persuaded the Kaiser to proceed with an army increase but to delay additions to the fleet.[114]

On 17 December 1912, just a week after Wilhelm II had assembled the *Kriegsrat*, a conference opened in London to attempt to conclude the Balkan War, in which Bulgaria, Serbia, and Greece had overwhelmed Turkey. The Serbs were adamant that they be awarded access to the Adriatic, but to this both the Austrians and the Italians, long used to having this sea as their sphere, were resolutely opposed. Wilhelm was determined to prevent Serbia from touching the Adriatic, but he had no intention of letting the issue drag Germany into war. The "Albanian she-goats (*Ziegenweiden*)," he declared, were not worth a war.[115] As far as the Kaiser was concerned, Russia's encouragement of Serbia and its allies had provoked the conflict. The tsar, however, was too ill-prepared to let the Balkan problem escalate into a European conflict, and Austria and Germany were therefore in a position to insist that *their* interests be respected.[116] A treaty arranged by an ambassadorial conference at London in May 1913 decreed that only Bulgaria would profit substantially from the war, gaining various parcels of formerly Turkish territory.[117] Serbia would obtain no part of Albania, and Greece would fail to make significant gains. The disaffected Greeks and Serbs, joined by Turkey and Rumania, thereupon went to war with Bulgaria, which was swiftly defeated by the end of July. Wilhelm II's sympathy in this second Balkan War was entirely with the coalition ranged against Bulgaria because of his intense dislike for Tsar Ferdinand in Sofia.[118] In defiance of the London conference, the Serbs attempted to retake Albania but submitted to an Austrian ultimatum to withdraw or face war. With that the Balkan crisis temporarily came to an end, but Serbia was bitterly resentful against Austria for preventing it from gaining access to the sea.

In 1913, as the problems in the faraway Balkans were gradually being resolved, Wilhelm faced another difficulty, one that also had been developing over many decades. This problem concerned Alsace-Lorraine, the two wealthy French provinces that had been taken by Germany in the war of 1870–71 and had been ruled thereafter as conquered satrapies. In 1911, responding to protests of his dissatisfied subjects there, Wilhelm rather grudgingly constituted the provinces as a single federal state and granted a constitution under which he continued to be the ultimate authority. Wilhelm acted through his viceroy, Count (later Prince) Karl von Wedel, a conservative but enlightened man who recognized that unless the Alsatians and Lorrainers were granted more concessions, they would remain in perpetual opposition to Berlin. Whenever Wedel attempted to urge the German government to adopt a conciliatory policy, he found himself opposed not only by Wilhelm II but also by the Berlin military establishment, which believed that the provinces were a hotbed of sedition and therefore were to be tightly controlled. The Kaiser appears to have decided that he had made a mistake in granting Alsace-Lorraine limited rights of autonomy in 1911 and that he should annex both of them to Prussia, which would govern them with an iron hand.[119]

At the end of October 1913, an incident at Zabern, a major garrison town in Alsace, provoked a crisis.[120] Lieutenant Baron von Forstner, in addressing his detachment, referred to the indigenous population as *Wackes*, a term of various opprobrious meanings such as "rowdies" or "loafers." Several soldiers quickly leaked Forstner's remarks to the local press, resulting in considerable unrest among the population. The army commanders, certain that widespread insurrection was about to break out, defended Forstner, arguing that he was merely referring to disruptive elements rather than the general population. Forstner and other officers then proceeded to arrest a number of protesters who were accused of violent and discourteous behavior toward German soldiers. The civilian authorities immediately freed those arrested. Wilhelm refused Count Wedel's request that Forstner be transferred in order to placate public opinion, for he entirely approved of the army's handling of the unruly Alsatians, whom he improbably imagined were being bribed by the British.[121]

The Zabern incident more than ever convinced the Kaiser that it had been an error to extend any privileges to the two provinces. The Alsatians and Lorrainers, always encouraged by French bribes to the local newspapers, had taken advantage of Germany's conciliatory gestures to make trouble. It would be altogether better if in the future Germany treated both areas as the British dealt with their colonies, with a firm military administration by officials of the crown, who, as they went about their work of subduing the *Wackes* in Alsace-Lorraine, would be caparisoned in uniforms that Wilhelm himself had designed.[122] A few days after the incident between Lieutenant Forstner and the citizenry of Zabern, the Reichstag took up the matter in an unusually quarrelsome session, and what had been a local affair now became a national concern. After hearing both Chancellor Bethmann and the war minister, General Erich von Falkenhayn, defend Forstner's behavior, the Reichstag voted overwhelmingly in favor of a resolution expressing no confidence in the chancellor. Wilhelm II, who was in Württemberg visiting Prince Max Egon Fürstenberg, made it clear he sympathized with Bethmann because of the chancellor's resoluteness in defending the military.[123] The Kaiser had Bethmann, Wedel, and General Berthold von Deimling, the commanding general in Alsace, come to Fürstenberg's palace at Donaueschingen for a brief conference, at which it was agreed that Forstner should face a court-martial to determine whether his forcible arrests had been justified.[124] Forstner was subsequently found guilty and sentenced to six weeks' imprisonment, but on appeal the charges were dismissed. Other officers, charged with having exceeded their authority in rounding up protesters, were declared innocent, and the Kaiser then ostentatiously decorated one of them. Wilhelm would not allow Colonel Ernst von Reuter, Forstner's commanding officer, to resign for personal reasons lest his departure be construed to be related to the controversy.[125]

What was at stake in the Zabern controversy from the perspective of parliamentary liberals was not so much the appropriate punishment for the army officers involved as it was the broader question of whether the military, not only in Alsace-Lorraine but in the rest of Germany, should be permitted to go its way independent, or even contemptuous, of the civilian instances of government. Although the Social Democrats in the Reichstag condemned what they considered to be a miscarriage of justice, the other parties, in spite of their earlier cooperation with the Socialists in declaring their lack of confidence in Bethmann, did nothing more than agree to the appointment of what proved to be an ineffectual special committee to investigate the situation in Alsace-Lorraine. The Kaiser nevertheless remained at the center of the controversy, for he had resolutely championed the right of his soldiers to deal harshly with the Alsatians. As far as Wilhelm was concerned, Bethmann was too inclined to favor civilian officials, especially Count Wedel, who had resented the high-handedness with which the army had acted in the Zabern affair.

The problem, in the Kaiser's opinion, was that no amount of conciliation would make the Alsatians and the Lorrainers into good Germans, for they were treacherous and would in the event of war immediately embrace the French. It was therefore pointless to indulge in conciliatory gestures such as the grant of a constitution. Furthermore, Wedel, an exponent of such a policy, would have to be replaced as viceroy with an official who realized that only a stern policy would be effective.[126] Wedel was indeed dismissed in May 1914, his successor being Johann von Dallwitz, the strictly conservative Prussian minister of interior who was known to have strongly supported the army's role at Zabern and who was, Wilhelm would years later declare, the only real statesman, along with Tirpitz, to serve the crown.[127] Dallwitz's appointment was another advertisement of the Kaiser's enthusiastic support for the military and, to the Left, another sign of his continuing determination to impose a personal regime on Germany. The Zabern affair also intensified Wilhelm's always great suspicion that French revanchism meant that a war across the Rhine was sooner or later inevitable, an attitude that the longtime French envoy in Berlin, Jules Cambon, was not long in reporting back to Paris.[128]

Domestic issues rarely interested Wilhelm II, whose tastes ran to the more dramatic course of foreign policy, in which he liked to position himself at center stage. He rarely even saw ministers responsible for the management of internal administration, although he was most generous with his time when it came to military officials or crises, such as the incident in Zabern, that affected his army. The Kaiser could on occasion deliver monologues on internal affairs, but these rarely betrayed any real understanding of the issues involved, and they disenchanted his audience.[129] The contest between the army and Parliament in the Zabern affair not only involved the military but also was, it appeared to Wilhelm, an unwarranted invasion of the crown's prerogative. An attack on the army, of which he was the supreme commander, was a challenge to the house of Hohenzollern, and for that reason the Kaiser had placed himself squarely in support of his officers at Zabern. The affair in Alsace deepened his hostility to the Reichstag, and this in turn affected Wilhelm's attitude to another domestic problem that at the time of the Zabern affair was of great interest to the German public: the question of the franchise for the

Landtag, the lower house of the Prussian legislature, which was part of the constitution of 1850. The Prussian constitution overwhelmingly favored wealth and therefore ensured the return of very conservative members. This was a matter of concern not only in Prussia but throughout Germany because Prussia, by virtue of its massive population and its influence on a number of smaller neighboring states, effectively was the governing force in the empire's political affairs. Virtual veto powers in the upper house of the imperial legislature meant that Prussia could nullify any bill that the Reichstag, which had a broad franchise and which had over the years become increasingly liberal in sentiment, elected to pass. Unless Prussia was reformed, there was little hope that the empire itself might be liberalized, and for that reason an alteration of the Prussian franchise had become a volatile political issue throughout Germany.

Although the Kaiser had agreed in January 1908 to make minor, liberalizing alterations in the franchise, the Prussian deputies had defeated a bill providing such a change later in the year and then in 1910 rejected a similar measure. The question of a franchise liberalization arose again in 1913, but Wilhelm II ruled it out, arguing that the behavior of the Reichstag in the Zabern affair clearly indicated that it was never to become the model for the legislature of his kingdom of Prussia.[130] His revered grandfather, Kaiser Wilhelm I, had erred in permitting the imperial constitution to grant the Reichstag such a liberal franchise, and he did not intend to have the chamber challenge his authority or that of any other regnant German prince. When, in 1913, Parliament debated whether or not the twenty-odd German rulers should be taxed, the Kaiser declared, "The German parliamentarians and politicians have over the years become pigs."[131] Stung by the Zabern incident, Wilhelm refused to budge, and the Prussian franchise, which liberals throughout Germany continued to denounce, remained in force, a monument of reaction in a nation that was a paragon of economic progress. This bizarre juxtaposition of modernity and reactionism, presided over by the Kaiser, his courtiers, and his military stalwarts, was increasingly challenged, as in the Zabern affair, by liberals, intellectuals, artists, the press, and all manner of Germans. They watched with dismay as Germany, first under Bülow and now under Bethmann, continued to forfeit its once paramount diplomatic position in Europe. Meanwhile the Fatherland remained enchained in a political system that was manifestly anachronistic and was under the rule of a man who seemed to be responsible for the many problems that afflicted the German Empire.

Nine

SO MANY ENEMIES: GERMANY AT WAR

O N 1 5 JUNE 1913 Wilhelm II celebrated the silver anniversary of his ascension as king of Prussia and German emperor, an occasion of much royal panoply that brought throngs of his subjects to Berlin. Elsewhere in Germany, statues were erected and commemorative volumes were issued extolling the accomplishments of the previous quarter of a century. The Kaiser was elated at this evidence of popularity and felt that at long last the public opprobrium that had followed the *Daily Telegraph* scandal almost five years earlier had been avenged.[1] Those who praised Wilhelm often lauded him as a sovereign who had helped to maintain the peace of Europe for a quarter of a century, and this was the honor he most appreciated. As the Kaiser told his friend Admiral Georg von Müller, the chief of the Naval Cabinet, he had come to the throne in 1888 determined that his reign be one of consolidation rather than expansion.[2] Wilhelm regretted that his efforts at preserving tranquility had not always been appreciated and that perhaps some of his subjects were disappointed that there had been no magnificent victories over foreign foes. His successor could fight wars should they be required, but Wilhelm declared that he would draw the sword only if the Fatherland was endangered. For preventive war, which he had briefly considered against Russia at the beginning of his reign, he had absolutely no interest.[3]

The Kaiser's opposition to war proceeded in part from a conviction that Germany could not afford to become engaged in foreign adventures as long as socialism represented a danger at home. The triumphant Reichstag elections of 1912 had indicated that its power as a political and social force in Germany was dramatically increasing, and Wilhelm believed that he therefore should keep his soldiers at home, where someday they might be needed. Nothing provoked the Kaiser's oratorical inflation more than socialism, and even before 1912 he allegedly had exclaimed to Chancellor Bernhard von Bülow that what was required was "first to shoot the socialists, behead them and make them innocuous, if necessary by means of a bloodbath." He added: "Then [we can have] war abroad. But not before and not too rashly!"[4] Wilhelm's personality also contributed to his reluctance to engage in war. Although he liked to strike military poses and was given to making bellicose statements in speech and writing, most people who knew the Kaiser recognized that he was by nature peaceful. There was also suspicion that, for all his bravado, he lacked the coolness and nerve requisite in a military commander.[5]

The prospect of war was something that could not be ruled out, however, and at the *Kriegsrat* of 8 December 1912 the Kaiser had ordered that Germany was to be made ready for war. Wilhelm did not foresee being put to the test in the near future. Although it was true that there would likely continue to be both difficulties with Socialists at home and diplomatic crises, some of which — like those in Morocco — had momentarily threatened to plunge Europe into conflict, the situation in Europe did not seem to Wilhelm to be especially threatening. The most likely troublespot was the Balkans, and the Kaiser, like Otto von Bismarck before him, believed that should war come, it would likely be from this corner of Europe. Germany's only ally, the Habsburg Empire, was faced by the intransigent Serbs and their ally Russia, who was, to the Kaiser's consternation, constantly increasing its armaments.[6] This potential danger could not be dismissed, but Wilhelm was somewhat reassured because he believed that the situation in western Europe did not present a similar level of danger. France was of course an implacable enemy and always would be, but the Kaiser was convinced that the French did not represent a real threat unless the British joined with them in fighting Germany.

If there was a thread that ran through Kaiser Wilhelm II's entire life, it was his exasperation at having failed to resolve his feelings for England, along with his puzzlement, always acute, as to why his royal relatives and their various governments behaved toward him and Germany the way they did. As Europe gradually crystallized diplomatically into rival camps — the Austrian-German-Italian league, which was established in the 1870s and 1880s, and the looser but increasingly solid entente among London, Paris, and St. Petersburg, which was forged shortly after the turn of the century — Wilhelm II engaged in the habitual speculation in Berlin about what England would do in the event of a war on the Continent. As on most subjects, the Kaiser's opinion frequently changed. Until the collapse of the mission to Berlin by Lord Haldane in February 1912, Wilhelm usually, but not invariably, thought that the British would never draw their swords against Germany in spite of the naval rivalry and the economic competition that existed between the two kindred peoples.[7] By the end of 1912, however, the Kaiser was not so sure, and the declaration by

Lord Haldane to Ambassador Lichnowsky in December of that year—
that Britain would not permit France to be destroyed—made him pessimistic. Although after 1912 Wilhelm on occasion would proclaim that an
Anglo-German war was "unthinkable," he had come to the conclusion
that if France got involved in hostilities with Germany, it would ultimately
have Britain as an ally.[8] But who could say with any certainty that there
would in fact be a war? At times, Wilhelm was convinced that Germany's
very strength was a guarantee against the other powers going to war, but
in the darker moments that often followed, he predicted that a war between the Slavs and the Germans was inevitable.[9] The Slavs, however,
could do nothing without Russia, which was utterly unprepared to fight.
And even if the tsar went to war against Germany, Britain would not feel
the same compulsion to aid the Russians as it would in the case of the
French.[10]

Wilhelm found it very difficult to deal with a situation that seemed so
ambiguous. Sometimes he would refuse to discuss the threatening future
and grasped at positive signs of good relations with his neighbors. But
clearly he was also alarmed, fearing that Germany might be suddenly
enveloped in war, and the Kaiser's determination to bring Germany's military and naval forces into readiness reflected his concern.[11] Throughout
1913 and early 1914 Wilhelm insisted that the navy be increased, placing
himself at the center of the parliamentary fray that centered on army
funding for 1913. When the Reichstag seemed to be on the verge of enact-
ing a budget that would result in a reduction of the number of cavalry
regiments, the Kaiser threatened to prorogue the chamber if it did not do
his will.[12] Chancellor Theobald von Bethmann Hollweg, always calmer
than his overlord, finally succeeded in effecting a compromise whereby the
regiments were retained but the number of military attachés was reduced.
This change was numerically insignificant, but it struck at the Kaiser's
prestige, since these officers were his personal representatives at foreign
capitals. Wilhelm was quite ungrateful for Bethmann's support, complaining that it had taken entirely too long to get the army budget passed.[13]
The army was equally displeased, not only at the chancellor but also at the
Kaiser. Ever since the turn of the century there had been resentment in the
officer corps at what was felt to be the ruler's preference for his navy.[14]
There was consternation among some of Wilhelm's generals that the Kaiser was regarded in Germany as an "Emperor of Peace" (*Friedenskaiser*),
one who failed to realize that his true role was to serve as a Prussian Mars,
a *Kriegsherr*.[15] Too often, military critics held, Wilhelm had held back
from drawing the sword: against German Socialists, against the French in

Morocco in 1911, or against Russia in the Balkan Wars in 1912–13. In 1909, General Friedrich von Bernhardi, the famous author of *Germany and the Next War* (1912), expressed regret that the Kaiser was obsessed with "peace *à tout prix.*"[16]

Wilhelm's failure to be imbued with what his generals thought to be an appropriate militaristic attitude was troublesome, since the Kaiser had for years made it very clear that he was the absolute commander of Germany's military forces. From the beginning of his reign in 1888, he had claimed for himself the leading role in the Prussian army, directing its maneuvers, designing its uniforms, promoting or retiring its generals and lesser officers, and declaring that in the event of war he would stand at the head of his troops.[17] The Kaiser was usually unreceptive to military advice unless it came from his adjutants, almost all of them men only too eager to cater to his vanity. Wilhelm in particular had no truck with his successive war ministers, whose office was a "poisonous den," and he also made the chief of the Military Cabinet subordinate to his adjutants.[18] General Helmuth von Moltke, the chief of the General Staff from 1905 until the first weeks of the war and a man celebrated more for his historic military name than for his ability, did not fare much better. The Kaiser liked Moltke and tried to bolster the general's faltering self-confidence, reassuring his friend, "The little work that is to be done in peacetime you can do, but in war I will be my own chief of staff."[19] Although retiring by nature, as chief of the General Staff, Moltke showed surprising firmness, insisting that maneuvers cease to be idle exercises contrived to ensure that the army, which Wilhelm invariably insisted on commanding, would prevail over its opponent.[20]

Together with some of his fellow generals, Moltke believed that Germany should launch a preventive war against France and Russia while the army possessed the advantage, and he had advanced this view at the *Kriegsrat* over which Wilhelm had presided in December 1912. As early as the turn of the century, and even more noticeably toward 1910, in the wake of deteriorating relations with France because of Morocco and with the British because of the *Daily Telegraph* affair, there had been other voices in the army who believed that war with France and Russia at that time was to be welcomed, since it would create an opportunity to deal effectively with internal and external problems.[21] This was not an opinion exclusively of the officer corps, for in the years leading up to 1914, there were also civilian figures who similarly believed that under favorable conditions, war was desirable, and there were others who did not necessarily want conflict but who believed that it was probably inevitable.[22] Although

in the *Kriegsrat* Wilhelm had ordered the swift construction of more submarines and the preparation, by the press, of public opinion for the likelihood of war with Russia, there is no indication whatsoever that between
1912 and 1914 he desired or even anticipated a conflagration between the
powers. Nothing in the Kaiser's behavior or his activities in the first six
months of 1914 betrayed any sense or conviction of approaching doom.
In the fall of 1913 Wilhelm carried out his traditional routine of hunting,
and in the spring of the next year he embarked on an extended voyage to
Corfu, where his attention was so squarely fixed on the ruins being excavated that his entourage was concerned about the lack of interest he paid
to European affairs.[23]

On the way back from Greece, Wilhelm visited the Archduke Franz
Ferdinand at his Bohemian estate at Konopischt. The two men, who frequently met one another at hunts, were similar in their vanity, their restlessness, and their ability, when they elected, to charm others. The association between Wilhelm and "Franzi" was based less on personal attraction
than on a mutual sense that Austria and Germany needed one another.[24]
Wilhelm wrote the archduke with uncharacteristic frequency, and often at
unusual length. There was suspicion in Vienna, even on Franz Ferdinand's
part, that the Kaiser was trying to prepare the archduke to be ready to
further Germany's interests when he succeeded the old emperor, Franz
Joseph.[25] In his correspondence with Franz Ferdinand, Wilhelm stressed
the value of a close Austro-German relationship, the dangers facing Europe at the hands of the yellow race and the Jews, the perfidy of Great
Britain, the menace represented by an aggressive pan-Slavism emanating
from Serbia and Russia, and the necessity of maintaining German-Magyar
hegemony within the Habsburg Empire. Franz Ferdinand agreed with
the Kaiser's analysis, especially of the Serbs, with whom he believed war
would ultimately be unavoidable. But there were often disagreements,
especially because of the archduke's belief that eventually the Slav subjects
of the Habsburg monarchy would have to be given a greater role in the
empire. It troubled Wilhelm that Franz Ferdinand was not more eager to
adopt his ideas.[26]

On Saturday, 20 June 1914, Wilhelm departed on the *Hohenzollern*
for Hamburg in order to be present at the christening of the Hamburg-
American Line liner the *Bismarck*, which he described in a wire to Franz
Ferdinand as a "majestic sight." When the Iron Chancellor's granddaughter failed to smash the bottle of champagne against the huge ship's side,
Wilhelm himself performed the task. He then went to Kiel for a sailing
regatta attended by a number of British and German pleasure boats as

well as a squadron of the Royal Navy. The Kaiser was suspicious that the British might attempt to pick up military secrets, and he ordered detectives sent to Kiel and foreign guests kept off his ships. As matters turned out, there were no difficulties, and when the British departed, the Kaiser expressed satisfaction at the "never failing comradeship and hospitality" his ships enjoyed whenever they met with the Royal Navy.[27] During the Kiel Week sailing competition, Wilhelm took the helm of his racing yacht *Meteor*, returning to dine and sleep on the larger *Hohenzollern*. He was aboard the *Hohenzollern* when, at 2:30 on Sunday afternoon, 28 June, a telegram was received announcing that Franz Ferdinand and his wife had been shot to death hours earlier in Sarajevo, the capital of Austrian Bosnia, where the archduke had gone to participate in maneuvers carried out by the Habsburg army.[28]

Wilhelm informed the British ambassador, Sir Edward Goschen, that the assassination of his friend was a blow because he and Franz Ferdinand had mapped out the future. That was an exaggeration, since he and the murdered archduke had not seen eye to eye on a number of problems. Nevertheless, Franz Ferdinand's death would mean more difficulties in the future between Berlin and Vienna, for the archduke's friendship with Wilhelm had helped to mollify the differences of opinion between the statesmen of the two empires.[29] Wilhelm declared in dismay that he neither knew nor cared now who would succeed the aged Franz Joseph, for it would undoubtedly be some young princeling hardly Franz Ferdinand's equal.[30] The Kaiser gave orders for an immediate return to Berlin so that he could, as he said, take the situation in hand and preserve the peace of Europe.[31] Arriving in the capital on the afternoon of the twenty-ninth, Wilhelm carried out an entirely normal routine for the next few days, spending over two hours on 1 July discussing the interior decoration scheme of his newly commissioned yacht, again to bear the name *Hohenzollern*. The Kaiser, however, was unsure whether he should leave on 6 July, as planned, on his annual cruise along the Norwegian coast.

The question that concerned Wilhelm, Chancellor Bethmann, and the German Foreign Office was not what Germany should do, since the murder did not directly involve Berlin. What was of concern was the effect the crime would have on Austria's relations with Serbia because the archduke's assassins, who were Serbian nationals, had crossed over into Bosnia from Belgrade outfitted with weapons. If the Serbian government could be shown to be complicit in facilitating the assassination, a convenient cause for a war of revenge would be at hand. The outrage in Sarajevo, as the

Austrian ambassador in Berlin, Count Ladislaus von Szögyényi-Marich, pointed out to former chancellor Bülow, was to be regarded as a "gracious coincidence of divine providence."[32] The Kaiser also felt that the time had providentially come to put Serbia in its place. Wilhelm by 1914 had for many years been concerned that the Habsburg Empire had become too listless and reluctant to defend its position in central Europe. He had therefore approved Austria's annexation in 1908 of the Ottoman provinces of Bosnia and Herzegovina, a triumph of the aggressive policy of the foreign minister, Baron Alois Lexa von Aehrenthal.[33] Aehrenthal, raised to the rank of count for his success in obtaining the provinces, died early in 1912, and Wilhelm found the new foreign minister, Count Leopold von Berchtold, less to his liking because, in the Kaiser's opinion, the minister worried too much about Russia.[34]

More to Wilhelm's taste was the dictatorial Hungarian prime minister, Count István Tisza, a man whose admirable willpower made him, in the Kaiser's view, unique among Habsburg officials. The Kaiser had advised Franz Ferdinand to form a closer tie with Tisza, but the archduke had been suspicious that Tisza aspired to rule Austria as well as Hungary.[35] To instill in the Habsburg government in Vienna a greater resolve and determination, Wilhelm had on many occasions, from the beginning of his reign, declared that if Russia provoked Vienna into a war, Germany would not leave its ally in the lurch.[36] The assassination at Sarajevo, an outrageous crime against the house of Habsburg as well as a major diplomatic crisis, would put Vienna's mettle to the test. Would the Austrians move in vigorous pursuit of Serbia, or would Berchtold dither and ultimately do nothing? The Kaiser need not have been concerned, for Count Berchtold and virtually the entire civil and military apparatus of the empire favored stern and immediate action against Serbia, whose complicity in the assassination had become increasingly apparent. Only Tisza favored a cautious policy, insisting on satisfaction from Serbia for the crime but preferring that it be obtained through diplomacy rather than war. Berchtold moreover had received information from Semlin, an Austrian border station on the Serb frontier close to Belgrade, that a band of assassins was en route to Berlin to assassinate the Kaiser, a fact that he hoped would make Berlin more acutely appreciative of Austria's dangerous situation.[37] The foreign minister was aware that Wilhelm and the German government had long deplored his indecisiveness, and therefore he was eager to prove to his ally that he was a man of resolve. To make this clear, he decided to send to Berlin as a special envoy his leading assistant in the Foreign Office,

Count Alexander von Hoyos, who ardently favored going to war with Serbia. Hoyos would have to leave for Germany quickly, since Wilhelm was scheduled to leave Berlin for Norway on 6 July.

In the Kaiser's opinion, the assassination was an affront against royalty and against the Habsburg monarchy, and therefore Serbia, which he held to be responsible for the outrage, had to be punished. "It is high time," Wilhelm declared on 2 July, "that a clean sweep was made of the Serbs." Two days later he added that the sooner this was done, the better.[38] On Sunday, 5 July, Hoyos arrived in Berlin, bringing with him a letter written by Emperor Franz Joseph and addressed to Wilhelm II; in it the aged sovereign declared that the Habsburg monarchy would in the future be safe from pan-Slav agitation only if Serbia was "eliminated" (*ausgeschaltet*).[39] Ambassador Szögyényi, invited to Potsdam for lunch, presented the letter to the Kaiser. Wilhelm responded to Franz Joseph's message by instructing the envoy to report to his sovereign that, subject to Bethmann's agreement, Vienna could reckon on "full support" from Germany. The Kaiser indicated that this would be the case not only in an Austro-Serbian war but also in one that involved Russia, a prospect Wilhelm did not think likely because of St. Petersburg's military unpreparedness. Furthermore, Wilhelm urged that Vienna undertake its punitive mission against the Serbs at once.[40]

From his audience with the Kaiser, Szögyényi derived the impression that Wilhelm wanted to incite Austria to take military action.[41] After lunch on 5 July, Wilhelm summoned his military and naval staffs to meet him at Potsdam at 5 P.M. in order to ascertain whether the army and the navy were ready for whatever eventualities might arise. In discussions that continued into the next morning, these assurances were forthcoming.[42] The Austrians were clearly to understand that Berlin expected them to make a firm intervention with Serbia and that failure to do so at such a propitious moment would be deplored.[43] Habsburg credibility required strong action, and Wilhelm was confident that Serbia would yield to Austria's demands and that within a week or so the situation would be clarified.[44] It was his expectation that the unfortunate matter could be settled without recourse to a European war, for Wilhelm continued to believe that the lack of readiness in both Paris and St. Petersburg would deter them from hostilities. Russia would do well, he warned, to recognize that the assassination in Sarajevo was a matter solely between the Habsburg Empire and Serbia and that if the tsar mobilized with an intention of intervening, the Kaiser would declare war at once. No one would be able to accuse him of a lack of resolution.[45] The Russians need not imagine that

Wilhelm would quail before the prospect of the French coming to the aid of their ally, for he was confident that Germany could defeat the French in a matter of five or six weeks. The prospect of Britain's entering the war does not seem at this juncture to have occurred to him.[46]

Bethmann, who had been on his estate in Brandenburg when the assassination occurred, was summoned to Berlin, meeting with the Kaiser at six o'clock on the evening of 5 July just after the military officials had left and some hours after Wilhelm had told the Austrian envoy that Germany would stand by Austria.[47] The chancellor concurred with these assurances. Bethmann wanted very much for Wilhelm not to delay leaving Germany for his Scandinavian cruise, since the vacation would advertise Berlin's confidence that the murder in Sarajevo was to be treated as a localized affair.[48] The Kaiser himself was eager to get on with his trip, especially because he believed that there was no prospect of "serious complications." Russia would recognize that it was not ready for war and that intervention in behalf of Serbia would undermine the monarchical principle supporting the Romanov crown.[49] He therefore departed as scheduled on 6 July, accompanied by the North Sea fleet, which would carry out exercises along the Norwegian coast. Bethmann made plans to return to the countryside toward the end of July, assuring a young relative who was to come to see him at Hohenfinow that "he did not believe that the cannons would prevent" the visit.[50]

Wilhelm proceeded first to Kiel for the annual regatta, in which a number of British vessels were taking part. The Kaiser and his friends among the officers of the Royal Navy visited back and forth. As he steamed out of port, Wilhelm expressed his appreciation for his guests' "never failing comradeship and hospitality," and Admiral Walker, in command of the British squadron, signaled in return, "Friends now and friends forever."[51] The Kaiser then proceeded, on 12 July, to Balholm on the Norwegian coast, where the *Hohenzollern* anchored until the twenty-fifth. The cruise was uneventful, and the Kaiser did not at first concern himself much with diplomatic affairs, instead hiking and listening to one of his generals lecture on the American Civil War. He did await with interest the official formulation of Austria's demands on Serbia. In his opinion, in retaliation for Franz Ferdinand's assassination, Vienna should insist on the cession of the Sanjak of Novi Bazaar, an enclave that, placed in Austrian hands, would prevent Serbia from joining Montenegro and thereby reaching the Adriatic. Wilhelm wrote on 14 July to Emperor Franz Joseph to assure him that he stood ready to fulfill his "joyful duty" in supporting the Habsburg Empire in its dispute with Serbia. Both rulers, he declared, had an obligation to stop Belgrade's propaganda mills and to prevent Russia from forming a league of the small Balkan powers against Austria-Hungary and Germany.[52] He fulminated to the Foreign Office that Serbia was not a nation in the European sense but only "a band of robbers that must be seized for its crimes" and that behind Belgrade stood Russia, "the perpetrator and *advocate* of regicide!!!"[53]

Bethmann was anxious not to give Wilhelm any cause for excitement because he feared that the Kaiser would then decide to return to Berlin, a homeward voyage that would surely alarm the powers.[54] It appears that Wilhelm felt no apprehension about the situation in the Balkans until 19 July, when he learned that Austria intended to present the Serbs with a forceful, and perhaps unacceptable, ultimatum three days later. This was exactly the sort of vigorous act Wilhelm had demanded from Vienna, but with strong measures now a reality, the Kaiser fell into what Admiral Müller described as a state of "high anxiety." Germany's preparedness for war became the vital concern of the moment, and Wilhelm debated whether German shipping lines should be alerted to take measures to protect their vessels and whether the fleet then conducting maneuvers in the North Sea should regroup and accompany his yacht back to Germany.[55] All this alarmed the chancellor, who feared Wilhelm might give some "disastrous" order to the fleet.[56] Bethmann succeeded in deterring the Kaiser from any "premature" action, and for the next few days Wilhelm made excursions on the mainland, admiring the local architecture. At dinner on 23 July, he received a telegram from Berlin informing him that, without taking the courtesy of alerting him, the Austrian ultimatum had been dispatched to Belgrade. This annoyed Wilhelm, who felt that he should have been given prior notice.[57] He had, however, no quarrel with the terms that Vienna had dictated to Belgrade, and to him they were not to be negotiable. "*Ultimata* are accepted nor not! But one does not *discuss* any longer! Thence the name!"[58] The time had come for the Habsburgs to preside over the Balkans, whether Tsar Nicholas II and his government liked it or not. Russia, he declared, was trying to make a European issue out of what was properly a local conflict to be settled by Austria-Hungary and Serbia.[59] Like the other Balkan peoples, the Serbs were savages who could not be measured by the same standards that applied to the civilized nations of Europe.[60] Vienna had therefore been completely justified in confronting the brigands with a strong ultimatum. "Just tread hard on the heels of that rabble," he wrote in approbation of Austria's demands.[61]

On 26 July, after receiving news that the Serbians had mobilized their army, the Kaiser, fearing that Russia might follow suit, ordered the fleet that had accompanied him to Norway to make the final preparations for the homeward voyage to Germany.[62] Bethmann protested to Wilhelm, who declared in return that the chancellor, whom he suspected of trying to shove him aside in this critical moment, had failed to keep him adequately informed and that, being a civilian, the chancellor had no comprehension of the situation.[63] Wilhelm was concerned that the Russian fleet, which had begun to group torpedo boat flotillas in the Baltic, might attempt a surprise attack on the *Hohenzollern* as it made for Kiel or might fall on German ports in the Baltic, just as the Japanese had suddenly blockaded Port Arthur in the Russo-Japanese War.[64] "My fleet has orders to sail for Kiel," he ordered, "and to Kiel it is going to sail!"[65] For good measure, Wilhelm spitefully refused the chancellor's request to meet him after docking in Germany. The *Hohenzollern*, which had sped ahead of the fleet, steamed into Kiel at 7 A.M on 27 July, and by three that afternoon the Kaiser was at Potsdam. Bethmann was at the Wildpark station that served the suburban palace, but Wilhelm received him curtly, annoyed because the chancellor had insisted that the Kaiser not proceed to Berlin, a move that might make the situation seem more ominous.[66]

Very early on the twenty-eighth, Wilhelm read the text of the Serbian reply to the ultimatum from Vienna, a reply that met most though not all of the Austrian conditions. He was elated, seeing in the answer from Belgrade an Austrian victory that not only humbled Serbia but also eliminated any cause for war. "A brilliant performance. . . . This is more than one could have expected! A great moral victory for Vienna."[67] The ultimatum was only a document, not an act, and Wilhelm reminded his state secretary at the Foreign Office, Gottlieb von Jagow, "The Serbs are Orientals, therefore liars, tricksters, and masters of evasion." Paper promises by such people were valueless, and what the Kaiser termed "*douce violence*," not arbitration, had to be used to convert worthless words into concrete deeds.[68] That meant not subtracting the Sanjak of Novi Bazaar from Serbia, Wilhelm's former demand, but rather requiring the surrender of Belgrade, the Serb capital, to Austria as a hostage for the fulfillment of the terms of the ultimatum. The Kaiser believed that if this was forthcoming, war would be unnecessary, and he planned to leave for his castle at Wilhelmshöhe in Hesse as soon as the situation was resolved.[69] His vacation never materialized, however, for Vienna found the Serb reply unacceptable. On 28 July the Habsburg Empire declared war on Serbia and began the bombardment of Belgrade.

Given the delay that was expected for Austria actually to occupy Serbian territory, there was no sense of frantic haste in Berlin but rather an expectation, which turned out to be false, that the slow mobilization of the opposing armies would provide an extended opportunity for diplomatic negotiation. During the last days of July the Kaiser believed that it was Britain on whom the maintenance of peace depended, for London had the ability to keep its allies, France and Russia, in line. Wilhelm was troubled, however, that before the dispatch of the Austrian ultimatum to Serbia, the British foreign secretary, Sir Edward Grey, had seemed somehow to believe that peace in fact depended on the Kaiser's impressing on his ally in Vienna the necessity of not imposing impossible conditions on Belgrade. That to Wilhelm was the same old story: the British were condescendingly telling him what to do.[70] Once Austria had thrown down the gauntlet to Serbia on 28 July, Grey continued to insist, to Wilhelm II's considerable annoyance, that the responsibility for what happened lay with Germany.

On 29 July, Grey informed Ambassador Lichnowsky, who was desperately trying to persuade the British to stay out of the conflict, that London would not become involved unless the Austro-Hungarian-Russian-Serb war widened to include France and Germany.[71] The Kaiser denounced Grey's declaration as "the worst and most scandalous piece of English pharisaism" that he had ever seen, his rage being due to the fact that this statement appeared to him to be at odds with King George V's remark made the day before to Prince Henry of Prussia, the Kaiser's brother who was vacationing in England. George V had said, "We shall try all we can to keep out of this and shall remain neutral."[72] To the Kaiser, Grey was a monument of bad faith, contradicting his own sovereign's promise and threatening Germany — as if it was "common as dirt" — with the specter of war if it did not desert Austria. In fact, Wilhelm declared, it was England who had only to instruct St. Petersburg and Paris that they were to calm down and negotiate. "That common crew of shopkeepers," Wilhelm ranted, "has tried to trick us with dinners and speeches." He insisted that it was that "common cur" Grey, and not his first cousin, the king, who was being duplicitous.[73] Always one to believe in the sanctity of crowns, Wilhelm declared to Admiral Alfred von Tirpitz, who by no means shared his confidence, "I have the word of a king and that is enough for me."[74]

George V's word was one thing to the Kaiser, but the word of Tsar Nicholas II was quite another. In spite of Wilhelm's bombardment of the tsar during the assassination crisis with telegrams appealing to his sense of monarchical solidarity, Nicholas on 29 July mobilized his army along Russia's frontier with Austria (though *not* along its frontier with Germany). To Wilhelm, this was an act of treachery by his Russian "colleague," who, as a Slav, was a partisan of the "bandits and regicides" in Serbia. It was the tsar, Wilhelm declared to Ambassador Szögyényi, who would be responsible should a world war develop.[75] On 28 July, Wilhelm wired Nicholas, reminding him that Austria's war with Serbia was a matter of principle, one in which politics played "no role at all." He was doing all that he could to encourage Vienna to behave in a way that would not force Russia to enter the conflict.[76] The tsar was not convinced, and in his reply he denounced Austria's attack on Serbia as "ignoble."[77] This infuriated the Kaiser, who assured Nicholas that Austria had no permanent designs on Serbian territory and that there was no need for Russia to enter the fray, since this would involve Europe in "the most horrible war" it had "ever witnessed."[78] To Wilhelm, Russia's mobilization was an act of betrayal, one engineered in cooperation with London and Paris in order to use the Austro-Serbian conflict to launch a "war of extermination" against Germany. The real architect of this treachery was his late but still despised uncle, King Edward VII, who had years before set it all in motion. Wilhelm declared of the king, "[He] is stronger after his death than I who am still alive!"[79]

The Kaiser was determined that England would pay for its deceit with the destruction of its empire, something that he believed Germany could bring about by urging King George's millions of Moslem subjects to rise up against this "hated, lying, conscienceless nation of shopkeepers." He added, "For if we are to bleed to death, England shall at least lose India."[80] Even so, Wilhelm resisted the bellicose insistence of his brother Henry and of four of his six sons, an argument forcefully advanced at a family dinner at Potsdam on 30 July, that should Russia mobilize on its *German* frontier, he should at once issue a similar order to his own army. Out of ancestral piety, the Kaiser had no desire to go to war with Russia, for his grandfather, Kaiser Wilhelm I, had on his deathbed commended his grandson to nurture Germany's long friendship with St. Petersburg.[81] Those sentiments became impossible to sustain when, on 31 July, Wilhelm received news of what he believed to be the final proof of the Anglo-Russian conspiracy ranged against him. Nicholas II, he was informed, had ordered the mobilization of the Russian army along the German border, an act that led the Kaiser to leave Potsdam for Berlin in order to direct the defense in the east.[82] At 1:45 P.M., Wilhelm, Bethmann, and Moltke decided to issue a notice that a "threatening danger of war" existed, which was understood to be the preamble to a general mobilization forty-eight hours later. This was followed within an hour and a half by a telegram to the German ambassador in St. Petersburg instructing him to insist that unless Russia stopped "every war measure" against Austria and Germany within twelve hours, Germany would mobilize along its eastern border, a move that in effect meant war. Fearful that Germany would soon be at war with Russia and France and perhaps with other powers as well, the Kaiser implored Nicholas, "Stop the military measures which must threaten Germany and Austria-Hungary."[83] Vainly trying to enforce the king of Italy's allegiance to the Triple Alliance, Wilhelm informed King Victor Emmanuel III, "War with Russia appears to me to be imminent and inevitable." He added that war with France appeared hardly less likely.[84]

That was why the Kaiser consented to the celebration, on 31 July, of the marriage of his son Oskar to a Prussian countess, a mésalliance that, in less troubled times, he might have protested. Wilhelm's mood on the wedding day was serious but calm, and he was confident that should a European war soon begin, Germany would be able to count on Rumania, Bulgaria, and Turkey as allies.[85] He continued to hope that his entreaties to Nicholas II might keep Russia out of the conflict, although he admitted to Ambassador Szögyényi that it seemed likely that Germany and Russia would soon be enemies.[86] England, Wilhelm also hoped, might be induced to stay out of a continental war, for George V had, on the thirty-first, inquired whether an offer of Franco-British neutrality would suffice to prevent Germany from attacking France. The Kaiser declared that once German mobilization had begun, as it had with the notification of a state of threatening danger, technical grounds prevented its revocation, but that if France offered neutrality that was guaranteed by Britain, Germany would not move against France.[87]

France's actions depended less on Britain than on Russia, but the tsar — in a final audience with the German ambassador, Count Friedrich von Pourtalès, early in the evening of 31 July — declared that Russia's mobilization could not for technical reasons be countermanded and, once again, called on Germany to put pressure on Austria to stop its campaign against Serbia. In the early afternoon of the next day, the mobilization order went out to the German army.[88] This did not mean, however, that German units would move over the Russian frontier, which General Moltke was eager to cross even though his army would not be completely prepared for hostilities for another two or three days. The French premier, René Viviani, in answer to the German ambassador's pointed question as to whether France would join with Russia in the war, would say only that it would, as the envoy reported to Berlin, "act in accordance with her interests."[89]

Wilhelm, backed by Admiral Tirpitz and State Secretary Jagow, ordered that there was to be no troop movement until receipt of a telegram expected from London. This arrived at about 5 P.M., and in it Grey declared that Britain and France would remain neutral if Germany made no military advances against France.[90] Wilhelm believed that if Grey's offer was not pursued, Germany could be branded as the aggressor, an opinion shared by Bethmann, Jagow, and Tirpitz.[91] General Moltke and the Prussian minister of war, General Erich von Falkenhayn, however, vehemently argued that if an attempt was made to alter the military campaign that mobilization had set in motion, the German army would be placed in a state of acute disorganization. According to Moltke, once the mobilization order had been given, it could not be changed to be directed against only Russia. This answer infuriated the Kaiser, who turned on Moltke with the bitter observation: "Your illustrious uncle would not have given me such an answer. If I order it, it must be possible."[92] A compromise was eventually agreed on whereby Grey would be informed that his wire had come too late to countermand the mobilization against France but that if France would agree to neutrality, Germany would not attack. Moltke then returned home in a rage, telling his wife that he would willingly fight against the enemy but not against "such a Kaiser as this one."[93]

Meanwhile, at ten o'clock on the evening of 1 August, a wire from Ambassador Lichnowsky in London arrived, describing the conversation he had had that afternoon with Grey. The foreign secretary had, throughout his remarks, emphasized that the vital question to the British was the neutrality of Belgium, to which all the powers were committed by a treaty signed in 1839. He was emphatic that any violation of Belgian territory would make it virtually impossible to keep Britain out of the war, adding, however, that he was not prepared to give Germany an absolute assurance of neutrality even if Germany did respect Belgium.[94] In the Kaiser's opinion this was all "drivel," duplicitous lies and "humbug," and when, on 2 August, the French mobilized, he and Bethmann recognized that peace in the West was virtually hopeless.[95]

At about one o'clock in the morning of 2 August, the German army invaded Luxembourg, alleging that it had done so to protect the German-controlled railroad system in the grand duchy in the event of a French attack. The battle orders of the German army dictated that Belgium would be next, and Lichnowsky continued to warn by telegraph that such a step would inevitably bring Britain into the war, whereas a German attack on France might not, provided that Germany did not impose too draconian a peace after the anticipated victory.[96] In the early hours of 2 August, the army had already sent reports that the French were firing across the border, the counterpart to French recriminations that the Germans had violated their frontier. Meanwhile military intelligence reported that French troops were being massed on the Belgian frontier, a development that would require German countermeasures. Wilhelm would later claim that Belgium had already forfeited its claim to neutrality by allowing the British and the French to stockpile war material on its territory and that he therefore had decided he must invade.[97] Late in the afternoon of 2 August, Jagow instructed Lichnowsky to inform the British that although French provocation would require the invasion of Belgium, once the war was over, its territory would be vacated with compensation for damage. The next day, a few minutes after 1 P.M., Bethmann instructed Ambassador Wilhelm von Schoen in Paris to inform the French government that as a result of hostile activity by French troops and aviators, a state of war was in effect.

Ambassador Lichnowsky in London nevertheless remained hopeful that the British would stay out of the war, his optimism dissipating only on the afternoon of the fourth, when he dolefully reported to Berlin, "Continuance of English neutrality can no longer be counted on and . . . a rupture of relations is imminent." "Poor Lichnowsky" had now at last come to his senses, the Kaiser noted.[98] The British declaration of war on Germany came just after 7 P.M. To Moltke, London had planned the war all along, and that fact now justified Germany in using the most ruthless means against its enemy across the channel. He rhapsodized that perhaps the United States, lured by a promise of Canada, might be brought into the war as Germany's ally. To Wilhelm, however, the fact that Germany was at war offered no cause for exhilaration. He was placid but downcast, regretting that his good name as a ruler of peace, a reputation bolstered by a reign of twenty-six years, was now forever destroyed. The Kaiserin, on the other hand, furiously ranted against Germany's enemies and reminded her husband that she had long predicted the war that was now a reality.[99]

The Kaiser was enraged at what he considered England's betrayal of his long attempts at friendship and his assurances of Germany's benign motives respecting Belgium. How, he asked, could the British have so easily forgotten their brotherhood with the Prussians a century earlier on the field at Waterloo?[100] But that was only a portion of his choler at the behavior of various powers he had considered to be his friends. Nicholas II, he declared, had shown "unscrupulous wantonness" (*gewissenlose Leichtfertigkeit*) in disregarding Wilhelm's stalwart attempts to preserve peace and thus had brought this "immense calamity" upon the world.[101] The Italians believed that Vienna's move against Serbia, backed if not abetted by Germany, was plainly an act of aggression and therefore one that did not activate their responsibility, under the Triple Alliance, to enter the war, a decision Wilhelm blamed on that "scoundrel," King Victor Emmanuel III.[102] King Carol of Rumania, a distant Hohenzollern kinsman of the Kaiser's, was commendably loyal and would have sent the Rumanian army into action against Serbia and Russia, but his government refused to become involved, much to Wilhelm II's irritation. "Our allies," he declared, ". . . are falling away from us like rotten apples!"[103] Germany was now locked in battle with the three greatest powers of Europe. "So many enemies," the Kaiser repeated over and over.[104] The only friend on whom Wilhelm could count was Austria-Hungary, in whose defense he had exposed Germany to the danger of war, one now realized. The Kaiser presciently recognized that Franz Joseph's empire might not prove capable of achieving victory over Serbia or of being much use against Russia. That would mean that Germany, beset with the awesome task of simultaneously repelling both the Russians and the French, would have to expend a good part of its energy and resources bailing out its one ally. From the moment that the war began, Wilhelm II had cause to wonder whether he would emerge crowned with the laurels of victory.

The Kaiser's first official act after Germany went to war was to summon the Reichstag to the palace to hear a royal address, which had been written in part by his friend the theologian Adolf von Harnack. The deputies, minus members of the Social Democrat faction who declined to come, assembled in the White Hall before the royal dais. Departing from the text, as he had been wont to do for years, the Kaiser made his famous pronouncement: "I no longer acknowledge parties; I know only Germans."[105] Wilhelm did not mean what he said, for throughout the four years of war that would ensue — a conflict far longer and more costly than he or his generals and admirals had ever imagined — his hostility toward the Reichstag did not abate, even toward the deputies of what he dismissed as the "so-called true-to-the-crown" Conservative Party.[106] Most distasteful to Wilhelm II was the Social Democratic Party, by 1914 the largest faction in the Reichstag, and although he recognized that it would be an essential element in the war effort, he expressed no gratitude when the Socialists joined the other factions in approving the extraordinary budgetary credits Bethmann requested to finance the conflict.[107]

The willingness of most Socialists to support the war reflected the sense of danger and the expectation of swift victory that in August 1914 exhilarated the German people and gave the Kaiser an enhanced status as commander-in-chief of a Fatherland under attack by a host of enemies. At last, it seemed, Wilhelm II, who for so many decades had postured as an intrepid general, would assume in fact the martial role that had distinguished his father and others of his ancestors and kinsmen.[108] Following the Prussian tradition that the king stood at the head of his troops, Wilhelm joined Moltke at the headquarters established early in August on the Rhine at Koblenz and then at the end of the month at Luxembourg, which had been invaded by the German army marching on Paris.[109] He took up residence in the Hotel Brasseur but moved in late September to Charleville, which was closer to the French front. Here Wilhelm would spend much of the war, periodically going out to the scene of battle, visiting hospitals, and inspecting arriving troops, all with little concern for his personal safety. There was a parade-like quality to the Kaiser's field visits, and since he traveled with a vast number of officers, it was difficult to bring him close to the front.[110] Wilhelm never in fact stood at the forefront of his armies, but he was occasionally exposed to enemy fire, crises he met with an exemplary bravery. He was delighted when he was close enough to the front to hear the roar of battle, and he would return to headquarters declaring that he had "joined in the fight."[111] The imperial regimen was not unlike the one that had prevailed in peacetime Berlin. Wilhelm rode early every morning, worked at his desk for two hours, carefully surveyed the daily press, and had lunch with his military staff, followed by an hour of conversation. In the afternoon, he was driven to see local monuments or battle sites, took walks, dined with his generals, and then talked and smoked until about eleven.[112] On many days the product of the Kaiser's energy was nothing more than a flurry of congratulatory telegrams or the award of decorations or gifts to officers who had been successful on the battlefield. It was as empty an existence as he had had in peacetime.

Wilhelm tended in war, as in peace, to dominate any group of which he was a part by inflicting a monologue on his audience.[113] The silence of flatterers should not be confused, as Wilhelm himself was prone to do, with the presence of actual leadership or real understanding of warfare. In peacetime he had told Moltke that should the Fatherland go to war, he would assume command, and Wilhelm's grandiloquence, to be sure, was replete with august proclamations of his forthcoming decisive role as supreme warlord. So the Kaiser could declare to his beloved First Foot Guards, the "first regiment of Christianity," as it departed for the front, "The sword is drawn, and I will not resheath it without victory and honor."[114] Yet no amount of bellicose rhetoric could conceal the fact that Wilhelm II's part in the war, especially as it concerned the army, took a secondary place behind the role of his officers. "Kaiser Wilhelm," Count

Ottokar Czernin, the Austro-Hungarian foreign minister during the latter part of the conflict, declared, "was from the beginning the prisoner of his generals."[115] Moltke and other military figures had long been worried that in the event of hostilities, the Kaiser would constantly intervene in military questions, but just as the fighting started, Wilhelm promised that he would not interfere in the conduct of military operations, and for once he abided by his word.[116]

The army was much relieved, for Wilhelm was too excitable and too superficial to be equal to the responsibilities ordinarily borne by a commander-in-chief. There was some concern, among civilian as well as military figures, that the Kaiser's tendency to nervous prostration, one that had on occasion in the past rendered him hors de combat, would not enable him to withstand the strains of warfare. Years before, the strongly conservative politician Georg von Köller, a man fixedly loyal to the Hohenzollern crown, had openly prayed, "God spare us a war as long as Wilhelm II is on the throne, for he's cowardly and will lose his nerves."[117] Wilhelm had witnessed the opening of the conflict with a measure of calm and earnestness, but he had slept only with the aid of Veronal and had been required to take to his bed. His pallid face acquired new lines, his eyes frequently brimmed with tears, and his conversational tone was often depressing.[118] The Kaiser's mood changed with astounding frequency, from elation at good news to the darkest pessimism when reports from the front were grim.[119] Wilhelm's military entourage had no wish to see him suffer any unnecessary anxiety, and for that reason, from the moment the war began, they shielded him whenever possible from any unpleasant information. In peacetime, the Kaiser's diplomats had suppressed reports that might cause him perturbation, and now in war he was coddled into believing that all was well. Victories were celebrated, but defeats were left unmentioned or minimized. He was shown only those battle reports that might promote optimism, the conversation at headquarters was deliberately cast in a positive tone no matter what news had come from the front, and letters that might have a discouraging effect were forbidden.[120] When in spite of this protective web the Kaiser anticipated that bad tidings might be coming his way, he became quite adept at avoiding serious, private conversation.[121] Generals and other prominent officials were to understand that part of their duties was to cheer up Wilhelm, and the army summoned to headquarters guests known as "lute players" (*Lautenschäger*), who could be depended on to be jolly and to perpetuate his "hurrah mood" (*Hurrastimmung*).[122] The retinue consequently made little objection when the Kaiser left his cares behind and sought relaxation in sawing wood, gardening, reading archaeological tracts, or even occasionally leaving headquarters to go on hunting expeditions.[123]

The Kaiser's ignorance of the true nature of the struggle in which Germany was engaged was profound and his utility to his military leaders quite limited. He could prevail on the excellent standing he enjoyed with Franz Joseph to obtain concessions from the Austrians, and he could effect the delivery of goods from occupied areas in Belgium or Russian Poland, both of which were technically under his personal command.[124] But on major issues, Wilhelm throughout the war deferred to his generals; he usually remained content merely to hear and endorse their opinions or to mediate between opposing positions. The Kaiser's obtrusiveness in military affairs, so prominent in peacetime, vanished in war, an uncharacteristic reticence due to his admiration for commanders such as General Falkenhayn or General Paul von Beneckendorff und von Hindenburg or to his fear of the temperamental General Erich Ludendorff.[125] Personnel questions were left to the General Staff, and field officers were free to issue orders in Wilhelm's name provided they secured his consent on vital issues, something that was almost always forthcoming.[126] Sometimes, however, Wilhelm was ignored and was informed only after the fact of critical decisions early in the war, such as the army's order early in October 1914 that General Hans von Beseler was to occupy not only the fortress of Antwerp but the entire city.[127] This diminution of royal prerogative distressed Wilhelm, and early in the war he began to complain that the General Staff told him very little and that he, unlike Hindenburg, was hardly ever mentioned in the press.[128] The man who in peace had believed himself omnipotent became in war a "shadow Kaiser" (*Schattenkaiser*), out of sight, neglected, and relegated to the sidelines in imperial Germany's hour of trial.

Ten

WAR WITHOUT VICTORY

WILHELM II'S generals had an easy time keeping him in good cheer as long as the news on the western front was favorable, for that theater of operations was always of more concern to him than was the east. It was the war in France, and particularly the fate of the British forces opposing his own army, that electrified Wilhelm. The struggle against Tsar Nicholas II's huge military machine did not interest him nearly so much, for that, in his opinion, was essentially Austria's war.[1] The Kaiser's emphasis on the western front reflected the strategic planning of the General Staff, which from 1897 had developed the "Schlieffen Plan," named after General Count Alfred von Schlieffen, chief of the General Staff from 1891 to 1905, which had envisioned the two-front war that Germany now found itself fighting. Schlieffen's tactic called for a lightning blow against France, one in which speed would be the essential factor. This would necessitate passage through neutral Belgium, and it was this maneuver that had made Britain enter the war. This was a dangerous but necessary development because the German strategists were certain that once the Kaiser's armies had moved through Belgium into France the war would soon be brought to a victorious conclusion. France would sue for peace when, within a matter of a few weeks, a pincers movement would engulf Paris, one arm moving to the north, seizing Calais, and then sweeping south to attack Paris from the west and the other arm driving through eastern France, crossing the Marne, and descending on the capital from the east. Once Paris fell to the Germans, French resistance would collapse, and the British would be unwilling to continue the war alone. With a victorious peace achieved on the western front, the German army could then wheel eastward and inflict a similar defeat on the Russians.

Once the war began, the plan was set into motion, and for a week in August 1914 it appeared that the long years of technical planning would yield precisely the rapid victory that Schlieffen had envisioned and of which both General Helmuth von Moltke and the Kaiser were confident.[2] Before the war began, Wilhelm had frequently told Sir Edward Grey, usually banging his fist on a table as he did so: "I know what France is worth. I have only at any moment to give the order for my troops to move, and within a fortnight—mark my words, within a fortnight—my army is in Paris."[3] The German juggernaut under the leadership of General Erich Ludendorff swept into Belgium and on 7 August, after a severe struggle, seized the great fortress of Liège; the Kaiser declared that this prize, along with the surrounding area, was to be annexed to Germany and settled by deserving NCOs and enlisted men.[4] Wilhelm, watching the progress of his army, was at first fearful of the outcome and berated Moltke, but then, realizing that victory was at hand, he exuberantly declared, "Within two weeks I will be able to send my troops home." That was perhaps not meant literally, for the Kaiser later amended his prediction to proclaim that when the leaves fell in the fall, the war would be over.[5] The war would end, at whatever moment, in military victory, and although Wilhelm declared that he was "most grateful" for Woodrow Wilson's offer made in the first days of the conflict to mediate between the belligerents, he made no move to help the U.S. president initiate such an undertaking.[6]

The Kaiser never developed any settled idea of what territory Germany should claim at the moment of victory, and one of his ministers regretted that he altered his war aims from day to day.[7] In general, Wilhelm was cautious about annexations, frequently asking his son Oskar: "What should Germany have as spoils of war? Slavic areas and people, French areas and people? What would we do with them? They would be only a source of discontent and of another war."[8] In spite of an occasional outburst about colonizing NCOs, the Kaiser did not want to annex Belgium, preferring to find a means that would make the kingdom dependent on Germany and therefore free of Britain's corrosive influence. King Albert might stay on the Belgian throne, but the Kaiser warned, "He will dance to my tune."[9] Extensive areas of Alsace-Lorraine, whose unruly inhabitants Wilhelm had long desired to punish, were to be attached to Prussia, and the rest was to be surrendered to Bavaria.[10] In the east, no matter the reservations he had expressed to his son Oskar, the Kaiser had a grander scheme. A Polish kingdom would be created from largely Russian territory, to be ruled as a client state by a German or Austrian prince, but the Baltic provinces of Lithuania, Latvia, and Estonia would be absorbed by Germany. After Rumania's entry into the war on the Allied side in 1916, Wilhelm decreed that the Fatherland was to take the kingdom and colonize it with Germans, and he had much the same plan for the enormous portions of Russia that were eventually occupied by the German army.[11]

Wilhelm's opinion on how the war should be fought and what lands were to be claimed in triumph also varied depending on the degree of influence the Kaiserin exercised on him at any given moment during the war. Augusta Victoria's authority had always increased at difficult moments, for she alone knew how to calm the Kaiser's distraught nerves. The war was a perpetual crisis, and the Kaiserin rose to the occasion. The counsel that she gave to her consort was that by land and by sea, he should relentlessly pursue the British, whom Augusta Victoria hated, that he should stiffen the Habsburg will to fight, that he should insist on the forceful prosecution of the war on all fronts, and that he should extract appropriate annexations to reward the Fatherland for its heroic sacrifices. The Kaiserin was also determined that Wilhelm's image in the eyes of his subjects be steadfastly upheld. She actively served as intermediary for General Paul von Beneckendorff und von Hindenburg, Admiral Alfred von Tirpitz, General Wilhelm Groener, and other important military figures, working to win the Kaiser's approval of their ideas or to keep them in his favor. They were glad to have her assistance. As one grateful general put it, "Now that's a strong woman!"[12]

Wilhelm and Augusta Victoria's heady visions of magnificent victory followed by a peace that heaped advantages on Germany while humiliating its foes vanished in the face of the resistance that General Moltke encountered as he drove across Belgium. Although Liège fell, it was only after a massive battle, and not only there but elsewhere, the Belgian army as well as the civilian population put up a heroic defense that slowed the German advance, enabling the French and the British to excavate trenches in France that would be used against the advancing German wave. The temerity of the Belgians in daring to resist the imperial army infuriated the Kaiser, who declared that their "crimes" differentiated them from the French, whom he once had condemned for feeding on revanchism but who, he now claimed, had in fact never wanted the war and would be happy to see Germany bring it to an end.[13] The prospect of humbling the arrogant British especially exhilarated the Kaiser, and any engagement that resulted in their defeat gave him such inordinate pleasure that his behavior, according to Rudolf von Valentini, the chief of the Civil Cabinet, bordered on being positively silly.[14] The Kaiserin outdid even her consort in loathing the British enemy. She gave no quarter, and when in October 1915 King Alfonso XIII of Spain appealed to her to intervene in behalf of Edith Cavell, an English nurse who had been condemned to death by a German court-martial in Belgium for aiding in the escape of enemy soldiers, she declined, coolly noting that if women behaved like men, they must be punished like men.[15] An opportunity to provide the

British an inkling of their doom came in late August 1914 when the Germans lay siege to the Belgian fortress of Namur, defended by Belgian, French, and British soldiers. On 25 August, after a severe bombardment, the citadel fell, and Wilhelm was overjoyed when he heard the news, especially since the British commander and most of his troops had been taken prisoner.[16]

The glorious victories registered along the western front in August 1914 unfortunately were not repeated in September. General Moltke, without consulting the Kaiser, amended the Schlieffen Plan, as its architect had years earlier predicted he would, reducing the strength of the northern salient and adding more divisions to the southern force that was marching toward the Marne.[17] This altered deployment of the invading army permitted the French and British forces to puncture the German line, thereby retarding Moltke's advance. Exaggerated estimates of the Allied forces blocking his way to Paris alarmed Moltke, and he decided that the prize could not be taken. He therefore had to calculate how his forces could be most effectively realigned in preparation for a renewed attack. Although Wilhelm had firmly declared that there was to be no retreat, on 8 September one of Moltke's aides, acting on behalf of the general, gave the order to pull back.[18] The infuriated Kaiser summoned Moltke and informed him that while he could formally remain chief of the General Staff, General Erich von Falkenhayn, the minister of war since 1913, would become quartermaster general with full responsibility for directing the western front. The Kaiser's "discovery" (*Erfindung*) of Falkenhayn surprised much of his entourage and found little resonance in the army, for the general had no claim to the post through seniority.[19] The Kaiser was oblivious to these objections and admired Falkenhayn's self-confidence, especially after dealing with the labile and uncertain Moltke. Falkenhayn, he was certain, was just the man to restore esprit on the western front.[20] On 3 November 1914 Wilhelm, with no show of regret, sent his erstwhile friend Moltke into retirement and appointed Falkenhayn as chief of the General Staff. If Falkenhayn did not succeed in rectifying the situation, the Kaiser declared that he was prepared to take to the field himself as commander. "Then," he declared, "the world will see something."[21]

Although the retreat at the Marne in mid-September had spoiled the southern wing of the Schlieffen Plan, the German army in the north of France continued its "drive to the sea" in the hope of taking Calais and thus preventing further British participation in the war. The route of advance lay through Antwerp, Ghent, Lille, and finally Ypres, all large, well-defended cities. Antwerp's garrison contained a small contingent of British troops, and when the city was taken on 9 October, Wilhelm was elated. "My relatives on the other side of the Channel will be upset by this," he declared with satisfaction, and he was confident that Antwerp's capitulation marked a turning point in the war.[22] Ghent fell on 11 October, Lille the following day. There remained only Ypres, against which General Falkenhayn now brought up a huge force, which was countered by an equally determined effort on the part of the British and French. Ypres played something of the role that Stalingrad would in the Second World War: depending on perspective, it had either to be taken at all costs or to be defended at all costs.[23] Falkenhayn assured the Kaiser that this prize would be in German hands in about a week's time, and on the opening day of the Ypres offense, 30 October, Wilhelm went to the front to witness the massive bombardment that was to be the prelude to the German investment of the city.[24] Although much of the handsome medieval city was destroyed, the defenders repulsed the Germans, whose losses after two weeks of savagery came to some eighty thousand men.

By mid-November, the Kaiser realized that Ypres would survive the German onslaught and that further assaults would be fruitless. He therefore agreed with Chancellor Theobald von Bethmann Hollweg and the General Staff, who argued that the German force in the Franco-Belgian sector should be reduced and such troops as could be spared transferred to the eastern front. Wilhelm's jubilation, sustained by earlier victories, now collapsed, and he became morose and depressed, his only consolation resting in his belief that Germany was economically better prepared than any other belligerent to face the long war of attrition that seemed now to loom in the future rather than the short victorious conflict that he had envisioned.[25] The failure only increased Wilhelm's fury against England, and in early December he told the chief of the Austro-Hungarian General Staff, General Count Franz Conrad von Hötzendorf, that his "ideal" — his "dream" — now was to make peace with France and then take the British expeditionary force into captivity.[26] A cessation of hostilities with the British was utterly impossible, he informed Albert Ballin, the head of the Hamburg-American Line. "I stand now alone with my God," he declared, "and I will make no peace with England (though I would with France or Russia) before she has been brought to her knees and all four corners of London devoured by flames and smoke."[27] Wilhelm's enmity was more than reciprocated in London, where at about this time Queen Alexandra, the widow of Edward VII and mother of George V, delighted in serving her guests a confectionery extravagance of chocolate cake with figures in white icing representing the Kaiser and his heir being blown to bits by an Allied bomb.[28]

The Kaiser did not disguise his displeasure at Falkenhayn's failure to redeem Moltke's error on the Marne, and he indicated quite plainly that new leadership would be required on the French front.[29] The panacea that Wilhelm II envisioned to atone for his army's disappointing failure to eliminate France from the war, first under Moltke and then under Falkenhayn, would be to place General Hindenburg in charge of the western front and repeat the attempt.[30] Wilhelm did not do so, however, because he realized that Hindenburg was at the moment indispensable in the conflict with Russia. The Kaiser's confidence in Hindenburg, one that would weather four years of war and a number of spirited disagreements, was due to the general's spectacular defense against the gigantic Russian army that had invaded Germany early in August 1914. Hindenburg was in fact not responsible for the German success in the east, for his tactical accomplishments were modest. It was his quartermaster, General Erich Ludendorff, the mastermind of the capture of Liège, and Ludendorff's assistant, Colonel Max Hoffmann, who were the real architects of Germany's eventual victory against Russia, in which the leading general proved to be August von Mackensen, a favorite of the Kaiser's. The Russian invasion in August 1914 brought the tsar's army within 150 miles of Berlin before Hindenburg was able to counterattack, but when he did so, his army achieved the two greatest victories Germany would score in the war, one at Tannenberg at the end of August and a week later at the Masurian Lakes, where Mackensen's brilliant maneuvers decimated the Russians. A German advance into Russian Poland ensued, culminating in December in the capture of the great Polish fortress of Lodz. Hindenburg and Ludendorff believed that they might have been able to accomplish even more had it not been for Falkenhayn's insistence on reserving enormous numbers of troops for his catastrophic assault on Ypres, and therein began the "war within the war," the battle that pitted the chief of the General Staff against Germany's two most popular and successful commanders. Falkenhayn was doomed eventually to lose the struggle, for Hindenburg and Ludendorff, regarded as an indivisible team, overnight became national heroes. Thereafter it was increasingly difficult for any authority, civilian or military, to prevail against the two victorious generals. Wilhelm had ignominiously cashiered Moltke and occasionally abused Falkenhayn for failing to produce a victory against France, but on his two victorious paladins in the east he showered honor after honor. Hindenburg was made a field marshal and Ludendorff raised to the rank of lieutenant general in November 1914, with Mackensen receiving his baton in May 1915.

The failure on the Marne and Falkenhayn's subsequent inability to take Ypres meant that as 1914 came to an end, Germany found itself involved in a war for which it had neither planned nor prepared. Instead of a lightning victory in the west, a protracted conflict would now have to be carried out in trenches and by siege, a process in which any movement by either side was likely to be accompanied by enormous human cost. In the east, although Hindenburg and Ludendorff had achieved impressive advances into Russian territory, a decisive victory had not been won, and Nicholas II seemed determined, as did his allies, to fight on. Instead of planning victory celebrations to mark the conclusion of a swift campaign, by the end of 1914 Wilhelm had to deal with the interrelated problems of military leadership, strategic planning, and war aims, on all three of which there was considerable division of opinion in the ranks of his army and naval officers. The inherent complexity of such a situation was complicated by the fact that the Kaiser's civilian statesmen insisted that both strategic planning for war and determination of war aims were matters of diplomacy that required the participation of civilian officials and thus the intrusion of ideas that by no means could be expected to coincide with those of the military. As the ultimate authority in imperial Germany, it would fall to Wilhelm II to resolve these debates. He would do so not by placing himself above the various parties and imposing his own policies but instead by yielding to the views of those who were able at one time or another to exercise the greatest degree of influence on him. The Kaiser's role from 1914 to 1918 was therefore not one of a supreme warlord but rather of an observer and listener who — when (and if) he was consulted — assented to or opposed plans and programs with which he had had no involvement. The once-vaunted *persönliches Regiment*, with its mighty throne and ruler, became in wartime a backseat occupied by a neglected, ill-informed, and increasingly inconsequential figurehead.

Since the land war on the western front was to the Kaiser always the Fatherland's principal conflict, it was to have priority in manpower and supplies. Even the war at sea, in which his much-prized navy was ready to participate, played a secondary role in Wilhelm II's calculations. Long before the war began, the Kaiser had declared that he would order his entire battle fleet to launch a ruthless attack on England.[31] This boast had assumed that Germany would have assembled an armada sufficient in size to realize Tirpitz's "risk theory," but the admiral himself had often declared that this goal would not be achieved until 1919 or 1920. Wilhelm, who had so often belittled the war-preparedness of the French and the Russians, now recognized that on the sea, Germany was ill-equipped to defeat its British foe. At the very end of July 1914, as the prospect of confronting Britain became increasingly imminent, he had confessed doubt about the fate of his navy. How the German fleet could effectively stand up to the numerically superior Royal Navy was a matter known, he told the Austro-Hungarian ambassador, by "God alone." Wilhelm sensed that the expenditure of millions upon millions of marks over many years had provided Germany with only a "parade fleet."[32] When war actually came in August 1914, the German battleship fleet, outnumbered by the Royal Navy, remained in port, its activity confined to sending out submarines and cruisers for rare, but often quite successful, attacks against British warships and ports. This corresponded to the Kaiser's view, supported by Admirals Friedrich von Ingenohl and Hugo von Pohl, respectively chief of the High Seas Fleet and chief of the Admiralty Staff, and by Chancellor Bethmann, who opposed engaging the enemy in the North Sea. Although Tirpitz admitted that Germany's strength in warships was less than desirable, he resolutely advocated seeking an encounter with the British. The Kaiser's opposition to Tirpitz's idea was based partly on a conviction that his ships were outnumbered and insufficiently armed, but he also believed that a German fleet that was strong and unscathed by fighting would give him a better chance to force an advantageous peace on the Allied powers.[33] His naval commanders, according to an order issued in the first month of the war, were not to attack but instead to practice "cool calculation and calm waiting."[34] Wilhelm's opposition, and his order in particular, enraged Tirpitz, who complained about the Kaiser's timorous lack of mettle and who contrasted his conduct with the valiant role of Wilhelm I in the war against France in 1870–71.[35] Tirpitz believed that his inability to determine the conduct of the war on sea was due to Wilhelm's jealous vanity. The Kaiser, bereft of any understanding of the naval situation, was a menace in command, and before the conflict was a year old, Tirpitz had come to the conclusion that Wilhelm had to be persuaded to surrender the direction of the war, on sea as well as on land, to General Hindenburg.[36]

Contrary to what Tirpitz believed, Wilhelm had not in fact assumed command of the wartime navy. Although he was regularly consulted, he was not always kept well informed of naval decisions. Perhaps that was quite satisfactory to the Kaiser, who told Admiral Georg von Müller that as a man who had no idea whether he would survive from one day to the next, he did not want to be burdened with details of naval policy.[37] That was particularly true if Tirpitz was involved, for Wilhelm was annoyed with him and saw him as little as possible and even then evaded any discussion of naval matters except to berate the admiral for the insufficient armor with which his ships were outfitted.[38] Although the Kaiserin was a strong advocate of Tirpitz's, he had few other friends at court, and Chancellor Bethmann, who, like Wilhelm, refused to put the battleship fleet into action, also avoided him. By February 1915, it was clear that Tirpitz's position with the Kaiser had seriously deteriorated, and the admiral himself felt that Wilhelm would have got rid of him had the Kaiser not been concerned about the effect on public opinion.[39]

The Kaiser's objections to Tirpitz concerned only battleships, for Wilhelm was willing to commit smaller vessels and submarines to action against the British.[40] In the early fall of 1914, German U-boats, which were approximately equal in number to those of the Royal Navy, had sunk several British cruisers and launched an attack on the British base at Scapa Flow. Unleashing the U-boats against belligerent ships was to be expected, but the Atlantic was full of vessels of neutral registry that regularly made their way back and forth to British and French ports carrying war matériel. International law regarding contraband abounded in murky contradictions, and all the powers at war resented the provisioning of their opponents by neutral vessels. Many of these ships flew the stars and stripes, and both Germany and Britain consequently ran the risk of provoking the entry of the United States into the war by sinking American merchant ships and passenger liners suspected of bearing military supplies. The prospect did not alarm Tirpitz, who was eager to make maximum use of his U-boats, even if this jeopardized German-American relations. Although Wilhelm agreed to permit his submarines to attack belligerent targets, the Kaiser was considerably more guarded than Tirpitz about their future as an arm of war. He was not convinced that German U-boats sent out into the North Sea would be effective against the Royal Navy, and besides, the extinction of civilians on the sea offended his notions of chivalry.[41] Late in November 1914 he expressed to Karl Helfferich, one of Germany's leading bankers, his relief that a large British liner had narrowly missed being sunk. He then turned to a group of admirals and said: "Gentlemen, always realize that our sword must remain clean. We are not waging war against women and children. We wish to fight this war as gentlemen, no matter what the other side may do. Take note of that!"[42] At the same time, he was very annoyed that the Americans were selling munitions and submarines to his enemies, and in February 1915, under considerable pressure from Tirpitz, he agreed, without demonstrable enthusiasm, that a policy of unrestricted submarine warfare might be instituted.

Any and all ships believed to be carrying contraband to the Allies would be torpedoed without warning, provided that "utmost caution" was exercised regarding ships of American and Italian registry.[43]

On 4 February 1915 Bethmann announced the implementation of unrestricted submarine warfare designed to subject Britain to absolute blockade. The result was the sinking of British ships, culminating on 7 May in the torpedoing without warning off the coast of Ireland of the White Star Line's *Lusitania* with the loss of 1,198 passengers, many of them U.S. citizens. Wilhelm believed, quite correctly, that the massive liner had been carrying arms in its hold, and he felt that Americans who traveled on the Atlantic were deliberately exposing themselves to danger.[44] He informed the American ambassador, James W. Gerard, that as a Christian and as head of the German church, he had tried to fight chivalrously but that the enemy had forced him to use dire means in retaliation. Even so, he told the envoy some months later, he was appalled by the deaths of innocent women and children; as a gentleman, he would not have countenanced the action had he known of their presence on board.[45]

So great was the outrage in America over the *Lusitania* incident that it became alarmingly clear in Berlin that unrestricted submarine warfare might well bring the United States into the war against Germany. That again did not bother Tirpitz, but Wilhelm, under the influence of Bethmann, Admiral Müller, and others, was fearful that unless the U-boats' targets were not chosen with more discrimination in the future, Germany might find itself contending with yet another enemy. On 1 June 1915 Wilhelm issued an order that *neutral* ships were to be spared and that his U-boats were not to attack unless they were absolutely certain that the intended victim was an enemy vessel.[46] That did little to satisfy the outrage of the Americans, who insisted that warning be given and that the safety and survival of all passengers be provided for. Throughout the summer of 1915, a duel was fought in Berlin between Tirpitz and his confederates, who urged that *unrestricted* submarine warfare be relentlessly pursued, and Wilhelm, Bethmann, and Müller, who wanted to formulate some limitation that would appease the Americans. By early August, Tirpitz knew that the Kaiser had deserted him.[47] The situation became even more critical when, on 19 August, a German submarine torpedoed, off southern Ireland without warning, the British White Star Line passenger ship *Arabic*, resulting in the death of three Americans. A few days later, Tirpitz was summoned to army headquarters at the palace of Prince Pless in Silesia and told that Wilhelm II had decided, against the admiral's advice, to issue an order declaring that in the future, submarines would give warning to passenger ships of impending attacks and would provide for the rescue of passengers and crews. This was entirely unacceptable to Tirpitz, who argued that the order would undermine public confidence at home and convince the enemy that Germany was weakening.[48] Although the Kaiserin urged Tirpitz not to desert Wilhelm, the admiral submitted a letter of resignation on 27 August. The Kaiser refused it, reminding Tirpitz that in time of war he could not permit an officer to quit a post because of a difference of opinion on naval policy, an area for which Wilhelm, as supreme commander, not Tirpitz, was ultimately responsible.[49] On 30 August 1915 Wilhelm issued an order that no passenger ships were to be sunk "without warning and saving of passengers and crew."[50] This calmed American feelings and eliminated, for the moment at least, any danger of the entry of the United States into the war.

Bethmann had less luck in Rome. At the outbreak of war, Italy had declined to support its partners in the Triple Alliance, arguing that this was a strictly defensive pact and that Austria's aggressive dealings with Serbia had provoked the ensuing French and Russian declarations of war. Italy therefore declared that it would remain neutral unless Austria agreed to cede portions of its Adriatic territories, a demand that Vienna rejected out of hand. Wilhelm had no intention of letting such a negligible, second-rate power, with its dwarfish king, interfere with Germany's winning of the war, but he could not deal with Italy until Hindenburg's campaign against the tsar had been concluded.[51] In spite of Hindenburg's monumental victory at Tannenberg and the triumph of Mackensen's forces at the Masurian lakes, Russia had not capitulated, and Italy therefore remained a problem. There was a strong suspicion in Berlin that rather than joining the Central Powers, Italy was ready to side with France and Britain, who were prepared to promise it the Adriatic properties Austria had refused to surrender. The Kaiser believed that to prevent this, Germany would need to persuade Vienna to be more amenable to Italy's territorial demands, and he tried in vain to persuade Emperor Franz Joseph to make the requisite concessions to the "traitor" king in Rome.[52] In spite of much diplomatic activity between Berlin and Rome, in May 1915 Italy declared war on Austria-Hungary, although not (as yet) on Germany, whereupon Wilhelm began to describe the punitive peace treaty he would one day have Austria exact from the Italians.[53]

As the Kaiser considered the war in which Germany was involved — one that, as 1915 began, seemed to be without much likelihood of immediate conclusion — it was not the question of whether Italy would remain neutral or join the Allied powers that was of paramount concern. The eastern front had demonstrated the superior military ability of the German army, and in the east, time would eventually wear down the Russians and remove them from the war. To Wilhelm, it was the western theater that was the heart of the conflict, but that campaign, in spite of thorough planning years before the assassination at Sarajevo and the employment of more than a million soldiers, had failed to deliver a German victory over the French and British. The fight had now settled into trenches that stretched mile after mile through northwestern France and Belgium, with the British still in control of the Channel, for Wilhelm's army had not succeeded in taking the ports of Dunkirk, Calais, or Boulogne along the Straits of Dover. That meant that the British could provision their large expeditionary force and supply the French as well, thereby enabling the Allies to sustain a war of attrition month after month, year after year.

Falkenhayn, who had devised the unsuccessful campaign in November 1914 to break through at Ypres and thus to put the Channel into German hands, was responsible for the deadlock in the west. Although the Kaiser was often critical of Falkenhayn, the general was a virtuoso at handling his master. Unlike Hindenburg and Ludendorff, he avoided tirades and threats to resign when his proposals were questioned. He not only managed to persuade Wilhelm not to replace him with Hindenburg but also avoided putting the sovereign in the position, which Wilhelm loathed, of having to decide between conflicting views. So deft was Falkenhayn's touch that he virtually eliminated the Kaiser as a factor in military decisions.[54] A man of considerable polish and unruffable demeanor, the general sometimes told Wilhelm nothing at all or, on other occasions, only what he thought would please the Kaiser. Careful to limit the access of other military figures to the Kaiser, Falkenhayn was exaggeratedly optimistic when conferring with Wilhelm and strengthened the Kaiser's predisposition to believe that the western front was the decisive theater of war.[55] This led the Kaiser to develop a false view of the situation and consequently to make many foolish observations that officers at the front resented.[56] As at Ypres, Falkenhayn continued to abound in false prophesies of victory, but Wilhelm, hoodwinked by such deceptiveness, readily passed along to others the evasions and half-truths that he had heard from Falkenhayn or anyone else.[57] Although the Kaiser realized that Falkenhayn was not keeping him fully informed, his confidence in the General Staff was enormous, especially after the great victories accomplished in May 1915 by General Mackensen against the Russians at Gorlice and Tarnow in northern Hungary. This was the beginning of a gigantic German advance into Russia, the first great success since Hindenburg and

Ludendorff's victories in eastern Prussia in the fall of 1914. Although Falkenhayn had little to do with the eastern front, Wilhelm accorded to him the laurels, and by July 1915 Kurt Riezler, Chancellor Bethmann's private secretary, declared that the "enormous position" that Falkenhayn enjoyed was due to a "mystic relationship" he had with the Kaiser.[58]

Wilhelm's confidence in Falkenhayn was not widely shared in any quarter of the government or the military. Bethmann led the civil opposition, admitting that the general had some military ability but deploring his character and his rude, overbearing manner.[59] From the moment in November 1914 that Falkenhayn succeeded Moltke as chief of the General Staff, he came under attack by many of his fellow generals, who believed that he lacked the superlative ability requisite for leading Germany to victory and who, like the chancellor, resented his brusque, superior air.[60] As a result, much of the energy of the leaders of Germany's military effort in the first two years of war was expended on personal rivalries and efforts to dethrone Falkenhayn. The general's most formidable and determined opponents were the popular heroes, Field Marshal Hindenburg and his quartermaster, General Ludendorff. Neither Hindenburg nor Ludendorff liked Falkenhayn; both had opposed his appointment as chief of the General Staff and were determined that he be sacked. Even as the two were involved late in 1914 in hurling the tsar's forces back into Russia, they had tried to have the Kaiser get rid of Falkenhayn. Their hope was that the rather phlegmatic Moltke would return to his old position and become their puppet, but if the Kaiser resisted that plan, Hindenburg and Ludendorff were both prepared to replace Falkenhayn.[61]

Such a notion had considerable support in both the army and the government, but except for Wilhelm's fleeting thought in November 1914 of naming Hindenburg chief of the General Staff, it failed to impress the Kaiser. The attempt by Hindenburg and Ludendorff to force Moltke or themselves on him enraged Wilhelm, and only the intervention of Kaiserin Augusta Victoria, who pointed out that the German public would not be able to understand the dismissal of a national hero, persuaded the Kaiser not to retaliate against Hindenburg.[62] Within a matter of weeks, however, Hindenburg and Ludendorff resumed their threats to resign, and again the field marshal enlisted the Kaiserin's help. It did no good, for Wilhelm was determined to retain Falkenhayn. Hindenburg, he declared, was trying to make himself into a Wallenstein, and he threatened to bring the field marshal before a military court for insubordination. Bethmann thereupon declared that should Hindenburg be dismissed, he could not accept responsibility for the future conduct of the war. Wilhelm backed down about punishing Hindenburg, but his loyalty to Falkenhayn remained unshakable.[63] The general was his protégé, and Falkenhayn's dismissal would therefore damage the crown's prestige. Worse, this would erode the Kaiser's authority in military affairs, since Hindenburg and Ludendorff, whose popularity far exceeded his own, would then be firmly in charge of the conduct of the war. Wilhelm, never one to let himself be outshone, found such a prospect intolerable. General Max Hoffmann, a close associate of Hindenburg's and Ludendorff's, recognized that the two generals "were just too popular, and no king allows that."[64]

Although Wilhelm had heaped honors on Hindenburg after his great victories against Russia in the fall of 1914, the Kaiser felt no personal attachment to him. Wilhelm had little to do with him before the war began, probably because on maneuvers, the general had not paid sufficient attention to the Kaiser's views.[65] Once Germany was at war, the Kaiser resented not only Hindenburg's popularity but also what Wilhelm considered to be the field marshal's touchiness and his tendency to propose military measures without proper preparation.[66] Wilhelm's lack of enthusiasm for Hindenburg was also due substantially to the field marshal's close attachment to Ludendorff, a man of bourgeois birth and inelegant manners and one ferociously insistent on having his own way. Hindenburg was inclined not only to let Ludendorff make most of the decisions regarding the eastern front but also to have his assistant defend or explain those conclusions when the Kaiser visited command headquarters in Poland (*Oberost*). Wilhelm therefore had ample opportunity to be exposed to Ludendorff's abrasiveness, and the Kaiser liked little about the quartermaster general, who was fearless in saying exactly what he thought. When, in January 1915, Bethmann proposed that Ludendorff succeed Falkenhayn, Wilhelm declared, not entirely inaccurately, that the quartermaster general was a "suspicious character corroded with personal ambition" and would therefore never receive such an appointment.[67]

The Kaiser's insistence on supporting Falkenhayn in the face of active opposition was revealed in a crisis that occurred in May 1915 at the height of the victorious drive by Germany against the Russians. Hindenburg and Ludendorff believed that if *Oberost* could be given enough troops, which would require diverting some from the relatively inactive western front, a successful campaign could be launched against St. Petersburg and would force Russia to sue for peace. Once that had been accomplished, Germany could turn its entire forces against the enemy in the west. Falkenhayn, however, was resolutely opposed to any diminution of his army poised against the British and French and indeed believed that every available

German soldier should be assembled on the western front to prepare for a forthcoming campaign to crush the Allied line. The question that had divided the Kaiser's generals was thus whether the eastern front, on which Germany could place only half the forces Russia possessed, should take precedence over the stalled attempt to defeat the Franco-British enemy in the west. "West or east?" Hindenburg wrote after the war was over. "That had to be the great question on the answer to which our fate depended."[68] There were not troops enough to pursue victory simultaneously on both fronts, and to Falkenhayn, as to Wilhelm II, Britain was *the* enemy.[69] The Kaiser therefore ordered that sufficient troops were to be maintained in the western trenches to repel the Allies and to prepare for an eventual attack, probably in 1916, that would end with German warriors marching along the avenues of Paris.

As for the eastern theater, Falkenhayn believed that the tsar could be forced to negotiate for peace if Germany seized Russian Poland, but he was opposed to an invasion of Russia proper as an utterly futile maneuver. In other words, in the west the solution eventually would be military, in the east diplomatic. Falkenhayn's viewpoint was grounded in pessimism, but to him it represented Germany's only chance. Bethmann concurred, but Hindenburg was utterly opposed. To the victor of Tannenberg, who, as a field marshal since December 1914, was superior in rank to Falkenhayn, Germany was in the war to win on the battlefield, and he was confident that this must and could be achieved in the east, where a victory would be a prelude to the final defeat of the western Allies.[70] Merely driving the Russians out of Poland would not bring them to the bargaining table; they had to be eliminated altogether by the capture of the Romanov capital. Once this had been accomplished, France and Britain could be successfully dealt with. Such a major difference of opinion required that the Kaiser be brought in to adjudicate the matter. So Wilhelm II, accompanied by the Kaiserin, went to western Poland in July 1915 to confer with Hindenburg, Ludendorff, and Falkenhayn.[71] In all decisions, whether in peace or in war, the Kaiser had a tendency to personalize problems and to be guided more by prejudice than by reason. He did so now. The Kaiser liked Falkenhayn greatly, and he felt considerable loyalty to Bethmann; on the other hand he was aggravated that Hindenburg had earlier in 1915 threatened to resign in hope of getting rid of Falkenhayn, and he thoroughly disliked Ludendorff. Not surprisingly, Falkenhayn and Bethmann therefore prevailed, and the Kaiser ordered Hindenburg to adhere to Falkenhayn's plan to restrict the advance in the north to Russian Poland.[72]

Although Falkenhayn retained his post, he was required to shift more troops than he thought prudent from the western front to Hindenburg's force soon to be deployed against the Russians. The campaign, waged with great ferocity from July until mid-September 1915, drove the enemy out of Russian Poland altogether and placed much of the tsar's Baltic provinces in the hands of the Germans. So great was the Russian defeat that in early September, just before the German advance came to a halt some 370 miles west of St. Petersburg, Tsar Nicholas II himself assumed command of the Russian army. The Kaiser, on the other hand, was pleased at the accomplishments of his army and more than ever delighted with Falkenhayn, to whom he once again gave credit for the victorious campaign. As summer turned to fall, the Kaiser was full of hope that the war might soon come to an end.[73] His optimism was unjustified, for the tsar showed no inclination to fulfill Falkenhayn's expectation that the loss of Poland would compel Russia to negotiate an exit from the war.

Hindenburg's drive into Russian Poland and the Baltic provinces in the summer of 1915 found a parallel in the joint Austro-German campaign waged with equal if not greater success along the southern Russian front. The combined army swept the Russians before it, first retrieving the parts of Austrian Poland and northern Hungary that Russia had taken in the fall of 1914 and then pressing eastward. This reduced Russia's southern frontier to a shambles and provided the Austrians with a much-needed dose of prestige. The successful advance also freed part of their army to turn at long last against the Serbs, leading to the fall of Belgrade to General Mackensen's Austro-German army on 9 October 1915. Neutral Rumania was now placed in an unenviable situation, for not only did King Ferdinand face a victorious Austro-German army on his western frontier, but to the east Turkey, which had joined Germany as an ally in November 1914, lay in wait down the Danube. Turkey's participation in the war meant that Russia could not be supplied through the Dardanelles and would have to divide its army between two fronts — one against Austria-Germany, the other against Turkey. Altogether, the Balkan situation in the late spring of 1915 appeared to be highly favorable for Austria and Germany except for the traitorous Italians, who had tied down a Habsburg army in an indecisive conflict in the Dolomites, fighting with astounding savagery but without any apparent prospect of success.

German conquests in Poland and the occupation of most of Belgium and a tenth of France did not, however, constitute victory. Although the campaign in Poland and in the Balkans in mid-1915, together with Hindenburg's confidence that victory was inevitable, had exhilarated the Kaiser, the war in the west remained a matter of considerable concern. In spite of the introduction in April 1915 of chlorine gas warfare, the Germans were unable to do more than retain their extensive foothold in France and Belgium. This stalemate deepened the already well-developed pessimism of Chancellor Bethmann, who by the end of 1915 had no confidence that Germany could win the war and whose only hope was that after peace was somehow established, Germany would emerge as Europe's economic leader.[74] The naval situation did not seem much more promising. The German high seas fleet was marooned in port, for the British navy had closed both the Channel and the North Sea, and because of Washington's protests, the policy of unrestricted submarine warfare, introduced in February 1915, had been abandoned late in the summer. Wilhelm believed that Germany must now bide its time and await a favorable moment to inflict against the British a sort of second Punic War.[75] Admiral Tirpitz found such inactivity little short of cowardice, and he used all his considerable powers of invective and propaganda to argue in vain for the reintroduction of a policy of ruthless submarine warfare. Germany should also proclaim its intention of retaining the Flanders coast, a demand that, in conjunction with the submarine attack, would make any peace negotiations with England impossible. The whip was what Great Britain needed, not enticement. Tirpitz grumbled that Wilhelm and Bethmann were foolishly obsessed with pursuing the phantom of peace with "bulldog" Britain rather than relentlessly attacking the British with every means at hand.[76]

The Kaiser found Tirpitz's opposition to his policy of watchful waiting annoying, for he had every intention of being the unquestioned leader of the German navy. "I run the huge army with my chief of the General Staff," Wilhelm informed the admiral in July 1915, "and I can certainly just so handle my little navy." This boast, Tirpitz noted, summed up the "cardinal error" (*Grundfehler*) of the war.[77] The Kaiser refused Tirpitz's attempts to reorganize the navy in such a way as to give him more authority, and instead Wilhelm began removing officers who were close to the admiral.[78] To make sure that the navy understood that no one, including Tirpitz, was to challenge the crown's leadership, in early September Wilhelm issued an order reminding his officers that he was the commander in chief and that he expected the navy loyally to support his leadership. To those who observed the duel between Wilhelm and his leading admiral, it seemed that Tirpitz might soon have to give way to someone who enjoyed more favor at court.[79]

The imperial navy needed a leader who could handle Wilhelm as expertly as did Hindenburg and Ludendorff, who had the Kaiser thoroughly in hand and who had come close to eliminating Bethmann and his government as a factor in military affairs. Internal politics in Germany had never interested Wilhelm as much as his army and navy, and that was even more true in wartime. Living at the front rather than in Berlin, he was completely out of touch with party affairs and for the most part had little contact with Bethmann after the first six months of the war, for the chancellor was in Berlin and the Kaiser was in the field. "They keep the emperor well surrounded," Bethmann complained of the Kaiser's entourage.[80] The representatives of the chancellor and the Foreign Office who were attached to the Kaiser were for the most part junior officials without much authority or influence, and consequently Wilhelm's awareness of internal questions was largely in the hands of the chief of the Civil Cabinet, a post occupied until early 1918 by Rudolf von Valentini, an able and conservative bureaucrat but not a person who would cause the Kaiser any distress. Wilhelm therefore was for practical purposes solely in the hands of a small number of military and naval figures, who were careful about what they told him. They did more or less as they pleased unless some issue among themselves or with the chancellor proved incapable of resolution. That included Hindenburg and Ludendorff, except when they crossed Falkenhayn on a major issue, which is what had required Wilhelm to go to Pless in July 1915 to arbitrate their disagreements about the forthcoming campaign in the east. Hindenburg described his and Ludendorff's relationship with the Kaiser: "In the case of more important decisions, I requested, *insofar as this was necessary*, imperial consent to our plans. The complete confidence of the Kaiser relieved us from a specific agreement from him in all non-critical questions."[81] Once a crisis passed, Wilhelm returned to the sidelines, was fed misinformation or half-truths, and was treated as a necessary bother rather than as a supreme warlord whose professional military figure had value.[82] Only when a new unresolvable difficulty arose did the Kaiser again assume any importance.

Wilhelm was not entirely happy with this situation, for he expected his army and navy to operate smoothly and to deliver victories. The problem was that he got neither, and indeed as 1915 turned to 1916, increasing friction developed between those, like Hindenburg and Tirpitz, who believed that the war could be won by force of arms and their opponents, notably Falkenhayn and Bethmann, who with more pessimism believed that the conflict would have to be brought to an end by a combination of diplomatic negotiation and limited warfare. Meanwhile at home, Wilhelm's subjects were becoming increasingly impatient, for the victories they had been promised in 1914 and for which they were now making significant sacrifices in their daily lives had not materialized, and the future appeared bleak. In August 1915, on the first anniversary of the declaration of war, Wilhelm had issued a proclamation in which he declared that Germany would fight on until it could secure a peace that would provide the Fatherland with the requisite political, military, and economic security, affording it untrammeled opportunity for development both at home and on "the free seas."[83] The Kaiser's bravado was only partially justified. To be sure, Germany occupied thousands of square miles of enemy territory, and no foreign troops stood on its European soil. But the Fatherland's colonies had vanished, its merchant marine had been lost at sea or marooned in home or neutral ports, its navy was rusting at anchor, its finances were heavily burdened, and its imports of raw materials and foodstuffs were imperiled. Every means to achieve victory, short of letting Tirpitz's fleet venture forth to battle the Royal Navy, had been tried, and none had provided the victory that Wilhelm insisted must be achieved. The war, so gloriously begun in 1914, by the beginning of 1916 was utterly bereft of glamour and perhaps had even lost any chance of being won.

Eleven

ONLY A SHADOW: WILHELM

AND HIS GENERALS

THROUGHOUT HIS long life, Wilhelm II tended to reduce all issues and problems to a matter of relations with other individuals, believing that he was capable of solving any problem if allowed to deal with a fellow sovereign.[1] No question was important enough to detach the Kaiser from his intensely personalized viewpoint, and thus much of the political history of imperial Germany involving the Kaiser is a chronicle of the attempts made by Wilhelm's advisers to ingratiate themselves so that he would endorse their ideas. Once captured, the Kaiser could then be exploited by feeding him only such information as would be convenient, by assuring him that in fact it was *he* who ruled Germany, and by demolishing the credibility of the opposition. Men of principle did not function well in such an environment, but courtiers replete with flattery and innuendo — Bernhard von Bülow was never eclipsed in this respect — usually succeeded in getting Wilhelm II to do what they wanted.

War did not change the Kaiser, and from 1914 to its disastrous conclusion in 1918 he continued to cling to people whom he liked, to be suspicious of others, and to be easily manipulated by almost all. The increasingly problematical situation in which Germany found itself after Europe exploded did not bring out in him a heightened sense of responsibility or a more deliberate judgment. Wilhelm identified the problems of a nation at arms with personalities and played favorites right down to the extinction of his empire, by which time he had become a cipher. The Kaiser's reduction even of war to a matter of prejudice was conspicuous in his attachment to General Erich von Falkenhayn, whom he had chosen in November 1914 to succeed the discredited General Helmuth von Moltke as chief of the General Staff and whom he had retained thereafter in spite of Falkenhayn's failure to shatter the Allied line in the west. At Christmas 1915, Falkenhayn persuaded the Kaiser to approve the army's war plans for the coming year. As far as the west was concerned, the aim would be once again to launch an attack against France, one that would eradicate its ability to help the British, who then would understand that they must retreat from the war and abandon their ambition to dominate the Continent economically. The campaign would be accomplished by combining, on land, a massive campaign against the French line centering on Verdun and, on sea, unrestricted submarine warfare against enemy shipping, even if that meant America's entry into the war.[2]

Falkenhayn thus finally allied himself with Admiral Alfred von Tirpitz, who stubbornly insisted that if his submarines were allowed to sink enemy merchant ships trying to provision the enemy, the war could be brought to an end within six or eight months.[3] Chancellor Theobald von Bethmann Hollweg, however, was certain that such a ruthless campaign on the water would only bring the United States into the conflict, an eventuality that had at all costs to be avoided in a war in which Germany's allies had become increasingly dependent for military help on Berlin and that was becoming more and more unpopular at home. The chancellor and Falkenhayn, once allies, had now drifted apart, and each wanted to see the other replaced.[4] In this division between the two men, insofar as it concerned the land attack on the western front, Falkenhayn had the advantage, since he was firmly in Wilhelm's favor, and the Kaiser disapproved of Bethmann's intruding himself into military opinions.[5] Falkenhayn succeeded in winning Wilhelm's consent to his 1916 war plans, and thereafter he no longer had much use for the Kaiser's opinion. The daily briefings were ritualistic, and Falkenhayn's interest in having Wilhelm stay at headquarters was probably not so that the general could hear his ideas but so that Bethmann and other officials in Berlin would have minimal influence on him.[6] The Kaiser felt a certain trepidation in front of the cool and self-confident general, so much so that he mounted no real protest when he realized that Falkenhayn had pushed him to the sidelines. "I'm only a shadow," the Kaiser complained to a junior officer. On realizing that much of his information was coming not from Falkenhayn but from the newspapers, he declared, "If I'm of so little use, then I can go back and live in Germany."[7]

The submarine contest with the Allies was a different matter. The Kaiser recognized that he stood confronted with "a choice between America and Verdun!" He was convinced that President Woodrow Wilson was searching for an issue that would galvanize his lagging popularity, and Germany would do well to encourage the president to grasp that the solution lay in becoming an apostle of peace rather than a captain of war.[8] He therefore shared Bethmann's concern about America's entry into the war and wanted to defer unleashing the U-boats until Verdun had fallen, even though Falkenhayn insisted that his forthcoming western campaign and the issue of unrestricted submarine warfare were inextricably connected.[9] As a result, in the summer of 1915 and on into early 1916 Wilhelm imposed a number of restrictions on what the U-boats might do, the most important being that no passenger ships were to be sunk before warning was given and all those aboard were rescued.[10]

The Kaiser did not like being placed in a situation in which his advisers did not agree, for that forced him to make the decision. He admitted, however, that the submarine warfare issue was one on which the war's outcome might well depend.[11] A series of conferences in the winter of 1915–16 made it clear that his advisers were divided, between those following Tirpitz, who insisted on unleashing the U-boats at once to search for prey, and those in a larger group, which wanted at least to delay the introduction of submarines until a better understanding of the consequences of the United States could be reached. The Kaiser, who had for years up to 1914 supported Tirpitz's advocacy of battleship-building only to find that these leviathans were in fact virtually useless in time of war, was skeptical about the admiral's new prophecies about the invincibility of his submarines. Wilhelm believed that Germany did not have enough U-boats to fulfill Tirpitz's assurances that England could be starved to death, and therefore the Kaiser felt that to set them loose on the water would be only to commit the "stupidity" of driving the United States into the war. The Kaiser was also concerned that even if America did not join the fight, it might stop permitting grain to be shipped to neutral ports in Europe, from which some of Germany's food supply was derived. The thing to do was to wait until England was economically in extremis and to make provisions to cover the eventuality that Holland and Denmark might abandon their neutrality. Meanwhile, Germany could perfect the design of its submarines. Wilhelm therefore elected to adopt a somewhat equivocal attitude, explaining in an address to a group of sailors in Wilhelmshaven that he would "fully" employ his submarines "once the political situation permitted."[12]

In August 1915, when Tirpitz had attempted to resign because of his disagreement with Bethmann over submarine warfare, Wilhelm had denied the request but had promised that the admiral would be consulted on all important naval matters in which the government was involved.[13] But in fact the Kaiser had failed to do so when, in February 1916, he and Bethmann had finally decided against unrestricted submarine warfare in favor of a more limited policy that exempted passenger liners. To Tirpitz this was treachery, and he again submitted his resignation as state secretary of the Imperial Naval Office.[14] Bethmann was determined that this would become the welcome opportunity for getting rid of the "father of lies," the man who had endlessly exaggerated the potency of battleships and, with their failure, now had fallen back on an equally bogus argument for submarines. Wilhelm raised no objections to dropping the admiral who had headed his navy for almost twenty years.[15] On 15 March 1916, Tirpitz bitterly went into retirement, much to Bethmann's satisfaction and without any sign of regret from the Kaiser, who never saw him again.

Tirpitz's dismissal did not please Falkenhayn, who had supported the admiral's demand for unrestricted submarine warfare, but he hoped that the more limited attacks Wilhelm had authorized on Allied shipping would be enough to undermine England's ability to help the French as they prepared to face his German juggernaut in the campaign planned for 1916. Falkenhayn calmly went about deploying more and more thousands of men against Verdun and laid out the western campaign without any serious consultation with the Kaiser. On 21 February 1916 the great offensive, with the crown prince as commander, got under way with the storming of Verdun. In a step short of unrestricted submarine warfare because it did not apply to passenger liners, the German government, with Wilhelm's assent, now notified the United States that any merchant ship, neutral or belligerent, that was armed and suspected of carrying contraband would be sunk on sight. On land, the Germans invested some of Verdun's outlying fortifications, much to the Kaiser's delight, but his enthusiasm soon waned as it became clear that the fortress itself would hold out. Both sides fought with utmost vigor, but by June the German advance, accomplished with horrendous cost in lives on both sides, had ceased, and the Allies now began an equally bloody, and equally unsuccessful, counteroffensive along the Somme River. Meanwhile, German submarines sank a number of Allied and neutral ships, with some loss of American lives. This evoked the expected protest from Washington, confirming Bethmann's fears that the United States was on the verge of entering the war. Falkenhayn continued to insist that unrestricted submarine warfare was essential to his campaign against Verdun, for the disrupted commerce in the Atlantic would mean that the Allies could not provision their armies.[16] But to this neither Bethmann nor Wilhelm would agree, for the general's failure at Verdun had made them both highly pessimistic about the chances for a satisfactory end to the war in the west. The entry of America would only make a dangerous situation intolerably worse. The chancellor saw no hope of a separate peace with any of the enemy powers, and Wilhelm spoke so negatively about the situation that even the most ardent monarchists were appalled.[17] In mid-May, the submarine campaign was called off, and the danger of war with the United States again subsided.

Much of Wilhelm's dark view of the future of the war was due to the Kaiser's quite belated realization of the falsity of Falkenhayn's assurances that if only he had enough men and submarines operating in his behalf, he could bring about victory. Wilhelm undoubtedly knew of the general's meager following in the army, support that declined after the failure before Ypres in 1914 and was all but destroyed when Verdun successfully resisted him two years later.[18] Bethmann's dislike of Falkenhayn, shared by Gottlieb von Jagow, the state secretary of the Foreign Office, and the fact that General Paul von Beneckendorff und von Hindenburg and General Erich Ludendorff had no reluctance to tell Wilhelm what they thought about Falkenhayn's mismanagement of the western front, cannot have improved his position with the Kaiser.[19] Wilhelm's frequent tirades against Falkenhayn made it seem that the general's position was ruined, but the Kaiser in fact remained doggedly loyal and refused all entreaties that a new chief of the General Staff be appointed, and only four days before the general was sacked, the Kaiser told him, "We will remain together until the end of the war."[20]

What finally brought about Falkenhayn's fall was not his own lack of success against the French and British, deplorable as that may have been, but rather the development of a situation that so acutely threatened Germany's position that Wilhelm II believed that only conferring supreme power on Hindenburg and Ludendorff could save the day. This was the entry on 28 August 1916 of Rumania into the war on the side of the Allies. The ruler in Bucharest was Wilhelm's distant Hohenzollern cousin King Ferdinand, who had engaged in a precarious neutrality ever since 1914. Essentially because of long-standing quarrels with the Habsburg Empire over disputed territory in Hungary, Rumania steadfastly resisted Germany's appeals to dynastic loyalty to entice it into the conflict. Russia, equally eager to secure Ferdinand as an ally, supported its Hungarian ambitions, and after the tsar's impressive successes against the Austrians in a summer campaign in 1916, the king seized on these assurances.

Rumania's equivocal position caused Wilhelm much anxiety, but he mistakenly believed, up to the night before Bucharest's entry into the war, that his "colleague" King Ferdinand would remain neutral.[21] The defection of this Balkan state in the camp of the enemy was an alarming development, especially because the large Rumanian army would very likely be able to overwhelm the war-weary force that the Austrians now placed in the field, all of which would mean that Germany would be called on once again to help Vienna fight its Balkan war. Wilhelm clearly appreciated how ominous this development was for Germany. He fell into a nervous depression and reportedly declared that Rumania's act sealed Germany's unhappy fate in the war. Peace would have to be made, and only Hindenburg and Ludendorff had the standing with the German people to bring about such a disappointing conclusion to the war.[22] This acute situation, which now transferred the fulcrum of the war to the east from the west, where under Falkenhayn nothing seemed to have succeeded, meant that the question of Germany's military leadership had to be reconsidered. Hindenburg and Ludendorff, whom Wilhelm had made virtually immune from interference from the General Staff, were becoming increasingly insistent that they be given authority to conduct the *entire* war, something that could be possible only if Hindenburg became chief of the General Staff. General Hans von Plessen, Wilhelm's adjutant and a voice to whom he was usually very responsive, as well as the chiefs of the Military and Civil Cabinets, General Baron Moritz von Lyncker and Rudolf von Valentini, argued that Falkenhayn had to go because he lacked any support in the army.[23]

On hearing of Rumania's declaration of war, Wilhelm summoned Falkenhayn to discuss how the German army might best deal with its new enemy. Wilhelm refused to accept Falkenhayn's proposed strategy, the first time that he had challenged his chief of staff. When, a little later, Falkenhayn heard that the Kaiser had then consulted Hindenburg about the same question, he submitted his resignation, which Wilhelm accepted after a rather chill talk, telling him that the crown must be free to consult whom it pleased.[24] Hindenburg became chief of the General Staff with Ludendorff as his quartermaster general, and Falkenhayn, who declined an offer to become ambassador in Constantinople, received the command of an army in Poland. The Kaiser declared that dismissing his friend Falkenhayn was as painful to him as Moltke's retirement in 1914, but both men, like so many of Wilhelm II's faithful servants, were shown the door without ceremony. Falkenhayn departed from Pless without a single member of the entourage in attendance.[25]

A month before being dismissed and aware of the intrigues at court working for his elimination, Falkenhayn had warned Wilhelm about the danger inherent in a change in command. "If Your Majesty takes Hindenburg and Ludendorff," Falkenhayn had warned, "then Your Majesty will cease to be Kaiser."[26] There was much truth in this prophesy, for after

29 August 1916, the day that Falkenhayn's resignation became effective, Wilhelm II no longer played even the already nominal role he had previously. Within a very short time, it became clear that the two leading generals had utterly overshadowed him in military affairs.[27] Wilhelm himself painfully realized that he was no longer (as Falkenhayn had adroitly but falsely convinced him that he was) Germany's warlord but instead was only the subaltern to the great hero Hindenburg, much the role that his own beloved grandfather Wilhelm I had played in the wars of unification led by the illustrious Helmuth von Moltke.[28] Everything and everyone, not only Wilhelm but also the chancellor and his civil officials, would have to bow before the will of Hindenburg, who in turn would be largely directed by Ludendorff. The Kaiser would continue to be advised and to be consulted; he would still have the final say in questions of personnel and in critical decisions affecting the course of the war. But the popularity of the two generals limited his freedom of choice, Hindenburg's fame and Ludendorff's imperious manner cowed him, and in the end he surrendered his authority to them and vanished into a world of empty dreams and futile hopes.[29]

Hans Delbrück, Wilhelmine Germany's greatest military historian, declared of the appointment of Hindenburg and Ludendorff on 29 August 1916, "On this day and with this decision the German empire was lost."[30] That was so, in his opinion, because the field marshal and his general did not share the sensible pessimism about the future that, at least by 1915, had begun to permeate the views of Bethmann, Falkenhayn, and Wilhelm II and that had eventually led them to believe that peace had to be negotiated. Instead Hindenburg and Ludendorff were blindly confident of victory, which would be pursued by employing every man, every weapon, and every diplomatic stratagem that Germany could muster. Once in command, they relentlessly widened the war, giving no quarter, accepting all dangers, unblinking at the prospect of adding additional powers to the long list of Germany's enemies. It would now be war à outrance, for better or for worse.

The war consequently took on for Wilhelm II an entirely different character. Although the daily round at headquarters—morning reports followed by a staff lunch—continued, Ludendorff rejected Falkenhayn's habit of disguising unpleasant news. Ludendorff consulted the Kaiser as he pleased, ignoring Wilhelm at times, but when they met he told the Kaiser exactly how matters stood, doing so with the blunt abrasiveness for which he was notorious. Ludendorff's brusqueness greatly alarmed the entourage, who had always tried to insulate the Kaiser from any sort of experience that might lead to depression, thus ordering visitors to head-quarters not to say anything that might be upsetting. The bourgeois and unpolished Ludendorff had little patience with these aristocratic courtiers and condemned the protective cocoon they had spun about their sovereign.[31] The general failed to pay the ceremonial courtesies that Wilhelm relished as signs, however empty, of his supreme authority. Wilhelm observed that compared with Ludendorff, Tirpitz, whose churlishness was legendary, was child's play. He took refuge by avoiding Ludendorff whenever possible, an unfortunate state that the general attributed to the fact that they were entirely different personalities.[32] The result was that the Kaiser abjectly approved whatever his generals wanted and soon was completely in the shade of Hindenburg and Ludendorff, "swimming," as Bethmann's confidant Kurt Riezler put it in November 1916, "in their wake without a will."[33] The Kaiser was reluctant to object to Hindenburg and Ludendorff's intrusion into civilian affairs, but he ordered Bethmann to stay out of military matters, thus maintaining the fiction that this was Wilhelm's domain as supreme warlord.[34]

Taking advantage of their independence, Hindenburg and Ludendorff turned to punish Rumania, whose entry into the war had been the cause of their promotion. Two large German forces, one commanded by Falkenhayn and the other by General August von Mackensen, invaded in September 1916, and by the end of the year King Ferdinand had been forced to flee from Bucharest, and most of his kingdom was occupied by German troops, who could now commandeer Rumanian agricultural produce and petroleum. Seized again with optimism, Wilhelm declared that this was a "decisive" development, and he awarded Hindenburg a special order of the Iron Cross, one not granted since the wars against Napoleon one hundred years earlier.[35] The Kaiser's satisfaction about the Rumanian campaign could not overcome his disappointment that Germany's efforts to roll over the enemy in the west had failed. Against this blow, Hindenburg's success in the east was cheerless to Wilhelm, for it inflicted no punishment on the British. To the Kaiser, Britain was inalterably *the* enemy and was a place, he declared in August 1916, that he would *never* again visit once the conflict was over.[36] Meanwhile it seemed to Wilhelm that something exceptional would be required to end the war on favorable terms. In the fall of 1916 he told his court chaplain, Ernst von Dryander: "I can only wait upon a wonder, just as the war broke out from a wonder. I also hope that it will end through a wonder."[37]

If there was a miraculous means that could end the conflict, it could be only the submarines, which Tirpitz had repeatedly predicted could paralyze oceanic commerce and starve the British into quitting the war before the United States and other powers could effectively enter in protest against the sinking of their ships. The Kaiser had long been reluctant to authorize the full employment of this weapon for fear of provoking the United States, yet by late 1916 it seemed that he now had no recourse but to authorize unrestricted submarine warfare. In 1915, Wilhelm noted, Germany had possessed too few U-boats to warrant introducing unrestricted submarine warfare and therefore had been forced to abandon such a policy. In the following year, food shortages and Germany's dependence on imports had dictated keeping the submarines in port, but 1917 would be different. An all-out U-boat campaign would have to be revived, with great care taken to assure the United States that Germany was doing so in order to uphold the principle, mutually endorsed by both nations, of freedom on the seas.[38] The Kaiser now found himself essentially in agreement with Hindenburg and Ludendorff but not with the chancellor, who was against such a U-boat campaign but who was reluctant to dispute military opinion. Bethmann would agree to an unrestricted campaign against all commerce destined for Britain but only if it was not instituted at once, as Tirpitz in retirement tirelessly advocated, but instead only when Germany's military position on the Continent was firmly established and the diplomatic terrain prepared to minimize the entry into the war of neutral powers. During this interval, Britain would become increasingly dependent on imports, and the navy could perfect the design of its increasingly large submarine fleet.[39]

The Kaiser was convinced that if Hindenburg and Ludendorff were the generals who could handle the military side of the problem, no one was likely to work out the diplomatic aspects of such a program more successfully than Bethmann. The chancellor had to coordinate his efforts with the army's demands, always firmly advanced by Ludendorff. The quartermaster general's perpetual intrusion into internal and diplomatic affairs disturbed the chancellor, who acknowledged that when he had agreed that the General Staff should be entrusted to Hindenburg and Ludendorff in August 1916, he had created a force that would probably cause him insuperable difficulties.[40] Even so, Bethmann got along reasonably well with both of the army leaders, although neither Hindenburg nor Ludendorff had much taste personally for him. For a few months after Falkenhayn's resignation, the devious military conspiracy against the chancellor, a situation that had characterized the first two years of the war, faded away. Wilhelm liked the calm that prevailed, since it relieved him of having to intervene, and in general his relations with the chancellor in the fall of 1916 and on into the winter of the next year were quite good.[41] Bethmann was careful not to give the Kaiser unnecessary cause for alarm, and he yielded to Wilhelm on personnel questions, in November 1916 removing Jagow as state secretary of the Foreign Office in favor of Arthur Zimmermann in order to please the Kaiser, who had no enthusiasm for Jagow.[42]

Bethmann's position was nevertheless fragile, for he had many enemies. None was more spiteful than Admiral Tirpitz, who blamed the chancellor for his fall and for Germany's failure to move energetically against the Royal Navy in the early years of the war. Tirpitz wanted to see Bülow, perennially eager to resume his old post, succeed Bethmann so that the war could be prosecuted with utmost vigor and liberalism would be thoroughly crushed at home. Tirpitz was out of power and out of favor, but he had friends in high places who advanced his anti-Bethmann viewpoint. The admiral found considerable support among other naval officers, who referred to Bethmann as "Judas Iscariot" and who worked hard to secure his downfall.[43] One of Tirpitz's confidants was the minister of the royal household, Count August zu Eulenburg, a man whom Wilhelm II saw almost every day and for whom he had a particular respect. Eulenburg agreed with Tirpitz that Bethmann had to go, although he did not believe that Bülow was the man to replace the current chancellor.[44] Among Tirpitz's most ardent supporters was the Kaiserin Augusta Victoria, who had fought hard to persuade Wilhelm not to dismiss the admiral and who continued, after Tirpitz's fall, to rally to his side. The Kaiserin, as ferocious an Anglophobe as was Tirpitz, attempted in vain to effect a reconciliation between her husband and the admiral.[45] As in the case with Falkenhayn, who had as many opponents as did Bethmann, Wilhelm was unmoved by criticism of his choice, and he dismissed all attempts to unseat Bethmann. It would require a great crisis, such as the entry of Rumania into the war, which had led to Falkenhayn's being jettisoned, to bring the Kaiser around to agreeing that a new chancellor had to be appointed.

Germany's diplomatic preparations for the reintroduction of unrestricted submarine warfare got under way in December 1916 when Bethmann, bolstered by the German army's success in Rumania, invited President Wilson to sound out the Allies as to whether they were ready to make peace, leaving unmentioned the terms that Germany would be prepared to accept. Wilhelm's motives in supporting this approach were based both on timing and on expediency. On the one hand his pessimism, shared by the chancellor, led him to doubt that Germany could win the war. But at this juncture no foreign soldier in Europe stood on German soil, and his armies held vast portions of enemy territory. Germany could therefore in the winter of 1916–17 psychologically afford to call for peace, doing so in a way that emphasized that it enjoyed the military advantage. "We all *pray (beten)* for peace," the Kaiser said, "but I will not have anything to do with *entreating (bitten)* it from our enemies."[46] At the same time, being the initiator of peace negotiations also had the advantage of investing Germany with moral superiority. "To propose to make peace is a moral act," the Kaiser at the end of October 1916 sententiously informed Karl Helfferich, the banker whom he had recently appointed to be state secretary of the interior. It would "free the world, including the neutrals, of the heavy burden" borne by all. He added: "Such an act is the province of a ruler, who has a conscience and feels himself responsible to God, who has a heart for his own people and those of the enemy, and the will to free the world from its suffering. I have the courage for all this and I will risk it for God's sake."[47] If Wilhelm and his government appealed to Wilson to ask the enemy for peace and if, as the Kaiser anticipated, the enemy declined, then it would be the Allies who would be saddled with the blame for continuing a ruinous war. Faced with a rejection, Germany could justifiably declare that it was now forced ruthlessly to employ its submarines, since they were the only means by which peace could be achieved.[48]

Wilson enthusiastically supported Bethmann's request to draw the belligerents into negotiations, but the Allies were suspicious of the absence of concrete terms and disinclined in any case to bargain with the Germans. The president's appeals to London and Paris to agree to a "peace without victory" met consequently with no response. Wilson did succeed late in January 1917 in persuading Bethmann to enumerate the peace conditions on which Germany would insist: a return to the status quo existing before the war, an increase in German colonial territory, indemnities for the losses incurred in the war, and freedom of the seas. As Wilhelm had suspected, the Allied powers denounced the German terms, leaving him feeling justified in pursuing the war with all available means. The decision to do so was taken at a meeting held on 9 January 1917 at the eastern front headquarters at Pless and chaired by the Kaiser, with Bethmann, Hindenburg, Ludendorff, and the chiefs of the Civil, Military, and Naval Cabinets present. Wilhelm already had made up his mind, and on the evening before had informed Admiral Georg von Müller that he would unshackle the submarines whether Bethmann liked it or not.[49] At the conference, Wilhelm declared that Germany now possessed sufficient U-boats to torpedo the British out of the war even if, as he expected, the United States entered. He was, as he put it, "not at all" interested in further mediation with President Wilson. If America broke off relations, it could not be helped. "We shall move ahead."[50] This was not the time for questioning but for action, he informed the chancellor. Bethmann was exceedingly reluctant to risk American entry into the war, but he declared that although he would not approve the decision, he was not prepared to contradict the opinion of the military experts.[51] Hindenburg was annoyed at Bethmann's resistance, but Wilhelm was unresponsive when the general demanded that the chancellor be forced to resign.[52] Bethmann never overcame his reservations about unrestricted submarine warfare, referring to it as the "Sicilian expedition," a reference to the disastrous naval campaign of Athens against Sicily that eventually led to the city-state's downfall.[53]

At the meeting at Pless, Wilhelm signed an order, kept secret for the moment, that unrestricted submarine warfare was to begin on 1 February. When the decision was announced on 31 January, there was an outcry in America, and on 3 February, diplomatic relations between the two countries were severed. Two months later the U.S. Congress declared that the United States and Germany were at war. Ludendorff was typically contemptuous. "The Americans are just bluffing," he magisterially assured Baron Kurt von Lersner, a young officer at headquarters. "They have no intention of declaring war against us. . . . I have no fear of American troops, for a nation that has no military education whatsoever is not proficient at war."[54] At first the U-boat campaign enjoyed a success even greater than its most optimistic adherents had predicted, and this gave Wilhelm extraordinary pleasure. Only a month after the submarines had been let loose, he informed the Austro-Hungarian ambassador that Britain was already beginning to feel the effect. What had happened, according to the Kaiser's analysis, was that unrestricted warfare on the seas had cut off Britain's supply of food, forcing it to buy goods in France in order to support its burgeoning army fighting there. Since the French were also running short, this would create difficulties between the Allies.[55] As time went on, U-boats continued to sink even more tonnage than the navy had predicted, and the Kaiser's confidence in his new weapon increased. The success indicated that God favored Germany's cause.[56]

Equally pleasing to the Kaiser was the news of the overthrow of his enemy, Tsar Nicholas II, who on 15 March 1917 abdicated in the face of a revolution that established a republic under the leadership of Prince Lvov, who declared that he would continue Russia's war against the Central Powers. Wilhelm typically saw the hand of London at work and was convinced that the tsar's overthrow had been masterminded by the British, who feared that Nicholas was on the verge of signing with Germany and

Austria a separate peace that would lengthen the war. "Cousin George" had enticed Nicholas into going to war against Germany but now had deserted him — "an irony of world history."[57] Bethmann would have to be wary of Britain's attempt to use the revolution against the Romanovs to stir up antimonarchical sentiments in Germany.[58] The Kaiser was not unduly concerned about the existence of a republic in Russia, even after its leadership passed in July 1917 from Lvov to the moderate socialist Alexander Kerensky. Wilhelm II was rightly convinced that Kerensky, who the Kaiser declared imagined himself to be a "second Napoleon," would not last long.[59] Wilhelm speculated on the military advantages of the new situation in the east, but he was oblivious to the effect the revolution in Petrograd might have on his own subjects. Bethmann was more perspicacious. Although the removal of the tsar seemed to suggest the same sort of "miracle" as the death in 1762 of the Empress Elizabeth, then pursuing a desperately outnumbered Frederick the Great in a war against Prussia, the chancellor recognized that what had happened in Russia would further polarize the Germans. The Kaiser's subjects would now be divided between those who insisted on an increasingly conservative regime to prevent a similar bloodbath in Germany and those who hoped that a Socialist Russia might influence the Germans if not to break out in revolution at least to introduce broad measures of political change.[60]

The question of internal reform had at least implicitly been raised with the outbreak of war, for the Kaiser's declaration in August 1914 that he no longer recognized parties but only Germans could be interpreted that he envisioned in the future a broader base for his monarchical regime, one that would recognize the wartime sacrifices of his subjects. He knew, as did all Germans, that ultimately only constitutional reform would sustain the support for the Hohenzollern crown that the fever of war had engendered. The revolutionary events in Petrograd had made the rhetorical assaults between parliamentarians of left and right, exchanges made in a protracted debate then in progress in the Prussian legislature, more pronounced than ever. The contest centered on two issues. One was a widespread demand that the government be composed of men more widely representative of the German people, a democratization of a state apparatus that had always been the bailiwick of the aristocracy. The other was the reduction of the Prussian predominance in imperial Germany, a position provided for in the imperial constitution of 1871. For forty-odd years the conservative nature of Prussia's parliamentary structure, built on a franchise that favored wealth, had been able to negate the increasingly liberal, indeed Socialist, character of the Reichstag. The only way, short of revolution, in which Germany could move to the Left was to end the conservative hegemony in Prussia by widening the franchise that applied in the lower house (*Abgeordnetenhaus*) of its legislature. These demands encountered formidable opposition from those who wanted tradition upheld, but their reactionism was exceeded by other conservatives who hoped that victory in war would lead to the introduction of an even more reactionary regime in Prussia and therefore in Germany at large.[61]

Wilhelm II was firmly opposed to any changes in Prussia, for he had no desire to see a greater degree of democracy spread into the parliamentary or bureaucratic machinery of the Hohenzollern kingdom. Although he had agreed in 1908 and again in 1910 to allow some alteration in the Prussian franchise, the behavior in 1913 of the Reichstag in condemning the government's role in the Zabern affair had changed him into an obdurate opponent.[62] War, however, meant that the people would have to be recompensed for the hardships forced on them. Early in 1915 the Kaiser agreed to a proposal made by Friedrich Wilhelm von Loebell, Prussian minister of interior, whereby at some unspecified time in the future the government would declare that once hostilities were over, a more democratic regime would be instituted in Prussia, without, however, specifying any details as to what would be changed.[63] Wilhelm was concerned that if an alteration of the constitution came about too quickly, the undesirable result might be a democratization in the Prussian officer corps. He believed that an army without aristocratic officers had been the ruin of France, and he did not intend to see this happen in his own country.[64]

As the war continued without decisive victory, the sacrifices of Wilhelm's subjects increased, and they began to experience increasingly acute deprivation. Cooper roofs were removed from buildings, church bells were melted down, food rationing was introduced, prices soared, and ordinary dietary fare became harder and harder to supply. By 1916, largely due to Bethmann's influence, the Kaiser rather reluctantly agreed that the Prussian franchise would have to be amended, but not until after the war's end.[65] He was unwilling to make an unambiguous promise on the matter, although in his speech from the throne in January 1916 Wilhelm declared that he hoped the German people's "mutual understanding and trust" that had prevailed during wartime might be perpetuated in peacetime by his awarding the people more adequate representation in the government.[66] Bethmann, like the Kaiser, believed that the franchise reform should await the conclusion of the war. By the spring of 1917, however, the increasingly acute shortages of food, the pressures exerted on German public opinion by the Russian revolution, and the propaganda introduced by the British and French to drive a cleft between the Germans and the Kaiser, by insinuating that the Allies' war was with the crown and not with Wilhelm's long-suffering subjects, had created a very volatile situation. In April 1917 the chancellor concluded that a promise of postwar constitutional reform, a promise that no longer indulged in vague generalities but instead specifically granted all Prussians equal voting rights, had to be made to the German people *at once*, especially because the bread ration was soon to be further reduced.[67]

The thought of a parliamentary regime horrified Wilhelm, who argued that it had proved bankrupt in Britain and was impossible in Germany because of the multiplicity of parties. It was also most unsuitable, for ministers should not come from the legislature, as in Britain, but instead should be appointed by the crown.[68] The Kaiser instead had another vision, that of a Fatherland unified in a crusade-like war, fighting, as his consort put it, for "law, religion, culture, and civilization," with all German women and men standing like a "steel wall" (*Stahlmauer*) around their sovereign.[69] The chancellor knew that the time for such vacuities had long since passed, and after much difficulty he finally succeeded in overcoming the Kaiser's reservations. On Easter Sunday, 7 April 1917, the "Easter Tidings" (*Osterbotschaft*), as Wilhelm had ordered it called, was issued in the Kaiser's name, to the delight of liberals and to the consternation of the Right and of the army. It announced that once the war was over, all Prussians would enjoy equal franchise rights in elections to the lower house and that the composition of the upper chamber would be revised in a more democratic fashion. The numerous addresses and resolutions approving the proclamation greatly pleased the Kaiser, but he was determined that what had been specified in his Easter proclamation was to be the extent of reform. Wilhelm reacted vehemently when, a few weeks later, the Reichstag demanded that in the future all military commissions and resignations were to be signed not only by the Kaiser but also by a responsible minister. Wilhelm declared that he would never consent to such a change, and the chancellor persuaded the party leaders to abandon the attempt. The Kaiser expressed his gratification to Bethmann but also pointedly noted that in the future he expected the chancellor strongly to resist any attempts to use the war to bring about a "so-called parliamentary system."[70]

Wilhelm's antipathy to radical political change found considerable support in the army. To Hindenburg the entire *Osterbotschaft* business was most distasteful, but there was consolation for him in his conviction that Bethmann would sooner or later be dismissed. Ludendorff, as usual, was more vivid in his opposition, declaring that the Kaiser's proclamation was kowtowing to the revolution in Petrograd.[71] Both the field marshal and his quartermaster general held the chancellor responsible not only for the "Easter Tidings" but also for Germany's failure to mobilize adequate personnel and resources, as well as for the labor disturbances that increasingly racked the Fatherland. Moreover, Bethmann showed a lamentable lack of confidence in victory and was deplorably reluctant to claim vast areas of Europe as spoils of war. Hindenburg was also, without reason, suspicious that the chancellor was plotting to remove him as chief of the General Staff, and for all these reasons both he and Ludendorff were determined to get rid of Bethmann as soon as possible.[72] One well-placed observer at headquarters early in July 1917 declared, "The hate against Bethmann is so fundamental that it no longer has any limits." Nevertheless, Wilhelm remained loyal, believing that the chancellor had the support of the working class and that getting rid of him would produce a general strike.[73] But even with the Kaiser's support, Bethmann was no match for his military opponents. The chancellor, one of his friends regretted, was a man whom no one feared, whereas Hindenburg and Ludendorff, both Olympian in manner, were national heroes before whom all Germany stood in awe.[74] The course of the war had shown that in military affairs, only the two great generals could provide effective leadership, and in the first half of 1917 they appeared to have the war situation well in hand. A modest but strategic retreat in the west had resulted in the establishment of the so-called Hindenburg Line, which in April and May 1917 successfully withstood an Allied offensive that proved so disastrous that some units of the French army mutinied rather than return to the front lines. Ludendorff was confident in May 1917 that Britain would give up within two or three months, overcome by Russia's collapse and the fearful attrition that Germany's submarines had caused in supplies from overseas.[75] To dismiss Bethmann might cause dismay in a few quarters, but this would soon subside. Hindenburg and Ludendorff could afford to urge the chancellor's removal, for they were virtually untouchable. Any move on the Kaiser's part to let them go would cause a public uproar throughout the length and breadth of Germany, and Bethmann himself acknowledged that it was impossible for Wilhelm to consider sacking the generals.[76]

The crisis between Wilhelm II's civil and military servants developed with full force early in July. The *Osterbotschaft* of 7 April 1917 promising an alteration of the Prussian franchise after the end of the war had proved insufficient to satisfy the increasing demands in the Reichstag for an *immediate* introduction of this reform. Bethmann concluded that to maintain political order, the Kaiser would have to issue such a decree at once, noting that he had never seen the Reichstag so roiled. On 5 July he asked Valentini, the chief of the Civil Cabinet, to tell Wilhelm that he must receive the parliamentary deputies and so inform them.[77] Hindenburg learned of this and was determined to stop the chancellor. He shared the Prussian aristocracy's disdain for parliamentary liberalism, and he was alarmed by the electrifying speech made before the Reichstag on 6 April by the Catholic Center deputy, Matthias Erzberger, who proposed for debate a "Peace Resolution" (*Friedensresolution*) calling for an end to war without annexations. This would become the subject of intense discussion in the course of the next several months. On 7 July, as Wilhelm II was en route from Vienna to Berlin to try to deal with the crisis, Hindenburg and Ludendorff left their headquarters at Pless to come to the capital to demand Bethmann's dismissal. They believed that a more conservative chancellor would be able to prevent the resolution from being adopted.[78] The chancellor was very annoyed, insisting that this was a political matter and therefore one in which the two generals had no right to intervene. Bethmann obtained the Kaiser's backing for this, and Wilhelm informed Hindenburg and Ludendorff that parliamentary affairs were not their business and indicated that they were to return at once to the front, which they did.[79]

Wilhelm realized that he was caught in a difficult position. He was attached to Bethmann, acknowledging that even the chancellor's ponderous manner, although admittedly irritating, was a mark of thoroughness. In any case, the Kaiser had no notion of who might succeed as chancellor. A general, for reasons Wilhelm did not divulge, was out of the question at this juncture, and in spite of entreaties, he absolutely refused to entertain any thought of Bülow's return to the office or of Admiral Tirpitz's appointment, both of whom had many advocates.[80] Bethmann would stay in office, and the Kaiser declared to the Bavarian envoy in Berlin, Count Hugo Lerchenfeld-Koefering, that he would have to inform the Reichstag that Erzberger's resolution was unacceptable. As for constitutional reform in Prussia, Wilhelm had no intention of allowing any changes until *after* the war was over and even then something that ideally might mark a retreat from the undesirable uniform, equal franchise promised in the "Easter Tidings."[81]

On 9 July, Wilhelm presided over a meeting, with Bethmann and all the imperial state secretaries and Prussian ministers in attendance, that dealt with the Prussian franchise and lasted for almost four hours.[82] After a dramatic debate, the officials were informally polled, and a majority sustained Bethmann's insistence on the immediate introduction of parliamentary reform in Prussia. At the conclusion of the meeting Wilhelm declared that he wanted to discuss the matter with the crown prince. His son and heir, who resented that Bethmann did not permit him to play a more influential role in politics, incongruously combined a preference for the bellicose Tirpitz as chancellor with an insistence that Germany sue for peace before the end of 1917.[83] The Kaiser informed the prince that a conclusion to the war would come only through a defeat of Germany's enemies on the battlefield but that Tirpitz, in spite of his extraordinary bellicosity, was impossible as chancellor. Little as the crown prince liked Bethmann, the Kaiser's son agreed that an immediate alteration of the Prussian franchise was necessary. This was most unwelcome to Wilhelm, but his son's opinion convinced him that change must come. He therefore announced on 11 July that a bill calling for an equal franchise would be laid before the lower house of the Prussian parliament in the near future. Now, the Kaiser believed, Bethmann's retention in office was secured.[84] Those state secretaries and ministers present at the 9 July meeting who had been in opposition submitted their resignations, holding that the Kaiser's decision had damaged the crown's prestige.

Although Bethmann had prevailed, he believed nonetheless that his position as chancellor was untenable, and he said so to the Kaiser on 10 July.[85] He had too many enemies among the conservative factions in the Reichstag, but it was the opposition of Hindenburg and Ludendorff, as Bethmann himself had long ago predicted, that was the insuperable difficulty. He therefore suggested to Wilhelm that the Kaiser appoint a new chancellor, but Wilhelm, backed by the crown prince, declined in spite of the fact that the Kaiserin had made an enormous scene, one that raged throughout the night, trying to persuade her husband to do otherwise.[86] He recognized that retaining Bethmann in the face of the chancellor's many foes would not be easy, but he was determined, whatever the cost, to do so.[87] The Kaiser soon discovered, however, that Bethmann's retention was in fact impossible. Just before 8 P.M. on 12 July, a telegram arrived from Hindenburg and Ludendorff announcing that they would no longer work with the chancellor and therefore were both in the process of writing letters of resignation. Wilhelm was enraged that his generals would place him in such a predicament, one that was quite unprecedented, for it seemed that the military was now moving to deprive him of his last shred of authority. He assured Bethmann of his support and declared that he would see Hindenburg and take care of the matter. But the field marshal, who came to Berlin on 13 July, was immovable, and Wilhelm capitulated.

"Now I can just abdicate," he dejectedly told the chancellor.[88] The German people would not tolerate the firing of the generals, but Bethmann, bereft of support in the Reichstag, was, as the Kaiser put it in a military metaphor, "a commander without troops."[89] Wilhelm got no argument from Bethmann, who realized that the hour for his departure had come. The Kaiser might decline the generals' resignations, as indeed he had to do because of the exigencies of war, but that would change nothing about the chancellor's inability to work with them, and they with him.[90]

"I have had to dismiss the very man who towers by heads over all the others," Wilhelm lamented on being forced to let Bethmann go.[91] The problem that had troubled Wilhelm for some time now became acute. If the chancellor went, and that was now inevitable, who could be found to replace him? The answer was not Tirpitz and was not Bülow, the one too reactionary and the other too untrustworthy. Hindenburg and Ludendorff, both of whom had their eye on either the Catholic General Max von Gallwitz or General Hermann von Stein, Prussian minister of war, indicated that they wanted a fellow officer as chancellor, but Wilhelm was opposed to a military figure.[92] In his letter of resignation, submitted to Wilhelm on 13 July, Bethmann had suggested the Catholic Bavarian minister-president, Count Georg von Hertling, who was in his seventies but nevertheless reasonably energetic, moderate in outlook, and generally popular not only in Germany but in Austria as well. Hertling, however, declined to be considered, citing his age and his disapproval of Hindenburg and Ludendorff's extensive war aims.[93] Bethmann then suggested Count Johann-Heinrich Bernstorff, until February 1917 the German ambassador in Washington. Wilhelm rejected this idea and told Valentini to ask Hindenburg whom he would recommend, but Valentini succeeded in convincing the Kaiser that it would be more suitable to deal with General Lyncker, the chief of the Military Cabinet. Valentini met with Lyncker and General Plessen, Wilhelm II's favorite among his military adjutants, and either Valentini or Plessen came up with the name of Georg Michaelis. This virtually unknown Prussian bureaucrat was in charge of provisioning both the army and the civilian population and in that capacity had recently been at supreme headquarters.[94] Baron Magnus von Braun, a junior official in the imperial Interior Ministry, had meanwhile suggested to Hindenburg and Ludendorff that Michaelis, who had impressed both officers, possessed sufficient decisiveness and optimism to be a suitable chancellor.[95] Hindenburg and the quartermaster general, perhaps delighted at the prospect of being able to dominate an inexperienced nonentity, agreed at once.

What led Valentini or Plessen or Braun to recommend Michaelis was certainly not his appearance or his bearing, neither of which could possibly attract a following, or his experience in diplomacy, which was nonexistent. What registered in Michaelis's favor was his skill in administration and his character, for he was known to be a person of great probity and profound religious beliefs.[96] It may be that the Kaiserin had a hand in the appointment, for she had dealt with Michaelis for many years in church affairs and admired his Moravian piety. She would be fiercely attached to him throughout his brief chancellorship.[97] Wilhelm had never met the man who was now to be foisted on him as his chancellor, and he was astonished that Bethmann's successor should be such an unknown and insignificant figure. The Kaiser received Michaelis gracelessly and invested him with the office.[98] On longer acquaintance, Michaelis would please Wilhelm greatly, and it is an illustration of the Kaiser's insignificance in the last year of Germany's war that the man whom he said he liked better than any of his other chancellors (except Bethmann) would inhabit the office barely three and a half months.[99] Bethmann's resignation, dictated by the army with little attention to Wilhelm's feelings and with virtually no acknowledgment of his prerogative, was the abdication in principle that would occur in fact in November 1918.

Twelve

MICHAELIS AND HERTLING:

THE SCARED RABBIT AND THE

WORN-OUT PROFESSOR

THE KAISER'S appointment of Georg Michaelis as chancellor at a desperate juncture in the war took Germany by surprise, since he was an unknown chosen for inscrutable reasons. The new chancellor was, to be sure, a man of great seriousness and considerable energy; he had a likable disposition and vast confidence that God would show him the way in which Germany was to be led. The choice, however astounding, did not prevent Michaelis's being at once desperately hailed as the German version of David Lloyd George, the dynamic prime minister who had taken office in December 1916 and then infused extraordinary determination into the British war effort.[1] Michaelis was in fact quite unlike Lloyd George, for he entirely lacked the charisma (and also the arrogance and immorality) that characterized the British premier. He could certainly advance no claim on the basis of experience, whereas Lloyd George had held a number of preeminent cabinet posts during his long service as a member of Parliament. Michaelis knew nothing of foreign affairs and little of warfare, all of which indicated that rather than being the prime minister's equal, he would in fact be General Paul von Beneckendorff und von Hindenburg and General Erich Ludendorff's puppet. On the day that he assumed office, the new chancellor, outfitted in a military uniform, admitted his lack of preparation to a group of Reichstag deputies: "I have tried to keep myself informed only as a newspaper reader might."[2] A week after Michaelis's appointment, General Hans von Beseler, the governor of Warsaw, spent two and a half hours with him at the eastern front headquarters at Pless and later declared that the new chancellor was "a little, insecure scared rabbit," in whom Beseler could not "detect the savior of the fatherland."[3] While at Pless, Michaelis did not demand that he be fully oriented about the strategic situation in order to be able to make his own conclusions, for he said that he intended to leave all military decisions in Hindenburg's hands.[4] The chancellor, like the Conservative Party to which he had many ties, was known to be a firm proponent of the field marshal's view that the war was being fought to be won and not to be bargained away through ill-advised peace negotiations.[5]

From the outset of his chancellorship, Michaelis and the Reichstag were set against one another. Parliament was shocked at his appointment and resentful that it had not been consulted. One deputy, on learning that Michaelis had succeeded Chancellor Theobald von Bethmann Hollweg, was certain that he had not correctly heard the name of the new chancellor.[6] Michaelis had never served in any parliament, and he believed that in time of war it was inadvisable to involve the Reichstag in state affairs, since to do so would make the conduct of business unmanageable and rob it of secrecy.[7] Government was the business of the chancellor, the General Staff, and the Kaiser, and he was determined to resist the Reichstag's "power hunger" (*Machthunger*).[8] The chancellor's tone toward Parliament, which he refused to take into his confidence, was Olympian, and almost at once he provided the chamber with a taste of his independent streak. On 19 July 1917, five days into his chancellorship, the Reichstag approved with a sound majority the "Peace Resolution" sponsored by Matthias Erzberger of the Catholic Center. The vaguely worded resolution called for a "peace of understanding," with no "forced territorial acquisitions," no economic penalties, freedom of the seas, and the rule of international law. Erzberger had discussed the wording of the text with Michaelis, who had indicated, although with reluctance, that he would support the resolution.[9] The chancellor, in his maiden speech to the chamber, nevertheless failed to give his support to the resolution but rather declared that the peace for which he would work was "attainable within the limits" of the resolution as he understood it, at which point he was interrupted by catcalls. The qualification "as I understand it" (*so wie ich sie auffasse*) seemed quite plainly to indicate that Michaelis did not consider himself bound by the language of the resolution and that, having been appointed to his post independent of the chamber, he would act as chancellor without its approval. From that moment on, Michaelis lost the confidence of the Reichstag, and speculation began as to who might replace him.[10]

Michaelis was by his own admission against the idea of a negotiated peace, and a few days after taking office he turned aside the pleas of Prince Hohenlohe, the Austro-Hungarian envoy in Berlin, who argued that the war must be concluded before the winter of 1917–18 if both the Habsburg and the Hohenzollern Empires were to avoid collapse.[11] To the chancellor, Erzberger's resolution resonated weakness, and he therefore was determined to circumvent it. He privately boasted that he would use the "notorious" document "to conclude any peace" he liked.[12] Michaelis's opposition to the Peace Resolution was directed less at its content, for like Erzberger, the chancellor disclaimed annexations, than at its implication that the Reichstag had the right to exert a role in diplomacy. Although Admiral Alfred von Tirpitz had founded a *Vaterlandspartei* to protest the Peace Resolution and call for the retention of the Channel coast and the areas of France and Belgium that were rich in coal and iron, Michaelis did not envision the permanent acquisition of land in this area but insisted, as had the Kaiser, that France and Belgium be required to subordinate their postwar economies to that of Germany. To effect this would mean holding only Liège and its industrial environs.[13]

The state secretary of the imperial Interior Office, Karl Helfferich, arranged for the Reichstag deputies, along with the state secretaries and Prussian ministers, to come to his official residence on 20 July to confer with Wilhelm II in the hope that this might foster better relations between the sovereign and Parliament. The deputies were in a truculent mood because the Reichstag had not been consulted in the choice of the new chancellor.[14] Erzberger in particular was angry, for on Hindenburg's orders the government had refused him a passport in order to curtail his speech-making in favor of a negotiated peace. Wilhelm was in no better frame of mind about the encounter, especially as far as Erzberger was concerned. Erzberger, condemned to begin with as a Catholic, had had the temerity to send an unsolicited letter to the Kaiserin, something that marked him as a "shameless fellow" (*unverschämter Kerl*). Although the Centrist leader was particularly objectionable, the entire Parliament was unpalatable to the Kaiser. "You Reichstag deputies are all wild men," he would tell a member later in the year, "and you don't even realize that there's a war on."[15] Like the chancellor, Wilhelm found the Peace Resolution quite deplorable, for the language adopted by Erzberger, who as a parliamentary deputy had no business meddling in diplomacy, made Germany seem weak when in fact the military situation in the summer of 1917, if short of victory on all fronts, was generally favorable.[16] He fulminated that once the Iron Cross–bedecked German soldiers returned home, they would know what to do with the Reichstag that had tried to force their Kaiser into a corner.[17]

The meeting, designed to promote reconciliation between crown and

Parliament, had precisely the opposite effect.[18] The Kaiser, resplendent in his guards uniform, spoke at some length, declaring that *he* sought not a "peace of understanding" as prescribed in the Peace Resolution but rather a "peace of compensation" (*Ausgleich*), Ludendorff's phrase for the delivery of those territories that Germany would receive as tribute from its defeated enemies. One of these foes was Rumania, which the Kaiser proposed to punish by rerouting the Danube. Turning to the western theater, he declared that although the British had not been brought to their knees, the eastern coast of England was nothing but a junkyard of sunken ships. German submarines would soon cause the British to make peace. Then one day he would fight a "second Punic War" against the British, a war that would as surely destroy them as thoroughly as Rome's legions had laid waste to Hannibal's Africa.[19] Speaking about a recent victory by the Prussian army against Alexander Kerensky's Russian republican force, the Kaiser also indicated his contempt for any sort of political liberalism: "Where the Garde marches, there is no democracy." The great triumphs of the army carried out by Hindenburg and Ludendorff, he boasted to Erzberger later on the same day, were due to the generals' utilization of campaign plans that he himself had drawn up.[20] When the inflated peroration came to an end, Wilhelm was certain that he had made a "great success" with the deputies, but almost all of them were in fact at first shocked and then horrified at the utter lack of reason or reality in his notions about peace. As one unidentified parliamentarian left Helfferich's residence he was heard to say, "Now finally we are convinced of the need of a parliamentary regime."[21] When other deputies who had not been present were told what the Kaiser had said they either wept or concluded that he must be insane.[22] It was altogether an unsettling performance by a sovereign whose erratic behavior had prompted Crown Prince Rupprecht of Bavaria to declare, only the day before Wilhelm's reception of the deputies, that reasonable men were becoming afraid that under such a ruler the Hohenzollern dynasty could not endure.[23]

Even though the Kaiser had contempt for the defeatist tone of the Peace Resolution passed by the Reichstag in July 1917, he was annoyed that the Allied powers, whose armies were then engaged in making a vain attempt to puncture the Hindenburg Line, made no response to the resolution. He was convinced that Great Britain was collapsing under the burden of Germany's resistance in the trenches and the U-boat campaign in the Atlantic at the moment reaching the apogee of its success. To Wilhelm the fierce and ultimately unsuccessful effort that the British were then conducting near Ypres was proof of the sense of desperation that affected the enemy. But at the same time he was concerned that once the United States began to send troops to France, it might be the Germans, and not the British, who would bleed to death.[24] Some additional initiative had to be taken to rekindle peace negotiations, and the Kaiser believed that the Vatican might serve as an intermediary with the Allies. At the end of July 1917, Wilhelm met with the papal legate to Germany, Eugenio Cardinal Pacelli, to whom in the past the Kaiser had showed marked attention, bestowing decorations on the prelate and granting him the use of a private railroad car. Wilhelm complained that since the enemy had rejected the Reichstag's peace feelers, he had no choice but to fight.[25] With President Woodrow Wilson, now at war with Germany, eliminated as a negotiator, it seemed to the Kaiser that only the Social Democrats of Europe, who were then holding an international convention in neutral Stockholm, were engaged in the peace movement. It was highly undesirable, however, that Socialists should get credit should an end to hostilities come about, so he urged Cardinal Pacelli to have Pope Benedict XV seize the initiative. "If the church forfeits the opportunity to negotiate a peace," the Kaiser had earlier informed Pacelli, "it will hurt itself and smooth the path for socialism."[26] Pacelli's assurances that England was interested in peace were clearly a sign that London knew it could not win the war. There was also the collapse of London's ally, imperial Russia, the dissatisfaction of the British working class, and the crop failures in both England and the United States in 1917. Besides, the British were alarmed that the longer the war went on, the greater was the danger that they might one day become dependent on America. This meant that Germany must adopt a resolute attitude toward the prospect of negotiations and have a firm notion of what, if anything, it expected to gain from Belgium.[27] There could be no talk of disarmament, Wilhelm declared, for no Prussian king or German kaiser could make such a concession.[28]

On 1 August 1917, the pontiff, responding to Wilhelm II's initiative, issued an appeal to the belligerents to agree to a peace that would restore all occupied territory, regard the future status of Alsace-Lorraine as a question subject to negotiation, renounce all indemnities, and institute a program of disarmament. The pope's peace offer launched days of tempestuous debate in the Reichstag. Wilhelm, who spent the summer traveling between the fronts, had little to do with the crisis in Berlin.[29] Michaelis found himself poised between the annexationist extremists, such as the crown prince, Tirpitz and his *Vaterlandspartei*, Hindenburg, and Ludendorff, and on the other side the Reichstag majority, supported by various figures in the Kaiser's retinue, notably Rudolf von Valentini, who were all prepared to accept a peace that returned Germany to the status quo existing before the war. The Kaiser informed Michaelis, who was at work on a response to the pope's appeal for peace, that ideally Germany would like to retain a significant portion of the Belgian coast. To do so, however, would only provoke insuperable problems with discontented Walloons and Catholic clergy, a point on which Felix Cardinal von Hartmann of Cologne had convinced him. Wilhelm was therefore prepared to reduce his Belgian claims to the single port of Zeebrugge.[30] Insisting on the retention of this fine harbor would appease the navy and prevent Tirpitz from claiming that the Kaiser was insufficiently resolute. The port would provide Germany with a useful point on the Channel from which to launch the "second Punic War" on which he so often dwelled. This conflict would require naval bases outside of Germany, not only Zeebrugge but also a Mediterranean outpost perhaps at Valona in Albania or at Corfu off the western coast of Greece. Coexistence with Britain was an impossibility, and there could be no peace in Europe until Germany and Britain had settled scores and one emerged the victor, just as in the 1860s no peace had been possible for the Germans until Prussia and Austria had dealt with one another by the sword.

To determine exactly how Michaelis should respond to the pope, Wilhelm summoned a crown council in Berlin on 11 September.[31] The debate was acrimonious, with both Michaelis and Richard von Kühlmann, who a month earlier had succeeded Arthur Zimmermann as state secretary of the Foreign Office, arguing that the Flanders coast must be jettisoned in order to secure peace. Ludendorff, however, insisted on the retention of the littoral as well as Liège, and Admiral Henning von Holtzendorff, the chief of the Admiralty Staff, was equally determined to see Germany have access to the channel. Wilhelm sided with his civilian advisers but noted that if Belgium remained intact, it would have to be in such a way as to guarantee that Germany would be paramount and the British without influence. If peace had not been concluded by the end of 1917, he would insist that the Belgian question be raised for renewed discussion. As for Alsace-Lorraine, the French insistence that both provinces be returned to it was a demand to which no German would ever submit. The response to the pope, an answer that Michaelis issued in Wilhelm II's name on 13 September 1917, provided no specific demands regarding Belgium and had nothing whatsoever to say about Alsace-Lorraine. There were instead only anodyne assurances that Germany was committed to a postwar Europe based not on strength but on morality.[32] The Fatherland would have to have "certain securities" (*gewisse Sicherheiten*) and "satisfactory conditions for existence" (*befriedigende Daseinsbedingungen*) for its future. "The imperial government," the answer read, "will support any proposal that is compatible with the vital interests of the German Empire and its people." That ambiguous response brought Benedict XV's efforts to an end.

The failure of the Michaelis government to support Erzberger's Peace Resolution or to respond more positively to the pope's efforts to encourage negotiation did nothing to improve the chancellor's already minimal popularity in the war-weary Reichstag. The chancellor's reputation for handling internal affairs was no more satisfactory to the deputies, for he had shown no interest in bringing the government into closer connection with Parliament even though he had appointed to cabinet posts several deputies or bureaucrats with close party ties. There was dissatisfaction that his preparations for a bill providing for a change in the Prussian franchise were moving too slowly, an objection that was true enough, since the chancellor was in fact opposed to this reform. Like Bethmann before him, Michaelis was also reproached for having failed to achieve any significant breakthrough in the military situation in the west.[33]

Early in October 1917, before his third month in office had been completed, Michaelis precipitated an additional crisis in his relationship with the Reichstag when the government imposed death sentences or long imprisonment terms on a number of sailors who had unsuccessfully attempted to promote revolution in the navy. In a speech on 9 October, the chancellor defended the sentences and suggested that Reichstag deputies from the pacifistic Independent Socialist faction had been involved in the matter. Admiral Eduard von Capelle, the state secretary of the Imperial Naval Office, was the next speaker, and abandoning all caution, he specifically identified three members of Parliament as coconspirators. That was too much for the Reichstag, which now closed ranks (except for the far Right) to denounce Michaelis and Capelle. The outburst culminated when Friedrich Ebert, the leader of the Majority Socialists, rose and declared that his party, the largest in the chamber, had no confidence in the chancellor and that the sooner Wilhelm dismissed Michaelis the better.[34] The Kaiser learned of this parliamentary insurrection while traveling in Bulgaria, where he was visiting his ally Tsar Ferdinand en route to Turkey to discuss military operations there with his generals. Wilhelm's reaction reflected the disdain he had always felt for the deputies. He told his confidant, Admiral Georg von Müller, on 9 October: "The Reichstag can do what it wants, it's all the same to me. I have the people and the army behind me, and Michaelis has the revolver, an order to dissolve the chamber, in his pocket."[35]

By the time Wilhelm returned to Berlin on 21 October, the chancellor's parliamentary position was utterly destroyed. Michaelis was prepared to resign should Wilhelm desire him to do so, but he seemed to think that he could nevertheless deal with the situation.[36] The Kaiser insisted that Michaelis remain in office and refused to accept the resignation of Admiral Capelle, both men continuing to be the object of vituperation by the Reichstag. The Kaiserin, always an influence on her consort in moments of crisis, urged Wilhelm to keep Michaelis no matter how great the price, and until the very end of the month Wilhelm resolutely intended to do so.[37] The only way to save the chancellor would be to dissolve Parliament, but this was an impossibility in time of war, for to do so would advertise the confusion that reigned in Berlin. The parties controlling a majority of the deputies had on 22 October agreed not only that Michaelis was to be dismissed at once but also that any prospective successor must give Parliament assurances that he supported the Peace Resolution unconditionally, not with Michaelis's reservation: "as I understand it." A deputation was sent to the palace to ask that Wilhelm be informed of this stand. It did not matter so much to the deputies *who* the new chancellor was, and they were prepared to leave the choice to the Kaiser provided that it was not the unpopular Helfferich.[38]

For several days the Kaiser dallied, avoiding a decision and instead busying himself with looking at films of his recent trip to Istanbul and entertaining various guests with graphic descriptions of the successful campaign being waged by German troops in Italy.[39] Among the many names that were proffered to Wilhelm, he rigorously excluded Bernhard von Bülow, for the former chancellor was still in 1917 unforgiven for having abandoned the Kaiser during the *Daily Telegraph* crisis nine years earlier, especially since the Kaiser knew that Erzberger and many other deputies preferred the former chancellor.[40] Count Georg von Hertling, the septuagenarian minister-president of Bavaria, was frequently mentioned, but he had already, on Bethmann's resignation in July 1917, declined to be considered for the chancellorship. Hertling recognized that, as a Roman Catholic and south German, he would encounter great difficulties in Berlin, but his real reservation was his realization that Hindenburg and Ludendorff would continue to intrude themselves into political decisions. That he was not prepared to accept. Wilhelm meanwhile attempted to salvage the situation by accepting Michaelis's proposal that he surrender the chancellorship but continue to serve as Prussian minister-president. Neither the Reichstag nor Hertling would agree to such a scheme.[41] The idea of appointing a Bavarian to serve both as chancellor and as minister-president of Prussia was distasteful to Wilhelm, and he considered all other available candidates.[42] In the end, however, a small band of Prussian advisers to whom he was very attached convinced him that Hertling was the only possible choice. This group included no parliamentarians other than Karl Helfferich, the member of the Reichstag probably most disliked by his brethren, and its leaders were Valentini, Paul von Breitenbach, minister for public works, and Count August zu Eulenburg, the minister of the royal household.[43]

Hertling had no desire to become chancellor, for he was old, almost legally blind, and very attached to Bavaria. He was in his own words "an old, worn-out philosophy professor."[44] To him, Berlin was a distasteful "witches' cauldron" (*Hexenkessel*), and he much disliked the way in which Wilhelm disdained Bavaria and its Wittelsbach dynasty.[45] Only a sense of duty led Hertling to accept, but on Helfferich's urging, he let it be known that he would want time to consider the appointment and to consult the party leaders to determine if they could agree on the policies that he, as chancellor, would be prepared to carry out. Hertling therefore came to Berlin to discuss his ideas with various deputies and government officials, leading the former to believe that should he become chancellor, he would represent, as Michaelis had utterly failed to do, the wishes of the Reichstag majority.[46] Satisfied with this negotiation and having received assurances from the Kaiser that Hindenburg and Ludendorff would refrain from interfering in political matters, Hertling accepted the appointment and took office on 1 November 1917.[47]

The aged aristocrat was in some respects a sensible choice, for he possessed the parliamentary connections and political experience that had been so singularly lacking in Michaelis. Hertling's appointment would have the advantage of calming the Reichstag, where he had served as a deputy for over thirty years, briefly as head of the Catholic Center faction. He had left the legislature in 1912 to go to Munich as minister-president, and in that capacity he had chaired the committee on foreign policy in the upper house of the imperial Parliament (*Bundesrat*). Moreover, Hertling's south German and Catholic identity, although perhaps unwelcome to Wilhelm II, would constitute an asset in dealing with Germany's Austrian ally, and at the same time his moderation and distinction would make a favorable opinion elsewhere in Europe.[48] Hertling was genuinely admired for his unquestioned probity and Christian earnestness, qualities that Michaelis had also possessed but that in Hertling were reinforced by the patina of age, the distinction of a long career, and a title of antiquity. He was an intellectual of some distinction, a doctor of philosophy who for many years had lectured on logic at the university in Munich. At the same time, the aged chancellor had to overcome the fact that as a Bavarian Catholic, he would be regarded in Berlin as an outsider; he seemed to be too old, blind, tired, and irenic by nature to be capable of entering effectively into contests with his younger opponents or even of managing the daily affairs of government. Hertling himself recognized his limitations. "To make an old professor like me chancellor in such an unspeakably difficult moment," he told a young friend, "is the worst thing one can do."[49] He had a tendency that was odd in time of war to seclude himself in order to read Thomas Aquinas and to rest, cleaving to his rule that evenings were not for working but for playing bridge. In the summer of 1918, as the war was at its most critical juncture, Hertling left Berlin for army headquarters on the western front in order, he said, that he might there (of all places) find an opportunity to relax.[50]

Like Michaelis, Hertling had the advantage of being thoroughly in Wilhelm II's graces. Throughout the year that Hertling served as chancellor, their relations were remarkably cordial, the Kaiser always striving to treat his elderly servant with consideration and Hertling, in return, concocting letters that were lavish with courtly folderol.[51] The new chancellor had an accommodating personality, which helped to avoid any conflicts with the Kaiser, and in any case there was little in his notions about war and peace that differed from Wilhelm's own ideas. In late October 1917, as Hertling took office, both were optimistic.[52] The Kaiser's armies had recently taken Riga and had won decisive victories against the Italians along the Isonzo River. In Russia, Germany's prospects had risen considerably when, in November 1917, the moderate socialist government of Kerensky, who had kept Russia in the war, fell, in a second revolution, to the Bolsheviks under Vladimir Lenin. The new leader's slogan was "peace, bread, and land," and within little more than a month he entered into an armistice with Germany and Austria-Hungary. Peace negotiations with Russia would soon be under way, and in the west the Allied attempt to push back the German line had been abandoned. The only ominous note was the failure of the unrestricted submarine warfare campaign begun in February 1917 to cripple the Allies. Throughout the summer the U-boats had had spectacular success, giving rise to hopes that Britain might in fact be forced to sue for peace. By the fall of 1917, however, the British and Americans had developed a convoy system that offered adequate defense against German submarines, and the number of Allied ships torpedoed began to fall drastically. The ultimate weapon had failed.

On domestic issues, Hertling and the Kaiser were reasonably close in attitude, for the chancellor no less than Wilhelm was an opponent of a parliamentary regime. Although Hertling recognized that a chancellor could not function successfully unless he commanded a majority in the chamber, he ideally preferred for Germany to exist as an enlightened absolutism. "Parliament is a device," Hertling once told his son, "designed to deal in the most difficult manner with the things that are the most simple in the life of a state."[53] But Wilhelm II did not possess the requisite talents to rule as the chancellor might have wanted, and even in small matters he showed an unsettling indifference to the sufferings of his people, eating reasonably well as they were subjected to increasing privation and burning up coal so that the royal train could take him to visit relatives. Although the German people gladly entrusted military decisions to Hindenburg and Ludendorff, by the time Hertling came to office the Reichstag, not the Kaiser or his government, was widely regarded as the defender of the national interest as far as political matters were concerned. Michaelis's fall from office had been due, for the first time in the history of the empire, not to a withdrawal of the Kaiser's confidence but to the chancellor's inability to satisfy Parliament. Whether Hertling, or Wilhelm, liked it or not, the new chancellor would have to do better than Michaelis in devising a way to deal with the Reichstag.

Although the chancellor did not much care for parliamentary monarchy and although the Reichstag resented not having been formally consulted in his nomination, they managed to get on remarkably well until the very end of Hertling's administration, which lasted just short of a year. Hertling consolidated his following among the deputies in the first few weeks of his chancellorship by dismissing the despised Helfferich as vice-chancellor and replacing him, to the Kaiserin's horror, with the popular Friedrich von Payer, who represented the Progressive Party in the Reichstag.[54] He also made Robert Friedberg, leader of the National Liberals in the Prussian lower house, deputy minister-president of Prussia, a move that, according to Valentini, had the effect of "winning over" the chamber. Thereafter, the chancellor was careful to receive parliamentarians very frequently at his official residence in the Wilhelmstrasse, which consequently lost much of the remoteness it had had under his predecessors. The deputies, emboldened by the novel attention they were accorded by the head of the government, now had the temerity to expect the same reception at court. The fastidious Valentini, whose Civil Cabinet handled access to the Kaiser, found any thought of trafficking with legislators quite distasteful, and few ever obtained audiences.[55]

The chancellor's nemesis was not the Reichstag but the Supreme Army Command (*Oberste Heeresleitung*, OHL) under Hindenburg and Ludendorff. Hertling had made it clear to Wilhelm II in July 1917, when he was being considered as successor to Bethmann, that he would not be the generals' puppet.[56] At the beginning of his chancellorship, he had secured the Kaiser's agreement to a regulation that prescribed how affairs of state would be conducted.[57] The OHL had the right to be consulted in political affairs, but if a decision by the government went against its wishes, it was to be required to accept the decision, for the chancellor, and no one else, was responsible for German policy. The OHL reluctantly accepted this limitation of its authority and then at once proceeded to attempt to negate the agreement. The problem was not Hindenburg but rather Ludendorff, who more and more towered over the field marshal and, unlike Hindenburg, believed that his responsibility embraced politics as well as war. Hertling, who had amicable relations with Hindenburg, disliked Ludendorff and therefore, like the Kaiser, avoided him whenever possible, a neglect that the quartermaster general found offensive.[58]

The quarrels between Hertling and Ludendorff were endemic, and they extended to several of the leading officials in the government and at court. Ludendorff relished expressing his violent dislike, and his malediction fell principally on two men, one Wilhelm's most trusted adviser and the other Hertling's most important subordinate, both of whom the general blamed for Germany's many problems. These two were Valentini, chief of the Civil Cabinet since 1908, and Kühlmann, the state secretary of the Foreign Office. Kühlmann was a rather arch and prideful diplomat who relished being called "the man in the iron mask." He got on well with the Kaiser, whom he once during the war oddly referred to as "the only wise man in all of Germany."[59] Kühlmann, like Hertling, thought Ludendorff an untutored oaf, incapable of seeing any issue except as a problem of military command, a man who lacked any cosmopolitan experience or breadth of learning but who nevertheless believed he should dominate German policy.[60] Since Hertling gave Kühlmann free rein in foreign affairs, Ludendorff identified him as the source of Germany's troublesome diplomatic situation everywhere in Europe.

The general's venom toward Russia concerned the peace negotiations at Brest-Litovsk in Russian Poland between Kühlmann and Lev Trotsky, the Bolshevik commissar of Foreign Affairs whom Lenin had deputized to negotiate Russia's exit from the war. Trotsky cleverly manufactured arguments designed to lengthen the discussions in the hope that, with time, Russia could create a successful revolutionary movement in Germany. This casuistry, however, did not intimidate Kühlmann, who realized that Bolshevik rhetoric could not conceal the utter collapse of Russia's military capability. Germany could therefore demand what it wanted and await Lenin's inevitable agreement to its terms. Ludendorff, on the other hand, had his own notion as to how Germany should deal with Russia. He was always intemperate in the face of opposition and therefore had no patience with Trotsky. Ludendorff was ready to abandon the Russo-German armistice reached in December 1917, seize European Russia, and annex much of the rest of the Continent, east and west.[61]

Like Ludendorff, Wilhelm was not satisfied with the way in which Kühlmann was conducting the negotiations with the Russians, and he eventually lost his patience with Trotsky, a Jew whom he identified as part of an international Hebraic conspiracy. The only way to deal with such a man was with the sword, and in late February 1918 the Kaiser, undoubtedly influenced by his ardently anti-Bolshevik wife, consented to a resumption of hostilities. The Bolsheviks, he declared, had to be trapped like a tiger flushed out of the jungle.[62] A strikingly successful assault by the German army ensued, and within ten days Trotsky had been forced back to the negotiating table. The victorious campaign in the east, swifter and more extensive than anyone had believed possible, ensured that within a matter of days or weeks, peace would be signed and Russia driven out of the war. That in turn would mean that hundreds of thousands of troops in the east could be diverted to the western front to prepare for a great campaign against the Allies in the spring of 1918. In February of that year, as German soldiers streamed into the grain-rich Ukraine, even those deputies in the Reichstag who had seven months earlier endorsed the Peace Resolution now began to waver in their opposition to an annexationist peace.

The Brest-Litovsk negotiations raised the question of what intentions Germany had in Poland and in the Baltic. Hindenburg and Ludendorff, mired at the moment in one war but full of apocalyptic visions of others the Fatherland might someday face, were insistent that Germany acquire formerly Romanov territory in the east that would offer adequate protection in a future conflict. They proposed extensive territorial annexations that would have added several million Slavs to Germany's population in order to create a "protective belt" against any enemy that in years to come might attack the Fatherland from the east. Kühlmann, who had Hertling's full support, believed that the acquisition of Polish territory would only weaken Germany, for the Poles were increasingly resentful because of the economic decline and regimentation that had characterized the German occupation that began late in 1914. They would be restless, disloyal, and a burden rather than an asset, and Kühlmann therefore insisted that the "protective belt" for which Ludendorff argued should be much reduced.[63]

General Max Hoffmann, a conspicuous opponent of Ludendorff and Hindenburg's who served as head of *Oberost*, the German command responsible for Polish territory, supported Kühlmann, arguing that Germany had enough problems with the one million Poles among the Kaiser's prewar subjects and that to add still more by agreeing to Ludendorff's annexationist proposals would be folly.[64] Wilhelm had a high opinion of General Hoffmann, whom he called "the best expert on the eastern question," and he agreed with Hoffmann and Kühlmann that the generals' plan for bringing more Poles into Germany was foolish.[65] In his quarrel with Hindenburg and Ludendorff on the question of eastern war aims, Kühlmann had the support of Count Ottokar Czernin, the Habsburg foreign minister, who was insistent that peace be negotiated before the Dual Monarchy collapsed. That meant not offending the Allies by claiming vast reaches of territory in central Europe and Russia, and both diplomats therefore favored creating an independent Polish kingdom that would be closely tied to both Germany and Austria-Hungary.[66]

The Kaiser had no desire for Poland, a people for whom he had always expressed an intense dislike. He was convinced that he had tried in vain to win over his Polish subjects living in Prussia, but they, like the British, had refused his entreaties. The "Polish danger" in Prussia's eastern provinces was a hazard no less acute than the "Yellow Peril" and no more to be tolerated.[67] Wilhelm was vigilant against any movement that he considered likely to advance Polish interests within Germany, and before the war he had favored buying out Polish proprietors and resettling their estates with Germans.[68] Ever since becoming Kaiser in 1888, Wilhelm had argued that the Polish problem could best be handled through detaching the Poles from Russia and creating an independent kingdom under a German prince. On occasion, he declared that he had no objection to letting an Austrian have the royal honor, but the Polish kingdom would have to be very strictly controlled by Germany.[69] The Baltic provinces of Lithuania, Latvia, and Estonia, which belonged to Russia but which had large numbers of Germans, were another matter. Even before the war, Wilhelm had been determined to join this area in personal union to the Hohenzollern crown. In February 1918, he rejected out of hand Hertling's suggestion that the provinces might become independent. "Nonsense!," the Kaiser wrote of the Baltic. "*I* will be its ruler and will tolerate no resistance. I have *conquered* it and no lawyer is going to take it away from me. . . . The Baltic [will be] a unit, in personal union under Prussia's king, who triumphed over it! Just as under Frid[ricus] Rex!"[70]

The tension between Kühlmann and Ludendorff over the question of eastern annexations finally became so severe that the Kaiser called a crown council to meet in Berlin on 2 January 1918.[71] Hindenburg and Ludendorff both spoke forcefully in favor of their plans, but when they had finished, Wilhelm declared in a calm and conciliatory tone that after considering both sides of the issue, he had to concur with Hoffmann rather than Ludendorff. He also indicated that he considered the OHL's objections to Kühlmann's conduct of the negotiations at Brest-Litovsk unjustified. At the conclusion of the council, Ludendorff left the room in a huff, slamming the door behind him. Hindenburg was more collected but no less annoyed that the Kaiser had preferred Hoffmann's viewpoint, which was not only a rejection of his own plans but offensive because it proceeded from a subordinate general known to be his enemy. The field marshal elected to advise the Kaiser, in writing, that in his opinion Kühlmann was bargaining away Germany's military security and thereby undermining the army's morale. He concluded with a vague hint that if he and Ludendorff did not get their way, they would resign.[72] Wilhelm had found Hindenburg and Ludendorff's truculent behavior at the crown council on 2 January very annoying, and he was determined that they be reminded that *he* was the head of Germany's military operations.[73] The Kaiser summoned Ludendorff to Berlin to meet with him and Hertling, and in the course of the discussion, the general declared that he would in fact resign unless Kühlmann was dismissed. Wilhelm rejected this out of hand, and after Ludendorff left he wrote to Hindenburg to reiterate that the military at any time had the right to express its opinions but that once the Kaiser had elected to side with Hertling and Kühlmann regarding Germany's eastern war aims, the matter was no longer subject to question.[74]

On 3 March 1918 Trotsky signed a humiliating peace treaty in Brest-Litovsk that left to Germany the fate of Poland, the Baltic states, Finland, and much of southern Russia. In fulfillment of the Kaiser's wishes, Poland was to become a monarchy, but one that existed only at Germany's sufferance. The occupation rights in the Baltic provinces granted by the treaty were to be used to force the population there to agree to a monarchy in personal union with Prussia. These provisions utterly failed to satisfy General Ludendorff, who believed that for strategic reasons Germany needed to annex large areas of Russia. He was therefore profoundly disappointed at what Kühlmann had negotiated at Brest-Litovsk and was ever more insistent that Kühlmann would have to be sacked.

Ludendorff would fail, at least for the moment, in disposing of Kühlmann, but he was more successful with his other enemy, Valentini. The campaign against Valentini, who was known in Berlin at this time as "*Ersatz Kühlmann*," was in fact carried out in compensation for not being able to get rid of Kühlmann.[75] Thoroughly conservative in attitude and unmistakably Prussian and aristocratic in behavior, Valentini had nevertheless run afoul of both Hindenburg and Ludendorff, who without foundation believed that the cabinet chief was attempting to undermine royal prerogative and turn Germany in a more democratic direction by keeping Wilhelm in the dark.[76]

Although the generals were prominent in Valentini's fall, the court played an even larger role. The Kaiserin, always a jealous partisan of her husband's authority, also believed that the leftward direction of German politics in wartime had depleted Wilhelm's dignity, something for which she too felt that Valentini, the good friend of the despised Bethmann, was responsible. "I would rather lay my head on the scaffold," Augusta Victoria proudly declared, "than to consent to any rights of the crown be diminished."[77] The crown prince, to whom Wilhelm had become more closely attached after the fall of Bethmann, was equally disenchanted, believing, like his mother, that the Civil Cabinet chief was responsible for the drift to the Left that had occurred under Bethmann. He even suspected, quite wrongly, that Valentini was trying to persuade Wilhelm to call the former chancellor back into office.[78] The matter came to a crisis in November 1917, when the Kaiserin and the crown prince demanded that Wilhelm sack Valentini, but the Kaiser emphatically refused to do so.[79] Two months later, in January 1918, Hindenburg and Ludendorff, who in their unsuccessful ambush of Kühlmann had merely intimated that they would resign if he was not fired, now baldly informed Wilhelm that unless Valentini was promptly cashiered, they would submit their resignations.[80] Hindenburg, so the Kaiser later told Valentini, had no intention of launching another major offensive against the west as long as his enemy was still at court.[81] The field marshal was not content merely to topple Valentini but also intended to dictate the replacement, and he had decided that this was to be Friedrich von Berg-Markienen. A friend of Wilhelm's from his military service when prince of Prussia at Berlin in the 1880s and one of the few men the Kaiser allowed to use the intimate *du* form of address, Berg was an unblemished reactionary very attached to both Hindenburg and Ludendorff.[82]

The demand made by the field marshal and his quartermaster was an unprecedented act, for although chancellors or generals had in the past resigned because of unresolvable differences with the sovereign, none had done so to secure the dismissal of another official. Wilhelm, who two months earlier had declared that he would not be pressured, now caved in. He was almost in tears as he dismissed Valentini on 16 January 1918, not only because he was personally attached to the cabinet chief but also because the pressure the military had brought to bear on him to renounce Valentini and to designate Berg as the successor was yet another invasion of his prerogative.[83] Berg was eager to have the position, for Berg felt Wilhelm needed to assume a more public role, to have his actions speak, at long last, as loud as his words. Berg was also inordinately jealous of any other influences on the Kaiser, and he refused to permit anyone to be in the royal presence unless he too was there.[84] In Wilhelm's opinion, it was Ludendorff who was the villain in the Valentini business, and he complained that the general had too little respect for the Kaiser. Wilhelm was not far from wrong, for Ludendorff did not hesitate to declare that what the German people (or at least those who agreed with him) thought was of more consequence to him than the Kaiser's opinion.[85] Valentini's sacking was a victory for the generals, but as Valentini himself had cautioned the crown prince a few days before his resignation, if Wilhelm let Hindenburg and Ludendorff tell the Kaiser what to do, the next installment in the dissolution of royal power would occur when the Reichstag also began to do so.[86]

With Valentini out of the way, the Kaiser was now securely in the hands of the generals, who could rely on Berg to carry out their desires. Hindenburg and Ludendorff had other enemies with whom scores were yet to be settled, especially Kühlmann and Admiral Müller, the chief of the Naval Cabinet whom they detested as defeatist. Hertling was not a problem, for he seemed to have the Reichstag well in hand, and the euphoria in Germany after the astounding Ukrainian campaign against Russia early in 1918 had deflated Parliament's enthusiasm for the fulfillment of the Peace Resolution. Hindenburg and Ludendorff had long insisted that Germany was fighting a war it expected to win, to be followed by a peace that would offer compensation for the protracted suffering of the Kaiser's subjects and that would secure for the Fatherland protection against Britain and France in the west and Russia in the east. The prosecution of the war and the arrangement of the peace required that those in Berlin who were liberals or pacifists, or who in any way lacked the army's determination to deliver victory, be eliminated from positions of influence. Bethmann had been hounded into retirement, Valentini had been dumped, and although Kühlmann and Müller would continue for some months to serve Wilhelm II, both the government and the court were by early 1918 more or less in sympathy with the army. It therefore seemed, as 1917 gave way to 1918 and winter turned to spring, that the moment had at long last arrived when Germany, freed from Russia's enmity, could place all its resources in a final, overwhelming blow against the Allied troops drawn up in their trenches in France and Belgium.

The Allies were no less determined that the contest to be fought with Germany in the devastated landscape along the western front would decide the war, for they had concluded that only military victory could force the Germans to abandon their hegemonic war aims. Early in January 1918 both the British and the Americans issued very clear statements of what they intended to exact from Germany by force of arms. Their viewpoint, summarized in President Wilson's so-called Fourteen Points, demanded the restitution of all conquered territory, the surrender to France of Alsace-Lorraine, and the dissolution of the Habsburg Empire in order to establish a number of ethnically determined states. Germany's ally would never consent to its own dismemberment, and even the most ardent advocates of the Peace Resolution of 1917 were not prepared to give up Alsace-Lorraine. As Bethmann had observed shortly before his fall, any sacrifice would be more bearable for Germany than giving up the two provinces, for their acquisition in the war against France in 1870–71 had been one of the most glorious moments in German history.[87]

The unacceptable Allied declaration instilled a greater degree of unity in the German population than had been known since the opening of the war in August 1914, and Wilhelm II stood at the head of his people in this respect. A week after Wilson's proclamation of his Fourteen Points, the Kaiser rejected any further negotiations. Queen Wilhelmina of the Netherlands had suggested that an international conference might be assembled to bring the belligerents to an agreement, but Wilhelm's answer left no doubt where he stood. "There will be no peace conference whatsoever," he declared. "Our enemies have no desire to do so. We must fight on until we have brought them to their knees and then dictate peace to them."[88] Hindenburg was sure that his armies were capable of inflicting such a defeat on the Allies. His expectation was that as soon as the snows melted and the ground hardened, the great western offensive would commence with a strike against the Allied line in Flanders, driving the British forces in the northern salient into the sea. Wilhelm gave his consent for the planning of the operation to begin, and he was kept fully informed of all developments.[89] The Kaiser's role in the military operations in the west during the last year of the war, however, was entirely passive: he listened and commented but never originated any ideas about what his armies were to do. When Wilhelm came to Berlin, an event of increasing rarity, his presence had no particular significance, and thus a group of Russian émigrés who arrived in the capital in June 1918 were struck with how unimportant the German sovereign seemed to be.[90]

Hindenburg informed the Kaiser that the campaign he envisioned to begin in Flanders in March 1918 would be the last possible hope for Germany, since American doughboys would begin pouring into the front lines by the following summer. Wilhelm agreed that this would be the decisive event of the war, but the crown prince was alarmed that his overly optimistic father did not realize that the offensive would be the Fatherland's "last trump" rather than merely another attempt to humble the enemy.[91] Hindenburg's great attack got under way on schedule on 21 March 1918, and just as in Russia a few weeks earlier, the German army astounded the world, sweeping back the Allied line, which had remained more or less fixed since October 1914, for some forty miles along a wide front. What was originally intended as a diversionary advance to the south in the direction of Paris proved to be so successful that this, rather than Flanders and the sea, became the primary sector of the campaign. Wilhelm was in a state of exultation throughout the spring as the German army rolled toward Paris, finally coming within about thirty-five miles, almost as close as General Helmuth von Moltke had advanced in the great western offensive at the outset of the war in 1914.[92] He signified his gratitude in April by renaming two bridges over the Rhine in honor of Hindenburg and Ludendorff, but he could not bring himself to contribute to a fund that was being collected throughout Germany to be presented to the quartermaster general.[93] The shaken Allies managed to consolidate their command under General Ferdinand Foch, an appointment that might have been foiled had not Wilhelm, on grounds of magnanimity, refused to endorse the General Staff's plan to have aircraft bomb Doullens, the site in northeastern France of an Allied meeting held on 26 March for the purpose of coordinating the resistance to the Germans.[94]

The critical nature of the campaign made Ludendorff ever more determined to get rid of those who did not share his confidence in a victory imposed by arms. His particular bête noire was still Kühlmann at the Foreign Office. The state secretary — devious, self-satisfied, and aloof — was not an especially likable man, and he was persistent in believing that Germany could not win the war and therefore had to make a peace that forswore annexations.[95] Wilhelm was not nearly so attached to Kühlmann as he had been to Valentini, Ludendorff's victim a few months earlier, but he had no desire to replace the state secretary. Ludendorff meanwhile had Valentini's successor, Berg, insinuate a press campaign against Kühlmann, reproaching him with a lack of confidence in Germany's prospects for victory.[96] Hertling fought in vain to save Kühlmann, but finally in early July, as the battle on the western front was reaching its zenith, the Kaiser summoned Kühlmann and informed him that, alas, he must resign, not because he did not have the crown's confidence but because he lacked Ludendorff and Hindenburg's.[97] A few days later, the chief of the Military Cabinet, General Baron Moritz von Lyncker, who had lost his two sons in the course of the war, was dismissed because he too had expressed doubt as to whether an advantageous military solution to Germany's situation was any longer possible.[98]

The appointment of Kühlmann's successor was carefully watched for what it indicated of the government's attitude toward peace. If an annexationist took the post, public opinion at home would be alarmed and Allied resistance stiffened; on the other hand, the naming of a moderate would advance the likelihood of a quick end to the war. Berg, who as chief of the Civil Cabinet was responsible for making personnel recommendations to the Kaiser, worked closely with Hindenburg and Ludendorff and proposed that the new state secretary be Paul von Hintze, a naval officer who was then serving as minister to Norway. He was a man whose conservative views left nothing to be desired and who could be expected to acquiesce in the generals' directions. Hintze's enemies perceptively detected in this smooth but essentially vacuous diplomat an ambitious office-seeker who was entirely unsuitable for such an exalted post, and even Hintze had doubts about his qualifications.[99] In the course of his career Hintze's intriguing manner had annoyed his superiors, and in the Foreign Office he was considered to be more a courtier than an experienced diplomat. He was known to have been in Wilhelm II's good graces ever since his service in St. Petersburg as naval attaché and military plenipotentiary. The Kaiser admired Hintze's ability to ferret out court gossip and found his reports to be admirable, so remarkable in fact that Wilhelm had Hintze transferred to the diplomatic service as minister to Mexico. Wilhelm considered him to be an expert on contemporary Russia, a man who would surely know how to deal with Lenin and Trotsky.[100] Although Hintze thus enjoyed great favor at court, the Reichstag found him compromised by his identity as a high-ranking officer, a conservative, and a favorite of the monarch's.

Wilhelm's record of capitulation to his generals thus remained unblemished. He approved their campaign plans, appointed the officials they nominated, and celebrated their military achievements. He had no real awareness of the state of affairs at the front, for, as the representative of the Foreign Office at headquarters regretted, the army's falsely confident reports to the Kaiser had by the summer of 1918 become nothing but "humbug" (*Spiegelfechterei*).[101] Wilhelm's confidence remained high, although there were signs by the beginning of July 1918 that he was beginning to waver. General Hans von Plessen, his oldest adjutant-general and a passionate believer in victory, was sufficiently worried about Wilhelm's morale to be pleased when the Kaiserin, always ready to replenish her husband's self-confidence in moments of crisis and herself imperturbably convinced of Germany's eventual victory, appeared at headquarters at Spa in Belgium.[102]

By the middle of July, Ludendorff believed that everything was in place for the German army, moving forward against the Allied front since March, to launch the ultimate drive across the Marne and, if all went as expected, to seize Paris. He was confident that his forces could achieve this goal, and Wilhelm was only slightly less so, even though the Kaiser had finally admitted that the submarine campaign against England had failed.[103] An Allied defeat in France, according to Hindenburg and Ludendorff, would not destroy England, but it would so greatly weaken the ability of the British to fight that they might be willing to grant Germany a satisfactory peace.[104] On 15 July, Ludendorff gave the order, earlier approved by the Kaiser, for his army to make for Paris, and shortly after midnight on the sixteenth the assault began. Wilhelm traveled to the front to observe the action, but before the day was over, Hindenburg's advance stalled and it never regained momentum. The Kaiser, however, was told nothing of this, and he consequently was full of optimism, airily describing the territorial gains and adjustments, in both east and west, that Germany would receive in a future peace.[105] The Allies, having withstood the German attack, managed only a few days later to begin a counteroffensive that steadily pushed the Germans back. The decisive moment came on 8 August near Amiens, where the Allies, moving under cover of a dense fog, launched a massive tank attack against the German lines and drove Hindenburg's troops steadily eastward across the Somme. Before the end of the day, the army had come to the realization that against the Allied mechanized force, Germany was powerless and that all that could be done was to retreat to the Hindenburg Line, which had been established in the fall of 1914 when the initial attempt to take Paris had failed. It was, as Ludendorff put it, "Germany's darkest day," less because of the loss of territory and the exposure of Germany's vulnerability to British tanks than because of his realization that in defeat he and Hindenburg would no longer be able to depend on the morale of their troops.[106]

Wilhelm was informed by his staff on 8 August that the war was lost and that peace must be made at once; in a visibly shaken state, he said that he had all along realized that this was going to happen.[107] A few days later, the Kaiser left Spa for the front to meet with Hindenburg and Ludendorff, who reiterated to him that disaster had struck, for not only were their troops demoralized but Austria-Hungary was virtually on the brink of collapse. Speaking to a room full of soldiers gripped in silence, the Kaiser declared: "The books must be balanced. The war must be concluded."[108] He ordered Hindenburg and Ludendorff to return with him to Spa to arrange the conclusion of a conflict, now utterly hopeless, that had begun four years earlier with such exuberant confidence.

Thirteen

NOVEMBER 1918:

THE GREAT LIQUIDATION

To determine how peace negotiations could best be undertaken, the Kaiser and his most important military and civilian advisers held a conference at Spa on 14 August.[1] Wilhelm's state of mind was pessimistic — "Look at me and you will see a defeated general," he had said a few days earlier — but he did not judge the situation to be so perilous that an immediate appeal needed to be made to the Allies. That could be deferred, at least for a while, until a favorable moment for negotiation presented itself.[2] He agreed with General Erich Ludendorff that although the military situation was grim, it was not hopeless, for German forces drawn up behind the Hindenburg Line could forestall any enemy attempt to attack Germany. The ever-solicitous state secretary Paul von Hintze soothingly minimized the danger by insisting that the recent military defeats were no more than "little setbacks" (*kleine Echecs*). The result of the Spa conference was negligible, the only agreement reached being that peace negotiations should be entered into not at once but instead when the Allied advance had been brought to a standstill. Measures were to be taken to create order in Germany, which was being rocked by strikes and dissent, to ensure the army's ability to continue the fight.[3] To all of this Wilhelm agreed, and he stressed that the resolve both of the home front, where lack of food and other rudimentary articles of daily life was creating exasperation, and of the army must be strengthened by a combination of flaming oratory and higher wages. Too many young Germans were to be seen lolling on the streets of Berlin, and the Kaiser declared that this sort of indolence was not to be tolerated in an hour of national crisis.[4]

As the conference concluded, the Habsburg emperor Karl, a weak, nervous princeling who had succeeded his great-uncle Franz Joseph in November 1916, arrived at Spa to plead for an instantaneous conclusion of hostilities to prevent the Dual Monarchy's collapse. This would require abandoning the extensive annexations that he and Foreign Minister Count Ottokar Czernin had identified with General Paul von Beneckendorff und von Hindenburg and General Ludendorff.[5] The visit was unwelcome to the Kaiser, who disliked Karl and his empress, Zita of Bourbon-Parma. In Wilhelm's opinion, Karl was the creature of his spiteful, anti-Hohenzollern wife, and the Kaiser found the royal couple untrustworthy and detestable. He complained that ever since coming to the throne, Karl had tried to end the war, efforts that had served only to increase the determination of the enemy to fight even harder.[6] The emperor and Czernin had been engaged since February 1917 in secret negotiations conducted through Karl's brother-in-law Prince Sixtus of Bourbon-Parma, an officer in the Belgian army. The prince in March 1918 had succeeded in securing from Karl a written promise that he would attempt to persuade Germany to surrender Alsace-Lorraine to France. The emperor's letter unfortunately became public knowledge, much to Wilhelm's outrage. The Kaiser demanded that Karl apologize, agree to end his efforts at mediation with the Allies, and tie the Habsburg Empire even more closely to Germany. In May 1918, Karl had come to Berlin, where he was subjected not only to Wilhelm's wrath but to that of the Kaiserin as well and where he had signed a document embodying the Kaiser's wishes.[7] Now Karl was back, again to plead for a swift end to the war. Wilhelm dismissed the entreaties of his visibly agitated guest, insisting that a peace initiative required waiting for the proper moment. The two rulers could not agree on Poland, which both wanted to control, Karl by establishing a personal union of Poland with the Habsburg crown and Wilhelm by having a newly constituted Polish kingdom be a satrap of Germany. The only issue settled was that the Habsburg crown would not make a unilateral appeal for peace.[8]

Once the Austrian deputation left Spa, Wilhelm and his wife, who had recently suffered a minor heart attack, departed for Wilhelmshöhe near Kassel, where he spent the next several weeks taking walks, visiting various points of interest, and inspecting war production plants in the area. The Kaiser's speech to the Krupp munitions workers at Essen, received in utter silence, was so awkward that it had to be recomposed before being made available to the press.[9] The entourage took pains to keep any depressing news from the trenches from Wilhelm, but on 2 September he heard that the Allies had penetrated a supposedly impregnable sector of the western front. The Kaiser summoned his staff and in a measured but full voice declared, "The war is lost!"[10] He managed to get through dinner but then suffered a nervous collapse. Wilhelm took to his bed, his doctor ordered complete rest, and the ailing Kaiserin took it on herself to revive his spirits. As usual, she succeeded, and by 5 September the Kaiser was well enough to receive Albert Ballin, the head of the Hamburg-American Line, who had come to Wilhelmshöhe to try to persuade the Kaiser to enter at once into negotiations with President Woodrow Wilson.[11] Wilhelm did not grasp the urgency of the situation, and the Civil Cabinet chief, Friedrich von Berg-Markienen, ever anxious to shield his master from anything unpleasant, prevented Ballin from telling the Kaiser the plain truth. Wilhelm instead put his trust in his old foe Ludendorff, who still believed that something might be salvaged. The Kaiser, insisting that the general must be relieved of some of his awesome responsibilities, noted, "He is worth more to us than a victory won."[12] Ludendorff's optimism was misplaced, for on 12 September Emperor Karl, violating his promise that was scarcely a week old, informed the enraged Kaiser that in two days' time he would seek a separate peace from the Allies. This overture received no encouragement from President Wilson and came to nothing. Furthermore, on the same day, the American divisions won their first independent campaign at Saint-Mihiel, a grave indication of the effect that the eventually limitless numbers of troops that President Wilson could put into the field would have on the war.[13] The Allies did not pursue their victory, however, and the battle lines once again hardened in opposing ranks of trenches.

On 24 September, Wilhelm journeyed to Kiel at the insistence of Admiral Reinhard Scheer, the chief of the Admiralty Staff, to inspect the naval yard there, the scene in recent weeks of rumblings of discontent. The workers showed little sign of appreciation of a royal visit, although the population of the city provided Wilhelm a courteous welcome.[14] While at Kiel, Wilhelm received the unwelcome news that his ally, Tsar Ferdinand of Bulgaria, whose army was being mercilessly pounded by the Allies, had appealed for an armistice, which was concluded on 30 September. The Kaiser recognized the ominous significance of Bulgaria's defection, for it would weaken Germany's hold over Rumania and increase the sense of war-weariness both in Austria-Hungary and in Germany.[15] At the end of September the Allies renewed their attack in the west, which proceeded slowly but successfully against the Germans, who were now forced along a wide front to abandon the Hindenburg Line and fall back toward Germany. For the first time in the war, Germany's western frontier appeared to be menaced by the advancing enemy. Faced now with a very grave emergency, Wilhelm summoned Chancellor Count Georg von Hertling and State Secretary Hintze to join him in Belgium at army headquarters in Spa on 29 September to discuss the situation.

Although the Kaiser began the day with a horseback ride during which he declared that he was hopeful the enemy advance could be successfully dealt with, the meeting with his advisers robbed him of all confidence.[16] In the morning session, since Hertling was still aboard his train making for Spa, Ludendorff took the leading role. The general, so assured in the spring of 1918 as his great offensive got under way, had fallen into despair in mid-August when it had failed, but he had recovered his confidence early in September. Ludendorff's always volatile nerves had meanwhile again suffered a collapse, and he was now, on 29 September, convinced that all was lost and that Germany was about to be devoured not only by military defeat but also by revolution. The home front, riddled by revolution, would not hold out until a new campaign could be organized. Backed by Hindenburg and Ludendorff, Hintze undertook to convince the Kaiser that an armistice must be concluded at once, followed by a peace to be negotiated with Wilson on the basis of the president's Fourteen Points. Furthermore, a new government, including a number of prominent Reichstag deputies, had to be formed and an order issued by the crown immediately instituting a secret, direct ballot in Prussia. All of this was unpalatable to Wilhelm, but he accepted Ludendorff's advice with surprising composure.

After a pause for lunch, the chancellor arrived and closeted himself with the Kaiser. Hertling was more optimistic than the generals and argued that seeking an armistice would undermine his negotiating position. Germany should not rush into either an armistice request or an ensuing peace negotiation based on the Fourteen Points. The chancellor was astounded that Hindenburg and Ludendorff, who were, like him, conservative and anti-democratic, had fallen in with Hintze's call for a parliamentary government, an idea with which Hertling had no sympathy whatsoever and that he refused to promote as chancellor.[17] Always susceptible to any news that was favorable, Wilhelm now seized on the chancellor's argument that the situation was by no means so critical that Germany had to seek peace at once. There was also an encouraging rumor that the French army was being decimated by an influenza epidemic, news that Ludendorff characterized as his "last hope."[18] The Kaiser therefore summoned Hintze and informed the state secretary that he intended to postpone for two weeks any decision on the diplomatic and political questions discussed that morning. Hintze, however, strongly protested this decision and in his determined way finally convinced Wilhelm once again that negotiations must begin at once.[19]

This was a repudiation of Hertling, who had never been able to realize the acute deterioration in Germany's strategic situation in the west. Nor did the chancellor have much sense of the increasing level of dissatisfaction with his regime both in public opinion and in the Reichstag.[20] Hertling had expected that he would remain as chancellor until the end of the war, but he had no intention whatsoever of presiding over a parliamentary regime in which, he claimed, ministers would be chosen not because of ability but because of their popularity with the people. He therefore submitted his resignation, to Wilhelm's distress, and the Kaiser accepted it on 30 September, but only as a provisional measure until a successor could be selected.[21] On the same day, Wilhelm took the step he had so long resisted and signed an order immediately instituting a modern franchise in Prussia and authorized Hintze to begin negotiations with President Wilson without delay. The Kaiser's rescript expressed the crown's intention that in the future the German people would "participate more effectively than heretofore in determining the history of the Fatherland." He also promised, "Men who enjoy the confidence of the people will participate to a greater degree in the rights and duties of the government."[22]

Hintze had, on the twenty-ninth, raised for discussion the prospect of replacing Hertling with a military dictatorship under Hindenburg and Ludendorff, but Wilhelm rejected this as nonsense. "*Diktatur ist Unsinn*," he declared.[23] Wilson would not negotiate with a military regime, and the German people, much as the two generals were revered, would not tolerate it. There were several civilian figures who seemed suitable and who were presumably acceptable to Wilhelm, with Prince Maximilian of Baden, heir to the reigning grand duke, appearing to be the leading, but as yet by no means certain, contender.[24] Ludendorff was in furious haste that the new chancellor be named at once, to which the Kaiser replied curtly: "I am no magician! You should have told me this two weeks ago."[25] Wilhelm approached the rebuilding of the government with distaste, for the thought of appointing Reichstag deputies, including even some from the ranks of the Social Democrats, to ministerial posts was anathema to him. But since Hintze and the generals were so insistent, he reluctantly agreed. Meanwhile, on the evening of 29 September, Admiral Scheer, having been told that the army could no longer offer the navy protective cover, advised Wilhelm that the bases being used by German submarines on the Belgian coast had to be abandoned. Although the Kaiser insisted that Germany continue to build U-boats, possession of which could eventually be useful in peace negotiations, he told Scheer that the war was lost and that he had known this ever since 8 August, when Hindenburg's campaign had failed.[26]

Everything that happened at Spa on 29 September was thoroughly depressing to the Kaiser, who was ambling about on a cane because of an attack of sciatica. In the course of a talk with Berg on the next day Wilhelm broke into tears, declaring that he had never wanted the war and yet had been held responsible for the bloodshed.[27] He wrote plaintively to the Kaiserin: "God has not permitted us to achieve the aim for which we hoped but rather has elected for us the way of suffering and misery. We submit to his holy will and approach him with the hope and prayer that he may give to *all* of us the power of his spirit to wander through this time of trial strong in belief that he wishes to call forth the best in us even when his ways appear difficult and incomprehensibly dark. . . . I will continue to do my duty toward Him and my fatherland so long as he allows me to."[28] There was nothing more that the Kaiser could do in Spa, where Hindenburg felt that Wilhelm and his retinue were an impediment, so on the evening of 1 October, with no successor for Hertling yet clearly in mind, the Kaiser departed for Potsdam.

Wilhelm had dispatched Berg to Berlin a day earlier, charging him with finding a suitable chancellor.[29] The leaders of the Reichstag resented Berg's intrusion, for in their opinion the day was over when the Kaiser could appoint a government.[30] This was a matter now for the legislature, but the chamber was not entirely of one mind as to who Hertling's successor should be. Whoever became chancellor would have to give unqualified endorsement to the Peace Resolution of April 1917, to the immediate introduction of Wilhelm's promised democratic franchise in Prussia, and to the formation of a government that included a number of deputies drawn from the parties of the center and the Left.[31] Prince Maximilian of Baden, who was prepared to accept these demands, seemed to have more support in the Reichstag than any other candidate, and it was known that Hindenburg and Ludendorff were willing to support him. The reactionary Berg, however, at first worked strenuously against Max, whom he considered too liberal and too inexperienced, a view with which the equally conservative Kaiserin entirely agreed.[32]

Max, often called "Badimax," was ready to be drafted as chancellor, and he came to Berlin on the afternoon of 1 October in anticipation of receiving the call. He would later declare the reason that he took the chancellorship: "All leading factors characterized me as the only person who was suitable for carrying out the great liquidation with some dignity."[33] Max at once saw Colonel Hans von Haeften, the head of the foreign division (*Auslandsabteilung*) of the OHL, who shocked him by describing a military situation so grave that an armistice had to be sought at once. He then talked to Berg, who coolly declared that Max was, unfortunately, the only person who appeared suitable to succeed Hertling. In the conversation that ensued, the prince declared that he would under no circumstances assume the chancellorship only to issue an armistice appeal to the Allies. What he would do was inform the enemy that Germany was prepared to make concessions regarding war aims but that if the Allies insisted on unworthy terms, Germany would continue to fight.[34] Berg found this course reasonable, and he therefore wired Wilhelm in Spa that Max was the person who should be appointed chancellor.[35]

On the evening of 2 October, the Kaiser came to Berlin to meet with Hindenburg, Hertling, Max, Berg, and other advisers about the formation of the new government. Insulated from unpleasant news by his entourage at Spa, the Kaiser had regained his confidence and was in a good humor as he strode into the room, asking the assembled crowd, "Why is it that I find such nervousness here in Berlin?"[36] After some discussion, Wilhelm agreed that Max should become chancellor on 4 October and that the new government would be composed of a number of parliamentarians, including Philipp Scheidemann of the Social Democratic Party. The question of negotiations with the Allies was then discussed, and although Max favored a delay in responding to Wilson, Hindenburg and Ludendorff insisted that he do so at once, accepting the president's Fourteen Points as the basis for negotiation.[37]

The new chancellor was elegant in manner and appearance, calm to the point of sometimes seeming devoid of passion or conviction. He had a streak of self-importance for which his modest accomplishments, notably his successful efforts to ameliorate the conditions under which prisoners of war of all belligerents were interned, provided little justification. Max was a strict monarchist, and as the leader of the upper house of the Baden legislature, he had firmly upheld royal prerogative in the face of parliamentary assaults. "I hate this word democratization," he had declared in 1917. Max felt that it was incumbent on Wilhelm to seize the peace initiative from the Reichstag and to show his subjects that "German freedom" was "better than western democracy."[38] Wilhelm II had known Max for many years and had not always approved of his reputation as a ladies' man and his disinclination to marry the Kaiserin's artistic sister Feodora. By 1918 these differences had long since faded, although the two men had never become more than casual friends.[39] Finding Max tolerable as a man did not translate into enthusiasm at the prospect of his becoming chancellor, and Wilhelm had in October 1917 repeatedly refused to heed advice that the prince should replace the discredited Michaelis, telling his retinue then that although he might take on a chancellor as aged as Hertling, he did not intend to permit a younger member of a royal house to serve in that capacity.[40] Early in September 1918, convinced that Hertling had no sense of Germany's critical situation, the prince had written to Wilhelm offering his services as chancellor; the Kaiser had replied gracefully but without any encouragement.[41] But now in October, not quite a month later, Wilhelm agreed to take on Max, not because he wanted to but because, as Berg had regretfully concluded, there was no one else. The parliamentary government established under Max on 4 October 1918 was an acknowledgment that Wilhelm's authority was now, for all practical purposes, subservient to that of the chancellor, who himself governed only at the sufferance of the Reichstag.

Max's first task, carried out with the assistance if not in fact the supervision of the majority parties in the parliament, was to form a new government. One of the first casualties was the unrepentantly conservative Hintze at the Foreign Office, whom the Kaiser wanted to keep but who was very unpopular with the Reichstag. His successor was Wilhelm Solf, formerly colonial secretary, a man who had good relations with Parliament and whose appointment would indicate to the Allies that Germany intended to retain its empire.[42] Six of Hertling's ministers stayed on, joined by seven new ones, all of them except Solf Reichstag deputies. Wilhelm granted Max's government an audience, at which he indulged in his habitual exaggeration. "No land in all the world," he informed his new ministers, "will be permitted to exceed Germany in political freedom." The Fatherland, he assured them, would if necessary fight "to its last breath and to its last blow."[43] The Kaiser remained in Berlin for almost all of the month of October, generally avoiding Max and other governmental officials, receiving few military reports, and nursing both his sciatica and his resentment at the diminution of his authority. This suited the chancellor, who wanted Wilhelm to keep out of sight in the hope that this would lead to less talk of abdication.[44] During this critical month, Wilhelm made few speeches, failed to attend a number of important meetings, and ratified, not always graciously, whatever Max told him needed royal assent. Unpalatable as change might be, the Kaiser considered it essential that the German people not be disappointed in the liberality of their ruler, as had been the case both in 1815 and again in 1848, when the kings of Prussia had reneged on promises of reform.[45]

Max proceeded without delay to enact, through orders issued by the Kaiser, various personnel changes as well as a number of reforms calculated to heighten popular approval of his regime.[46] Of the former, the most important was the removal on 7 October of the arch-reactionary

Berg as chief of the Civil Cabinet. Berg's replacement was the universally admired Clemens von Delbrück, a moderate who had served from 1909 to 1916 as state secretary of the interior.[47] Max's reforms brought about a limitation of military authority in civil matters and an amnesty for all political prisoners, but he declined to move forward with the critically important alteration of the Prussian franchise, the change that Wilhelm had finally agreed to implement. This was profoundly dismaying to the German people; by October 1918 only military success could have revived their will to fight on, and that was not forthcoming. Nor was it to be expected, for Germany utterly lacked the ability to place enough men on the western front to provide adequate challenge to the tens of thousands of American soldiers arriving in Europe every month. Oil was in very short supply, food was meager, and many of the Kaiser's exhausted troops were suspected of no longer being disposed to fight. Germany's allies were in the process of negotiating their own armistices with the enemy, and in Bavaria a separatist movement in favor of proclaiming independence from the German Empire was rapidly gaining strength. In addition to all these seemingly insuperable problems, Max's government had to negotiate first an armistice and then a peace with Wilson and his allies, all of whom by now believed that Germany was defeated and should be shorn of all its power.

In both Germany and the Allied camp, Wilhelm II emerged by mid-October as a central consideration in any vision of Germany's future form. To the enemy, the Kaiser and the autocratic system of rule identified with him had caused the war, and such a tyrant would surely confound Europe once again as soon as an armistice expired and Germany had caught its breath. As chancellor, Theobald von Bethmann Hollweg had predicted in April 1917, as America entered the war, that one day the Allies would declare that they would negotiate with the German people but not with the Hohenzollerns.[48] To the Germans, who recognized that their ruler was detested everywhere in Europe as well as in America, Wilhelm II was not only an impediment to the peace for which almost everyone yearned but also the logical scapegoat for all the frustrations, disappointments, and privations his subjects had suffered in four long years of relentless war. Although censorship prevented any mention of abdication in the press, it had existed underground since early in 1917 and was open and wide-spread by the fall of 1918.[49] After Max became chancellor on 4 October and exchanged one note after another with Woodrow Wilson to try to bring about an end to hostilities, the demands for Wilhelm's abdication became prominent even among people, notably industrialists and their allies in conservative political circles, who had traditionally been among the Kaiser's supporters.[50] Wilhelm himself realized that his giving up the throne might be the price Wilson would try to exact in return for an armistice, a thought that to his wife was the zenith of America's vulgar ignorance of the historic position of the house of Hohenzollern.[51] The Kaiser was under no illusions: he knew that many of his subjects were clamoring for him to abdicate, but he told the chancellor that no successor of Frederick the Great would ever think of doing so.[52]

The matter of Wilhelm's continuation on the throne reached an acute phase when, on 23 October, Wilson issued the third of his notes to the chancellor, complaining that the Kaiser's vast authority remained intact and noting that the Allies would negotiate only with emissaries who were "authentic representatives of the German people." Wilson's language was interpreted in Berlin as a demand for the Kaiser's abdication, although unbeknownst to Max and the government, the president might still have been willing to tolerate Wilhelm on the throne had he been shorn of his prerogative.[53] The Kaiser acutely resented what he too perceived to be Wilson's call for his removal. "With every note more is demanded, and every time we give in," he complained. "Wilson wants to prescribe what sort of constitution Germany should adopt and he wants the complete subjection and abdication of the German federal princes. I'm not going."[54] The president, he declared, was an "impudent lout" and his note "unadulterated Bolshevism [and] a declaration of war against the monarchical principle."[55] The Kaiser demanded that Max, whose ability he thought to be unequal to the massive difficulties facing Germany, immediately denounce this "piece of immitigated [*sic*] frivolous insolence" and use Wilson's arrogance to stir up the German people to an impassioned defense of their ruler.[56]

By October 1918 very few Germans were likely to rise to protect Wilhelm, for by this time he had lost whatever popularity he had enjoyed at the beginning of the war. Only those who were bound to him by oath, as were all Prussian officers, or by long service, as were his elderly courtiers, were prepared to stand by the Kaiser to the end, and even their confidence was shaken. Although Max's cabinet had agreed, in a meeting just after he took office in early October, that any Allied demands for Wilhelm's abdication would be resisted "to the utmost" *(mit Hörnern und Klauen)*, Scheidemann pointed out that if the question — peace or the Hohenzollern dynasty? — was put to the German people, they would opt for peace.[57] Although Wilhelm was conveniently present in Berlin as the abdication crisis prompted by Wilson's third note of 23 October broke out, Max was reluctant to discuss the matter with him. The chancellor's position was delicate, for as heir to the Baden throne, he could not easily advocate another German ruler's abdication, especially since he might be suspected of desiring to have the imperial crown transferred to himself.[58] He wanted to inform Wilhelm of the "unfavorable implication" (*ungünstige Deutung*) of Wilson's note but could not bring himself to do so. Nor could the chancellor find anyone among the Kaiser's entourage — Court Chaplain Ernst von Dryander, House Minister Count August zu Eulenburg, or a favorite adjutant such as Oskar von Chelius — who was prepared to try gently to make him understand that the question could not be avoided.[59] As a result, Max did not bring up the subject with Wilhelm, and it was left in abeyance until the very end of October, by which time the forces calling for the Kaiser's overthrow had grown much more powerful.

When Max received Wilson's note on 23 October, he was involved in a struggle with General Ludendorff that threatened his continuation as chancellor. Colonel Haeften, a General Staff officer who was close to Ludendorff, urged both Hindenburg and Ludendorff to come to Berlin to argue that Wilson's note, which the generals held to be incompatible with Germany's honor because of its refusal to negotiate with the Kaiser, be rejected and the war continued.[60] Hindenburg, acting for Ludendorff as well as himself and without any prior consultation with either Max or the Kaiser, on 24 October sent a message to his commanding officers describing Wilson's note as a demand for "military capitulation." He added, "It is therefore unacceptable to us soldiers."[61] The military had thus intruded itself into a decision that constitutionally was the chancellor's and the sovereign's to make. Wilhelm agreed with the generals' point of view, but he was furious that he had not been consulted. It was Ludendorff, not Hindenburg, who in his opinion was to blame, and the quartermaster general would have to go, before he cost Wilhelm his crown.[62] The chancellor was equally enraged, both at the army's uninvited intervention in a diplomatic matter and at its departure for Berlin, where it had no proper business to transact. Max informed the Kaiser that he would resign if this "double government" (*Doppelregierung*) continued. Ludendorff would have to be dismissed and Hindenburg ordered back to headquarters at Spa in Belgium if an armistice was to be arranged and the Hohenzollern dynasty salvaged.[63]

On the generals' arrival in Berlin on 25 October, they at once saw the Kaiser, who had no notion of how desperate the situation on the western front was. Ludendorff, who did most of the talking, lost no time overruling Max's objections and insisted that Wilson's note be rejected, indicating, with his accustomed brusqueness, that if he did not get his way, he would resign.[64] Ludendorff, always excitable and irascible in expression, had overstepped the bounds of propriety in talking as he did to the Kaiser, who, although appearing collected, was not one who gladly heard such lecturing, especially from someone he thoroughly disliked. Early the next morning, the two generals were back at the Bellevue palace for a second audience, and this time the Kaiser, who had meanwhile been convinced by Delbrück that Ludendorff had to be sacked, was irate.[65] Wilhelm expressed his rage at Hindenburg's improper communication to his generals urging them to reject President Wilson's note. In September, the Kaiser reminded them, they had insisted that Germany had to conclude an armistice with all due speed, but now they took quite the opposite view, all without bothering to consult him or the chancellor. Ludendorff then insisted on resigning, doing so in language so lacking in courtly manners that Wilhelm was forced to remind him that he was speaking to his sovereign. Max urged that the Kaiser remove the quartermaster general, who had opposed the government at every turn. Hindenburg, who thus far had participated very little in the discussion, now declared rather halfheartedly that he too would have to go. The exasperated Kaiser, who declared that he no longer had any confidence in the General Staff, accepted Ludendorff's request but denied Hindenburg's, telling him curtly, "You stay."[66] The field marshal persuaded Wilhelm to appoint General Wilhelm Groener, the able head of the General Staff's transportation division, to Ludendorff's position as quartermaster general. Ludendorff was so angry with Hindenburg for having failed also to resign that he refused to ride back to the General Staff building in the same vehicle with his superior. Wilhelm was happy to have the business of disposing of Ludendorff out of the way. He complained to a group of officers that Hindenburg and Ludendorff had come to Berlin unbid, "like elephants in a porcelain shop breaking up everything." The "Siamese twins" were now sundered, Wilhelm declared with pleasure, and he was at last rid of that "fellow" (*Kerl*) Ludendorff.[67]

By the time of Ludendorff's resignation on 26 October, Berlin was rife with calls for the Kaiser's abdication. On the day before, the respectably conservative newspaper *Frankfurter Allgemeine Zeitung*, in defiance of the censors and pleas for silence by the government, had raised the issue in its editorial columns.[68] There were also rumors that Wilhelm was no longer safe in Berlin, a city notorious for its belligerent Socialist population, and the Kaiser seems to have believed that his life was in jeopardy there.[69] In his confrontation in Berlin with Hindenburg and Ludendorff on 26 October, neither Wilhelm nor the generals had said anything about his coming to Spa, and indeed the Kaiser's disagreement with the Supreme Command might have made him feel uncomfortable in their presence. Hindenburg, however, believed that the notification received in Berlin on 27 October from Emperor Karl in Vienna, who stated that once again he intended to seek a separate peace, was of such enormous significance that it required Wilhelm's presence at headquarters. This act of Habsburg ingratitude left the Kaiser very shaken, and he declared: "Now we stand alone against the entire world! We have had to endure this war in order not to leave Austria in the lurch, and she has done so to us!"[70]

There were considerations besides Emperor Karl's defection that inclined Wilhelm to join his beleaguered troops at the front. Although none of the Kaiser's courtiers or generals had the temerity to talk to him about the eventuality of abdication, they were ready to urge Wilhelm to raise his martial image with the army, exactly the opposite of the chancellor's desire to keep him out of sight. Especially prominent in efforts to restore Wilhelm's repute was Berg, who had remained in close contact with the Kaiser after Max had forced his resignation as chief of the Civil Cabinet in early October. Berg believed that Wilhelm's willpower would be increased by imbibing some of the fortitude exuded by Hindenburg and that at Spa, surrounded by his loyal generals, he would be more resistant to attempts to persuade him to abdicate.[71] General Max von Gallwitz, of whom the Kaiser had a high opinion, also encouraged Wilhelm to assume a more vigorous role among his troops, who the general noted were increasingly asking, "Where is the Kaiser?"[72] Gallwitz believed that Wilson's demands should be resisted and that if the Kaiser would assume leadership, the army and the people would follow. His prescription, tendered in an audience on 27 October, was that Wilhelm should issue an appeal to the army for increased courage and loyalty. The senior and most conservative adjutant, General Hans von Plessen, very probably joined Berg in pleading with the Kaiser to leave Berlin, for the general had long believed that the sovereign's sense of confidence was greater when he was with his fellow officers.[73]

It was certainly not fear that led Wilhelm to leave Berlin, whatever the danger that lurked there, for even his enemies admitted that he was brave.[74] He believed that he could more effectively challenge those who were at work to dethrone him by going to Spa and calling on the help of his generals, who were bound to him by oath and by conviction, rather than remaining in Berlin with Max, whom he bitterly but mistakenly identified as the leading figure in the abdication party.[75] Once at Spa, he could stiffen German resistance to the Allies and inspire his troops to keep on with their heroic fight. The Kaiser was convinced that without him, morale at the front would collapse, but this salutary influence, according to General Baron Ulrich von Marschall, Baron Moritz von Lyncker's successor as chief of the Military Cabinet, could be achieved only if Wilhelm went to Spa.[76] Although the official explanation for the Kaiser's departure from Berlin was that he did so "at Hindenburg's wish," Marschall apparently was the principal force in the decision. It was he who put out the story that Wilhelm was not safe in Berlin, who duplicitously kept the Kaiser's departure a secret, and who later declared that it was Hindenburg who had desired to have Wilhelm at the front.[77]

Late in the afternoon of 29 October, Max was told about Wilhelm's impending departure by Baron Werner von Grünau, the representative of the Foreign Office in the retinue, who in turn had learned of this from Major Alfred Niemann, a General Staff officer in attendance on the Kaiser. Max at once tried, over the telephone, to persuade Wilhelm to remain in Berlin and asked for permission to see him at Potsdam. The Kaiser declined to receive the chancellor and refused to abandon his forthcoming trip, reminding Max that it was he who had insisted on Ludendorff's resignation, which in turn now made it imperative for Wilhelm to go to Spa to introduce the new quartermaster, General Groener, into his responsibilities. This was of course nonsense, for as Max pointed out, Hindenburg was the only person who could inform Groener what his new role was to be. Max also tried again, for the second time without success, to persuade Dryander and August Eulenburg to help him, but both refused to intervene, and so Wilhelm left Berlin, never to return.[78] He reached Spa late in the afternoon of 30 October, declaring on arrival that he had done so to confound the attempts being made by Max to dethrone him.[79] Hindenburg, who for several weeks had argued that Wilhelm's place was with the army, had not been informed that the royal train was en route for Belgium and consequently was quite surprised to see the Kaiser, whom one general who had not seen him in recent months described as a little more serious but otherwise his usual self.[80]

Once at headquarters, the Kaiser had a full schedule of audiences, but he also had time to find relaxation in chopping down trees.[81] In Berlin the Reichstag deputies were sure that he had gone to Spa to plot Max's removal as chancellor, and since the prince had taken office at the behest of Parliament, Wilhelm's entraining for Belgium to closet himself with Hindenburg could be seen only as defiance of the Reichstag's authority.[82] The presence in Spa of the Kaiser's friend Paul von Hintze, who had come to consult with Hindenburg, was unsettling to the deputies, who had never liked this very conservative favorite. State Secretary Solf would later declare that it was Wilhelm's departure for Spa on 29 October, and not his flight to Holland two weeks later, that sealed the fate of the Hohenzollern monarchy.[83] To Max, Wilhelm's decamping to headquarters sundered their relationship and brought to an end his attempts to preserve the Kaiser on the throne. The chancellor was convinced that Wilson was determined to destroy Germany, and to prevent that debacle, war would have to be waged to the utmost in the hope of extracting honorable peace terms. But the German people would do this only if Wilhelm II and the crown prince abdicated.[84]

Although Max had come to the conclusion that the Kaiser had to surrender the crown, he insisted that this be a voluntary act.[85] After meeting with various advisers, the chancellor decided that someone would have to go to Spa to inform Wilhelm that his abdication was essential to ensure that the German army and the civilian population would continue to fight for an honorable end to the war. As heir to a crown, Max could not go himself, and he would therefore have to find a "neutral" figure to conduct the unpleasant task.[86] Enlisting a willing spokesman proved very difficult, however, and the task finally was entrusted to the Prussian minister of interior, Wilhelm Drews, who appeared in Spa on 1 November.[87] The Kaiser berated Drews, who as a Prussian official in the "so-called government" had taken an oath of loyalty to his sovereign, for having suggested that Wilhelm consider giving up the throne. Wilhelm warned Drews that if he abdicated, the army would collapse and return to Germany as pirates, leaving the enemy free to stream across the frontier. Wilhelm declared that he had no intention of abandoning his crown because of the demands of several hundred Jews and several thousand Socialist workers. "I too have sworn an oath," he reminded Drews, "and I will honor it."[88]

The day after his unsatisfactory exchange with Drews, the Kaiser informed Hintze that he would return to Berlin but only after an armistice was signed. According to Wilhelm's scenario, the army in the west would march back to Germany and restore order in Berlin by crushing the revolutionary outbreaks that had begun to occur in the last days of October. The most serious of these was at the naval base at Kiel, where a number of Socialist sailors had mutinied on 28 October. This was to Wilhelm rank ingratitude for all he had done for the navy, and he did not intend to tolerate such insolence. The German army, unbridled against his subjects, would soon humble the sailors and the errant bourgeoisie, whereupon his soldiers could then move against Vladimir Lenin and his Bolsheviks and the Japanese, perhaps even enlisting British help in this endeavor to repel these enemies of Western civilization.[89] Germany, he informed Hintze on 3 November, would experience a revolution from above that would bring into line (*kanalisieren*) the revolution from below. He was confident that the troops in German cities were loyal and that millions of his subjects would support him.[90]

General Groener believed that if the Kaiser was to save the dynasty and avoid abdication, the place for him to be was not at headquarters but at the actual front in the midst of the fight, where the possibility of death would await him. If Wilhelm was wounded, he would win a hero's laurels and thereby retain his throne, and if death should be his fate, the Hohenzollern dynasty would be saved for his heirs.[91] Hindenburg, however, would have nothing to do with such a plan. As Plessen remarked some years later, "A monarch has higher duties than to seek death or wounds in the trenches."[92] But on 4 November, Hintze took it on himself to bring up the matter with Wilhelm, who replied that he had already talked to Hindenburg about such a plan. The field marshal, he claimed, had consented, and he intended to go to the front later that day.[93] The Kaiser did in fact on 4 November travel by train to a portion of the line between Brussels and Liège, where the German army was in the process of making an orderly retreat, and he then returned to Spa, full of satisfaction at the greeting he had received from the troops. Wilhelm was deluded, for others who were along reported an unfriendly, even disrespectful, reception or noted that soldiers who cheered in public later privately had scurrilous things to say about their ruler. In any case, the Kaiser had not been exposed to any danger, for he had been taken to recruit and communication stations well to the rear rather than to the front line.[94] On the following day, 5 November, a number of younger officers at Spa were at work to find a suitable place in the trenches where Wilhelm might find a heroic death by making an attack on the Allied line. Volunteers were in the process of being solicited for such a suicide mission, scheduled for 7 November.[95] The project collapsed because Hindenburg and Plessen were opposed and because no one had any desire to bring the matter up with the Kaiser, who in any case had no intention of sacrificing himself. Wilhelm was no coward, but to him, suicide would have been an admission of failure and was, besides, contrary to his religious views.[96]

In Berlin, Max and his government continued to press for the Kaiser to relinquish the throne but only if he would do so voluntarily. What Wilhelm should do, the chancellor telephoned from Berlin on 8 November, was to declare that he would abdicate as soon as elections could be held, thus creating an impression that his departure was a free act and not one forced by Scheidemann and his Socialists, who were openly demanding that Wilhelm give up his crown at once. Time was running out, however, and not only were many German cities now openly engaged in Socialist revolution, but the Social Democrat leaders in the Reichstag had declared that unless Wilhelm surrendered the throne before the day was out, they would resign from the government, effectively leaving the chancellor incapable of governing in the face of opposition from the largest faction in the chamber.[97] Secretary Solf meanwhile wrote to warn that if the Kaiser did abdicate at once, the Socialist bolt from the government would bring civilian authority to an end. In such an impasse, only a military dictatorship could rule Germany, but in that case the Allies would refuse to negotiate.[98]

None of these developments made much impression on the Kaiser, who persisted in refusing to give up the crown. Wilhelm had written to the Kaiserin on 7 November that the "situation was truly dreadful" (*wahrhaft grauenhafte Zustände*), what with the naval mutinies, the treacherous connivance of the Social Democrats with the revolutionaries, and the "deplorable" (*jammervolle*) government that did nothing to prevent all this. There were loyal troops, however, ready to defend the Fatherland and to march under his command back into Germany and defeat the revolution, and he ordered his royal train outfitted with additional machine guns for the forthcoming trip to Berlin.[99] Wilhelm, who was in a state of considerable agitation and sleeping only with the aid of medication, now busied himself arranging to try to persuade Felix Cardinal von Hartmann of Cologne to come to his aid, for the route of his return to Germany had to lie through the Rhineland. The Kaiser informed the prelate that there was a masonic conspiracy of Frenchmen and Jews plotting to overthrow all the crowned heads of Europe. Hartmann must inform the pope and order the clergy in the Rhineland that they were to rally to Wilhelm's support.

Whether they would have done so did not matter, for Soviet revolutionaries prevented the messenger from delivering the Kaiser's appeal to the cardinal, and Cologne itself, as well as other great transportation centers in western Germany, was now convulsed by revolution.[100] That fact, if the Kaiser was told about it, did not deter his determination to return to Germany. On 8 November he informed his wife that he would soon be en route, and at his customary morning conference that day with Hindenburg and Groener, he ordered them to prepare the assembling of a force "for the reconquest of the homeland" to march under his command.[101]

Wilhelm seemed to think that his presence alone would galvanize the Germans and overthrow the revolution, and he continued to reject, calmly but firmly, Max's entreaties by telephone that he abdicate.[102] When the Kaiser was informed that Socialists had seized part of the royal palace in the heart of Berlin, he pounded his fist on the table and asked, "Where are sufficient troops to be found in order that I can reconquer my castle?"[103] That indeed was the question: would the Kaiser be able to find loyal officers and men prepared to join with him in putting down the revolution? Hindenburg himself was not sure of the answer, so he had summoned to Spa a group of thirty-nine officers from the various armies along the front to give their opinion on the question. They were expected on the morning of 9 November.[104] On their arrival, Hindenburg assembled the officers and glumly described the revolutionary unrest in Germany, of which most seemed to have been unaware, and pointed out the logistical difficulties that would be entailed in attempting to march the army back to Germany. Everything he said seemed calculated to produce a negative reaction.[105] The officers were then polled as to whether or not Wilhelm could count on a body of troops to accompany him in retreat. Only one officer declared that such a scheme would succeed, fifteen were doubtful that the Kaiser could command a following, and the remaining twenty-three flatly denied that anyone would be willing to march behind the sovereign, not because they were personally hostile to Wilhelm but because they were indifferent about his future. The thirty-nine officers were unanimous that even if the Kaiser could muster a detachment, no German soldier would fight in a civil war against the revolutionaries at home.[106]

As this opinion was being ascertained, Wilhelm was beginning what would prove to be the last day of his reign, unaware that he had no army and would soon have no crown. His first visitor, Adjutant Major Niemann, found that the Kaiser's nerves were quite steady and that he was concerned not about the western front but about the infiltration of bolshevism into Germany from Austria-Hungary, which on 3 November, beset with revolution, had entered into an armistice with the Allies. Wilhelm informed Niemann that it was his responsibility as the Kaiser to eradicate this godless peril and that the Allies must be made to understand that if Germany also fell to bolshevism, all European culture would be imperiled.[107] Shortly after talking to Niemann, Wilhelm had a conference with Hindenburg, Groener, and various other officers and diplomats, who all morning had been besieged with telephone calls and wires informing them that Berlin was awash in revolution. Hindenburg was notably silent and left it to Groener to inform the Kaiser bluntly that German troops might march home under their generals but not under royal command.[108] General Count Friedrich von der Schulenburg-Tressow, the chief of staff of the army commanded by the crown prince, disputed this and then proposed an idea that had circulated for some time: Wilhelm could abdicate as kaiser but retain his position as king of Prussia, in which capacity he was commander-in-chief of its army.[109]

Later in the morning, Colonel Wilhelm Heye, a General Staff officer whose task was to make daily reports to Wilhelm II, appeared at the Villa Fraineuse, the Kaiser's residence on a hill outside Spa. Wilhelm, on seeing him, asked, "So, Heye, how does it stand: can I reckon on my army?"[110] Heye answered that the troops were tired and that they would not march home under Wilhelm or under anyone else in order to engage in civil war. He indicated that although the Kaiser might march *with* the army, he could not lead it even if its sole purpose was a peaceable return to Germany. At this juncture Hintze brought the news that Berlin was "flowing in blood" and that Max must have Wilhelm's abdication within a matter of minutes, for even troops ordered to Berlin because of their supposed reliability were deserting.[111] Stating that he was prepared to give up only his dignity as the Kaiser, Wilhelm told Hintze to inform Berlin that Hintze, together with Generals Schulenburg, Plessen, and Marschall, was in the process of drawing up a document stating that Wilhelm was *ready* to abdicate if such a step would avoid civil war. He would remain king of Prussia and, in that dignity, contrary to what Heye had told him, would lead his army home.[112] The four officers got to work at once, and the Kaiser, ashen and tightlipped, led his staff into the villa for a solemn and taciturn lunch.

Just as everyone rose from the table, shortly after 2 P.M., Hintze brought the completed document for Wilhelm's signature. After the Kaiser signed, Berlin was at once informed, but the answer received at Spa was that this act, so long resisted, had come too late.[113] An hour earlier Max had proclaimed that Wilhelm had renounced both of his thrones, and the crown prince his rights of succession, and that he, Max, had handed over the government to the Social Democrat leader Philipp Scheidemann, who in turn had proclaimed from a balcony of the Reichstag building the establishment of a German republic. On being informed, the Kaiser denounced Max's act: "Betrayal, shameless, disgraceful betrayal!"[114] He then retreated to an armchair in front of the fireplace, smoking one cigarette after the other, saying very little. Meanwhile, there were reports that even the bodyguard units at Spa could no longer be depended on, for the soldiers had declared that although they would not harm Wilhelm, they would not make any effort to defend him.[115]

Shortly before five on the afternoon of 9 November, Hindenburg and his staff again appeared before Wilhelm and informed him that since the army could no longer be counted on, he must abdicate as king of Prussia. They could not be responsible for letting him be captured by the revolutionaries and transported to Berlin as their prisoner.[116] The field marshal and his fellow officers had discussed among themselves the dangerous situation in Spa and the even greater peril that awaited Wilhelm across the border in Germany. They thereupon had decided that the Kaiser must leave Spa at once and that Holland, only fifty kilometers away and monarchical in sentiment, was preferable to Switzerland, the only — but far more distant — alternative. In Wilhelm's presence, Hindenburg, deferential by nature and reluctant bluntly to tell his ruler that the Kaiser *had* to leave Germany, took the rather oblique line that if the situation warranted abandoning Spa, Holland would be the place to which Wilhelm would have to flee.[117]

Informed of this decision, the entourage ordered the royal train to be made ready, for the Villa Fraineuse was not easily defensible. Wilhelm could dwell in his wagon-lit until the order was given to proceed to the Dutch border. Plessen agreed that the Kaiser should board his train but this was in order to protect him not until he could leave for Holland but until the railroad line to Cologne was cleared of revolutionaries and thus his return to Germany could be effected, a utopian notion with which the Kaiser enthusiastically concurred.[118] So Wilhelm refused to budge, declaring that he would remain with his troops. He ordered the villa to be stockpiled with arms, but he must have realized that he would not be there long, for he proceeded to burn a collection of personal papers.[119] In the early evening, General Plessen and Hintze finally succeeded in convincing the Kaiser that remaining in the villa was impossible and that to avoid capture, he must board the royal train. Wilhelm agreed, protesting that he would nevertheless rally his troops.[120]

With Wilhelm on the train were Hintze and Baron von Grünau, the representative of the Foreign Office attached to the Kaiser, as well as Adjutants Plessen and Sigurd von Ilsemann, Military Cabinet Chief General Marschall, and Major Niemann. Hindenburg remained at headquarters and, after their meeting on the afternoon of 9 November, never again saw Wilhelm. The Kaiser dined on the train, receiving reports about the deteriorating military situation because of which there was not only no possibility that he could proceed by rail to Germany but also less and less likelihood that the short passage to Holland would be open for long. At about 9 P.M. Hintze instructed Grünau to inform the Kaiser that in the opinion of both Hintze and Hindenburg, an escape to Holland had to be undertaken immediately or not at all. Wilhelm should be reminded that once safely there, he would be in a position to negotiate passage to Holland for his wife, who with her entourage was in the palace in Berlin under the guard of the revolutionary soldier and worker Soviet.[121] Shortly before 10 P.M. Grünau delivered this message to the Kaiser, who received it in the presence of General Plessen, whose dogged optimism, still alive only hours before, had finally collapsed. He too now knew that it was Holland for which the Kaiser must entrain. Wilhelm responded: "If I must! But not before early tomorrow morning."[122]

With that command, Wilhelm retired to his sleeping car, writing a letter to the Kaiserin and two unaddressed notes and then, at 2 A.M., having a short rest.[123] Two hours later, at 4 A.M. on 10 November, he reappeared in the dining car, with an hour to go until the appointed departure at 5. Wilhelm, however, had not accepted the fate that stood before him. "I just cannot bring myself to accept the decision to go to Holland!" he told his retinue. "What if Bolshevism also breaks out there?"[124] Only after Grünau and Plessen had reassured him that this was not likely did the Kaiser agree to leave. He solemnly shook hands with those officers who were to remain at Spa, and after they disembarked, the train got up steam. Twenty-five soldiers, armed with machine guns, rifles, and hand grenades, lined the corridor outside Wilhelm's compartment. In about ten minutes, the train halted at La Reide, for it was apparent that the revolutionaries had control of Liège and that continuation by rail was impossible. Several automobiles had therefore been dispatched to the tiny depot, with drivers who knew the route to the Dutch frontier. The vehicles proceeded without difficulty to the border village of Eysden, crossing over by convincing the guard that the party consisted of a German general and his staff. Once safely in Holland, Wilhelm lit a cigarette and urged his companions to do the same. "You've deserved it," he declared.[125] After Wilhelm's true identity had been discovered, the mayor of Eysden received him with courtesy, asking him to promise that he would not attempt to leave Holland, to which the Kaiser acceded with a handshake.[126] Several hours later, Friedrich Rosen, the German minister to Holland whom Hintze had alerted about the flight, arrived. "I am a broken man," Wilhelm told his old acquaintance. "How can I start again in life? There is no hope left for me and nothing remains for me save despair." The inventive Rosen suggested that the Kaiser could vindicate himself by writing his memoirs, and Wilhelm, with the characteristic electric change in temperament for which he was notorious, cried out with delight, "I'll start tomorrow!"[127]

The Dutch government had been informed that Wilhelm wanted to seek safety in Holland, but it apparently had no knowledge at what point along the border he would attempt to cross.[128] It ordered that from whatever place the Kaiser arrived he was to be taken temporarily to Amerongen, in the province of Utrecht in central Holland. Here Count Godard Bentinck, like the Kaiser a descendant of William the Silent, had been enlisted to provide shelter on his estate. At half past nine on the morning of 10 November, a Dutch train pulled into Eysden to transport Wilhelm to Maarn, the station nearest Amerongen. The trip took six hours, with thousands of hostile people lining the route. At three in the afternoon, the train reached its destination, where a crowd had assembled. Wilhelm, who had had almost no sleep in the last twenty-four hours, was pale, but he walked toward Count Bentinck's waiting automobile with a firm step, impervious to the prolonged booing. At Amerongen, there was also an unfriendly multitude. It included the wife of the British envoy at The Hague, a woman who had once known the Kaiser in better days in Berlin, where her husband had been posted.[129] She now undiplomatically stationed herself at the castle gate alongside curiosity seekers and members of the press in order to indicate, by her presence, the delight she felt at the fall of England's hated enemy.

Fourteen

IN EXILE: I BIDE MY TIME

ILHELM DROVE through the rain for thirty minutes to Count Godard Bentinck's estate at Amerongen, where arrangements had hurriedly been made to receive the fallen ruler and the thirty-odd members of his retinue. On arrival, the Kaiser's first request was for "a cup of real good English tea."[1] Wilhelm felt relieved to be with Bentinck and his wife, whose piety he greatly admired, but he recognized that this could be only a temporary residence. "Everything is very uncertain here," he wrote on 13 November to the Kaiserin, still a prisoner of the revolutionaries in Berlin. He was confined to the grounds of the house, and there was nothing to do but read, make archaeological drawings, and begin writing his memoirs.[2] Neither the Kaiser nor anyone else knew whether he would remain in Holland and, if so, where or whether he would be delivered over to the victorious Allies or to his own former subjects, now engulfed in a civil war that pitted communist revolutionaries against the army and the moderate socialist government. Wilhelm was in fact to remain as Count Bentinck's increasingly unwelcome guest until May 1920, when he established at nearby Doorn what would prove to be his domicile for the rest of his long life.

At the very end of November 1918, the republican government in Berlin allowed the Kaiserin to leave the capital and join her husband in Amerongen. Dona arrived in Holland on the twenty-eighth broken in health but still determined to shield the Kaiser from anyone who would do him harm. The royal couple believed that the prospect of Wilhelm's extradition was imminent, and at Christmas 1918 she wrote a letter to their children as a last greeting in the event that they would never see one another again.[3] The Kaiserin assured their sons and daughter that neither she nor their father would permit themselves to be delivered to the enemy, but even if that fate was avoided, there was no certainty as to where they could wile away their old age. The hostile reception Wilhelm encountered as he crossed over the border at Maarn on 10 November indicated how detested he was in Holland, and he himself recognized that his presence created difficulties for the Dutch government and for Count Bentinck. The French were determined to drag him before an international tribunal, but the Kaiserin hoped that once President Woodrow Wilson arrived in Europe to sign a peace treaty with the German republic, a less vindictive attitude might win the upper hand among the Allies.[4]

Wilhelm's uncertainty about the future was due first to his fear that assassins or kidnappers were lying in wait to deal with him, even though Count Bentinck's castle, surrounded by not one but two moats, had guard towers and iron gates that could provide considerable security. The Dutch government assigned a detail of fourteen policemen, a detective, and a large number of constables to patrol the grounds.[5] There was also grave concern at Amerongen during the first few days after the Kaiser's arrival that a Communist revolution was on the verge of toppling Queen Wilhelmina, a development that would almost certainly lead to Wilhelm's arrest. The Kaiser therefore might need to flee to save his life. The walled moats of the castle, surrounded by police who broke up the ice every night, made any sort of secret escape virtually impossible. If Wilhelm was to vanish from Holland, it would have to be from some place other than Amerongen. For that reason, in mid-December the Kaiser began to feign a recurrence of his lifelong ear affliction, keeping to his room for two weeks and then swaddling his head in bandages.[6] The ruse, kept up until the end of 1918, not only would create sympathy among the Dutch but also would serve as the pretext for Wilhelm's transfer to a clinic located in a place from which an escape might be more easily carried out.

On 8 December, Count Lynden van Sandenburg, the governor of the province of Utrecht, formally asked Wilhelm to leave the country. The Kaiser declared that he was prepared to do so in order to avoid embarrassing the Dutch, but where could he go? The overland route to neutral nations, notably Switzerland or Spain or Sweden, lay, in the first two cases, through France, a path that Wilhelm feared would lead to his murder. Traveling to Sweden would require passing through Germany, for which permission from the republican regime would have to be obtained. There was also the question of whether, and under what conditions, the Socialist government in Berlin might permit the former Kaiser to take up residence permanently in Germany. Wilhelm did not rule out this possibility and apparently contemplated asking his former high court marshal, Count August zu Eulenburg, who had remained in Berlin, to enter into negotiations with the Socialist cabinet. Eulenburg was to propose that the Kaiser, in return for residential rights in Germany, would forswear any future political activity.[7] This came to nothing.

There was considerable sentiment in Holland that Wilhelm II, who had never officially renounced either his Prussian citizenship or his imperial throne and thus could not technically be regarded as a private citizen, should be extradited to Germany. The Kaiser's concern on this point led him, probably at his wife's urging, to sign an instrument of abdication as both king and kaiser on 28 November, but this did nothing to dispel the insistence, especially strong among Dutch Socialists, that Wilhelm should leave the country so that Holland could avoid being confronted with an Allied demand that he be evicted, an insistence that, if resisted, might then be effected by force.[8] The conservative government in The Hague insisted, however, on enforcing the law of the land that prohibited handing over aliens who had sought refuge in Holland for political reasons. Wilhelm and his entourage decided that there was nothing to do but to await developments, and the Dutch government, hopeful that popular interest in the Kaiser's fate would eventually abate, abandoned its earlier insistence that Wilhelm leave Holland and insisted that he remain quietly at Amerongen, since any change of residence would instantly attract widespread attention. So Count Bentinck was prevailed upon to extend his hospitality for an indefinite period, a solution that pleased the Kaiser because he and the count had become quite friendly. Even so, there were periodic scares, leading to much activity between Amerongen and groups of the Kaiser's adherents in Germany who were prepared to do whatever was necessary to prevent his falling into enemy hands. One plan was to spirit Wilhelm to his hunting lodge at Rominten, hard on the Polish border, where an armed detachment would defend him.[9] The problem with such a scheme, other than the enormous logistical difficulties of carrying it out, was that if the Kaiser left Holland, it would appear to be his *second* flight from peril, and for that reason Friedrich von Berg-Markienen, Wilhelm's former Civil Cabinet chief, as well as Hans von Seeckt, a prominent republican general, insisted that he remain at Amerongen.[10] A better alternative, the two monarchists believed, would be to try to enlist King George V and other sovereigns to protest the extradition of their fellow ruler. The British king was very opposed to his first cousin's being treated as a war criminal, but on being approached by several dethroned German rulers to speak out in the Kaiser's behalf, he declined to intervene.[11] He argued that since his German cousin's fate was to be determined in the Allies' peace treaty with Germany, it was a matter with which all the victorious powers would soon have to deal.

The Allied plenipotentiaries assembled at Versailles in January 1919 to draw up the peace terms that would be dictated to Germany, one issue being whether the former Kaiser should be extradited and tried as a war criminal for having premeditated the war by urging Austria-Hungary to attack Serbia. The situation was unique, for historically military leaders defeated in war had either died in battle or surrendered. The French premier, Georges Clemenceau, led the demand for extradition, and the British prime minister, David Lloyd George, whose coalition government had won an impressive electoral victory on 14 December 1918 on a platform of bringing the Kaiser to trial, offered very voluble support, arguing that Dover Castle would be just the place for the legal proceedings.[12] To indict Wilhelm would raise a number of formidable legal questions. A German court was an impossible venue, since by tradition a sovereign, as maker of law, could not be tried by his own creation. Any non-German tribunal would have to wrestle with the fact that to bring the Kaiser to justice would be a proceeding for which existing international law provided neither a legal code nor a scale of penalties.[13] Wilson stood in opposition to his Allied partners, opposing a trial not because of such legal difficulties but because of fear that it would make a martyr of the former Kaiser and lead eventually to a Hohenzollern restoration. Instead Wilson argued that the Kaiser should "be judged by the contempt of the whole world," which the president considered to be the "worst punishment."[14]

After considerable debate that lasted into March 1919, a committee responsible for devising a judicial means of charging various enemy figures with perpetrating the war reported that the Kaiser's alleged role in deliberately inciting Austria in 1914 was not a charge that would be sustainable in a court of law. Wilhelm II and others might, however, be brought before the bar for perpetrating acts in violation of the "laws of humanity."[15] At the beginning of April, Clemenceau and Lloyd George pressed this rather amorphous charge, with Belgium to be the plaintiff as well as the scene of the trial and Wilhelm extradited from Holland to Brussels to meet his judges. On 8 May, the Kaiser learned that the peace terms being drawn up by the victors would include such provisions, to which he protested that he was guilty of nothing and that he was not subject to any tribunal.[16] The Belgian government, however, had no wish to antagonize King Albert, a very popular sovereign who was opposed to any arraignment of the Kaiser, or to offend the Dutch, who would declare that extradition was incompatible with their laws and was an affront to their sovereignty. In the end, the Allies had to be content with the inclusion, as article 227, in the Versailles treaty of 28 June 1919 — to Wilhelm, a "criminal abomination" — of an unenforceable statement that the former sovereign would be tried "for a supreme offence against international morality and the sanctity of treaties." On 16 January 1920, the Allies formally requested Holland to surrender the Kaiser, but the Dutch government at once declared that since it was not a signatory of the Versailles treaty, it was bound not by article 227 but only by the law and custom of the land, which traditionally had always granted "refuge for the vanquished in international conflicts."[17] Wilhelm would remain in Holland.

Although a patient and generous host, Count Bentinck was anxious for Wilhelm to establish his own abode. Even before the Dutch rebuffed the Allies' demand to hand over the Kaiser so that he could be tried, Wilhelm had come to the conclusion that unless his former enemies were prepared to use force, which seemed unlikely, he could expect to live in Holland with impunity, indefinitely and perhaps forever. That being the case, in August 1919, with the consent of the Dutch government, he bought a small castle set in unkempt grounds at Doorn, about eight kilometers from Amerongen.[18] The main building was antiquated and in need of repair, but on 15 May 1920, after the completion of considerable renovation, Wilhelm, the Kaiserin, and their retinue took their final leave of Count Bentinck and the town of Amerongen.[19] Awaiting them in Doorn were about a dozen servants brought from Germany, including "Vater" Wilhelm Schulze, who since 1879 had served as Wilhelm's valet.

By the time of the move to Doorn, Augusta Victoria's heart condition had become much worse, and she kept largely to her bedroom or often moved about the rest of the house or the garden in a wheelchair. Wilhelm, whose health was splendid, at once established a daily routine that would continue with almost no variation until his death many years later.[20] He arose at seven and took a walk, ending at the castle entrance to feed the ducks in the moat. The household was then assembled in the hall to hear him lead prayers, a custom the Kaiser had adopted from the pious Count Bentinck's ménage at Amerongen. After breakfast, along with the adjutants on duty and any guests who might be present, he returned to the garden to saw trees. This was a pastime he had developed during the war and had continued at Amerongen, where he had decimated Count Bentinck's forest. By 1929, Wilhelm had felled his twenty-thousandth tree at Doorn. Logs were sawed, first by hand but later with a machine, into three-foot lengths and taken to the castle, where they were chopped into firewood or distributed to the poor. Wilhelm also busied himself with planting trees and tending two rose gardens, one consisting entirely of American roots and the other, located near the road and occasionally open to the public, maturing eventually into the most spectacular rosarium in all of Holland. The Kaiser's dendrological projects were partly financed by his old friend Prince Max Egon von Fürstenberg, who periodically sent to Doorn specimen trees or money to be used for plantings.[21] Lunch was simple and brief, and after Wilhelm's nap there was tea, an interval for working at his desk on the saddle stool brought from the palace in Berlin. Dinner was at eight, followed by the party's retiring to a drawing room to hear the Kaiser read or talk until 10:30 or later. If Wilhelm was annoyed with his entourage, he punished them by reading extended passages from P. G. Wodehouse, whose comic tales amused him greatly but baffled the retinue, who lacked the Kaiser's acquaintance with the arcana of English landed society.[22] The entire routine was carried out with traditional, if somewhat reduced, Hohenzollern ceremonial, and like the court in Berlin in the better days before the war, it was stiflingly dull for those in attendance.[23]

Although Wilhelm had arrived in Holland on 10 November 1918 with a large entourage, the Dutch government eventually required him to limit his staff very severely. During his two decades at Doorn, the Kaiser consequently had only two adjutants on duty at any one time, a physician, and his house servants. They were housed in a large gatehouse built to Wilhelm's designs at the entrance to the Doorn property. Everyone found serving the loquacious Kaiser very taxing, and the adjutants and physicians, who received no pay other than their railroad fares to and from Holland, for the most part rotated duty every three months and after a few years usually opted to return permanently to Germany. An indication of how difficult it was to remain constantly exposed to the Kaiser is pathetically apparent in the departure of "Vater" Schulze, who after forty-three years decided in October 1922 that he could take no more and fled Doorn in tears without taking leave of his master of so many decades.[24]

Of all the Kaiser's staff, the only person who was on permanent duty at Doorn was Sigurd von Ilsemann, a young officer who in August 1918 had become one of Wilhelm's adjutants and had crossed over the border to Holland in the Kaiser's automobile three months later. The handsome and polished Ilsemann in October 1920 married Count Bentinck's daughter, who, like her husband, kept a very informative diary. Ilsemann recognized Wilhelm's unfortunate qualities and often chafed at the suffocating regime in Doorn, but like the other members of the retinue, he was not inclined to register much opposition. The crown prince was correct in reproaching his father's adjutants in Doorn for their sycophancy and for thereby perpetuating Wilhelm's "world of illusion."[25] Certainly no corrective could be expected from the Kaiserin and her entourage, the chief fixture of which was Countess Mathilde von Keller, who had served Augusta Victoria since Dona's marriage in 1881. "Aunt Ke," as she was called behind her back, was fanatically, even absurdly, insistent that life at Doorn should be a copy in miniature of the old days in Berlin and Potsdam. Although the countess had the virtue of fierce loyalty, Ilsemann's future wife declared, "One notices quickly that she isn't very bright."[26] It was altogether a somber, flat household, gripped by the Kaiserin's ever-worsening health.

After Augusta Victoria's arrival at Amerongen late in November 1918, she had sacrificed her own declining strength to cheer her husband, disguising how exhausted she was as long as that was possible. The trials of her children, to whom she was exceedingly attached, were an additional burden. She was separated from her favorite son, the crown prince, who in November 1918 had sought refuge in Holland and had been exiled by the Dutch government to the remote island of Wieringen. Another son, August Wilhelm, was in the throes of obtaining a divorce, something to which Augusta Victoria had always been resolutely opposed. The most overpowering calamity was the suicide in July 1920 of her youngest son, Prince Joachim, who had been in a state of despair over the lost war and his own dissolving marriage. The Kaiser and his wife were told that their son's death was an accident, although Wilhelm later discovered the sad truth.[27] In the Kaiser's opinion, Joachim's fate was the result of the betrayal of the German people in November 1918 by a "rabble of Jews" (*Judengesindel*), and he was sure that this same misfortune precipitated the final decline in his wife's condition.[28] After months of increasing debility, the Kaiserin died on 11 April 1921. She had expressed a wish to be buried in Germany, and the republican government in Berlin agreed that she could be interred in the royal mausoleum in the grounds of the New Palace at Potsdam. Wilhelm accompanied Augusta Victoria's body to the Dutch frontier and there said farewell to his wife of forty years.[29] On his return, Doorn took on an even more funereal character, with the Kaiserin's chamber closed off (as it remains even today) and the bed strewn every day with fresh flowers gathered by the Kaiser. Augusta Victoria's death further exacerbated Wilhelm's relations, never very good, with his sons, for he expected them piously to recall each anniversary of their mother's death. When, almost without exception, they failed to do so, he became very annoyed.[30] "My loneliness was indescribable," Wilhelm later wrote. "It bore me down. It was hell."[31]

The gloom that pervaded Doorn had financial as well as personal causes, for Wilhelm had arrived in Holland virtually penniless, without any civilian clothing or valuable possessions of note. The recovery of his fortune depended entirely on the goodwill of the republican government in Berlin. On the fall of the monarchy, all the royal palaces and other estates, together with their contents, had been seized. A distinction had to be made between what was the personal property of the Hohenzollerns and what were crown possessions that had legally devolved on the republic after the flight of the Kaiser. Wilhelm's thrift during his thirty-year reign had enabled him to save approximately fifty million marks, and there were dozens of properties that were considered family rather than state assets.[32] On 30 November 1918 the Socialist government, headed by Philipp Scheidemann, eager to convince the anxious electorate that private ownership of property would continue to be permitted, freed the Kaiser's personal belongings. The transfer of both goods and cash to the former sovereign soon began, and vast sums of money as well as some 1,565 pieces of table silver, 118 Oriental rugs, and dozens of paintings and pieces of furniture were eventually sent to Holland.[33] In spite of this settlement, Wilhelm continued to be financially strapped, not having enough to outfit himself with a decent supply of mufti to replace the wardrobe stolen from the Berlin palace in November 1918.[34] The Kaiser held that he was entitled not only to his personal fortune but also to an entail established by his Hohenzollern ancestors consisting of real estate in Berlin. The Weimar government eventually acknowledged this claim and between November 1918 and October 1920 paid Wilhelm slightly more than sixty-nine million marks, a sum equal to approximately $1,750,000 at the time.[35] From this, Wilhelm was expected to be able to support himself, his family, and his entourage and to purchase and maintain his residence in Doorn. The Kaiser, predictably, was ungrateful and rejected requests for financial assistance from other people and organizations in real need by declaring that he had been "plundered" by his former subjects.[36] The hyperinflation that overwhelmed Germany late in 1923 had a disastrous impact on the royal finances, reducing Wilhelm to selling some of the late Kaiserin's pearls and leaving him, according to his second wife, "practically wiped out."[37]

In November 1925, in preparation for a plebiscite as to whether or not the Hohenzollerns and the other former German rulers should be dispossessed, the family's landed estates were appraised and found to have a value of five hundred million marks. "That's democracy, damn it!" the Kaiser complained to a friend regarding the forthcoming vote.[38] The polling in June 1926 failed, however, to achieve the necessary majority, and four months later the Weimar Republic made a final financial settlement with Wilhelm, under which he received title to a number of urban palaces and rural castles and farms, some forest property rich in income, thirty million marks in cash, and between ten and twelve million in stocks and bonds.[39] The Kaiser, once again, did not think this nearly enough to enable him to live in state and to sustain what, by his reckoning, was a body of fifty Hohenzollern princes, some of them hugely in debt, who depended on his largesse for their existence. In spite of his complaints, the 1926 settlement proved sufficient to weather further disasters in the late 1920s, when the Kaiser was the victim of fraud perpetrated by a bank to which one of his entourage had connections.[40] The depression that began in October 1929 severely buffeted the royal fortune, and to cope, the Kaiser reduced salaries at Doorn or left vacant positions unfilled. Nevertheless, the miniature court continued to live in some semblance of pomp. Wilhelm more often than not had enough spare money to support his favorite literary, archaeological, or horticultural projects, and when he died in 1941 his estate came to almost fourteen million marks, the largest portion of which was in German and Dutch shares in which he had made a considerable profit.[41]

In his lonely but attractive refuge at Doorn, of which the Kaiser over the years became quite fond, he concentrated the brunt of his attention on a single issue: his return to the throne. This would preoccupy Wilhelm to the point of obsession until the mid-1930s, long after the ascent of Adolf Hitler had effectively put an end to his dreams. He did not expect much help in this from his ungrateful former subjects. The German masses, who had turned him out in 1918, were undeserving of his leadership, for he considered them to be stupid canaille, *Schweinehunde*, bereft of true national patriotism and sunk in gluttony and corruption. Here and there a noble German might rise up, but the herd itself was miserable.[42] In November 1918 the Germans had in his opinion committed the "*most enormous betrayal* that ever in the history of the world a people had committed against its own self, its dynasty, its traditions and its history."[43] For such a miserable and unworthy people, only one form of government was suitable, and that was the leadership of a strong personality, perhaps temporarily a dictator but ultimately a monarch.[44] The Germans had to realize that the western European notion of parliamentary constitutionalism was passé and unsuitable for the Fatherland, whose doltish citizens were incapable of sustaining such an institution and which, unlike the divine Hohenzollern monarchy, would not have as its cardinal purpose providing each and every citizen with a decent life.[45] A republic was, in Wilhelm's definition, a public-assistance institution (*Versorgungsanstalt*) appropriated by Socialists, Bolsheviks, Jews, and profiteers "who would feed at the trough while the *Volk* was left to suffer."[46] Its leaders were pirates, its political parties were cowardly, and its military fortitude was utterly deficient. The constitution adopted at Weimar in 1919 had created what he often declared was a "pig's republic" (*Saurepublik*), and anyone who supported it inexorably sank beneath the Kaiser's notice. That included the almost twenty-six million Germans, two-thirds of those voting in the first republican election in 1919, who cast their ballots for manifestly republican candidates.[47] Forgetting for the moment his xenophobic contempt for Orientals, Wilhelm declared that the Germans should turn for inspiration to the autocratic regimes of the East.[48] Although the Kaiser declared that the West had nothing to teach Germany, there were a few individuals, gleaned here and there from both sides of the Atlantic, who were worthy of emulation. "Dictatorship by the Monarch is the best remedy," he wrote to an American journalist in 1924, "with a mixture of Mussolini, Trotski, Sitting Bull, Arminius & Charles the Great! Don't you think so?"[49]

Wilhelm's contempt for the Weimar republic was limitless, not only because he so abhorred republicanism in principle but also because he despised the leaders who had come to the fore on 9 November 1918 and who had assumed the responsibilities that, of course, he himself had abandoned. Friedrich Ebert, a decent man, leader of the moderate wing of the Socialist Democratic Party, and eventually the initial president of the republic, was to the Kaiser a certified Bolshevik. The Socialists, whom Wilhelm had despised throughout his thirty-year reign (and indeed even before coming to the throne), were uniformly "without honor, lying, stealing, unpatriotic criminals, fit for the dung-heap." In their filth, they were worthy followers of Lenin, whom the Kaiser castigated as a "fiend, a true son of Satan and, like all his Jewish fellow trash, the born enemy of Christian culture."[50] For the Kaiser, all this was true of Ebert's associates Matthias Erzberger and Philipp Scheidemann, one a Roman Catholic and the other a cautious Socialist, but the Kaiser's real bête noire was not a Socialist but a liberal who had never opposed the Hohenzollern monarchy, even in exile. This was Gustav Stresemann, who from 1923 until his untimely death in 1929 was Germany's leading statesman and an admirer of the fallen Kaiser. Stresemann, so Wilhelm told Ilsemann, was the greatest traitor ever known and therefore deserved to be shot and quartered.[51] Stresemann's policy was to restore the German economy by fulfilling the peace terms signed at Versailles but at the same time cultivating the Russians in order secretly to engage in rearmament, which was prohibited by the treaty. To effect this, Stresemann ended the passive resistance that had begun in Germany early in 1923 in protest against the terms imposed on

Germany and that had led to the Allied occupation of the Rhineland. He also agreed to the limitation of Germany's armed forces, persuaded the Allies to permit Germany to join the League of Nations, lightened the burden of reparations in 1924 by negotiating an agreement with the American banker Charles G. Dawes, and signed the Locarno treaty of 1925 that outlawed war and acknowledged France's possession of Alsace-Lorraine. The award to Stresemann in the following year of the Nobel Peace Prize signified Germany's return to diplomatic respectability, and the Kellogg Pact of 1929 renouncing aggressive war crowned his career.

Wilhelm was at the ready to denounce each and every one of Stresemann's accomplishments. The Kellogg Pact was an "idioticy [*sic*]"; joining the League and agreeing to disarmament, to the Dawes "swindle," and to the alienation of imperial Germany's borderlands were all shameless acts that made a mockery of the Fatherland. Republican Germany, Wilhelm declared, had sunk to the disgraceful status of a banana republic.[52] Locarno, the peace conference in 1919, and the Washington disarmament conference of 1922 (a "colossal swindle") were three instances of the "Versaillesization" of Germany (*versaillisiertes Deutschland*).[53] Instead of this sort of abject capitulation, a real German leader would have slammed his fist on the table and declared that he would fight rather than be enslaved by the Allies. The French, for whom Wilhelm had an especially deep hate, should be driven out of Germany, where their Senegalese soldiers had raped white women and pillaged the land. But alas, the Germans had meekly given in, and that, the Kaiser pointedly noted, was because they had no monarch to take command.[54] Stresemann's accommodation with Russia in the east, which he worked hard to obscure because it conflicted with the terms of the Versailles treaty, was to Wilhelm just as sordid as his cowardly behavior in the west. Like Alexander Kerensky in his day, Stresemann was only the herald of the Bolsheviks and let the Russians take advantage of him with the result that Germany's honor, in the east no less than in the west, was lost.[55]

Wilhelm thus conceived as his mission the revival of national dignity. Without an army at his command, he could not force himself on the Germans; he had to be called home. He seems oddly enough to have had no doubt whatsoever that the very people he had mercilessly castigated for stupidity, greed, and worthlessness would one day summon him to Berlin to sit again on his ancient throne. "I [will] return when the People of Germany *beg me* to come & save them, *recall me*, as they rejected me!" he told an American friend. He would have nothing to do with sudden gestures calculated to engender the rising of a monarchical fronde, such as those vainly attempted by ex-Kaiser Karl when he twice appeared in Hungary. "All must be made in a loyal, open, gentlemanlike way. Heaven will indicate the right moment, & move the hearts of my countrymen. . . . Thy Will be done, & until then I bide my time!"[56] But for Wilhelm II to be brought back to Germany, a monarchical movement would have to be nurtured. This in turn would require a campaign designed to remove the doubts and reservations that existed about his qualifications once again to lead Germany. Many Germans, to say nothing of millions of other Europeans, held the Kaiser responsible for the outbreak of the war, and he, after all, had been at least in a formal sense the architect of defeat in 1918. Then Wilhelm had fled the country, thus avoiding altogether the humiliation and hardship inflicted on the vanquished Fatherland. The Kaiser's first task was therefore to establish a creditable case that it was not *he* who had been responsible for either 1914 or 1918, that indeed he had been blameless in both instances. The past would have to be pictured in such a way that Wilhelm, like his former subjects for whom he expressed such contempt, would emerge as a victim, one ready to avenge the wrongs done both to him and to Germany in November 1918 and at Versailles.

Stresemann and the other republican traitors could not be expected to take the lead in clearing Wilhelm II's record, for if it could be shown that the Kaiser had not been responsible for the war or Germany's defeat, then the Weimar Republic was the usurper of the Hohenzollerns' ancient rights and thus had no right to exist. Wilhelm consequently was eager to enlist in his cause any person, or any group, who was prepared to interpret the past in a way that exonerated him. The Kaiser himself produced two volumes of memoirs, both of which were tendentious rationalizations of his life that testified amply to his subjective obtuseness. *Ereignisse und Gestalten (Events and Figures)*, which appeared in 1922, was written at Amerongen in the first year of exile. Although the Kaiser composed the body of the manuscript, Eugen Zimmermann, editor-in-chief of the Scherl publishing house in Berlin, thoroughly rewrote it.[57] The Kaiser believed that his memoir would serve as an "arm of truth against the lies of Versailles."[58] In 1927, Wilhelm published *Aus Meinem Leben (From My Life)*, which dealt with his life before he came to the throne. The Kaiser's family and friends found both volumes embarrassing to the monarchical cause, and although the books brought Wilhelm handsome royalties, he was disappointed that they were not more widely read in Germany.[59] Both memoirs were fulsome targets for critics, who mercilessly pointed out the innumerable distortions and evasions committed by the author.

The Kaiser claimed that from youth he had been a "fanatical historian" and that in Holland he had worked day and night accumulating material for his books, but he could not alone absolve Germany and himself from the responsibility for the war, a battle that he declared was more important than the solution of all of Germany's contemporary problems.[60] One protégé he enlisted was Alfred Niemann, a young General Staff officer who from early August 1918 until the end of the war had been a member of Wilhelm's entourage. Niemann wrote four cheaply produced books that were full of defensive comments by the Kaiser about his reign, but the works failed to win much popular success.[61] In addition to Niemann, another of Wilhelm's literary confidants was the outspoken polemicist George S. Viereck, editor of the *American Monthly* and a kinsman of sorts of the Kaiser's, Viereck being an illegitimate descendant of Wilhelm I. The Kaiser had read Viereck's revisionist accounts minimizing Germany's role in causing the war and thereupon entered into an extensive correspondence with him. In the mid-1920s, Viereck published a number of articles in the *Saturday Evening Post*, full of exculpations provided by the Kaiser, who received half of the author's royalties. Wilhelm eventually became disenchanted with his friend, complaining alternately that he did not get enough of his material published or that Viereck made improper use of it. The friendship, once quite warm, faded, but Wilhelm continued to allow Viereck to correspond with him and to come to Doorn.[62]

The Kaiser was annoyed that few German historians showed an interest in sounding him out on the events of his long reign.[63] Neglect had always perturbed Wilhelm, and he was eager to find a defender. After a number of overtures to German historians failed, a young Austrian journalist with historical aspirations, Karl Nowak, was invited to come to Holland. Wilhelm was soon infatuated and permitted Nowak to have access to his papers.[64] Nowak, he declared, was a "ruthless searcher after truth, with the aim of destroying once and for all the infamies" made against the Kaiser.[65] He was in fact, like Viereck, a rank polemicist whose books sought to demote the importance of all other figures, civilian and military, and to present Wilhelm as an inspired but unappreciated ruler. The Kaiser was appropriately grateful, in spite of efforts of his staff to convince him that Nowak's books, like the Kaiser's own, would lead to ridicule. As Wilhelm fell more and more under Nowak's spell he refused to see any other literary figures, and until Nowak's sudden death in 1932 the journalist enjoyed almost a monopoly of access to the Kaiser. The demise of his vindicator depressed the Kaiser greatly, and he declared that now the true history of his reign could not be completed.[66] Nowak's books enjoyed only limited popularity, and the author had been forced to cajole Wilhelm into buying back the unsold copies of his first book, *Kaiser und Kanzler* (1929), which was largely a spiteful and unconvincing attack on Otto von Bismarck, who Nowak claimed had vainly imagined himself to be "the chosen of the Lord."[67]

In addition to sponsoring or contributing to various works defending his historical role, Wilhelm read some of the vast tide of literature on the war, and even if the portrayal made of him was often unfavorable, he was delighted to be the center of attention.[68] It was nevertheless very distressing to the Kaiser that a great many of his former officials or their literary executors had wasted no time after imperial Germany's fall in writing memoirs that justified their own positions but unflatteringly pictured their sovereign as either incompetent or bellicose. Such revelations would only intensify the conviction among the Allies that he had been responsible for the war and would thereby revive the question of extradition. The Kaiser took criticism by his former lieges very hard, on occasion bursting into tears and requiring medical treatment to restore his nerves.[69] Only a few accounts published in the 1920s were generous to Wilhelm II, one being Admiral Alfred von Tirpitz's *Erinnerungen* (*Memoirs*, 1919), in which Tirpitz deliberately contrived to portray the Kaiser in a more favorable light than the actual record justified.[70] The admiral's subsequent two-volume *Politische Dokumente* (1924–26) was another matter. This was largely a compilation of archival material, and the admiral therefore could not so readily conceal Wilhelm's bombastic and impetuous nature. The Kaiser found the admiral's volumes "perfectly outrageous" and threatened to relieve him of his order of the Black Eagle.[71]

The Kaiser approved of the "eminent historian" Harry Elmer Barnes, whose *The Genesis of the War* (1926) exonerated Germany from the stain of guilt for 1914.[72] Barnes was bid to Doorn, and Wilhelm subsequently declared that his newly discovered apologist was a "splendid specimen of a clear minded, open, veracious, energetic warden of truth. A fine character and thorough gentleman!" Wilhelm added, "We became great friends!"[73] He was also delighted with any books that would promote his popularity with various groups in Germany who might lobby for his restoration. For that reason he provided financial support to Max Buchner, a conservative professor of history at Würzburg, who in 1929 published a book extolling Wilhelm's behavior toward German Catholics, a group that the Kaiser had long detested but with whom he was eager to reconcile in order to return to the throne.[74] Wilhelm was confident enough of his position reflected in these revisionist writings to declare in 1930, "History has already given her verdict in my favour."[75] But in fact historical revisionism never succeeded in overcoming the general view that Germany had been largely responsible for the war and that, among Germans, Wilhelm II was the most culpable figure. History did not, the Kaiser's conviction notwithstanding, render a verdict in his favor, nor did anything that Wilhelm did in exile work to promote his return to Germany and to the throne. Some of his own family believed that Wilhelm's flight to Holland and the condemnatory memoirs written by his former officials had robbed him of any chance of regaining his crown.[76] Even ardent conservatives, such as Admiral Tirpitz or Wolfgang Kapp, who in 1920 staged an unsuccessful coup against the republic, a coup that was believed to be aimed at a restoration of the monarchy, did not envision Wilhelm's return to Berlin as kaiser.[77] Wilhelm's brother-in-law, the deposed duke of Saxe-Meiningen, who had never liked the Kaiser, was undoubtedly right when he declared in 1920, "There is no one who would have him back, not even the most blue-blooded conservative."[78] The Kaiser was oblivious to the lack of enthusiasm for him in Germany and confident that he would be recalled to his crown. "He would like to play Mussolini, but he's overlooked the fact that his people are not Italians," the duke sneered.[79] In 1924, believing the ground was fertile for a restoration, the Kaiser recruited Magnus von Levetzow, a retired admiral with strong monarchist sympathies, to be his agent in Germany in charge of promoting his return to the throne.[80]

Awaiting the call that would never come, Wilhelm bided his time by berating all those who failed to appreciate his genius, who had been responsible for his having been forced to give up his crown, and who now wantonly prevented his return to the throne. Never once, not in so much as a single instance, did the Kaiser acknowledge that he himself should be heavily accountable for the extinction of the Hohenzollern monarchy. He declared that, like Pericles, he too suffered from the ingratitude of his people. He liked to quote another famous martyr, the unhappy Pope Gregory VII, who was driven from his papal throne and later died in desolation in southern Italy in 1085. "I have loved what was right and hated what was not," the pope regretted, "and because of that I perished in exile."[81] And it certainly never occurred to Wilhelm II that it was *his* record, and *his* personality, that guaranteed that neither he nor his descendants would ever again mount the throne. His faithful adjutant Ilsemann, who loyally struggled to detect virtue in the Kaiser, noted with exasperation that Wilhelm "always believed what he does is right but what others do is wrong."[82]

The Kaiser was certain that he had almost succeeded in winning the war only to have been betrayed by his own army in that General Paul von

Beneckendorff und von Hindenburg had encouraged, even forced, him to abandon his troops and flee to Holland before dawn on 10 November 1918. The field marshal was the chief personal agent of his fall, but the underlying cause of Germany's collapse, and therefore of the Kaiser's forfeiture of his crown, was a broad conspiracy that had been percolating in Germany and in Europe for decades. The Jews, Wilhelm declared, were at the heart of all the evil of 1918 and were responsible for the Weimar republic, which he declared was "prepared by the *Jews*, made by the *Jews*, [and] maintained by *Jewish pay*."[83] This was no wonder, since the Jews were to Wilhelm an alien and unworthy race, like the French of Negroid descent, and therefore without any claim to a European identity.[84] Frenchmen, who disguised their basic filth with perfume, were essentially weak and feminine in nature and, through miscegenation with Jews, blacks, and other races, had created a society characterized by the rule of the masses.[85] France's conspiracy with the Africans was creating a "black peril" that represented a danger of "gigantic proportions" to Caucasian civilization.[86] The British seemed incapable of recognizing this racial danger and, as he informed Viereck in his ungrammatical English, allowed "the Niggerboys to march shoulder to shoulder with the Lords son and the squires boy in the Boy-Scout companies. The beginning of treason to their Race formerly only executed by the French Negroids!"[87] Masculine nations, such as Germany or Holland, on the other hand, were racially pure and were therefore destined to be governed by great individual leaders.[88]

The Gospel might instruct men and women to love their brethren, but that was not an injunction that appealed to the Kaiser. "My brother," he assured a Catholic friend in 1929, "is first and always foremost my fellow German."[89] That excluded Jews, who were alien to German civilization, and the Kaiser viewed with approbation the attack on Jewish shops in Berlin during the height of the hyperinflation in 1923.[90] Catholics, no matter what Professor Buchner had written about Wilhelm's conciliatory views, were also to be rejected according to the Kaiser, for they were working arm in arm with the Jews to destroy Protestantism. The Catholic Center Party, which Wilhelm had loathed even before coming to the throne in 1888, was a hotbed of Jewish and Bolshevik sedition, and Wilhelm believed that its leader, Matthias Erzberger, a "Catholic Jew" who had signed the Versailles treaty, was conspiring with the former Habsburg empress Zita to form a Catholic-German empire.[91] The Catholics were not the only allies of the Jews. There were also the German Socialists and Russian Bolsheviks, who were equally eager to obliterate Germany, and almost equally dangerous were the "white Zionists," as Wilhelm referred to Masons.[92] Europe, the Kaiser steadily proclaimed from 1918 on, had an obligation to destroy the Bolsheviks, who, as Russians allied (he believed) with the Chinese, represented the realization of his warnings made for decades about a "Yellow Peril."[93] The reds, "a goddamned race of peoples' parasites," were embroiled with the Africans, also a lesser race.[94] Wilhelm repeatedly called for the formation of a great alliance under the leadership of a German monarch to relieve Europe of this pestilence led by Vladimir Lenin, that "worthy son of Satan and sworn enemy, like his Jewish riffraff, of Christian culture."[95] The Kaiser envisioned that this holy campaign would be "a pogrom without mercy and without indulgence." When there was no response whatsoever to Wilhelm's jeremiads, he blamed this on the fact that the Foreign Office in Berlin had been captured by the Bolsheviks.[96]

Wilhelm was enraged that the Jews, armed with their ubiquitous press, were relentlessly hostile to the house of Hohenzollern, and he believed that the road to Berlin would remain closed to him until they had changed their attitude.[97] The Jews and their scum were responsible for all the misfortunes that had beset Germany, and the Kaiser, since 1914. "Satan's servants" included Attila the Hun, Genghis Khan, Nero, Napoleon, and finally Edward VII, who with the help of the Jews and the Masons had set the stage for the First World War.[98] Germany might have won that great encounter had it not been for the treachery of the Jews, whom Wilhelm held accountable, in collusion with his own former subjects, for bringing down the Hohenzollern dynasty. It had all begun in 1908 with the charge of homosexuality brought by the Jewish literary lion, Maximilian Harden, a "loathsome, dirty, Jewish fiend," against Wilhelm's closest friend, Count Philipp zu Eulenburg, whom the Kaiser had then abruptly abandoned but who, he claimed some years after Eulenburg's death in 1921, had been in fact innocent.[99] The revolution of 1918 was an act of "betrayal by the German people, deceived and lied to by a pack of Jews, of their royal house and their army."[100] The ignominious Versailles treaty of 1919, no less than the revolution of the year before, was also treachery, and the same was true of the Weimar constitution. Christian tradition, the Kaiser intoned, did not allow for the concept of a sovereign people, and this absurd notion was in fact the creation of Jews and Masons during the French Revolution of 1789.[101] The Jews, Wilhelm regretted, had no tradition in their mythology that told of the return of dispossessed rulers to their rightful thrones, and for that reason they worked against the Hohenzollerns and instead supported the inferior Wittelsbachs of Bavaria.[102]

As a result of this conspiracy of Jews, Bolsheviks, Catholics, and Socialists, the Kaiser was forced to wile away his time in Doorn, desperately unhappy at being now entirely alone, without wife or children and with only a handful of retainers. His entourage thought that he might remarry after the customary two-year period of royal mourning, and they believed that the Kaiser's childhood friend Frau Gabriele von Rochow, only a year younger than he and an occasional guest in Holland, would be suitable.[103] Nothing came of this matrimonial project, but the dreariness that pervaded Doorn was in any case not to last long. On 5 November 1922, a little more than a year and a half after the Kaiserin's death, Wilhelm remarried. He was ecstatic at the prospect, wiring his friend Prince Fürstenberg, "How happy I am that I have found a woman who is ready to share my loneliness with a warm love and again to bring sunshine into this house."[104] Wilhelm wrote at greater length to Countess Therese von Brockdorff-Kletkamp, for decades the chief lady-in-waiting to the late Kaiserin. What he needed, Wilhelm declared, was "a sympathetic soul," a heart in which he could confide, a person to whom he could bare his soul. He added: "No adjutant or relative or acquaintance of either sex can do that! Beyond merely a wife, I must have a comrade, a friend, and that my bride will be to me. The memory of the late empress will as before be sacredly upheld and nourished, and my bride will do all that she can to imitate her. We have both at once emphasized this in standing bowed in prayer at the Kaiserin's bed."[105]

The bride was Princess Hermine von Schönaich-Carolath, born into the elder line of the Reuss dynasty, rulers of one of imperial Germany's most inconsequential federal states. At the time of her marriage, Hermine, whom Wilhelm called "Hermo," was not quite thirty-five, short and rather swarthy, dignified but lively, shrewd, and not without charm.[106] She had been married to Prince Johann-Georg von Schönaich-Carolath, who was rich but of a family ennobled only in the eighteenth century and by no means equal to the regnant Reusses. She and the prince, who died in April 1920, had five children, of whom two sons and two daughters survived. In 1908 Hermine had been Wilhelm's partner at a luncheon but otherwise had never spoken to him. She was a woman who knew what she wanted, telling a woman friend that it was her "duty" to share the Kaiser's sad life, and she set forth to capture him. An English visitor to Doorn thought that the phrase "tough cookie" summed her up, and that seems to have been an accurate assessment.[107] Hermine contrived to have her fifteen-year-old son write to Wilhelm sympathizing with his loneliness and offering to bring his mother's Easter cakes to Doorn. Wilhelm replied, Hermine answered, and an invitation was soon forthcoming.[108] Hermine handled her brief courtship with Wilhelm with premeditated skill, and he was soon cast in the role of the nervous suitor; he was in a state of constant agitation as her first visit to Doorn approached, and he was enraptured from the moment that she arrived. According to the bride-to-be, Wilhelm saw in her "the messenger of love sent . . . by heaven!"[109] There was probably an element of financial calculation in Hermine's campaign, for although she owned several estates in eastern Germany, they were mismanaged and she had fallen into debt. The prenuptial agreement signed by the two provided that Wilhelm would maintain Hermine, and on marriage she received an appanage of slightly more than 90,000 marks a year. Wilhelm additionally advanced her some 773,000 marks over the years to help bail out her landed properties, and he also periodically made grants to her improvident children.[110]

No one in Doorn or in Wilhelm's family expected Wilhelm to live alone, and the crown prince and the Kaiser's brother Heinrich indeed wanted him to remarry.[111] Hermine's ambitions were ill-concealed, however, and neither the entourage nor the Hohenzollern family favored the match, one that came indecently soon after the Kaiserin's death and that involved a woman who seemed inappropriately young, too ambitious, and genealogically not of the first water.[112] The alarm increased when Wilhelm ordered that his new wife was to be referred to as the Kaiserin Hermine, pointing out that it was German tradition for wives to bear their husband's titles, be it *Ihre Exzellenz* or *Deutsche Kaiserin*. Although the German government insisted on inscribing her passport as "wife of the former German Kaiser," Hermine took great satisfaction in being addressed at Doorn as an empress. She was understandably annoyed, however, by the Kaiser's unfeeling habit of using the phrase "my wife" to refer to his deceased consort.[113] Wilhelm managed to be oblivious to all objections made to his marriage, declaring that in fact his match met with almost universal approbation. He insisted that there was a Hohenzollern precedent in the nuptials in 1824 of his great-grandfather, King Frederick Wilhelm III of Prussia, to an Austrian princess.[114] On the wedding day, two of his five surviving sons and his only daughter were conspicuously absent at the simple service, with the bride outfitted in a gown designed by her groom. There was, of course, nowhere to go for a honeymoon.

Hermine at once settled into the role of mistress of the house, and if her motives in marrying Wilhelm were perhaps grasping, she was scrupulously loyal to her husband, gracefully deferring to him in all decisions and resigning herself to the difficult role of living in a house that was a temple to the memory of her predecessor.[115] It is not easy to differentiate Hermine's ambitions from her feelings, but it seems that like everyone else, she found living with Wilhelm a trial. She admired her husband's refusal to sink into misanthropy in spite of all the humiliations he had suffered since 1918, but at the same time she admitted that he was childish and impetuous.[116] Wilhelm and Hermine exuded a superficial impression of compatibility, but appearances were deceiving, and there was friction from the start. They both complained about the other, and Ilsemann, who was the one adjutant on perpetual duty at Doorn and who therefore observed the couple every day, concluded that after five years of marriage, the sort of conjugal partnership that could be considered normal had failed to materialize.[117] Hermine handled the Kaiser's disaffected children with skill, promising to Wilhelm's daughter that she would "in piety and reverence uphold the memory of the dear, irreplaceable Kaiserin and respect the inner and essential ties between father and children [existing because of] the death of the noble Kaiserin."[118] She had a picture of Augusta Victoria hung in her boudoir next to one of her husband and later suggested that a biography be written of the late empress, a hagiographical study that pleased Wilhelm greatly.[119] Hermine's efforts to ingratiate herself were not very successful. The crown prince never warmed to her, and his wife, the preeminent female Hohenzollern after the Kaiserin's death in 1921, resented Hermine's regal pretensions and habitually referred to her as "the new wife."[120] No one in the retinue at Doorn ever liked the chatelaine, whose judgment they found all too often mistaken and whose dignity was, for all her efforts, bogus. Hermine in turn was wary of the Hohenzollerns and was jealous of anyone who appeared to have a rival influence with her husband.[121]

Remarriage solved the problem of Wilhelm's loneliness, but at a price, and after Hermine's arrival, Doorn was a hotbed of backbiting. One of Wilhelm's doctors early described the situation at the little castle: "The one intrigues against the others, the men among themselves, the women among themselves, and both against one another."[122] Yet even though there was some marital conflict, life became happier for Wilhelm, since Hermine liked to entertain. Queen Wilhelmina carefully avoided the Kaiser, and she never received him during the twenty-two years he lived in Holland. Her government, on the other hand, was accommodating and gradually lifted the restrictions imposed in 1918 on the Kaiser's freedom of movement so that he and his bride could now frequently tour the countryside in Wilhelm's gigantic Mercedes cabriolet. The royal pair occasionally visited a small group of Dutch friends, visitors appeared regularly from Germany, and now and then relatives came to stay.

In spite of their occasional quarrels, the Kaiser and his wife had in common a fixed determination that one day the Hohenzollern monarchy would be restored, if not under Wilhelm himself, then with one of his descendants as sovereign. Hermine from the beginning saw herself as the leading advocate of restoration, for she, unlike the Kaiser or the crown prince, could travel to Germany. There was a personal motive in her calculations. She resented the cult of Wilhelm's dead consort that was so prominent a feature of Doorn and the fact that many German monarchists did not acknowledge her as more than a morganatic wife, one who should be deprived of the imperial title.[123] A restoration of the empire would make her *the* Kaiserin and put these critics in their place. Moreover, it offended Hermine that Wilhelm II's former subjects did not treat him with appropriate respect and took insufficient interest in his plight as an exile. Like millions of other Germans, Hermine felt an acute sense of dissatisfaction with the Weimar Republic and its bourgeois leaders. She was therefore very susceptible to the blandishments of anyone who showed interest in trying to effect Wilhelm II's return at least to Germany, if not to his ancient throne, and in granting her officially the dignity of empress. A resourceful and determined woman, Hermine set to work not only to make Doorn more lively for the Kaiser but also to cultivate and encourage those in Germany who shared her imperial ambitions.

Fifteen

HOHENZOLLERNS AND NAZIS:

THE PATH TO THE PALACE

WILHELM II's miniature court at Doorn, enlivened through his marriage to Hermine, provided him with an agreeable setting from which he could pursue his cultural interests and political ambitions. The grounds at Doorn, denuded by the Kaiser's woodchopping only to be reforested, were subjected to the sort of archaeological excavations he had once enjoyed at Corfu, with his occasional finds sent to the provincial museum in Utrecht. Wilhelm was an eager host, and during his long residence in Holland a steady stream of guests appeared at Doorn, welcomed cordially and then ensnared in protracted royal monologues.[1] There were a few, but not many, old friends from better days, a horde of curiosity seekers, and a few adventurers who claimed that, for money, they could arrange Wilhelm's return to the throne.[2] A procession of historians, cultural anthropologists, and pastors paid homage to the Kaiser, who in spite of his protestations of financial debility, occasionally funded digs and museum exhibitions dealing with the Greco-Roman era, as well as anthropological expeditions to Africa.[3]

The Kaiser's most eagerly expected guest was Leo Frobenius, the president of the Research Institute for Cultural Morphology at Frankfort on the Main, who was, Wilhelm declared, a universal intellect devoid of the arid specialization that dessicated less talented professors. Frobenius was an accomplished courtier always ready to encourage Wilhelm's hopes of a Hohenzollern restoration, to praise Wilhelm's archaeological expertise, and to share his strongly anti-Socialist views.[4] Frobenius was famous for his ethnological explorations and for his theory that human civilization had developed organically in a way similar to plants and animals. Wilhelm, however, was less interested in these theories than he was in having the learned professor give ballast to his own ideas through their "close, intellectual connection."[5] He was therefore happy to help Frobenius financially, to have intermediaries enlist Henry Ford (even though Wilhelm believed the automotive magnate to be a Jew) to provide automobiles for an African expedition, or to have one of his adjutants intervene in Frobenius's behalf with Field Marshal Paul von Beneckendorff und von Hindenburg after the army officer became president of the Weimar Republic in 1925.[6]

What was important to Wilhelm was Frobenius's interest in tracing the connection among the civilizations of Europe, the Near East, India, and Africa, for Frobenius's discoveries confirmed the Kaiser's view that navigation was the force that had united humankind in prehistoric times.[7] Frobenius's findings were also of importance for contemporary political as well as religious thought. Since the Greeks, and by inheritance the Germans, were inextricably bound to the civilizations of the Near East, they had no reason to fear the prophesy made by Oswald Spengler, in his *Decline of the West: Outline of a Morphology of World History* (1918–22), that Europe's star was falling. The future lay to the East, which created some momentary embarrassment given Wilhelm's once passionate advocacy of a "Yellow Peril" and his habit of writing on postcards emblazoned with Professor Hermann Knackfuss's pictorial admonition: "People of Europe, Protect Your Most Sacred Possessions!" The drawing would simply have to be revised, he declared. "We belong on the other side!"[8] Was not Germany, as Frobenius had taught, "the face of the east turned toward the west," and thus unlike the Berber-Hamitic French, who, as the professor pointed out, were to be numbered among the colored races?[9]

In a religious sense, Wilhelm believed that Frobenius's work would help to free Christianity from the evil toils of Judaism, for archaeology was the proper means through which the origins of religion might be revealed. If Western culture, passing from the East to the Greeks and thence to Germany, was thus a mixture of Oriental and Hellenic elements, the religious expression of that Western civilization must also reveal its similar development from the East. That, most assuredly to the Kaiser, did not mean that it had developed from the Semitic Jews, who had killed God's Son and therefore merited eternal damnation.[10] Jesus was a Galilean by nativity; he had not been born in Bethlehem and therefore was not a Jew, nor, being a man of uncommon handsomeness, with blond hair and with hands and arms of aristocratic stamp, did he resemble a Jew.[11] "The Jews," Wilhelm triumphantly declared in 1923 to his friend the polemicist Houston Stewart Chamberlain, who needed no encouragement on this point, "are *not our religious predecessors* but rather Zoroaster and the Persians, thus Aryans [are]!"[12] It was unfortunate that Luther in the Old Testament of

his German Bible had not used "Yahweh" rather than "God" to differentiate the Jewish from the Christian deity, for Yahweh was "atrocious" (*ent-
setzlich*).[13] A revised Bible would do well simply to commence with the
New Testament, but if the Old Testament was to be retained, Jewish
national history and legends should be expunged, along with "harem
romances" such as the book of Esther. A critical look should be leveled at
the songs of Solomon and at the psalms, some of which, Wilhelm held,
were assuredly not the work of David.[14] Once men and women had rejected the raging, vengeful Yahweh, they would become united in love;
Chamberlain, the Kaiser's "second Luther," and Frobenius, with his in-
spirational style and belief in the interconnectedness of civilizations, were
the men to lead the way. This sense of commonality obviously contained,
in Wilhelm II's view, no place for the hated Jews, nor could the revival of
piety on earth for which he hoped be expected to obliterate national
borders and patriotic sentiments. "Nationalism is in itself *good*," the Kaiser wrote to Frobenius at the end of 1931, provided that it did not run
amok as was the case in the imperial appetites of France, Great Britain,
and the United States.[15] Although Wilhelm was confident that there would
one day exist a philosophical, cultural, and racial unity stretching from
India to the Atlantic, God would favor those who faithfully followed
him.[16]

On 1 June 1925, Wilhelm, together with Frobenius and Alfred Jeremias, an eminent anthropologist from the University of Leipzig whom
the Kaiser had known for twenty years, founded the "Doorn Academy"
(*Doorner Akademie*). Until 1931, this group held annual meetings that
lasted several days, but in the next year the academy was disbanded in
favor of a new group known as the "Doorn Work Group" (*Doorner
Arbeits-Gemeinschaft*), with Wilhelm as president.[17] The purpose of the
organization was to assemble an archive of pictures and writings dealing
with Mediterranean and Indian civilizations, the prologue to a great syn-
thesis of world culture. The membership, largely drawn from academic
colleagues or friends of Frobenius's, included Jeremias, Dr. Julius Jordan,
director of antiquities for the government of Iraq, a number of German
and Dutch scholars, and one or two members of Wilhelm's entourage. The
Kaiser served as a sort of clearinghouse for the ideas of other members,
forwarding material sent to him to those who might have an interest in the
contents. He opened the annual meetings of the group, often providing a
comment at the conclusion of the papers and on occasion presenting an
address, not always of his own composition. One such address, delivered
in 1933 and written by Frobenius, was entitled "History of the Chinese

Monads Yin and Yang," but the Kaiser did not always keep to cultural topics and sometimes managed to conflate his material with denunciations of socialism and bolshevism.[18]

Wilhelm often raised before his colleagues the interpretation of Greek statuary, a subject that had intrigued him since his university days at Bonn sixty years earlier. Under Frobenius's influence, he had become greatly interested in the relation of the Greeks to other ancient civilizations, and the discovery in 1911 of an ancient Doric temple excavated on the island of Corfu not far from his summer palace, the Achilleion, became a matter of acute interest to him. Wilhelm had helped finance the dig and had Professor Wilhelm Dörpfeld, an eminent archaeologist who had been the great Heinrich Schliemann's assistant at the discovery of Troy and Mycenae many years earlier, come to Corfu to direct the excavations and to discuss the significance of the statuary group in the ruin's pediment. Wilhelm had returned to Corfu in 1912 and again in 1914 to investigate the progress that was being made and to help arrange for the display of the find in a local museum. This was the beginning of a long association between the Kaiser and Dörpfeld, who until his death in 1940 continued to write to the Kaiser at Doorn.[19] The excavation at Corfu fascinated Wilhelm because it seemed to offer an indubitable confirmation of his notions of the integrality of civilizations. The temple's eastern pediment contained a number of human and animal figures, but presiding at the center was the likeness of a snake-encrusted Amazon poised between two massive lions.[20] Dörpfeld and Wilhelm both believed that the female figure was meant to be one of the three Gorgons, the serpent-haired women of Homeric mythology whose very glance could turn men to stone. The Gorgons, although first presented in literature through Homer, were not, in the Kaiser's opinion, of Greek origin but rather were derived from the sun goddess of the southern Arabians. This could be shown by tracing the evolution of the swastika, the symbol of the movement of the heavenly bodies and the Gorgons' sign.[21] Phoenician seafarers had taken the motif from Arabia to various sites in the Mediterranean, and the Greeks, on becoming aware of it, had associated the Gorgons with their goddess Artemis.[22]

In retirement in Doorn, unable to continue his active participation in the Corfu digs, Wilhelm spent considerable time reading professional archaeological literature on the Gorgons' repeated appearance in sculpture and mythology, discussing the subject with visitors, and designing an insignia for the Doorn Work Group as well as a ceremonial cup featuring the Gorgons. With Frobenius's help, he wrote a brief pamphlet entitled

"Gorgo Studies," which reiterated his views, and in 1934 he presented his findings in a slide show to his colleagues. Wilhelm's last address before the assembly came in 1937, when he dealt again with the Gorgons, whom he claimed personified the "heavenly secrets of the centuries." As it happened, this was the next to last meeting of the society, for Frobenius, who was its mainspring as well as the provider of almost all of Wilhelm's own material presented before it, died in August 1938. Even had he lived, it is doubtful that the Doorn Work Group would have long endured, for the Kaiser had become convinced, with characteristic suspicion, that Frobenius was insufficiently grateful for his financial and intellectual help and was appropriating his ideas on the Gorgons.[23]

Wilhelm's fellowship with Frobenius and his circle helped relieve a social desert that Hermine's presence could not repair. The Kaiser did not complain about being bored — he had his wood sawing and archaeology, his memoir writing, and his newspaper reading to fill the day — but Hermine regretted that there were not more visitors, some of whom announced their intention to come to Doorn only to fail to appear, hardly the courtesy due to kings.[24] There was an occasional royal guest, but rarely did a once sovereign German prince find his way to Doorn. There seem to have been no French visitors whatsoever, and Wilhelm would admit no one from England to Doorn so long as British troops occupied the Rhineland.[25] There were a few loyal friends from the period before 1918 who found their way to Holland, one being Ernst von Dryander, Wilhelm's chief court preacher and devoted follower. Another was the American journalist Poultney Bigelow, the son of John Bigelow, the American minister in Paris in the 1860s. Sent to Berlin to be educated, Poultney had played with Wilhelm as a boy and now revived their old friendship, coming to Doorn many times, frequently exchanging letters, and arranging for one of the Kaiser's grandsons traveling in America to be introduced to important people.[26] Wilhelm resented the fierce anti-German propaganda that Bigelow had made during the war, and he did not at all like the fact that Bigelow had declared that the Kaiser would be willing to appear before an international court to prove that he had not been responsible for starting the conflict. The Kaiser forgave Bigelow after the journalist recanted the things he had said, and the only sign of a residual misgiving about this "thorough gentleman" was an unnecessarily formal insistence on addressing him as "Mr. Bigelow."[27] Another of the Kaiser's friends was Countess Elisabeth zu Salm, a sister of Prince Fürstenberg's, who had known Wilhelm since childhood and who shared his interest in the connection between German and Eastern culture. "Essi" came to Doorn frequently for long visits, and the Kaiser greatly enjoyed her company, quite oblivious to the fact that his frenetic behavior wore her out.[28]

A particular favorite of the Kaiser's was General Wallscourt H.-H. Waters, who had served as British military attaché in Berlin early in the century. He had ingratiated himself by writing a letter of condolence when the Kaiserin died in 1921 and thereafter was frequently invited to be a guest at Doorn for extended periods of time.[29] At the encouragement of his friend Bigelow, Waters wrote several volumes of memoirs, which were favorable to the Kaiser. To Wilhelm, this was very welcome, for he felt the avalanche of hostile commentary about him and his reign, commentary proceeding from Britain, was slanderous. "An ocean of abuse, vilification, infamy, slanders and lies has rolled over me coming from London," he wrote to Waters in 1928, "disclosing a spirit of debased venomous hatred I never imagined possible in the British People, once so proud of their 'fair play'!"[30] Wilhelm for years was resentful of his English relatives because, with the exception of his Aunt Beatrice, Princess Battenberg, they had failed to write to him on the Kaiserin's death. The Kaiser's scorn, as usual, was directed in particular against King Edward VII, who had been laid to rest in his marble tomb in St. George's Windsor in 1910, yet even so, after the Kaiser had the funds to purchase a civilian wardrobe, he ordered clothes that had an unmistakable Edwardian cut, replete with an enormous tiepin featuring a miniature of Queen Victoria. His speech was full of somewhat dated British expressions such as "a damned topping good fellow," and one visitor to Doorn thought he looked like a slimmer version of the late king.[31] Wilhelm continued to blame his uncle's alleged encirclement of Germany for the war, poor payment for the Kaiser's having (so he falsely claimed) prevented the powers from attacking Britain during the Boer War.[32] Even in the postwar period the king continued his evil, according to the Kaiser, this time in the person of his official biographer, Sir Sidney Lee, whose definitive work appeared between 1925 and 1927. Wilhelm denounced Lee for being a Jew, which he was, and for falsifying the record, which he did not, in order to blacken Wilhelm. The Kaiser never forgave his uncle, declaring that of all Englishmen, Edward VII was the only one whom he did not love.[33]

Before 1914 Wilhelm had found Edward VII's son and successor, George V, to be pleasant and peace-loving, but in his letters to General Waters the Kaiser was swift to denounce his first cousin for having gone to war to continue the encirclement policy of Edward VII and for behaving with indecent discourtesy in drumming Wilhelm out of the chapter of the knights of the Garter.[34] On the day that Wilhelm fled to Holland,

George V declared that his German cousin was "the greatest criminal known for having plunged the world into this ghastly war," although he strenuously opposed the Kaiser's extradition from Holland.[35] In 1928, the king authorized the publication of the correspondence of the Empress Frederick, his aunt and Wilhelm's mother. These letters contained many passages that were highly critical of the Kaiser, who was anxious to prevent the book's appearance. Wilhelm contemplated taking legal action against the British publisher, since the copyright of the letters was legally his, but he was persuaded instead to write an introduction to the German edition of the letters, one that attempted, not entirely successfully, to defend himself against his mother's criticisms.[36]

The gravamen of Wilhelm's correspondence with General Waters was not so much the behavior of members of the British royal family as it was the political situation in Germany and in the world at large. It was on this subject that the Kaiser made a vast daily collection of newspaper clippings, dutifully typed and placed in volumes, that became the staple of his correspondence and his conversation. Talk was one thing, active involvement another, for Wilhelm had acceded to the insistence of the Dutch government that as a condition of exile, he would not engage in political activity. He also did not want to jeopardize his property in Germany by giving the republican government in Berlin any cause for offense. In 1922 he therefore informed all his guests at Doorn, in writing, that after their departure, they were not to ascribe political views to him.[37] Any political involvement by the Kaiser in the Fatherland's affairs would have to be conducted through other figures, such as Hermine, who to be sure found no pleasure whatsoever in her husband's absorption in the archaeological work group but who was fiercely interested in Weimar politics and was free to travel back and forth to Germany. Wilhelm's various adjutants, who often returned home between their tours of duty at Doorn, could also be of service.

Wilhelm's all-absorbing concern was the restoration of the monarchy, not under one of his heirs but with himself returned to his ancient throne. There was nothing that indicated, in or after 1918, that this was more than a remote possibility, and it was a possibility that steadily became less and less likely. This attenuation was due in part to Wilhelm's own rude behavior toward those who once had faithfully attended him, to his self-serving memoirs that were swift to criticize everyone but himself, and to his marriage so soon after the Kaiserin's death to an unsuitable woman widely believed to be a conniver.[38] Even Hermine herself, on her return from a trip to Germany in the late summer of 1923, admitted that there was no enthusiasm in Germany for the Kaiser and, in a confession that must have been painful, noted that it was due to his remarriage.[39] Wilhelm knew almost nothing of this negative opinion, for he refused to read anything that was critical, and his entourage, as was the case before 1918, was reluctant to tell him unpleasant truths. Furthermore, in exile as during his reign, Wilhelm had a limited interest in public opinion and internal affairs in Germany, matters that he discussed only in order to denounce the republic and its leaders.[40]

One of the few men who dared to speak openly to Wilhelm was Professor Frobenius, who on the occasion of his first trip to Doorn in October 1923 bluntly told the Kaiser that a restoration might take years to accomplish.[41] This Wilhelm seemed to realize, for the existence of the Versailles treaty that proclaimed him a criminal and demanded his extradition meant that for the time being, he had prudently to remain in the protective hospitality of the Dutch. Furthermore, a "law for the protection of the republic," enacted by the Reichstag in 1925, explicitly outlawed the Kaiser's crossing the German border. *If* and *when* circumstances should ever allow his return to Germany, there was some feeling that even should Wilhelm do so as kaiser and king of Prussia, it would have to be for only the briefest interval, with an immediate abdication in favor of a younger member of his family.[42]

Many monarchists as well as members of the Hohenzollern family were therefore eager to advance their own candidacies rather than Wilhelm's. The crown prince was sure that although the Germans would never take his father back, they might well be willing to have him or one of his sons, and for that reason he was eager to leave Holland for his native land, a move to which Wilhelm II was inalterably opposed.[43] The crown prince was indeed far more popular in Weimar Germany than was his father, the crown princess inestimably better liked than Hermine; the prince's volume of memoirs, in which he had registered considerable criticism of the Kaiser, had been well received.[44]

The dispute within the Hohenzollern clan surfaced in 1923, when the French invaded the Rhineland to deal with the passive resistance that had erupted in protest against the Versailles treaty. The crown prince was determined to use this affront as justification for his homecoming, for Germany now faced an hour of great crisis that he believed would soon lead to war. The Kaiser was no less certain that conflict was on the horizon, and if so, *he*, and not his son, must captain the Fatherland's battle against the enemy. He had no intention of letting the crown prince usurp his prerogatives. "If one of us two is to return," the Kaiser is said to have declared, "then by all means I should be the first."[45] The crown prince, without informing his father, in September 1923 secured Chancellor Gustav Stresemann's agreement to his coming home, and on 9 November, the fifth anniversary of the proclamation of the German republic, he crossed the border. Wilhelm was enraged that his son had stooped to plead with the despised Stresemann, but he was powerless to do anything about it.

In his longing to be reinvested with monarchical dignity, Wilhelm was perceptive enough to realize that the old autocratic empire could not be restored in one fell swoop. A transitional dictatorship, perhaps *before* the crown was delivered to the Hohenzollerns or even for a period after this had occurred, was not to be ruled out. For the first few years in exile, Wilhelm declared that he was prepared to share authority, and from exile in Holland he did not proclaim, as he so often had before 1914, that the monarch was to rule alone. What Wilhelm clearly had in mind for Germany was a variant of fascism, which had emerged in the early 1920s with notable success in Italy and with many imitations in other parts of Europe. "Everywhere there is a leader!" the Kaiser exclaimed in 1924. "Fascism is everywhere becoming active and freeing people from the yoke of affairs being run by party cliques." But alas, in the Fatherland there was only apathy, according to Wilhelm, for the Germans were selfish, negative, and unadventurous.[46] No leader had emerged, but as Wilhelm told his entourage in September 1924, it worked to his advantage that after almost six years in power, the revolution of 1918 had failed to provide Germany with a man whom the people could follow.[47] Although the Kaiser might cooperate temporarily with a Fascist leader, eventually the Hohenzollern crown must be supreme, and he intended to rule again, he warned, with the total power of a Japanese shogun.[48]

Wilhelm recognized that he would need help in recovering the crown, and for that reason he had recruited apologists and supplied them with material favorable to his cause. Historians and journalists were not endowed with the seignorial manner, however, and the Kaiser had hoped that the nobility would respond to its hereditary duty and take the lead in infusing a heightened monarchical spirit in the Germans. Unfortunately, the aristocracy, like the bourgeoisie, no longer venerated the Hohenzollerns and would not work for their return. The working class was, happily, another matter, and the Kaiser declared in 1926, "I need only to whistle and I'll have tens of thousands behind me!" Although this was a view of patent absurdity, it was one that he nevertheless repeatedly trumpeted.[49] These loyal Germans needed, however, to be organized, and Wilhelm believed that there were a number of aristocratic military figures who could impose their formidable personalities on the population and prepare it to support a reentry of the monarch into his ancient capital. "Everywhere," he noted, pointing to Germany as the exception, "a man has emerged."[50] Admiral Alfred von Tirpitz, whom Wilhelm had removed from office in 1916 but who was a highly popular and ferociously conservative figure, would be serviceable, as would be Field Marshal August von Mackensen, next to Hindenburg the most beloved officer of the imperial army. General Hans von Seeckt, during the war Mackensen's chief of staff and since 1920 commander-in-chief of the dwarf republican army, had all of Tirpitz's Caesarean manner and commanded widespread support. Finally there was General Erich Ludendorff, who, ever since the collapse of the monarchy, had been tirelessly active in various rightist movements in Bavaria.[51] Mackensen was the only one of the four who was truly loyal and ready to serve the Kaiser unquestioningly, but he had little interest in politics and no desire to preside over Germany. The other three would probably gladly have seized the opportunity, but they did not see monarchism as their path to power. Seeckt's ambition was boundless, but he avoided the Kaiser, and neither Tirpitz nor Ludendorff seemed inclined to call him home.[52]

What Wilhelm clearly was looking for in men such as Seeckt or the others was someone similar to that "real man," Benito Mussolini. The Kaiser admired the energetic Fascist for his success in restoring order in postwar Italy and for his sense of national grandeur that dreamed of the reestablishment of the Roman Empire.[53] The Germans, if electrified, might also become determined to restore their Fatherland to glory, but Wilhelm felt that this was hardly likely to happen under Stresemann, with his ignoble kowtowing to the victorious Allies. To the Kaiser, no less than to other contemporaries, Stresemann appeared to be the "good European," one who put peace before power and who believed in open diplomacy rather than in the labyrinthine web of secret treaties and deals that had abounded before 1914. Wilhelm preferred Mussolini precisely because he was pursuing not a policy of capitulation to the West but rather a "free hand" diplomacy that was willing to consort with Communist Russia and to do so as an equal rather than let himself be used, as Stresemann had, by the Kremlin. Mussolini, to the Kaiser's satisfaction, had been willing to end the long quarrel between the Italian state and the pope if that was necessary to re-create the empire of the Caesars. Wilhelm correctly predicted that one day Italy's *sacro egismo* would lead to war, and when Mussolini attacked Ethiopia in 1935, the Kaiser declared, again accurately, that the duce would be unstoppable.[54]

In the Kaiser's opinion, Mussolini had wisely allowed King Victor Emmanuel III to continue to occupy his powerless throne and to perform, with a show of regality that paled beside *il Duce*'s own imitations of Roman imperial splendor, the traditional pageantry of the house of Savoy. Mussolini had his own views about how a Hohenzollern restoration might be effected, but his prescription was not one that Wilhelm II, had he known, would have approved. *Il Duce* thought that should the dynasty return to the throne, the most desirable candidate would be neither the crown prince nor one of his heirs but instead the Kaiser's fourth son, Prince Oskar, a personality quite as lackluster (and thus entirely as manageable) as Victor Emmanuel.[55] What Wilhelm saw, to his delight, in Mussolini was the dictator's pioneering role in reviving the European monarchies. The Kaiser declared in 1923, as General Miguel Primo de Rivera established a rightist government in Spain, that these new regimes, following in *il Duce*'s wake, showed that Europe had finally recognized that parliamentarism was bankrupt.[56] Even the Germans would eventually embrace this truth, and Wilhelm would be fully prepared to provide the requisite leadership. If the Germans could not find a leader in their own ranks, the Kaiser declared in a transparent allusion to Doorn, then they should look abroad for a savior.[57]

In the early summer of 1924, when Wilhelm rhetorically asked why Tirpitz, or Mackensen, or Seeckt, or Ludendorff had not come to the fore to provide Germany with the Fascist leadership he welcomed elsewhere in Europe, he had curiously omitted the name of Field Marshal Hindenburg, the man universally acclaimed as the Fatherland's greatest public figure. The reason undoubtedly lay in the Kaiser's belief that it was because of pressure from Hindenburg that he had unwillingly fled to Holland on 10 November 1918. The field marshal, notoriously laconic by nature, had let other military figures do most of the talking at Spa in the last hours of the monarchy, and during the early years of the republic he declined to accept any responsibility for the Kaiser's flight. In the summer of 1922 Hindenburg finally wrote to Wilhelm a widely published letter in which he somewhat self-servingly declared that although he and all of the Kaiser's other advisers had recommended that Wilhelm leave for Holland, he had not meant that the Kaiser was to have done so at once.[58] Wilhelm was not blind to the circumventions in the letter, and he waited for two months to reply, informing Hindenburg that he had gone to Holland against his "convictions" because of the bad advice he had received.[59] All further contact between the two men was ceremonial and distant. Hindenburg never asked to be received at Doorn, nor did he write to Wilhelm after his

1922 letter about the November 1918 events that had led to the Kaiser's abrupt departure for Holland. The Kaiser persistently insisted, up to Hindenburg's death in 1934, that the field marshal's apology was not enough and that full atonement could come only through his active promotion of the restoration of the monarchy.[60]

Hindenburg was a devoted monarchist and was scrupulously deferential to Wilhelm, refusing to become a candidate for president of the republic after the death of Friedrich Ebert in 1925 until the Kaiser had grudgingly signified his assent. Hindenburg declared that the position ought properly to belong to the crown and that he would hold the office as a sort of trustee for Wilhelm.[61] Hindenburg's position throughout the 1920s and until his death was that the Hohenzollern monarchy should be restored and that propriety required that Wilhelm II himself, and no one else, should mount the throne.[62] Furthermore, the Kaiser was to have the full panoply of authority he had enjoyed under the empire, an expectation that was entirely incapable of being fulfilled in postwar Germany but on which Hindenburg refused to budge.[63] The aged field marshal, loyal to Wilhelm though he was, recognized that a premature attempt to restore the Hohenzollerns would be fatal to the cause, and for that reason he advised against monarchical coups.[64]

Hindenburg's performance as president from 1925 until 1934 did not satisfy the Kaiser, who was dismayed that the field marshal did not move at once to enable Wilhelm to return to Germany and claim his throne but instead supported the anti-Hohenzollern Catholic Center Party and the hated Stresemann. Furthermore, not content to betray the Kaiser once in November 1918, he had done so again in 1925, according to Wilhelm, by signing the Reichstag's "law for the protection of the republic" that forbade Wilhelm's return to Germany.[65] The Kaiser, full of pique and outrage at Hindenburg, became obsessed with proving that it was not the field marshal but rather other generals who had been responsible for Germany's victory over Russia in the fall of 1914. *When* Wilhelm returned to the throne, the Kaiser declared, he would never again permit any officer to have the supreme command that Hindenburg had held from 1916 until the end of the war but instead would have his royal headquarters run the army.[66] Wilhelm clearly was jealous of the adulation that the field marshal received in Germany, a worship that, in his opinion, was appropriate only for a sovereign. Although Wilhelm would send the president a message as Hindenburg lay dying in 1934, he never forgave Hindenburg, and a visitor to Doorn in 1939 reported that the Kaiser's "greatest hate" was for the deceased hero.[67]

Although Wilhelm was quite dismayed that Hindenburg could not bring himself to fight for an instantaneous restoration of the monarchy, in the first years of exile the Kaiser had no such objections to the field marshal's erstwhile subaltern, General Ludendorff. After his precipitous resignation as quartermaster general in late October 1918, Ludendorff had fled in disguise to Sweden but then returned to Germany and became active in monarchical movements that aimed at overthrowing the Weimar republic. During the war the Kaiser had thoroughly disliked Ludendorff, but in exile Wilhelm was prepared to use him. The Kaiser believed that Ludendorff, although working in Bavaria, intended to coopt the southern German monarchist element into a movement for the restoration of the Prussian Hohenzollerns rather than the Catholic Wittelsbachs. Ludendorff had every military virtue, and he therefore was qualified to stand, along with Tirpitz, Seeckt, and Mackensen, as one of the Kaiser's putative leaders of a revitalized Germany. Furthermore, the general shared Wilhelm's prejudices against Jews, Catholics, and Masons, and indeed did so with a virulence that far exceeded even the Kaiser's.[68]

Wilhelm and Ludendorff also shared a detestation for the Weimar republic. The general's unbridled hatred for democratic government brought him into the camp of Adolf Hitler, the demagogic leader of the National Socialist German Workers', or Nazi, Party, which called for the overthrow of the republican government. In the fall of 1923, as the ministry headed by Stresemann collapsed and while Hitler was still a marginal political figure, the Kaiser, in what was his first reference to the Nazi leader, declared that Hitler's egoism would make him unsuitable to participate in a coalition government.[69] On 9 November 1923, just as the crown prince was driving across the German frontier and ending his long exile in Holland, Ludendorff and Hitler attempted an armed putsch against the Munich government, in which Gustav von Kahr, head of the Bavarian security forces, was the most prominent figure. Kahr, who was very close to Prince Rupprecht, once crown prince of Bavaria and now the leading candidate of a Wittelsbach restoration, was himself an enemy of the republic, but he had no enthusiasm for letting radical competitors such as Hitler, Ludendorff, and their Nazi minions win any prominence. The putsch was quickly stamped out, and Hitler was convicted for treason and imprisoned. Ludendorff's military fame protected him from persecution, and in the next year he was elected to the Reichstag as a Nazi deputy.

The Kaiser, observing this Bavarian frenzy from Doorn, applauded the botched attempt by Hitler and Ludendorff to destroy the republic. They had been defeated because they had overestimated their power and had no sense of the strength wielded by Kahr and his allies, all of them parochial Catholics trading in small, Wittelsbachian coin and lacking the larger, German-nationalist vision that Hitler and Ludendorff had unsuccessfully championed.[70] Wilhelm correctly believed that the failure of the putsch would bring Ludendorff's political career to an end, although as a military leader, the general still might play a role, according to Wilhelm, in the future deliverance of the Fatherland.[71] After Munich, Wilhelm became more and more disenchanted with Ludendorff, finally turning against him altogether. The general was, after all, only an adventurer who, the Kaiser imagined, was conspiring against him.[72] As for Hitler, the Kaiser saw in the collapse of the conspiracy in Munich a sign that the would-be deliverer of Germany had lost his touch, so much so that even Ludendorff no longer seemed to be much concerned with his fellow Nazis.[73]

While in prison, Hitler wrote his testamentary *Mein Kampf* (1925), in which he was careful to steer an ambivalent course concerning the exiled Kaiser. He did not categorically rule out the restoration of the monarchy in Germany, but in what was, from the perspective of Doorn, an ominous warning, he declared in chapter 12 of his interminable work, "Anything less folkish than most of the Germanic monarchic state formations can hardly be imagined." The mission of the Nazi movement, he baldly declared in the same chapter, lay "not in the foundation of a monarchy or in the reinforcement of a republic, but in the creation of a Germanic state." In a few passages in *Mein Kampf* Hitler pitied Wilhelm as a victim of Jewish press abuse in the *Daily Telegraph* affair, but on the other hand he reproached the Kaiser for being too enamored of Jews and capitalists and too inclined to surround himself with sycophants. Hitler declared that good monarchs were few and far between, and when he listed those who had served the Germans well in the past, Wilhelm II was conspicuously absent.[74] Indeed, Hitler drew a pointed distinction between the Kaiser and his grandfather, noting that Wilhelm I had been a grand seigneur, whereas the last Kaiser was only a "strutting puppet of no character." What Hitler disliked in Wilhelm, exactly what King Edward VII and many others had found objectionable, was his rude behavior, his backslapping his fellow sovereigns and belittling his entourage in a way inappropriate for a ruler and all the while making wild speeches that were "as tactless as they were stupid."[75] In private, Hitler was explicit about his indifference to the former German ruling houses and was frank to declare that he would use them as a means to elevate himself to power. Monarchy was "an absurdity," he told an American military officer in 1922, three years before *Mein Kampf* appeared, and was of "fifth or sixth importance." Someday the

Germans might decide whether they wanted a monarchy or a republic, but Hitler declared that this would occur only after his nationalist front had come to power.[76]

Wilhelm never read *Mein Kampf* and was unaware of Hitler's reservations expressed there and elsewhere, but he entirely approved of the would-be leader's statements opposing the sequestration of property of the Hohenzollerns and the other German dynasties, a ploy that Hitler hoped would embellish his conservative credentials.[77] Hitler was aware that a connection with the Hohenzollerns could invest the rowdy and unpolished Nazis with a needed measure of respectability. Therefore he occasionally rose to protect Wilhelm II against postwar critics, arguing in 1929, for example, that the Kaiser's regime had not been responsible for the fall of the empire.[78] For six or seven years after the 1923 putsch, Wilhelm had little to say about Hitler though much about Ludendorff, whom he turned against and blamed, along with Hindenburg, for having set in motion the events that had led to his abdication.[79] Only in 1930, with the astounding increase in the Nazis' popularity that occurred following the economic difficulties created by the October 1929 crash of the New York stock exchange a few weeks later, did the Kaiser's interest in Hitler, the movement's self-proclaimed "Führer," began to revive.

Wilhelm's descendants, however, had somewhat earlier displayed perceptible eagerness to exploit the advantages of a Nazi connection. Of the Kaiser's sons, Prince August Wilhelm ("Auwi") had occasional contact with Hitler, whom he met in 1927 through the veterans' organization *Stahlhelm* when both mourned a fellow member who had been killed by a Communist. A year later, Auwi joined the SA (*Sturmabteilung*), a sort of private Nazi army, and thereafter became one of Dr. Joseph Goebbels's propagandists for Hitler's cause.[80] In April 1930 Auwi, together with his brother Oskar, joined the Nazi Party, a move their father vainly protested not because they had enrolled under Hitler's flag but because they had done so without seeking Wilhelm's permission. The Kaiser gave his ex post facto consent, explaining to one of his grandsons that this departure from the tradition that Hohenzollerns did not participate in politics was justified because "special times and circumstances require special measures."[81] Auwi's oldest brother, the crown prince, who would later become the most visible Hohenzollern connection with the Nazi movement, was attracted to the Nazis through his acquaintance with the convivial Hermann Göring, one of Hitler's closest lieutenants, who invited the crown prince to his soirées in Berlin. Here on several occasions after 1928 the prince met Hitler, "who," he wrote to a friend in April 1932, "once again" pleased him "greatly."[82] The Kaiser's only daughter, Princess Victoria Louise of Brunswick, saw Hitler and his subalterns from time to time in the early 1930s and for several years supported the Nazi aim of restoring Germany's former wealth and power.[83]

The Nazis, wide as their contacts with the Hohenzollerns might have been, had neither the power nor the desire in the 1920s or early 1930s to bring the Kaiser back to Berlin. Wilhelm took a very reserved position toward the party that so fascinated some of his sons, showing no enthusiasm for either the movement or its Führer. The Kaiser's only interest, invariable in his every encounter, was in how Hitler might contribute to his reclaiming his throne. By the late 1920s, the prospect was becoming increasingly dim, but Wilhelm, despite occasional despair, did not lose heart in the possibility of his restoration. The failure in 1926 of the plebiscite to dispossess the former German ruling houses of their property was a sign that the fires of monarchism still burned brightly, but in the following year when the Reichstag, with the rightist parties in the majority, extended the "law for the protection of the republic," with its clause prohibiting Wilhelm from living in Germany, his spirits fell. Within a few weeks, however, the Kaiser was again full of talk of his return to the throne, believing that Europe would soon erupt in another great war, this time one directed against bolshevism.[84] Most of Wilhelm's family as well as most of the gentlemen in his retinue felt by the late 1920s that there was no hope of his returning to Germany as kaiser and that at best he might someday do so as a private individual.[85] Even his adjutants, however, were not prepared to controvert this view and attempted instead to point out, insofar as the Kaiser's temperament would allow them to do so, how unpropitious circumstances in Germany were for a restoration.[86] Wilhelm, however, made it clear that he would come back as sovereign or not at all.

There were a few men in Wilhelm's entourage in Doorn or in the House Ministry, located in Berlin and responsible for Wilhelm's financial affairs in Germany, who in fact encouraged the Kaiser in these aspirations. The most redoubtable was *Hofrat* Nitz, who managed the Kaiser's money; he flattered the Kaiser and Hermine shamelessly and assured Wilhelm that restoration was imminent.[87] The Reichstag elections of May 1928, in which the parties of the Right lost ground to both the Communists and the Socialists in a clear repudiation of monarchism, did not deflate Wilhelm's hopes, which were revealed quite ostensibly on the occasion of his seventieth birthday celebration on 27 January 1929.[88] The festivities began with an assembly in Doorn of the Kaiser's former generals, who presented their old commander with an address read by Field Marshal Mackensen. In his extemporaneous reply, Wilhelm declared that he and no one else was the head of the Hohenzollern family (a warning to would-be claimants to his vacated throne) and concluded by asking the officers whether they would follow him faithfully. "I ask for your answer, gentlemen!" to which there was a less than resounding "*Ja*."[89] For the birthday dinner on the twenty-seventh, almost the entire Hohenzollern family was present, with little regret on the part of Wilhelm's relations that Hermine was confined to her bedroom with a case of measles. The once-reigning German princes, however, were embarrassingly underrepresented, with the king of Saxony, the grand duke of Mecklenburg-Schwerin, and the Kaiser's son-in-law, the duke of Brunswick, being the only former rulers to appear. Wilhelm did not care for the ceremonial speech the king made because it failed to refer to the Kaiser's resumption of the imperial and Prussian thrones.[90] Wilhelm was not much more pleased at Admiral Tirpitz's efforts on this occasion to heal the breach that had occurred between them after Tirpitz's dismissal from office as state secretary of the Imperial Naval Office in 1916. The admiral sent birthday congratulations, and Wilhelm answered civilly but refused the advice of one of his adjutants to invite Tirpitz to pay a visit to Doorn. When the old admiral died early in 1930, the Kaiser's expression of regret was perfunctory.[91]

On 14 September 1930, the widening financial crisis, arising in America and now gripping all of Europe, forced Heinrich Brüning, the conservative chancellor, to hold new elections to the Reichstag. The result was an extraordinary victory for the National Socialist Party, now second only to the Majority Socialists in parliamentary strength, and for Hitler, who with this election became the most important political figure in Germany. The choice made by German voters would indicate to any reasonable person that the cause of monarchy in Germany — whether under Wilhelm, another Hohenzollern, or indeed any other princeling — was now a dead issue, for the Communists and Socialists, who took slightly more than a third of the votes, were doctrinarily opposed to monarchy, and neither the Nazis, with a further 18 percent of the vote, nor the Catholic Center, with a little more than 10 percent, had given the least indication that they wanted to have anything to do with a restoration. Wilhelm II, however, always somehow confident that his day was about to dawn, was hopeful that in Adolf Hitler and his Nazis the path to the palace in Berlin could now at last be prepared.

The Hitler phenomenon, welcome as it might have been, nonetheless put the Kaiser in a difficult position. On the one hand, the Führer's low birth and inelegant manners hardly made him suitable even for a government position, much less a dominating role. "The new Reich," Wilhelm had written Field Marshal Mackensen in December 1923 after Hitler's Munich putsch, "will not come from a beer joint."[92] The Kaiser disdained Hitler's pretentiousness in calling himself the *Führer*, for that was a word that was properly used to refer only to God Almighty.[93] A Hohenzollern, quite apart from promises Wilhelm had made to the Dutch government in 1918 not to involve himself in German politics, could hardly be expected to have any traffic with such an odious creature. At the same time, Hitler's increasing hold on the German people meant that in the future he might be the critical player in a restoration of the monarchy, a step that Hitler had not ruled out, at least not with rigid explicitness, in what he had said and written. His German-nationalist ideas and his racist demonology, embracing especially Jews but also Slavs and anyone who was yellow or black, were all ideas that the Kaiser fervently endorsed. Herr Adolf Hitler, the descendant of Austrian peasants, could pave the way for the return to the throne of Wilhelm Hohenzollern.

This was exactly the view of Magnus von Levetzow, the former naval officer whom Wilhelm in 1924 had made his unpaid political agent in Berlin. Levetzow had served at Spa in the last months of the monarchy and then in March 1922 came to Doorn as a "duty-drawing guest" (*diensttuender Gast*). In September 1928, by which time he had been put on the Kaiser's payroll, Levetzow proposed to Wilhelm that the restoration could be brought about by allying the monarchical cause with the business and intellectual leadership of the Weimar republic. Bankers, industrialists, and professors of history could all be marshalled, and to their number could be added the glorious names of Germany's military leadership from the imperial era, especially Tirpitz and Hindenburg.[94] This plan won the Kaiser's approval, and Levetzow set to work, without notable success, in drumming up a group of supporters. In May 1930, well before Hitler's great electoral victory the following September, Levetzow urged that steps be taken to coopt the burgeoning Nazi movement into a monarchical nationalist front. That presumably would result in Hitler's elimination, for, the fastidious Levetzow added, he was hardly the person to lead such a body.[95]

Hermine meanwhile convinced the Kaiser that the person through whom Hitler could be utilized was the "silver fox," Alfred Hugenberg.[96] This enormously wealthy businessman had in the late 1920s become engaged in an attempt to establish a united nationalist movement of all parties on the Right, the so-called Harzburg Front. Hugenberg was bit-

terly indignant at the Versailles treaty, at Stresemann's policy of fulfillment, and at the adjustment of reparations, the so-called Young Plan,
that Hindenburg had urged the Reichstag to approve in December 1929
shortly after Stresemann's death. Wilhelm entirely agreed and declared
that even the Hottentots knew how to govern themselves better than
the Germans, who must certainly realize that the payments scheduled in
the plan could never be fulfilled.[97] On the very day that elections for the
Reichstag took place, 14 September 1930, but before he knew of the
sizable Nazi gains, the Kaiser indicated that he would approve the absorption of Hitler's followers into the Harzburg Front. This came as a surprise
to Adjutant Sigurd von Ilsemann, who noted that until that point, Wilhelm had been "very opposed" to the Nazis.[98] The seal of approval accorded to Hugenberg was also odd, since Wilhelm thought him quite
commonplace although better than some of the incompetents among the
leaders of the Right.[99]

Wilhelm's change of heart about the Nazis, since it came before Hitler's
election victories, must have been due to the pro-Nazi, and pro-Hugen-
berg, influences that had already been at work in Doorn in the late 1920s
and on into 1930. Of these the most important was his wife, Hermine,
who, long before the Kaiser, had envisioned a future in which Hitler and
his cohorts would be used to place Wilhelm back on the throne. Although
Hermine often expressed doubt that Wilhelm would regain his crown, she
never fully abandoned hope for a restoration, an act through which her
own standing would be greatly enhanced, since then she would be the
Kaiserin in fact rather than merely in name. Hermine, however, was not a
successful emissary for the royal cause, for she did not possess sufficient
charm or royal bearing to enlist adherents in Wilhelm's behalf. From the
beginning she was, to her outrage, rudely ignored in Germany. Hermine
nevertheless doggedly sought out politicians and journalists to burnish
Wilhelm's image, and in doing so, she was brought into contact with many
people who were also enemies of the Weimar Republic, including Hugenberg and Franz von Papen, a member of the Prussian legislature who
yearned to become a national figure. Hermine was exposed to the Nazis
through her two sons, both of whom were involved in the movement. She
occasionally saw Hitler, Papen, and other political figures in the Berlin
nationalist salons of Baroness von Tiele-Winckler and Frau Viktoria von
Dirksen. There is no indication that Hermine attracted any recruits among
the Nazi elite or that she in any way impressed Hitler, who was usually
awkward in aristocratic society and who found all the bowing and scrap-
ing before the "empress" alarming.[100] In 1929 Hermine attended the Nazi

Party day ceremonies at Nürnberg, and her sons arranged for her to meet the Führer. The two spoke only briefly, but long enough for Hermine to ask the bachelor Hitler a question whose rude directness reveals why her company was not sought after. Why, she tactlessly inquired, had he never married? The future Führer replied that it was because *he* had no desire to found a dynasty. She also received a negative response to her inquiry as to whether Hitler could effect Wilhelm's return to Germany.[101]

After the astounding Nazi victory in the September 1930 elections, Levetzow urged that a personal contact between Doorn and the Nazis should now be made, but he argued that it not be through the oafish Hitler. Instead Göring, a former officer with a heroic war record and the husband of a Scandinavian baroness, should be invited to call at Doorn.[102] The visit occurred on 18–19 January 1931, with both the Kaiser and Göring anxious to please the other.[103] The wily Göring courteously endured Wilhelm's expansive conversation on archaeology and politics, but he was careful to speak only in generalities when the subject of the restoration was raised. Although Göring declared that someday Wilhelm must return to Germany, he was evasive about the conditions under which this might happen. He did, to the Kaiser's distress, declare that the minor German princes were never to retrieve their thrones. Otherwise all proceeded smoothly, but Göring had impressed Hermine — who referred to him as a "true and respectable (*anständig*) man" — more than he had the Kaiser. At the time of the 1923 putsch in Munich, Wilhelm had found Hitler too full of himself, and that was now, almost a decade later, still the impression he had not only of the would-be Führer but also of Göring, a vain creature, a mere army captain who would be consigned to obscurity once the Kaiser remounted his throne.[104] The Nazis might help the Hohenzollerns regain their ancestral crown, but there would be no place for them under the approaching reign of Kaiser Wilhelm II.

Sixteen

THE KINGDOM OF DAMP

WILHELM WATCHED with perverse satisfaction as Germany sank in the late 1920s into increasing financial distress and political instability, for he was convinced that when the Fatherland came to the brink of destruction, as it seemed to be surely headed from 1930 to 1932 under what he considered to be the incompetent leadership of the conservative Catholic chancellor Heinrich Brüning, it would call him back as kaiser.[1]

Although Wilhelm had little use for either Adolf Hitler or Hermann Göring, their movement was quite another matter. The rightist German National Party and the militantly antirepublican *Stahlhelm*, a veterans' organization, had utterly failed to promote his candidacy, whereas Hitler, he believed, was prepared to do so. He argued that the Führer's silence about his monarchical sentiments proceeded purely from tactical considerations.[2] In February 1932, the Kaiser gave his son Auwi permission to stand as a Nazi candidate for the Reichstag, but only after his pro-Nazi house minister in Berlin, Leopold von Kleist, sought out Hitler and ascertained that the Führer agreed.[3] In the course of his conversation with Kleist, Hitler had declared that he favored a restoration, but not under Wilhelm II or the crown prince, both of whom were too unpopular. Kleist probably did not tell the Kaiser what Hitler had said about him, but in any case Wilhelm was adamant that no one would come to the throne but himself. In late April 1932, he warned his son Oskar that if any of the Kaiser's other sons attempted to advance themselves as candidates, they would be expelled from the family.[4] In his tirade, Wilhelm specifically referred to the crown prince, at whom he was violently angry because of his suspicion that his eldest son and the crown princess were conniving to make themselves Germany's future monarchs. The Kaiser's wrath had been excited at the end of March when the crown prince told his father that he intended to stand as a candidate in the second round of the presidential elections scheduled for 10 April 1932 and that he had written to Hitler to ask for the support of the Nazis.[5] In March Paul von Beneckendorff und von Hindenburg, running for reelection even though he was almost eighty-five, had been pitted against Hitler and a Communist candidate, but when the old field marshal narrowly failed to achieve a majority, a second election had to take place on 10 April. The crown prince's decision to present himself as a candidate arose from an overture made to him by members of the Nazi Party acting without Hitler's knowledge, and the prince was ready, for he believed that he was the most suitable royal figure for the throne. For years he had considered running for president in the event of Hindenburg's death, but he had finally grown weary of waiting for the octogenarian field marshal to vacate his high office. If elected, he would appoint Hitler chancellor, Brüning foreign minister, and Alfred Hugenberg minister of finance.[6]

Wilhelm could not stomach the thought that his son was prepared to take the presidential oath to support the republic, and the Kaiser refused outright to allow the crown prince to become a candidate. Hermine joined ranks, declaring that her stepson's candidacy would be a fatal blow to the monarchical principle and to any chance of her husband's returning to Berlin as kaiser. This would come not by the crown prince's election, should he enter the race and win, but rather by Hitler, in whom she put her trust.[7] The prince bowed to his father's opposition and publicly declared that he would vote for Hitler. Hindenburg was reelected, but given the chancellor's great age, the crown prince did not abandon his hopes to succeed the aged president. Göring, always eager to cut the proper figure socially, declared that he was a strict legitimist and therefore could support no one for the throne other than the Kaiser.[8] Wilhelm was eager to reinforce this view and therefore invited Göring to pay a second visit to Doorn, where he was treated to an extensive indictment of the crown prince's ambitions. Pleased with how smoothly this encounter had gone, Kleist now began to plan for an invitation to Doorn to be extended to Hitler himself.[9] Wilhelm meanwhile told Kleist to agree — "well why not?" he asked — to a request from Magnus von Levetzow to stand as a Nazi candidate in the July 1932 Reichstag elections.[10]

A few days after Göring returned to Berlin, Brüning's government fell because of a disagreement the chancellor had with Hindenburg. The president now appointed as chancellor Franz von Papen, who formed a government that excluded the Nazis. Papen had once visited Doorn and had encountered Hermine several times on her trips to Germany. Snobbish and self-impressed, he imagined for no good reason that he was a master of political manipulation and would therefore be able to control Hitler. The Reichstag elections held on 31 July 1932 resulted in a sensational victory for the Nazis, but Hitler refused on 13 August to let his party join with Papen in a coalition government, nor would he accede to Hindenburg's request that Hitler agree to become vice-chancellor. This was the decision that began Wilhelm II's final disenchantment with Hitler and his movement, for it revealed that the Führer was not a devoted German who would put the nation first but was instead a mere egomaniac, interested only in himself and therefore not in the monarchy. What Hitler should have done, the Kaiser declared, was boldly to have created an uprising in the name of a restoration, unseated Papen and Hindenburg, and obliterated the republic.[11] Hitler had not done so, and this failure would now cause many of his followers to turn to the Communists, that internationalist rabble with no allegiance to Germany. Göring was also involved in this folly, according to the Kaiser, for he had rounded up a huge Reichstag majority to support a Communist motion of no confidence in Papen, whom Hitler would neither support nor attempt to overthrow. This failure meant that the radical Left might find an opening through which to seize power. Wilhelm considered Göring's maneuver to be "first unworthy, second laughable, third absolutely *revolutionary*!" The Nazis clearly had no conscience and no sense of history, and in his vanity Hitler was prepared to destroy the nationalist movement grouped on the Right if he could not have the chancellorship. "He is no statesman," the Kaiser wrote to the crown prince at the end of September.[12] Wilhelm's effusion somehow became known to Göring, who threatened to inform Hitler, an act that would end forever any hope of Nazi support (such as it was) for a restoration. The Kaiser became enraged at Göring, an ingrate to whom the many courtesies extended to him on his visits to Doorn clearly meant nothing and whose repeated promises to support the Kaiser's return to the throne were now shown unmasked as empty and worthless.[13]

Hitler's failure to unseat Papen and Hindenburg was not the Kaiser's only disappointment in the Führer. In October 1932 Hitler had written an irate letter to the crown prince rejecting his suggestion that the Nazis draw closer to the rightist parties and to the *Stahlhelm*. In frenzied language Hitler had declared that he demanded total power for himself and that he would fight on until he had achieved that goal. Nowhere was there any reference to a restoration, and the Kaiser again detected in Hitler's fanfaronade unmistakable signs of the sort of megalomania from which the Führer's friend General Erich Ludendorff also suffered. Wilhelm declared that the crown's association with the Nazis was now over, and there was nothing to do but to call all monarchists to rally not to Hitler but to Hugenberg.[14] The Kaiser's realization by early October 1932, long suspected but now undeniable, that the egotistical Hitler had no interest in restoring him to his throne led to a number of alterations in the staff at Doorn. One was the dismissal, at the crown prince's urging, of the only ardent pro-Nazi in the entourage, Berlin House Minister Kleist, who was cashiered on 9 December, to be replaced by General Wilhelm von Dommes, an anti-Nazi who denounced Hitler as a would-be Caesar.[15] A second victim was Admiral Levetzow, who, like Kleist, believed that the Nazis should be cultivated. He was relieved of his duties in Berlin later in the month, a step that Levetzow warned the Kaiser would be regarded as yet another hostile gesture from Holland against the Führer and therefore one that would do the cause of restoration no good whatsoever.[16]

The Papen government fell on 17 November 1932, replaced by a cabinet headed by General Kurt von Schleicher, who proved unable to produce a stable majority in the Reichstag. President Hindenburg therefore finally felt compelled to invite Hitler to assume the chancellorship, installing him on 30 January 1933 in a ceremony in the Garrison Church in Potsdam. Hitler might be chancellor, but Wilhelm was determined that there was to be no "Nazi-state."[17] Writing to his friend General Karl von Einem, a fanatical monarchist as well as an admirer of Hitler's, Wilhelm stated, "A dictator can be a transitional figure but never a form of government." He declared, "The welfare of our people is best assured by a return of the legitimate hereditary monarchy that stands *above* parties!"[18] But Hitler, now enthroned as chancellor, had less interest than ever in the prospect of a restoration. In a meeting on 15 May 1933, arranged by Hindenburg to bring the Führer together with Wilhelm's old friend and former cabinet chief and minister Friedrich von Berg-Markienen, Hitler declared that he saw as the end of his life's work the return of the Hohenzollern monarchy but that, for internal and diplomatic reasons, this could not happen at once but only after the conclusion of a victorious war.[19] Indeed, the Führer declared that there could be no restoration as long as he lived, for the German people would have no ruler other than himself.[20] An equally discouraging message went to General Dommes in an audience with the Führer on 24 October 1933, a meeting that Dommes had requested to discuss the anti-Hohenzollern tone of the Nazi-controlled press. The talk, which lasted only fifteen minutes, was friendly in tone but devoid of promise.[21] Hitler refused to commit himself to any future form of government, noting that he had enough to do with saving Germany from the Bolsheviks and the Jews, enemies whom the Hohenzollerns would be incapable of combating successfully. The Führer directed Dommes to his deputy,

Rudolf Hess, in the event that there were further problems involving Wilhelm, but Dommes was to find that Hess never had time to see him.

Hermine, indefatigable in her pursuit of a crown and resistant to all signs of Nazi hostility to the Hohenzollern cause, now spent increasingly long periods of time in Berlin, blithely informing her husband that the cause of the monarchy was making steady progress under Hitler. The truth was that few of the Nazis whom she courted had anything to do with her, since Hitler was said to have declared that he had no interest in her "petticoat politics."[22] Hermine was not easily deflated, but Wilhelm's disillusion with the Third Reich was steadily increasing. Before the Nazis had been in power two months he realized that Hitler's aims were neither monarchical nor republican but rather were focused on the establishment of a party state. In the new Germany there would be no place for him; it was, he complained, as though he had been buried alive.[23] The Austrian Hitler falsely paraded about as the great national leader, oblivious to the fact that it was not he but the Hohenzollerns who had created Germany. Captain Göring, newly minted by the Führer as a general, had the temerity to sit on ceremonial occasions in Frederick the Great's chair in the Garrison Church in Potsdam, and the hated Hindenburg held court from the royal loge at the opera house. It was too much for the Kaiser.[24]

Wilhelm was prepared to avoid deliberately insulting the Nazis in order to keep alive, however barely, the hope of restoration and to preserve his fortune in Germany. Hermine and her confederate in the entourage, Baron Alexander von Senarclens-Grancy, both blindly obtuse about the hostile attitude of the Nazis toward the house of Hohenzollern, continued to be confident that Hitler could somehow be persuaded to restore the monarchy. The difference of opinion created considerable tension between Hermine and the Kaiser, who rightly deplored his wife's running after the Nazis with unseemly eagerness.[25] It was especially grievous to the Kaiser that his former military officers, abjuring the oaths they had once sworn to the crown, were transferring their loyalty to the new regime. To Wilhelm no one was more guilty of this base ingratitude than Hindenburg. Like the Nazis, who refused to accord the Hohenzollerns their due, so the aged field marshal, in an address in 1933 before thousands of Nazis at the monument to the great World War I battle in 1914 at Tannenberg in East Prussia, had failed to declare that Wilhelm himself should rightly be considered one of the geniuses of this momentous engagement, almost the only conspicuous victory of the imperial army in the four years of war. "They treat me at home as though I were dead," he told his adjutant

Sigurd von Ilsemann about Hindenburg's speech.[26] Wilhelm was further annoyed when, in October 1933, Hindenburg, speaking to another adjutant sent from Doorn to determine the president's views, declared that although he desired to see the Kaiser remount the throne, this was impossible because of political circumstance and public opinion.[27] In spite of this rebuff, Adjutant Dommes, who believed that internal or diplomatic difficulties would eventually force Hitler to recall Wilhelm to the throne, persuaded the Kaiser to send President Hindenburg a birthday greeting in October 1933 and urged Wilhelm to be very careful to preserve a neutral position toward the Nazis.[28] To all that, the Kaiser agreed.

In January 1934, Wilhelm observed his seventy-fifth birthday, and one of his adjutants, General August von Cramon, pleaded in vain with Hindenburg that this would be a most suitable opportunity for the restoration, pointing out that the eighty-six-year-old president should do this while he was still alive rather than by posthumously supporting the act in his will.[29] Cramon was undoubtedly carrying out instructions provided by the Kaiser, who continued to feel that Hindenburg had not sufficiently atoned for having advised him to flee to Holland in November 1918. That sin could be propitiated through bringing Wilhelm back to his throne.[30] Cramon argued unconvincingly that Hindenburg would "give eternity to the accomplishment of Adolf Hitler if he would restore the immortal monarchy by bringing the Kaiser home." Hindenburg disregarded Cramon's request, but in May 1934 the ailing president did draw up a document, one intended for publication, that was both a survey of his presidential career and an expression of his hopes for Germany's future. He declared that it was his wish that the monarchy someday be restored, leaving to Hitler the determination as to when the proper time might be.[31] How unlikely that was can be detected in a remark the Führer made to Benito Mussolini during his first trip to Italy in June 1934. Hitler observed that *il Duce* would have done well to have got rid of King Victor Emmanuel III, for a king inevitably interfered with a dictator's authority, and this represented a danger for fascism.[32]

Hindenburg died early in August 1934, his last words being "my Kaiser," a farewell that to Wilhelm, cold and unforgiving as ever, were proof only of a bad conscience. Speaking at the funeral at Tannenberg, Hitler pointedly implied that had Wilhelm more promptly recognized the field marshal's abilities, the First World War might have had a successful conclusion.[33] By the time that Hindenburg died, the Kaiser had long since abandoned Hitler and his regime, but prudence led Wilhelm to keep this detestation to himself. A major cause of the Kaiser's repugnance was the

Führer's breaking up of several celebrations in Germany honoring the Kaiser's seventy-fifth birthday, accompanied by an order to the press to minimize coverage of the event. "The Nazis have dropped their mask," Wilhelm declared, "and revealed that they are a socialist party."[34] The Kaiser's alienation became complete when, in the course of celebrating the first anniversary of coming to power, the Führer delivered a violent diatribe against the throne and a few days later, on 2 February 1934, outlawed all monarchical institutions. This was to the Kaiser a "declaration of war against the house of Hohenzollern."[35]

Not all of the Kaiser's family shared his rejection of the Führer. Prince Auwi continued to serve in the SA and signed his letters to his father "Heil Hitler." A British observer noted that Wilhelm's daughter and her husband appeared in 1936 to be "pro-Nazi." The crown prince, still true to Hitler, wrote articles for the British press praising the new regime and worked strenuously, though not successfully, to ingratiate himself with the leaders of the party.[36] The crown princess, although rumored to have ordered all the windows opened after the allegedly malodorous Hitler had come to drink tea, intoned to a group of women a few months after the Führer became chancellor, "[Hitler] has our gratitude that our patriotic duties can again be performed."[37] Gradually the ardor of the younger Hohenzollerns waned, for Hitler refused to offer the dynasty even crumbs of recognition. By 1935 the crown prince began to dissolve his contacts with the party leadership and thereafter lived a private existence, disparaging the Nazis in conversations with his family and friends. Except for Auwi, the Kaiser's other sons had little connection with the Nazi elite after 1935, although Eitel Friedrich and Oskar, to their father's dismay, had, as members of the party, pledged their loyalty to the Führer. Prince Adalbert, who loathed the new regime, moved to Switzerland in protest.

Hermine was the last holdout. She continued to conclude her letters *"für Deutschland und mit Hitler!"* or *"Mit deutschem Gruß,"* an expression that Wilhelm especially disliked.[38] In her opinion, the Führer was a genius to whom all Germans should feel grateful for having snatched the Fatherland back from the abyss. She regretted that there were those, some of them monarchists, who did not feel this indebtedness, and their "grotesque" hope that the Nazi movement might be toppled was not only an idiocy but a crime as well.[39] Hitler's venomous speeches about monarchy and his hostile attitude toward the Kaiser's seventy-fifth birthday celebrations in January 1934 wounded Hermine, but nevertheless a few days later she wrote to the Kaiser's old friend Field Marshal August von Mackensen, "I remain loyally rooted in my attachment and am confident that he

[Hitler] as well as Göring will steer the good ship Germany wisely and correctly."[40] She continued on for several years with unabated enthusiasm for the Führer, with whom she perceived "striking parallels" to Wilhelm in that their common purity was not fully appreciated or understood.[41]

Although after 1934 Wilhelm was determined to reject Hitler as the means of his return to the throne, he steadfastly believed that millions of Germans, in fact two out of every three, desired his restoration to the throne. He continued to insist, as he had from 1919 on, that he would return only when his former subjects called him home.[42] This was a hope, unreasonable from the outset and increasingly unlikely, that the Kaiser nurtured well into the 1930s, but thereafter he seldom mentioned the possibility and seems to have thought of either the crown prince or one of his grandsons as being Germany's future kaiser. This sense of futility was evident in Wilhelm's declaration, made in September 1935, that if he could not return to the fatherland as sovereign, he would prefer to be buried in Holland.[43] Even though Hitler had no intention of reestablishing the monarchy, the Kaiser was full of speculation, some of it quite visionary, as to how it might be done. The German people, dissatisfied with their lot, might overthrow the Führer, or the British might force Hitler out and bring Wilhelm back, or the Germans might follow the lead of the French, who in the wake of the rioting in 1934 over the Stavisky scandals might soon abolish their republic and select a king. Or might not a union of German Protestants and Catholics, a prospect that the Kaiser imagined but that other Germans had not seriously entertained for centuries, result in both camps insisting on a restoration of the Hohenzollern monarchy?[44]

In the meantime, the Kaiser could do little but indulge in denouncing Hitler to his entourage. The Führer was nothing but an Austrian house-painter or busboy (*Küchen-Ordonnanz*) who vainly imagined that he could occupy the place the Hohenzollerns had held since the Middle Ages.[45] There was to the Kaiser something unseemly in the way the Nazis behaved, especially in the carnage of the "Night of the Long Knives" on 30 June 1934, in which Hitler's minions killed the crown prince's friend, the SA leader Ernst Röhm, and many other enemies. This reminded Wilhelm of Chicago gangsterism, and his disdain increased when, a few days later, Hitler required all army officers to retake their oaths of loyalty, this time to him.[46] The Kaiser could not understand how his former comrades could traffic with a man like Hitler, and even Mackensen, the soldier whom Wilhelm most liked and admired, had demeaned himself by accepting a landed estate and an honorary military command from the Nazis.[47] Wilhelm had from his youth complained about the influence of the Jews in

Germany and, after 1918, about their complicity with the Bolsheviks and Masons in the collapse of his empire. He continued long after 1933 to condemn the Jews, who, he declared, were incapable of assimilation. But Hitler went too far in his attacks, and the Kaiser utterly disapproved of the infamous *Kristallnacht* of 9 November 1938, in which Nazi gangs destroyed Jewish shops and stores. This was to him only another excrescence of hooliganism and an outrage against which every German should protest, but alas they did nothing. "I am absolutely *horrified* at the late events at home," he wrote. "Pure bolshevism!"[48]

Hermine's attachment to the Nazis was only one strain in her relations with the Kaiser, relations that by the 1930s no longer had much apparent warmth. The marriage, happily entered into in 1922 by both parties, had soon foundered, for neither partner found what he or she had hoped for. Wilhelm began by treating Hermine with exaggerated deference, but this turned to neglect and finally to outright indignation, and the "Kaiserin," at first most solicitous of her husband, before long was going behind his back and asserting a degree of independence that Wilhelm had always found undesirable in anyone, of either sex, in his immediate company. The Kaiser's children, especially the crown prince and his wife, never overcame their reservations about their father's second marriage. Hermine had an inordinate sense of her own importance, flattery swayed her easily, and she had an unattractive way of forcing her opinions on Wilhelm and his entourage. Life at Doorn was frustrating for Hermine, who hated the wet climate at Doorn — the "kingdom of damp," a British guest described it — and who resented the guests with whom Wilhelm liked to talk about the old days. Just as Wilhelm's first wife had in her day complained, the Kaiser preferred to be with his male friends, leaving women to their own devices. Hermine therefore stayed in Germany for increasingly long periods, and the retinue, happy to see her depart, encouraged her not to rush back to Holland when Wilhelm fell sick or other emergencies occurred.

Hermine liked to surround herself with people who she believed shared her dedication to monarchism but who were in fact using her to ferret out information about the Kaiser, a task that her volubility and indiscretion facilitated. This exposed her to manipulation and might well have endangered the royal house. Wilhelm recognized that his wife's behavior was potentially dangerous and that he therefore had to be careful in what he said to her. "Around my wife I must place every word on the scales," he complained to his trusted Ilsemann (who intensely disliked Hermine). "May I say something or must I not be silent? In the end I don't any longer know what I should say."[49] In April 1937, for reasons that are not clear,

Hermine quite suddenly became disenchanted with the Nazis and broke off all relations with her Berlin contacts in the party. She would later say that although Hitler had done some good things, his movement was evil and he was ill-served by Heinrich Himmler and others. Yet it may have been that she abandoned the Nazis at the moment that she realized, quite belatedly, that they had no intention of restoring Wilhelm to his throne. She eventually came to hate the Third Reich even more than did her husband, and she worked to bring Wilhelm to her level of outrage against Hitler.[50]

The Führer and his regime could hardly have been less interested in what Wilhelm and Hermine thought about them, and they made no effort whatsoever to treat the exiled household in Doorn with dignity. Mail coming from and going to Holland was opened, the Kaiser's adjutants were sometimes roughly questioned as they made their way across the German border, and the press was ordered to disregard the activities of the Hohenzollern family. In Germany there were other insults to the royal house. Stores were no longer allowed to carry pictures of the Kaiser or of any other member of the royal family, but to Wilhelm the greatest outrage of all was the order, given at the Nazi Party day in Nürnberg in 1935, that the old red, white, and black imperial flag that had been retained under the Third Reich was now to give way to a Nazi swastika standard. That meant, to the Kaiser's mortification and fury, that the buildings the crown still owned in Berlin now had to fly this hated ensign.[51]

The abandonment of all hope that he would ever be able to return to Germany to claim his throne depressed the Kaiser, but only momentarily. He had always had an ability to spring back quickly from emotional trials, and Ilsemann and his other adjutants noted that this attribute had not deserted Wilhelm in old age. The Kaiser simply ignored what did not please him, always ready to believe things depending on their intersection with his convictions and judging events and people, as he always had, from his own personal perspective.[52] In the late 1930s, with Hermine happily often away in Germany managing her estates and visiting her children, the Kaiser created a pleasant enough life for himself, often entirely oblivious to the darkening state of international relations. Old friends continued to come to Doorn, among them Prince Max Egon von Fürstenberg, now a Nazi sympathizer, who found the Kaiser's diatribes against Hitler very unsettling.[53] Wilhelm, as was his wont, did not show much consideration to Fürstenberg or his other old comrades, for the appalling streak of cold-bloodedness that his mother had deplored sixty years earlier was still one of his unfortunate qualities.[54]

On the other hand, the Kaiser made a conspicuous effort to end the enmity that existed between himself and his English relatives, a discord that stretched back even before 1914. Although Wilhelm would continue to speak contemptuously of Britain to his entourage, in January 1936 he initiated a revival of relations when he wrote a letter of consolation to Queen Mary on the death of his first cousin, King George V, even though he had long resented the king's silence when the Kaiserin had died in 1921.[55] The queen in return sent him a gold box from the late king's desk, and from that point on, Wilhelm wrote quite cordially not only to her but also to other members of the royal family.[56] Another funereal correspondent of the Kaiser's was the widow of Admiral John Jellicoe, who had commanded the British fleet at the battle of Dogger Bank, the one great naval encounter between the German and the British navies in the First World War. There was, and is, debate as to which side could be accorded the victory, but Wilhelm always believed that his battleships had won the day. It was Dogger Bank, he declared, that had forever ruined England's status as a great power, and not surprisingly but quite falsely he claimed that it was he who had devised the plan whereby Germany had achieved this dubious victory.[57] Wilhelm nevertheless wrote handsomely to Lady Jellicoe, praising "the illustrious admiral" and his "sterling qualities, as gallant leader, splendid sailor, chivalrous antagonist and British gentleman."[58]

The Kaiser had always imagined that he was not only as brilliant a sailor as Jellicoe but also an equally talented general, and for that reason he took much interest in the wars that involved one or another of the European states in the 1930s. From the moment that Mussolini seized power in Italy in 1922, the Italian leader had always been an object of the Kaiser's admiration and often the subject of his conversation. *Il Duce*'s success in bringing order to Italy, exactly what Wilhelm boasted he would do for Germany when and if restored to his throne, was splendid. Mussolini was, Wilhelm declared, "a kingly Lenin," adept at the merciless methods of the Bolsheviks but at the same time wise enough to retain the monarchy.[59] In 1935, the dictator became involved in a victorious war in Abyssinia, but his success did not entirely please the Kaiser. Britain, gutted of great-power status by the Dogger Bank encounter with the German navy in 1916, so Wilhelm argued, should have acted to prevent the Italian invasion by fomenting a Muslim uprising to help the Christian Abyssinians, with whom he sympathized. The British, however, had done nothing, and so Mussolini had created his empire. On reflection, the Kaiser decided that *il Duce* was not to be begrudged this victory because it was after all a Caucasian triumph over the black race and because Mussolini had proclaimed the innocuous King Victor Emmanuel III to be emperor of Ethiopia. That would show the world, Wilhelm illogically proclaimed, "that Mussolini without the King" was "nothing." The same, of course, was true of Hitler and himself.[60] Of even greater interest to Wilhelm was the Spanish civil war that erupted just a year after the Italian victory in Africa. From the beginning, the Kaiser's sympathies were entirely with General Francisco Franco's antirepublican Falange movement, and he was delighted when Hitler granted diplomatic and financial support to the caudillo.[61] He followed each step of the conflict with the closest interest, placing pins on hand-colored maps, and nothing brought him more pleasure than news of a Falangist success. When Franco brought the conflict to a successful conclusion in March 1939, Wilhelm was distraught that he no longer had war games to play.[62]

Closer to home and of immediate concern to Germany was the situation in central and eastern Europe, the area that Hitler had proclaimed in *Mein Kampf* must one day belong to Germany. In the late 1930s, the Führer proceeded to fulfill this desire, and his first victim was the republic of Austria, which he bloodlessly invaded on 12 March 1938 and then incorporated into the Third Reich. Wilhelm expressed approval, but not because it increased Germany's prestige (for that would redound to Hitler's glory) but because England's failure to move against the Führer was another sign that its days as a great power were over. But Wilhelm later came to the conclusion that Hitler's appropriation of Austria was an act that an ogre such as Joseph Stalin, of whom he greatly disapproved, might have committed, and he incorrectly predicted that the Austrians, like the inhabitants of Alsace-Lorraine, who had been so unhappy when ruled by imperial Germany, would soon demand autonomy.[63] The Czechoslovakia crisis, which seemed to bring Europe to the brink of war in September, was of little concern to the Kaiser, perhaps because he had always had a vast contempt for Slavs. The British prime minister, Neville Chamberlain, flew to Munich to meet with Hitler at the end of the month and capitulated to the Führer's demand that the largely German Sudetenland be ceded to Germany. Wilhelm was happy that war had thus been averted, and he wrote to Queen Mary that he had "not the slightest doubt that Mr. Chamberlain was inspired by Heaven & guided by God. . . . God bless him."[64] He was, however, not entirely confident that the peace thus gained would be permanent. At Christmas the Kaiser wrote what would prove to be the last of many letters to his old English friend General Wallscourt H.-H. Waters, again attributing the deceptive calm in Europe to Chamberlain and to divine providence but adding "*pourvu que cela dure!*" — if it could in fact last.[65] It did not, of course. Hitler, confident that neither London nor Paris would offer any resistance, took the Slavic remainder of Czechoslovakia, an act of unclad aggression that could not be defended on nationalist grounds. Hermine was delighted, but the news apparently made no impression on Wilhelm. Word had made its way to Doorn, through Mackensen, that the Führer was annoyed that his accomplishments had failed to produce any recognition from the Kaiser, and General Dommes tried in vain to coax Wilhelm into sending Hitler at least some guarded expression of approval.[66] The Führer's deeds might seem to be mighty, but Wilhelm reminded the guests assembled at Doorn for his eightieth birthday on 27 January 1939 that God had a way of humbling those who imagined that they could have whatever they wanted.[67] Swallowing Czechoslovakia might appear a great coup, but he predicted that if Germany went to war with the rest of Europe, it would go down to defeat. That was because Hitler's *Wehrmacht*, unlike the Kaiser's imperial army, had a heterogeneous officer corps and poor NCOs.[68]

Poland was clearly the Führer's next victim, but this too was a country of Slavic people for whom Wilhelm had never had the least sympathy. He did not intend to raise his voice now in their defense. In March 1939 Hitler declared that the largely German port of Danzig, defined somewhat dichotomously in the Versailles treaty as a free city in which Poland would have certain economic privileges, would become German territory. The Poles were also to grant Hitler the right to construct roads and railways across the Polish "corridor" that would link the main body of Germany to the sundered province of East Prussia. The British and the French, enraged by the Führer's seizure of Czechoslovakia, promised the Poles that the two countries would come to their defense in the event of military intimidation from Hitler. The scene was set for war unless Hitler backed down or the British and the French disavowed their guarantees to Warsaw.

Wilhelm thought Hitler's demands regarding Danzig and the corridor not only justifiable but in fact modest, yet he was very fearful that the Polish crisis might result in war, a development to which he was absolutely opposed.[69] On 22 August 1939, Hitler and Stalin electrified the world by signing a nonaggression pact. The Kaiser at first found this to be a masterstroke of diplomacy, but he soon changed his mind, declaring that no one would ever trust Germany in the future. He fantasized that perhaps Hitler's treachery in allying with the "archenemy" in the Kremlin would bring the German people to their senses and lead to the Führer's overthrow.[70] He realized now that Europe stood at the brink of war, and on 30 August 1939, he wrote again to Queen Mary in a lame attempt to combine humor with pathos. "Yes," he assured the queen, "you are right, the world is sorely troubled! I suggest that the World's [League of] nations committee at Geneva is dissolved, their Palace may be turned into an asylum for Political lunacy to recieve [*sic*] all the Europ. statesmen for a cure till they recover their senses! May Heaven preserve us from the worst!"[71]

On 1 September 1939, Hitler invaded Poland, and two days later both Britain and France made good their promises to enter the war on behalf of the Poles, who fought valiantly but in vain against the Führer's superior forces. Wilhelm followed each German victory with gusto, happy again to have maps on which to trace the order of battle and proud that of his progeny, one son and eight grandsons were serving in the *Wehrmacht*. A grandson was killed in Poland on the fifth day of the war, another in May 1940 during the invasion of France, and a third, grousing in Scotland with the Duke of Buccleuch, was interned for the duration. The Kaiser felt that Hitler's military tactics had been splendid, and he was delighted that the Führer had not encountered the insurmountable problems that had bedeviled the imperial army throughout the First World War.[72] Since Holland was neutral, he could not express his pleasure in public, but General Dommes was ordered to write a memo summarizing his sentiments and to send it to the chief of Hitler's *Reichskanzlei*, Dr. Hans Lammers.[73]

To Wilhelm, the conflict that began in 1939 was ordained for the settling of old scores, especially the grievances that Germany had suffered at the hands of England. Divine providence would reward the righteous, and thus the victory of the pious Finns over the godless Russians in the "Winter War" of 1940 was to him God's reward to Christian people. This war, like the first in 1914, was the work of his hated uncle, King Edward VII, and the king's plutocratic retinue. It was not the British people against whom the war was directed, Wilhelm declared, but against the "*reigning upper class of free masons* completely poisoned and ruled by Jewry."[74] For years the British elite, with their Hebraic and Masonic satellites, had played one power off the other, but now the day of reckoning had come, and they would be humbled. When England was forced to beg for peace, it would have to surrender parts of its empire and be made to understand that its future lay in cooperating with a German-dominated Europe and not with the United States.[75]

On 10 May 1940, the "phoney war" came to an end with Hitler's invasion of France and also of Holland, Belgium, and Luxembourg. This instantly altered Wilhelm's situation in Doorn, which was located between the advancing Germans and the Dutch defensive force. Although it was out of the direct line of battle, cannonades could easily be heard from the house.[76] The Kaiser had informed the Dutch government in May 1939 that in the event of war, he intended to remain firmly put in Doorn unless it was threatened by the enemy, in which case he would return to Germany.[77] So Wilhelm and Hermine stayed put, but the Dutch deprived them of all but four of their German servants, confiscated their radios, and cut the telephone wires. The grounds of the castle were closely patrolled, with orders to shoot anyone moving outside the house after 8 P.M. Wilhelm was required to sign a document that he would do nothing to harm the Dutch government or the country. Hitler sent a letter to Wilhelm, one that Hermine described as "handsome [and] worthy," requesting the Kaiser and his wife to come to whatever place in Germany they might choose, an offer that pleased them both but that they indirectly declined.[78] A similar offer arrived from the British government on 12 May, but Wilhelm sharply rejected it, saying that he would rather be shot than flee to England, where he would be forced to be photographed with his old nemesis Winston Churchill. "I considered the British offer as a temptation of Satan, [and] therefore refused it placing my whole confidence and trust in *God alone*. His answer to this resolve was: the Germans [appeared] in Doorn and [effected] our immediate deliverance the next day! Direct acts of Providence! . . . The old Prussian spirit of Fredericus Rex, of Clausewitz, Blücher, Yorck, Gneisenau etc. has again manifested itself." He continued, with consummate vanity: "The brilliant leading Generals in this war come from *my* school, they fought under my command in the World War as lieutenants, captains or young majors. Educated by Schlieffen they put the plans he had worked out under me into practice."[79]

On 13 May 1940 the *Wehrmacht* entered Doorn, to Wilhelm's jubilation. His servants were freed from internment, and a German patrol was detailed to guard the former Kaiser. He ordered that champagne be served with dinner, and raising his glass he declared with tears in his eyes this glorious moment that recalled Frederick the Great's annihilation of the Austrian army at Leuthen in 1757 and Wilhelm I's victory over France a hundred-odd years later.[80] A month later, the French, whose forces had proved incapable of mounting a successful resistance to the German tide, sued for an armistice. It was the moment of revenge for 1918. The Kaiser now at last provided the Führer with the congratulations that Hitler had theretofore sought in vain. On the day that France requested an armistice, Wilhelm wired Hitler extolling him and the army on this "powerful victory sent by God." Wilhelm repeated the Lutheran chorale that Frederick had ordered sung at Leuthen: "Now thank we all our God." The Führer's reply, for which Wilhelm had to wait a week, was strictly ceremonial, for

Hitler had long since rejected the Kaiser and his family as irrelevant to the great German Empire that was now being built.[81] German soldiers in Doorn were ordered to have no contact with the monarch, and after two of Wilhelm's grandsons had been killed in action, the Führer ordered that the remaining princes be retired from the service in order to forestall the growth of a cult of Hohenzollern martyrdom. Hitler's dismissiveness of the Kaiser also characterized Dr. Joseph Goebbels, who in 1940 declared that Wilhelm was an "incorrigible fool" who quite probably had Jewish blood in his veins.[82]

Although the Kaiser was well past his eightieth birthday when Hitler's war began in September 1939, his doctors were generally satisfied with the state of his health. As a young man, the Kaiser had feared that he would die early, and he did not like to be near people from whom he might contract diseases.[83] Wilhelm had especially worried that he would be stricken with cancer, which had killed both his mother and his father, and that the malignancy would settle in his throat, as it had with Frederick III. Cancer, he believed, was caused by unhealthy food such as vegetables grown in earth containing sewage and also by meat that had been transported over a long distance, and he was therefore careful about what was served at his table.[84] As it happened, Wilhelm, the oldest of eight children, survived all but his youngest sibling, Princess Margaret of Hesse, who was thirteen years his junior, and it was not cancer but heart disease that finally killed him. In spite of Doorn's execrable climate for most of the year, the Kaiser had flourished during his twenty-odd years in Holland, exercising regularly and eating carefully. He had always been a cautious drinker, but on the advice of one of his physicians at Doorn he began having a spot of whiskey every evening after dinner as a precaution against catching a cold. Until his early seventies, Wilhelm II was a model of health, but in January 1932, a few days before he turned seventy-three, he suffered a slight heart attack brought on by bronchitis and accompanied by some swelling in the legs.[85] Although the Kaiser recovered quickly, this unmistakable intimation of mortality, together with his increasing distaste for the Nazis, led him to dictate, on Christmas Day 1933, the directions for his funeral, plans that superseded the program he had drawn up thirty-two years earlier, after his mother's death. If a restoration had occurred by the time he died, he was to be interred in Potsdam between his two empresses; if not, Doorn would be his "provisional" resting place. In either case the funeral was to have no Nazi vestiges.[86] Once he was gone, the Fatherland would have to make its way as best it could. Not long before writing these directions, he coolly told one of his adjutants that he was "rather indifferent" about what happened to Germany after his death.[87]

Wilhelm's health remained remarkably good until 1938, when he suffered a brief episode in which his speech became very confused. Three years later, on the first day of March 1941, during his daily gardening exercise, he was, as he put it, "rather overcome" and had to take to his bed.[88] The Kaiser's condition was actually quite serious, and he was forced to stay in bed or use a wheelchair for much of the time, his failing heart requiring vitalization by injections. On 24 May 1941 an intestinal obstruction, along with signs of vascular deterioration, developed, alarming the doctors, who insisted that Wilhelm's children be called to Doorn.[89] The crown prince, his sister, Auwi, and Oskar hurried to Holland (illness prevented the two other sons from coming), and they found their father weak but entirely rational. Wilhelm told them of his love for Germany, his pride in the recent accomplishments of German arms, his delight — "It's fabulous!" (*Das is ja fabelhaft!*) — in the sinking of the British battleship *Hood* by the German *Bismarck* and in the conquest of Crete. "Bring me more good news like that and I'll soon start to get well."[90] The Kaiser did begin to improve, and most of the family, for whom in any case there was inadequate food in Doorn, left for Germany. On Tuesday afternoon, 3 June 1941, the Kaiser suffered another heart attack. He realized that this was the end and said to Hermine, who sat on one side of his bed, that he was ready to die. He then lapsed into unconsciousness and died at half past eleven on the following morning.

On hearing that Wilhelm's death was approaching, Goebbels had cynically declared that it would "provide some interest for a day at the most" and ordered that the event be relegated to the back pages in the German press.[91] Hitler, however, saw more clearly than his propaganda chief that the Kaiser's death represented an opportunity for the Third Reich to bury forever the Hohenzollern monarchy along with its last ruler. This was to be symbolized in a great state funeral in Berlin in which the Führer, walking behind the imperial coffin, would represent the successor to the German kaisers.[92] Hitler's scenario, along with his condolences, was telephoned to Doorn, but the crown prince and the rest of the family insisted on adhering loyally to the Kaiser's 1933 testamentary instructions that if Germany was not a monarchy, he was to be buried in Doorn. At the same time, the heirs were not eager to offer the Führer any gratuitous provocation, for they resided in Germany and were dependent on him for the preservation of their lives and property. After hurried negotiations between Doorn and Berlin, a compromise was arrived at whereby the burial would take place in Holland but a deputation of Nazi military officers headed by Arthur Seyss-Inquart, Nazi high commissioner in the Netherlands, would be invited.

On Monday, 9 June 1941, a glorious warm day under a brilliant blue sky—what in happier times had been known as "Hohenzollern weather"—Wilhelm's funeral took place before a large assemblage of family members. They had been brought to Holland on a special train, to which Himmler's private car had been added to accommodate the ninety-two-year-old Field Marshal Mackensen, but the trip had been ominously delayed near Dortmund because of a British air raid.[93] Wilhelm lay in state in the dining room at Doorn, his coffin covered by an imperial ensign. One hundred and seventy-one wreaths, including an arrangement of lilies of the valley and orchids sent by the Führer, surrounded the coffin, before which there were two pillows, on which the Kaiser's field marshal's baton and decorations were displayed. The service, at which Wilhelm had ordered there was to be no eulogy, lasted a bare half hour, and at its conclusion the Kaiser's body was borne in his gray Mercedes to a mortuary chapel that a former owner of the estate had erected near the gatehouse. The crown prince had ordered that Seyss-Inquart and his officers were to be placed markedly by themselves to one side, with Mackensen and the Hohenzollerns composing a distinctly separate group, but in fact the Nazi cohort stationed itself close to the assembled royalty. A second, very brief service was held at the chapel, and at its conclusion three scoops of earth dug from Potsdam were sprinkled on the coffin. Then only Mackensen accompanied the body into the chapel, remaining there in prayer for a minute or so.

Within a year after Wilhelm's death, Doorn was empty. Hermine, to whom Wilhelm left a generous allowance, retreated to her Silesian estates, where in 1945 she was captured by the advancing Russians and forced to live in penury until her death two years later. The Kaiser's papers were sent to the regional archive in Utrecht, and in 1942 the castle was converted into a museum full of memorabilia of its last occupant. On the first anniversary of his death, Wilhelm's body was transferred to a modest chapel built in the garden near the house. There it rests today, almost sixty years after his death. Flowers continue to be deposited at his feet, and the coffin is still covered with his flag of the great empire whose last sovereign he was destined to be. Since he had once decreed that if the monarchy was not reestablished, he preferred to rest in Holland, it seems likely that the last of the German kaisers will lie forever in a foreign field across the Rhine from the German land over which he once had ruled.

Had a eulogy been allowed on that June day of 1941 that marked Wilhelm II's passage into history, to what great accomplishments, what lofty visions, might it have referred? On many occasions after he lost his throne, the Kaiser had written or spoken his own laudation, for he was anxious that he be remembered and given a valued place in history. In the spring of 1937 he wrote out by hand a statement, without a title or a specific recipient, in which he declared that the welfare of the Fatherland had been his life's work and that for the love of his people he had left Germany on 10 November 1918, thereby bringing them "the greatest and most difficult sacrifice" that he "in any wise could have made and through that step taking" upon himself "every known misinterpretation, mockery, and filth."[94] Here Wilhelm sounded the same forlorn note that had figured in his self-defense ever since he had come to the throne in 1888. He had, he believed, worked hard and done his best to protect and enrich his people and to maintain peace. No one — not his family, or his people, or England, or his generals, statesmen, and admirals, or the Nazis in more recent times — had appreciated these efforts. If he had failed to achieve what he had wanted, it had not been his fault but theirs, and therefore with him might rightly repose the praise that comes to good men, with the blame distributed among those who had perversely refused to recognize him as their exemplar. He therefore would die, though a man without a country and without a crown, nonetheless a noble victim, a martyr, a Christian hero bereft of all but honor, and therefore surely deserving of the hymn that the bells of the Garrison Church at Potsdam tolled — "Be ever true and honest, unto thy cold grave" (*Üb' immer Treu und Redlichkeit, bis an dein kühles Grab*).

That was the vision that Kaiser Wilhelm II had of himself throughout his long life, and one of the few constant elements throughout all these decades was the fixity with which he believed in himself. Like all else, his conviction of his own worth was a fantasy, a creation proceeding not from evidence but from vanity, one that he alone believed and that few of his subjects and still fewer of those who have reviewed his role in history could endorse. It may be written on Wilhelm's funerary tablet that he was a moral man granted a fulsome intelligence who worshiped God and hated war. But there the letters run out, and one is left with only the unelevating spectacle of a mortal called through destiny to immeasurable glory and great power but one who, with what seems like a relentless perversity, squandered these gifts and made such a travesty of authority that the wreckage not only of a life but of a once mighty nation was the unhappy consequence. A longtime British diplomat at his court, who had for years struggled in vain to detect virtue in the Kaiser, found himself reminded of the poet Alexander Pope's lines on the Duke of Buckingham, another disaster.

A man so various that he seemed to be,
Not one, but all mankind's epitome
Fixed in opinion, ever in the wrong
Was all by fits and starts, and nothing long.[95]

Wilhelm Hohenzollern, on whom the trials at birth of bodily affliction and in youth of familial alienation were blamelessly laid and for which understanding and allowance should be granted, failed as a son, as a husband, as a father, as a friend, as a commander, as a statesman, and as an emperor because in all of his roles, he was falsely confident that he possessed truly uncommon talent and perception. For that reason, he never listened to anyone, and he believed that those who stood with him were right and those who opposed him were wrong. Had this Olympian conception been accurate, Wilhelm II might have had a glorious life: loved and admired by his subjects, revered throughout the world as a great lord, and in death praised by the concourse of nations. Instead, the pattern of his life was descendant — through parental alienation, marital tyranny, paternal frigidity, martial pretension, political obtuseness, diplomatic maladroitness, and finally, military inconsequence. What debts do Germans of today owe to their last kaiser? What Ozymandian remnants of his empire still exist to proclaim his praise? What memories of an engaging, or admirable, or imposing figure might be unearthed to conjure up a commendatory image of those Wilhelmine decades over which he presided so disastrously? Unhappily, there are none. It would seem that the last of the kaisers deserves, for his own time and place in history, the brutal envoi that the Duke of Wellington paid to King George IV, an inglorious king who had ruled England long before his kinsman Wilhelm was born. He was a sovereign, the Iron Duke regretfully concluded, who lived and died without having been able to assert so much as a single claim on the gratitude of posterity.

Notes

The following abbreviations are used for printed works cited in the notes.

BD	G. P. Gooch and H. W. V. Temperley, eds. *British Documents on the Origins of the War, 1898–1914.* 11 vols. London, 1925–38.
Briefwechsel	Ernst Deuerlein, ed. *Briefwechsel Hertling-Lerchenfeld, 1912–1917: Dienstliche Privatkorrespondenz.* 2 vols. Boppard, 1973.
Bülow	Bernhard von Bülow. *Denkwürdigkeiten.* 4 vols. Berlin, 1930–31.
DDF	France, Ministry of Foreign Affairs. *Documents Diplomatiques Français, 1871–1914.* 40 vols. Paris, 1929–59.
GP	Johannes Lepsius, Albrecht Mendelssohn-Bartholdy, and Friedrich Thimme, eds. *Die Grosse Politik der Europäischen Kabinette.* 40 vols. Berlin, 1922–27.
HP	Norman Rich and M. H. Fisher, eds. *The Holstein Papers.* 4 vols. Cambridge, 1955–63.
Ilsemann	Harald von Koenigswald, ed. *Sigurd von Ilsemann. Der Kaiser in Holland. Aufzeichnungen des Letzten Flügeladjutanten Kaiser Wilhelms II.* 2 vols. Munich, 1967–68.
Kiderlen	Ernst Jäckh, ed. *Kiderlen-Wächter, der Staatsmann und Mensch: Briefwechsel und Nachlass.* 2 vols. Berlin, 1924.
Max von Baden	Prince Max von Baden. *Erinnerungen und Dokumente.* Berlin, 1927.
Montgelas and Schücking	Count Max von Montgelas and Walther Schücking, eds. *Outbreak of the World War. German Documents Collected by Karl Kautsky.* New York, 1924.
PD	Alfred von Tirpitz. *Politische Dokumente.* 2 vols. Stuttgart, 1924–26.
Röhl	John C. G. Röhl, ed. *Philipp Eulenburgs Politische Korrespondenz.* 3 vols. Boppard, 1976–83.
Schulthess	*Schulthess' Europäischer Geschichtskalender.* 82 vols. Munich, 1860–1941.
Ursachen	Germany, Nationalversammlung. *Die Ursachen des Deutschen Zusammenbruchs im Jahre 1918.* 4th ser. *Das*

<table>
<tr><td></td><td>Werk des Untersuchungsausschusses. 12 vols. Berlin, 1925–29.</td></tr>
<tr><td>Valentini</td><td>Bernhard Schwertfeger, ed. Kaiser und Kabinettschef: Nach Eigenen Aufzeichnungen und dem Briefwechsel des Wirklichen Geheimen Rats Rudolf von Valentini. Oldenburg i.O., 1931.</td></tr>
<tr><td>W2:PE</td><td>Lamar Cecil. Wilhelm II: Prince and Emperor, 1859–1900. Chapel Hill, 1989.</td></tr>
<tr><td>Zedlitz-Trützschler</td><td>Count Robert Zedlitz-Trützschler, Zwölf Jahre am Deutschen Kaiserhof: Aufzeichnungen. Berlin, 1924.</td></tr>
</table>

Abbreviations for manuscript sources used in the notes are located at the beginning of the bibliography.

CHAPTER I

1. On Wilhelm's lifelong immaturity, see Zedlitz-Trützschler, p. 201; Rudolf von Valentini, notes on a Mediterranean trip with Wilhelm in 1904, Schwertfeger Papers, no. 206; Vierhaus, *Tagebuch*, p. 469; DDF, 1st ser., 8:374; Ilsemann, 1:266, 2:22.

2. Iciness, see Mutius Papers, p. 168; Knodt, *Ernst Ludwig*, p. 124; Ilsemann, 2:87–88.

3. See W2:PE, pp. 43–45, 68–86.

4. Louise, Princess of Tuscany, *Own Story*, p. 163.

5. Morel, *Eastern Embassy*, pp. 132–33. Dislike of corpulence, see Davis, *The Kaiser*, p. 167; see also Redwitz, *Hofchronik*, p. 64.

6. Dona's provinciality: Bülow, 1:262–63; Louise, Duchess of Coburg, *Throne*, p. 187; Duke of Saxe-Meiningen to Gossler (20 Sept. 1922), Gossler Papers, no. 7. Wilhelm's role in her clothes: Eulalia, *Memoirs*, p. 73; Topham, *Memories*, pp. 121–22; Philipp Eulenburg to his wife (13 Dec. 1893), Eulenburg Papers, no. 26, p. 574.

7. Pless, *Better Left Unsaid*, p. 72; a similar observation is in Paget, *Tower*, 2:410; also Howe, *Meyer*, p. 74. On Dona, who was born three months before Wilhelm, looking older: Mannix, *Old Navy*, p. 104; Beyens, *Deux Années*, 1:138. On Wilhelm's preference for mature women, see Dona to Philipp Eulenburg (5 Nov. 1898), Eulenburg Papers, no. 52, pp. 315–17. For negative views on her appearance: Meister, *Yesterdays*, p. 46; Salburg, *Erinnerungen*, 2:18–19. More positive estimations are in Townley, *"Indiscretions,"* pp. 54–55; Zobeltitz, *Chronik*, 1:121; Braun, *Ostpreussen bis Texas*, p. 80. For her improvement over the years: Fanny von Wilamowitz-Moellendorff, *Erinnerungen*, p. 103; Morel, *Eastern Embassy*, p. 37; Louise, Duchess of Coburg, *Throne*, p. 187.

8. Bunsen, *Zeitgenossen*, p. 193.

9. Formality: Ebart, *Herzogshofe*, p. 87; Johannes Kessler, *Ewige Jugend*, p. 143; Kleinmichel, *Memories*, p. 283; Marie, *Life*, 2:227–28; Erbach-Schönberg, *Erklugenes*, p. 225; Arthur Lee, *Empress Writes to Sophie*, pp. 96, 131; Brabant, *Hausen*, p. 233. On her boredom and uncomfortableness, see Raschdau, *Bismarck*

und Caprivi, p. 299, and Taube, *Buch der Keyserlinge,* p. 258, but see also: Freytag-Loringhoven, *Menschen und Dinge,* p. 183; Bunsen, *Lost Courts,* pp. 243–45; Olfers, *Briefe,* 2:254. On Dona's prosaic nature: Salburg, *Erinnerungen,* 2:18–19; Louise, Duchess of Coburg, *Throne,* p. 185. There are some positive views of Dona, most of them by people who did not know her well. See Moltke, *Moltke Erinnerungen,* pp. 147–48; Kiderlen, 1:79; Christopher Howard, *Goschen,* p. 199; Senden notes, Senden Papers, p. 36; Stephanie, *Empress,* p. 194.

10. Duke of Saxe-Meiningen to Gossler (8 July 1920), and same to same (8 June 1920, 24 May 1921), Gossler Papers, no. 19; same to same (20 Sept. 1922), ibid., no. 7.

11. On her limited role in society: Townley, *"Indiscretions,"* pp. 54–55; Herbert von Hindenburg, *Am Rande,* p. 219; Haller, *50 Jahre,* pp. 136–37.

12. Meisner, *Denkwürdigkeiten,* 3:192; Bülow, 1:262.

13. Her Protestant rigidity: Beyens, *Germany,* p. 59; Radziwill, *Lettres,* 1:158–59, 2:78, 3:59, 97; Louise, Duchess of Coburg, *Throne,* p. 185; Paget, *Tower,* 2:410. On her entourage's religiosity, see Victoria, *Memories,* p. 51. Wilhelm's annoyance at the "donkeys": Raschdau, *Bismarck und Caprivi,* pp. 303–4; Zedlitz-Trützschler, pp. 44–45, 67–68, 211, 242–43; Janssen, *Graue Exzellenz,* p. 107.

14. Herbette: Lascelles to Salisbury (7 Feb. 1896), FO 64/1376. On the prince of Wales: Bülow, 1:261–62; Widenmann, *Marine-Attaché,* p. 92; on Leopold of the Belgians, see Bülow 1:17; on Russia: ibid., 1:261–62; Raschdau, *Bismarck und Caprivi,* p. 263. She also despised the Danish royal family for having denied her father the ducal throne of Schleswig-Holstein. Eulenburg's notes (13 Oct. 1894), Eulenburg Papers, no. 32, p. 774; Bülow, 2:304. See W2:PE, pp. 77–78, 277–78, for Dona's dislike of England.

15. Herbert von Hindenburg, *Am Rande,* p. 63; Wagemann, *Feodora,* p. 114; Rheinbaben, *Kaiser Kanzler Präsidenten,* p. 69; Topham, *Chronicles,* pp. 158, 162; Rogge, *Holstein Lebensbekenntnis,* p. 216; Bing, *Secret Letters,* pp. 128–30; Zedlitz-Trützschler, p. 138; Marie Louise, *Memories,* pp. 89–90.

16. Röhl, 1:510; Holstein to Eulenburg (n.d. [June 1895]), Eulenburg Papers, no. 36, pp. 445–47.

17. Keen, *Seven Years,* p. 115; Bülow 1:504–6, 2:128; Kiderlen, 1:131; Lascelles to Lansdowne (13 Sept. 1905), FO 800/130; Pless, *Better Left Unsaid,* p. 194.

18. Ilsemann, 1:68–69 (diary of Countess Elisabeth Bentinck, 30 Nov. 1918).

19. Obliqueness: Meisner, *Denkwürdigkeiten,* 2:194; deference: Athlone, *Grandchildren,* pp. 92–93; Eulenburg Papers, no. 81, part 1, p. 197; Bülow, 1:261; Topham, *Chronicles,* p. 127.

20. Johannes Kessler, *Ewige Jugend,* p. 143.

21. Marie, *Life,* 2:222.

22. Dona to Hohenlohe (29 July 1896), Chlodwig Hohenlohe Papers; same to Eulenburg (5 Nov. 1898), Eulenburg Papers, no. 52, pp. 315–17; Eulenburg, *Mit dem Kaiser,* 1:101; Lerchenfeld-Koefering, *Wilhelm II.,* p. 19.

23. Count August zu Eulenburg to Eulenburg (16 Oct. 1891), Eulenburg Papers, no. 16, pp. 313–14; Johannes Kessler, *Ewige Jugend,* p. 146; Bunsen, *Zeitgenossen,* p. 197; Keller, *Vierzig Jahre,* p. 29.

24. Eulenburg to wife (4 July 1898), Eulenburg Papers, no. 53, p. 101; Rudolf

von Valentini to wife (1 Aug. 1908), KE, no. 341/2. For the lone courtier who seems to have enjoyed having Dona aboard ship, see Janssen, *Graue Exzellenz*, p. 107.

25. Röhl, 2:1245.

26. Kiderlen, 1:96, 139.

27. Johannes Kessler, *Ewige Jugend*, p. 145. Wilhelm did not like his wife to accompany him on his morning horseback rides. Rheinbaben, *Kaiser Kanzler Präsidenten*, p. 33.

28. Szögyényi to Aehrenthal (1 Sept. 1911), HHStA, no. 169(B); Eulenburg Papers, no. 81, part 1, pp. 286–87; Wilhelm to grand duke (3 Mar. 1906), Fuchs, *Friedrich I.*, 4:628.

29. Holstein diary (1 Sept. 1885), Holstein Papers, 3861/H196091–92. For his brusqueness to Dona: Holstein diary (23 Sept. 1884), ibid., 3860/H195944; Eulenburg diary (12 Apr. 1894), Eulenburg Papers, no. 29, p. 392; Zedlitz-Trützschler, pp. 109, 222; Janssen, *Graue Exzellenz*, pp. 108–9; Bülow, 1:230, 534. For the resentment of a cousin at the way Wilhelm took advantage of Dona's devotion, see Athlone, *Grandchildren*, pp. 92–93.

30. Bülow, 1:262.

31. Kleinmichel, *Memories*, p. 282.

32. Bülow, 1:248–49. On the disappointment of German feminists, see Lange, *Lebenserinnerungen*, p. 169, and also Rosebrock, *Frauenfrage*. For the influence of Wilhelm's childhood tutor on this attitude, see W2:PE, p. 56.

33. Topham, *Chronicles*, p. 131; Christopher Howard, *Goschen*, p. 39; BD, 10/2:699–701.

34. Speech in Königsberg on 25 Aug. 1910 before an assembly of East Prussian notables, in Schulthess (1910), p. 339. I am indebted to Dr. Karen Offen for this reference.

35. Louise, Duchess of Coburg, *Throne*, p. 181.

36. Pless, *Better Left Unsaid*, p. 288; Eulenburg notes (28 Oct. 1892), Eulenburg Papers, no. 22, pp. 695–96; ibid., no. 80, p. 15 n. 1; Marie, *Life*, 2:169, 229; Wentzcke, *Neuen Reich*, 2:444–45; Münz, *Edward VII*, p. 233; Winterfeldt-Menkin, *Jahreszeiten*, p. 115; Haller, *50 Jahre*, p. 176. Some women, however, found the Kaiser charming: Erbach-Schönberg, *Erklugenes*, p. 99; Princess Ludwig Ferdinand of Bavaria, *Four Revolutions*, pp. 224–25; Eulalia, *Memoirs*, p. 73; Hegermann-Lindencrone, *Diplomatic Life*, p. 313. Wilhelm's second wife declared, "It was not always easy, especially for women, to engage him in conversation." Hermine, *Empress in Exile*, p. 299. He was, however, sympathetic to women in the first pangs of widowhood. See Bunsen, *Welt*, pp. 189–90.

37. Taube, *Buch der Keyserlinge*, p. 258; Lascelles to Grey (1 Nov. 1907), FO 800/61; Bülow, 2:68, 270; Einem, *Erinnerungen*, pp. 126–27.

38. The decline began in 1894. See Röhl, 2:1245 n. 10; Nostitz-Rieneck, *Briefe Kaiser*, 1:386; Deines diary (5 July 1895), Deines Papers, no. 13; Eulenburg, *Mit dem Kaiser*, 1:321–22; Meisner, *Denkwürdigkeiten*, 2:355.

39. Eulenburg to Bülow (20 July 1898), Röhl, 3:1909; Eulenburg notes, Eulenburg Papers, no. 37, pp. 507–9; August Eulenburg to Eulenburg (31 Aug. 1895), ibid., pp. 578–79.

40. Eulenburg to Bülow (25 Sept. 1900), Röhl, 3:1995–96.

41. Rosner, *Erinnerungen des Kronprinzen*, pp. 3–4, 268; Viktoria Luise, *Tochter des Kaisers*, pp. 14–16. On her indulgence: Deines diary (22 Mar. 1895), Deines Papers, no. 13; Bunsen, *Zeitgenossen*, pp. 192–93.

42. Deines diary (22 Mar. 1895, 2 Oct. 1896), Deines Papers, no. 13.

43. Eulenburg to Bülow (22 and 23 Sept. 1900), Röhl 3:1992–97. Later Prince Adalbert also was educated at Plön.

44. Wilhelm's relationship with the crown prince: Zedlitz-Trützschler, p. 49; Meisner, *Denkwürdigkeiten*, 2:196; Bülow, 1:617–18; Rogge, *Holstein Lebensbekenntnis*, p. 279; Janssen, *Graue Exzellenz*, pp. 139, 149–51; Cecilie, *Erinnerungen an den Kronprinzen*, pp. 57–61; Rosner, *Erinnerungen des Kronprinzen*, pp. 14–16. The crown prince's second son noted how different in personality the Kaiser and his father were. Louis Ferdinand, *Kaiserenkel*, pp. 251–53. Wilhelm was a difficult father, but the crown prince's character alarmed many people. See Vierhaus, *Tagebuch*, p. 435; Waters, *Potsdam and Doorn*, p. 77; Redlich, 1:220; Austen Chamberlain, *Down the Years*, pp. 65–66; Rogge, *Holstein Lebensbekenntnis*, p. 279. The only person who seems to have had a high opinion of the crown prince was Friedrich von Berg-Markienen, a notable reactionary. See KE, no. 331/2, p. 23.

45. Thimme Papers, no. 16, pp. 12–13; Bülow, 1:617–18; Rosner, *Erinnerungen des Kronprinzen*, pp. 12–13; Röhl, 3:2033; Waters, *Potsdam and Doorn*, pp. 76–77; Janssen, *Graue Exzellenz*, pp. 149–51; Briefwechsel, 1:257.

46. On popularity in the army, see *DDF*, 3d ser., 3:61; on the uniform, see Goschen to Sir Arthur Nicolson (17 Mar. 1911), FO 371/1123. Jealousy of the Kaiser: Rattigan, *Diversions*, p. 127; Tresckow, *Fürsten*, p. 107.

47. Rosner, *Erinnerungen des Kronprinzen*, p. 4; Zorn, *Universitätsleben*, p. 109. For a rare dispute, see Röhl 3:2031–33.

48. Faramond, *Souvenirs*, p. 44; Viktoria Luise, *Tochter des Kaisers*, pp. 59, 239; Röhl, 3:2031–33.

49. On being alone with his sons, see KE, no. 331/2, p. 53. On the relationship in general: ibid., p. 24; Rosner, *Erinnerungen des Kronprinzen*, p. 10; Ethel Howard, *Potsdam Princess*, p. 135; Waters, *Potsdam and Doorn*, pp. 76–77. Adjutant-General Kessel, who saw the family daily for years, said that Wilhelm was cold to everyone, including his own children. Ilsemann, 1:67.

50. Rosner, *Erinnerungen des Kronprinzen*, p. 5; Ethel Howard, *Potsdam Princess*, p. 135; Wagemann, *Feodora*, p. 165.

51. Dullness: Szögyényi to Goluchowski (20 Dec. 1897), HHStA, no. 148(V); Eulenburg's observation in Eulenburg Papers, no. 17, p. 8 n, and in ibid., no. 80, p. 24; Radziwill, *Lettres*, 1:117. On Henry's deference to Wilhelm: Eulenburg to Count Herbert von Bismarck (15 Jan. 1889), Eulenburg Papers, no. 5, p. 15; Radziwill, *Lettres*, 2:107; Brauer, *Dienste Bismarcks*, p. 239; Bunsen, *Welt*, p. 79. On the navy: Zedlitz-Trützschler, p. 100; Brett, *Journals and Letters*, 2:414.

52. "Political child" in Widenmann, *Marine-Attaché*, pp. 70–71. On the Hohenzollern-Hessian relationship: Corbett to Grey (22 Apr. 1913), FO 800/1650; Knodt, *Ernst Ludwig*, p. 124; Holstein to Eulenburg (28 Dec. 1895), Eulenburg Papers, no. 76, pp. 84–85; Eulenburg's notes (12–13 Oct. 1895), ibid., no. 38, pp. 727–32; Radziwill, *Lettres*, 1:58; Bülow, 1:454–55; Röhl, 2:844. For the tsar's fondness for Henry, see Grierson to Gough (8 Dec. 1897), FO 64/1412.

53. For Charlotte's relationship with her brother and Dona: Marie, *Life*, 2:81; Radziwill, *Lettres*, 1:174–75, 223–24, 3:20; Wilke, *Erinnerungen*, p. 139; Raschdau, *Weimar*, pp. 92–93; *DDF*, 1st ser., 8:323; Eulenburg notes (12–13 Oct. 1895), Eulenburg Papers, no. 38, pp. 727–32; Senden notes, Senden Papers, no. 11, pp. 38–39.

54. Duke of Saxe-Meiningen to Gossler (3 Dec. 1918, 7 July 1924), Gossler Papers, no. 7; same to same (8 June 1920, 24 May 1921,), ibid., no. 19.

55. *W2:PE*, pp. 7, 119–23.

56. Hardinge, *Old Diplomacy*, p. 127. See also Arthur Lee, *Empress Writes to Sophie*.

57. *W2:PE*, p. 321; Wedel, *Kaiser und Kanzler*, pp. 166, 173; Rogge, *Holstein und Hohenlohe*, pp. 345–47; Feder, *Bismarcks Grosses Spiel*, pp. 450–51; Radziwill, *Lettres*, 1:53, 2:167; Ponsonby, *Letters of the Empress Frederick*, pp. 420–21. On their shaky reconciliation: Topham, *Chronicles*, pp. 172–73; Radziwill, *Lettres*, 2:134–35.

58. On the Baden relationship: Brauer, *Dienste Bismarcks*, pp. 378, 431; Jagemann, *Fünfundsiebzig Jahre*, p. 115; Feder, *Bismarcks Grosses Spiel*, p. 467; Radziwill, *Lettres*, 1:29; Topham, *Chronicles*, p. 162. See also Fuchs, *Friedrich I.*, vol. 4.

59. On Wilhelm's alienation from the federal princes: Ernst Ludwig, *Erinnertes*, pp. 138–39; Bunsen, *Zeitgenossen*, pp. 34–35; Schlözer, *Jugendzeit*, p. 231; Bülow Papers, no. 34, p. 37; *HP*, 3:611–13, 619–20; Knodt, *Ernst Ludwig*, p. 117; Bülow, 2:86. A few *Bundesfürsten* liked the Kaiser. See Haller, *Aus dem Leben*, pp. 56–57; Viktoria Luise, *Glanz der Krone*, pp. 257–58; Brabant, *Hausen*, pp. 237–38.

60. Ernst Heinrich, *Lebensweg*, p. 65; Fuchs, *Friedrich I.*, 4:227; Swaine to Barrington (3 Sept. 1895), Salisbury Papers, no. A122; Hohenlohe-Schillingsfürst, *Reichskanzlerzeit*, pp. 227, 236–40; Tambach Papers, no. 31/19, 00032–33; Herwig, *"Luxury Fleet,"* p. 19; Raschdau, *"Zum Kapitel Holstein,"* p. 245; Lerchenfeld-Koefering, *Wilhelm II.*, pp. 30–31.

61. Eulenburg Papers, no. 80, pp. 65–66. He refused to enable his uncle, the grand duke of Baden, to realize his fervent desire to be made king. Fuchs, *Friedrich I.*, 4:357.

62. Rodd to Hardinge (12 May 1908), Hardinge Papers, no. 12; Ernst Ludwig, *Erinnertes*, pp. 98, 101, 138–39; Knodt, *Ernst Ludwig*, p. 117.

63. Haller Papers, no. 13, p. 10.

64. Deichmann, *Impressions*, p. 119.

65. Wilhelm to Eulenburg (29 Mar. 1888), Röhl, 1:281. On the Wittelsbachs and Wilhelm II, see Möckl, *Prinzregentenzeit*, esp. pp. 377 n. 100, 417–20.

66. Hohenlohe diary (7 Mar. 1897), Hohenlohe-Schillingsfürst, *Reichskanzlerzeit*, p. 311.

67. Gutsche, *Wilhelm II.*, p. 112. On the superiority of monarchs in diplomacy: *GP*, 39:550–54; Bülow, 1:80.

68. *W2:PE*, pp. 286–90.

69. Buckle, *Letters of Queen Victoria*, 3:336–37.

70. Ibid., 3:336, 343–44.

71. On the entourage, see Kenneth Young, *Balfour*, pp. 121–22; Christopher Howard, *Goschen*, p. 170; Chilston, *W. H. Smith*, p. 350.

72. Newton, *Lansdowne*, p. 330.

73. Lamar Cecil, "William II and His Russian 'Colleagues,' " pp. 114–31.

74. Notes of conversation with Wilhelm II at Sandringham (1901), FO 800/130; Eulenburg notes (8 Nov. 1896), Eulenburg Papers, no. 44, pp. 753–55; Bülow, 1:454–55.

75. Lascelles to Salisbury (9 Mar. 1900), Salisbury Papers, no. A121; same to same (24 Nov. 1896), FO 64/1379.

76. Vogel, *Russlandpolitik*, p. 109.

77. Youssoupoff, *Lost Splendour*, pp. 158–59. Also Mossolov, *Court of the Last Tsar*, p. 203; Sazonov, *Fateful Years*, p. 75; Waters, *Potsdam and Doorn*, pp. 193–94; Görlitz, *Der Kaiser*, p. 76.

78. Bing, *Secret Letters*, p. 120.

79. Korostowetz, *Graf Witte*, p. 124.

80. S. Lee, *Edward VII*, 2:565.

81. Ibid., 2:593; Hardinge, *Old Diplomacy*, p. 157; Mossolov, *Court of the Last Tsar*, pp. 202–3.

82. Franz Joseph's annoyance at Wilhelm: Christopher Howard, *Goschen*, p. 170; Nostitz-Rieneck, *Briefe Kaiser*, 2:216; Steinitz, *Erinnerungen an Franz Joseph*, p. 271; Stürgkh, *Erinnerungen*, pp. 193–94; Kynzlmann de Beauchamps to Haller (4 Mar. 1931), Haller Papers, no. 13. For his appreciation of Wilhelm, see Nostitz-Rieneck, *Briefe Kaiser*, 1:282, 396, 2:35–36, 84, 165. For Wilhelm and the old emperor: Viktoria Luise, *Tochter des Kaisers*, pp. 31–33; Wilhelm II, *Meinem Leben*, pp. 86, 277–78. On Frau Schratt, see Holstein to Eulenburg (3 Mar. 1897), Bülow Papers, no. 92.

83. Wilhelm and Sophie: Eulenburg to Franz Ferdinand (26 June 1900), HA, Rep. 53a, no. 63; Nikitsch-Boulles, *Vor dem Sturm*, pp. 32–33; Röhl, 3:1979; Eulenburg, *Erlebnisse*, pp. 282–309. The Kaiserin never made Sophie welcome. Sosnosky, *Franz Ferdinand*, p. 29; Schoen, *Erlebtes*, p. 122; Nikitsch-Boulles, *Vor dem Sturm*, pp. 32–33. Cf. Topham, *Memories*, p. 289.

84. Franz Ferdinand's gratitude in Eulenburg, *Erlebnisse*, pp. 305–6. On the similarity of views and personality: Chlumecky, *Franz Ferdinands*, pp. 357–62; Conrad von Hötzendorf, *Dienstzeit*, 1:159; Kielmansegg, *Kaiserhaus*, p. 168. On their differences: Röhl, 3:1937–40; Bülow, 1:400–401. Franz Ferdinand's reservations about Wilhelm: Chlumecky, *Franz Ferdinands*, pp. 75–79, 91–92; Conrad von Hötzendorf, *Dienstzeit*, 1:69–70; Nikitsch-Boulles, *Vor dem Sturm*, pp. 147–48, 194–95.

85. Extract of report by Sir Horace Rumbold to the Foreign Office (10 June 1892), RA, I 59, no. 84. On the tulips, Wilhelm to Franz Ferdinand (25 May 1914), Franz Ferdinand Papers.

86. Röhl, 3:1837–38; Szögyényi to Goluchowski (2 July 1897), HHStA, no. 148(V). Cecil Rhodes compared Wilhelm unfavorably with Leopold, a man of "broad ideas" although one who "haggled like a Jew." Lascelles to Bertie (17 Mar. 1899), Salisbury Papers, no. A121.

87. Bülow, 2:72–75; also Wilhelm, *Meinem Leben*, p. 174. Leopold thought Wilhelm dangerously warlike. See Louise, Duchess of Coburg, *Throne*, p. 176.

88. Wilhelm's rudeness: Feder, *Bismarcks Grosses Spiel*, p. 430; Tirpitz diary (4 Jan. 1905), Tirpitz Papers, no. 21; Duke of Saxe-Meiningen to Gossler (26 Dec.

1918), Gossler Papers, no. 7; Bülow, 1:132–33. For the Italian king's consequent distaste for Wilhelm: DDF, 2d ser., 10:89–90; 3d ser., 10:61; Paléologue, Three Critical Years, p. 34; HP, 4:210–11. See also Kiderlen, 2:164.

89. Carol and Marie's dislike of Wilhelm: Hutten-Czapski, Sechzig Jahre, 2:60; Jonescu, Impressions, pp. 114–15; Bülow's undated notice, Bülow Papers, no. 39; Bülow, 2:129; Marie, Life, 2:226–27. Wilhelm's disaffected sister, Charlotte of Saxe-Meiningen, took revenge on her brother by creating animosity between the two royal houses. See Marie, Life, 2:81, 239.

90. Wilhelm's behavior to Ferdinand: Waters, "Secret and Confidential," p. 331; Schelking, Recollections, pp. 219–20; Vierhaus, Tagebuch, p. 517; Mensdorff to Vienna (7 May 1910), Bittner and Uebersberger, Aussenpolitik, 2:878–79.

91. Wilhelm's low opinion of Ferdinand: Szögyényi to Goluchowski (20 Aug. 1897, 2 July 1903), HHStA, no. 148(V), 159(B); Wilhelm to Nicholas II (19 Nov. 1903), Goetz, Briefe, p. 331; Wilhelm's marginalia on Jenisch to Berlin (26 Sept. 1908), GFO Papers, 240/00167; Goschen to London and to Grey (27–28 May 1913), FO 800/62; Lascelles to Grey (21 Sept. 1906), ibid., 371/79; Szögyényi to Vienna (18 Aug 1910), HHStA, no. 169(V); Bülow, 2:341. He did acknowledge that Ferdinand had made Bulgaria the most important of the small Slavic states. Szögyényi to Goluchowski (31 Jan. 1905), HHStA, no. 162(B).

92. Wilhelm II's notes (28 Mar. 1927), HA, Rep. 53a, no. 33; Bülow, 2:79; Moltke, Moltke Erinnerungen, pp. 331–32; Paget, Embassies, 2:488; Hegermann-Lindencrone, Diplomatic Life, pp. 295, 300. For the contrast in Wilhelm's deference to older rulers and the domineering tone he took toward those who were younger, see DDF, 2d ser., 10:69.

93. Radziwill, Lettres, 2:65–66; Hohenlohe-Schillingsfürst, Reichskanzlerzeit, p. 7; Egan, Ten Years, pp. 112–13. On Wilhelm and the Danish connection, see Lamar Cecil, "Wilhelm II and His Russian 'Colleagues,'" pp. 119–21.

94. Christopher Howard, Goschen, p. 75.

95. Marschall, Reisen und Regieren, pp. 158–59, also pp. 144–45, 166.

96. Battersea, Reminiscences, p. 319; Findlay to Stamfordham (5 Aug. 1913), RA, Geo V P 452, no. 20; Szögyényi to Goluchowski (1 Aug. 1905), HHStA, no. 162(B); GP, 20/2:648–49.

97. Huret, Berlin, pp. 89–91; Vierhaus, Tagebuch, p. 274; Schwering, Berlin Court, pp. 141–42; Gebhard Blücher von Wahlstatt, Memoirs, pp. 76–77, 149; Count Harry Kessler, Gesichter und Zeiten, p. 176; Bülow, 1:138–39.

98. Baron Roman Rosen, Forty Years, 1:180.

99. Zorn, Universitätsleben, p. 77. The Bavarian noble, Baron Otto von Dungern, declared that he was one of the world's parvenu rulers. Dungern, Kaiser und Kanzlern, p. 33.

100. On how few friends the Kaiser had in the nobility: Monts to Bülow (27 Mar. 1896), Bülow Papers, no. 106; also Schiffer, Leben, p. 179. On avoiding Berlin: Beyens, Deux Années, 1:159; Radziwill, Lettres, 1:134; Scheffler, Berlin, p. 151. This was also due to financial exigencies: Faramond, Souvenirs, p. 38; Gleichen, Memoirs, p. 255; Moritz Bonn, Scholar, p. 292.

101. Eulenburg notes of a conversation with Wilhelm (29 Sept. 1903), Eulenburg Papers, no. 74, part 2, pp. 40–41; Szögyényi to Goluchowski (26. Mar. 1901), HHStA, no. 155(B); Wilhelm to Bülow (20 Aug. 1899), Bülow Papers, no.

154; Hohenlohe, *Leben*, pp. 357–59; Radziwill, *Lettres*, 1:203; Meisner, *Denkwürdigkeiten*, 2:306, 3:181–82, 493; Wedel, *Kaiser und Kanzler*, pp. 159–60, 184; Thimme, *Front wider Bülow*, p. 126; Hohenlohe-Schillingsfürst, *Reichskanzlerzeit*, pp. 508, 517–18, 523–24; Hohenlohe-Schillingsfürst, *Denkwürdigkeiten*, 2:483. On Junker hostility to the Kaiser: Westarp, *Konservative Politik*, 1:348–49; Valentini, p. 233; Meisner, *Denkwürdigkeiten*, 3:181–82. For Junker pride in an antiquity superior to that of the Hohenzollerns, see Ayme, *Kaiser Wilhelm II.*, p. 94. Deplorable as their politics were, Wilhelm acknowledged the Junkers' merits as soldiers. See *DDF*, 1st ser., 1:627.

102. Bülow to Wolff (7 Feb. 1925), Wolff Papers.

103. On the selection of adjutants, see Treutler Papers, no. 7/16; Schönburg-Waldenburg, *Erinnerungen*, pp. 134–35, 196–97; Bülow, 2:183–84; Einem, *Erinnerungen*, pp. 148–49. For Wilhelm's wish to be the smartest man in any group: Eulenburg, "Kaiser Wilhelm II.," Eulenburg Papers, no. 80, p. 16; *DDF*, 1st ser., 13:489–90. On his treatment of the adjutants: Fürstenberg, *Lebensgeschichte*, p. 440; Czernin von und zu Chudenitz, *Weltkriege*, p. 75.

104. Eulenburg to his wife (4 July 1898), Eulenburg Papers, no. 53, p. 102; also Raschdau, *Bismarck und Caprivi*, p. 51; Czernin von und zu Chudenitz, *Weltkriege*, pp. 81–82.

105. Mutius Papers, pp. 167–68.

106. Wedel, *Kaiser und Kanzler*, p. 185. On the supinenes of the entourage: Schönburg-Waldenburg, *Erinnerungen*, p. 140; Hohenlohe, *Leben*, pp. 371–72; Ponsonby, *Letters of the Empress Frederick*, p. 405; Raschdau, *Bismarck und Caprivi*, p. 51; Raschdau, *Weimar*, p. 128; Zedlitz-Trützschler, pp. 79, 149, 177–79. For two examples, see Janssen, *Graue Exzellenz*, pp. 104, 123.

107. Zedlitz-Trützschler, p. 81.

108. Raschdau, *Weimar*, p. 128; for examples, see Schiffer, *Leben*, p. 95, and W2:PE, pp. 185–86.

109. Topham, *Chronicles*, p. 233; Röhl, 3:1857, for Bülow; similar resignation is expressed by General Friedrich von Bernhardi in his *Denkwürdigkeiten*, p. 156.

110. On the desirability of seeing Wilhelm alone: Westarp, *Konservative Politik*, 2:312–13; Groener, *Lebenserinnerungen*, p. 245; Janssen, *Graue Exzellenz*, pp. 120–21; Tirpitz, *Erinnerungen*, p. 135. On the adjutants' protectiveness of Wilhelm: Eulenburg Papers, no. 75, p. 43; Einem, *Erinnerungen*, p. 52; Kiderlen, 2:138; Groener, *Lebenserinnerungen*, pp. 366–67. For an example, see Lamar Cecil, *Ballin*, pp. 336–38.

111. Eulenburg Papers, no. 80, p. 18. On the difficulty of speaking to the Kaiser: Schönburg-Waldenburg, *Erinnerungen*, p. 140; Kiderlen, 2:138; Einem, *Erinnerungen*, pp. 139–41; Johannes Kessler, *Ewige Jugend*, p. 160; Friedrich Rosen, *Wanderleben*, 1:11–12; Viktoria Luise, *Glanz der Krone*, pp. 236–37. On Wilhelm's preference for gossipy diplomatic and military reports, see Lamar Cecil, *Diplomatic Service*, pp. 214–16; Zedlitz-Trützschler, p. 244.

112. Eulenburg notes, Eulenburg Papers, no. 58, pp. 27–29. On Wilhelm's conversational prowess: Czernin von und zu Chudenitz, *Weltkriege*, p. 86; Swaine to Malet (30 Aug. 1895), FO 64/1351; Eulenburg Papers no. 80, p. 68, no. 84, p. 53. For the difficulty that this created for diplomats in trying to report the Kaiser's

mood accurately, see Lascelles to Grey (24. Jan. 1907), FO 371/260; Jagow to Thimme (21 Oct. 1921), Thimme Papers, no. 9.

113. On the navy, see Friedrich Rosen, *Wanderleben*, 3/4:14. There is disagreement over Wilhelm's imperviousness to advice on all other subjects. For those who felt he would listen: Einem, *Erinnerungen*, pp. 139–41; Moltke, *Moltke Erinnerungen*, pp. 254, 303–13; Friedrich Rosen, *Wanderleben*, 1:10–11; Schoen, *Erlebtes*, pp. 125–26; Monts, *Erinnerungen*, p. 441; Johannes Kessler, *Ewige Jugend*, p. 160; Viktoria Luise, *Glanz der Krone*, pp. 236–37; Waters, *Potsdam and Doorn*, p. xiii; Bernhardi, *Denkwürdigkeiten*, p. 322; Schnee, *Gouverneur*, p. 106. For the opposite view: Raschdau, *Bismarck und Caprivi*, p. 51; Zedlitz-Trützschler, p. 81; Topham, *Chronicles*, p. 233.

114. Monts, *Erinnerungen*, p. 140; similarly, Rosner, *Erinnerungen des Kronprinzen*, pp. 13–14.

115. Bülow, 2:99.

116. Eulenburg Papers, no. 74, part 2, p. 39.

117. KE, no. 317/2, p. 161; Fürstenberg, *Lebensgeschichte*, pp. 440–41; Vasili, *Société*, pp. 162–63; Zedlitz-Trützschler, p. 50; Bülow, 1:76, 495; Hutten-Czapski, *Sechzig Jahre*, 1:407; Viktoria Luise, *Tochter des Kaisers*, p. 229; Kühlmann, *Erinnerungen*, p. 128; Schmidt-Ott, *Erlebtes*, p. 97; Schiffer, *Leben*, p. 110; Delbrück, *Mobilmachung*, p. 280. The only carping note came from one of Wilhelm's English cousins, who found Eulenburg pompous. Athlone, *Grandchildren*, p. 94.

118. Viktoria Luise, *Glanz der Krone*, p. 239.

119. Eulenburg Papers, no. 75, pp. 57–60, no. 76, part 3, p. 9. For Wilhelm's disregard of what he said, see KE, no. 331/2, p. 12.

120. Eulenburg notes, Eulenburg Papers, no. 42, p. 377; Szögyényi to Kálnoky (29 Dec. 1888), HHStA, no. 134(B).

121. *HP*, 3:560–61; Meisner, *Denkwürdigkeiten*, 3:140–41. See also Wilhelm II, *Leben*, pp. 236–38.

122. For her dislike, see Ponsonby, *Recollections*, p. 162. On Kessel's activity: Eulenburg notes, Eulenburg Papers, no. 81, part 2, pp. 15–49, no. 30, pp. 474–75; no. 1, p. 59; *HP*, 1:143; Zedlitz-Trützschler, p. 231–32.

123. Empress Frederick to Queen Victoria (10 Nov. 1888), RA, Z 43, no. 36.

124. Scorn: Eulenburg to Holstein (23 Sept. 1895, 1 Feb. 1897), Eulenburg Papers, no. 37, p. 627, no. 45, pp. 80–82; Herbert von Hindenburg, *Am Rande*, p. 58; Bülow, 1:64; *HP*, 3:593–94; Röhl, 3:1493–94. Fear of Lucanus's power: Hohenlohe, *Leben*, pp. 306–7; Brauer, *Dienste Bismarcks*, pp. 373–74; Schmidt-Ott, *Erlebtes*, p. 97; Hohenlohe-Schillingsfürst, *Reichskanzlerzeit*, p. 137.

125. Holstein noted that the influence of the entourage increased because it was constant whereas ministers came and went. Holstein to Bülow (8 Jan. 1897), Bülow Papers, no. 90. There are a number of valuable treatments of the Hohenzollern court: Röhl, *Kaiser, Hof und Staat*, esp. chaps. 3 and 4, and Röhl and Sombart, *Kaiser Wilhelm II*, esp. chaps. 6–8; Hull, "Prussian Dynastic Ritual," in Fink, Hull, and Knox, *German Nationalism*, and Hull, *Entourage*. See also Fehrenbach, *Kaisergedankens*, and Lerchenfeld-Koefering, *Wilhelm II.*, pp. 10–11.

126. Bülow Papers, no. 30.

127. Morel, *Eastern Embassy*, p. 161, for the fever. On Wilhelm II's inflation of honors: Holstein diary (27 Feb. 1907), Holstein Papers, 3861/H196437; Tres-

ckow, *Fürsten*, pp. 172–73; Vierhaus, *Tagebuch*, pp. 392, 456, 530; Raschdau, *Weimar*, p. 126; Hohenlohe, *Leben*, pp. 327–28; Schwering, *Berlin Court*, p. 160; Schmidt-Ott, *Erlebtes*, p. 82; Whitman, *German Memories*, p. 196; Zedlitz-Trützschler, p. 75; Wilke, *Erinnerungen*, pp. 233–34; Germany, *Verhandlungen des Reichstages* 236 (29. Mar. 1909): 7830 (Liebermann von Sonnenberg). See also Lamar Cecil, "Creation of Nobles," for comparison of Wilhelm II's awards with those of Wilhelm I and Friedrich III.

128. On the parvenu nature of Wilhelm II's court: Paula von Bülow, *Lebenserinnerungen*, pp. 49–50; Fanny von Wilamowitz-Moellendorff, *Erinnerungen*, p. 258; Hohenlohe, *Leben*, p. 348; Louise, Princess of Belgium, *Own Affairs*, pp. 161–62; Marie, *Life*, 2:225–26; Kiderlen, 1:81; Meisner, *Denkwürdigkeiten*, 2:80; Bunsen, *Lost Courts*, p. 107; Schwering, *Berlin Court*, pp. 250–58; Huret, *Berlin*, pp. 89–91.

129. On Bavaria: Röhl, 1:281; Fuchs, *Friedrich I.*, 4:227. Resentment at lack of foreign guests: Allenby to Lascelles (16 Jan. 1906), FO 371/75; *BD*, 3:369, 7:20–22.

130. Townley, *"Indiscretions,"* p. 53. Wilhelm on Berlin's lack of interest: Eulenburg, *Erlebnisse*, pp. 63–64; Bülow, 3:63.

131. Cartwright to Grey (28 Feb. 1907), FO 371/257; Howe, *Meyer*, p. 85 n. 1; Ponsonby, *Recollections*, p. 362.

132. Military as dancers: Howe, *Meyer*, p. 86; dancing: Erbach-Schönberg, *Erklugenes*, pp. 90–91; Russell, "Reminiscences," pp. 60–61; Meister, *Yesterdays*, pp. 106–7.

133. Wilson, *Campbell-Bannerman*, p. 187; Tresckow, *Fürsten*, p. 177.

134. Cahén, *Weg nach Versailles*, p. 123; also Louise, Duchess of Coburg, *Throne*, pp. 187–88; Eulalia, *Memoirs*, p. 73; Topham, *Memories*, pp. 121–22.

135. On the inelegance of the Berlin court: Christopher Howard, *Goschen*, pp. 182, 188; Fugger, *Glanz der Kaiserzeit*, pp. 10–11, 411; Ebart, *Herzogshofe*, pp. 85–86; Marie, *Life*, 2:225–26; Braun, *Ostpreussen bis Texas*, p. 80; Reynoso, *50 Jahre*, pp. 160–61; Howe, *Meyer*, p. 86; Athlone, *Grandchildren*, p. 96; Louise, Princess of Belgium, *Throne*, pp. 161–62; Faramond, *Souvenirs*, p. 155; Marie Louise, *Memories*, p. 65. A few observers took a more positive view: Townley, *"Indiscretions,"* p. 54; Einem, *Erinnerungen*, p. 124; Freytag-Loringhoven, *Menschen und Dinge*, pp. 68–69; Wermuth, *Beamtenleben*, p. 298.

136. Röhl, 2:765. Lerchenfeld's elegance intimidated the Kaiser. See Bunsen, *Zeitgenossen*, p. 93. On the application of the word "parvenu" for Wilhelm's surroundings, see Wahlendorf, *Erinnerungen*, p. 50; *BD*, 7:51–52.

137. Schmidt-Ott, *Erlebtes*, p. 195.

CHAPTER 2

1. Princess Ludwig Ferdinand of Bavaria, *Four Revolutions*, pp. 224–25; Eulenburg Papers, no. 74, part 2, p. 36.

2. Wilhelm to Chamberlain (23 Dec. 1907), H. S. Chamberlain, *Briefe*, 2:226–27.

3. Eulenburg Papers, no. 80, p. 76. Similar condemnation of Wilhelm's laziness:

KE, no. 576/1, p. 13; Meisner, *Denkwürdigkeiten*, 2:6, 77, 153, 370; Bussmann, *Herbert von Bismarck*, pp. 539–40; Wertheimer, "Militärattaché," p. 268; Zedlitz-Trützschler, pp. 222–23, 244; *HP*, 3:280, 291, 323; Ilsemann, 1:67.

4. On marginalia: Meisner, *Denkwürdigkeiten*, 2:425; Thimme, *Front wider Bülow*, p. 110. Wilhelm himself once said, "One should not tie me down to my marginal comments." Tirpitz, *Erinnerungen*, p. 137. Wilhelm was not the author of some of his correspondence with Tsar Nicholas II. See Friedrich Rosen, *Wanderleben*, 1:11.

5. Wilhelm on his trips: Ernst, *Reden des Kaisers*, pp. 118–19; Gauss, *German Emperor*, p. 250; Raschdau, *Weimar*, p. 64.

6. Zedlitz-Trützschler, pp. 67–68, 94–95.

7. Eulenburg Papers, no. 74, part 2, p. 39; also Viktoria Luise, *Tochter des Kaisers*, p. 27. Boelcke, *Krupp und die Hohenzollern*, argues for a close relationship between Wilhelm and the Krupps but presents material that shows the contacts to be in fact largely ceremonial. For Wilhelm's refusal to intervene in Krupp family affairs, see Margarethe Krupp to August Eulenburg (5 Dec. 1902), Bülow Papers, no. 74. On the retinue, see in general Hull, *Entourage*, and on the minuscule Jewish element, see Mosse, *German-Jewish Economic Elite*.

8. Moritz Bonn, *Scholar*, p. 146; Schnee, *Gouverneur*, p. 112; Hutten-Czapski, *Sechzig Jahre*, 2:25–26; Topham, *Memories*, p. 25; Bülow, 2:267. For other examples of Wilhelm's rudeness: Rogge, *Holstein und Hohenlohe*, pp. 347, 374–75; Georg Hertling, *Erinnerungen*, 2:204–5; Pastor, *Tagebücher*, p. 550; Mossolov, *Court of the Last Tsar*, pp. 205–6; Widenmann, *Marine-Attaché*, p. 107; Bülow, 2:38.

9. Janssen, *Graue Exzellenz*, p. 132, for the crown prince's opinion; also Ilsemann, 2:87.

10. Röhl, 1:34, speaks of murky circumstances in the decline of the friendship; Hull, "Kaiser Wilhelm II," pp. 210–11, is more explicit about the scandal as the cause.

11. On Wilhelm's friendship with Fürstenberg, see KE, no. 331/2, p. 27; Fürstenberg, *Carl-Fürstenburg-Anekdoten*, p. 31; Vierhaus, *Tagebuch*, p. 564; Zedlitz-Trützschler, pp. 231–32; Bülow, 1:153, 542, 2:351; Viktoria Luise, *Glanz der Krone*, pp. 225–26; Fugger, *Glanz der Kaiserzeit*, pp. 431–37; Wilke, *Erinnerungen*, pp. 174–75; Szögyényi to Berchtold (8 Apr. 1914), HHStA, no. 171(B).

12. See Lerman, *Chancellor as Courtier*, and Lerman, "Decisive Relationship"; Cole, "*Daily Telegraph* Affair."

13. Meisner, *Denkwürdigkeiten*, 2:416–17; Raeder, *Leben*, 1:62. See Persius, *Menschen und Schiffe*, p. 42, on how the costliness of the gilding annoyed the navy.

14. Gutsche, *Wilhelm II.*, p. 112.

15. Malet to Salisbury (14 Oct. 1889), Salisbury Papers, no. A62.

16. Marschall, *Reisen und Regieren*, pp. 221–24, lists the companions. See also Eulenburg's *Mit dem Kaiser*, Güssfeldt's *Kaiser Wilhelms II.*, and Stöwer's *Pinsel und Palette*; Kiderlen, 1:94–95; Kiderlen-Wächter's notes (1892), Kiderlen Papers, Box 4/004, 0166/000 7306–7; Schönburg-Waldenburg, *Erinnerungen*, pp. 170–71.

17. Cleinow, "Diplomaten-Erziehung," pp. 76–79, for the statutes.

18. Hopman diary (9 May 1914), Hopman Papers, no. 10; Valentini diary (Mar. 1904), KE, no. 341/1.

19. Eulenburg Papers, no. 74, part 2, pp. 3–6. For Dr. Leuthold's concern during a 1903 cruise, see Röhl, 3:2091.

20. Wilhelm Michaelis Papers, no. 4, p. 27. For Wilhelm's indiscretions in front of sailors, see Röhl, 3:1984.

21. Dissatisfaction by travelers: Müller to Hintze (15 May 1914), Hintze Papers, no. 105; same to Tirpitz (6 July 1911), Tirpitz Papers, no. 24b; Wilhelm Michaelis Papers, no. 4, p. 26; Röhl, 3:1983; Moltke, *Moltke Erinnerungen*, p. 287; Kiderlen, 1:124; Eulenburg Papers, no. 74, part 1, pp. 30–31, part 2, pp. 12–13; Janssen, *Graue Exzellenz*, pp. 102–9. On Wilhelm's bad humor: Eulenburg Papers, no. 58, pp. 156–57, no. 74, part 2, pp. 31–33; Büchsel to Tirpitz (2 July 1899), Tirpitz Papers, no. 200; Röhl, 3:1984–85.

22. English crews: KE, no. 814; on aristocratic German yachtsmen: Fürstenberg, *Lebensgeschichte*, pp. 442–43; Herbert von Hindenburg, *Am Rande*, p. 136; Mosse, *German-Jewish Economic Elite*, p. 201.

23. Dumas to Whitehead (29 June 1906), FO 371/78; Widenmann Papers, p. 9. On Wilhelm's considering yachting as a means of making himself popular and on his reputation for poor sportsmanship, see Lerchenfeld-Koefering, *Wilhelm II.*, p. 23.

24. *Jacht-Besitz* is in Eulenburg Papers, no. 74, part 1, p. 2. For Wilhelm's intoxication at wealth, especially American: ibid., no. 80, pp. 23, 32–33, no. 52, pp. 262–63; Röhl, 3:1952–54; Czernin von und zu Chudenitz, *Weltkriege*, p. 82; Kühlmann, *Erinnerungen*, p. 73; Hohenlohe, *Leben*, pp. 348–49; David Hill, *Impressions*, pp. 44–46, 48, 68; Beyens, *Deux Années*, 1:167; Bülow, 1:573; Pückler, *Diplomatenleben*; Raschdau, *Weimar*, p. 40; Janssen, *Graue Exzellenz*, p. 121.

25. Davis, *The Kaiser*, pp. 156–58, 232.

26. Corey, *House of Morgan*, p. 12; Vierhaus, *Tagebuch*, p. 570. Wilhelm's claim that he improved relations: Moltke, *Moltke Erinnerungen*, pp. 296–97; Beyens, *Germany*, pp. 18–19.

27. Redlich, *Schicksalsjahre*, 1:117; Meisner, *Denkwürdigkeiten*, 2:269. Wilhelm was, even by the redoubtable standards of his time, a crack shot. Brett, *Journals and Letters*, 1:244; Lucius von Ballhausen, *Bismarck-Erinnerungen*, p. 223; Bussmann, *Herbert von Bismarck*, p. 554; Meisner, *Denkwürdigkeiten*, 1:229.

28. Eulenburg Papers, no. 56, pp. 301–2; Schönburg-Waldenburg, *Erinnerungen*, p. 158; Roloff, *Zwei Welten*, pp. 51–52; Zedlitz-Trützschler, p. 174; Röhl, *Kaiser, Hof und Staat*, p. 105; Röhl, 2:1576; Lerchenfeld-Koefering, *Wilhelm II.*, p. 10.

29. Eulenburg Papers, no. 22, pp. 695–96; Eulenburg to Holstein (1 Aug. 1890), ibid., no. 12, pp. 517–21, which reads "without feminine conversation, which he does not like," has been altered somewhat in *HP*, 3:353. On exotic game, see Treuberg, *Memoiren*, p. 3. Portraits of Wilhelm hunting are in Gerlach, *Erinnerungen*, pp. 243–45; Kluck, *Wanderjahre*, pp. 166–68; Haller, *50 Jahre*, p. 46.

30. Kaulisch, *Tirpitz*, p. 118.

31. Tirpitz notes (4 Jan. 1905), Tirpitz Papers, no. 21.

32. Eulenburg Papers: no. 22, pp. 689–91, no. 73, pp. 4–5, no. 74, part 2, pp. 43–46, no. 81, part 1, p. 60, part 2, pp. 5–6. Dona admitted that he was a flatterer: Schönburg-Waldenburg, *Erinnerungen*, p. 150.

33. Eulenburg notes (21 Sept. 1900), HA, Rep. 53a, no. 63.

34. On the Plesses: Meister, *Yesterdays*, pp. 109–10; Schwering, *Berlin Court*, pp. 172–73; Townley, *"Indiscretions,"* pp. 57–61; Waters, *Potsdam and Doorn*, pp. 173–74; Bülow, 2:425, 3:254. See also Pless, *Daisy, Princess of Pless*, and Pless, *Better Left Unsaid*. Wilhelm on the prince's neglibility: KE, no. 331/2, p. 22.

35. Schönburg-Waldenburg, *Erinnerungen*, p. 159; Holstein to Kiderlen-Wächter (9 May 1907), Kiderlen Papers, Box 4/004 0144/000 7033.

36. On Wilhelm's falling out with Henckel: Kleinmichel, *Memories*, pp. 281–83; Meisner, *Denkwürdigkeiten*, 2:151, 312, 416–19; Eckardstein, *Lebenserinnerungen*, 1:224–30. On their reconciliation and subsequent closeness: Buchanan, *Diplomacy*, pp. 56–57; Meisner, *Denkwürdigkeiten*, 3:173–74, 194; Schwering, *Berlin Court*, pp. 178–81; Bode, *Leben*, 2:156. On the sumptuous life at Neudeck, see Meister, *Yesterdays*, p. 133.

37. Hutten-Czapski, *Sechzig Jahre*, 1:94; Kardorff, *Kardorff*, pp. 298–99.

38. Eulenburg described his role in his *Mit dem Kaiser*, pp. 321–23; on the hostility of the military group to Eulenburg, see Eulenburg Papers, no. 75, pp. 57–60, no. 74, part 1, p. 7, no. 81, part 2, pp. 89–90.

39. Zedlitz-Trützschler, pp. 122–23; see also Kürenberg, *War Alles Falsch?*, pp. 228–29.

40. Count Harry Kessler, *Tagebücher*, p. 86; Swaine, *Camp and Chancery*, p. 220; Feder diary (1 Apr. 1926), Feder, *Heute Sprach Ich*, p. 30.

41. Seidel, *Kaiser*, pp. 98, 104–5, 182, 243.

42. Zechlin, *Deutsche Politik*, p. 48; Wilhelm to Bigelow (28 June 1937), Bigelow Papers, no. 34a. On his claim to have turned Jews to the arts, see Dommes Papers, no. 17.

43. White, *Autobiography*, 2:224–27; Pallat, *Schöne*, pp. 327–28; Paret, *Berlin Secession*, p. 86.

44. Ernst Ludwig, *Erinnertes*, p. 101.

45. Pallat, *Schöne*, pp. 234–35; similarly in Schott, *Künstler-Leben*, p. 142. As an example, in 1894 Wilhelm endowed an annual prize for the study of classical art, constituting himself as the sole judge. Seidel, *Kaiser*, pp. 181–82. On the Kaiser's munificence in purchasing a building in Munich to house the art collection of Count Adolf von Schack, see Röhl, 2:1286–87, 1301, 1308.

46. KE, no. 317/2, p. 167; also Bunsen, *Welt*, p. 192; Gauss, *German Emperor*, pp. 195–97. When the distinguished novelist Theodor Fontane turned seventy in 1889, Wilhelm awarded him the order of the Red Eagle, fourth class. This led the popular journalist Fedor von Zobeltitz to comment, "Our Medicis seem to care nothing for literature." Zobeltitz, *Chronik*, 2:211–13. The allegedly German descent of Italian artists was an idea of Houston Stewart Chamberlain's, an idea with which Wilhelm apparently agreed. H. S. Chamberlain, *Briefe*, 2:213, 216.

47. Bode, *Leben*, 1:180, 2:150–56, 181; Bode, *Fünfzig Jahre*, pp. 8–10; Zedlitz-Trützschler, p. 51.

48. Hohenlohe-Schillingsfürst, *Reichskanzlerzeit*, p. 24; Scheffler, *Berlin*, pp.

53–55. See Velde, *Geschichte meines Lebens*, p. 180, for the unique strength of the German protest against tradition.

49. Osborn, *Bunte Spiegel*, p. 137; KE, no. 814.

50. Morel, *Eastern Embassy*, p. 166; Schönberg-Waldenburg, *Erinnerungen*, p. 193; Zobeltitz, *Chronik*, 1:189.

51. Rogge, *Holstein Lebensbekenntnis*, p. 267; Hohenlohe-Schillingsfürst, *Reichskanzlerzeit*, p. 24. Wilhelm's decision that a statue of Frederick the Great would be a suitable gift to the United States led to derision. Bülow Papers, no. 34, p. 33. On Wilhelm's relations with art lovers and patrons: Hohenlohe, *Leben*, pp. 347–48, 360; Count Harry Kessler, *Tagebücher*, pp. 86, 651; Pallat, *Schöne*, p. 290; Eulenburg Papers, no. 80, p. 48. For the opinion of artists on Wilhelm: Osborn, *Bunte Spiegel*, p. 137; Topham, *Chronicles*, pp. 191–92. One artist whose work Wilhelm did not like was his sister-in-law. See Wagemann, *Feodora*.

52. Schott, *Künstler-Leben*, p. 184; Hohenlohe-Schillingsfürst, *Reichskanzlerzeit*, p. 24.

53. Mossolov, *Court of the Last Tsar*, p. 204, and Shaw, *William of Germany*, p. 233, on choreography; on architecture: Valentini, pp. 49–50; Schmidt-Ott, *Erlebtes*, p. 55; Taylor, *Hohenzollern Berlin*, esp. chap. 9. The great Belgian pioneer of art nouveau, Henry van de Velde, visited Berlin in 1900 and declared with dismay that the Kaiser unfailingly chose the worst of everything: Werner in art, Begas in sculpture, and Ihne in architecture. Velde, *Geschichte meines Lebens*, p. 165. On Wilhelm's talent in painting: Schmidt-Ott, *Erlebtes*, p. 62, for Liebermann's opinion; also Seidel, *Kaiser*, pp. 236–37, and p. 25, illustrating one of Wilhelm's pictures.

54. Schiffer, *Leben*, pp. 94–95; Eulenburg Papers, no. 81, part 2, pp. 19–20; Valentini, pp. 49–50; Shaw, *William of Germany*, pp. 232–33; Seidel, *Kaiser*, pp. 215–16; Russell to Wade (Feb. 4, 1911), FO 371/1123.

55. Widenmann, *Marine-Attaché*, p. 108.

56. Mosse, "Wilhelm II," p. 184.

57. Saltzmann: Luckner, *Sea Chest*, p. 78; Eulenburg, *Mit dem Kaiser*, 1:109; Seidel, *Kaiser*, pp. 222, 234–36. On Stöwer, see his *Pinsel und Palette*. Koner: Fuchs, *Friedrich I.*, 3:41; Ssuworin, *Geheimtagebuch*, p. 62. He also admired Adalbert von Kossak, a military panoramist, one of whose dreadful pictures is reproduced in Schönburg-Waldenburg, *Erinnerungen*, p. 192, and in Seidel, *Kaiser*, p. 193. On Kossak, see Stürgkh, *Erinnerungen*, pp. 238–39.

58. For Wilhelm's veneration of Menzel: Dickie, *Kaiser's Capital*, p. 130; Cecilie, *Erinnerungen an den Kronprinzen*, pp. 126–27; Viktoria Luise, *Glanz der Krone*, pp. 130–32; Schmidt-Ott, *Erlebtes*, p. 67; Seidel, *Kaiser*, pp. 13, 58, 124.

59. Zedlitz-Trützschler, p. 148; Bunsen, *Lost Courts*, pp. 234–35; Schmidt-Ott, *Erlebtes*, p. 62; Pallat, *Schöne*, pp. 327–28; Herzfeld, *Miquel*, 2:632.

60. Wilhelm's explanations of the picture's iconography: Malet to Salisbury (26 Oct. 1895), Salisbury Papers, no. A120; Goetz, *Briefe*, pp. 294–95. Wilhelm's sketch for the picture is in Seidel, *Kaiser*, p. 13; see Goetz, *Briefe*, pp. 393–94, for his predictions coming true. For an art expert's opinion that Wilhelm's contribution was superior to Knackfuss's, see Gosselin to Salisbury (29 Nov. 1895), Salisbury Papers, no. A120.

61. Radolin to Holstein (28 Sept. 1895), Holstein Papers, 3859/H195173–74, partially printed in *HP*, 3:545–46; Hohenlohe to Münster (15 Jan. 1896), Münster Papers; Raschdau, *Weimar*, pp. 35–36, 45. Wilhelm, with Knackfuss's assistance, designed another iconographical picture representing Russia and Germany as "sentinels . . . of the Gospel of Truth and Light in the East." Goetz, *Briefe*, p. 306.

62. Bismarck: Raschdau, *Weimar*, p. 47; Tolstoi: Ssuworin, *Geheimtagebuch*, p. 62.

63. Lascelles to Lansdowne (19 Oct. 1904), FO 64/1595; Schierbrand, *Kaiser's Speeches*, pp. 234–35.

64. Gauss, *German Emperor*, p. 200 (speech of 18 Dec. 1901).

65. Liebermann: Paret, *Berlin Secession*, pp. 60, 159–60; Bülow, 2:377–78; Bode, *Leben*, 2:198–99; Deshmukh, "Liebermann," pp. 196–97.

66. With, "The Emperor," pp. 87, 91; Arnhold, *Gedenkbuch*, pp. 271–72.

67. On Wilhelm's contradictory opinions on the Munich Secession: Cartwright to Grey (17 May 1907), FO 371/260; Paret, *Berlin Secession*, p. 34; Eulenburg Papers, no. 22, pp. 773–75; Glum, *Erlebtes*, pp. 81, 108; Makela, *Munich Secession*, p. 15 n. 43.

68. Deshmukh, "Liebermann," p. 190. On the Secession, see Pfefferkorn, *Berliner Secession*, and Doede, *Berliner Secession*.

69. Shaw, *William of Germany*, p. 211; Paret, *Berlin Secession*, p. 34.

70. Schmidt-Ott, *Erlebtes*, pp. 60–61; also Rogge, *Holstein Lebensbekenntnis*, pp. 221–22; Schiffer, *Leben*, p. 95; Bode, *Leben*, 2:230–35; Eulenburg Papers, no. 74, part 1, p. 7. For Wilhelm's dislike of Henry van de Velde, the pioneer of art nouveau in Germany who had close connections with the Secession, see Bodenhausen-Degener, *Bodenhausen*, p. 207, and Velde, *Geschichte meines Lebens*, pp. 239–40.

71. Pallat, *Schöne*, pp. 327–28; also With, "The Emperor," p. 89.

72. Bode, *Leben*, 1:89–90, 107. See also Bode, *Fünfzig Jahre*, pp. 7–8.

73. See Schmidt-Ott, *Erlebtes*, pp. 65–66, on the Kaiser; on Augusta Victoria, see Scheffler, *Fetten und die Mageren Jahre*, p. 237.

74. With, "The Emperor," p. 90. On Meissonier: Paret, *Berlin Secession*, pp. 160–61; Nostitz, *Bismarcks*, p. 196; *DDF*, 1st ser., 1:359.

75. On the quarrel: Paret, "Tschudi Affair"; Lenman, "Politics and Culture"; Makela, *Munich Secession*, pp. 5, 15.

76. Shaw, *William of Germany*, p. 234.

77. See Fürstenberg Papers, "Briefe vom Gefolge," for a design by Wilhelm of a fountain that was subsequently built at Donaueschingen; see Schott, *Künstler-Leben*, p. 136, and Seidel, *Kaiser*, for other, presumably unrealized, designs by the Kaiser.

78. Arnhold, *Gedenkbuch*, p. 46; Bunsen, *Welt*, 192; Doede, *Berliner Secession*, p. 38.

79. Görtz: Wilhelm II, *Erinnerungen an Korfu*, p. 27; Zedlitz-Trützschler, pp. 110–11. Schott: Schott, *Künstler-Leben*, pp. 100–146; Müller diary (30 Oct. 1905), Müller Papers, no. 3.

80. Doede, *Berliner Secession*, pp. 60–61. On Begas and Wilhelm: Scheffler, *Fetten und die Mageren Jahre*, p. 127; Ssuworin, *Geheimtagebuch*, p. 52; Bunsen, *Lost Courts*, pp. 234–35.

81. With, "The Emperor," p. 90. Also Wilhelm's speech (27 Jan. 1895) on the *Siegesallée*, in Seidel, *Kaiser*, pp. 162–63.

82. HA, Rep. 53a, no. 63, "Liebenberger Jagd, 1900," p. 11/6; Schott, *Künstler-Leben*, p. 127.

83. Ambassador Lascelles's observation is in Friedrich Rosen, *Wanderleben*, 1:30; patriotism: White, *Autobiography*, 2:224–25; noses: Topham, *Chronicles*, pp. 191–92.

84. Kinsky, *Wilczek Erzählt*, pp. 181–82; Seidel, *Kaiser*, pp. 49–71.

85. Ihne: KE, no. 814; Schmidt-Ott, *Erlebtes*, pp. 55, 70–71; Fürstenberg, *Carl-Fürstenberg-Anekdoten*, p. 31; Bunsen, *Welt*, p. 192. On Hoffmann: Bode, *Leben*, 2:76, and Bode, *Fünfzig Jahre*, p. 9; Fechter, *Wende*, pp. 456–58.

86. For a denunciation, see Bartning, "Baugeschichte."

87. Schiffer, *Leben*, p. 21; Gurlitt, "Wallotbau," p. 340; Hohenlohe-Schillingsfürst, *Reichskanzlerzeit*, pp. 11–12; Zobeltitz, *Chronik*, 1:51. Wilhelm also did not like the domes on the Berlin cathedral. Fechter, *Wende*, pp. 186–87.

88. Bode, *Leben*, 2:182–83, 192; Schmidt-Ott, *Erlebtes*, pp. 55, 71; Pogge von Strandmann, *Rathenau Tagebuch*, p. 476 n. 4, for Messel's practice. Wilhelm's dislike of Jugendstil architecture: Schiffer, *Leben*, p. 95; Rogge, *Holstein Lebensbekenntnis*, pp. 221–22.

89. Shaw, *William of Germany*, p. 234. On Leoncavallo: Bunsen, *Welt*, pp. 192–93; Friedrich Rosen, *Wanderleben*, 1:30, 192; Gleichen, *Memoirs*, p. 277

90. Hegermann-Lindencrone, *Diplomatic Life*, p. 331; Kürenberg, *War Alles Falsch?*, pp. 222–23.

91. The two quotations are in Bunsen, *Welt*, p. 193, and Davis, *The Kaiser*, pp. 92–93.

92. Del Mar, *Strauss*, 1:280–81. Strauss on Wilhelm's musical compositions: Krause, *Strauss*, pp. 189–90.

93. Krause, *Strauss*, pp. 52–53.

94. Zobeltitz, *Ich Hab so Gern Gelebt*, pp. 107–8; Del Mar, *Strauss*, 1:236. For another sudden exit by the Kaiserin, this one caused by ballerinas in too abbreviated tutus, see Bariatinsky, *Russian Life*, pp. 82–83.

95. Szögyényi to Kálnoky (10 June 1894), HHStA, no. 145(V). Zelinsky, "Wilhelm II.," p. 349, argued that Wilhelm avoided Bayreuth because of his dislike for the Bavarian prince regent but remained a supporter of Wagner's. Two of Wilhelm's Wagnerian friends in youth were Countesses Dönhoff and Schleinitz. See W2:PE, p. 47.

96. Eulenburg Papers, no. 2, pp. 57–58.

97. Tuchman, *Proud Tower*, p. 306.

98. Bülow, 1:550.

99. Ibid., 1:149.

100. Ibid. 1:175.

101. Zedlitz-Trützschler, p. 47. See also Butler, *Across the Busy Years*, 2:64, for Wilhelm's "strong dislike" of Wagner in 1905.

102. On the statue, see Zelinsky, "Wilhelm II.," p. 349; the horn is in Panofsky, "Apothéose du Festival," p. 260.

103. Music: Meister, *Yesterdays*, p. 129; Eulenburg, *Mit dem Kaiser*, 1:223; Eulenburg Papers, no. 74, p. 17. Folksinging: Göhler, "Volks-Liederbuch," pp.

70–72; Schmidt-Ott, *Erlebtes*, 90; Müller to Tirpitz (5 June 1905), Tirpitz Papers, no. 207. See also Wilhelm's address to a prize singing contest in Frankfort on the Main (6 June 1903) in Francke, *German Classics*, 15:500–504.

104. Stanislavsky, *My Life*, p. 44.

105. Shaw, *William of Germany*, p. 234. On moral quality of theater: White, *Autobiography*, 2:227; speech to royal theater company (1898), in Elkind, *German Emperor's Speeches*, p. 18.

106. Audience with Marguerite Durand, editor of the Paris feminist paper *La Fronde* (1902), in Elkind, *German Emperor's Speeches*, p. 182.

107. Shakespeare: Münz, *Edward VII*, pp. 154–55; White, *Autobiography*, 2:227; Russell, "Reminiscences," p. 60. French plays: Zobeltitz, *Chronik*, 1:51; Schönburg-Waldenburg, *Erinnerungen*, pp. 192–93.

108. On Lauff: Szögyényi to Goluchowski (10 Apr. 1897), HHStA, no. 148(V); Bülow, 1:175–76, 2:377–79; Ebart, *Herzogshofe*, p. 119.

109. On Wilhelm and Wildenbruch: Boelcke, *Krupp und die Hohenzollern*, p. 102 n. 85; Litzmann, *Wildenbruch*, 1:287–88, 300, 315, 2:60, 112–13.

110. Ernst Ludwig, *Erinnertes*, p. 110; Fuchs, *Friedrich I.*, 3:626 n. 3.

111. On Wilhelm's involvement with Wildenbruch's plays: Brauer, *Dienste Bismarcks*, pp. 278–79; Fuchs, *Friedrich I.*, 3:502; Röhl, 1:355, 358; Litzmann, *Wildenbruch*, 2:70–80. On the Kaiserin: Rogge, *Holstein Lebensbekenntnis*, p. 216. On Wilhelm's neglect of Wildenbruch, see Bunsen, *Zeitgenossen*, pp. 46–47.

112. Wahlendorff, *Erinnerungen*, p. 80; KE, no. 814; Eulenburg Papers, no. 81, part 2, pp. 17–18; Wilhelm II, *Erinnerungen an Korfu*, p. 77. On Hülsen's sycophany: Zobeltitz, *Ich Hab so Gern Gelebt*, pp. 107–8; Zedlitz-Trützschler, p. 124; Hutten-Czapski, *Sechzig Jahre*, 1:411.

113. Elkind, *German Emperor's Speeches*, p. 182.

114. Ferdinand Bonn, *Künstlerleben*, p. 122.

115. Wilhelm to Persius (5 Oct. 1894), KE, no. 330; also Durieux, *Neunzig Jahre*, p. 90.

116. Vierhaus, *Tagebuch*, p. 349. Wilhelm's opposition only increased interest in such plays. See Osborn, *Bunte Spiegel*, p. 137.

CHAPTER 3

1. Intellectual acuity: Tirpitz, *Erinnerungen*, p. 132; Schoenaich, *Damaskus*, p. 85; Radziwill, *Lettres*, 1:168; Meisner, *Denkwürdigkeiten*, 1:223, 238; Einem, *Erinnerungen*, pp. 138–39; Dryander, *Erinnerungen*, p. 198; Eulenburg, *Mit dem Kaiser*, 1:282; Valentini, p. 55; Paget, *Tower*, 2:409. On Wilhelm's phenomenal memory: Monts, *Erinnerungen*, p. 140; Brett, *Journals and Letters*, 2:266–67; Johannes Kessler, *Ewige Jugend*, p. 157; Raschdau, *Bismarck und Caprivi*, p. 176; Fürstenberg, *Lebensgeschichte*, pp. 439–40.

2. Freytag, *Menschen und Dinge*, p. 64; Hohenlohe, *Leben*, p. 359; Brett, *Journals and Letters*, 2:266, 344.

3. Müller diary (15 Jan. 1912), Görlitz, *Der Kaiser*, p. 109; Lamar Cecil, *Diplomatic Service*, p. 212 n. 53, for other attacks on diplomats. A diplomat once noted

that of all the professions, Wilhelm respected only the military. Janssen, *Graue Exzellenz*, p. 125.

4. Foulke, *Autobiography*, p. 133; also Schönburg-Waldenburg, *Erinnerungen*, p. 193.

5. Cf. the manuscript of Wilhelm's "Erinnerungen an Korfu" in Rijksarchief Papers, no. 301, with the published version; on his *Geschichtstabellen* and *Meine Vorfahren*, see Ilsemann, 1:96, 108, 117, 122, 312; on his *Meinem Leben*, see ibid., 1:264, 293–94; on his *Gorgo Studien*, see Rijksarchief Papers, no. 287, p. 9. Many of Wilhelm's sermons delivered aboard the *Hohenzollern* were also ghostwritten. Bell, *Davidson*, pp. 239–40.

6. Eulenburg Papers, no. 20, pp. 476–77; Eulalia, *Memoirs*, p. 72; Ulrich von Wilamowitz-Moellendorff, *Erinnerungen*, pp. 45–46.

7. *DDF*, 1st ser., 8:31, 566; Tirpitz, *Erinnerungen*, p. 160 n. 1; Ssuworin, *Geheimtagebuch*, p. 51. Wilhelm once had Mark Twain come to court but was disappointed by his silence. Hermine, *Empress in Exile*, pp. 287–88.

8. Wilhelm's admiration for Schiemann: Wilhelm II, *Ereignisse und Gestalten*, pp. 165–66; Freytag, *Menschen und Dinge*, p. 170; Meyer, *Schiemann*, pp. 57–58. On Schiemann's flattery: Janssen, *Graue Exzellenz*, pp. 106–7; Bülow, 1:144, 2:15, 245, 529.

9. Widenmann, *Marine-Attaché*, p. 83; Meyer, *Schiemann*, p. 247; Hohenlohe-Schillingsfürst, *Reichskanzlerzeit*, p. 88.

10. Schmidt-Ott, *Erlebtes*, p. 101; also Bunsen, *Welt*, p. 194.

11. Ulrich von Wilamowitz-Moellendorff, *Erinnerungen*, pp. 257–59. On Dörpfeld, see his letters to Wilhelm in Rijksarchief, no. 40; Wilhelm, *Ereignisse und Gestalten*, pp. 169–70, and his *Erinnerungen an Korfu*, esp. pp. 82–83. He had a high opinion of Wilhelm's intelligence. See Bunsen, *Welt*, p. 191.

12. Müller to Tirpitz (26 Apr. 1914), Tirpitz Papers, no. 207; Freytag, *Menschen und Dinge*, p. 168; Kiderlen, 1:80; Valentini, p. 114. On Wilhelm's interest in archaeology elsewhere: Bussmann, *Herbert von Bismarck*, pp. 528–29; Moltke, *Moltke Erinnerungen*, p. 303; White, *Autobiography*, 2:228–29; Schmidt-Ott, *Erlebtes*, p. 93.

13. Kiderlen, 1:80. Kiderlen Papers, box 4/004 0186/000 7896, notes that after Wilhelm's departure, the excavations were *"verbüddelt,"* the German slang for "to dig" being *"buddeln."* This account is corroborated in Ilsemann, 1:117. For a more charitable account of the Kaiser's participation in digs on Corfu, see Bunsen, *Welt*, pp. 191–92.

14. Rumors persisted about spiritualism: *BD*, 6:7–8; Röhl, 3:1998. Admiral Müller, a religious zealot known as "Rasputin," was suspected of leading the Kaiser in this direction. See Reischach, *Unter Drei Kaisern*, p. 242.

15. Moltke, *Moltke Erinnerungen*, pp. 361–62; also Zedlitz-Trützschler, p. 149; Fitzroy, *Memoirs*, 2:446; Bell, *Davidson*, pp. 239–40. On the Kaiserin's fanaticism see above.

16. Janssen, *Graue Exzellenz*, pp. 139–40.

17. W2:PE, pp. 104–7, on his efforts to combat socialism through the Christian-Social movement headed by Adolf Stöcker.

18. Zedlitz-Trützschler, p. 121, on soldiers; on Milton and Goethe, see Schneller, *Königs-Erinnerungen*, pp. 248–49.

19. Schiffer, *Leben*, pp. 93–94; also Bell, *Davidson*, pp. 239–40.

20. *Berlin Post*, 2 Sept. 1897. On the exclusive possession of divine right by the Hohenzollerns, see Wilhelm's speech at Königsberg (25 Aug. 1910), in Schulthess (1910), pp. 338–39. For the negative reaction in Bavaria, see Cartwright to Hardinge (1 Sept. 1910), FO 800/907. On Wilhelm's claims to Hohenzollern divinity, see Treutler Papers, no. 15, part 2, p. 3; Szögyényi to Kálnoky (2 Feb. 1895), HHStA, no. 146(V).

21. Letter of 27 Dec. 1906, Boyd Carpenter Papers, Add MS 46721.

22. Goetz, *Briefe*, pp. 297–300; Bülow, 2:72–75.

23. Wilhelm to Boyd Carpenter (22 Dec. 1909), Boyd Carpenter Papers, Add MS 46721; Boyd Carpenter diary (8 Dec. 1900), ibid., Add MS 46741, and (20 May 1910), ibid., Add MS 46751.

24. Wilhelm on Dryander: Eulenburg Papers, no. 84, p. 77; Wilhelm, *Ereignisse und Gestalten*, pp. 179–80. On Dryander's flattery: Zedlitz-Trützschler, p. 90, and pp. 79, 149, on the flattery of *all* court preachers.

25. Boyd Carpenter diary (16 May 1910), Boyd Carpenter Papers, Add MS 46752. On Boyd Carpenter and the Kaiser: Topham, *Memories*, p. 293; Janssen, *Graue Exzellenz*, p. 257.

26. Fitzroy, *Memoirs*, 2:446; Wilhelm to Boyd Carpenter (6 Feb 1910, 8 Jan. 1912), Boyd Carpenter Papers, Add MS 46721; H. S. Chamberlain, *Briefe*, 2:242–43.

27. Boyd Carpenter diary (8 Dec. 1900, 31 Jan. 1901), Boyd Carpenter Papers, Add MS, 46741–42.

28. On Harnack's flattery: Bülow to Wolff (7 Feb. 1925), Wolff Papers; Bülow, 1:526–27, 3:90.

29. Wilhelm, *Ereignisse und Gestalten*, p. 165. For concern in orthodox circles about Harnack's influence, see Meisner, *Denkwürdigkeiten*, 3:200–201, 204. Wilhelm on Harnack's errors: Wilhelm's notes (20 Nov. 1929), Rijksarchief, no. 268; Pastor, *Tagebücher*, p. 427.

30. Zahn-Harnack, *Harnack*, p. 262.

31. See H. S. Chamberlain, *Briefe*, 2:131–275, and H. S. Chamberlain, "Kaiser Wilhelm II."; Anna Chamberlain, *Erinnerungen*, pp. 133–39; also Field, *Evangelist of Race*, esp. chap. 3.

32. Eulenburg Papers, no. 84, pp. 69–70; Anna Chamberlain, *Erinnerungen*, pp. 134–35; Wilhelm's appreciation of the meaning of Chamberlain's work for the destiny of Germany is in Eulenburg Papers, no. 58, pp. 191–93.

33. Asquith, *Genesis of the War*, p. 88.

34. Eulenburg, *Erlebnisse*, pp. 330–36; Eulenburg Papers, no. 58, pp. 27–29; Röhl, 2:2039–40.

35. Anna Chamberlain, *Erinnerungen*, pp. 134–35.

36. Field, *Evangelist of Race*, p. 241.

37. H. S. Chamberlain, *Briefe*, 1:237–38, claims that he saw Wilhelm frequently thereafter, but this is contradicted by his wife, who says they met only twice, and by the absence of any evidence other than the questionable account in Kürenberg, *War Alles Falsch?*, pp. 254–55. See Anna Chamberlain, *Erinnerungen*, p. 139. On

Anglo-Saxon mammonism, see Wilhelm to Bigelow (17 Nov. 1927), Bigelow Papers, no. 34.

38. Wilhelm to Chamberlain (31 Dec. 1901), H. S. Chamberlain, *Briefe*, 2:141–43; Field, *Evangelist of Race*, p. 251.

39. See Lamar Cecil, "Jew and Junker," and "Wilhelm II. und die Juden."

40. Meisner, *Denkwürdigkeiten*, 2:6.

41. On the press: Zechlin, *Deutsche Politik*, p. 48; Schmidt-Ott, *Erlebtes*, p. 195; on politics: Hohenlohe-Schillingsfürst, *Reichskanzlerzeit*, p. 92.

42. A special favorite was Albert Ballin, head of the Hamburg-American Line. See Lamar Cecil, *Ballin*, esp. pp. 102–8, 353–56; Schelking, *Recollections*, p. 70; Mosse, "Wilhelm II," pp. 181, 189 nn. 91, 93; Viktoria Luise, *Tochter des Kaisers*, p. 27. For other Jews Wilhelm liked: Bülow, 4:28–29, 405–6; Princess Friedrich Leopold of Prussia, *Behind the Scenes*, p. 85. On the great art collector James Simon, see Friedländer, *Reminiscences*, pp. 103–4; Mosse, "Wilhelm II," pp. 183–84.

43. Townley, *"Indiscretions,"* p. 45.

44. Brett, *Journals and Letters*, 2:255.

45. On the controversy, see Larsen, "Orientalism."

46. On the women, see Schönburg-Waldenburg, *Erinnerungen*, p. 192. For Wilhelm on the speech: H. S. Chamberlain, *Briefe*, 2:165–68; Szögyényi to Goluchowski (27 Jan. and 25 Feb. 1903), HHStA, no. 159(B); Dryander, *Erinnerungen*, pp. 228–29; memoir by Franz Böhl (10 Dec. 1938), Rijksarchief, no. 273.

47. H. S. Chamberlain, *Briefe*, 2:188–92; Count Emil Schlitz zu Görtz (1 Mar. 1903), HA, Rep. 53, no. 180.

48. Printed in Réal, "Lettre à l'Amiral Hollmann"; also printed in part in Wilhelm, *Ereignisse und Gestalten*, pp. 183–86. On Wilhelm and the society, see Simon, "Kaiser Wilhelm II.," p. 97.

49. Zahn-Harnack, *Harnack*, pp. 266–67.

50. The fourth and lowest rank of Prussia's Pour le Mérite order was designated "for learning and art." See Laforgue, *Berlin*, pp. 72–74.

51. Eulenburg Papers, no. 80, p. 16. Eulenburg decided against trying to establish a salon that would bring Wilhelm into contact with intellectuals. Röhl, *Germany without Bismarck*, p. 131.

52. On Studt: Brocke, "System Althoff," p. 39; Zedlitz-Trützschler, pp. 161–62.

53. Brocke, "System Althoff," p. 97. Cf. Dryander, *Erinnerungen*, pp. 209–10.

54. Hohenlohe-Schillingsfürst, *Reichskanzlerzeit*, p. 88.

55. Brocke, "System Althoff," p. 99.

56. Kiaulehn, *Berlin*, p. 379. On the servility of the professoriat, see Czernin von und zu Chudenitz, *Weltkriege*, p. 79.

57. Gutsche, *Wilhelm II.*, p. 114. Other distinguished scientists sometimes invited to court were Wilhelm Wundt, Emil Fischer, Wilhelm von Waldeyer-Hartz, and Adolf Slaby.

58. Roentgen: Radziwill, *Lettres*, 2:11; Zeppelin: Flotow to Aehrenthal (31 Aug. 1909), HHStA, no. 167(B).

59. Haller, *Aus dem Leben*, p. 172. Zedlitz-Trützschler, who knew Wilhelm well, noted the curious dichotomy in a man who on the one hand wanted Germany

to be the quintessence of industrial modernity and yet at the same time wanted it to be ruled in a medieval, autocratic manner. Zedlitz-Trützschler, p. 85.

60. See Pachnicke, *Führende Männer*, p. 202, on machines. On ships: Bülow, 1:69, but cf. Eulenburg Papers, no. 80, p. 46.

61. Brocke, "System Althoff," p. 24; McClelland, *State, Society and the University*, p. 306; Wilhelm, *Ereignisse und Gestalten*, pp. 163–65; Simon, "Kaiser Wilhelm II.," p. 93; Schmidt-Ott, *Erlebtes*, pp. 110–24; Burchardt, *Wissenschaftspolitik*, p. 21. Rudolf von Valentini's role in founding the society has largely been overlooked. See Valentini to Harnack (17 Dec. 1922), and Schmidt-Ott to Frau von Valentini (20 Dec. 1925), Schwertfeger Papers, no. 206.

62. Burchardt, *Wissenschaftspolitik*, p. 33.

63. Zahn-Harnack, *Harnack*, p. 334.

64. Röhl, *Kaiser, Hof und Staat*, pp. 29–32, and Röhl, *Wilhelm II.*, 1:67–71, 320–28.

65. Townley, *"Indiscretions,"* p. 40; Hohenlohe-Schillingsfürst, *Reichskanzlerzeit*, p. 151; Zedlitz-Trützschler, p. 46; Topham, *Chronicles*, p. 233.

66. See *DDF*, 1st ser., 8:374, on the tics; Hinzpeter in *W2:PE*, p. 35.

67. *DDF*, 1st ser., 8:374. Also Röhl, *Kaiser, Hof und Staat*, pp. 29–30.

68. Comparison by Bismarck: Busch, *Bismarck*, 3:314, and chap. 3 of the third volume of Bismarck-Schönhausen, *Gedanken und Erinnerungen*, in which he depicts the dead sovereign as more talented than Wilhelm; by Waldersee in Meisner, *Denkwürdigkeiten*, 2:287, 333–34. Others who saw similarities: Monts to Bülow (24 Mar. 1896), Bülow Papers, no. 106; Bülow, 1:34; Kardorff, *Kardorff*, p. 302; Raschdau, *Weimar*, pp. 23, 172; *HP*, 4:548, 606; Röhl, 1:65.

69. Dove, *Gustav Freytag*, p. 204; Raschdau, *Weimar*, pp. 132–33; Treitschke was punished by being deprived of access to the royal archives. Zobeltitz, *Chronik*, 1:41–45. The historian Johannes Haller in the 1920s found Wilhelm to be a "kitchy reproduction" (*kitschige Reproduktion*) of Friedrich Wilhelm IV. See Röhl, 1:65. For Treitschke's low opinion of Wilhelm: Breysig, *Tagen und Träumen*, p. 75; Dove, *Gustav Freytag*, pp. 111, 598, 623–24.

70. *Caligula: Eine Studie in Cäsarenwahnsinn* (Leipzig, n.d. [1894]).

71. Bunsen, *Zeitgenossen*, pp. 104–5.

72. Bunsen, *Lost Courts*, p. 197; Röhl, *Kaiser, Hof und Staat*, p. 140; Vierhaus, *Tagebuch*, for the similar opinion of Bodo von dem Knesebeck, the vice-master of ceremonies at the court.

73. Radziwill, *Lettres*, 4:47; Röhl, *Kaiser, Hof und Staat*, p. 140.

74. Monts, *Erinnerungen*, p. 372; Röhl, 1:537, 560, 730. Lerchenfeld, who knew both, was emphatic that Wilhelm in no way resembled Ludwig II. Lerchenfeld-Koefering, *Wilhelm II.*, p. 58.

75. Röhl, 2:1405. For a comparison by Adjutant-General Adolf von Wittich, who knew Wilhelm quite well, see Bismarck Papers, no. FC 3018/0270. See also the opinion of Bismarck's physician, Ernst Schweninger, in Kardorff, *Kardorff*, p. 278.

76. Public discussion: Count Harry Kessler, *Gesichter und Zeiten*, pp. 250–51; *DDF*, 1st ser., 8:374; Holstein to Bülow (2 Apr. 1897), Bülow Papers, no. 90; Bülow notes (7 Apr. 1897), ibid., no. 76; Caprivi memo (1 Sept. 1892), Reichskanzlei Papers, no. 1466; KE, 317/2, pp. 193–94; Raschdau, *Weimar*, p. 124.

77. See Bunsen, *Lost Courts*, p. 197, for the Empress Frederick; for Charlotte, see Wilke, *Erinnerungen*, p. 139. Another relative, one of the Kaiserin's sisters, thought Wilhelm unbalanced. See Princess Friedrich Leopold of Prussia, *Behind the Scenes*, p. 249.

78. Queen Victoria to Salisbury (15 Oct. 1888), Buckle, *Letters of Queen Victoria*, 1:440–41; for the prince, see Waters, *"Private and Personal,"* p. 256. For a British cousin, see Athlone, *Grandchildren*, p. 99.

79. See Monts to Bülow (23 Mar. 1897), Bülow Papers, no. 106, for the grand duke; for the duke of Saxe-Meiningen, see his letters to Gossler (8 June 1920, 24 May 1921), Gossler Papers, no. 19.

80. Mossolov, *Court of the Last Tsar*, p. 202.

81. Bülow, 1:139–40, for Hohenlohe; Tirpitz, *Erinnerungen*, p. 132; Holstein in *HP*, 3:66–69, 641; Röhl, 1:669; for Eulenburg, see, inter alia, Röhl, 1:391, 530, 537, 560, 626, 640, 665, 730; Marschall von Bieberstein, in Raschdau, *Bismarck und Caprivi*, p. 369; Roedern, in *KE*, no. 317/2, pp. 193–94.

82. Lansdowne to Lascelles (1 Apr. 1901), FO 800/128; *BD*, 6:6.

83. Lady Gwendolen Cecil, *Salisbury*, 4:367; *W2:PE*, p. 280; Asquith to Knollys (24 May 1911), RA, Geo V O 2580, no. 2; Gray in Brett, *Journals and Letters*, 2:344. On Taft, see Bryce to Grey (12 July 1909), FO 371/675; on Roosevelt: Lee of Fareham, *"Good Innings,"* pp. 83, 117; Foulke, *Autobiography*, p. 133; *BD*, 6:278. See also Gosselin to Salisbury (29 Nov. 1895), Salisbury Papers, no. A120, for gossip about Wilhelm's odd behavior.

84. Memo by Lord Salisbury's private secretary, Sir Schomberg McDonnell (26 Oct. 1914), who had been told this by Sir John Erichsen, one of Queen Victoria's physicians, who in turn heard it from a German doctor who had examined Wilhelm. RA, Geo V M 688a, no. 1. On Wilhelm's otitis media, see Röhl, *Wilhelm II.*, 1:320–38.

85. On Wilhelm's bad health in the 1880s: Lucius von Ballhausen, *Bismarck-Erinnerungen*, p. 326; Janssen, *Graue Exzellenz*, pp. 46–47; Eulenburg Papers, no. 80, p. 14; Rogge, *Holstein und Hohenlohe*, p. 257; Eulenburg's notes on his letter from Wilhelm (8 Sept. 1896, printed in Röhl, 1:198–99), Eulenburg Papers, no. 1, pp. 51–52.

86. Röhl 1:347, 391; for another doctor (name illegible), see Caprivi memo (1 Sept. 1892), Reichskanzlei Papers, no. 1466.

87. Röhl, 2:800.

88. Radziwill, *Lettres*, 1:116–17.

89. Letter (15. Mar. 1892), in Buckle, *Letters of Queen Victoria*, 2:106 n. 2.

90. Ibid., and Salisbury to the queen (14 Apr. 1892), ibid., p. 110.

91. Holstein to Karl von Lindenau (29 July 1896), *HP*, 3:636–39. Note that Holstein speaks of Semon's opinion "four or five years ago."

92. Kardorff, *Kardorff*, p. 278. Wilhelm is not mentioned by name, but it is clear that it is he who is being discussed.

93. Eulenburg notes (30 July 1893), Eulenburg Papers, no. 25, pp. 326–28.

94. Röhl, 3:1718–19, 1740, 1811; also Raschdau, *Bismarck und Caprivi*, p. 175. For an ailment in 1896, see Meisner, *Denkwürdigkeiten*, 2:374; Rogge, *Holstein und Hohenlohe*, p. 258.

95. Raschdau, *Weimar*, p. 124 (emphasis added).

96. Röhl, 3:1984.

97. Ibid., 3:1991–98.

98. Ibid., 3:2091, 2095; for Eulenburg's concern, see ibid., 3:2096–99.

99. Bülow, 2:421–23.

100. Ibid.

101. Janssen, *Graue Exzellenz*, p. 171; Monts to Harden (26 Sept. 1909), Harden Papers, no. 75.

102. On Bülow's lack of interest and weakness in internal affairs: Loebell Papers, no. 26, part 1, p. 140; Fuchs, *Friedrich I.*, 4:209; Hutten-Czapski, *Sechzig Jahre*, 1:399, 503; Monts, *Erinnerungen*, pp. 20, 152. On Wilhelm's lack of interest: Valentini, p. 73 n. 1; Schiffer, *Leben*, p. 91.

103. Monts, *Erinnerungen*, pp. 421–22. Other similar opinion: Raschdau, *Weimar*, p. 154; Hohenlohe-Schillingsfürst, *Reichskanzlerzeit*, p. 375; Zedlitz-Trützschler, pp. 236–40; *HP*, 4:244–46; Janssen, *Graue Exzellenz*, pp. 170–71. A positive estimate of Bülow is in Lerchenfeld-Koefering, *Erinnerungen*, pp. 374–75, which nevertheless explains that Bülow's polished manners tended to give a false impression.

104. Thimme, *Front wider Bülow*, p. 156. Also GFO Papers, 280/00259; Janssen, *Graue Exzellenz*, p. 171.

105. Flotow, "Bülows Römische Mission," p. 400; Princess Herbert Bismarck, "Erinnerungen an Bülow," Bismarck Papers, no. FC 2958/979–80. He was apparently more interested in his own verbiage than he was in listening. Mutius Papers, p. 130.

106. Pogge von Strandmann, *Rathenau Tagebuch*, p. 143.

107. Röhl, 1:146; Eulenburg to Bülow (23 Sept. 1900), HA 53a, no. 63; for an example of Eulenburg's intervention with the Kaiser in Bülow's behalf, see Röhl, 2:1060–62.

108. Raschdau, *Weimar*, p. 41; Kiderlen, 2:18. Wilhelm liked his reports very much. Raschdau, *Bismarck und Caprivi*, pp. 309–10.

109. Haller, *Aus dem Leben*, p. 225.

110. Pogge von Strandmann, *Rathenau Tagebuch*, p. 143.

111. Röhl, 3:1858. On Bülow's talent as a flatterer of the Kaiser: Meisner, *Denkwürdigkeiten*, 2:433; Valentini, p. 73 n. 1.

112. Bülow indicted Wilhelm for conceit in Tirpitz diary (4 Jan. 1905), Tirpitz Papers, no. 21; for volubility in Fuchs, *Friedrich I.*, 4:257; for exaggeration in Lascelles to Salisbury (23 Dec. 1898), FO 64/1439; for hypersensitivity in same to same (11 Mar. 1899), Salisbury Papers, no. A121; for tactlessness in same to Lansdowne (12 June 1905), FO 800/130; for impulsiveness in Zedlitz-Trützschler, p. 88. Bülow concluded that the Kaiser hurt his own reputation. See Röhl, 3:1656.

113. Pless, *Better Left Unsaid*, p. 286; Vietsch, *Bethmann Hollweg*, pp. 157–58.

114. Röhl, 3:1707, 1714.

115. Zedlitz-Trützschler, p. 88.

116. Fuchs, *Friedrich I.*, 4:222; also Hammann, "Aufzeichnungen," p. 549.

117. Röhl, 3:2096. On Bülow's clever manner of handling Wilhelm: Meisner, *Denkwürdigkeiten*, 2:433; Zedlitz-Trützschler, pp. 181–82; Valentini, p. 73 n. 1.

118. On Hohenlohe, see Hohenlohe-Schillingsfürst, *Reichskanzlerzeit*, p. 375; on Holstein, see *HP*, 4:234–35, 425–26.

119. Wilhelm to Eulenburg (20 Aug. 1897), Eulenburg Papers, no. 48, pp. 453–57.

120. Szögyényi to Vienna (15 Jan. 1902), HHStA, no. 157(B); Wilhelm to Fürstenberg (23 Dec. 1908), Fürstenberg Papers, "Wilhelm II c. 1908–1918." For the Kaiser's irritation at Bülow: Zedlitz-Trützschler, p. 37; *HP*, 4:234–35.

121. Bülow, 2:242.

122. Monts, *Erinnerungen*, pp. 153–54.

123. Wilhelm's initial opposition: Herbert Bismarck's diary (1 Jan. 1885), Bismarck Papers, no. FC 3018/0522; Dona's is in Röhl, 1:512. For Eulenburg's role in the reconciliation, see Haller, *Aus dem Leben*, p. 224. Wilhelm's admiration for the princess: Gwynn, *Spring Rice*, 1:245; Bunsen, *Zeitgenossen*, p. 198; Bülow, 3:63; Loebell Papers, no. 27, part 2, p. 68.

124. Thimme, *Front wider Bülow*, p. 223; Hammann, *Vorgeschichte*, pp. 108–9; Hutten-Czapski, *Sechzig Jahre*, 1:553.

CHAPTER 4

1. Mutius to Thimme (11 Feb. 1930), Thimme Papers, no. 17; Goschen to Hardinge (4 Dec. 1908), Hardinge Papers, no. 11.

2. For the suspicions of Gottlieb von Jagow, Count Paul von Hatzfeldt, Friedrich von Holstein, and Baron Hermann von Eckardstein, see Gebhard Blücher von Wahlstatt, *Memoirs*, p. 218; *BD*, 7:437; Rogge, *Holstein Lebensbekenntnis*, p. 214; Eckardstein, *Entlassung*, p. 37.

3. Lascelles to Salisbury (17 Feb. 1898), FO 64/1437; see Howe, *Meyer*, p. 127, for Sir Cecil Spring-Ricze; see Gebhard Blücher von Wahlstatt, *Memoirs*, p. 218, for Sir William Tyrrell; Austen Chamberlain, *Politics*, p. 95; Sir Fairfax Cartwright in *BD*, 7:51–52; Bunsen, *Zeitgenossen*, p. 80.

4. Bülow was recognized as being versatile in concealing his feelings. See Sonntag, *Begegnungen mit Bülow*, p. 21; Lerchenfeld-Koefering, *Erinnerungen*, p. 415. On being forced to embrace Russia: Lascelles to Lansdowne (28 Dec. 1904), FO 64/1594; Rosner, *Erinnerungen des Kronprinzen*, p. 78. After the war, Bülow would blame the failure of England and Germany to form good relations on Joseph Chamberlain, Edward VII, and Wilhelm II. See his letter to Wolff (10 July 1923), Wolff Papers.

5. Loebell Papers, no. 27, part 2, p. 30. How early in his career Bülow developed this idea can be seen in his letter to Eulenburg (8 Feb. 1892), in Röhl, 1:761–63. On Austria-Hungary, see Lascelles to Lansdowne (25 Aug. 1901), FO 64/1521.

6. Holstein diary (7 Nov. 1902), *HP*, 4:270.

7. Lascelles to Lansdowne (28 Feb. 1901), FO 64/1520. Similar language by Wilhelm to the Austro-Hungarian envoy is in Szögyényi to Vienna (15 Jan. 1902), HHStA, no. 157(B), and in a letter to Edward VII (30 Dec. 1901), in RA, X 37, no. 51.

8. Raschdau, *Weimar*, p. 153; Rogge, *Holstein Lebensbekenntnis*, p. 214.

9. On the Teutonic brotherhood: Swaine to Bigge (23 Dec. 1900), RA, I 62, no. 113; Wilhelm to Edward VII (30 Dec. 1901), ibid., X 37, no. 51; Boyd Carpenter

diary (20, 26 May 1910), Boyd Carpenter Papers, Add MS 46751–52. On religious cohesion: Wilhelm to Boyd Carpenter, ibid., Add MS 46721; Boyd Carpenter diary (20 May 1910), ibid., Add MS 46751; Malet to Kimberley (16 Jan. 1895), FO 64/1350; Swaine to Lascelles (20 Dec. 1895), ibid., 1351.

10. This was revealed to Wilhelm in what he falsely believed to be English support for the great Hamburg dock strike of 1896. See Lascelles to Salisbury (28 Nov., 2 Dec. 1896), FO 64/1379; Szögyényi to Vienna (28 Nov. 1896), HHStA, no. 147(B); Queen Victoria's Journal (2 Dec. 1896), RA.

11. On Venezuela: Gosselin to Foreign Office (4 Nov. 1895), Salisbury Papers, no. A120; on materialism; Boyd Carpenter diary (8 Aug. 1901), Boyd Carpenter Papers, Add MS 46741; Meisner, *Denkwürdigkeiten*, 2:17; Topham, *Chronicles*, p. 232; on bossiness: Swaine to Lascelles (20 Dec. 1895), FO 64/1351; *BD*, 1:117; Lascelles to Foreign Office (26 May 1899), RA, I 62, no. 12; Wilhelm to Queen Victoria (27 May 1899), ibid., no. 14.

12. *HP*, 3:307; Bülow, 1:80, 2:62, 397. The crown prince also thought so. See Rosner, *Erinnerungen des Kronprinzen*, p. 84.

13. Malet to Salisbury (4 July 1888), FO 64/1187.

14. Salisbury to the Empress Frederick (1 Aug. 1898), RA, I 61, no. 57, referring to Wilhelm's letter to his mother (1 Jun. 1898), printed in *HP*, 4:82–84. For Wilhelm's resentment at the disregard of his efforts at improving relations: Wilhelm to Edward VII (31 July 1900), RA, T 10, no. 126; Grierson to Lascelles and to Bigge (3, 4 May 1899), ibid., I 62, no. 10, 10a; *HP*, 4:82–84; Lascelles to Salisbury (19 Feb. 1900), FO 64/1492; same to Lansdowne (11 Apr. 1901), ibid. 1495; *BD*, 1:117.

15. Irritation: Malet to Kimberley (16 Jan. 1895), FO 64/1350; Swaine to Lascelles (19 Jan. 1896), ibid., 1376; draft of Wilhelm to Edward VII (31 Jan. 1910), GFO, England 81/1 geheim, T149/240/00432–33; Bülow, 2:27; Goetz, *Briefe*, p. 297; Zedlitz-Trützschler, p. 97; Brett, *Journals and Letters*, 2:136–38; Newton, *Lansdowne*, p. 335. Wilhelm's claim that he never read papers is in Zedlitz-Trützschler, p. 204; Radziwill, *Lettres*, 3:276. Schönburg-Waldenburg, *Erinnerungen*, p. 157, and Ssuworin, *Geheimtagebuch*, p. 52, on the other hand, depict Wilhelm as a close reader of the press.

16. Waters, *Potsdam and Doorn*, p. 52; also Raulff, *Machtpolitik und Imperialismus*, p. 31.

17. Grierson to Lascelles (3 Mar. and 5 May 1896), FO 64/1376–77.

18. Conspiracy: Lascelles to Wilhelm (28 Oct. 1899), Salisbury Papers, Class E; same to Salisbury (2 Mar. 1900), FO 64/1492. On the role of Jews: Bigelow to Wilhelm (28 Feb. 1898), Bülow Papers, no. 112; Goetz, *Briefe*, p. 387.

19. Malet to Salisbury (5 Jan. 1889), Salisbury Papers, no. A62; Newton, *Lansdowne*, p. 335; Lascelles to Grey (3 Jan. 1906), FO 371/75; Szögyényi to Goluchowski (2 Jan. 1906), HHStA, no. 163(B); Zedlitz-Trützschler, p. 153.

20. Lascelles to Salisbury (11 Mar. 1899), Salisbury Papers, no. A121.

21. Letter of 10 June 1897, RA, Z 500, no. 7.

22. Queen Victoria to the Empress Frederick (25 Nov. 1899), RA, Add MS U/32, p. 754.

23. Imprudence: Queen Victoria's diary (27 Jan. 1899), in Buckle, *Letters of Queen Victoria*, 3:336; comparison to the tsar: Queen Victoria to Salisbury (3 Oct.

1896), Salisbury Papers, no. A46. On the queen's irritation at her grandson, see Queen Victoria's Journal (3 Jan. 1896, 8 and 13 May 1897), RA.

24. *W2:PE*, pp. 326–28; note dictated by the queen (12 Apr. 1900), Salisbury Papers, no. A121.

25. Buckle, *Queen Victoria's Letters*, 3:360; Queen Victoria's Journal (1 June 1899), RA. Wilhelm, who wanted Coburg to go to his uncle Arthur, Duke of Connaught, was annoyed that it went instead to a first cousin, the Duke of Albany. See Lascelles to Salisbury (31 Mar. 1899) and Grierson to Lascelles (3 May 1899), RA, I 62, nos. 9, 10; on his "threats": Buckle, *Letters of Queen Victoria*, 3:360.

26. Wilhelm to Lascelles (19 Jan. 1901), FO 800/128.

27. Kaiserin Auguste Viktoria to her sister (25 Jan. 1901), Glücksburg Papers, no. 22. Accounts of the deathbed and aftermath: Wilhelm, *Ereignisse und Gestalten*, pp. 74–76; Reid, *Ask Sir James*, pp. 210–11; *HP*, 4:217–18.

28. Reid, *Ask Sir James*, p. 216; Leslie, *Long Shadows*, pp. 74–75.

29. Duchess of Cornwall and York, wife of Edward VII's son and heir, to Grandduchess Augusta of Mecklenburg-Strelitz (27 Jan. 1901), RA, Geo V CC 22, no. 55. On the approval in England of Wilhelm's performance: Lansdowne to Lascelles (23 Jan. 1901), FO 800/128; Ponsonby, *Recollections*, pp. 127–28. A few days after the funeral the new king referred to the Kaiser as his "difficult nephew." J. G. Lockhart, *Cosmo Gordon Lang*, p.143.

30. Wilhelm to George V (15 Feb. 1911), RA, Geo V AA 43, no. 152.

31. Lascelles to Edward VII (13 Apr. 1901), FO 800/128. For the king's largely successful visit to Germany later in 1901, see Szögyényi to Goluchowski (6 Mar. 1901), HHStA, no. 155(B) and S. Lee, *Edward VII*, 2:136–40.

32. Lamar Cecil, "History as Family Chronicle," p. 105.

33. On the king's standing as a diplomat: Gleichen, *Memoirs*, p. 337; *GP*, 24:10–12. Wilhelm consequently did not like to be left alone with his uncle. Roddie, *Peace Patrol*, p. 217.

34. Zedlitz-Trütschler, p. 153; Howe, *Meyer*, pp. 217, 339.

35. Lister, *Reminiscences*, p. 196.

36. Wilhelm's castigations of the king's amorality, which do not specifically mention Mrs. Keppel: Metternich to Bülow (4 Feb. 1903), GFO, England 81/1 geheim, T149/240/00417–18; Duke of Saxe-Meiningen to Gossler (26 Dec. 1918), Gossler Papers, no. 7; Erbach-Schönberg, *Erklugenes*, p. 225. Reid, *Ask Sir James*, p. 238, reports that Wilhelm refused Mrs. Keppel's request for an audience at the time of Edward VII's death.

37. The quotation combines Johnston, *Life and Letters*, p. 175, and Rose, *George V*, p. 164. See also Princess of Wales to her son Prince George (30 Aug. 1890), RA, Geo V AA 31, no. 14; same to same (28 Apr. 1900), ibid., AA.32, no. 21; Athlone, *Grandchildren*, p. 148; *W2:PE*, pp. 266–67. Wilhelm considered Alexandra to be anti-German. Szögyényi to Goluchowski (Dec. 12, 1902), HHStA, no. 158(V).

38. The Kaiser's military attaché in London from 1902 to 1906, Count Friedrich von der Schulenburg-Tressow, believed that the entourages of both sovereigns worked to worsen Anglo-German relations. Schulenburg Papers, p. 26. This was also the belief of the astute British minister in Munich, Sir Fairfax Cartwright, as far as the German entourage was concerned. See *BD*, 6:51.

39. Lamar Cecil, "History as Family Chronicle," p. 107.

40. Szögyényi to Aehrenthal (19 Aug. 1908), HHstA, no. 166(B); Watson to Goschen (9 Oct. 1913), FO 371/1986.

41. Heath to Goschen (7 Mar. 1910), FO 371/900; Hardinge to Lascelles (26 Feb. 1906 and 22 Feb 1908), FO 800/11, 13.

42. Brett, *Journals and Letters*, 2:182–83.

43. Knollys to Ponsonby (22 Jan. 1894), RA, I 60, no. 31. See also Howe, *Meyer*, p. 239.

44. Bülow, 2:38–39; Leslie, *Long Shadows*, p. 55; Wilhelm's marginalia on Metternich to Bülow (16 Mar. 1903), GFO, England 81/1, T149/239/00541; Pless, *Better Left Unsaid*, p. 86; BD, 6:51.

45. Widenmann, *Marine-Attaché*, p. 38; HP, 4:275, for the differing attitudes of the Berlin and London courts to Jews. Wilhelm did like Baroness Mathilde Rothschild, a notable philanthropist. See Bülow, 4:28–29, 405–6.

46. Hardinge to Lascelles (26 Feb. 1906) and Knollys to Lascelles (21 Mar. 1905), FO 800/13; Edward VII to Knollys (15 Nov. 1908), RA, W 53, no. 37; Zedlitz-Trützschler, p. 132.

47. On Edward VII's resentment at his nephew having preceded him on a throne, see Czernin von und zu Chudenitz, *Weltkriege*, pp. 82–83, relating Kiderlen-Wächter's view.

48. Viktoria Luise, *Tochter des Kaisers*, p. 37; see Lascelles to Grey (18 May 1906), FO 800/61, for gushiness. He also found Wilhelm rude and excessively nervous. Rudeness: Knollys to Lascelles (27 Jul. 1904, 23 Sept. 1905), FO 800/12; Widenmann, *Marine-Attaché*, p. 107; nervousness: Fitzroy, *Memoirs*, 1:264; Rosner, *Erinnerungen des Kronprinzen*, p. 84.

49. Christopher Howard, *Goschen*, p. 154; DDF, 2d ser., 3:68, 10:305; Athlone, *Grandchildren*, p. 148.

50. Edward VII's dislike of Lonsdale: Edward VII to Hardinge (1 Sept. 1907), Hardinge Papers, no. 8; Bülow, 1:70–71, 2:30, 155–56; Lonsdale's dislike of the king's Rothschild friends: HP, 4:275; Bülow's regret at Wilhelm's friendship with Lonsdale: BD, 7:45. Another bête noire was Admiral Baron Gustav von Senden und Bibran, whom the king correctly perceived as working to undermine good Anglo-German relations. See Eckardstein, *Lebenserinnerungen*, 2:79–87; HP, 4:146–47; Bülow, 1:68–70, 342–43. The king's hostility to Senden greatly irritated Wilhelm. See Bigge to Queen Victoria (14 Mar. 1898) and Lascelles to Edward VII (25 Mar. 1898), RA, I 61, no. 37, 39.

51. Goschen to Grey (10 Jan. 1912), FO 800/1372. See also Lascelles to Hardinge (31 Aug. 1907), Hardinge Papers, no. 10; Blunt, *Diaries*, p. 752; Eulenburg Papers, no. 80, pp. 63–64.

52. Thurn to Goluchowski (21 Oct. 1903), HHstA, no. 160(B); Lansdowne to Lascelles (17 Jan. 1902), FO 800/129.

53. Ponsonby, *Recollections*, pp. 260, 363. On fraudulent outward cordiality, see ibid., pp. 178–79, and Rosner, *Erinnerungen des Kronprinzen*, p. 84.

54. Lansdowne to Lascelles (25 Sept. 1905), FO 800/130; Ponsonby, *Recollections*, pp. 178–79; Meister, *Yesterdays*, p. 159; Widenmann, *Marine-Attaché*, p. 109; Christopher Howard, *Goschen*, pp. 167–68; Bülow, 2:306–7, 399. Eckardstein, who knew both sovereigns well, thought Wilhelm to blame: see

Erinnerungen an König Eduard, pp. 14–15, and *Lebenserinnerungen*, 1:207. Eckardstein's memoirs abound in exaggeration, but Richard von Kühlmann (*Erinnerungen*, p. 311) believed that what he wrote about Edward VII should be taken seriously. Waters, who knew both rulers, declared that although they got on well in one another's presence, when the two separated, friction arose. See Waters, *Potsdam and Doorn*, pp. 43–44, and also Szögyényi to Goluchowski (19 Aug. 1906), HHStA, no. 162 (V).

55. Bülow, 1:341–42.

56. Meister, *Yesterdays*, p. 159.

57. Holstein in *HP*, 4:415; Schoen in Szögyényi to Vienna (14 Feb. 1909), HHStA, no. 167(B); Lascelles in his telegram to Salisbury (19 Feb. 1898), Salisbury Papers, no. A121. See also Ernst Ludwig, *Erinnertes*, p. 101.

58. Wilhelm's "Bemerkungen" (1934), Beseler Papers. The Kaiser's Englishness in mannerisms and appearance: Lamar Cecil, "History as Family Chronicle," p. 106, and also Paget, *Tower*, 2:409; Mohl, *Fünfzig Jahre*, pp. 316–17; Marie Louise, *Memories*, pp. 68–69.

59. See Zedlitz-Trützschler, p. 235, on decadence.

60. See Bülow, 2:30, for how Edward VII used the "tea king," Sir Thomas Lipton; on the sovereign's demimonde company: Erbach-Schönberg, *Erklugenes*, p. 225; Haller, *Aus dem Leben*, p. 177; Eulenburg Papers, no. 81, part 1, pp. 184–85; Meisner, *Denkwürdigkeiten*, 2:35; Zedlitz-Trützschler, p. 140.

61. Bülow, 1:573.

62. Ibid., 1:261–62, 290–91, 342, 398, 504–6, 2:246–47, 529–30, 3:198–99; Fitzroy, *Memoirs*, 1:263; Topham, *Chronicles*, p. 227; Eulenburg Papers, no. 81, part 1, p. 197; for her dislike of her husband and sons being in England: Bülow, 1:290–91, 504–6; the Kaiserin to Bülow (14 Mar. 1899), Bülow Papers, no. 109; Lascelles to Lansdowne (26 Jan. 1901), FO 800/128; Pless, *Better Left Unsaid*, p. 72.

63. Bülow Papers, no. 153, p. 140.

64. Bülow, 1:342; Münz, *Edward VII*, p. 101; Szögyényi to Goluchowski (6 Mar. 1901), HHStA, no. 155(B).

65. Keller, *Vierzig Jahre*, p. 259; Bülow, 1:246, 303; Topham, *Chronicles*, pp. 36, 50, 187–88. For anti-English gentlemen in the Kaiserin's suite: Deines to his father (3 Nov. 1899), Deines Papers, no. 14; Bülow, 1:339; Topham, *Chronicles*, p. 197.

66. Lascelles to Lansdowne (26 Jan. 1901), FO 800/128; Ebel, *Hatzfeldt*, 2:1362; *BD*, 7:51–52; Zobeltitz, *Chronik*, 1:336–37.

67. *HP*, 3:511–12. For Eulenburg's one trip to England in 1891 and the distaste it caused, see his *Mit dem Kaiser*, 1:145–48, and also 119–20, 2:68, 77.

68. Röhl, 3:2013.

69. Ponsonby, *Letters of the Empress Frederick*, p. 363; also Ponsonby, *Recollections*, p. 162.

70. Ebel, *Hatzfeldt*, 2:1326 n. 6; see also Lascelles to Bertie (22 Feb. 1901), ibid., 2:1363.

71. This was also true for two other generals, August von Mackensen and Helmuth von Moltke, whom Wilhelm especially liked. Russell, "Reminiscences," p. 67; Moltke, *Moltke Erinnerungen*, pp. 330–32. Other Anglophobes were the

chief of the Civil Cabinet, Rudolf von Valentini, and in the navy, Admiral Alfred von Tirpitz and the naval attaché in London from 1907 to 1912, Wilhelm Widenmann.

72. Bülow on his motives in the speech: Lascelles to Lansdowne (31 Jan. 1902), FO 64/1551; German opinion on the speech: *HP*, 4:236–37, 244, 247; Rogge, *Holstein Lebensbekenntnis*, p. 214; Hammann, *Vorgeschichte*, pp. 141–42.

73. Hötzsch, *Bülows Reden*, 1:244–45.

74. Waters, *Potsdam and Doorn*, p. 68. Also Lascelles to Salisbury (28 Feb. 1901), FO 64/1495; Grierson to Lascelles (3 May 1899), Salisbury Papers, no. A121; same to Bigge (4 May 1899), RA, I 62, no. 10a.

75. Szögyényi to Goluchowski (29 Jan. 1902), HHStA, no. 158(V).

76. Lascelles to Knollys (17 Jan. 1902), FO 800/10; similarly Szögyényi to Vienna (15 Jan. 1902), HHStA, no. 157(B).

77. RA, X 37, no. 52.

78. Ibid., no. 51.

79. Szögyényi to Goluchowski (12 Dec. 1902), HHStA, no. 158(V); Sommer, *Haldane*, pp. 183–84. The Kaiser precipitated a diplomatic crisis in 1896 by congratulating President Paul Kruger of the Transvaal Republic for repulsing an invasion of the republic by British mercenaries. See *W2:PE*, chap. 12.

80. Sommer, *Haldane*, pp. 183–84.

81. See Szögyényi to Goluchowsky (16 Jan. 1900), HHStA, no. 153(B), on naval strength; on closing down free trade: Bülow, 1:55–56; Lascelles to Salisbury (19 Feb. 1900), FO 64/1492; same to Lansdowne (28 Feb. 1901), ibid., 1495.

82. Swaine to Bigge (28 Dec. 1900), RA, I 62, no. 113; also same to Lascelles (20 Dec. 1895), FO 64/1351. Wilhelm believed that sooner or later Britain would be forced to join in a continental alliance. See Grierson to Bigge (21 Jan. 1898), RA, I 61, no. 32a; *HP*, 4:236.

83. Speech by Wilhelm to the War Academy (8 Feb. 1895), p. 22, Tambach Papers; Lascelles to Salisbury (21 Dec. 1898), FO 64/1439. See *W2:PE*, p. 299, for Wilhelm and Mahan.

84. Szögyényi to Goluchowski (2 July 1903), HHStA, no. 159(B).

85. Wilhelm to Theodor Schiemann (Jan. 1907), Schiemann Papers. On food: Wilhelm's speech to the War Academy (8 Feb. 1895), p. 22, Tambach Papers. Wilhelm's belief that Germany was powerless without a fleet dated to the Kruger telegram crisis of 1896. See *W2:PE*, pp. 304–5.

86. Treutler Papers, XV, part 7, p. 2; Eulenburg Papers, no. 74, part 2, p. 56; Vierhaus, *Tagebuch*, p. 428; Wilhelm's notes (3 July 1924), Rijksarchief Papers, no. 649;

87. Lascelles to Foreign Office (26 May 1899), RA, I 62, no. 12; Szögyényi to Goluchowski (16 Jan. 1900), HHStA, no. 153(B); Eckardstein, *Lebenserinnerungen*, 1:106.

88. Eulenburg Papers, no. 74, part 2, pp. 51–53; Valentini, p. 72.

89. Letter of 26 Feb. 1902, RA, X 37, no. 55.

90. Lascelles to Lansdowne (8 Feb. 1902), FO 800/129. He had used the term earlier to refer to the British cabinet. See Waters, *Potsdam and Doorn*, p. 115.

91. *BD*, 2:80–83. See, for background, Monger, *End of Isolation*, p. 66; Gren-

ville, *Salisbury and Foreign Policy*, chaps. 7, 12, 15; Kennedy, *Anglo-German Antagonism*, chap. 13.

92. Kennedy, *Anglo-German Antagonism*, pp. 253, 270; Grenville, *Salisbury and Foreign Policy*, p. 361.

93. Schulenburg-Tressow Papers, p. 33.

94. Bülow speech (12 Apr. 1904), in Kennedy, *Anglo-German Antagonism*, p. 267. For dismay at the entente elsewhere in the Wilhelmstrasse, see Vierhaus, *Tagebuch*, p. 439.

95. Lascelles to Lansdowne (7 Feb. 1905), FO 64/1616. By 1906, Wilhelm had decided that the entente would in fact promote good Franco-German relations. See Haldane, *Autobiography*, pp. 218–19.

96. Letter of 6 June 1904, Goetz, *Briefe*, p. 341.

97. Lansdowne notes (1901) of talk with Wilhelm II at Sandringham, FO 800/130. See also Lamar Cecil, "Wilhelm II and His Russian 'Colleagues,'" p. 123.

98. Bülow, 2:98–99; notes by Prince Louis Battenberg (3 May 1911), RA, Geo V O 2580, no. 1; Müller to Tirpitz (4 June 1905), Tirpitz Papers, no. 21.

99. On Nicholas II yielding to the Kaiser's efforts, see *DDF*, 2d ser., 4:506. On the two empresses, see Lamar Cecil, "William II and His Russian 'Colleagues,'" pp. 117–23.

100. Lambsdorff to Nelidov (38 Sept. 1905), "Björkö," 7:99.

101. On the HAPAG involvement, see Lamar Cecil, "Coal for the Fleet That Had to Die."

102. Ibid., p. 1000.

103. Hötzsch, *Bülows Reden*, 2:74.

104. Lichnowsky memo (23 Apr. 1904), *GP*, 20/1:202–3.

105. Bülow, 2:107–8; *GP* 20/1:262–63. On the terms being nonbinding on Germany, see *DDF*, 2d ser., 6:217–21. Baron von Eckardstein's highly colored memoirs report an account, otherwise unverified, by Prince Max Egon von Fürstenberg that Wilhelm believed Bülow wanted to make war over Morocco in order that victory would gain for him a great title and a dotation from the Kaiser. Eckardstein, *Entlassung*, p. 66.

106. Hohenlohe-Schillingsfürst, *Reichskanzlerzeit*, p. 185. The notion apparently was Kiderlen's. See Kiderlen to Foreign Office (13 Jul 1895), GFO Papers, 26/66.

107. See Rich, *Holstein*, 2:684, 692, on assurances to Alfonso. The same were also made to Edward VII in 1901. See Lansdowne memo (21 Aug. 1901), FO 800/128.

108. Bülow to Radolin (21 July 1904, 28 Apr. 1905), *GP*, 20/1:210–14, 20/2:346–47; same to Tschirschky (6 Apr. 1904), ibid., 20/1:201. See also Rich, *Holstein*, 2:684. Bülow, 2:103–4.

109. *GP*, 20/1:207–53.

110. Rich, *Holstein*, 2:681–84, 692; *GP*, 20/1:207–9. Holstein in turn was influenced by Richard von Kühlmann, chargé in Tangiers. See Kühlmann, *Erinnerungen*, p. 219.

111. Rich, *Holstein*, 2:700–703.

112. Einem, *Erinnerungen*, p. 111; report by Alfred Beit (29 Dec. 1905), FO 800/13.

113. Schoen, "Tangerfahrt des Kaisers," pp. 393–94, which is identical to the account in Schoen, *Erlebtes*, pp. 18–19.

114. Wilhelm's reluctance to land in Tangiers was quite marked, and the idea therefore can hardly have originated with him. See Howe, *Meyer*, p. 216; Valentini, p. 79; Kühlmann, *Erinnerungen*, pp. 229–30; Bülow, 2:106; Hammann, *Vorgeschichte*, pp. 204–5; *GP*, 20/1:285. Zedlitz-Trützschler, pp. 126–27, provides the sole argument that the inspiration was Wilhelm's.

115. Wilhelm's concern about his safety: Rogge, *Holstein Lebensbekenntnis*, p. 239; Schoen, *Erlebtes*, p. 19; *GP*, 20/1:279.

116. Kühlmann, *Erinnerungen*, pp. 229–30; *GP*, 20/1:285.

117. Plessen to Fürstenberg (28 Apr. 1905), Fürstenberg Papers, "Briefe vom Gefolge."

118. Eyewitness accounts: ibid.; memo by Lord Louis Battenberg (1 Apr. 1905), FO 800/130, relating Wilhelm's description; Kühlmann, *Erinnerungen*, pp. 225–36; Schöne, *Erlebtes*, pp. 20–22; Stöwer, *Pinsel und Palette*, pp. 147–51; Valentini, pp. 79–81; Valentini to his wife (1 Apr. 1905), KE, no. 341/2; *DDF*, 2d ser., 6:265–84; Karow, *Neun Jahre*, pp. 107–17; *BD*, 3:63.

119. Bülow to Wilhelm (26 Mar. 1905), *GP*, 20/1:273–77.

120. Chérisey to Delcassé (31 Mar. 1905), *DDF*, 2d ser., 6:265–66, which does not agree with Schoen's account in *GP*, 20/1:286–87, of a much more contentious conversation. On Tunis, see Battenberg memo (1 Apr. 1905), FO 800/130. On Wilhelm's talk with Mulay Abdul, see *DDF*, 2d ser., 6:283–84.

121. Schoen (at Gibraltar) to Foreign Office (31 Mar. 1905), *GP*, 20/1:286–87.

122. Schoen, *Erlebtes*, p. 22; Valentini, p. 76. Wilhelm was said to have declared later that he had planned a return to Germany on land via Italy and Austria in the event that the British, enraged over his stop at Tangiers, closed the Mediterranean. Szögyényi to Goluchowski (28 Nov. 1905), HHStA, no. 161(V).

123. On the Kaiser's ruffled sense of dignity: Lascelles to Lansdowne (7 Apr. 1905) and Lansdowne's reply (9 Apr.), FO 800/130; *DDF*, 2d ser., 8:23–24, 372–76.

124. *DDF*, 2d ser., 6:475–76.

125. Letter of 13 May 1905 in Morison, *Letters of Theodore Roosevelt*, 4:1177–79; see also Roosevelt to Taft (8 Apr. 1905), ibid., 4:1159, and to Arthur Lee (17 Oct. 1908), ibid., 6:1293; *DDF*, 2d ser., 6:511–12, 7:7–8, 126–27, 8:11–12.

126. Lansdowne to Lascelles (7 Apr. 1905), FO 800/130; S. Lee, *Edward VII*, 2:340. The king was suspicious of Wilhelm's intentions in going to Morocco before it was even certain that the Kaiser would do so. See Knollys to Lansdowne (21 Mar. 1905), FO 800/12.

127. For Wilhelm's blaming the king: Szögyényi to Goluchowski (23 Jan. 1906), HHStA, no. 163(B); Howe, *Meyer*, p. 217; his dislike for Delcassé: ibid., pp. 126–27, 216; Haldane diary (2 Sept. 1906), FO 800/13; *GP*, 21/1:9–11.

128. On France's position: Szögyényi to Goluchowski (23 Jan. 1906), HHStA, no. 163(B); Wilhelm to the grand duke of Baden (1 Mar. 1906), Fuchs, *Friedrich I.*, 4:627; on Wilhlem's being treated as a nullity: Lascelles to Lansdowne (7 Apr. 1905), FO 800/130; *GP*, 20/2:325 n.

129. Alfred Beit report (29 Dec. 1905), FO 800/13.

130. Einem, *Erinnerungen*, pp. 114–15; Bülow, 2:198, 209; also Bernhardi, *Denkwürdigkeiten*, pp. 273–74.

131. Anderson, *First Moroccan Crisis*, pp. 199–200.

132. Rich, *Holstein*, 2:707; Wilhelm to Nicholas II (27 Oct. 1904), "Björkö," 6:438–40. On the desire of both for an international conference, see *GP*, 20/2: 386–87.

133. Roosevelt to Speck von Sternburg (23 June 1905), Morison, *Letters of Theodore Roosevelt*, 4:1251.

134. Röhl, 3:2110 n. 3; a similar observation to another French officer is in Zedlitz-Trützschler, p. 174. On Wilhelm's jubilation at Delcassé's fall, see *DDF*, 2d ser., 7:66–67.

CHAPTER 5

1. Hammann, *Um den Kaiser*, pp. 1–2.

2. *GP*, 20/2:646–56.

3. Wilhelm's marginalia on a letter from Bülow (3 Dec. 1905), ibid., 679–81.

4. *DDF*, 2d ser., 7:7–8, 90, 135, 8:11–12.

5. See ibid., 7:243–44, for the queen. On Alfonso: ibid., 8:86, 429–32. For Wilhelm's annoyance at Alfonso's failure to help him, see *HP*, 4:395.

6. Lamar Cecil, "Coal for the Fleet," pp. 992–93, 998.

7. Nicholas's comment is on an undated letter from Lambsdorff (ca. 27 Oct. 1904), "Björkö," 6:440; *GP*, 19/1:303 n.

8. *GP*, 20/1:316–19; Bernstein, *Willy-Nicky Correspondence*, pp. 85–86.

9. See Wilhelm to Nicholas II (30 Oct. 1904), "Björkö," 6:443–46, and Nicholas to Lambsdorff (20 Oct. 1905 O.S.), ibid., 446–48, for drafts.

10. "Björkö," 6:457–61; Goetz, *Briefe*, pp. 351, 354 ("they not being Princes or Emperors I am unable to place them . . . on the same footing as you my equal, my cousin and friend"); *GP*, 19/1:317, 322–23.

11. Vogel, *Deutsche Russlandpolitik*, p. 99.

12. Tschirschky to Bülow (24 July 1905), *GP*, 19/2:454–56. Accounts of Björkö by those present: ibid., 452, 458–64, 502–3 (Wilhelm II), 454–56 (Tschirschky); Tower to Lansdowne (13 Aug. 1905), FO 800/130, relating an account by Prince Otto Wittgenstein; Moltke, *Moltke Erinnerungen*, pp. 325–30; Melgunoff, *Tagebuch des Letzten Zaren*, pp. 250–51.

13. *GP*, 19/2:458–64.

14. The treaty, in facsimile in Wilhelm's hand, is in Bülow, 2:140, and is also in *GP*, 19/2:465.

15. *GP*, 19/2:471.

16. Wilhelm to Nicholas (27 July 1905), in Goetz, *Briefe*, pp. 373–75.

17. Nekludov, "Entrevue de Bjoerkoe," pp. 136–38; "Björkö," 7:99–100, 105–6.

18. Wegerer, "Björkoe," pp. 477–78, 481–82.

19. Bülow, 2:139–44. See also *GP*, 19/2:467, 488–90, for Bülow's concern expressed to other German diplomats.

20. See their exchange in Bülow, 2:138–47.

21. *GP*, 19/2:499–500.

22. See *DDF*, 2d ser., 9:821, for the comparison to Delcassé. For Wilhelm and Lambsdorff's mutual suspicion: ibid., 7:304–5; "Björkö," 7:99, 105–7; *GP*, 19/2:493–96, 21:316–20.

23. *GP*, 19/2:513–14.

24. Ibid., 522–25.

25. Letter of 1 Feb. 1906, RA, X 37.

26. Bülow, 2:137.

27. Bülow's irritation at the Kaiser during the Moroccan crisis: Bülow, 2:198, 207; *GP*, 20/2:429–30; Holstein's irritation: Rogge, *Holstein Lebensbekenntnis*, p. 245; *HP*, 4:392–93.

28. *GP*, 21/1:14–15, 38–41.

29. Bülow, 2:206–10.

30. *DDF*, 2d ser., 9:387–88. The Kaiser admitted that he wanted to save face. Ibid., 9:522–23.

31. Wilhelm's marginalia on Metternich to Foreign Office (1 Mar. 1906), GFO, 239/00862.

32. *GP*, 21/1:267–68.

33. Goschen to Grey (21 Feb. 1909), FO 371/672.

34. Hötzsch, *Bülows Reden*, 2:303.

35. Szögyényi to Goluchowski (1 Aug. 1905), HHStA, no. 162(B). Szögyényi noted that Balfour and Lansdowne, formerly inclined to try to moderate the king's negative view of the Kaiser, now had come to share his mistrust.

36. Szögyényi to Goluchowski (23 Jan. 1906), HHStA, no. 163(B), and same to same (30 Jan. 1906), ibid., no. 162(V); Röhl, 3:2115.

37. *DDF*, 2d ser., 8:359–64.

38. *GP*, 21/1:125, 188, 198–201.

39. Wilhelm to Bülow (26 June 1907), ibid., 21/1:571–74.

40. Morison, *Letters of Theodore Roosevelt*, 4:242–49, 252, 319, 358.

41. *DDF*, 2d ser., 9:356–57, 399–400.

42. On the tsar's weakness: *GP*, 21/1:251–56; *DDF*, 2d ser., 8:372–76.

43. *GP*, 21/1:251–56, 316–20.

44. Lamar Cecil, "William and His Russian 'Colleagues,'" pp. 130–31.

45. *DDF*, 2d ser., 6:333–34, 389–90, 7:191–93, 8:204–5, 9:41; Hammann, *Um den Kaiser*, p. 3.

46. *GP*, 21/1:286–90, 21/2:353–56, 371–72.

47. *DDF*, 2d ser., 9:428–29. The French ambassador is in ibid., 9:533–34.

48. Ibid., 9:533–34.

49. *GP*, 21/2:360–62.

50. *DDF*, 3d ser., 1:407–8; Hammann, *Um den Kaiser*, pp. 2–3. Wilhelm's wire to Goluchowski is in *GP*, 21/1:332 n. He was still using the unfortunate phrase a month later. Hammann, "Aufzeichnungen," p. 543.

51. Szögyényi to Goluchowski (11 Dec. 1908), HHStA, no. 168(B); *GP*, 21/2: 564–67.

52. Szögyényi to Goluchowski (9 Dec. 1908), HHStA, no. 167(V).

53. Röhl, 2:2115; Wheeler-Bennett, *Knaves, Fools, and Heroes*, p. 184.

54. Röhl, 3:2137 n. 2; Rogge, *Holstein und Harden*, pp. 99–104. Lerman, *Chancellor as Courtier*, pp. 148–55, notes that 1906 marked the "watershed" of his relations with the Kaiser, which is also the argument in Cole, "Kaiser versus Chancellor."

55. Röhl, 3:2118–19; Monts, *Erinnerungen*, p. 445.

56. Bülow, 2:151.

57. Brauer, *Dienste Bismarcks*, p. 420. Holstein's assistant, Richard von Kühlmann, thought that he was "only pathologically to be explained." See Bunsen, *Zeitgenossen*, p. 86.

58. Holstein's account is in Rogge, *Holstein Lebensbekenntnis*, pp. 236–37, *HP*, 4:312–13, and Friedrich von Trotha, *Holstein*, p. 78; secondhand accounts are in Hohenlohe, *Leben*, p. 318; Friedrich Rosen, *Wanderleben*, 1:86–88.

59. Eulenburg notes (5 May 1906), Eulenburg Papers, no. 78, part 1, no. 76, part 8, p. 7; Lascelles to Grey (16 Aug. 1906), FO 371/77. Holstein made a second but unsuccessful attempt to meet Wilhelm in early April 1906 but it was too late, since his resignation had already been sent to the palace. See Meyer, *Schiemann*, p. 148.

60. Bülow, 1:372.

61. Pückler, *Diplomatenleben*, p. 65; on General Kessel, see Haller, *Aus dem Leben*, p. 299; Eulenburg Papers, no. 78, parts 3 and (together with General Plessen) 9; also on Plessen, Eulenburg Papers, nos. 75, 57–60; General Hülsen in ibid., no. 81, part 3, pp. 65–66, and Tresckow, *Fürsten*, pp. 207–8. Eulenburg believed that the military entourage was jealous of him because of his relative wealth and his access to the Kaiser. Eulenburg Papers, no. 75, pp. 39–43, 57–60.

62. *W2:PE*, pp. 237–39.

63. Holstein to the Radolins (31 Jan. and 24. Mar. 1902), *HP*, 4:250–51, 255; Waldersee diary (12 Oct. 1902), Meisner, *Denkwürdigkeiten*, 3:191; Eulenburg to Wilhelm (23 May 1902), Röhl, 2:1066 and also n. 3.

64. Hull, *Entourage*, pp. 109–11; Röhl, *Kaiser, Hof und Staat*, pp. 62–63. See Röhl, 3:2083–85, on the marriage of his son to a Roman Catholic in 1902 as an additional cause of friction.

65. Radziwill to de Robilant (31. Jan. 1904), Radziwill, *Lettres*, 3:229; see also *HP*, 4:397 n. 1.

66. Rogge, *Holstein Lebensbekenntnis*, p. 252.

67. Ibid., p. 294; Meisner, "Gespräche und Briefe Holsteins," p. 11.

68. See Eulenburg's notes (5 May 1906), Eulenburg Papers, no. 78, indicating that he believed that Bülow exaggerated the seriousness of his illness in order to stay in the background.

69. *HP*, 4:414, 419. Not quite a month after his dismissal, Holstein was convinced that Bülow had opposed it. Hammann, "Aufzeichnungen," pp. 542–43.

70. The presence of the Kaiser at Liebenberg revived memories of 1894, when Wilhelm, then Eulenburg's guest and with his participation, had decided on the removal of General Leo von Caprivi as chancellor. See *W2:PE*, pp. 208–11, and also Fuchs, *Friedrich I.*, 4:660–61.

71. Röhl, 3:2165 n. 5, 3:2137 n. 2; Rich, *Holstein*, 2:774–75.

72. Monts, *Erinnerungen*, p. 158; Hutten-Czapski, *Sechzig Jahre*, 1:471. After Wilhelm's visit to Liebenberg in early November, General Moltke, the chief of the

General Staff, emerged in rumor as likely to be the new chancellor, but there is no evidence that the Kaiser ever approached or even considered him. His candidacy, as well as the imminence of Bülow's resignation, was denied in the semi-official newspaper *Norddeutsche Allgemeine Zeitung*. See Röhl, 3:2137 n. 2.

73. Monts, *Erinnerungen*, pp. 430–31; Hutten-Czapski, *Sechzig Jahre*, 1:467. For background, see Hellige, *Rathenau Maximilian Harden*, pp. 520–23.

74. Rich, *Holstein*, 2:763.

75. Cartwright to Grey (18 June 1907), FO 371/260. For another opinion that Lecomte's invitation to Liebenberg was a mistake, see Röhl, 2:2139 n. 6.

76. Bülow Papers, no. 153, p. 19. Excerpts of the Harden articles are in Röhl, 2:2144 n. 2. See Bunsen, *Zeitgenossen*, pp. 37–38, for an interesting assessment of the gift for theatricality that Wilhelm II and Harden shared.

77. Ssuworin, *Geheimtagebuch*, p. 50. Eulenburg's denial of such rumors is in Eulenburg Papers, no. 78, part 6, p. 6; for Eulenburg's insistence that he was *not* homosexual, see ibid., no. 75, p. 73, and for his insistence that the Kaiser was not, see ibid., p. 228.

78. For arrangements on all three, see Eulenburg Papers, no. 75, p. 231, and also on Rominten, see ibid., no. 78, part 6, p. 6. Harden claimed that late in 1907 he had a letter, written by Eulenburg's physician to a medical colleague, stating that Eulenburg had bragged that he and Wilhelm had slept in the same room. See Hellige, *Rathenau Maximilian Harden*, pp. 553–54.

79. Rosner, *Erinnerungen des Kronprinzen*, p. 13; Tresckow, *Fürsten*, p. 172. For Eulenburg's belief that the generals were responsible for igniting the scandal, see Eulenburg Papers, no. 75, pp. 65, 213, 236.

80. Rich, *Holstein*, 2:778. He informed Bülow that no matter how much Eulenburg might be hurt, justice must be pursued. See Wilhelm to Bülow (18 July 1908), Bülow Papers, no. 153, p. 143.

81. Cartwright to Grey (18 June 1907), FO 371/260.

82. Letter of 4 May 1907 in Röhl, 3:2144–45.

83. Ibid., 3:2145–46.

84. This was Zedlitz's opinion. See Zedlitz-Trützschler, p. 160.

85. Röhl, 3:2160–63.

86. Wilhelm to Bülow (20 Nov. 1907), Rogge, *Holstein und Harden*, pp. 246–47. For the *Lumpenpack*, see Zedlitz-Trützschler, pp. 181–82. See Bülow, 2:308, for Wilhelm's irritation at the chancellor.

87. Zedlitz-Trützschler, pp. 183–84.

88. Hellige, *Rathenau Maximilian Harden*, p. 552.

89. Rogge, *Holstein und Harden*, p. 275.

90. Ibid., p. 290.

91. Bülow Papers, no. 153, p. 143; Röhl, 3:2184 n. 2.

92. Röhl, 3:2183 n. 3. Eulenburg had long suspected that his friendship with Wilhelm might end this way. See Haller, *Aus dem Leben*, p. 330.

93. Holstein declared in September 1907 that Bülow was "entirely consumed by the thought of remaining chancellor as long as possible." Rogge, *Holstein Lebensbekenntnis*, p. 290. For rumors of Bülow's declining position with the Kaiser, see Vierhaus, *Tagebuch*, pp. 472, 480; Rogge, *Holstein und Harden*, pp. 99–104; Cartwright to Grey (12 Jan. 1907), BD, 6:5.

94. See chap. 3, n. 112, above.

95. Bülow, 2:97; Westarp, *Konservative Politik*, 1:351.

96. Meisner, *Denkwürdigkeiten*, 3:493; Westarp, *Konservative Politik*, 1:39–50.

97. For Wilhelm on Heydebrand, see Thimme, *Front wider Bülow*, p. 126; Westarp, *Konservative Politik*, 1:348, 2:111–12. For the Kaiser's dislike of the *Kreuzzeitung*, see Bussmann, *Herbert von Bismarck*, pp. 554–55; Meisner, *Denkwürdigkeiten*, 2:88. See also Gerlach, *Erinnerungen*, pp. 82–84.

98. Röhl, 3:2020; Bülow to Holstein (4 Oct. 1902), *HP*, 4:265–66. On embracing the liberals, see Bülow, 1:456–57.

99. Radziwill, *Lettres*, 3:94–95; Hutten-Czapski, *Sechzig Jahre*, 1:256; Hohenlohe, *Leben*, pp. 91–93. Leo XIII, pope from 1878 to 1903, greatly admired Wilhelm. See Pastor, *Tagebücher*, p. 427, and Benson, *English Relations*, p. 185 n.

100. On officers, see *HP*, 3:497; also Bülow, 2:97. Wilhelm's anti-Catholic utterances are listed in Bachem, *Vorgeschichte*, 4:262–70. On the lower clergy: Möckl, *Prinzregentenzeit*. p. 470; H. S. Chamberlain, *Briefe*, 2:141–43. For his dislike of the allies of the Jesuits, the Redemptorist Order, see Raschdau, *Bismarck und Caprivi*, pp. 93–94; on his dislike of the Jesuits: Bülow, 2:11; Zedlitz-Trützschler, pp. 85–86.

101. Rogge, *Holstein Lebensbekenntnis*, p. 157; Bülow, 3:253.

102. Ziekursch, *Geschichte*, 3:3, 9, and Bülow, 2:7 on apes; for Wilhelm's peremptory manner with deputies, see Pachnicke, *Führende Männer*, p. 223; Payer, *Bethmann Hollweg bis Ebert*, p. 16; Schiffer, *Leben*, pp. 58–59. The deputies, he declared in 1907, were "absolutely not mature enough for a constitution." Zedlitz-Trützschler, pp. 181–82.

103. There had been an earlier crisis with the Catholic Center when Bülow had publicly defended the army officer corp's use of dueling. See Cole, "Kaiser versus Chancellor," p. 42.

104. Ibid., pp. 48–51; see also Zedlitz-Trützschler, pp. 185–86; Radziwill, *Lettres*, 3:273.

105. Bülow, 2:272–73; Crothers, *Elections of 1907*, chap. 3.

106. Crothers, *Elections of 1907*, p. 181.

107. Szögyény to Aehrenthal (5 Feb. 1907), HHStA, no. 165(V); Keim, *Erlebtes*, p. 118.

108. Crothers, *Elections of 1907*, p. 182. The painting by Friedrich Skarbina depicting this moment is reproduced in Bülow, 2:280.

109. Bülow, 2:279.

110. Lerman, *Chancellor as Courtier*, pp. 174–86; Bunsen, *Zeitgenossen*, p. 90.

111. Zedlitz-Trützschler, pp. 161–62; Brocke, "System Althoff," p. 39.

112. Portrait of Posadowsky is in Bunsen, *Zeitgenossen*, p. 90; Bülow, 1:470–71; on how he bored Wilhelm, see Kiderlen, 2:34–35. Wilhelm also disliked Posadowsky's wife, whom he found meddlesome. Lerman, *Chancellor as Courtier*, p. 176.

113. Hammann, *Um den Kaiser*, p. 3; Monts, *Erinnerungen*, pp. 245–46; Bülow, 2:214–15, 256–57, 300–301; Pogge von Strandmann, *Rathenau Tagebuch*, p. 141.

114. Brauer, *Dienste Bismarcks*, p. 416.

115. Monts, *Erinnerungen*, pp. 441–42; Bülow, 2:256–57.

116. Kiderlen, 2:32–37. See Lamar Cecil, *Diplomatic Service*, p. 301, for Schoen's relations with Wilhelm.

117. Müller diary (9 Apr. 1905), Müller Papers, no. 3. The Austrian envoy, Count Szögyényi, summed Schoen up as invariably pleasant, hard-working, of modest talent, and lacking in independence and energy. Szögyényi to Aehrenthal (7 July 1910), HHStA, no. 168(B).

118. Nostitz, *Bismarcks*, p. 163.

CHAPTER 6

1. "H.M.'s conversations with ambassadors: for that no one less suitable." Bülow's undated notes, Bülow Papers, no. 33; Bülow to Loebell (21 Aug. 1909), Loebell Papers, no. 5. For an example of Wilhelm II's obtuse diplomatic style and the alarm it caused the chancellor, see Bülow to Wolff (16 May 1924), Wolff Papers.

2. Lascelles to Lansdowne (12 June 1905), FO 800/130. See also Tirpitz's notes (4 Jan. 1905), Tirpitz Papers, no. 21; Lascelles to Salisbury (23 Dec. 1898), FO 64/1439. For other criticism of the Kaiser's personality as an obstruction to diplomacy: Eulenburg Papers, no. 80, p. 68; Goschen to Nicolson (21 Oct. 1910), FO 800/62, registering Kiderlen's dismay; Grey to Goschen (6 Jan. 1913), FO 800/62, for Ambassador Lichnowsky; Goschen to Grey (10 Jan. 1913), ibid., for Bethmann.

3. Bülow's notes (30 Oct. 1905), Bülow Papers, no. 153, p. 116; Meisner, "Gespräche," p. 8. See also Bülow to Wilhelm II (17 June 1908), Bülow Papers, no. 33, in which the chancellor warns him about the unfortunate effect of his indiscretions.

4. See, for example, Christopher Howard, *Goschen*, p. 200. Bülow made much the same claim. See Lascelles to Lansdowne (31 Jan. 1902, 28 Dec. 1904), FO 64/1551, 1594.

5. For representative expressions of the desire for good relations on the part of Metternich, see *HP*, 4:244–46; for Holstein: Rogge, *Holstein Lebensbekenntnis*, p. 231; *HP*, 4:376–77; Eckardstein, *Entlassung*, p. 37; Kühlmann, *Erinnerungen*, p. 373; Kiderlen, 2:41–78; Lerchenfeld-Koefering, *Erinnerungen*, pp. 410–11.

6. Christopher Howard, *Goschen*, pp. 184–85; *HP*, 4:254.

7. Pless, *Better Left Unsaid*, p. 193, for the king; Hardinge to Lascelles (19 May 1908), FO 800/11.

8. Metternich to Bülow (1 Aug. 1908), Metternich notes (27 Nov. 1908), Tirpitz Papers, no. 54; Bülow, 2:432–35. On Metternich's outspokenness, see Meisner, *Denkwürdigkeiten*, 2:431; Einem, *Erinnerungen*, p. 131. On Widenmann, see his *Marine-Attaché* and his correspondence with naval authorities in Berlin in Tambach Papers, no. 26, 91/00628–31, 00695–700, 00756–66. See also Tirpitz, *Erinnerungen*, pp. 177–78; *PD*, 1:42–43, 51, 72.

9. Bülow, 2:438; for Metternich on Bülow, see *HP*, 4:244–46.

10. For Wilhelm's opinion on Metternich expressed to his uncle, see *GP*, 15:559–60. For his reservations about the envoy, see his marginalia on a Metternich

report (3 Mar. 1909), Tirpitz Papers, no. 54; Wilhelm to Bülow (3 Apr. 1909), ibid.; Wilhelm's marginalia on Widenmann to Reichsmarineamt (27 Mar. 1909), Tambach Papers, no. 26, 91/00756–66; Bülow, 2:429–30; Görlitz, *Der Kaiser*, pp. 91–92.

11. *BD*, 6:139; Bunsen, *Zeitgenossen*, p. 80.

12. Swaine to Bigge (1 Jan. 1901), RA, I 62, no. 114; Szögyényi to Goluchowski (29 Jan. 1902), HHStA, no. 158(V).

13. Szögyényi to Goluchowski (3 Jan. 1906), HHStA, no. 162(V).

14. Zedlitz-Trützschler, pp. 132–33. When a point arose on which Lascelles and Wilhelm did not agree, their exchanges could become quite pointed, with the ambassador baiting the Kaiser and getting the same in return. See Davidson to Bigge (25 Aug. 1912), RA, Geo V O 320A, no. 1.

15. Radziwill, *Lettres*, 3:7; Szögyényi to Aehrenthal (19 Aug. 1907), HHStA, no. 166(B); Harry Young, *Lichnowsky*, p. 206 n. 40. For the general disappointment in Berlin that a more distinguished figure had not been sent to Berlin, see Szögyényi to Aehrenthal (16 Aug. 1908), HHStA, no. 167(V).

16. Esher to Bigge (9 May 1909), RA, Geo V Q 724, no. 1. Milner, *Picture Gallery*, p. 233.

17. Lansdowne to Lascelles (1 Apr. 1901), FO 800/128; Paléologue, *Three Critical Years*, pp. 119–20; also Lansdowne to Lascelles (9 Apr. 1905), and Lascelles to Tower (20 Aug. 1905), FO 800/130; *GP*, 17:28.

18. Wilson, *Campbell-Bannerman*, pp. 537–38.

19. Minute by Grey (19 Apr. 1909), FO 371/672; Grey to Lascelles (1 Jan. 1906), FO 800/61; Brett, *Journals and Letters*, 2:344; Grey to Goschen (6 Jan. 1913), FO 800/62.

20. Gleichen, *Memoirs*, pp. 262–65, and see pp. 282–83, for Gleichen's dislike of the Kaiser. Knollys to Lascelles (27 July 1904), FO 800/12, for Wilhelm's criticism of Gleichen. Colonel Frederick Trench was the British military attaché from 1906 to 1910, but his five audiences with the Kaiser were inconsequential. See *BD*, 6:20–21, 109, 176–78, 234–36, 252–53, a source that also indicates how rarely Wilhelm saw Captains Dumas, Heath, and Watson, the British naval attachés from 1906 to 1913. He much admired Admiral John Jellicoe. See Wilhelm to Lady Jellicoe (n.d. [ca. 1936]), Jellicoe Papers. He corresponded with Adm. the hon. Victor Montagu: RMA papers, no. 123. Wilhelm liked Admiral E. Commerell, an officer of German descent. See Waters, *Potsdam and Doorn*, pp. 175–76. Another friend was Captain Mark Ker, for whom see Admiral Müller to Montagu (22 May 1908), RMA Papers, no. 123; Ker to Wilhelm (7 Aug. 1908, 4 Jan. 1911), Tambach Papers, no. 31, 19/00048–55, 00098–99.

21. On "Copenhagening": Glücksburg papers, no. 36-B/1; Lascelles to Lansdowne (28 Dec. 1904), FO 64/1594; Beit report (29 Dec. 1905), ibid., 800/13; Müller diary (18 Mar. 1911), Müller Papers, no. 4; also Moltke, *Moltke Erinnerungen*, pp. 304–7.

22. Letter of Nov. 1906 in S. Lee, *Edward VII*, 2:333; Newton, *Lansdowne*, pp. 334–35; Fisher, *Memories*, 1:22, 34–35, 49; report by Alfred Beit (29 Dec. 1905), FO 800/13, is the basis for Esher's memo to Edward VII (18 Jan. 1906), in Brett, *Journals and Letters*, 2:136–38. See also Marder, *Fear God and Dreadnought*, 2:146.

23. Hardinge to Lascelles (26 Feb. 1906), Hardinge Papers, no. 13.

24. Note by Lecomte (n.d. [ca. Mar. 1907]), *DDF*, 2d ser., 10:704.

25. Gleichen, *Memoirs*, p. 337.

26. See Bülow, 1:115–16 and also his *Deutsche Politik*, pp. 19–20, for his analysis of the problem. On the chancellor and Tirpitz, see Bülow, 2:245. Bülow's halfhearted praise of Tirpitz, often mixed with criticism, is in ibid., 1:414, 432, 2:229, 3:122; Steinberg, *Yesterday's Deterrent*, p. 116. For Tirpitz's opinion of Bülow, see his *Erinnerungen*, p. 117, and *PD* 1:161–62; Thimme, *Front wider Bülow*, p. 185. Bülow's extensive *Denkwürdigkeiten* do not reveal much interest in the navy.

27. The essential study is Berghahn, *Tirpitz-Plan*; see also Deist, *Flottenpolitik*; Kaulisch, *Tirpitz*; Lambi, *German Power Politics*.

28. Rogge, *Holstein Lebensbekenntnis*, p. 292; *PD*, 1:51, 94–96, 100–104, 112–15; Bülow, 2:432. For Holstein's influence, see Lambi, *German Power Politics*, pp. 282–83.

29. Lambi, *German Power Politics*, p. 295; *PD*, 1:117–20.

30. Wilhelm to Schiemann (1 Jan. 1907), Schiemann Papers. On the cost of ships and wars, see Wilhelm's comments on a letter from Montagu (11 Apr. 1907), RMA Papers, no. 123.

31. Szögyényi to Goluchowski (2 July 1903), HHStA, no. 159(B); Eulenburg Papers, no. 74, part 2, pp. 51–53; Wilhelm's marginalia on Coerper to Reichsmarineamt (17 Feb. 1903), Tambach Papers, no. 26, 91/00280.

32. On Wilhlem's support of Tirpitz within the navy: Tirpitz to Hollmann (13 May 1901), Tirpitz to Wilhelm (n.d. [ca. May 1901]), Wilhelm to Bülow (n.d. [ca. June 1901]), Tirpitz notes of his visit to Wilhelm at Huburtusstock (10 Dec. 1903), all in Tirpitz Papers, no. 20. For Tirpitz's acknowledgment of the Kaiser's crucial role in navalism, see his letter to the crown prince (15 Apr. 1909), ibid., no. 8, and his *Erinnerungen*, p. 134.

33. For examples of Wilhelm's technical advice to Tirpitz, see his letters to the admiral (28 Apr., 7 May, and 20 July 1905), Müller to same (4 June 1905), Tirpitz to Wilhelm (30 July 1905), all in Tirpitz Papers, no. 22; Tirpitz diary (11 Sept. 1904), ibid., no. 21; Müller to Tirpitz (9 Mar. 1905), ibid., no. 207; Trampold to Tirpitz (8 May 1907), RMA Papers, no. 2009; Müller diary (4 Jun. 1905), Müller Papers, no. 3; Görlitz, *Der Kaiser*, pp. 62–63. For competitions, see Wilhelm's order (17 Mar. 1906), Tirpitz Papers, no. 23. For an interesting account of Wilhelm's nature and how Tirpitz constituted an exception among his courtiers, see Mutius to Thimme (1 Nov. 1933), Thimme Papers, no. 18. See also Monts, *Erinnerungen*, p. 195.

34. Tirpitz notes (16 June 1897), Tirpitz Papers, no. 4; Tirpitz notes (12 Oct. 1903), ibid., no. 20; Tirpitz to Trotha (n.d. [ca. 27 July 1915]), ibid., no. 169.

35. The letter is printed in *GP*, 24:32–34. For Wilhelm's annoyance at Esher, see Lascelles to Grey (17 Feb. 1908), FO 800/61.

36. The original of the letter to Tweedmouth is in the Tweedmouth Papers. On the affair, see Repington, *Vestigia*, chap. 21; *BD*, 6:132–41; *GP*, 24:32–35; S. Lee, *Edward VII*, 2:604–10.

37. Letter of 20 Feb. 1908 in Tweedmouth Papers; see also Grey to Tweedmouth (18 Feb. 1908), *BD*, 6:133.

38. Hardinge to Davidson (7 Mar. 1908), Hardinge Papers, no. 14; Brett, *Journals and Letters*, 2:344; see Widenmann, *Marine-Attaché*, pp. 105–6, for Tweedmouth's indiscretion.

39. Repington, *Vestigia*, pp. 284–85. Bülow also favored publication. See Bülow to Wilhelm (18 Mar. 1908), RMA Papers, no. 118; *GP*, 24:40.

40. The king's annoyance at Wilhelm: Hardinge to Lascelles (25 Feb. 1908), FO 800/11; Brett, *Journals and Letters*, 2:285–86, 288–89; S. Lee, *Edward VII*, 2:606; at Esher, *GP*, 24:44–46; at the *Times*: Edward VII to Admiral Fisher (10 Mar. 1908), RA, Vic Add MSS U 38, no. 8; Ballin to Müller (11 Mar. 1908), RMA Papers, no. 118.

41. Prince of Wales letter (24 Aug. 1908), Hardinge Papers, no. 14.

42. *BD*, 7:140; also Grey to Lascelles (22 Feb. 1908), FO 800/11.

43. Hardinge memo of talk with Bülow (11 Feb. 1909), RA, W 55, no. 2; Cranley to Tyrrell (9 Apr. 1908), FO 800/61.

44. Bülow's denial of knowledge in Lascelles to Grey (28 Feb. 1908), FO 800/61; see Bülow to Wilhelm (7 Mar. 1908), Tambach Papers, no. 31, 19/00035–36, for Metternich. The state secretary of the Foreign Office, Baron Wilhelm von Schoen, was also careful to deny being privy to the letter. See Lascelles to Grey (6 Mar. 1908), FO 800/61; *BD*, 7:141. See also *GP*, 24:39.

45. Szögyényi to Aehrenthal (3, 18 Mar. 1908), HHStA, no. 166(B).

46. August Eulenburg to Müller (30 Aug. 1908), RMA Papers, no. 118.

47. Diary entry (11 Mar. 1908), Vierhaus, *Tagebuch*, p. 481; similar language is in Holstein's letter to Bülow (6 Mar. 1908), *HP*, 4:516. See Bülow, 2:325, for his belief that there would soon be another crisis.

48. *BD*, 6:184–90.

49. Goetz, *Briefe*, p. 394; the king's annoyance is in *BD*, 6:200 n. B.

50. Bülow, 1:454. Eulenburg Papers, no. 74, part 2, pp. 48–49, makes a similar observation about the verbal indiscretions; see Hardinge memo (11 Feb. 1909), RA, W 55, no. 2, on Bülow's assurances that in the future there would be no more such outbursts from Wilhelm.

51. Clark, *A Good Innings*, p. 116; also Bülow, 1:340; Repington, *Vestigia*, p. 86. See Lamar Cecil, "History as Family Chronicle," pp. 105–6, for a fuller discussion.

52. See reverse of letter of Tyrrell to Stuart-Wortley (8 Nov. 1907), Montagu-Stuart-Wortley Papers, on the arrangements; on the stay, see Stuart-Wortley to wife (1, 2, 7 Dec. 1907), ibid.; Gleichen, *Memoirs*, pp. 317–18; Müller diary (21 Nov. 1907), Müller Papers, no. 3; on the Kaiser's friendship with Stuart-Wortley, see Radziwill, *Lettres*, 4:51.

53. Several sources show Wilhelm, while at Highcliffe, keeping Bülow informed: Stemrich to Kiderlen-Wächter (10 June 1909), Kiderlen Papers, Box 4/004 0155/000 7060; Meyer, *Schiemann*, pp. 163–65; Thimme, *Front wider Bülow*, p. 315; Valentini, p. 100 n. 1. Bülow denied this in his memo (25 June 1910), Loebell Papers, no. 6; Meyer, *Schiemann*, p. 164; Bülow, 3:52.

54. Hiller von Gaertringen, *Bülows Denkwürdigkeiten*, p. 124. Wilhelm apparently did not inform the chancellor about the content of these talks.

55. Ibid., p. 127, argues that the initiator of the interview cannot be determined but that most people believed it to be Wilhelm. Evidence that the idea in fact

originated with the Kaiser can be found in Hardinge to Edward VII (28 Oct. 1908), RA, W 54, no. 124, and in Gleichen, *Memoirs*, pp. 317–18.

56. Trefz, "Bülows Denkwürdigkeiten," p. 381.

57. Bülow's complaints in Bülow Papers, no. 34, pp. 2–4; *HP*, 4:565; Münz, *Bülow*, p. 228; Bülow, 2:337–39; see also Hiller von Gaertringen, *Bülows Denkwürdigkeiten*, pp. 129–30.

58. Vierhaus, *Tagebuch*, p. 494; Hammann, *Um den Kaiser*, pp. 66–67; Flotow to Aehrenthal (3 Nov. 1908), HHStA, no. 166(B). The document was typed or neatly written, contrary to Bülow's claim in Bülow, 2:338. See ibid., p. 382; Gleichen, *Memoirs*, p. 319 n. 1; Bülow to Jenisch (11 Oct. 1908), Bülow Papers, no. 35; Thimme, *Front wider Bülow*, pp. 391–92.

59. Bülow Papers, no. 34, pp. 7–8.

60. Jenisch to Wilhelm (15 Oct. 1908), HA, Rep. 53a, no. 58. This important letter has been deposited here, as though to hide it, in a file otherwise concerned with Gustav Adolf Cardinal von Hohenlohe-Schillingsfürst, brother of the former chancellor. See also Bülow to Jenisch (11, 15 Nov. 1908), Bülow Papers, no. 33.

61. Bülow to Jenisch (11 Nov. 1908), Bülow Papers, no. 33.

62. Bülow, 2:339.

63. Bülow to Jenisch (11 Oct. 1908), Bülow Papers, no. 35. These reflected Jenisch's advice. See his letter to Wilhelm (15 Oct. 1908), HA, Rep. 53a, no. 58.

64. Bernhardi, *Denkwürdigkeiten*, p. 332; Bülow, 2:339, 353. Müller's reply is unknown, but it seems likely that he warned against publication.

65. Wilhelm to Stuart-Wortley (15 Oct. 1908), Montagu-Stuart-Wortley Papers. See also Szögyényi to Aehrenthal (9 Dec. 1908), HHStA, no. 167(V).

66. A facsimile is printed in Bülow, 2:353.

67. Wilhelm to Stuart-Wortley (15 Oct. 1908), Montagu-Stuart-Wortley Papers; *GP*, 24:168.

68. Letter (31 Oct. 1908), Montagu-Stuart-Wortley Papers.

69. *BD*, 6:225. On the reaction in Britain, see *BD*, 6:165; Bülow, 2:355. The only sympathetic note sounded in London was by Mary Montagu, the daughter of Wilhelm's friend Admiral Montagu. See HA, Rep. 53, no. 190.

70. *BD*, 6:201, 209.

71. Findlay to Hardinge (11 Nov. 1908), Hardinge Papers, no. 11.

72. Vierhaus, *Tagebuch*, p. 489. A similar observation is in Radziwill, *Lettres*, 4:45–46. For a sampling of other opinion, all of it negative, see *HP*, 4:591; Weber, *Max Weber*, pp. 447–48; Westarp, *Konservative Politik*, 1:49–50.

73. Bülow, 2:353–54.

74. Hiller von Gaertringen, *Bülows Denkwürdigkeiten*, pp. 134–35, argues against this; also Schoen, *Erlebtes*, p. 108.

75. On lèse-majesté, see Flotow to Aehrenthal (10 Nov. 1908), HHStA, no. 167(V); on Wilhelm's demeanor on receiving the news, see Wilhelm to Bülow (4 Nov. 1908), Reichskanzlei Papers, no. 810, p. 10; Bülow to Wilhelm (4 Nov. 1908), Bülow Papers, no. 33.

76. Eyewitness accounts are in Bunsen, *Zeitgenossen*, pp. 82–83; Hiller von Gaertringen, *Bülows Denkwürdigkeiten*, p. 16 n. 251; *BD*, 6:212–15. For the chancellor's worry, see Szögyényi to Vienna (16 Nov. 1908). Wilhelm had Bülow

informed that when he addressed the Reichstag he was very pointedly to remind the deputies that the Kaiser's sole aim in granting the interview had been to improve Anglo-German relations. Jenisch to Bülow (4 Nov. 1908), Bülow Papers, no. 33. On Bülow's reluctance to rise in defense of Wilhelm, see Hammann, "Aufzeichnungen," pp. 545–47; Hammann, *Um den Kaiser*, p. 71; Thimme, *Front wider Bülow*, p. 120; Loebell Papers, no. 27, part 2, p. 55.

77. The Kaiserin, who disliked her husband's intimacy with Fürstenberg, did not want him to go to Donaueschingen. Bülow Papers, no. 34, p. 64. On the Austrian visit, see Findlay to Hardinge (8 Dec. 1908), Hardinge Papers, no. 11; Wilhelm to Franz Ferdinand (16 Dec. 1908), Franz Ferdinand Papers.

78. Radziwill, *Lettres*, 4:46–47; Findlay to Hardinge (11 Nov. 1908), Hardinge Papers, no. 11.

79. "*Justiz-Mord*" in Kessel diary (19 Nov. 1908), HA, Rep. 53a, no. 27; Findlay to Hardinge (8 Dec. 1908), Hardinge Papers, no. 11.

80. Jenisch to Bülow (13, 14 Nov. 1908), Bülow Papers, no. 33; Valentini, pp. 101–2.

81. There is some evidence that Bülow deliberately wanted Wilhelm to stay at Donaueschingen so that he could be reproached for avoiding Berlin in a time of crisis. See Eckardstein, *Entlassung*, pp. 64–65; Brabant, *Hausen*, pp. 238–40. For efforts by the retinue to persuade Wilhelm to return to Berlin, see Müller diary (6 Nov. 1908), Müller Papers, no. 3; Görlitz, *Der Kaiser*, p. 70; Valentini, pp. 101–2. On Wilhelm's agitated state, see also Zedlitz-Trützschler, p. 194; Findlay to Hardinge (8 Dec. 1908), Hardinge Papers, no. 11.

82. On the dancing tradition: Schönburg-Waldenburg, *Erinnerungen*, pp. 171–72; Eulenburg, *Mit dem Kaiser*, 1:79, 111.

83. Zedlitz-Trützschler, pp. 216–17, says the costume was a tutu, but his account is spiteful and incorret in various details. Valentini's account seems to be the most reliable. See his "Das Drama von Donaueschingen," in KE, no. 341/1, pp. 15–22; his diary (14 Nov. 1908) in Thimme Papers, no. 26; and Valentini, p. 103. Kessel is erroneous in his diary (11–14 Nov. 1908) in HA, Rep. 53a, no. 27.

84. On Hülsen's swift rise, see Zobeltitz, *Chronik*, 1:348. On their relations: ibid.; Hutten-Czapski, *Sechzig Jahre*, 1:410–13; Meyer, *Schiemann*, pp. 156, 160; Radziwill, *Lettres*, 1:108; Janssen, *Graue Exzellenz*, p. 105; Eulenburg, *Mit dem Kaiser*, 1:63, 2:176; Raschdau, *Bismarck und Caprivi*, p. 200; Bülow, 1:175. On new faces in the entourage, see Schönburg-Waldenburg, *Erinnerungen*, p. 199; on desire to please, see Raschdau, *Weimar*, p. 128. For Wilhelm's estimation of Hülsen: Zedlitz-Trützschler, p. 195; Valentini, "Das Drama von Donaueschingen," in KE, no. 341/1, pp. 15–22.

85. On the sense of expectancy about the meeting: Vierhaus, *Tagebuch*, p. 492; Hammann, *Um den Kaiser*, p. 72. For Bülow's preparation for the encounter, see Meyer, *Schiemann*, pp. 159–61; see also Ballin to Francke (29 Oct. 1908), Francke Papers, no. 6. For Wilhelm on the eve of the meeting, see Szögyényi to Aehrenthal (9 Dec. 1908), HHStA, no. 167(V); for Bülow, see *HP*, 4:594–96. For Holstein's role in advising the chancellor, see Rogge, *Holstein und Harden*, pp. 360–65, 386–90.

86. Bülow's contemporaneous accounts are in Szögyényi to Vienna (26 Nov. 1908), HHStA, no. 166(B), and in same to Aehrenthal (18 Nov. 1908), ibid.; *HP*,

4:596; Hammann, *Um den Kaiser*, p. 73, and his "Aufzeichnungen," pp. 545–46. The chancellor's later account, *Denkwürdigkeiten* (Bülow 2:377–81), is often fanciful.

87. Bülow, 2:380.

88. The icy reception is in Radziwill, *Lettres*, 4:49.

89. Szögyényi to Aehrenthal (18 Nov. 1908), HHStA, no. 167(V).

90. Thimme, *Front wider Bülow*, p. 123.

91. For Wilhelm's description of his state, see his letter to Prince Fürstenberg (25 Nov. 1908), Fürstenberg Papers, miscellany. Other depictions are in Oppenheimer to Grey (16 Jan. 1909), FO 471/671; Valentini, p. 105; Valentini diary (15 Nov. 1908), Thimme Papers, no. 26; Zedlitz-Trützschler, p. 194; Viktoria Luise, *Tochter des Kaisers*, pp. 58–59; Rosner, *Erinnerungen des Kronprinzen*, pp. 92–94; Topham, *Memories*, pp. 156–57, and Topham, *Chronicles*, pp. 200–201. Bülow's account of the crisis is in Bülow, 2:382–87, and in Bülow Papers, no. 34, p. 134.

92. Rosner, *Erinnerungen des Kronprinzen*, pp. 92–94; also Meister, *Yesterdays*, p. 161; Bunsen, *Zeitgenossen*, p. 85; Bülow, 2:386–88.

93. Wilhelm to Fürstenberg and Plessen to same (25 Nov. 1908), Fürstenberg Papers, miscellany; August Eulenburg to Bülow (25, 26 Nov., 3 Dec. 1908), Bülow Papers, no. 33, and Bülow's memoir on the crisis, no. 34, p. 134. Szögyényi to Vienna (3 Dec. 1908), HHStA, no. 166(B); Topham, *Chronicles*, pp. 200–201; also see Topham, *Fatherland*, pp. 156–57.

94. Wilhelm to Franz Ferdinand (16 Dec. 1908), Franz Ferdinand Papers.

95. Hardinge to Findlay (17 Dec. 1908), Hardinge Papers, no. 13. The queen wrote in response to Wilhelm's inquiry about Edward VII's health. See also Hardinge, *Old Diplomacy*, p. 171.

96. Wilhelm to Franz Ferdinand (16 Dec. 1908), Franz Ferdinand Papers.

97. Wilhelm to Fürstenberg (23 Dec. 1908), Fürstenberg Papers, miscellany; Szögyényi to Vienna (3 Dec. 1908), HHStA, no. 166(B); Kessel diary (9 Nov. 1908), HA, Rep. 53a, no. 27; Zedlitz-Trützschler, pp. 194, 196, 198–99.

98. Wilhelm to Fürstenberg (23 Dec. 1908), Fürstenberg Papers, miscellany.

99. Szögyényi to Aehrenthal (9 Dec. 1908), HHStA, no. 166(B).

100. Radziwill, *Lettres*, 4:54, 64, 70; Valentini, p. 105; Loebell Papers, no. 27, part 2, p. 56; Augusta Victoria to Bülow (13, 24 Nov. 1908), Bülow Papers, no. 33.

101. Wilhelm to the dowager grand duchess of Baden (5 Feb. 1909), HA, Rep. 53a, no. 20.

102. Radziwill, *Lettres*, 4:59–60.

103. Undated, unsigned memo of a talk with Hale, FO 371/462; Hammann, *Um den Kaiser*, pp. 73–74; Johnson, *Remembered Yesterdays*, pp. 229–37.

104. Johnson, *Remembered Yesterdays*, p. 229. For Roosevelt's view of the interview, see Morison, *Letters of Theodore Roosevelt*, 6:1163–64, 1292–93, 1466–67.

105. Northcliffe to Tyrrell (21 Aug. 1908), FO 371/462.

106. Undated, unsigned memo of talk with Hale, FO 371/462; Johnson, *Remembered Yesterdays*, pp. 229–32.

107. Northcliffe to Tyrrell (21 Aug. 1908), FO 371/462.

108. On the payoff, see Bülow to Wilhelm (21 Oct. 1908), Bülow Papers, no. 112; Bülow Papers, no. 34, p. 115. On Roosevelt's role in preventing publication,

see his letter to Arthur Lee (17 Oct. 1908), Morison, *Letters of Theodore Roosevelt*, 6:1292–93.

109. Hardinge to Goschen (17 Nov. 1908), Hardinge Papers, no. 13.

110. Metternich to Knollys (24 Nov. 1908), Hardinge Papers, no. 14; Goschen to Hardinge (26 Feb. 1909), ibid., no. 15. The interview was published in part in *Nineteenth Century* 64 (1908): 903–23.

111. Einem, *Erinnerungen*, p. 122.

112. Szögyényi to Aehrenthal (17 Feb. 1909), HHStA, no. 168(B); Metternich to Bülow (17 Nov. 1908), Tirpitz Papers, no. 54. Wilhelm was pleased with the visit. See Müller diary (13 Feb. 1909), Müller Papers, no. 3. Bülow, 2:419–23, claims that the king was agreeable with him. On the king's reaction to the interview, see his minute on an unsigned, undated memo of a talk with Hale, FO 371/462; Edward VII to Knollys (25 Nov. 1908), RA, W 53, no. 37; S. Lee, *Edward VII*, 2:622–23.

113. S. Lee, *Edward VII*, 2:672–77; on the amazement of the British guests, see Wilhelm to Franz Ferdinand (12 Feb. 1909), Franz Ferdinand Papers. On Hardinge's efforts with Northcliffe, see Hardinge to Knollys (20 Nov. 1908), RA, W 54, no. 132.

114. Hardinge memo (11 Feb. 1909), *BD*, 6:232.

115. Wilhelm to Fürstenberg (23 Dec. 1908), Fürstenberg Papers, miscellany.

116. Valentini, p. 106. The Kaiserin, House Minister Count August zu Eulenburg, and Maximilian Beseler, Prussian minister of justice, were also probably involved in arranging this. See Vierhaus, *Tagebuch*, pp. 502–3; Eulenburg to Bülow (18 Dec. 1908), Bülow Papers, no. 74; Loebell Papers, part 2, p. 56.

117. Accounts by Wilhelm: Valentini, pp. 106–8; Meyer, *Schiemann*, pp. 159–61; Reischach to Fürstenberg (12 Mar. and 12 Apr. 1909), Fürstenberg Papers, "Briefe vom Gefolge." Bülow's account is in Bülow, 2:446–49. Other accounts, none of them very informative, are August Eulenburg to Fürstenberg (12 Mar. 1909), Fürstenberg Papers, "Briefe vom Gefolge"; Szögyényi to Vienna (13 Mar. 1909), HHStA no. 167(B); Valentini diary (11 Mar. 1909), Thimme Papers, no. 26; Zedlitz-Trützschler, pp. 223–24.

118. Valentini, p. 108 n.

119. Radziwill, *Lettres*, 4:71; Goschen to Grey (1 Apr. 1909), FO 371/670; Zedlitz-Trützschler, p. 224.

120. Lerman, *Chancellor as Courtier*, p. 234. Bülow believed Fürstenberg, who allegedly had come to Berlin with detectives to shadow the chancellor, was working against him. See Bülow, 2:268, and Eckardstein, *Entlassung*, pp. 75–76.

121. Vierhaus, *Tagebuch*, p. 521; Valentini, p. 121. Lerman, *Chancellor as Courtier*, pp. 229–34, discusses the opposition to Bülow of various powerful figures. See *BD*, 7:437, for Hatzfeldt; on Chelius, see his letter to Fürstenberg (3 Oct. 1909), Fürstenberg Papers, "Bethmann, Jagow . . ."; on Reischach, see his letter to Fürstenberg (2 Jan. 1913), ibid., "Briefe vom Gefolge"; Bunsen, *Zeitgenossen*, p. 62; for Fürstenberg, see Bülow Papers, no. 153, p. 89; Bülow, 3:27; for Count von Seckendorff, see Vierhaus, *Tagebuch*, p. 499; Christopher Howard, *Goschen*, pp. 184–85; *BD*, 7:51–52.

122. Valentini, p. 105.

123. On the financial reforms: Witt, *Finanzpolitik*; Reinhold von Sydow, "Fürst

Bülow und die Reichsfinanzreform 1908/09," in Thimme, *Front wider Bülow*, pp. 105–35; Westarp, "Konservative Partei"; Westarp, *Konservative Politik*, 1:51–78. 124. Bülow, 2:514; Radziwill, *Lettres*, 4:86–87; Eckardstein, *Entlassung*, pp. 70–72; Monts, *Erinnerungen*, pp. 25–26, 145–46, 150–51.

125. Monts's spurning of the office is in Hutten-Czapski, *Sechzig Jahre*, 2:1. On the mutual dislike, see Bülow, 1:27–28, 125–28, 2:99–100, 3:468–69; Valentini, pp. 110, 121–22; Monts, *Erinnerungen*, p. 158.

126. Valentini, p. 121.

127. Ibid., p. 122; Widenmann, *Marine-Attaché*, p. 66.

128. Bülow to Loebell (29 Jan. 1912), Loebell Papers, no. 7. Bülow later claimed that Bethmann was third on his list of three candidates. See Hiltebrandt, *Erinnerungen*, p. 32. For Bethmann's reluctance, see Loebell Papers, no. 27, part 2, p. 61.

129. Liebert, *Erinnerungen*, p. 186.

130. Bülow to Loebell (11 Aug. 1909), Loebell Papers, no. 6.

CHAPTER 7

1. Spitzemberg diary (29 June 1910), Vierhaus, *Tagebuch*, p. 523; Wilhelm, *Ereignisse und Gestalten*, p. 105; Mutius Papers, p. 191.

2. Thimme Papers, no. 17, pp. 10–11; Wilhelm, *Ereignisse und Gestalten*, p. 105; Vietsch, *Bethmann Hollweg*, pp. 27–28.

3. Westarp, *Konservative Politik*, 1:378; Spitzemberg diary (14 Mar. 1903, 23 Mar. 1905) Vierhaus, *Tagebuch*, pp. 427–28, 446.

4. Jarausch, *Enigmatic Chancellor*, p. 66. For Bethmann's angst, see Pless, *Better Left Unsaid*, p. 286.

5. Lichnowsky to Bülow (8 Apr. 1910), Bülow Papers, no. 98; Zimmermann to Kiderlen (25 Aug. 1909), Kiderlen, 2:34–35. On his humorlessness, see Schiffer, *Leben*, pp. 188–89.

6. Müller diary (2 Oct. 1912, 23 Apr. 1914), Müller Papers, no. 4; Vietsch, *Bethmann Hollweg*, pp. 156, 159.

7. Görlitz, *Der Kaiser*, p. 96.

8. Kiderlen, 2:32–33; Radziwill, *Lettres*, 4:85; also Vierhaus, *Tagebuch*, pp. 508–9. For the tempering of Wilhelm's behavior in the aftermath of the *Daily Telegraph* crisis, see Rosner, *Erinnerungen des Kronprinzen*, pp. 20, 82, 94.

9. Bethmann's admission of inexperience in diplomacy is in Szögyényi to Aehrenthal (3 Aug. 1909), HHStA, no. 167(V); his interest in learning more is in Kiderlen, 2:34. For a view that depicts Bethmann as deluded with a belief that he was a masterful diplomat, see Liebert, *Erinnerungen*, p. 186.

10. See Lamar Cecil, *Diplomatic Service*, p. 213, for the quotation. Wilhelm's like for Schoen is in Pogge von Strandman, *Rathenau Tagebuch*, p. 141, and Kiderlen, 2:34. For Bethmann's meager opinion of Schoen, see Kiderlen, 2:173.

11. Lamar Cecil, *Diplomatic Service*, p. 309.

12. Hutten-Czapski, *Sechzig Jahre*, 2:28; Mutius Papers, p. 108. On Wilhelm's lack of enthusiasm, see Hutten-Czapski, *Sechzig Jahre*, 2:29; Kiderlen, 2:6, 15.

13. On the Kaiserin's dislike, and its reciprocation by Kiderlen: Beyens, *Ger-

many, pp. 60–61; Raschdau, *Bismarck und Caprivi*, p. 175; Monts, *Erinnerungen*, pp. 44–45. "China shop" remark is in Redlich, *Schicksalsjahre*, 1:117. His like for Kiderlen's anecdotal talent is in Kiderlen, 1:90. Wilhelm was less happy to discover that he was sometimes the butt of the jokes, nor did he approve Kiderlen's living openly with his mistress, Hedwig Kypke. See Friedrich Rosen, *Wanderleben*, 2:10; Bittner and Uebersberger, *Aussenpolitik*, 2:94.

14. "Kypke Anekdoten von Kiderlen, 1891," in Kiderlen Papers, Box 4/004 0186/000 7895; Mutius Papers, p. 109.

15. Kiderlen, 2:80.

16. Ibid., 2:41–78.

17. Goschen diary (2 July 1910), Christopher Howard, *Goschen*, p. 206.

18. Kiderlen, 2:82; Hutten-Czapski, *Sechzig Jahre*, 2:29. Max von Mutius, an adjutant and military-attaché, noted that Kiderlen had very few friends. Mutius Papers, p. 191. Kiderlen was very critical of his colleagues. See Sonntag, *Begegnungen mit Bülow*, p. 29.

19. Kiderlen's complaints about Bethmann are in Kiderlen, 2:144; on his keeping information from the chancellor, see Hutten-Czapski, *Sechzig Jahre*, 2:29.

20. BD, 7:546, 622; Kiderlen, 2:34–35, 122.

21. Kiderlen, 2:36.

22. Müller to Tirpitz (17 Apr. 1909), Tirpitz Papers, no. 54.

23. Szögyényi to Aehrenthal (3 Aug. 1909), HHStA, no. 167(V).

24. Loebell Papers, no. 27, part 2, p. 90.

25. Oettingen diary (9 June 1912), KE, no. 517/5; SpitzembergVierhaus, *Tagebuch*, p. 496; Vietsch, *Bethmann Hollweg*, p. 159.

26. Müller diary (13 Oct. 1911), Müller Papers, no. 4; Görlitz, *Der Kaiser*, pp. 96–97.

27. On the Kaiserin's preference for Bülow, see Vietsch, *Bethmann Hollweg*, pp. 161–62; the crown prince's opinion is in his letter to Bülow (3 May 1924), Bülow Papers, no. 113. Bethmann's reservations about the crown prince are in Vierhaus, *Tagebuch*, p. 496, and Vietsch, *Bethmann Hollweg*, pp. 161–62. Wilhelm's younger son Adalbert also did not like Bethmann. See Hopman notes for Tirpitz (8 Apr. 1912), Tirpitz Papers, no. 27a.

28. Johannes Kessler, *Ewige Jugend*, pp. 209–10.

29. Wermuth, *Beamtenleben*, pp. 260–61, 313; Schiffer, *Leben*, p. 191; Tirpitz to Bülow (15 June 1919), Bülow Papers, no. 126.

30. Wermuth, *Beamtenleben*, p. 187; Schiffer, *Leben*, p. 192; also Oldenburg-Januschau, *Erinnerungen*, p. 107.

31. Wilhelm, *Ereignisse und Gestalten*, p. 111; Zmarzlik, *Bethmann*, p. 30.

32. Müller diary (11 Nov. 1911), Müller Papers, no. 4.

33. Zmarzlik, *Bethmann*, p. 28.

34. For an example, see Müller diary (3 July 1913), Müller Papers, no. 4.

35. Bethmann Hollweg, *Betrachtungen*, 1:19–20, 96–98; Bülow, 3:121; Einem, *Erinnerungen*, pp. 155–61; Jarausch, *Enigmatic Chancellor*, p. 91.

36. On Bethmann's misperception of the Reichstag, see Schiffer, *Leben*, p. 198; on the parties, see Jarausch, *Enigmatic Chancellor*, pp. 85–91. See KE, no. 517/5, in which Bethmann admits he also should have more effectively cultivated Wilhelm.

37. Jarausch, *Enigmatic Chancellor*, pp. 74–79.

38. Einem, *Erinnerungen*, p. 161. Einem was opposed to Bethmann for his failure to defend the Kaiser in the *Daily Telegraph* affair. Ibid., pp. 119–21.

39. Loebell Papers, part 2, p. 84; Kluck, *Wanderjahre*, pp. 169–70.

40. Vietsch, *Bethmann Hollweg*, p. 160; on his lack of enthusiasm for the army, see Thimme Papers, no. 17, p. 4. On Bethmann's unpopularity in the army, see Loebell Papers, no. 27, part 2, p. 84; Bethmann to Falkenhayn (4 Dec. 1911), Reichskanzlei Papers, no. 951/1.

41. Oldenburg-Januschau, *Erinnerungen*, p. 111, relating General Schlieffen's criticisms. Bethmann was not entirely comfortable dealing with other Prussian nobles. Thimme Papers, no. 17, p. 4.

42. Oldenburg-Januschau, *Erinnerungen*, pp. 108–10.

43. On the connection of the fleet and good Anglo-German relations: Müller diary (13 Sept. 1911), Müller Papers, no. 4; *PD*, 1:159. On Bethmann's determination to improve the relationship, see Szögyényi to Aehrenthal (3 Aug. 1909), HHStA, no. 167(V); Kiderlen, 2:36.

44. Müller to Tirpitz (17 Apr. 1909), Tirpitz Papers, no. 54; *PD*, 1:183.

45. Persius, *Menschen und Schiffe*, pp. 35, 118.

46. Dallwitz, "Erinnerungen," p. 12, in Thimme Papers, no. 16; Glücksburg Papers, no. 36-B/1; also *PD*, 1:183. On Tirpitz's planning, see Berghahn, *Tirpitz-Plan*, and Epkenhaus, *Flottenrüstung*.

47. Tirpitz, *Erinnerungen*, p. 179; *PD*, 1:162, 168–69.

48. Vierhaus, *Tagebuch*, pp. 545–46.

49. Christopher Howard, *Goschen*, p. 200; Heath to Goschen (7 Mar. 1910), FO 371/900.

50. Wilhelm to Fürstenberg (17 Mar. 1910), Fürstenberg Papers, "Wilhelm II. c. 1908–1918."

51. Leonidas E. Hill, *Weizsäcker-Papiere*, p. 131; Szögyényi to Berchtold (21 May 1912), HHStA, no. 170(B); *BD*, 9/2:504.

52. Monts, *Erinnerungen*, pp. 145–47.

53. The Russian ambassador admitted Wilhelm behaved well at the funeral at Windsor but felt that he had "encore une fois trop joué le *chief mourner* pendant la procession à travers London. Une fois encore cela a choqué le public." Iswolsky, *Service de la Russie*, 2:267. For Wilhelm's relief at the king's death, see Meister, *Yesterdays*, pp. 166–68, and Wilhelm to Bethmann (7 May 1910), GFO, reel 62.

54. Meister, *Yesterdays*, pp. 166–68.

55. On their problems with one another, see Rose, *George V*, p. 165; Bülow to Rosen (16 Aug. 1921), Bülow Papers, no. 117; Nicolson, *George the Fifth*, pp. 175, 181–82; Pope-Hennessy, *Queen Mary*, p. 281.

56. Prince Heinrich of Prussia to Wilhelm (11 Dec. 1912), *PD*, 1:363–64. That was also Ambassador Lascelles's opinion. See Bunsen, *Zeitgenossen*, p. 80.

57. Asquith to Knollys (24 May 1911), RA, Geo V o 2580, no. 2.

58. Leonidas E. Hill, *Weizsäcker-Papiere*, p. 137; Szögyényi to Aehrenthal (19 Jan. 1912), HHStA, no. 170(B).

59. Dryander, *Erinnerungen*, pp. 248–49; Wilhelm's marginalia on an article, "Topics for the Day," in *Spectator* (9 Dec. 1911), Tirpitz Papers, no. 26a. For Wilhelm's views on Anglo-German economic cooperation, see Swaine to Bigge (28

Dec. 1900), RA, I 62, no. 113; Sommer, *Haldane*, pp. 183–84; Thimme Papers, no. 16, p. 12. For opinion in Germany that commercial rivalry was not the principal cause of Anglo-German discord, see Lerchenfeld-Koefering, *Erinnerungen*, pp. 402–3; Persius, *Menschen und Schiffe*, pp. 118–19; *HP*, 1:159–60.

60. Tirpitz to Bülow (15 June 1919), Bülow Papers, no. 126. The same qualities were to be observed in Tirpitz. See Einem, *Erinnerungen*, pp. 151–52; *BD*, 6:507.

61. KE, no. 342/3. On Kiderlen, see Kiderlen, 2:31, 153, 155. For Tirpitz's other opponents among diplomats: Vierhaus, *Tagebuch*, p. 542, for Count Wilhelm von Mirbach; Bunsen, *Zeitgenossen*, p. 197, for Baron von Rosen; Kühlmann, *Erinnerungen*, p. 292.

62. Einem, *Erinnerungen*, p. 160.

63. On the friction, see Görlitz, *Der Kaiser*, pp. 62–64; Bernhardi, *Denkwürdigkeiten*, p. 272; Schönburg-Waldenburg, *Erinnerungen*, p. 195; Einem, *Erinnerungen*, pp. 151–53; Bülow, 1:113, 2:244.

64. Kühlmann, *Erinnerungen*, pp. 334–35; Monts, *Erinnerungen*, p. 195. Wilhelm's jealousy is in Bülow, 1:113.

65. Wilhelm's rudeness; Wilhelm Michaelis Papers, no. 4, pp. 26–27; on his awareness of Tirpitz's position, see Lans to Scheer (17 Apr. 1906), Tirpitz Papers, no. 23.

66. Bülow, 2:512–13.

67. *PD*, 1:183.

68. On honor, see "Auszug aus den Akten über die Agreement-Frage" (12 Aug. 1908), Tirpitz Papers, no. 24b; Wilhelm to Bülow (13 Aug. 1908), Hammann, *Bilder*, pp. 143–44. On Germany's freedom, see Wilhelm's marginalia on an article in *Spectator* (9 Dec. 1911), Tirpitz Papers, no. 26a; Lambsdorff, *Militärbevollmächtigten*, pp. 337–38.

69. Glücksburg Papers, no. 36-B/1; Wilhelm to Fürstenberg (18 Feb. 1910), Fürstenberg Papers, "Wilhelm II. c. 1908–1918"; Görlitz, *Der Kaiser*, p. 106.

70. Christopher Howard, *Goschen*, pp. 203–4.

71. See Kiderlen, 2:59–67, 69–74, for his talks with Goschen (14 Oct., 4 Nov. 1909), and Flotow to Kiderlen (11 Nov. 1909) for the Kaiser's viewpoint.

72. Goschen in Kiderlen, 2:73.

73. *BD*, 6:291.

74. Ibid., 6:283–84, 289.

75. Bülow, 2:319.

76. Wilhelm to Franz Ferdinand (6 Dec. 1911), Franz Ferdinand Papers.

77. Hammann, *Bilder*, p. 141; Brett, *Journals and Letters*, 2:343; *BD*, 6:184–90.

78. Bülow, 2:429–31; *PD*, 1:147–49.

79. Bülow, 2:438–39.

80. *PD*, 1:147–49.

81. Dülffer, *Friedenskonferenzen*, pp. 93, 126–27; *GP*, 15:149, 300–305.

82. Nostitz, *Bismarcks*, p. 247.

83. *GP*, 23/1:213–17. Wilhelm to Bethmann (25 Nov. 1909), *GP*, 29:33–35.

84. *PD*, 1:156–57.

85. Wilhelm's marginalia on Metternich to Bülow (1 Nov. 1911), ibid., 1:241. Wilhelm's criticism of Metternich is in his comments on a Metternich report (3

Mar. 1909) and in Wilhelm to Bülow (3 Apr. 1909), Tirpitz Papers, no. 54; Wilhelm's comments on a letter by Bülow (28 July 1908), Bülow Papers, no. 150.

86. *PD*, 1:160.

87. Ibid., 1:263, 294; *GP*, 31:199–200.

88. *BD*, 6:294, 296–97, 304–13.

89. Goschen to Grey (1 Jan. 1910), ibid., 6:434.

90. There are two accounts, which differ somewhat. Goschen's is in *BD*, 6:530–33, and there is a misdated account by Admiral Müller, who was present, in *PD*, 1:182–84. Both contain material not found in the other. Memo by Wilhelm (28 Mar. 1927), HA, Rep. 53a, no. 33.

91. Wilhelm to Bethmann (25 Nov. 1909), *GP*, 29:33–35.

92. Memo by Wilhelm (28 Mar. 1927), HA, Rep. 53a, no. 33.

93. Wilhelm to Bethmann (22 Apr. 1911), *GP*, 29:89; also Jenisch to Foreign Office (26 May 1911), ibid., 29:93–94; same to Kiderlen (30 Apr. 1911), ibid., 29:101.

94. Bethmann memo (23 May 1911), ibid., 29:120–21; Glücksburg Papers, no. 36-B/1; *PD*, 1:203.

95. Kiderlen, 2:233.

96. See Wilhelm's comment on Bethmann letter to him (10 July 1911), *GP*, 20:177.

97. See Wilhelm Michaelis Papers, no. 4, p. 35, for the "blare of trumpets." Bethmann's concern at Kiderlen is in Hammann, "Aufzeichnungen," pp. 547–48. *PD*, 1:202, holds that Kiderlen neither expected nor wanted war. See also Kiderlen, 2:122, and *GP*, 29:142–49.

98. Oettingen diary (14 Nov. 1911), KE, no. 517/5.

99. Glücksburg Papers, no. 36-B/1.

100. *GP*, 29:152; Kiderlen, 2:122, 127. For Wilhelm's concern about the reaction in London, see Görlitz, *Der Kaiser*, p. 106.

101. Görlitz, *Der Kaiser*, p. 89. See also *GP*, 29:177.

102. The *Panther* was replaced by the cruiser *Berlin* on 7 July. It and the gunboat *Eber* remained alternately or together at Agadir until the very end of November 1911.

103. *BD*, 7:323–25.

104. Caillaux, *Agadir*, p. 107.

105. *GP*, 29:177, 184–88.

106. Fürstenberg, *Lebensgeschichte*, p. 551; Kiderlen, 2:127; Eckardstein, *Erinnerungen an König Eduard*, p. 101.

107. *GP*, 29:184–86, 189–93.

108. Ibid., 29:193; Kiderlen, 2:129, 134. On the Kaiserin's hawkish role, see Kiderlen, 2:138, 235–36; Beyens, *Germany*, pp. 60–61.

109. A partial text is in *BD*, 7:392.

110. *GP*, 29:206 n. 2, 227–28. Grey admitted in a speech in the House of Commons on 27 Nov. that he and Asquith had participated in composing the speech.

111. *BD*, 7:450–52, 462–63.

112. *GP*, 29:227–30.

113. See Görlitz, *Der Kaiser*, pp. 86–87, for the alarm.

114. On the colonies, see Tirpitz's notes (12 Aug. 1911) and an unsigned note (20 Aug. 1911), in Tirpitz Papers, no. 25a. On Wilhelm's annoyance, see *GP*, 29:311–16, 345. On his concern about public opinion, see ibid., 34:386.

115. Ibid., 29:413.

116. Hammann, "Aufzeichnungen," pp. 548–50.

117. Zobeltitz, *Chronik*, 2:258–59; Moltke, *Moltke Erinnerungen*, p. 362.

118. Wilhelm's marginalia on Metternich to Foreign Office (28 Nov. 1912), GFO, reel 53.

119. Balfour, *Kaiser and His Times*, p. 317; KE, no. 317/2, p. 168.

120. Granville to Grey (29 Dec. 1911), FO 800/1370.

121. Wilhelm's note on Metternich to Bethmann (20 Dec. 1911), *GP*, 31:81–86.

122. Wilhelm's comments on a report by Kühlmann, Tirpitz Papers, no. 26a.

123. Bülow, 2:512–13; Wilhelm's comments on Metternich to Bülow (16 July 1908), *GP*, 24:103–4.

124. *PD*, 1:270, 274–75.

125. Ibid., 1:213, 220, 223.

126. Ibid., 1:217, and also 1:215.

127. Ibid., 1:217. For Wilhelm on naval costs, see his letter to Fürstenberg (18 Feb. 1910), Fürstenberg Papers, "Wilhelm II c. 1908–1918."

128. KE, no. 342/3; Tirpitz, *Erinnerungen*, p. 452.

129. Widenmann, probably to Tirpitz (4 Dec. 1911), Tirpitz Papers, no. 25b; Bethmann to Metternich (22 Nov. 1911), *GP*, 31:31–32. On Wilhelm's agreeing to a delay, see *PD*, 1:216–18.

130. Müller diary (9 Dec. 1911), Müller Paper, no. 4; *PD*, 1:226.

131. *GP*, 31:31–32.

CHAPTER 8

1. Lamar Cecil, *Ballin*, pp. 180–86.

2. Ballin's notes on his meeting with Cassel (10 July 1909), Tirpitz Papers, no. 54; "Bemerkungen" by Wilhelm, HA 192, no. 20, p. 291; *PD*, 1:163–64.

3. *GP*, 31:97–98.

4. Winston Churchill, *World Crisis*, 1:96–97.

5. *GP*, 31:97–98, 104.

6. Ballin to Wilhelm (7 Feb. 1912), RMA Papers, no. 1764; on Grey's reluctance to go to Berlin, see *BD*, 6:668, 670.

7. Koss, *Haldane*, p. 77.

8. *BD*, 6:669.

9. Ibid., 6:676–77.

10. *GP*, 21:110 n.

11. Müller diary (8 Feb. 1912), Müller Papers, no. 4; Tirpitz, *Erinnerungen*, pp. 188–89; Briefwechsel, 1:132–33.

12. Wilhelm Michaelis Papers, no. 4, pp. 33–34.

13. Wilhelm's remarks on Kühlmann report (11 Jan. 1912), Tirpitz Papers, no. 26a; *PD*, 1:274–75.

14. On the Mission, see Epkenhaus, *Flottenrüstung*, pp. 113–37; Koss, *Hal-*

dane, chap. 3; Lamar Cecil, *Ballin*, pp. 181–90. Haldane's account is in *BD*, 6:676–84; Tirpitz's is in *PD*, 1:279–89, and Tirpitz, *Erinnerungen*, pp. 185–99; Wilhelm's is in his *Ereignisse und Gestalten*, pp. 122–33.

15. On Kiderlen, see Briefwechsel, 1:142; Tirpitz in his *Erinnerungen*, p. 192; Bethmann in Vierhaus, *Tagebuch*, p. 545.

16. *BD*, 6:680–81.

17. Wilhelm to Müller (2 Feb. 1912), RMA, no. 1764.

18. Lerchenfeld's notes of a talk with Wilhelm and his letter to Hertling (12, 13 Mar. 1912), in Briefwechsel, 1:139 n. 1, 139–40; Müller diary (28 Feb. 1912), Müller Papers, no. 4.

19. Wilhelm to Kiderlen (24 Feb. 1912), Kiderlen Papers, 4/004 0174/000 7554.

20. *PD*, 1:307.

21. *GP*, 31:205–10; also *PD*, 1:292, 307–8; Lamar Cecil, *Diplomatic Service*, p. 212.

22. Widenmann, *Marine-Attaché*, pp. 225–26; *GP*, 31:181–83, 191–93, 205–10; Müller diary (26 Feb., 14 Mar. 1912), Müller Papers, no. 4.

23. Müller diary (14 Oct. 1911, 10 Jan., 28 Feb. 1912), Müller Papers, no. 4; Briefwechsel, 1:139–40.

24. Stamfordham memo (10 June 1912), RA, Geo V M 450, no. 16.

25. Vierhaus, *Tagebuch*, p. 545.

26. Mosse, "Wilhelm II," p. 185.

27. Franz Ferdinand Papers. Other complaints by the Kasier about British interference in the Balkans are in Wilhelm to Franz Ferdinand (8 Nov. 1908, 9 Dec. 1912), ibid.; Wilhelm to Fürstenberg (17 Mar. 1910), Fürstenberg Papers, "Wilhelm II. c. 1908–1918"; Wilhelm's marginalia on Jenisch to Foreign Office (26 Sept. 1908), GFO Papers, 240/00167.

28. See Siebert, *Benckendorff*, 1:163–65, for Wilhelm's attachment to Austria being caused by his fears of diplomatic encirclement.

29. Münz, *Bülow*, p. 55; on Bethmann and Kiderlen, see Westarp, *Konservative Politik*, 1:165.

30. On Wilhelm's approbation of Aehrenthal, see his letter to Franz Ferdinand (9 Apr. 1909), Franz Ferdinand Papers; Redlich, *Schicksalsjahre*, 1:50; Szögyényi to Aehrenthal (25 Oct. 1906), HHStA, no. 162(V); Wilhelm's notes on a letter from Hintze (9 Oct. 1908), Hintze Papers, no. 13. For the Kaiser's support of Aehrenthal in the 1908 Bosnian crisis: Lambsdorff, *Militärbevollmächtigten*, pp. 296–99; Bittner and Uebersberger, *Aussenpolitik*, 2:212.

31. Franckenstein report on talk with Wilhelm (23 Nov. 1909), Bittner and Uebersberger, *Aussenpolitik*, 2:557–58.

32. Notes by Hausen of a talk with Wilhelm (1 Mar. 1909), in Brabant, *Hausen*, p. 241.

33. Kiderlen, 2:11, 188–89; Westarp, *Konservative Politik*, 1:164–65.

34. Berchtold on Wilhelm: Hantsch, *Berchtold*, 1:160. Wilhelm approved of Berchtold's conduct of affairs but apparently was not at all personally attracted to him.

35. Steinitz, *Erinnerungen an Franz Joseph*, p. 270. See also Szögyényi to Vienna (16. Mar. 1909), HHStA, no. 167(B); Hantsch, *Berchtold*, 2:530.

36. Wilhelm to Franz Ferdinand (12 Feb. 1909), Franz Ferdinand Papers;

Szögyényi to Vienna (16 Mar. 1909), HHStA, no. 167(B); Franckenstein report of a talk with Wilhelm (23 Nov. 1909), Bittner and Uebersberger, *Aussenpolitik,* 2:557–58.

37. Hantsch, *Berchtold,* 2:506, 522; Baernreither, *Fragments of a Political Diary,* p. 277.

38. The quote is from Szögyényi to Vienna (18 Aug. 1913), HHStA, no. 170(B). See also same to same (16 Mar. 1909), ibid., no. 167(B); Brabant, *Hausen,* p. 241; Hantsch, *Berchtold,* 1:261–62, 350, 2:506.

39. Kiderlen, 2:189–90; Hantsch, *Berchtold,* 2:503.

40. Wilhelm to Franz Ferdinand (9 Dec. 1912), Franz Ferdinand Papers.

41. Same to same (9 Apr. and 13 Aug. 1909), ibid.

42. Same to same (1 Oct. 1913), ibid.; also Szögyényi to Vienna (11 Dec. 1912), HHStA, no. 170(B). Conrad found the Kaiser charming but sometimes wrongheaded. See Conrad von Hötzendorf, *Dienstzeit,* 1:69–70, 3:169.

43. Mosse, "Wilhelm II," p. 185. For an impression that Wilhelm was against war in 1912, see Leonidas E. Hill, *Weizsäcker-Papiere,* p. 141.

44. Wilhelm to Franz Ferdinand (18 Jan. and 8 Nov. 1908), Franz Ferdinand Papers.

45. Brabant, *Hausen,* p. 241.

46. Wilhelm to Franz Ferdinand (18 Jan. and 8 Nov. 1908), Franz Ferdinand Papers.

47. Wilhelm admitted Ferdinand's ability but did not like him at all. See Szögyényi to Goluchowski (31 Jan. 1905), HHStA, no. 162(B); Wilhelm to Fürstenberg (17 Mar. 1910), Fürstenberg Papers, "Wilhelm II. c. 1908–1918"; same to Franz Ferdinand (27 May 1913), Franz Ferdinand Papers.

48. On Ferdinand, see Wilhelm to Nicholas II (9 Nov. 1903, 22 Aug. 1905), Goetz, *Briefe,* pp. 331, 377. For the connection between the two, see Jenisch to Berlin (26 Sept. 1908), GFO Papers, 240/00167.

49. Wilhelm to Franz Ferdinand (31 Dec. 1908, 12 Feb, 13. Aug. 1909), Franz Ferdinand Papers; Berchtold to Aehrenthal (15 Feb. 1909), Bittner and Uebersberger, *Aussenpolitik,* 1:828–29.

50. Meyer, *Schiemann,* pp. 254–55.

51. For Wilhelm's low opinion of Iswolsky: Sazonov, *Fateful Years,* p. 27; Wilhelm to Franz Ferdinand (31 Dec. 1908), Franz Ferdinand Papers. In 1905, however, Wilhelm had wanted Iswolsky named envoy in Berlin, believing that he would work well with Bülow. See Wilhelm to Nicholas II (15 Jan. 1905), Goetz, *Briefe,* p. 357.

52. Szögyényi to Berchtold (12 Mar. 1914), HHStA, no. 171(B); Bompard to Bourgeois (16 May 1906), DDF, 2d ser., 10:89–90; Lamar Cecil, "William II and His Russian 'Colleagues,'" pp. 130–31.

53. Hantsch, *Berchtold,* 2:539; Szögyényi to Berchtold (12 Mar. 1914), HHStA, no. 171(B). He was, however, concerned about Russia's increasing armaments. See Meyer, *Schiemann,* p. 184 n. 559.

54. See Granville memo (18 Feb. 1913), BD, 9/2:504, on the British alliance; on Russia, see Szögyényi to Berchtold (19 Aug. 1912), HHStA, no. 170(V).

55. Louis to Pichon (5 Jan. 1911), DDF, 2d ser., 13:200; Buchanan to Grey (3 Apr. 1914), BD, 10/2:781.

56. Hantsch, *Berchtold*, 1:158.

57. Hohenlohe-Schillingsfürst, *Reichskanzlerzeit*, p. 327; Bülow, 2:509–11.

58. Kenneth Young, *Balfour*, p. 121.

59. Hammann, "Aufzeichnungen," p. 544.

60. Ziekursch, *Geschichte*, 2:3, 9; Bülow, 2:7; *HP*, 3:657–58; Gurlitt, "Wallotbau," p. 340; Milner, *Picture Gallery*, p. 233.

61. Schönburg-Waldenburg, *Erinnerungen*, p. 196.

62. Bülow, 2:279, 509–11; Zmarzlik, *Bethmann*, p. 40.

63. *HP*, 2:382. On Wilhelm's rudeness, see Pachnicke, *Führende Männer*, p. 233; Payer, *Bethmann Hollweg bis Ebert*, pp. 16, 173–74; Schiffer, *Leben*, pp. 58–59.

64. Hutten-Czapski, *Sechzig Jahre*, 1:62, 258; Gerlach, *Erinnerungen*, pp. 32–33.

65. Westarp, *Konservative Politik*, 1:338, 351.

66. Ibid., 1:39–50, 349–50; Vierhaus, *Tagebuch*, p. 493.

67. On the trade treaties, see Hohenlohe, *Leben*, pp. 357–58; Radziwill, *Lettres*, 1:203; Meisner, *Denkwürdigkeiten*, 2:306. For the canal: Thimme Papers, no. 16; Moltke, *Moltke Erinnerungen*, p. 239; Bülow, 2:256–57.

68. On the reluctance of the Conservatives to intrude into diplomatic affairs, see Westarp, *Konservative Politik*, 1:154–57; on the party's stand in the *Daily Telegraph* affair, see ibid., 1:349, and Zedlitz-Trützschler, pp. 240–41; on the party's position during the Moroccan crisis, see Hammann, "Aufzeichnungen," pp. 548–50.

69. Bülow, 2:97; Westarp, *Konservative Politik*, 1:351.

70. Vierhaus, *Tagebuch*, p. 428; Meisner, *Denkwürdigkeiten*, 3:206–7.

71. Bülow, 1:456–57; for Wilhelm on ruling with the Conservatives, see *HP*, 4:265–66. On the Kaiser's efforts at reconciliation, see Westarp, *Konservative Politik*, 1:350.

72. See Bülow, 2:97, for the Hundebande; for his special hate of Centrist deputies, see ibid, 1:479.

73. Radziwill, *Lettres*, 3:273; Bülow, 2:256–57.

74. On authority, see Radziwill, *Lettres*, 3:94–95; on pomp and mysticism, see Hohenlohe, *Leben*, pp. 91–93.

75. Wilhelm to Chamberlain (31 Dec. 1901), H. S. Chamberlain, *Briefe*, 2:141–43; same to Nicholas II (7 Feb. 1895), Goetz, *Briefe*, p. 290.

76. He liked Georg Cardinal Kopp of Breslau and Antonius Cardinal Fischer of Cologne. See Hutten-Czapski, *Sechzig Jahre*, 1:256; Pastor, *Tagebücher*, p. 427. On the lower clergy, see Möckl, *Prinzregentenzeit*, p. 470; on the Jesuits, see Bülow, 2:11.

77. *HP*, 4:165.

78. Zobeltitz, *Chronik*, 2:120; Schoenaich, *Damaskus*, p. 138.

79. Lascelles to Salisbury (28 Nov. 1896), Salisbury Papers, no. A120.

80. Riezler diary (4 Aug. 1911), Erdmann, *Riezler*, p. 174.

81. Wilhelm's marginalia on Siegel to Tirpitz (7 May 1904), Raulff, *Machtpolitik und Imperialismus*, p. 33.

82. Zedlitz-Trützschler, p. 204; on Wilhelm's attention to the press, see Ssuworin, *Geheimtagebuch*, p. 52; Schönburg-Waldenburg, *Erinnerungen*, p. 157; Waters, *Potsdam and Doorn*, pp. 64–65.

83. Radziwill, *Lettres*, 3:276.

84. On Wilhelm's like for some journalists, see August Stein, *Ganz Anders*, p. 180; on the British press, see Zedlitz-Trützschler, p. 97; Brett, *Journals and Letters*, 2:136–38; Newton, *Lansdowne*, p. 335. On Edward VII, see see Zedlitz-Trützschler, p. 153.

85. Raulff, *Machtpolitik und Imperialismus*, p. 31.

86. On his intentions before being crowned, see Lucius von Ballhausen, *Bismarck-Erinnerungen*, pp. 409–11. The connection of Jews to the Socialist press was implied rather than clearly stated. See Hohenlohe-Schillingsfürst, *Reichskanzlerzeit*, p. 92; Zechlin, *Deutsche Politik*, p. 48. On the Jews' pernicious influence on the Reichstag Socialists, see Wilhelm's letter to Nicholas II (7 Feb. 1895), Goetz, *Briefe*, p. 290.

87. Westarp, *Konservative Politik*, 1:340.

88. Oettingen diary (9 June 1912), KE, no. 517/5.

89. Lerchenfeld to Hertling (8 Mar. 1912), Briefwechsel, 1:134.

90. Hutten-Czapski, *Sechzig Jahre*, 2:2. The crown prince and the Kaiserin were two prominent opponents. For the former, see Zmarzlik, *Bethmann*, pp. 30, 36–37; on the Kaiserin: Widenmann, *Marine-Attaché*, pp. 278–79; Vietsch, *Bethmann Hollweg*, pp. 161–62.

91. See Bethmann's correspondence with Wilhelm and others (1 Dec. 1911 through 29 Feb. 1912) in Reichskanzlei Papers, nos. 951/1, 952; Glücksburg Papers, no. 36-B/1; Wilhelm to Fürstenberg (18 Feb. 1910), Fürstenberg Papers, "Wilhelm II. c. 1908–1918"; Müller diary (9 Jan. 1912), Görlitz, *Der Kaiser*, p. 106. For Bethmann's concern, see Hopman diary (6 Jan., 5 Feb. 1913), Hopman Papers, no. 10.

92. Randolph Churchill, *Churchill*, companion vol. 2/2:1108; see also *BD*, 6:587.

93. Tirpitz to Posadowsky (5 July 1912), Tirpitz Papers, no. 27a; Müller diary (1 July 1912, 15 June 1913), Müller Papers, no. 4; Fürstenberg, *Lebensgeschichte*, pp. 442–43.

94. Wilhelm's notes on a letter from Tirpitz (20 July 1908), Bülow Papers, no. 150, p. 10. On the linkage in the Kaiser's mind between the navy and his and Germany's honor, see Wilhelm's note on an article in the London *Times* (18 Aug. 1911), in Hecker, *Rathenau*, p. 129; Schulenburg-Tressow Papers, pp. 34–35; Meyer, *Schiemann*, pp. 255–56; Hohenlohe-Schillingsfürst, *Reichskanzlerzeit*, p. 159; Bülow, 2:512–13; *GP*, 24:103–4, 126–27; Zedlitz-Trützschler, p. 225.

95. Wilhelm to Fürstenberg (17 Mar. 1910), Fürstenberg Papers, "Wilhelm II. c. 1908–1918."

96. Szögyényi to Berchtold (21 May 1912), HHStA, no. 170(B); same to same (19 Aug. 1912), ibid., no. 170(V); Leonidas E. Hill, *Weizsäcker-Papiere*, pp. 123, 131; Granville memo (12 May 1913), *BD*, 9/2:504.

97. Mountbatten to George V (23 May 1911), in Hough, *Louis and Victoria*, p. 242.

98. Franckenstein report of a talk with the Kiaser (23 Nov. 1909), Bittner and Uebersberger, *Aussenpolitik*, 2:557–58; Brabant, *Hausen*, pp. 141–42; Hantsch, *Berchtold*, 2:530.

99. The perceptive Russian envoy in Berlin, Count Nicholas Osten-Sacken,

believed in late 1909 that the Austrians had succeeded in capturing Wilhelm for their purposes. See Siebert, *Benckendorff*, 1:163–65. Jagow was concerned that Austria was taking the leading role in the Dual Alliance. See Lerchenfeld to Hertling (2 Feb. 1913), *Briefwechsel*, 1:221–22; see Kiderlen, 2:11, for concern in about 1909 by both Kiderlen and Count Monts, German ambassador in Rome. See also Bethmann Hollweg, *Betrachtungen*, 1:82–83; Wilhelm to Kiderlen and Wilhelm's memo (7, 11 Nov. 1912), *GP*, 33:295, 302–4. For Wilhelm's reluctance in early 1913 to help Austria, see Conrad von Hötzendorf, *Dienstzeit*, 4:39.

100. On the unpreparedness of the other major European powers: *GP*, 33:147–48; Kiderlen, 2:189–90. On Turkey's weakness, see *GP*, 33:253, 339–40.

101. Wilhelm's memo (11 Nov. 1912), *GP*, 33:302–4.

102. Ibid., 33:359–60, 373–74; Röhl, "Schwelle zum Weltkrieg," pp. 81–82.

103. *GP*, 33:372–73. Wilhelm also compared the situation to the unsettled state of Europe in 1877, when Russia had declared war on Turkey. Ibid., 33:387.

104. Röhl, "Schwelle zum Weltkrieg," p. 84.

105. Ibid., p. 125. This is from George V's account of the conversation as he reported it to the Austrian ambassador in London on 22 Dec. 1912, and there is no reason to doubt its accuracy. Henry, however, does not mention the king as having said this — either in his diary for 6/7 Dec., when he saw George V, or in a letter to Wilhelm II of 11 Dec. Henry suppressed the remarks at the king's request, but that he did so was remarkably obtuse. Perhaps this was to avoid agitating his ever-excitable brother. See Henry to George V (14 Dec. 1912), ibid., p. 110.

106. Wilhelm to Henry (12 Dec. 1912), ibid., p. 105; the same phrase was used in a letter to Eisendecher written on the same day (ibid., p. 106).

107. Wilhelm to Kiderlen-Wächter (8 Dec. 1912) and to Eisendecher (12 Dec. 1912), ibid., pp. 101, 106; Meyer, *Schiemann*, p. 181 n. 537.

108. The critical source for this meeting is Röhl, "Schwelle zum Weltkrieg." Tirpitz does not mention the meeting in his otherwise extensive *Politische Dokumente*, but he gave an account of the proceedings to Admiral Hopman, who recorded them in his diary for 9 Dec. See Hopman Papers, no. 9. On Wilhelm's not inviting Bethmann and Kiderlen, see *Briefwechsel*, 1:189–92; see also Wilhelm to Franz Ferdinand (9 Dec. 1912), Franz Ferdinand Papers; same to Prince Henry of Prussia (12 Dec 1912), Röhl, "Schwelle zum Weltkrieg," p. 105.

109. Müller diary (8 Dec. 1912), Müller Papers, no. 4. Tirpitz described Moltke as using the same phrase. See Hopman diary (9 Dec. 1912), Hopman Papers, no. 9. A few years earlier, in 1908 or 1909, Moltke had told Bülow that he would rather regard Britain as an open enemy than as an unfriendly observer in war. Bülow to Tirpitz (11 June 1922), Tirpitz Papers, no. 173.

110. Wilhelm to Franz Ferdinand (9 Dec. 1912), Franz Ferdinand Papers; also same to Prince Henry of Prussia (23 Dec. 1912), Röhl, "Schwelle zum Weltkrieg," p. 105.

111. Bethmann to Eisendecher (20 Dec. 1912), Röhl, "Schwelle zum Weltkrieg," pp. 124–25; same to Wilhelm (18 Dec. 1912), ibid., pp. 122–23; Tirpitz's notes (19 Dec. 1912), *PD*, 1:370.

112. Wilhelm's comments on Lichnowsky to Bethmann (13 Feb., 25 Mar. 1913), *GP*, 9:21–22, 127.

113. Wilhelm to Franz Ferdinand (6 Dec. 1911), Franz Ferdinand Papers.

114. *GP*, 39:177–78; *PD*, 1:370.

115. Conrad von Hötzendorf, *Dienstzeit*, 3:156.

116. Ibid., 3:155; Wilhelm to Franz Ferdinand (9 Dec. 1912, 24 Feb. 1913), Franz Ferdinand Papers; Szögyényi to Berchtold (27 Dec. 1912), HHStA, no. 170(V).

117. Wilhelm falsely claimed that he and Nicholas had been able to resolve the situation in the Balkans "because stupid diplomats were not involved." See Vietsch, *Bethmann Hollweg*, p. 159.

118. Szögyényi to Vienna (18, 19 Aug. 1913), HHStA, no. 170(B).

119. Schoenbaum, *Zabern*, p. 92.

120. On the affair, see ibid.; Kitchen, *Officer Corps*, chap. 8; Deimling, *Lebenserinnerungen*, chap. 8.

121. Kitchen, *Officer Corps*, p. 207.

122. For Wilhelm's view of the provinces at the time of the Zabern incident, see Szögyényi to Berchtold (23 Jan. 1914), HHStA, no. 171(V); transcript of address by Wilhelm II to the Bavarian house of deputies (17 Dec. 1913), in Briefwechsel, 1:262 n. 4; Iswolsky, *Memoirs*, p. 78. For his long-standing hostility to Alsace-Lorraine: Radziwill, *Lettres*, 1:13–14; Hohenlohe, *Leben*, pp. 142–47. On modeling the provinces on the British Empire, see Meyer, *Schiemann*, p. 245; on the uniforms the Kiaser designed, see Hohenlohe, *Leben*, p. 195.

123. Spitzemberg diary (8 Dec. 1913), Vierhaus, *Tagebuch*, p. 565.

124. Kitchen, *Officer Corps*, p. 210.

125. Deimling, *Lebenserinnerungen*, p. 150.

126. Szögyényi to Berchtold (23 Jan. 1913), HHStA, no. 171(V).

127. Mutius Papers, p. 192.

128. Cambon to Pichon (24 and 27 Nov. 1913), *DDF*, 3d ser., 8:653–54, 660–61.

129. On the excessive time given to military affairs, see Schmidt-Bückeburg, *Militärkabinett*, p. 178. On the Kaiser's lack of interest in internal affairs, see Mutius to Thimme (23 Dec. 1929), Thimme Papers, no. 16, pp. 8–9; KE, no. 317/2, p. 176, no. 576/1, p. 13; Raulff, *Machtpolitik und Imperialismus*, p. 27.

130. Westarp, *Konservative Politik*, 1:123.

131. Zmarzlik, *Bethmann*, p. 40; Wilhelm to Bethmann (23 Jan. 1911), KE, no. 331/1.

CHAPTER 9

1. Vietsch, *Bethmann Hollweg*, p. 156. The jubilation was by no means universal. For an example of dismay, see Vierhaus, *Tagebuch*, p. 558.

2. Müller diary (13 Dec. 1913), Müller Papers, no. 4.

3. Thimme, *Front wider Bülow*, p. 239; Briefwechsel, 1:295–98; see also Albert von Mutius to Thimme (8 June [1936?]), Thimme Papers, no. 16.

4. Bülow, 2:197–98.

5. On Nicholas II, see *DDF*, 3d ser., 9:415–16; on Albert of Belgium, see ibid., 8:653–54; on Ambassadors Cambon and Paléologue, see ibid., 9:395, 10:300; on Ambassador Goschen, see *BD*, 10:377–78. For the views of German officials:

Bülow, 2:197–98; Wilhelm von Stumm, a diplomat, in a report (2 Aug. 1911), Tirpitz Papers, no. 25a; Thimme Papers, no. 16, p. 12; Valentini in Bernhardi, *Denkwürdigkeiten*, p. 294.

6. Meyer, *Schiemann*, p. 184.

7. For his belief that England and Germany would not go to war: Thimme Papers, no. 16, p. 12; Leonidas E. Hill, *Weizsäcker-Papiere*, p. 131; for his fear, expressed in 1908, that they might, see *GP*, 24:68.

8. *BD*, 9/2:503–5; Davis, *The Kaiser*, pp. 130, 134–35; Meyer, *Schiemann*, p. 181 n. 537; Leonidas E. Hill, *Weizsäcker-Papiere*, p. 146; Briefwechsel, 1:189–92.

9. Eulalia, *Memoirs*, p. 212; Hantsch, *Berchtold*, 2:530.

10. Hantsch, *Berchtold*, 2:529; Meyer, *Schiemann*, p. 184 n. 559.

11. Janssen, *Graue Exzellenz*, pp. 112–13.

12. Westarp, *Konservative Politik*, 1:238–40.

13. Müller diary (3 July 1913), Müller Papers, no. 4.

14. *PD*, 1:266; Waldersee, *Denkwürdigkeiten*, 2:126–27; Hinzpeter, *Wilhelm II.*, p. 7; Einem, *Erinnerungen*, pp. 60–61.

15. Zobeltitz, *Chronik*, 2:258–59; *DDF*, 3d ser., 3:61.

16. Bernhardi, *Denkwürdigkeiten*, p. 335.

17. For Wilhelm on his leadership in war: Hermann von Stein, *Erlebnisse und Betrachtungen*, pp. 36–37; *BD*, 7:62–63; for uniforms, see Schoenaich, *Damaskus*, pp. 86–87.

18. Schoenaich, *Damaskus*, p. 85; on the cabinet, see Schmidt-Bückeburg, *Militärkabinett*.

19. Hermann von Stein, *Erlebnisse und Betrachtungen*, pp. 36–37. On Moltke's lack of self-confidence: Freytag-Loringhoven, *Menschen und Dinge*, p. 135; Schiffer, *Leben*, p. 40; Bülow, 2:83–84. For opposition in the army to his appointment as chief, see Einem, *Erinnerungen*, pp. 148–49, 161.

20. Schiffer, *Leben*, p. 40; Bernhardi, *Denkwürdigkeiten*, p. 263; Deimling, *Lebenserinnerungen*, p. 49.

21. In chronological order, beginning in 1898, see Brabant, *Hausen*, p. 133; Goltz, *Denkwürdigkeiten*, p. 331; Zobeltitz, *Chronik*, 2:58–59; Zedlitz-Trützschler, p. 226; *DDF*, 3d ser., 3:1; Vierhaus, *Tagebuch*, p. 563.

22. Morel, *Eastern Embassy*, p. 158; Vierhaus, *Tagebuch*, pp. 501, 519; Keller, *Vierzig Jahre*, pp. 235–36, 247; Topham, *Chronicles*, p. 239.

23. Müller to Tirpitz (26 Apr. 1914), Tirpitz Papers, no. 207.

24. Stürgkh, *Erinnerungen*, pp. 301–2; Conrad von Hötzendorf, *Dienstzeit*, 1:159.

25. See Nikitsch-Boulles, *Vor dem Sturm*, p. 114, on the letters; on the suspicions: Siebert, *Benckendorff*, 1:163–65; Conrad von Hötzendorf, *Dienstzeit*, 1:69–70, 3:169.

26. On the inevitability of war with Serbia, see Cecilie, *Erinnerungen an den Kronprinzen*, p. 49; see Chlumecky, *Franz Ferdinands*, pp. 75–76, on their disagreements; on the Kaiser's regret that Franz Ferdinand did not adopt his ideas, see KE, no. 659, p. 27.

27. Wilhelm to Admiral Warrender (4 July 1914), RMA, 2/1940.

28. Eyewitness accounts on the *Meteor* are in Tambach Papers, no. 31,

19/00171–72 (Admiral Karpf); Lichnowsky memo, KE, no. 659, p. 27; HA, Rep. 53, no. 342, p. 1; Müller diary (28 June 1914), Müller Papers, no. 4.

29. This was Lerchenfeld's opinion. See Briefwechsel, 1:302.

30. Christopher Howard, *Goschen*, p. 289.

31. Admiral Karpf to Foreign Office (12 Dec. 1919), Tambach Papers, no. 31, 19/00171–72.

32. Bülow, 3:136–37.

33. Szögyényi to Vienna (16 Mar. 1909), HHStA, no. 167(B); Franckenstein to same (23 Nov. 1909) and Wilhelm to Franz Joseph (14 Oct. 1908), Bittner and Uebersberger, *Aussenpolitik*, 2:212, 557–58; Lambsdorff, *Militärbevollmächtigten*, pp. 296–99. Wilhelm was very annoyed that he had not been given prior notification of the deal. See Bülow, 2:336; Szögyényi to Vienna (8 Oct. 1908), Bittner and Uebersberger, *Aussenpolitik*, 2:155–56.

34. Treutler to Foreign Office (24 Mar. 1914) and Tschirschky to Bethmann (8 May 1914), *GP*, 39:336–37, 405–6.

35. For the Kaiser's high opinion of Tisza, see ibid., 39:333–37, 341–43, 358–59, 365–69.

36. See an account of Wilhelm's visit to Vienna in 1889 in Glaise-Horstenau, *Franz Josephs Weggefährte*, pp. 337–38; record of a talk with Wilhelm (1 Mar. 1909), Brabant, *Hausen*, p. 241; Szögyényi to Vienna (16 Mar. 1909), HHStA, no. 167(B). See also *GP*, 33:295, 302–4, 373–74, for Wilhelm's instructions to Bethmann and Kiderlen on this point.

37. Berchtold notes of his talk with Tschirschky (3 July 1914), in Austria-Hungary, *Dokumente zum Kriegsausbruch*, p. 14.

38. Fischer, *Griff nach der Weltmacht*, p. 58; see also KE, no. 659, "Briefe des früheren Kruppdirektors Mühlon," p. 1.

39. Fischer, *Griff nach der Weltmacht*, p. 59.

40. Szögyényi to Berchtold (5 July 1914), Austria-Hungary, *Dokumente zum Kriegsausbruch*, pp. 17–18.

41. Albertini, *Origins of the War*, 2:156, 175–76; Hantsch, *Berchtold*, 2:571.

42. Fischer, *Griff nach der Weltmacht*, pp. 60–61.

43. Hopman diary (6 July 1914), Hopman Papers, no. 11; Captain Z. S. Zenker note (8 Nov. 1919), Montgelas and Schücking, p. 49; Berchtold to Szögyényi (8 July 1914), Austria-Hungary, *Dokumente zum Kriegsausbruch*, p. 31; Hantsch, *Berchtold*, 2:583.

44. Hopman to Tirpitz (6 July 1914), Tirpitz Papers, no. 100; Tschirschky to Foreing Office, 2 wires (7 July 1914), Montgelas and Schücking, pp. 112–14; "Briefe des früheren Kruppdirektors Mühlon," KE, no. 659, p. 1; also Hopman diary (6 July 1914), Hopman Papers, no. 11.

45. "Briefe des früheren Kruppdirektors Mühlon," KE, no. 659, p. 1, reporting a conversation, between Wilhelm and Karl Helfferich, that took place before Wilhelm's departure on his cruise on 6 July. As early as 1909 the Kaiser had said that if Russia mobilized, he would do the same. See Albertini, *Origins of the War*, 2:121.

46. Fischer, *Griff nach der Weltmacht*, p. 61. On 6 July Wilhelm had a talk with Admiral Capelle in which the possibility of war was discussed, but he made no mention of Britain. Hopman to Tirpitz (6 July 1914), Tirpitz Papers, no. 100.

47. On this talk, see the account by Zimmermann, also present, in Thimme, *Front wider Bülow*, p. 231; Bethmann Hollweg, *Betrachtungen*, 1:135–36.

48. Görlitz, *Regierte der Kaiser?*, p. 31; Albertini, *Origins of the War*, 2:142; Delbrück, *Mobilmachung*, p. 96. Wilhelm later reproached Bethmann for deliberately keeping him out of Berlin during the crisis. See Hammann, *Um den Kaiser*, p. 89.

49. Bertrab to Foreign Office (26 Oct. 1919), Montgelas and Schücking, p. 47; Hopman diary (6 July 1914), Hopman Papers, no. 11.

50. Mutius Papers, p. 200.

51. Wilhelm to Admiral Warrender (4 July 1914), RMA, 2/1940; KE, no. 708/1, p. 82.

52. Montgelas and Schücking, pp. 89–90. Szögyényi noted two days earlier that, based on his long experience with the Kaiser, he never doubted that Wilhelm would stand fast by the Habsburg monarchy, with the Kaiser motivated in part by his admiration for Franz Joseph. See Austria-Hungary, *Dokumente zum Kriegsausbruch*, pp. 37–39.

53. Wilhelm's marginalia on Pourtalès to Bethmann (21 July 1914) and on Jagow to Wilhelm (23 July 1914), Montgelas and Schücking, pp. 159–63.

54. Jagow to Wilhelm's retinue (18 July 1914), ibid., p. 128. Jagow, however, is recorded three days later as beginning to doubt the wisdom of having the Kaiser so far away. See Hopman diary (21 July 1914), Hopman Papers, no. 11.

55. See Montgelas and Schücking, p. 128, on the shipping lines; on the navy regrouping, see Müller diary (additions to entry for 28 June 1914), Müller Papers, no. 4; Wilhelm's notes (8 June 1924), Rijksarchief Papers, no. 649, p. 3; the order to the fleet (19 July 1914) is in RMA, no. 1756. See also Müller to Jagow (20 July 1914), in Montgelas and Schücking, p. 137.

56. Hopman to Tirpitz (22, 24, 25 July 1914), Tirpitz Papers, no. 100; Bethmann to Foreign Office (21 July 1914), Montgelas and Schücking, p. 150.

57. Müller diary (24 July 1914), Müller Papers, no. 4. Wilhelm later falsely claimed that he had first read of the ultimatum in a Norwegian newspaper. See Rijksarchief Papers, no. 649, p. 3; Wilhelm to Foreign Office (26 July 1914), Montgelas and Schücking, p. 227.

58. Schoen to Foreign Office (24 July 1914), Lichnowsky to same on same date, and Griesinger to same on same date, all in Montgelas and Schücking, pp. 181, 183–86; Bach, *Gesandtschaftsberichte*, pp. 20–21.

59. Tschirschky to Foreign Office (24 July 1914), Montgelas and Schücking, p. 182; Freytag-Loringhoven, *Menschen und Dinge*, pp. 188–89.

60. Wilhelm's note on Lichnowsky to Foreign Office (24 July 1914), Montgelas and Schücking, pp. 183–85.

61. Wilhelm's notes on Griesinger to Foreign Office (24 July 1914), ibid., p. 186.

62. Zimmermann memo (25 July 1914), ibid., p. 196; Wilhelm to Foreign Office (26 July 1914), ibid., p. 227; Müller diary (25 July 1914), Müller Papers, no. 11.

63. Roddie, *Peace Patrol*, pp. 214–15; Müller diary (26 July 1914), Müller Papers, no. 11; Bethmann to Wilhelm (25 July 1914), Montgelas and Schücking, pp. 201–2.

64. Freytag-Loringhoven, *Menschen und Dinge*, p. 187.

65. Wilhelm's notes on a letter from Bethmann (26 July 1914), Montgelas and Schücking, p. 223.

66. Müller diary (27 July 1914), Müller Papers, no. 11; Leonidas E. Hill, *Weizsäcker-Papiere*, p. 147. Bülow claimed that Wilhelm said that he was so upset that on his arrival he had been forced to take "a little nerves rest cure" by staying in bed for fourteen hours. Bülow, 3:146–47.

67. Montgelas and Schücking, pp. 252–54.

68. Wilhelm'a marginalia on Chelius to Wilhelm (28 July 1914), in Lambsdorff, *Militärbevollmächtigten*, pp. 436–37; Wilhelm to Jagow (28 July 1914), Montgelas and Schücking, pp. 273–74.

69. Wilhelm to Jagow and to Nicholas II (both 28 July 1914), Montgelas and Schücking, pp. 273–74, 296–97. On Wilhelm's travel plans, see his letter to the Kaiserin (27 July 1914), Bach, *Gesandschaftsberichte*, p. 21; Valentini to his wife (29 July 1914), KE, no. 341/4.

70. Wilhelm's comments on a letter from Jagow (23 July 1914), Montegelas and Schücking, pp. 162–63.

71. Lichnowsky to Foreign Office (29 July 1914), ibid., pp. 321–22.

72. Wilhelm's comments on ibid.; Henry to Wilhelm (28 July 1914), ibid., pp. 328–29.

73. Wilhelm's comments on Lichnowsky to Foreign Office (29 July 1914), ibid., pp. 321–22.

74. *PD*, 2:3; Tirpitz, *Erinnerungen*, p. 238.

75. Wilhelm on Pourtalès to Bethmann (26 July 1914), Montgelas and Schücking, pp. 266–68; Szögyényi to Berchtold (31 July 1914), Austria-Hungary, *Dokumente zum Kriegsausbruch*, pp. 45–46; Wilhelm's comments on a letter from Chelius (31 July 1914), Lambsdorff, *Militärbevollmächtigten*, p. 440.

76. Wilhelm to Nicholas II (28 July 1914), Montgelas and Schücking, pp. 296–97.

77. Telegram (29 July 1914), ibid., p. 295.

78. Wilhelm to Nicholas II (29 July 1914), ibid., p. 315.

79. Wilhelm's marginalia on Pourtalès to Foreign Office (30 July 1914), ibid., pp. 349–50. "The World's War was King Edward VII's," Wilhelm wrote in 1929. "He engineered it." Wilhelm to Bigelow (Christmas 1929), Bigelow Papers, no. 34.

80. Wilhelm's notes on Pourtalès to Foreign Office (30 July 1914), Montgelas and Schücking, pp. 349–50.

81. Valentini to his wife (31 July 1914), KE no. 341/4; Valentini diary (30 July 1914), Thimme Papers, no. 26; Valentini, pp. 126–27; Mutius diary (30 July 1914), Mutius Papers, p. 201. On Wilhelm I, see Beseler to his wife (16 Sept. 1915), Beseler Papers, no. 53.

82. Mutius diary (31 July 1914), Mutius Papers, pp. 202–3.

83. Wilhelm to Nicholas II and the tsar's response (both 31 July 1914), Montgelas and Schücking, pp. 399, 402–3.

84. Wilhelm to Victor Emmanuel III (31 July 1914), ibid., pp. 424–25. Wilhelm also sent one of his adjutants to Rome to work on the king. Szögyényi to Berchtold (31 July 1914), Austria-Hungary, *Dokumente zum Kriegsausbruch*, pp. 46–47.

85. Regele, *Conrad*, p. 228; Briefwechsel, 1:322.

86. Rosner, *Erinnerungen des Kronprinzen*, p. 136; Wilhelm to Franz Joseph (31 July 1914), Montgelas and Schücking, pp. 419–20.

87. Wilhelm to George V (1 Aug. 1914), RA, Geo V Q 1549, no. 12; Lichnowsky to Bethmann and Bethmann to Lichnowsky (1 Aug. 1914), Monteglas and Schücking, pp. 444, 452; Rosner, *Erinnerungen des Kronprinzen*, p. 136.

88. This is printed in Montgelas and Schücking, p. 441, and given in facsimile in Wrisberg, *Erinnerungen*, 2:3.

89. Schoen to Foreign Office (1 Aug. 1914), Montgelas and Schücking, p. 448; on Moltke, see Tirpitz's notes (1 Aug. 1914), Tirpitz Papers, no. 100.

90. Tirpitz's notes (1 Aug. 1914), Tirpitz Papers, no. 100.

91. Valentini, pp. 126–27; *PD*, 2:16–18.

92. Haeften Papers, no. 1, p. 33.

93. Ibid., pp. 34–35.

94. Lichowsky to Foreign Office (1 Aug. 1914), Montgelas and Schücking, pp. 460–62.

95. Lichowsky to Foreign Office (1 Aug. 1914) and Bethmann to Schoen (2 Aug. 1914), ibid., pp. 479–80.

96. Lichnowsky to Foreign Office (2 Aug. 1914), ibid., p. 483. When, just before 7 P.M. on 3 Aug., Ambassador Szögyényi pointed out to the German Foreign Office that an invasion of Belgium would only increase the likelihood of Britain's intervention, he was told that the military "were now in charge and one could not contradict them." See Austria-Hungary, *Dokumente zum Kriegsausbruch*, p. 95.

97. Waters, *Potsdam and Doorn*, pp. 122–23, relating a conversation in 1928 with Wilhelm.

98. Lichnowsky to Foreign Office (4 Aug. 1914), Montgelas and Schücking, p. 580.

99. Goschen to Nicolson (1 Aug. 1914), *BD*, 11:284, reporting what Jagow had told him; also HA, Rep. 94, no. 975.

100. Cambon to Doumergue (22 Aug. 1914), *DDF*, 3d ser., 11:589–90. He would later declare that he could not understand how the course of events had prevailed against the word of kings. See Groener diary (30 Oct. 1914), Groener *Lebenserinnerungen*, p. 527.

101. Eggeling, *Russische Mobilmachung*, p. 52.

102. See Montgelas and Schücking, pp. 514, 543, 587.

103. Ibid., p. 570. For Wilhelm's expectation that Rumania would help, see Szögyényi to Berchtold (31 July 1914), Austria-Hungary, *Dokumente zum Kriegsausbruch*, pp. 45–46.

104. Viktoria Luise, *Tochter des Kaisers*, pp. 134–36.

105. On Harnack's authorship: Zahn-Harnack, *Harnack*, p. 345; Braun, *Weg durch 4. Zeitepochen*, p. 101. Two other addresses, to the German people and to the army and navy, were also ghostwritten. See Haeften diary (1 Aug. 1914), Haften Papers, no. 1, pp. 3–4. Note that they were prepared two days before Germany went to war.

106. Wilhelm's marginalia on the *Norddeutsche Allgemeine Zeitung* (7 July 1909), Bülow Papers, no. 35.

107. Delbrück, *Mobilmachung*, pp. 28–29.

108. Groener, *Lebenserinnerungen*, p. 150.

109. This was because in theory, if not in practice, all military orders proceeded by command of the monarch, the usage in the Franco-Prussian War of 1870–71. The Kaiser's entourage succeeded until 11 Sept. in convincing Moltke that he therefore could not leave for the front. See Tappen to Reichsarchiv (5 July 1920), Tappen Papers, no. 6.

110. Mutius Papers, p. 210; Groener Papers, no. 75, frame 238; Valentini to his wife (4 Oct. 1914), KE, no. 341/4.

111. Valentini to his wife (6 Sept., 4 Oct. 1914), KE, no. 341/4; Görlitz, *Regierte der Kaiser?*, p. 55; Seeckt, *Leben*, pp. 186–87; Thaer, *Generalstabsdienst*, pp. 231–32; Eisenhart-Rothe, *Persönlichkeit*, pp. 175–77, Janssen, *Graue Exzellenz*, pp. 117–19.

112. KE, no. 317/2, pp. 173–74.

113. Hopman diary (19 Oct. 1914), Hopman Papers, no. 12; Payer, *Bethmann Hollweg bis Ebert*, pp. 174–75.

114. Schiffer Papers, no. 5, p. 1030. There is a very similar quotation from the same period in Schulenburg-Tressow Papers, p. 77.

115. Czernin von und zu Chudenitz, *Weltkriege*, p. 24.

116. Schönburg-Waldenburg, *Erinnerungen*, p. 224; Tappen to Reichsarchiv (30 Sept. 1920), Tappen Papers, no. 6; Groener, *Lebenserinnerungen*, p. 172; Müller to Thimme (17 Jan. 1923), Thimme Papers, no. 14; Lerchenfeld-Koefering, *Wilhelm II.*, p. 39.

117. Alexander Hohenlohe, *Leben*, 338. Other doubts about the Kaiser's martial role are in Tirpitz, *Erinnerungen*, p. 415; Bülow, 1:57, 2:152.

118. Schönburg-Waldenburg, *Erinnerungen*, p. 225; Pohl diary (6, 19 Aug. 1914), Pohl, *Aufzeichnungen*, pp. 5, 20.

119. Wedel to Bülow (16 Feb. 1915), Bülow Papers, no. 39; Freytag-Loringhoven, *Menschen und Dinge*, pp. 272–73.

120. Moltke, *Moltke Erinnerungen*, p. 449; Nicolai, *Nachrichtendienst*, p. 213; Niemann, *Kaiser und Revolution*, p. 32; Czernin von und zu Chudenitz, *Im Weltkriege*, p. 75.

121. Czernin von und zu Chudenitz, *Weltkriege*, p. 75

122. See Groener Papers, no. 75, p. 238, and Groener, *Lebenserinnerungen*, p. 187, on the lute players. Two of these were Wilhelm's childhood friend General Adolf Wild von Hohenborn and General Prince von Schönburg-Waldenburg. See Janssen, *Kanzler*, p. 40, and Schönburg-Waldenburg, *Erinnerungen*, p. 226.

123. See Wild von Hohenborn Papers, no. 2, p. 10, for hunting; gardening is in a memo by H. N. Anderson of talk with Wilhelm (19 Mar. 1915), RA, Geo V O 1177, no. 22; Schönburg-Waldenburg, *Erinnerungen*, p. 247, depicts him sawing wood. Valentini's diary (30 June 1916) notes that Wilhelm was decoding the Hittite tongue ("more important than the entire war"). See Thimme Papers, no. 4.

124. Ludendorff, *Own Story*, 1:106, 307.

125. Schulenburg-Tressow Papers, p. 262; Groener Papers, no. 75, pp. 235–36; memo by Hans von Below (1920), in Below Papers, no. 2; Freytag-Loringhoven, *Menschen und Dinge*, p. 276; Deist, *Militär und Innenpolitik*, 2:425 n. 5; Czernin von und zu Chudenitz, *Weltkriege*, pp. 86–87. Max von Mutius, one of Wilhelm's

adjutants during the first year of the war, noted that although the Kaiser was more reserved in what he said, the willfulness that characterized his personality remained unbroken. Mutius to Thimme (1 Nov. 1933), Thimme Papers, no. 18.

126. Falkenhayn, *Oberste Kriegsleitung*, p. 3; Paul von Hindenburg, *Leben*, p. 170. Freytag-Loringhoven, *Menschen und Dinge*, p. 276, deals with personnel.

127. Pohl to his wife (13 Oct. 1914), Pohl, *Aufzeichnungen*, p. 77.

128. Wild von Hohenborn to his wife (27 Aug. 1915), Wild von Hohenborn Papers, no. 3; Groener, *Lebenserinnerungen*, p. 528. For efforts to increase coverage of the Kaiser in the press, see Deist, *Militär und Innenpolitik*, 2:832, and Ilsemann, 1:59.

CHAPTER 10

1. Gen. Baron Ferdinand von Marlerer to Conrad von Hötzendorf (4 Nov. 1914), noting that all Wilhelm was interested in was the war against England, in Regele, *Conrad*, p. 335; also Hoffmann diary (30 May 1916), Hoffmann, *Aufzeichnungen*, 1:119.

2. Regele, *Conrad*, p. 268, reporting a meeting of 22 Nov. 1912 at which Wilhelm did not contradict Moltke's estimate of a war of four to five weeks.

3. Chirol to Hardinge (24 Aug. 1914), Hardinge Papers, no. 93.

4. Janssen, *Macht und Verblendung*, p. 30; Erdmann, *Riezler*, p. 201 n. 25.

5. Hermann von Stein, *Erlebnisse und Betrachtungen*, pp. 38–39; Pastor, *Tagebücher*, p. 626. He is recorded only once in the early stages of the war as believing it would be long-lasting. See Ambassador Gerard's notes of a talk with Wilhelm on 10 Aug. 1914, in which he somewhat dejectedly declared that Britain's entry would make the conflict protracted. Gerard, *Four Years*, p. 206.

6. Wilhelm to Wilson (10 Aug. 1914), in Gerard, *Four Years*, pp. 200–202.

7. KE, no. 317/2, p. 183; Czernin von und zu Chudenitz, *Weltkriege*, p. 93.

8. Dommes Papers, no. 15.

9. Bülow, 3:253; Crown Prince Rupprecht of Bavaria's diary (11 July 1917), Rupprecht, *Kriegstagebuch*, 2:227; Leonidas E. Hill, *Weizsäcker-Papiere*, pp. 192–93.

10. Valentini, p. 239.

11. On the Baltic and Russia, see Schiffer, *Leben*, pp. 67, 72; Meyer, *Schiemann*, p. 232; on Rumania, see Thaer, *Generalstabsdienst*, p. 156; on Poland, see ibid., as well as Hutten-Czapski, *Sechzig Jahre*, 2:145, 288; Braun, *Weg durch 4. Zeitepochen*, p. 151; Leonidas E. Hill, *Weizsäcker-Papiere*, pp. 192–93.

12. Wild von Hohenborn notes (17 Nov. 1915), Wild von Hohenborn Papers, no. 2, pp. 24–25. For the Kaiserin's intervention in behalf of Hindenburg: Tirpitz, *Erinnerungen*, p. 138; Mutius Papers, p. 211; Janssen, *Kanzler*, pp. 77–79, 156; in behalf of Groener, see Groener, *Lebenserinnerungen*, pp. 361, 366–67; in behalf of Tirpitz, see Tirpitz, *Erinnerungen*, pp. 474–75. She also intervened to help the East Elbian aristocracy, who wanted troops moved from the west to the east to offer them greater protection. See Schiffer, *Leben*, p. 36. For her wartime prejudices, which were that Austria was too weak and that Great Britain was *the* hated

enemy: Cramon, *Bundesgenosse*, p. 161; Ballin to Bülow (9 Dec. 1914), Bülow Papers, no. 60. Wilhelm sometimes resented his wife's obtrusive activity. See Janssen, *Kanzler*, pp. 78–79; Mutius Papers, p. 211.

13. Pohl to his wife (14 Sept. 1914), Pohl, *Aufzeichnungen*, p. 48.

14. On his determination to defeat the British, see Görlitz, *Regierte der Kaiser?*, p. 59; for his delight at British defeats; Seeckt, *Leben*, pp. 186–87; Valentini to his wife (27 Oct. 1914), KE, no. 341/4.

15. Princess Evelyn Blücher von Wahlstatt, *English Wife in Berlin*, p. 86.

16. Valentini to his wife (25 Aug. 1914), KE, no. 341/1, and his diary of the same date in Thimme Papers, no. 26; Schönburg-Waldenburg, *Erinnerungen*, p. 231; Helfferich, *Weltkrieg*, p. 143.

17. On Schlieffen's belief that Moltke would one day spoil his plan, see Hahnke to the crown prince of Prussia (2 Apr. 1922), Hahnke Papers.

18. Wilhelm's version, dating from 1925, is in Cramon Papers, no. 31; see also Groener, *Lebenserinnerungen*, p. 172; Groener Papers, no. 75, frame 237.

19. Lossberg, *Tätigkeit im Weltkriege*, pp. 141, 166. Colonel Nicolai, head of the *Nachrichtendienst* at the General Staff, declared that Wilhelm had less to do with the General Staff once Falkenhayn took over. See HA, Rep. 53, no. 342, p. 43. For opinion in the army on Wilhelm and his attachment to Falkenhayn, see Wedel to Bülow (16 Feb. 1915), Bülow Papers, no. 39; Mutius Papers, p. 210; Cramon, *Bundesgenosse*, p. 23. On Falkenhayn's being promoted over the heads of other generals, see Zwehl, *Falkenhayn*, p. 71.

20. Schönburg-Waldenburg, *Erinnerungen*, pp. 233–34.

21. Hopman diary (15 Sept. 1914), Hopman Papers, no. 11.

22. Tirpitz to his wife (9 Oct. 1914), Tirpitz, *Erinnerungen*, p. 416.

23. Janssen, *Kanzler*, p. 39; Erdmann, *Riezler*, pp. 226–27.

24. Falkenhayn's assurances are in Schönburg-Waldenburg, *Erinnerungen*, p. 252.

25. For the Kaiser's depression, see Valentini to his wife (4 Nov. 1914), KE, no. 341/4; for his confidence in Germany's economy see, Pohl to his wife (26 Nov. 1914), Pohl, *Aufzeichnungen*, p. 92.

26. Conrad von Hötzendorf's notes on a meeting with Wilhelm (2 Dec. 1914), Conrad von Hötzendorf, *Dienstzeit*, 5:655. On the Kaiserin's equally great rage, see Ballin to Bülow (9 Dec. 1914), Bülow Papers, no. 60; KE, no. 317/2, p. 184.

27. Kessel diary (4 Dec. 1914), HA, 53a, no. 29. Furthermore, the British would have to "lay Japan at [his] feet" in revenge for Tokyo's attempt to take the German colony at Kiaochow in China, whose possession in the 1890s Wilhelm considered to be his own achievement. Wilhelm also admired Bethmann's very anti-British speech in the Reichstag (2 Dec. 1914). See Bunsen, *Zeitgenossen*, p. 135.

28. J. G. Lockhart, *Halifax*, 2:239.

29. Wild von Hohenborn to Falkenhayn (11/12 Nov. 1914), in Janssen, *Kanzler*, p. 40 n. 54.

30. Groener diary (20 Nov. 1914), Groener, *Lebenserinnerungen*, p. 204.

31. Admiralty Staff to Tirpitz (22 Dec. 1909), Tambach Papers, no. 31, 4/00745–46.

32. Szögyényi to Berchtold (31 July 1914), Austria-Hungary, *Dokumente zum*

Kriegsausbruch, pp. 46–47. "Parade fleet" is Admiral Pohl's expression, with which Wilhelm agreed. See Pohl to his wife (15 Nov. 1914), Pohl, *Aufzeichnungen*, pp. 87–88.

33. Pohl to his wife (6, 29 Aug., 13, 17 Sept., 16 Oct. 1914), Pohl *Aufzeichnungen*, pp. 5, 35–36, 58, 66, 78–79; Hopman diary (2 Aug, 3 Sept. 1914), Hopman Papers, no. 12; Tirpitz, *Erinnerungen*, pp. 310–11. See also Niemann's report of a talk with Wilhelm (17 Dec. 1926), Rijksarchief Papers, no. 253.

34. Pohl to his wife (30 Aug. 1914), Pohl, *Aufzeichnungen*, pp. 37–38; Tirpitz, *Erinnerungen*, pp. 397–98, 444. The chief of the Military Cabinet, General Lyncker, declared after the war that Tirpitz had in August 1914 opposed putting the fleet on the water to ensure its being intact at the end of the conflict. See Lyncker to Tirpitz (20 Dec. 1926), Capelle Papers, no. 5.

35. Tirpitz, *Erinnerungen*, p. 415.

36. Ibid., p. 432, 460–61. The Kaiser's health was to be alleged as the reason.

37. Tirpitz to his wife (9 Apr. 1915), ibid., p. 468. The Kaiser, for example, did not know of the conditions of the policy of unrestricted submarine warfare, initiated on 1 Feb. 1915, until three days later. See Pohl, *Aufzeichnungen*, p. 106.

38. Tirpitz's complaints about how isolated he is from the Kaiser are in his letter to Capelle (19 Mar. 1915), Capelle Papers, no. 1; Tirpitz to Wild von Hohenborn (26 Mar. 1916), Wild von Hohenborn Papers, no. 7; Tirpitz, *Erinnerungen*, pp. 415, 442; Wilhelm's criticism of the admiral's ships is in Pohl, *Aufzeichnungen*, pp. 52, 75.

39. On the admiral's descendant star, see Pohl, *Aufzeichnungen*, pp. 86, 93–94; for Tirpitz on his various enemies, see his letter to Trotha (mid-Sept. 1915), Tirpitz Papers, no. 169. The Kaiserin was one of his most ardent supporters. See Widenmann, *Marine-Attaché*, pp. 66–67, 227, 278–79.

40. Tirpitz, *Erinnerungen*, p. 444; Pohl, *Aufzeichnungen*, p. 5.

41. Wilhelm expressed his fears of submarine inadequacy in a talk with Tirpitz in mid-June 1914. See *Berliner Monatsschrift* 3 (Aug. 1925): 561–62.

42. Helfferich, *Weltkrieg*, p. 309.

43. Doerries, *Imperial Challenge*, p. 284 n. 30; Wilhelm's annoyance is in Gerard, *Four Years*, pp. 219, 251–53; Davis, *The Kaiser*, p. 85.

44. *PD*, 2:335; Davis, *The Kaiser*, pp. 84–85, for Wilhelm's reaction. To the end of his life the Kaiser believed that the *Lusitania* had been heavily laden with munitions. See his notes (1934) in HA, Rep. 192, no. 20.

45. Doerries, *Imperial Challenge*, p. 126; Gerard, *Four Years*, pp. 251–53.

46. *PD*, 2:348.

47. Tirpitz's unaddressed letter (7 Aug. 1915), Tirpitz, *Erinnerungen*, p. 490.

48. *PD*, 2:404–6; Tirpitz, *Erinnerungen*, pp. 358–59; Tirpitz to Müller (9 May 1915), Tirpitz Papers, no. 207.

49. *PD*, 2:409–17.

50. Ibid., 2:411–12.

51. Conrad von Hötzendorf, *Dienstzeit*, 4:197.

52. Erzberger, *Erlebnisse im Weltkrieg*, pp. 49–52; also Chelius to Bülow (3 Feb. 1915), Bülow Papers, no. 39.

53. Lerchenfeld to Hertling (30 June 1915), Briefwechsel, 1:471–72.

54. On Falkenhayn's surefootedness in dealing with Wilhelm, see ibid., 2:712;

Janssen, *Kanzler*, p. 165; Groener Papers, no. 75, frames 31, 237; Groener, *Lebenserinnerungen*, p. 187; Hoffmann, *Aufzeichnungen*, pp. 62, 69–70. Falkenhayn's elimination of Wilhelm's influence is in Brauer, *Grosse Krieg*, p. 72.

55. Hoffmann, *Aufzeichnungen*, p. 100; Groener, *Lebenserinnerungen*, p. 528; Janssen, *Kanzler*, p. 189; Ilsemann, 1:59; Gerard, *Face to Face with Kaiserism*, p. 65. For the primacy of the western front, see Kraft, *Staatsräson*, pp. 42–43.

56. Lossberg, *Tätigkeit im Weltkriege*, pp. 164–65.

57. Groener, *Lebenserinnerungen*, p. 216.

58. Erdmann, *Riezler*, p. 283; Hoffmann, *Aufzeichnungen*, p. 79. Groener declared, with some concern, that his trust in Falkenhayn was "unshakable and incapable of being shaken." Groener, *Lebenserinnerungen*, p. 245. See also Freytag-Loringhoven, *Menschen und Dinge*, p. 273.

59. Janssen, *Graue Exzellenz*, p. 228; Briefwechsel, 1:405.

60. Wild von Hohenborn to wife (24 Aug. 1916), Wild von Hohenborn Papers, no. 2, p. 101; Groener Papers, no. 75, frames 31, 36; memo by Hans von Below (1920), Below Papers, no. 2; Lossberg, *Tätigkeit im Weltkriege*, p. 141; Wedel to Bülow (16 Feb. 1915), Bülow Papers, no. 39; Gallwitz, *Führertätigkeit*, p. 145; Moltke, *Moltke Erinnerungen*, pp. 413–16; Hoffmann, *Aufzeichnungen*, p. 62.

61. Haeften (?) to Bethmann (12 Jan. 1915), KE, no. 342/1; Janssen, *Kanzler*, p. 77; Kraft, *Staatsräson*, pp. 42–43.

62. Hopman, *Kriegstagebuch*, p. 68.

63. Kraft, *Staatsräson*, pp. 42–43; Janssen, *Kanzler*, pp. 77–79. Albrecht von Wallenstein (1583–1634) was an Austrian general of great ability but also notorious for cruelty and avarice.

64. Hoffmann to wife (30 May 1915), Hoffmann Papers, no. 2. On Wilhelm's jealousy of the two generals, see Wild von Hohenborn to wife (27 Aug. 1915), Wild von Hohenborn Papers, no. 3; Mutius Papers, p. 211; KE, no. 331/2, pp. 2–3; Regele, *Conrad*, p. 351; Groener, *Lebenserinnerungen*, pp. 214–15.

65. For Wilhelm's dislike of Hindenburg, see Groener, *Lebenserinnerungen*, p. 245; Mutius Papers, p. 162.

66. Tappen diary (15 Apr., 27 July 1915), Tappen Papers, no. 1.

67. Hecker, *Rathenau*, p. 272. For Wilhelm's dislike of Ludendorff, see Groener, *Lebenserinnerungen*, pp. 214–15, 245. For Ludendorff's fearlessness in telling the Kaiser what he thought, see Czernin von und zu Chudenitz, *Weltkriege*, p. 79.

68. Paul von Hindenburg, *Leben*, p. 119.

69. Lossberg, *Tätigkeit im Weltkriege*, p. 203.

70. Paul von Hindenburg, *Leben*, p. 120.

71. Accounts of the meeting are in ibid., p. 119; Hoffmann, *Versäumten Gelegenheiten*, p. 137, misdating the meeting as having occurred in May.

72. General Bernhardi thought this was the decisive decision of the war because it abandoned the attempt to destroy the Russian army and thus eliminate the eastern front. See Bernhardi, *Denkwürdigkeiten*, pp. 408–9.

73. Groener diary (11 Oct. 1915), Groener, *Lebenserinnerungen*, p. 542. In June, even before the campaign got under way, he believed that Russia was finished. See Marwitz, *Weltkriegsbriefe*, p. 141.

74. Oettingen diary (4 Nov. 1915), KE, no. 517/5.

75. Tirpitz to Trotha (2 Aug. 1915), Tirpitz Papers, no. 169.

76. Ibid.; Tirpitz to Trotha (n.d. [mid-Sept.. 1915]), ibid.; Tirpitz, *Erinnerungen*, p. 324.

77. Tirpitz to Trotha (n.d. [ca. 20/27 July 1915]), Tirpitz Papers, no. 169; same to same (22 July 1916), ibid.

78. Tirpitz to Trotha (22 July 1916), ibid.

79. Hohenlohe to Burián (6 Sept. 1915), HHStA, no. 171(B).

80. Gerard, *Face to Face with Kaiserism*, p. 66. See also KE, no. 317/2, p. 176.

81. Paul von Hindenburg, *Leben*, p. 170 (italics added).

82. On the personal regime in wartime, see Freytag-Loringhoven, *Menschen und Dinge*, p. 276; Alter, *Armeeführer*, p. 249; Bethmann Hollweg, *Betrachtungen*, 2:19–25; Payer, *Bethmann Hollweg bis Ebert*, p. 174; Westarp, *Konservative Politik*, 2:662; Baron Roman Rosen, *Forty Years*, 2:297.

83. Schulthess (1915/1), pp. 335–36; Erdmann, *Riezler*, p. 287 note 1.

CHAPTER 11

1. Rosner, *Erinnerungen des Kronprinzen*, pp. 18–19; *HP*, 3:307; Bülow, 1:80, 2:62, 397. Wilhelm's mother also recognized this. Bülow, 1:212.

2. Zwehl, *Falkenhayn*, p. 210; Lossberg, *Tätigkeit im Weltkriege*, pp. 205–7.

3. *PD*, 2:450–61; Leonidas E. Hill, *Weizsäcker-Papiere*, p. 194.

4. Zwehl, *Falkenhayn*, p. 210.

5. Bethmann to Valentini (14 June 1916), KE, no. 341/2. For the Kaiser's hostility to *any* advice on military matters, see Janssen, *Kanzler*, p. 292.

6. Grünau to Bethmann (10 May 1916), Reichskanzlei Papers, no. 806/6.

7. HA, Rep. 53, no. 342, p. 38; Wild von Hohenborn diary (25 June 1916), Wild von Hohenborn Papers, no. 2, p. 77. For Wilhelm's angst at Falkenhayn, see Erdmann, *Riezler*, p. 338.

8. Helfferich, *Weltkrieg*, p. 331.

9. Janssen, *Kanzler*, p. 192; Scheer, *Hochseeflotte im Weltkrieg*, pp. 127–28; *Briefwechsel*, 2:628–29.

10. *PD*, 2:411–12, 461.

11. Leonidas E. Hill, *Weizsäcker-Papiere*, p. 188, 192; Tirpitz's notes of a talk with Admiral Holtzendorff (21 Aug. 1916), Tirpitz Papers, no. 205.

12. Leonidas E. Hill, *Weizsäcker-Papiere*, p. 188; Hohenlohe to Vienna (3 Mar. 1917), HHStA, no. 172(B); Bethmann to Jagow (5 Mar. 1916), KE, no. 342/1; Tirpitz's notes of a talk with Holtzendorff (21 Aug. 1916), Tirpitz Papers, no. 205; *Briefwechsel*, 2:579; Janssen, *Graue Exzellenz*, pp. 238–39.

13. Wilhelm's promise is in a cabinet order (19 Sept. 1915), *PD*, 2:437; on the Kaiser's failure to consult, see Schiffer diary (30 Mar. 1916), Schiffer Papers, no. 3, p. 466; Hopman, *Kriegstagebuch*, p. 159.

14. *PD*, 2:508–10.

15. Oettingen diary (22 Mar. 1916), KE, no. 517/5. The Kaiserin was acutely disappointed, to her husband's annoyance. See *PD*, 2:512–13; Widenmann, *Marine-Attaché*, p. 227; Janssen, *Graue Exzellenz*, pp. 238–39.

16. Janssen, *Kanzler*, pp. 192, 196.

17. Bethmann to Loebell (9 May 1916), Loebell Papers, no. 5; unaddressed

letter (16 May 1916) describing the Kaiser by General Thaer in his *Generalstabs-dienst*, p. 69.

18. Lerchenfeld to Hertling (30 Aug. 1916), Briefwechsel, 2:687.

19. Bethmann's dislike of Falkenhayn is in Oettingen diary (13 Nov. 1916), KE, no. 517/5; Lossberg, *Tätigkeit im Weltkriege*, p. 240; Jagow's dislike is in Hohen-lohe to Vienna (24 May 1916), HHStA, no. 172(B). The Kaiserin was also a foe. See Schiffer, *Leben*, p. 125.

20. Groener, *Lebenserinnerungen*, p. 320.

21. On his fixation, see Hantsch, *Berchtold*, 2:803–4; his confidence in Ruma-nia's neutrality is in Bauer notes (27 Aug. 1916), Bauer, *Grosser Krieg*, p. 104.

22. Wilhelm's depression is in Valentini diary (27 Aug. 1916), Thimme Papers, no. 26; Valentini, p. 139; Valentini to his wife (30 Aug. 1916), KE, no. 341/6; Falkenhayn's diary (31 Aug. 1916), in Zwehl, *Falkenhayn*, pp. 211–12; Janssen, *Kanzler*, p. 249. On the fateful situation Germany now found itself in, see Regele, *Conrad*, p. 533.

23. Plessen diary (29 Aug. 1916), HA, Rep. 192, no. 22; Valentini, p. 139; Wild von Hohenborn diary (28 Aug. 1916), Wild von Hohenborn Papers, no. 2, pp. 102–4. On Wilhelm's consent to an increase of Hindenburg and Ludendorff's authority in the east in the month leading up to Falkenhayn's dismissal, see Wild von Hohenborn diary (24, 27 July, 6, 12–13 Aug. 1916), Wild von Hohenborn Papers, no. 2, pp. 86, 89–90, 94, 97–98.

24. Zwehl, *Falkenhayn*, pp. 211–12. Wilhelm claimed that the parting was quite painful for him.

25. Wild von Hohenborn diary (28 Aug. 1916), Wild von Hohenborn Papers, no. 2, pp. 102–4; Janssen, *Kanzler*, p. 256.

26. Janssen, *Kanzler*, p. 235.

27. Riezler diary (22 Nov. 1916), Erdmann, *Riezler*, pp. 383–84; Tirpitz notes of a talk with Count August zu Eulenburg (24 Nov. 1916), Tirpitz Papers, no. 203; HA, Rep. 53, no. 342, p. 43.

28. Lerchenfeld to Hertling (20 Sept. 1916), Briefwechsel, 2:712.

29. The Kaiser, for example, saw to it that his childhood friend General Wild von Hohenborn retained his position as minister of war. See Briefwechsel, 2:764. On how the generals intimidated him, see Payer, *Bethmann Hollweg bis Ebert*, p. 174.

30. Janssen, *Kanzler*, p. 256.

31. Ludendorff, *Own Story*, 2:61. The crown prince agreed. See Einem, *Ar-meeführer*, pp. 269–70. On the entourage's alarm at Ludendorff's frankness, see Hofmann, *Aufzeichnungen*, 1:149–50.

32. For the comparison to Tirpitz, see Leonidas E. Hill, *Weizsäcker-Papiere*, p. 272. On Wilhelm's avoiding Ludendorff, see Hoffmann, *Aufzeichnungen*, 1:149–50; Pogge von Strandmann, *Rathenau Tagebuch*, p. 222. The general regretted being shut out. See Bauer, *Grosse Krieg*, p. 111.

33. Riezler diary (22 Nov. 1916), Erdmann, *Riezler*, pp. 383–84. One of Wil-helm's adjutants agreed. See Niemann, *Kaiser und Revolution*, p. 39.

34. On keeping the chancellor out of military affairs, see Erdmann, *Riezler*, p. 361 n. 6.

35. Valentini diary (3, 9 Dec. 1916), Thimme Papers, no. 26.

36. Tirpitz's notes of a talk with Admiral Holtzendorff (21 Aug. 1916), Tirpitz Papers, no. 205.

37. Dryander, *Erinnerungen*, p. 304.

38. Tirpitz's notes of a talk with Admiral Holtzendorff (21 Aug. 1916), Tirpitz Papers, no. 205.

39. See ibid. for the Kaiser; on the generals, see Paul von Hindenburg, *Leben*, pp. 230–33; on Bethmann, see Oettingen diary (13 Nov. 1916), KE, no. 517/5.

40. Thimme Papers, no. 61, p. 66.

41. Haussmann to wife (11 Nov. 1916), Haussmann, *Schlaglichter*, p. 76.

42. Tirpitz's notes of a talk with Count August zu Eulenburg (24 Nov. 1916), Tirpitz Papers, no. 203. Tirpitz favored getting rid of Jagow. See his notes of a talk with Eulenburg (6 Mar. 1917), ibid.

43. Hertling to Lerchenfeld (4 Aug. 1916), Briefwechsel, 2:657.

44. Tirpitz's notes of talks with Eulenburg (10 Oct., 24 Nov. 1916) and of a talk with Widenmann (20 Oct. 1916), Tirpitz Papers, no. 203.

45. Tirpitz's notes of a talk with Widenmann (20 Oct. 1916), ibid.; Widenmann, *Marine-Attaché*, pp. 278–79.

46. Cramon, *Bundesgenosse*, pp. 94–95; Lerchenfeld to Hertling (11 Dec. 1916), Briefwechsel, 2:781.

47. Helfferich, *Weltkrieg*, p. 339.

48. Bethmann to Hindenburg (1 Oct. 1916), in Doerries, *Imperial Challenge*, pp. 198–99; Czernin von und zu Chudenitz, *Weltkriege*, p. 152.

49. Valentini diary (9 Jan. 1917), Thimme Papers, no. 26; Müller diary (9 Jan. 1917), *Regierte der Kaiser?*, pp. 248–49; Bethmann Hollweg, *Betrachtungen*, 2:131–32; Paul von Hindenburg, *Leben*, p. 233; PD, 2:592–93. Helfferich, *Weltkrieg*, p. 368, says that Wilhelm resolved to do this only after great personal struggles.

50. Doerries, *Imperial Challenge*, p. 209.

51. Görlitz, *Regierte der Kaiser?*, p. 248.

52. Valentini, pp. 146–47; Valentini diary (9 Jan. 1917), Thimme Papers, no. 26. Wilhelm's behavior toward Bethmann was cordial in the next month or so. See KE, no. 317/2, p. 181; Müller diary (22 Mar. 1917), Görlitz, *Regierte der Kaiser?*, p. 267.

53. Brecht, *Nächster Nähe*, p. 141.

54. KE, no. 591/11, p. 207.

55. Hohenlohe to Vienna (13 Mar. 1917), HHSDtA, no. 172(B).

56. Trotha to Tirpitz (n.d. [ca. 20/27 July 1915]), Tirpitz Papers, no. 169; Czernin von und zu Chudenitz, *Weltkriege*, pp. 196–97.

57. Wilhelm to Schiemann (16 Mar. 1917), Schiemann Papers.

58. Deist, *Militär und Innenpolitik*, 2:689.

59. Davis, *The Kaiser*, p. 162.

60. Bethmann Hollweg, *Betrachtungen*, 2:174; Thimme Papers, no. 61, p. 14; see also Erdmann, *Riezler*, pp. 419–20. Hindenburg and Ludendorff also feared that the revolution in Russia might lead to pacifism and "greediness" (*Begehrlichkeit*) in German politicians. Braun diary (16 Apr. 1917), Braun, *Weg durch 4. Zeitepochen*, p. 104.

61. Hopman to Reichsmarineamt (27 Oct. 1914), Deist, *Militär und Innenpolitik*, 1:206.

62. See chapter 8.

63. In the spring of 1915 Wilhelm agreed that the Prussian ministry might vote on the draft of a revised franchise but that any action would be tabled for eighteen months. Westarp, *Konservative Politik*, 2:256–57. In his *Ereignisse und Gestalten*, p. 114, the Kaiser claimed that he wanted the change considered only after the conclusion of the war.

64. Erzberger, *Erlebnisse im Weltkrieg*, pp. 49–52. Wilhelm also felt that electoral reform would have enhanced the influence of Prussia's western provinces, which were very densely populated and more liberal in sentiment than the East Elbian agrarian provinces. Niemann, *Wanderungen*, p. 75.

65. Haussmann to his wife (11 Nov. 1916), Haussmann, *Schlaglichter*, pp. 106–7. Bülow tells a tale, perhaps spurious, that in the fall of 1916 Wilhelm told him that the Germans were fed up with parliamentarism and would prefer to be ruled by generals representing the Kaiser. Bülow, 3:253, 265.

66. Bethmann Hollweg, *Betrachtungen*, 2:179–80.

67. Bethmann to Loebell (11 Apr. 1917), Loebell Papers, no. 5.

68. Wilhelm to Bethmann (12 May 1917), Deist, *Militär und Innenpolitik*, 2:748–50.

69. Augusta Victoria to her sister (16 Jan. 1917), Glücksburg Papers, no. 36.

70. Wilhelm to Bethmann (12 May 1917), Westarp, *Konservative Politik*, 2:244; Thimme Papers, no. 61, pp. 43–44; Bethmann Hollweg, *Betrachtungen*, 2:192–93.

71. On Hindenburg, see Einem to his wife (20/21 May 1917), Einem, *Armeeführer*, pp. 312–13; on Ludendorff, see Bethmann Hollweg, *Betrachtungen*, 2:191.

72. Grünau to Foreign Office (14 Mar. 1917), Deist, *Militär und Innenpolitik*, 2:670–71.

73. The quotation is from a memo by Hermann Mertz von Quirnheim (9 July 1917), in ibid., 2:785. On the danger of strikes, see Gallwitz, *Erleben*, p. 189.

74. Weizsäcker's observation is in Janssen, *Macht und Verblendung*, p. 269 n. 555.

75. Deist, *Militär und Innenpolitik*, 2:744–45.

76. Bethmann Hollweg, *Betrachtungen*, 2:235–36.

77. Dülffer, *Bethmann Hollweg*, pp. 391–93.

78. Ibid., pp. 407–8.

79. On Wilhelm, see Haussmann diary (8 July 1917), Hausmann, *Schlaglichter*, pp 106–7; Dülffer, *Bethmann Hollweg*, pp. 408–9; Mertz von Quirnheim, "Im Grossen Hauptquartier," in Deist, *Militär und Innenpolitik*, 2:785; Bauer diary (7 July 1917), Bauer Papers, no. 16.

80. Lerchenfeld to King Ludwig III (8 July 1917) and to Lössl (9 July 1917), Briefwechsel, 2:860–63, 870–72.

81. Ibid., 2:860–63.

82. There are accounts by Bethmann in Dülffer, *Bethmann Hollweg*, p. 397; Valentini, pp. 158–59; Valentini diary (9 July 1917), Thimme Papers, no. 26; Helfferich, *Weltkrieg*, pp. 445–46.

83. Lerchenfeld to Ludwig III (12 July 1917), Briefwechsel, 2:875–77; Schulen-burg-Tressow Papers, p. 152. For the crown prince's resentment of Bethmann, see Zorn, *Universitätsleben*, pp. 123–24.

84. Dülffer, *Bethmann Hollweg*, p. 396; Briefwechsel, 2:874–80; *Ursachen*, 2:152–55; Karl Hertling, *Ein Jahr*, p. 12.

85. Dülffer, *Bethmann Hollweg*, pp. 395–97; Bethmann's notes (11 July 1917), *Ursachen*, 2:152–53.

86. Bethmann's notes (11 July 1917), *Ursachen*, 2:152–53; Valentini diary (10 July 1917), Thimme Papers, no. 26. See also Payer, *Bethmann Hollweg bis Ebert*, p. 32.

87. Hohenlohe to Vienna (10 July 1917), HHStA, no. 172(B).

88. Hammann, *Bilder*, p. 77. See also Valentini, p. 166; Helfferich, *Weltkrieg*, pp. 452–53; Bethmann Hollweg, *Betrachtungen*, 2:235–36.

89. Undated memoir by Breitenbach, Thimme Papers, no. 28; also Lerchenfeld to King Ludwig III (14 July 1917), Briefwechsel, 2:878–80.

90. Valentini, p. 166; Bethmann's notes (14 July 1917), *Ursachen*, 2:153–55.

91. Valentini, p. 162; Valentini diary (10 July 1917), Thimme Papers, no. 26.

92. Tirpitz's notes of a talk with Count August zu Eulenburg (19 May 1917), Tirpitz Papers, no. 203. Tirpitz also liked Gallwitz. See his notes of talk with Eulenburg (early Oct. and 26 Oct. 1918), ibid.

93. Bethmann's notes (14 July 1917), *Ursachen*, 2:153–55.

94. On the origins of Michaelis's appointment, see the following: ibid.; Deist, *Militär und Innenpolitik*, 2:797; KE, no. 591/11, pp. 216–17; Valentini diary (13 July 1917), Thimme Papers, no. 26; Bülow, 3.267–68; KE, no. 331/2, p. 21; Müller diary (7 Aug. 1917), Müller Papers, no. 6; Michaelis, *Staat und Volk*, pp. 320–21; Briefwechsel, 2:878–80; Kühlmann, *Erinnerungen*, pp. 501–2.

95. Kühlmann, *Erinnerungen*, pp. 501–2; see Braun, *Ostpreussen bis Texas*, pp. 113–16, on Hindenburg. On Ludendorff's liking Michaelis, see KE, no. 591/11, pp. 216–17, and Bethmann notes (14 July 1917), *Ursachen*, 2:153–55.

96. Lerchenfeld to King Ludwig III (1 July 17), Briefwechsel, 2:878–80. Wilhelm would tell Kühlmann that before Michaelis's appointment he had not known Michaelis at all. Wilhelm added, "But the field marshal repeatedly assured me that he was such an upright, god-fearing man so that I selected him in God's name." Kühlmann, *Erinnerungen*, pp. 501–2.

97. Schiffer, *Leben*, p. 200; Rheinbaben, *Kaiser Kanzler Präsidenten*, p. 49.

98. Valentini described Wilhelm's behavior as "dreadful" (*schrecklich*), but Michaelis himself made no mention of the fact. Valentini diary (13 July 1917), Thimme Papers, no. 26; Michaelis, *Staat und Volk*, pp. 323–24. See also Hauss-mann, *Schlaglichter*, pp. 150–51.

99. Bülow, 3:272–73.

CHAPTER 12

1. Ballin to Francke (15 July 1917), Francke Papers, no. 7.

2. Haussmann diary (14 July 1917), Haussmann, *Schlaglichter*, p. 131.

3. Beseler to wife (25 July 1917), Beseler Papers, no. 55.

4. Schulenburg-Tressow Papers, p. 153.

5. Kühlmann, *Erinnerungen*, p. 477; Braun, *Ostpreussen bis Texas*, p. 146.

6. Schiffer, *Leben*, p. 200.

7. Michaelis, *Staat und Volk*, pp. 358–60. See Payer, *Bethmann Hollweg bis Ebert*, for how deeply ignorant of politics Michaelis was.

8. Görlitz, *Regierte der Kaiser?*, p. 315; Max von Baden, p. 140; Braun, *Ostpreussen bis Texas*, pp. 125, 145. Braun's diary (24 Aug. 1917) describes the Reichstag as "drunk in its appetite for power." Ibid., p. 124.

9. Scheidemann, *New Germany*, 2:38–40.

10. Schiffer, *Leben*, p. 201; also Braun, *Ostpreussen bis Texas*, pp. 123–24; Payer, *Bethmann Hollweg bis Ebert*, p. 42; Max von Baden, p. 117.

11. Hohenlohe to Czernin von und zu Chudenitz (17 July 1917), HHStA, no. 172(B); Michaelis, *Staat und Volk*, pp. 352–56.

12. Gatzke, *Germany's Drive to the West*, p. 201; Michaelis, *Staat und Volk*, pp. 326, 330.

13. Michaelis, *Staat und Volk*, pp. 352–56.

14. Background is in ibid., p. 324; Braun, *Weg durch 4. Zeitepochen*, p. 119; Westarp, *Konservative Politik*, 2:473–74.

15. Schiffer, *Leben*, pp. 60–61. The contents of Erzberger's letter are unknown, but the Austro-Hungarian envoy thought its purpose was to advertise Erzberger's alleged influence at court. Hohenlohe to Vienna (20 July 1917), HHStA, no. 172(B).

16. See Michaelis, *Staat und Volk*, p. 323, for his audience with Wilhelm (13 July 1917).

17. Müller diary (16 Nov. 1917), *Regierte der Kaiser?*, p. 333.

18. There are accounts in Payer, *Bethmann Hollweg bis Ebert*, pp. 42–44; Erzberger, *Erlebnisse im Weltkrieg*, pp. 52–54; Scheidemann, *Memoirs*, 2:96–97 (reporting Erzberger's account); KE, no. 317/2, p. 183; Westarp, *Konservative Politik*, 2:473; Braun, *Ostpreussen bis Texas*, pp. 120, 145; Braun, *Weg durch 4. Zeitepochen*, pp. 119–21.

19. Wilhelm had used the Punic War theme as early as 1915. Tirpitz diary (8 Apr. 1915), Tirpitz, *Erinnerungen*, pp. 467–68. He would use it again several times: Schiffer, *Leben*, p. 61; Wilhelm to Michaelis (10 Sept. 1917), KE, no. 283/49.

20. Erzberger notes of an audience with Wilhelm (20 July 1917), Erzberger, *Erlebnisse im Weltkrieg*, pp. 52–54.

21. KE, no. 317/2, p. 183. See John G. Williamson, *Helfferich*, p. 234, on "great success," which is what Helfferich and Braun also thought. See Braun, *Ostpreussen bis Texas*, p. 120.

22. Scheidemann, *Memoirs*, 2:96–97; Schiffer Papers, no. 5, p. 1358.

23. Rupprecht, *Kriegstagebuch*, 3:18.

24. Briefwechsel, 2:906–11.

25. Ibid., 2:890–93; Wilhelm, *Ereignisse und Gestalten*, pp. 225–30.

26. KE, no. 591/11, pp. 229–30.

27. Wilhelm to Michaelis (10 Sept. 1917), Georg Michaelis Papers, no. 49; same to same (17 Sept. 1926), ibid., no. 48; Michaelis, *Staat und Volk*, pp. 349–50.

28. Wilhelm's marginalia on a letter from Michaelis (13 Sept. 1917), Georg Michaelis Papers, no. 49.

29. Görlitz, *Regierte der Kaiser?*, p. 312; Braun, *Ostpreussen bis Texas*, p. 151.

30. Georg Michaelis Papers, no. 49, and memo by Michaelis of audience with Wilhelm (12 Sept. 1917), ibid.; Michaelis notes (11 Sept. 1917), KE, no. 283/49; Michaelis, *Staat und Volk*, pp. 345–46.

31. Accounts of participants are in Michaelis, *Staat und Volk*, pp. 344–45; Kühlmann, *Erinnerungen*, pp. 481–82; Görlitz, *Regierte der Kaiser?*, pp. 319–20, relating accounts by Admiral Holtzendorff and by Wilhelm.

32. Michaelis's draft, to which the Kaiser signified his agreement, is in Michaelis to Wilhelm (13 Sept. 1917), Georg Michaelis Papers, no. 49. See also Helfferich, *Weltkrieg*, p. 479.

33. Michaelis, *Staat und Volk*, p. 361, enumerates the appointments.

34. Epstein, *Erzberger*, p. 222; Michaelis, *Staat und Volk*, p. 365; Kühlmann, *Erinnerungen*, pp. 494–95.

35. Görlitz, *Regierte der Kaiser?*, p. 324.

36. Hertling to his wife (30 Oct. 1917), Hertling Papers, no. 23; Braun, *Ostpreussen bis Texas*, pp. 153–54.

37. See Hohenlohe to Vienna (24 Oct. 1917), HHStA, no. 172(B), on the Kaiserin; on keeping Michaelis, see Hertling to his wife (30 Oct. 1917), Hertling Papers, no. 23; Müller diary (21 Oct. 1917), Görlitz, *Regierte der Kaiser?*, p. 326.

38. Max von Baden, p. 148; Karl Hertling, *Ein Jahr*, p. 12; Görlitz, *Regierte der Kaiser?*, p. 327; Braun, *Ostpreusen bis Texas*, p. 155.

39. Müller diary (31 Oct. 1917), Görlitz, *Regierte der Kaiser?*, pp. 328–29.

40. Bernhardi, *Denkwürdigkeiten*, p. 480; Morsey and Matthias, *Ausschuss*, p. 476; Epstein, *Erzberger*, p. 227. The Kaiser had also refused to consider Bülow in July 1917 as Bethmann's successor. Valentini, p. 159.

41. John G. Williamson, *Helfferich*, pp. 249–50; Braun, *Ostpreussen bis Texas*, pp. 155–57; Karl Hertling, *Ein Jahr*, p. 14.

42. Hohenlohe to Czernin von und zu Chudenitz (3 Nov. 1917), HHStA, no. 172(B).

43. Briefwechsel, 2:955–56.

44. Kühlmann, *Erinnerungen*, p. 577.

45. See Naumann, *Dokumente und Argumente*, pp. 71–72, for Hertling's resentment at the way Wilhelm treated King Ludwig III.

46. Karl Hertling, *Ein Jahr*, p. 43; Valentini, p. 183; Kühlmann, *Erinnerungen*, p. 511; Helfferich, *Weltkrieg*, p. 509.

47. Karl Hertling, *Ein Jahre*, pp. 11–14.

48. Ibid., p. 12. Wilhelm valued the fact that his Austrian ally would like the Catholic Hertling. Czernin von und zu Chudenitz, *Weltkrieg*, p. 270.

49. KE, no. 591/11, p. 236.

50. See *Ursachen*, 2:381, on coming to Spa for health; see Schiffer, *Leben*, p. 202, for Aquinas; see Karl Hertling, *Ein Jahr*, p. 46, for bridge.

51. On the relationship, see KE, no. 317/12, p. 191; Karl Hertling, *Ein Jahr*, pp. 17–18. For a truly fulsome example of Hertling's epistolary style, see his letter to Wilhelm (31 Dec. 1917), Reichskanzlei Papers, no. 806/6.

52. For Hertling's optimism, see Max von Baden, p. 231; Karl Hertling, *Ein Jahr*, pp. 15–17.

53. Karl Hertling, *Ein Jahr*, pp. 43–44.

54. Valentini, pp. 183, 211.

55. Ibid., p. 183.

56. Karl Hertling, *Ein Jahr*, pp. 12–13.

57. Ibid., p. 59; also Kühlmann, *Erinnerungen*, pp. 514–15.

58. Karl Hertling, *Ein Jahr*, pp. 13, 18–19.

59. Czernin von und zu Chudenitz, *Weltkriege*, p. 312.

60. Kühlmann, *Erinnerungen*, p. 514.

61. Ibid., pp. 524–25, 534.

62. Baumgart, *Ostpolitik 1918*, p. 25; Payer, *Bethmann Hollweg bis Ebert*, pp. 61–65; Morsey and Matthias, *Ausschusses*, p. 241 n. 5; KE, no. 331/2, p. 16; Paul von Hindenburg, *Leben*, p. 306; Czernin von und zu Chudenitz, *Weltkriege*, p. 336. On the Kaiserin, see her letter to her sister (25 Feb. 1918), Glücksburg Papers, no. 38.

63. See Ludendorff, *Own Story*, 2:156, for Hindenburg; Kühlmann, *Erinnerungen*, pp. 522–24. For the increasing anti-German feeling among the Poles, see Braun, *Ostpreussen bis Texas*, pp. 133–34.

64. Hoffmann, *Versäumten Gelegenheiten*, pp. 203–4; Kühlmann, *Erinnerungen*, pp. 526–27.

65. Ludendorff, *Own Story*, 2:156, 170–71; Hoffmann, *Versäumten Gelegenheiten*, pp. 203–4. Wilhelm's admiration for Hoffmann is in Czernin von und zu Chudenitz, *Weltkriege*, p. 314.

66. Kühlmann, *Erinnerungen*, pp. 516, 566.

67. Szögyényi to Goluchowski (29 Jan. 1902), HHStA, no. 158(V).

68. Monts, *Erinnerungen*, p. 356; Bülow, 2:489–90.

69. Waldersee diary (8 Dec. 1889), Waldersee, *Denkwürdigkeiten*, 2:81; Hutten-Czapski to Wilhelm (5 Nov. 1916), Beseler Papers, no. 54; Hutten-Czapski, *Sechzig Jahre*, 2:145, 288; Braun, *Ostpreussen bis Texas*, p. 151; Bülow, 2:243.

70. Baumgart, *Ostpolitik 1918*, p. 68.

71. Accounts are in Hoffmann, *Versäumten Gelegenheiten*, p. 205; Ludendorff, *Own Story*, 2:170–71; Kühlmann, *Erinnerungen*, pp. 527–29.

72. Hindenburg to Wilhelm (7 Jan. 1918), *Ursachen*, 2:123–25; an even less veiled threat went to Hertling. See Kühlmann, *Erinnerungen*, p. 537.

73. Müller diary (8 Jan. 1918), Görlitz, *Regierte der Kaiser?*, p. 342. Wilhelm complained that the generals did not consult him sufficiently. See his comments on a newspaper article (9 Jan. 1918), *Ursachen*, 1:123.

74. Wilhelm to Hindenburg (n.d.), Kühlmann, *Erinnerungen*, pp. 538–39. See also ibid., pp. 537, 540–42, 563.

75. Ibid., p. 548.

76. Deist, *Militär und Innenpolitik*, 2:1124–26; on Hindenburg, see his letter to Wilhelm (16 Jan. 1918), Bauer Papers, no. 18; Görlitz, *Regierte der Kaiser?*, p. 344; on Ludendorff: KE, no. 317/2, p. 179; Karl Hertling, *Ein Jahr*, pp. 55–56. On both generals, see Valentini diary (13 Jan. 1918), Thimme Papers, no. 26. For Valentini on the enmity he faced from the generals, see KE, no. 331/2, p. 2.

77. Valentini memo (10 Oct. 1918), Schwertfeger Papers, no. 206. See also Görlitz, *Regierte der Kaiser?*, p. 331; Valentini diary (16 Nov. 1917), Thimme Papers, no. 26; KE, no. 331/2, p. 2; Einem, *Armeeführer*, p. 353.

78. Valentini diary (16 Nov. 1917), Thimme Papers, no. 26; Görlitz, *Regierte der Kaiser?*, p. 331; Valentini, pp. 185–86.

79. Wilhelm to the crown prince (22 Nov. 1917), Schwertfeger Papers, no. 206; Valentini diary (16 Nov. 1917), Thimme Papers, no. 26; Valentini, pp. 183–84.

80. KE, no. 341/1, notebook containing Valentini's account of his dismissal; Deist, *Militär und Innenpolitik*, 2:1124–27; Valentini memo (10 Oct. 1918), Schwertfeger Papers, no. 206; Valentini, pp. 190–91.

81. Valentini to Hindenburg (unsent, Jan. 1918), Schwertfeger Papers, no. 206.

82. On Berg's relations with the generals, see KE, no. 317/2, pp. 180–81, no. 331/2, p. 2; Hohenlohe to Vienna (17 Jan. 1918), HHStA, no. 174(B).

83. On his prerogative, see KE, no. 331/2, pp. 2–3, 6–7; his unhappiness at letting Valentini go is in Valentini diary (15 Jan. 1918), Thimme Papers, no. 26; Karl Hertling diary (22 Jan. 1918), Hertling Papers, no. 40; Haussmann, *Schlaglichter*, p. 226.

84. Deist, *Militär und Innenpolitik*, 2:1293 n. 18; KE, no. 317/2, pp. 180–81.

85. Müller diary (14 Jan. 1918), Müller Papers, no. 7; KE, no. 331/2, pp. 6–7.

86. Valentini memo (10 Oct. 1918), Schwertfeger Papers, no. 206.

87. Czernin von und zu Chudenitz, *Weltkriege*, p. 96.

88. Friedrich Rosen, *Wanderleben*, 3/4:136. At about the same time (14 Jan. 1918), Wilhelm was in favor of following a peace feeler from the king of Denmark before the great western offensive got under way. It came to nothing. Karl Hertling, *Ein Jahr*, pp. 56–58.

89. *Ursachen*, 2:438–40.

90. Baron Roman Rosen, *Forty Years*, 2:297.

91. Naumann, *Profile*, p. 151. On Wilhelm's optimism, see *Ursachen*, 2:438–40.

92. Hertling notes (16 Apr. 1918), Hertling Papers, no. 41.

93. KE, no. 382, Anlage p. 11, no. 331/2, pp. 34–35.

94. Thaer, *Generalstabsdienst*, p. 212.

95. For an indictment of Kühlmann, see Vietsch, *Gegen die Unvernunft*, p. 111.

96. Deutelmoser notes (14 Sept. 1918), Hertling Papers, no. 41.

97. Hohenlohe to Vienna (9 July 1918), HHStA, no. 174(B); Reichskanzlei memo, probably by Hertling (2 July 1918), Hintze Papers, no. 42; Kühlmann to Hertling (10 July 1918), Hertling Papers, no. 41; Kühlmann, *Erinnerungen*, pp. 579–80; KE, no. 331/2, pp. 38–39.

98. KE, no. 331/2, p. 42. Baron Marschall von Bieberstein, a Baden bureaucrat, took the post.

99. For Hintze's doubts about himself, see Hertling to unknown correspondent (8 July 1918), Hertling Papers, no. 41. For estimations, generally negative, of Hintze, see KE, no. 591/12, p. 386; Kühlmann, *Erinnerungen*, p. 581; Westarp, *Ende der Monarchie*, p. 165; Karl Hertling, *Ein Jahr*, p. 133.

100. Niemann, *Kaiser und Revolution*, p. 62; notes on Hintze to Reichsmarineamt (28 Jan. 1907), Tambach Papers, no. 26/89, vol. 1; Lambsdorff, *Militärbevollmächtigten*, pp. 170–80.

101. Mühleisen, *Lersner*, pp. 27–28.

102. Plessen diary (22 June 1918), HA, Rep. 192, no. 22.

103. Reichskanzlei notes (19 July 1918), in *Ursachen*, 2:348–52.

104. Schönburg-Waldenburg diary (11 July 1918), Schönburg-Waldenburg, *Erinnerungen*, p. 296

105. Schiffer, *Leben*, p. 67; Baumgart, *Ostpolitik 1918*, p. 187, pictures Wilhelm at this time dividing Russia into four empires: the Ukraine, a southeastern monarchy with its capital at Tiflis, Great Russia, and Siberia. He was not being kept informed by his generals. See Mühleisen, *Lersner*, pp. 27–28. Niemann, *Kaiser und Revolution*, p. 32, depicts General Plessen insisting that the situation be presented to the Kaiser as optimistically as possible. See also Deist, *Militär und Innenpolitik*, 2:1306.

106. Max von Baden, p. 285; Ludendorff memo (31 Oct. 1918), *Ursachen*, 2:361–68.

107. Niemann, *Kaiser und Revolution*, pp. 40–41. Only a few days earlier he had still had some optimism. See Lersner's diary (5 Aug. 1918), KE, no. 591/11, p. 326.

108. Niemann, *Kaiser und Revolution*, pp. 41–43. See also Ludendorff, *Own Story*, 2:335.

CHAPTER 13

1. There are accounts of the meeting in Hintze Papers, no. 42; *Ursachen*, 2:389–90; Bauer, *Grosse Krieg*, p. 210; Ludendorff, *Leben*, 2:335; KE, no. 331/2, p. 46.

2. Weizsäcker to his parents (11 Aug. 1918), Leonidas E. Hill, *Weizsäcker-Papiere*, p. 273. Waiting for a suitable moment is in KE, no. 591/12, p. 338; *Ursachen*, 2:389–90.

3. Bauer, *Grosse Krieg*, p. 210. On Hintze: Max von Baden, p. 288; Niemann, *Kaiser und Revolution*, p. 58. Hertling was also optimistic. Max von Baden, p. 303.

4. Hintze Papers, no. 42.

5. KE, no. 591/12, p. 338; Niemann, *Kaiser und Revolution*, pp. 60–61; Kühlmann, *Erinnerungen*, p. 516.

6. Hertling notes (16 Apr. 1918), Hertling Papers, no. 40; Sauerbruch, *Leben*, pp. 216–20. See also Cramon, *Bundesgenosse*, pp. 111, 150; KE, no. 591/11, p. 193; Niemann, *Kaiser und Revolution*, pp. 60–61; Kühlmann, *Erinnerungen*, pp. 565–66.

7. Cramon, *Bundesgenosse*, pp. 155–56.

8. Niemann, *Kaiser und Revolution*, pp. 60–61; KE, no. 591/12, p. 338.

9. Niemann, *Kaiser und Revolution*, pp. 78–81; KE, no. 331/2, p. 51; Görlitz, *Regierte der Kaiser?*, pp. 410–11; Ilsemann, 1:17; KE, no. 591/12, pp. 354–55. On the care of the retinue to avoid anything serious at Wilhelmshöhe, see Niemann, *Kaiser und Revolution*, p. 65.

10. KE, no. 591/12, pp. 350–51; Ilsemann, 1:16.

11. On the Kaiser's collapse: Niemann, *Kaiser und Revolution*, pp. 69–70; KE, no. 591/12, pp. 35–51, no. 331/2, p. 50. On Ballin: his letter to Francke (10 Sept. 1918), Francke Papers, no. 7; KE, no. 331/2, p. 50; Niemann, *Kaiser und Revolution*, pp. 75–77; Ilsemann, 1:16; Hermine, *Empress in Exile*, p. 23; Lamar Cecil, *Ballin*, pp. 336–38.

12. Heye diary (11 Sept. 1918), Heye Papers, no. 4, p. 384.

13. On the army's reaction to Saint-Mihiel see ibid., p. 385; Max von Baden, p. 289; Wilhelm was very upset at the Austrian decision. Niemann, *Kaiser und Revolution*, p. 82.

14. Niemann, *Kaiser und Revolution*, pp. 83–85.

15. Ibid., p. 85; Niemann, *Revolution von Oben*, pp. 104–5.

16. See Niemann, *Kaiser und Revolution*, pp. 87–88, on the ride. On the conference: Wilhelm to Augusta Victoria (30 Sept. 1918), in Viktoria Luise, *Tochter des Kaisers*, p. 179; Rosner, *Erinnerungen des Kronprinzen*, pp. 243–46; Hintze Papers, no. 63, pp. 19–23; *Ursachen*, 2:409–10, 418–19, which are Hintze's and Roedern's accounts; Heye Papers, no. 6, pp. 404–6; Karl Hertling, *Ein Jahr*, pp. 180–81. See also KE, no. 331/2, p. 57.

17. *Ursachen*, 2:410; Karl Hertling, *Ein Jahr*, pp. 177–80; Payer, *Bethmann Hollweg bis Ebert*, pp. 82–83.

18. Müller diary (30 Sept. 1918), Görlitz, *Regierte der Kaiser?*, p. 423. Ludendorff described the pestilence as "my last hope." Haeften Papers, no. 4, pp. 50–51.

19. *Ursachen*, 2:410. By that evening, however, he seems to have lapsed back into pessimism. Granier, *Levetzow*, pp. 229–30; Leonidas E. Hill, *Weizsäcker-Papiere*, p. 290.

20. Payer, *Bethmann Hollweg bis Ebert*, p. 83.

21. Wilhelm's regret is in Karl Hertling's diary (30 Sept. 1918), Hertling Papers, no. 40; Hertling's disgust at a parliamentary regime is in Karl Hertling, *Ein Jahr*, pp. 185–87.

22. Printed in Max von Baden, p. 329. On Hintze, see Granier, *Levetzow*, pp. 229–30.

23. "Dictatorship is absurdity." *Ursachen*, 2:409–10; Heye Papers, no. 4, pp. 404–6.

24. Karl Hertling, *Ein Jahr*, p. 182.

25. Ibid., p. 183.

26. Granier, *Levetzow*, pp. 229–30.

27. KE, no. 331/2, p. 60.

28. Letter (30 Sept. 1918), Viktoria Luise, *Tochter des Kaisers*, p. 179.

29. Ibid.

30. Berg's choice was Count Siegfried von Roedern, the conservative but capable state secretary of the Imperial Treasury Office. See Payer, *Bethmann Hollweg bis Ebert*, pp. 92–93; *Ursachen*, 2:423; Morsey and Matthias, *Max von Baden*, pp. 15–16

31. Epstein, *Erzberger*, p. 259.

32. On the generals and other officers at headquarters: Max von Baden, p. 330; Niemann, *Kaiser und Revolution*, p. 93. Delbrück, *Mobilmachung*, p. 267, notes that the expectation in Berlin was that the liberal vice-chancellor Friedrich von Payer would become chancellor, governing with the majority parties. But Payer preferred Max of Baden to lead the government. See Payer, *Bethmann Hollweg bis Ebert*, p. 84. On Berg, see KE, no. 331/2, p. 57; on the Kaiserin, see Niemann, *Kaiser und Revolution*, p. 74.

33. Max to the grand duke of Baden (15 Oct. 1918), Max von Baden, p. 405.

34. Ibid., pp. 331–32.

35. KE, no. 331/2, p. 62.

36. Max von Baden, p. 346.

37. Ibid., pp. 346–52; Payer, *Bethmann Hollweg bis Ebert*, pp. 107–11; KE, no. 331/2, p. 64.

38. The quotes are from letters by Max to Colonel Haeften (7 July 1917) and to Wilhelm (15 Aug. 1918), Max von Baden, pp. 107, 292.

39. Eulenburg, *Erlebnisse*, p. 250; see Wilke, *Alt Berliner Erinnerungen*, p. 86, for Wilhelm's disapproval. For the improvement: Eulenburg to Wilhelm (17 Feb. 1900), Eulenburg, *Erlebnisse*, p. 255; Viktoria Luise, *Tochter des Kaisers*, p. 75. The Kaiserin had doubts about Max's suitability as chancellor. See Niemann, *Kaiser und Revolution*, p. 101.

40. Max von Baden, p. 148; Valentini, pp. 177–78.

41. Max von Baden, pp. 315–16. See Morsey and Matthias, *Max von Baden*, pp. xvi–xxix, on Max's ascent to the chancellorship.

42. Max von Baden, p. 357; Payer, *Bethmann Hollweg bis Ebert*, pp. 107–8.

43. Haussmann, *Schlaglichter*, pp. 258–59.

44. See Niemann, *Kaiser und Revolution*, p. 99, on the Kaiser's withdrawal, and Max von Baden, p. 474, on the chancellor's desire to keep him out of sight.

45. Delbrück, *Mobilmachung*, p. 289.

46. Payer, *Bethmann Hollweg bis Ebert*, pp. 126–27.

47. The Kaiserin was furious. See Niemann, *Kaiser und Revolution*, p. 97. Delbrück and the Kaiser never developed any rapport. Ibid., p. 105.

48. Bethmann to Loebell (11 Apr. 1917), Loebell Papers, no. 5.

49. In April 1917 the Military Cabinet had received letters demanding Wilhelm's abdication and the renunciation of his sons' rights to the throne. Deist, *Militär und Innenpolitik*, 2:813.

50. Industrialists: Payer, *Bethmann Hollweg bis Ebert*, pp. 146–47; Haussmann diary (13 Oct. 1918), Haussmann, *Schlaglichter*, p. 250; Friedrich Rosen's account of an audience with Wilhelm (20 Oct. 1918), Rosen, *Wanderleben*, 3/4:212–13. On the Conservatives: Max von Baden, p. 405. On Bavaria: Gustav Freytag, professor of medicine at Munich, to Solf (12 Oct. 1918), Solf Papers, no. 56; intellectuals: Max Weber to von Schulze-Gävernitz (11 Oct. 1918), Weber, *Max Weber*, p. 670.

51. On the Kaiserin, see Neumann, *Kaiser und Revolution*, pp. 100–102.

52. Max von Baden, p. 467; Lerchenfeld-Koefering, *Wilhelm II.*, p. 52.

53. Schwabe, *Woodrow Wilson*, pp. 95, 433 n. 77.

54. Ilsemann diary (25 Oct. 1918), Ilsemann, 1:25.

55. Schwabe, *Woodrow Wilson*, pp. 95, 439 n. 2.

56. Morsey and Matthias, *Max von Baden*, p. 218 n. 3; Ilsemann, 1:27.

57. Max von Baden, pp. 367–68.

58. Payer, *Bethmann Hollweg bis Ebert*, pp. 147–48.

59. Max von Baden, p. 517; Haeften Papers, no. 6, p. 56; Dryander, *Erinnerungen*, p. 316.

60. Haeften notes (24 Oct. 1918), Haeften Papers, no. 6, pp. 2–5.

61. Printed in Niemann, *Kaiser und Revolution*, p. 112 n.

62. Ibid., pp. 110–13; Ilsemann, 2:28.

63. Letter (25 Oct. 1918), Morsey and Matthias, *Max von Baden*, pp. 359–60.

64. See accounts of the meeting in Haeften Papers, no. 6, pp. 28–29, on Hindenburg. Ludendorff, *Own Story*, 2:421; *Ursachen*, 2:367; Ilsemann, 1:28; and Niemann, *Kaiser und Revolution*, pp. 113–15, give Wilhlem's version; Paul von Hindenburg, *Leben*, p. 396. A secondhand account is in Leonidas E. Hill, *Weizsäcker-Papiere*, pp. 308–9.

65. See accounts of this meeting in Haeften Papers, no. 6, pp. 23–28, giving Ludendorff's account; Groener, *Lebenserinnerungen*, p. 440, giving Hindenburg's; Ludendorff, *Leben*, 2:425; Thaer, *Generalstabsdienst*, pp. 247–48, relating Ludendorff's version.

66. Haeften Papers, no. 6, pp. 23–28.

67. Leonidas E. Hill, *Weizsäcker-Papiere*, pp. 308–9.

68. Calls for abdication are reported in Gallwitz diary (30 Oct. 1918), Gallwitz, *Führertätigkeit*, p. 443; Groener, *Lebenserinnerungen*, p. 443; Scheidemann, *Memoirs*, 2:200, 203, 215. On newpaper discussion of the question: Sweetman, "Unforgotten Crowns," p. 20; Max von Baden, p. 512.

69. Weizsäcker to his parents (30 Oct. 1918), Leonidas E. Hill, *Weizsäcker-Papiere*, p. 311.

70. Ilsemann diary (27 Oct. 1918), Ilsemann, 2:30; on Hindenburg, see Niemann, *Kaiser und Revolution*, p. 121.

71. Heye notes (ca. 17 Oct. 1918), Heye Papers, no. 4; General Scheüch to General Baron Marschall (21 May 1922) and Groener to Scheüch (31 May 1922), Schwertfeger Papers, no. 545.

72. Gallwitz notes (27 Oct. 1918), Gallwitz, *Führertätigkeit*, p. 437; also Max von Baden, pp. 519–23.

73. Gallwitz, *Führertätigkeit*, p. 189.

74. See the testimony in Thaer, *Generalstabsdienst*, pp. 231–32; Eulenburg, *Mit dem Kaiser*, 1:38; Schönburg-Waldenburg, *Erinnerungen*, p. 135; Seeckt, *Leben*, p. 81; Eisenhardt-Rothe, *Bann der Persönlichkeit*, pp. 175–77; Kosposth, *Erinnerungen*, p. 37; Janssen, *Graue Exzellenz*, pp. 117–19; Schneller, *Königs-Erinnerungen*, p. 159.

75. Hintze Papers, no. 56, p. 1. The Kaiserin urged him to go so that he would not be so much under Max's influence. Dorpalen, "Auguste Victoria," p. 36.

76. Scheüch to General Marschall (21 May 1922), Schwertfeger Papers, no. 545.

77. Scheüch to Schwertfeger (17 Dec. 1927), ibid., on Marschall's secretiveness; on the Supreme Command's desire that Wilhelm come to Spa: Haeften Papers, no. 6, pp. 56–57; Granier, *Levetzow*, p. 59 n. 199; Max von Baden, pp. 428–29; Görlitz, *Regierte der Kaiser?*, p. 442. However, Scheüch claimed after the war that Hindenburg and Ludendorff did not make such a request, and Groener declared that headquarters at Spa was surprised when Wilhelm arrived there. It may be that the Kaiser's presence was surprising only because he had come more quickly than anticipated. Scheüch notes (1 June 1922), Schwertfeger Papers, no. 545; Groener, *Lebenserinnerungen*, p. 441.

78. Max von Baden, p. 528.

79. Ibid., 527–29; on Dryander and Delbrück, see Hammann, *Bilder*, pp. 135–38.

80. Wilhelm's appearance is in Gündell diary (31 Oct. 1918), Obkircher, *Gün-*

dell, p. 305. On Hindenburg's surprise, see Groener Papers, no. 63, copy of Mertz von Quirnheim diary (30 Oct. 1918); Groener, *Lebenserinnerungen*, p. 441.

81. See Ilsemann, 1:30, on trees; also Lieutenant Colonel W. Stewart Roddie memo, recording a conversation with Groener (29 June 1921), RA, Geo V M 1515, no. 36.

82. Wilhelm's declaration is reported in a memo by Hintze (1919), Niemann, *Revolution von Oben*, p. 366; on the Reichstag, see Payer, *Bethmann Hollweg bis Ebert*, p. 148; on the negative public response, see Max von Baden, pp. 536–37.

83. Solf to Hammann (23 Jan. 1919), Hammann, *Bilder*, pp. 135–38.

84. Max von Baden, p. 534.

85. For accounts of the meeting: ibid., pp. 536–40; Payer, *Bethmann Hollweg bis Ebert*, pp. 148–50; Erzberger, *Erlebnisse im Weltkrieg*, pp. 323–24. The protocol is in Deist, *Militär und Innenpolitik*, 2:1350–55.

86. Max von Baden, pp. 555–56; Niemann, *Kaiser und Revolution*, p. 121 n.

87. See Max von Baden, pp. 551–60, for Max's unsuccessful attempt to enlist the Kaiser's brother-in-law Prince Friedrich Karl of Hesse to go to Spa.

88. HA, Rep. 53a, no. 435, pp. 6–7; Hintze Papers, no. 56, p. 2. For the Kaiser's version of Drews's visit: notes of court preacher Dr. Vogel of a talk with Wilhelm (3 Nov. 1918), Mackensen Papers, no. 39; Schiffer, *Leben*, pp. 135–37; Ilsemann, 1:30; and Deist, *Militär und Innenpolitik*, 2:1397 n. 6. See also memos by Plessen and Hintze (both from 1919): Niemann, *Revolution von Oben*, pp. 361–63, 366–67; Niemann, *Kaiser und Revolution*, p. 123. There is a sketchy report of Drews's own impressions in KE, no. 591/13, p. 420.

89. Hintze notes (2 Nov. 1918), Hintze Papers, no. 56; Niemann, *Revolution von Oben*, pp. 388–89. British help is mentioned in Müller diary (29 Oct. 1918), Görlitz, *Regierte der Kaiser?*, p. 441.

90. Hintze Papers, no. 56, pp. 3–4.

91. Groener said so to Wilhelm's adjutants on 1 Nov. See Plessen note (14 Nov. 1925), Dommes Papers, no. 18; Groener Papers, no. 75, p. 243; Roddie memo of a talk with Groener (29 June 1921), RA, Geo V M 1515, no. 36.

92. Plessen note (14 Nov. 1925), Dommes Papers, no. 18; Groener-Geyer, *Groener*, p. 96. Hindenburg's opposition is in Groener Papers, no. 75, frame 243.

93. Hintze Papers, no. 56, pp. 3–4.

94. Ibid., p. 6; Niemann, *Revolution von Oben*, p. 367; HA, Rep. 53a, no. 435, pp. 6–7; Ilsemann, 1:32. The sullen attitude of many of the troops Wilhelm saw is in Niemann, *Revolution von Oben*, p. 389, and Niemann, *Kaiser und Revolution*, pp. 126–27.

95. Thaer diary (5 Nov. 1918) and his memo (2 Dec. 1919), Thaer, *Generalstabsdienst*, pp. 252, 259–64; Groener, *Lebenserinnerungen*, p. 451; Delbrück, *Mobilmachung*, p. 283.

96. See article by Viereck, "The Kaiser and the Fourteen Points," p. 5, Rijksarchief Papers, no. 242, on Wilhelm's religious reservations; on Plessen: Feder, *Heute Sprach Ich*, p. 169; Thaer, *Generalstabsdienst*, p. 263.

97. Max von Baden, pp. 616–17; Max von Baden, "Der 9. November 1918" (30 July 1919), Glücksburg Papers, no. 36-B/2, p. 35; Payer, *Bethmann Hollweg bis Ebert*, pp. 158–59; Groener, *Lebenserinnerungen*, pp. 450–51; Hintze Papers, no. 56, pp. 6–7; Feder, *Heute Sprach Ich*, p. 169.

98. Viktoria Luise, *Tochter des Kaisers*, pp. 205–6; Ilsemann, 1:35.

99. See Hintze Papers, no. 56, pp. 7–9, for Max's wire; Solf's letter, which Wilhelm apparently did not receive, is in Solf Papers, no. 58.

100. Gallwitz, *Führertätigkeit*, p. 488; also Bülow, 3:297.

101. Heye Papers, no. 6, pp. 7–8; Groener, *Lebenserinnerungen*, pp. 454–56.

102. Niemann, *Revolution von Oben*, pp. 369–70; Dryander, *Erinnerungen*, p. 318; Max von Baden, "Der 9. November 1918," Glücksburg Papers, no. 36-B/2, p. 35; Hintze Papers, no. 56, pp. 7–9; Ilsemann, 1:35; Max von Baden, pp. 623–24.

103. Heye Papers, no. 6, p. 7.

104. Ibid.

105. Rosner, *Erinnerungen des Kronprinzen*, pp. 298–99; Niemann, *Revolution von Oben*, pp. 345–60, 437–44.

106. On the polling: Heye Papers, no. 6, p. 11; Groener, *Lebenserinnerungen*, pp. 456–57; Niemann, *Revolution von Oben*, pp. 350–51; Rosner, *Erinnerungen des Kronprinzen*, pp. 295–301. On the officers' refusal to participate in a civil war: Below Papers, no. 35; Heye Papers, no. 6, p. 14; Groener, *Lebenserinnerungen*, p. 456.

107. Niemann, *Kaiser und Revolution*, p. 133.

108. HA, Rep. 53a, no. 435, pp. 8–9; Rosner, *Erinnerungen des Kronprinzen*, p. 277; Schulenburg "Denkschrift," Glücksburg Papers, no. 36-B/2, pp. 5–6.

109. Groener, *Lebenserinnerungen*, pp. 459–60; Rosner, *Erinnerungen des Kronprinzen*, p. 279; Hintze Papers, no. 56, pp. 15–18. Hindenburg noted in 1919 that he and Groener were careful not to tell Wilhelm that it was necessary for him to abdicate. Hindenburg memo (16 Apr. 1919), Hubatsch, *Hindenburg und der Staat*, pp. 183–87.

110. Heye Papers, no. 6, p. 14. See also Groener, *Lebenserinnerungen*, pp. 459–62; Rosner, *Erinnerungen des Kronprinzen*, pp. 183–85.

111. Hintze Papers, no. 56, pp. 9–12, no. 65, Kleist to Hintze (29 Nov. 1926) and Plessen to same (8 Sept. 1919); Max von Baden, "Der 9. November 1918," Glücksburg Papers, no. 36-B/2, p. 38; Rosner, *Erinnerungen des Kronprinzen*, pp. 271–72; Niemann, *Revolution von Oben*, p. 325.

112. Heye Papers, no. 6, p. 17; Rosner, *Erinnerungen des Kronprinzen*, p. 286; Groener, *Lebenserinnerungen*, p. 461; Niemann, *Revolution von Oben*, p. 325.

113. Ilsemann, 1:37.

114. Niemann, *Kaiser und Revolution*, pp. 139–41.

115. HA, Rep. 53a, no. 435, p. 10; also Niemann, *Revolution von Oben*, p. 325.

116. Rosner, *Erinnerungen des Kronprinzen*, pp. 304–5; Groener, *Lebenserinnerungen*, pp. 462–63; Niemann, *Kaiser und Revolution*, pp. 141–42.

117. Notes by Maltzahn (15 Feb. 1922), relating a conversation on that day with Hindenburg, HA, Rep. 53a, no. 62.

118. Plessen notes in Below Papers, no. 35.

119. Dommes Papers, no. 18; KE, no. 591/13, pp. 440–43.

120. Dommes Papers, no. 18; Niemann, *Revolution von Oben*, pp. 343–44.

121. Dommes Papers, no. 18; Niemann, *Revolution von Oben*, pp. 311–12; Niemann, *Kaiser und Revolution*, pp. 144–45. On the Kaiserin's travails in Berlin: Dryander, *Erinnerungen*, pp. 318–19; KE, no. 381; Keller, *Vierzig Jahre*, pp. 334–39.

122. Niemann, *Kaiser und Revolution*, pp. 144–45.

123. The letter to the Kaiserin and the unaddressed notes are reproduced in: Niemann, *Revolution von Oben*, pp. 311–12; Westarp, *Ende der Monarchie*, pp. 128–29; Viktoria Luise, *Tochter des Kaisers*, p. 209.

124. Ilsemann, 1:43.

125. Ibid., 1:44–45; HA, Rep. 53a, no. 435, pp. 11–12.

126. HA, Rep. 53a, no. 435, pp. 11–12.

127. Friedrich Rosen, *Wanderleben*, 3/4:218–21.

128. Benoist, "Guillaume II en Hollande," pp. 388–90.

129. Townley, *"Indiscretions,"* pp. 283–89; HA, Rep. 53a, no. 435, pp. 11–14; Kenneth Young, *Diaries*, pp. 316–17.

CHAPTER 14

1. Bentinck, *Ex-Kaiser in Exile*, p. 23.

2. See Viktoria Luise, *Tochter des Kaisers*, pp. 212–13, for the letters; see KE, no. 578/1, for his archaeological pursuits. Wilhelm's complaints about his physical confinement are in a letter to Schiemann (17 June 1919), Schiemann Papers.

3. Letter dated Dec. 1918 in HA, Rep. 53a, no. 77.

4. Ibid.

5. Ilsemann, 1:60, 68, 87–88. For a frustrated kidnapping attempt, see Silverman, "Kidnapping the Kaiser."

6. Marks, "Ozymandias," p. 135.

7. Ilsemann, 1:70–71, 85. On Eulenburg, see the draft of a statement by Wilhelm (1919), Dommes Papers, no. 21.

8. Ilsemann, 1:66–67.

9. Heye to Groener (n.d. [ca. 15 June 1919]), Groener Papers, no. 162.

10. Seeckt to Berg (8 July 1919), Seeckt Papers.

11. Nicolson, *George the Fifth*, p. 337.

12. For the Kaiser's lasting hatred of Lloyd George, see Wilhelm's notes (19 June 1925), Rijksarchief Papers, no. 651.

13. House and Seymour, *What Really Happened at Paris*, p. 248. On the prospect of trying the Kaiser: Clarke, "Allied Demand"; Baldwin, "Proposed Trial"; Menken, *Trial of the Kaiser*; Peignot, "Châtiment."

14. Walworth, *Wilson and His Peacemakers*, p. 215.

15. Marks, "Ozymandias," p. 137.

16. Ilsemann, 1:319–20. Wilhelm continued to express this view for years afterward. See his letter to Waters (12 July 1930), RA, Geo V O 2578, no. 19.

17. For Wilhelm on Versailles, see his letter to Bigelow (17 Nov. 1927), Bigelow Papers, no. 34. Undated memo, "Gutachten über die Zulässigkeit einer Strafverfolgung sowie einer Auslieferung des Kaisers aus Anlass des Weltkrieges," Dommes Papers, no. 21; Marks, "Ozymandias," pp. 150–65; House and Seymour, *What Really Happened at Paris*, pp. 243–47; Walworth, *Wilson and His Peacemakers*, pp. 213–16. On 17 Mar. 1920 Queen Wilhelmina issued an order that the Kaiser was to be permitted to live in the province of Utrecht.

18. On the purchase of Doorn, see Rijksarchief Papers, no. 422.

19. As parting gifts Bentinck got a bust, the town a small clinic. Ilsemann, 1:114, 324–25.

20. The best account of the Kaiser's regimen is in Cecilie, *Erinnerungen an den Kronprinzen*, pp. 98–100; for others: Schneller, *Königs-Erinnerungen*, pp. 226–27; Ilsemann, esp. 1:160; Louis Ferdinand, *Kaiserenkel*, pp. 240–48.

21. Wilhelm to Fürstenberg (16 Mar. 1928), Rijksarchief Papers, no. 6; same to same (27 Jan. 1933), Fürstenberg Papers, "Wilhelm II. c. 1908–1918"; Louis Ferdinand, *Kaiserenkel*, p. 244.

22. Wheeler-Bennett, *Knaves, Fools, and Heroes*, pp. 175–76; Kenneth Young, *Diaries*, p. 240.

23. See Ilsemann, 1:138, 156, on how delighted adjutants were when it was time for them to be relieved. See also ibid., 1:236, 240.

24. Ibid., 1:242. Wilhelm's adjutants were General Count Eberhard von Schmettow, General Wilhelm von Dommes, Colonel Hans von Tschirschky und Bögendorff, Admiral Hubert von Rebeur-Paschwitz, General Count Conrad Finck von Finckenstein, Count Detlef von Moltke, Colonel Alfred Niemann, General August von Cramon, Major Baron Ulrich von Sell, naval Captain Baron Alexander von Senarclens-Grancy. In addition, at Berlin were Friedrich von Berg, head of the *Generalverwaltung* of the Kaiser's properties, who in 1926 was succeeded by Leopold von Kleist. A very influential figure was *Geheim Hofrat* Nitz, president of the Schatullen und- Vermögensverwaltung, which handled the Kaiser's financial interests in Germany.

25. Crown Prince Wilhelm of Prussia to Hahnke (26 Oct. 1922), Hahnke Papers; also same to Mackensen (24 May 1921), Mackensen Papers, no. 40; Schramm, "Notizen."

26. Ilsemann, 1:124–25; Ilsemann agreed with his wife. Ibid., 1:184.

27. Prince Eitel Friedrich of Prussia to Wilhelm (18 July 1920), Glücksburg Papers, no. 39; Wilhelm to Mackensen (2 Dec. 1919), Mackensen Papers, no. 39.

28. Wilhelm to Mackensen (2 Dec. 1919), Mackensen Papers, no. 39.

29. On the Kaiserin's death and burial, see Rijksarchief Papers, nos. 151, 152. Wilhelm requested permission to be allowed to go to Potsdam with the crown prince for the funeral, but the Dutch cabinet, encouraged by Paris and Berlin, refused. Benoist, "Guillaume II en Hollande," p. 402. Wilhelm later blamed his wife's death on her distress with Lloyd George's "hang the Kaiser" motto in the "Khaki" election campaign in December 1918. See Wilhelm to Bigelow (30 Aug. 1930), Bigelow Papers, no. 34a.

30. Wilhelm to Countess Brockdorff (3 May 1923), in HA, Rep. 192, no. 20; Ilsemann, 2:17. On the gloom at Doorn, see Kurt Ernst von Bülow, *Kaiser Wie Er Wirklich War*, p. 16; Hermine, *Empress in Exile*, pp. 1–3; Meister, *Yesterdays*, pp. 207–8.

31. Hermine, *Empress in Exile*, pp. 9–11; also Viktoria Luise, *Tochter des Kaisers*, p. 236.

32. Heinig, *Hohenzollern*, p. 20.

33. Rijksarchief Papers, no. 437.

34. Crown Prince to Selasen-Selasinsky (17 Nov. 1921), Selasen-Selasinsky Papers, no. 1; Baron von Loën [Hausmarschallamt Doorn] to Selasen-Selasinsky (14

Apr. 1923), ibid., no. 7. The Kaiser's Dutch bank accounts are listed in Rijks-archief Papers, no. 572. At the time of his flight to Holland, Wilhelm had 650,000 marks on deposit in Dutch banks. Gutsche, *Kaiser im Exil*, p. 31.

35. Heinig, *Hohenzollern*, p. 141. There is information on transfers of cash to Wilhelm from Germany in Mar. and Apr. 1919 in PRO Papers.

36. Wilhelm to Dörpfeld (9 Mar. 1921), HA, Rep. 53, no. 24; Wilhelm to Waters (24 Sept. 1930), RA, Geo V O 2578, no. 16.

37. Hermine, *Empress in Exile*, pp. 279–80.

38. Wilhelm to Viereck (18 Nov. 1925), Viereck Papers.

39. *Wilhelm II. und Hermine*, pp. 151–54. The 1926 settlement also reserved as a residence to Wilhelm and his second wife, Hermine, in the event they ever returned to Germany, the royal castle at Homburg vor der Höhe. Gutsche, *Kaiser im Exil*, p. 81.

40. On Wilhelm's charity to other royals, see Kenneth Young, *Diaries*, p. 246. Baron von der Heydt, a friend of the crown prince's, mismanaged some of Wilhelm's money, and Nitz, in charge of the Kaiser's German funds, made bad loans to his son-in-law. Nitz was fired in June 1929. Kurowsky Papers, no. 6.

41. HA, Rep. 192, no. 18; Gutsche and Petzold, "Verhältnis der Hohenzollern zum Faschismus," p. 919, gives the figure as 12 million marks.

42. Wilhelm's "Einige Reflexionen" (28 Aug. 1934), HA, Rep. 192, no. 19; Wilhelm to Schiemann (6 Feb. 1919), Schiemann Papers; Wilhelm's notes (20 Oct. 1923, 9 Jan. 1925), Rijksarchief Papers, nos. 646, 650; Ilsemann, 2:40; see a sermon by Wilhelm to his household, Spring 1925, KE, no. 809, for his indictment of his former subjects.

43. Wilhelm's notes (2 Jan. 1924), Rijksarchief Papers, no. 647.

44. Wilhelm's notes (5 June 1924), ibid., no. 649; Wilhelm to Einem (12 June 1933), Einem Papers; Wilhelm to Schiemann (6 Feb. 1919), Schiemann Papers; Wilhelm to Viereck (4 Dec. 1923), Viereck Papers.

45. See Wilhelm to Viereck (4 Dec.1923), Viereck Papers, on the collapse of parliamentarism; on intellectual incapacity, see same to Schiemann (6 Feb. 1919), Schiemann Papers; on the federal principle, see Wilhelm's notes (24 Oct. 1923), Rijksarchief Papers, no. 646; on the lives of the citizenry, see his notes (2 Jan. 1924), ibid., no. 647.

46. Wilhelm's notes (2, 23 Jan. 1924), Rijksarchief Papers, no. 647.

47. In Mar. 1928 Wilhelm was asked if flowers should be sent to the wedding of young Prince Bismarck. The Kaiser replied, "As long as the prince is an *active official* of the German sow-republic (*Saurepublik*) I will have nothing to do with him *directly*." Wilhelm's comment is on a memo by his adjutant, Baron von Grancy (29 Mar. 1928), Rijksarchief Papers, no. 6.

48. Wilhelm to Viereck (4, 20 Dec. 1923), Viereck Papers.

49. Same to same (27 Apr. 1924), ibid.

50. Wilhelm's notes (24 Jan., 3 Feb. 1924) on Lenin and Ebert respectively, Rijksarchief Papers, no. 647.

51. Wilhelm's notes (2 Jan. 1924), ibid.; Ilsemann, 1:290. For Stresemann's opinion of the Kaiser see, Kenneth Young, *Diaries*, p. 82.

52. Wilhelm to Viereck (24 June 1924), Viereck Papers; Ilsemann, 2:14; Wilhelm's notes (22 Sept. 1924), Rijksarchief Papers, no. 649, express opposition to

the League of Nations and/or the Washington Disarmament Conference. On the Kellogg Pact, see Wilhelm to Bigelow (12 Feb. 1929), Bigelow Papers, no. 34. The Dawes Plan is condemned in marginalia on a letter from John Kümpel, an American student (21 Feb. 1929), Rijksarchief Papers, no. 8. The banana republic remark is in Wilhelm's notes (21 Aug. 1924), ibid., no. 649.

53. Wilhelm to Bigelow (17 Nov. 1927), Bigelow Papers, no. 34; same to Reischach (25 Nov., 13 Dec. 1925), Mackensen Papers, no. 256.

54. See Wilhelm's notes (25 Apr. 1924), Rijksarchief Papers, no. 647, on how Germany should behave. On the French: Wilhelm's notes (2 Feb. 1924), ibid.; Wilhelm to Bigelow (17 Nov. 1927), Bigelow Papers, no. 34; Ilsemann, 2:34; Wilhelm to Viereck (27 Apr. 1924), Viereck Papers; Waters, *Potsdam and Doorn*, p. 143.

55. Wilhelm's notes (3 Sept. 1923, 9, 22 May 1924), Rijksarchief Papers, nos. 646, 649.

56. Wilhelm to Viereck (4 Dec. 1923), Viereck Papers; similar language in 1928 is in Waters, *Potsdam and Doorn*, p. 116, and in 1929 in Robert H. Bruce Lockhart, *Retreat from Glory*, p. 323.

57. Ilsemann, 1:264, 293–94.

58. Niemann, *Wanderungen*, p. 33. This was to complement Wilhelm's ghostwritten *Comparative Historical Tables*.

59. Objections by General Baron Lyncker are in Schwertfeger Papers, no. 206; the crown prince's opinion is in his letter to Hahnke (26 Oct. 1922), Hahnke Papers; Ilsemann, 1:293. Popular success is noted in Kurt Koehler (the Kaiser's publisher) to Wilhelm (17 Oct. 1923), Rijksarchief Papers, no. 240, and in Wilhelm to Viereck (13 May 1924), Viereck Papers. The Kaiser's disappointment: Niemann, *Wanderungen*, pp. 30–33; Ilsemann, 2:11.

60. Niemann, *Wanderungen*, p. 30.

61. Ilsemann, 2:41. Niemann's works nevertheless have considerable value, since he knew Wilhelm quite well and on occasion printed documents not found elsewhere.

62. Wilhelm to Viereck (26 Mar., 6 Nov. 1928), Viereck Papers; Ilsemann, 2:231, 300, 310.

63. Robert H. Bruce Lockhart, *Comes the Reckoning*, pp. 39–40; Ilsemann, 2:47, 131.

64. See Ilsemann, 2:41, 140, on Friedrich von Berg in Berlin being the one who recommended him to Wilhelm. Hermine declared that Nowak was given material at Doorn because no other historian had expressed such a wish. See her letter to Haller (1 May 1930), Haller Papers, no. 20.

65. Wilhelm to Fürstenberg (3 July 1927), Fürstenberg Papers, "Briefe von I.I.M.M. Kaiser Wilhelm II. von 1909–1940"; also Robert H. Bruce Lockhart, *Retreat from Glory*, p. 327.

66. Ilsemann, 2:136, 138–41, 210.

67. The quotation is from Nowak's *Kaiser und Chancellor*, p. ix; on the buyback, see Ilsemann, 2:148–49. Nowak was also involved in producing a film in which Wilhelm appeared. Hans von Below to Otto von Below (14 Feb. 1933), Below Papers, no. 2, in which Below says that the film will make Wilhelm a laughingstock abroad.

68. Schneller, *Königs-Erinnerungen*, p. 238.

69. Ilsemann, 1:123–24. Among the most damaging were the memoirs of Zedlitz-Trützschler and the serialized reminiscences of Hammann and Raschdau.

70. Tirpitz to Chamberlain (10 Nov. 1926), Tirpitz Papers, no. 177. On the appearance of Tirpitz's *Erinnerungen* in 1919, Wilhelm wrote an article in "Deutsche Politik" (21 Nov. 1919) correcting the admiral's account.

71. Wilhelm to Viereck (26 Oct. 1926), Viereck Papers; Ilsemann, 2:41, 123.

72. Captain Gr[ancy] to the editor of *Current History* (5 Apr. 1928), Rijksarchief Papers, no. 251; Schneller, *Königs-Erinnerungen*, p. 238.

73. Wilhelm to Viereck (9 Sept. 1926), Viereck Papers.

74. *Kaiser Wilhelm II., seine Weltanschauung und die Deutschen Katholiken* (Leipzig, 1929), dedicated to the memory of Chancellor Hertling. Hermine, Wilhelm, and Buchner were regular correspondents. See Buchner Papers, nos. 112–115, 122.

75. Wilhelm to Waters (12 July 1930), RA, Geo V O 2578, no. 19.

76. See Hans von Below to Otto von Below (14 Feb. 1933), noting the opinion of the Kaiser's late aunt, the grand duchess of Baden. Below Papers, no. 2; his brother-in-law, the duke of Meiningen, had the same view. Duke to Gossler (3 Dec. 1918, 11 Apr. 1922), Gossler Papers, no. 7.

77. Tirpitz in his letter to Bachmann (1 May 1925), Tirpitz Papers, no. 198; Kapp in Roddie, *Peace Patrol*, p. 150.

78. Duke to Gossler (8 June 1920), Gossler Papers, no. 19.

79. Same to same (27 May 1924), ibid.

80. See Granier, *Levetzow*, esp. pp. 120–21.

81. Niemann, *Wanderungen*, p. 107. For the comparison with Pericles, see Wilhelm to Bigelow (7 Jan. 1941), Bigelow Papers, no. 34a.

82. Ilsemann, 2:139.

83. Wilhelm to Viereck (9 Feb. 1925), Viereck Papers.

84. Wilhelm's notes (8 Nov., 21 Dec. 1923), Rijksarchief Papers, no. 646; Wilhelm to Viereck (21 Apr. 1926), Viereck Papers.

85. Berbers in Wilhelm's notes (20 Oct., 8 Nov. 1923), Rijksarchief Papers, no. 646; Wilhelm to Viereck (20 Dec. 1923, 20 Feb. 1925), Viereck Papers. On perfume, see Wilhelm to Anna Chamberlain, widow of Houston Stewart Chamberlain (7 June 1931), Rijksarchief Papers, no. 288; on femininity, see Wilhelm, "Sex of Nations," p. 130.

86. Wilhelm to Viereck (20 Dec. 1923, 27 Apr. 1925), Viereck Papers.

87. Same to same (20 Feb. 1925), ibid.

88. Wilhelm, "Sex of Nations," pp. 130–31.

89. Wilhelm to Professor Bluhner (29 Aug. 1929), HA, Rep. 53, no. 352.

90. Wilhelm's notes (6 Nov. 1923), Rijksarchief Papers, no. 646; also Wilhelm to Viereck (9 Feb. 1925), Viereck Papers.

91. The "Catholic Jew" is in Wilhelm to Viereck (30 Dec. 1925), Viereck Papers; Zita is in same to Schiemann (30 June 1919), Schiemann Papers. The Kaiser's low opinion of the Center is in his notes (26 May 1924, 16 Jan. 1925), Rijksarchief Papers, nos. 649–50. On Catholic collusion with Jews, Communists, and Socialists: Wilhelm to the crown prince (17 Sept. 1932), HA, Rep. 53a, no. 176; same to Schiemann (30 June 1919), Schiemann Papers; same to Mackensen (2 Dec. 1919),

Mackensen, no. 39; same to Fürstenberg (31 Jan. 1923), Fürstenberg Papers, "Briefe von I.I.M.M. Kaiser Wilhelm II. von 1909–1940."

92. Wilhelm's notes (3, 22 Sept., 8 Nov. 1923), Rijksarchief Papers, no. 646 (4 Dec. 1924), no. 650.

93. Wilhelm to Dörpfeld (14 Feb. 1920), KE, no. 578/1; same to Viereck (20 Feb. 1925), Viereck Papers.

94. Wilhelm's notes (4 Dec. 1924), Rijksarchief Papers, no. 650; Wilhelm to Viereck (27 Apr. 1925), Viereck Papers.

95. Wilhelm's notes (24 Jan. 1924), Rijksarchief Papers, no. 647. On the Alliance: Wilhelm to Viereck (27 Apr. 1925), Viereck Papers; Wilhelm's notes (4 Dec. 1924), Rijksarchief Papers, no. 650; Wilhelm to Schiemann (27 Feb. 1920), Schiemann Papers; Dommes diary (28 Feb. 1920), Dommes Papers, no. 3/3.

96. Wilhelm's notes (27 Dec. 1924), Rijksarchief Papers, no. 650.

97. Buchner to Hermine (9 Jan. 1933), Buchner Papers, no. 114. On the Dutch press: Wilhelm's notes (7 Aug. 1940), Rijksarchief Papers, no. 263; Wilhelm to Waters (27 Aug. 1933), RA, Geo V O 2578, no. 42; on the German press, see same to Viereck (30 Dec. 1925), and on the *New York Times*, see same to same (18 Apr. 1927), Viereck Papers.

98. Wilhelm to Marianne Geibel (28 July 1940), Rijksarchief Papers, no. 263.

99. On Harden, see Wilhelm to Viereck (29 Jan. 1926), Viereck Papers; on Eulenburg's innocence, see Wilhelm on a memo by Eulenburg's physician, Dr. Saar (2 Sept. 1927), Rijksarchief Papers, no. 6.

100. Wilhelm to Mackensen (12 Aug. 1920), Mackensen Papers, no. 39; Wilhelm to Buchner (5 Feb. 1930), Rijksarchief Papers, no. 273.

101. Wilhelm to Buchner (5 Feb. 1930), Rijksarchief Papers, no. 273.

102. On Jewish myths, see Wilhelm to a young pastor (n.d. [ca. 1930]), Mackensen Papers, no. 263. Wilhelm sometimes thought that the Bavarian Wittelsbachs might be destined to sweep away the German republic, but usually he insisted that only the Hohenzollerns could do this. See Wilhelm's notes (24 Oct. 1923, 26 May 1924), Rijksarchief Papers, nos. 646, 649; undated letter by same to Professor Jeremiah, ibid., no. 266; Wilhelm to Viereck (4 Dec. 1923), Viereck Papers.

103. *Wilhelm II. und Hermine*, pp. 109–10, 146; Ilsemann, 1:186, 188, 207, 210; Friedrich Leopold of Prussia, *Behind the Scenes*, p. 136. Wilhelm in 1921 showed some interest in Baroness Lili von Heemstra, whose family had once owned Haus Doorn. Ilsemann, 1:191, 194.

104. Wilhelm to Fürstenberg (14 Oct. 1922), Fürstenberg Papers, "Briefe von I.I.M.M. Kaiser Wilelm II. von 1909–1940." See also same to Viereck (22 Oct. 1924), in which Wilhelm describes Hermine as "a trusted and able comrade, a splendid incarnation of loving and adorable womanhood, in fact 'the ideal' wife for a man in a position like [his] at the time."

105. Letter of 15 Oct. 1922 in HA, Rep. 192, no. 20. This was in response to a letter from the countess, who told Wilhelm that in August 1918 the Kaiserin had confided that she hoped the Kaiser would remarry. Hermine, *Empress in Exile*, pp. 26, 178.

106. On Hermine, see her *Empress in Exile* and her "Unsrem Heim." There are favorable estimations of her: Robert H. Bruce Lockhart, *Retreat from Glory*, p.

324; Kenneth Young, *Diaries*, p. 75; Ilsemann, 1:219; Naso, *Ich Liebe das Leben*, pp. 641–42.

107. Wheeler-Bennett, *Knaves, Fools, and Heroes*, pp. 182–83; also *Wilhelm II. und Hermine*, p. 204. For her designs on capturing Wilhelm: Tschirschky, *Erinnerungen*, p. 125; Ilsemann, 1:2.

108. Wilhelm's account of the letter is in Hermine, *Empress in Exile*, pp. 11–12; Hermine's is in ibid., pp. 197–200, where it is printed. See also Ilsemann, 1:233.

109. On the courtship: Hermine, *Empress in Exile*, pp. 209–23; Ilsemann, 1:218–22.

110. The nuptial agreement is in HA, Rep. 53, no. 399; Dommes Papers, no. 23, gives details of Wilhelm's gifts to her.

111. Ilsemann, 1:187–88.

112. Viktoria Luise, *Tochter des Kaisers*, pp. 242–43; Ilsemann, 1:218–25.

113. On "my wife," see Ilsemann, 2:39; on her satisfaction in her title, see ibid., 1:247–50, 257. Visitors to Doorn were instructed to address her as *"Majestät."* Wilhelm did not relish being called "ex-Kaiser" or "former Kaiser." See his letter to Viereck (18 Apr. 1927), Viereck Papers, protesting that the *New York Times* had done so, and see H. C. Burman (United Press) to Dommes (11 Dec. 1934), saying he would try to see that the expression was not used. Rijksarchief Papers, no. 39. Wilhelm preferred for relatives to address him formally as *"Euer Majestät."* See Ernst Heinrich, *Lebensweg*, p. 67.

114. Kürenberg, *War Alles Falsch?*, p. 20. On this, see Viktoria Luise, *Tochter des Kaisers*, p. 242, and Ilsemann 1:247.

115. Wheeler-Bennett, *Knaves, Fools, and Heroes*, pp. 182–83. On her daily life, see Hermine, *Empress in Exile*, pp. 270–76.

116. Hermine to Haller (24 Jan. 1931), Haller Papers, no. 20; Ilsemann, 1:266–67, 2:22.

117. Ilsemann, 2:88. They complained about one another. Ibid. 1:282, 2:93.

118. Viktoria Luise, *Tochter des Kaisers*, p. 242.

119. Wilhelm to Viereck (26 Oct. 1926), Viereck Papers. The book is Paul Lindenburg's *Das Buch der Kaiserin Auguste Viktoria* (Berlin, 1927).

120. On the "new wife," see Ilsemann, 1:269. For the crown princess's resentment, see ibid., 1:247–48, 257, 269, 274, and for Hermine's dislike of her, see 2:207. On the crown prince: ibid., 2:33, 99; Jonas, *Crown Prince William*, pp. 145–46. See also Viktoria Luise, *Tochter des Kaisers*, p. 243.

121. Ilsemann, esp. vol. 2, is rich in detail on this.

122. Ibid., 1:274.

123. Wheeler-Bennett, *Knaves, Fools, and Heroes*, pp. 182–83.

CHAPTER 15

1. There are guest books for Doorn in Rijksarchief Papers, no. 392 (1913–33) and no. 366 (1930–38).

2. For examples of adventurers, see Ilsemann, 2:38, 54–55.

3. Wilhelm to Dörpfeld (7 Aug. 1924), KE, no. 578/1; same to Viereck (20 Dec. 1923), Viereck Papers.

4. Wilhelm to Frobenius (29 June 1933), Rijksarchief Papers, no. 276; Ilsemann, 2:22, 104, 137, 308.

5. Wilhelm's address to the *Doorner Arbeits-Gemeinschaft* (28 Oct. 1937), Rijksarchief Papers, no. 296.

6. On Ford the Jew, see Wilhelm's notes (15 Sept. 1923), ibid., no. 646; on obtaining automobiles for Frobenius, see Wilhelm's notes (27 Feb. 1934), ibid., no. 276; on General Cramon's intervention with Hindenburg, see ibid., no. 287, p. 29. On financial help to Frobenius, see Wilhelm to Viereck (20 Dec. 1923), Viereck Papers.

7. Wilhelm to Frobenius (22 May 1932) and to Countess Elisabeth zu Salm (6 July 1932), Rijksarchief Papers, no. 276.

8. Ilsemann, 1:287. Wilhelm kept on handcoloring Knackfuss postcards and continued to warn of the rise of Japan, which unfortunately had displaced Caucasian influence in Asia but which might be a potential ally against the Bolsheviks. For warnings against the "Yellow Peril": Wilhelm to Waters (27 Aug. 1933), RA, Geo V O 2578, no. 42; same to Viereck (18 June 1925), Viereck Papers.

9. Hermine, *Empress in Exile*, p. 170; Wilhelm to Viereck (20 Dec. 1923), Viereck Papers.

10. Wilhelm's undated letter to an unnamed cleric in Rijksarchief Papers, no. 266.

11. Wilhelm to Chamberlain (3 June 1923), H. S. Chamberlain, *Briefe*, 2:274.

12. Same to same (12 Mar. 1923), ibid., 2:269; same to Blüher (8 Feb. 1932), Rijksarchief Papers, no. 267.

13. Same to Chamberlain (21 Nov. 1931, 12 Mar. 1923), H. S. Chamberlain, *Briefe*, 2:260, 267; Wilhelm's notes (2 May 1927) concerning a second edition of Chamberlain's *Mensch und Gott*, Rijksarchief Papers, no. 263.

14. Wilhelm to Viereck (29 Jan. 1926), Viereck Papers.

15. Same to Frobenius (27 Dec. 1931), Rijksarchief Papers, no. 275.

16. The voluminous correspondence between Wilhelm and Jeremias is in ibid., no. 268.

17. History of the *Gemeinschaft* is in ibid., no. 277 and no. 287, and a list of members (8 May 1933) is in ibid., no. 275. Wilhelm related the history of the organization in an address during a meeting on 28 Oct. 1937, ibid., no. 296.

18. Wilhelm acknowledged Frobenius's authorship in ibid., no. 287, p. 52. Another of Frobenius's ghostwritten papers for the Kaiser, dated 12 Feb. 1931, is in ibid., no. 288.

19. There are a number of letters by Dörpfeld but only one by Wilhelm in ibid., no. 40. On the relationship, see also Wilhelm, *Erinnerungen an Korfu*, p. 82; Dryander, *Erinnerungen*, pp. 329–30.

20. Wilhelm, *Erinnerungen an Korfu*, p. 72, has a drawing of the pediment.

21. Ibid., p. 121; Wilhelm to Frobenius (17 July 1933), Rijksarchief Papers, no. 276.

22. Wilhelm, *Erinnerungen an Korfu*, pp. 109–14, and also pp. 102, 105.

23. Wilhelm's marginalia on a letter from Frobenius (4 July 1938), Rijksarchief Papers, no. 277; see Wilhelm to Dörpfeld (7 Aug. 1924), KE, no. 578/1, on appropriation of ideas.

24. Hermine to Buchner (26 Oct., 1935), Buchner Papers, no. 114.

25. Robert H. Bruce Lockhart, *Retreat from Glory*, pp. 318–19. The Kaiser made an exception for his old friend Colonel Waters. See Waters, *Potsdam and Doorn*, p. 97.

26. Dryander, *Erinnerungen*, 328–32. There is correspondence between the two men in Rijksarchief Papers, no. 39, that is not found in among Bigelow's papers in New York.

27. On the court proceedings, see Wilhelm to Waters (12 July 1930), RA, Geo V O 2578, no. 19. In a letter to Bigelow at Christmas 1929, Wilhelm urged him to publish an apology for all the anti-German things he had written, and when Bigelow did so, the Kaiser told Waters that Bigelow was "setting a good example by his recantation." See Wilhelm to Bigelow, Bigelow Papers, no. 34, and to Waters (15 June 1930), in RA, Geo V O 2578, no. 18.

28. Wilhelm to Countess Salm (6 July 1932), Rijksarchief Papers, no. 75; same to Fürstenberg (4 Feb., 1 June 1922), Fürstenberg Papers, "Briefe von I.I.M.M. Kaiser Wilhelm II. von 1909–1940"; Ilsemann, 1:218, 246, 2:144.

29. There is correspondence between them in RA, Geo V O 2578, and in Rijksarchief Papers, no. 249. Robert Bruce Lockhart, who knew the Kaiser well, called Waters Wilhelm's closest English friend. See Robert H. Bruce Lockhart, *Retreat from Glory*, p. 321. For Wilhelm on Waters, see Ilsemann, 2:101.

30. Letter of 24 Apr. 1928, RA, Geo V, O 2578, no. 2.

31. Robert H. Bruce Lockhart, *Retreat from Glory*, p. 321. On Wilhelm's resemblance to his uncle: Schramm, "Notizen," p. 945; Bentinck, *Ex-Kaiser in Exile*, p. 50; on his language, see Wheeler-Bennett, *Knaves, Fools, and Heroes*, p. 181.

32. Robert H. Bruce Lockhart, *Comes the Reckoning*, p. 37; resentment at the king in Wilhelm to Waters (24 Sept. 1930), RA, Geo V O 2578, no. 16.

33. Wheeler-Bennett, *Knaves, Fools, and Heroes*, p. 184; Robert H. Bruce Lockhart, *Comes the Reckoning*, p. 37.

34. Wilhelm to Waters (24 Apr. 1932), Rijksarchief Papers, no. 249. Waters, *Potsdam and Doorn*, reports Wilhelm saying that no one can in fact remove him from the order.

35. George V's diary in Rose, *George V*, p. 229.

36. Robert H. Bruce Lockhart, *Retreat from Glory*, pp. 318–19; on the Kaiser's efforts to prevent publication, see Ilsemann, 2:106–7.

37. Ilsemann, 1:325. Ilsemann was concerned that the Kaiser himself would be indiscreet. Ibid., 1:180.

38. Ibid., 1:267, and also the testimony of Chelius, ibid., 1:270, of Schulenburg, ibid., 1:172, of Berg, ibid., 1:281, of the Kaiser's childhood friend Frau von Leipzig, ibid., 1:303, and of Cramon, ibid. 2:13.

39. Ibid., 1:282, also 2:91–92.

40. Ibid., 1:235.

41. Ibid., 1:289.

42. Ibid., 1:279, reporting Colonel Niemann's view.

43. Ibid., 1:116, 278, 2:91.

44. Ibid., 1:268. The prince's *Erinnerungen* (1922), like most of his father's works, was ghostwritten. See Ilsemann, 1:265.

45. Jonas, *Crown Prince William*, p. 150. See also Ilsemann, 1:286–87, 299–301, for the Kaiser's disapproval of his son's return.

46. Wilhelm's notes (5 June 1924), Rijksarchief Papers, no. 649. On German apathy: his notes (6 June 1924), ibid.; Wilhelm to Schiemann (6 Feb. 1919), Schiemann Papers.

47. Ilsemann, 2:15.

48. Ibid., 2:36, on the shogun. On the Kaiser's view of a dictatorship: his letter to Schiemann (6 Feb. 1919), Schiemann Papers; Ilsemann, 1:184, 302–3; the Kaiser's letter to Einem (12 June 1933), Einem Papers.

49. Ilsemann, 2:11, 36, 89, 144.

50. Wilhelm's notes (5 June 1924), Rijksarchief Papers, no. 649.

51. On Seeckt, see Ilsemann 2:10; on Ludendorff and Tirpitz, see ibid., 13.

52. Robert H. Bruce Lockhart, *Retreat from Glory*, p. 326; Sherrill, *Bismarck and Mussolini*, pp. 113–14; Wilhelm to Viereck (29 Jan. 1926), Viereck Papers.

53. The Kaiser did not at all approve of Mussolini's dealings with the Kremlin, but he nevertheless had a grudging admiration for Mussolini's diplomatic verve. See Wilhelm's notes, "Was soll Locarno" (20 Nov. 1925), Schwertfeger Papers, no. 443, and his letter to Reischach (25 Nov. 1925), in which he argues that Germany should employ a freehand policy "like Mussolini!" Mackensen Papers, no. 256. See Waters, *Potsdam and Doorn*, pp. 178–79, for the Kaiser's appreciation of *il Duce*'s Vatican diplomacy.

54. Lochner, *Always the Unexpected*, pp. 254–55; Wilhelm's notes, "Was soll Locarno" (1925), Schwertfeger Papers, no. 443.

55. Mussolini to the British ambassador, Sir Ronald Graham (14 Nov. 1932), Sweetman, "Unforgotten Crowns," p. 354.

56. Wilhelm's notes (15 Sept. 1923), Rijksarchief Papers, no. 646.

57. Wilhelm's marginalia on a letter from General Enckenvort (23 Dec. 1929), ibid., no. 248.

58. Letter (28 July 1922), Niemann, *Revolution von Oben*, p. 445, and Wheeler-Bennett, *Wooden Titan*, p. 242. In January 1922, six months before Hindenburg sent his letter, Wilhelm was trying to round up witnesses who would testify to the field marshal's responsibility. See Wilhelm to Lyncker (21 Jan. 1922), HA, Rep. 53, no. 2. Hindenburg was incorrect in holding that *everyone* had advised Wilhelm to flee, for that was not true of either Groener or Schulenburg.

59. See Ilsemann, 1:317–18, for Wilhelm's letter to Hindenburg (21 Sept. 1922).

60. Wilhelm to Levetzow (17 Oct. 1932), Granier, *Levetzow*, p. 346 n. 5. For Wilhelm's condescension, see Dorpalen, *Hindenburg*, pp. 132–33.

61. Hindenburg to Cramon (27 Mar. 1925), Cramon Papers, no. 22; Wheeler-Bennett, *Wooden Titan*, p. 355. On Hindenburg's lack of enthusiasm for Wilhelm's restoration, see his letter to Cramon (23 Oct. 1933), Cramon Papers, no. 22.

62. Jonas, *Crown Prince William*, p. 170.

63. Wheeler-Bennett, *Wooden Titan*, pp. 355–56.

64. Hindenburg to Cramon (23 Oct. 1933), Cramon Papers, no. 22.

65. Ilsemann, 2:49, 142; Granier, *Levetzow*, p. 346 n. 5; Wilhelm to the crown prince (17 Sept. 1932), HA, Rep. 53a, no. 176; Dorpalen, *Hindenburg*, pp. 132–33.

66. Ilsemann, 2:66–67, 71, 94, 118, 123–24.

67. Wheeler-Bennett, *Knaves, Fools, and Heroes*, p. 184; Ilsemann, 2:73, 146.

68. Ludendorff to Wilhelm (9 Aug. 1927) and Wilhelm response (26 Aug. 1927), in which the Kaiser applauds an anti-Semitic tract by Ludendorff. Mackensen Papers, no. 39.

69. Wilhelm's notes (13 Oct. 1923), Rijksarchief Papers, no. 646.

70. Wilhelm's notes (12 Nov. 1923), ibid.; Wilhelm to Mackensen (19 Dec. 1923), Mackensen Papers, no. 39; Ilsemann, 1:298.

71. Wilhelm's notes (12 Nov. 1923), Rijksarchief Papers, no. 646.

72. Ilsemann, 2:20.

73. Wilhelm's notes (18 July 1924), Rijksarchief Papers, no. 649.

74. Hitler expresses sympathy in chapter 11 but strong criticism in chapter 10. On Wilhelm and *Mein Kampf*, see Ilsemann, 2:255.

75. Trevor Roper, *Hitler's Secret Conversations*, talk of 31 May 1942, pp. 411–12.

76. Dietrich, *12 Jahre*, pp. 244–46; Smith, *Berlin Alert*, p. 61.

77. Gutsche and Petzold, "Verhältnis der Hohenzollern zum Faschismus," p. 919.

78. Ibid., p. 920.

79. Ilsemann, 2:69.

80. On Auwi and the Nazis: Sweetman, "Unforgotten Crowns," pp. 258, 280, 290; Ilsesmann, 2:134, 155, 191; Jonas, *Crown Prince William*, p. 171; Gutsche and Petzold, "Verhältnis der Hohenzollern zum Faschismus," p. 919; Viktoria Luise, *Tochter des Kaisers*, pp. 267–72.

81. Wilhelm to Louis Ferdinand of Prussia (23 Feb. 1932), Bigelow Papers, no. 34a. On Oskar, see Viktoria Luise, *Tochter des Kaisers*, p. 267.

82. Crown Prince to Selasen-Selasinsky (20 Apr. 1932), Selasen-Selasinsky Papers, no. 10; Ilsemann, 2:155; Jonas, *Crown Prince William*, pp. 162, 171.

83. To an English observer in 1936, she and her husband still appeared to be "pro-Nazi." Kenneth Young, *Diaries*, p. 348. On the princess's association with the Nazi movement, see Viktoria Luise, *Tochter des Kaisers*, pp. 265, 275–78, 287.

84. Ilsemann, 2:40, 56, 64–65, 74.

85. Ibid., 2:107–8.

86. Ibid., 2:78–79, 90–92.

87. Others were General Unruh, Kleist, and Lersner. See ibid., esp. 2:63–64, 79.

88. Ibid., 2:98.

89. Ibid., 2:115.

90. Ibid., 2:122.

91. Ibid., 2:136.

92. Letter of 19 Dec. 1923, Mackensen Papers, no. 39.

93. Sermon by Wilhelm at Doorn (18 May 1930), Mackensen Papers, no. 263.

94. Levetzow to Wilhelm (22 Dec. 1932), HA, Rep. 53, no. 168; Granier, *Levetzow*, pp. 120, 257.

95. Granier, *Levetzow*, p. 269.

96. Hermine to Buchner (9 Sept. 1930), Buchner Papers, no. 113.

97. Ilsemann, 2:137.

98. Ibid., 2:145.

99. Ibid., 2:143.

100. On the negative Nazi reaction to Hermine, see Fromm, *Blood and Banquets*, p. 59; see Ilsemann, 1:282, for her complaints at neglect; on Papen, see her letters to Buchner (3 Feb. 1928, 13 May 1930), Buchner Papers, no. 112. For Hitler's awkwardness, see Dietrich, *12 Jahre*, pp. 245–46. On the Tiele-Winckler and Dirksen salons, see Granier, *Levetzow*, p. 312 and n. 5.

101. Schneider, *Verhüllter Tag*, p. 104; also Sweetmann, "Unforgotten Crowns," pp. 280–82.

102. Granier, *Levetzow*, pp. 287–88, 297–98. On the belief in the entourage that in the Nazis lay the hope of a restoration, see Ilsemann 2:152, 162.

103. Ilsemann, 2:153–56, 158–59.

104. Ibid., 2:158, 171. To secure the avaricious Göring's future cooperation, he was given furniture and silk hangings from the royal collections. Gutsche, *Kaiser im Exil*, p. 131.

CHAPTER 16

1. Ilsemann, 2:172.

2. Ibid., 2:189.

3. Ibid., 2:183.

4. Ibid., 2:189–90. See Kenneth Young, *Diaries*, p. 348 (14 July 1936), for Wilhelm's belief, apparently unfounded, that his daughter and her husband were currying favor with Hitler in order to take the throne.

5. See Jonas, *Crown Prince William*, pp. 173–74, for the prince's letters to Hitler and to Wilhelm (both 29 Mar. 1932). On the prince's candidacy, see Friedrich, *Wer Spielte*, pp. 8–17, and Selasen-Selasinsky Papers, no. 10.

6. Ilsemann, 2:91; Viktoria Luise, *Tochter des Kaisers*, p. 269.

7. Mary von Selasinsky to "Teechen" (31 Mar. 1932), Selasen-Selasinsky Papers, no. 10.

8. Ilsemann, 2:192.

9. Ibid., 1:193–95.

10. Levetzow to Wilhelm (22 Dec. 1932), and Dommes to Levetzow (14 Jan. 1933), HA, Rep. 53, no. 168; Granier, *Levetzow*, p. 186. Wilhelm claimed that his remark reflected not approval of the Nazis but rather the fact that Levetzow was no longer in his employ.

11. Gutsche and Petzold, "Verhältnis der Hohenzollern zum Faschismus," p. 924; Ilsemann, 2:201–3.

12. Letter of 27 Sept. 1932, Sweetman, "Unforgotten Crowns," p. 350.

13. On the leak, for which the Kaiser suspected the crown princess, see Ilsemann, 2:204.

14. Ibid., 2:202, 205–7.

15. Dommes to an unnamed count (26 Apr. 1932), Rijksarchief Papers, no. 251; on the crown prince's role: Gutsche and Petzold, "Verhältnis der Hohenzollern zum Faschismus," pp. 932–34; Ilsemann, 2:207.

16. Levetzow to Wilhelm (22 Dec. 1932), HA, Rep. 53, no. 168.

17. Ilsemann, 2:215.

18. Letter of 12 June 1933, Einem Papers; see also Ilsemann, 2:215.

19. Gutsche and Petzold, "Verhältnis der Hohenzollern zum Faschismus," p. 935; Ilsemann, 2:281.

20. Ilsemann, 2:281.

21. Gutsche and Petzold, "Verhältnis der Hohenzollern zum Faschismus," pp. 937–39; Dommes to Hitler (24 Oct. 1933), HA, Rep. 192, no. 13.

22. Ilsemann, 2:217–18. For Hermine's approval of the Nazis: her letters to Schwertfeger (4 Jan. 1934, 22 May 1935), Schwertfeger Papers, no. 443; same to Mackensen (4 Dec. 1937), Mackensen Papers, no. 40; Ilsemann, 2:272. "Petticoat politics" is in Ilsemann, 2:239.

23. Ilsemann, 2:216.

24. Ibid., 2:228–31, 241. The only good thing that Wilhelm had to say about Hitler was that he did not plunder the state, taking no salary and living from his publication royalties. Waters, *Potsdam and Doorn*, p. 202.

25. Ilsemann, 2:222. For Hermine's contacts with the SA leader, see Ernst Roehm, ibid., and 2:217.

26. Ibid., 2:229.

27. Ibid., 2:232.

28. Ibid., 2:234–35.

29. Cramon memo (Oct 1933), Cramon Papers, no. 46.

30. Wilhelm to Levetzow (27 Oct. 1932), Granier, *Levetzow*, p. 346 note 5.

31. The instrument is dated 11 May 1934 and is printed in Wheeler-Bennett, *Wooden Titan*, pp. 470–73, and in Dorpalen, *Hindenburg*, pp. 476–77. Wilhelm was very disappointed that Hindenburg had said nothing about a restoration. Ilsemann, 2:273.

32. Dietrich, *12 Jahre*, p. 246.

33. Dorpalen, *Hindenburg*, p. 481; Ilsemann, 2:269–72.

34. Ilsemann, 2:248. For the Nazi prohibition of the birthday celebrations, see Cramon to Leeres, a newspaperman (27 Jan. 1934), and the order by Hitler's *Pressereferat* that any notices of the birthday in the press must be modest and not indulge in monarchist propaganda. Both are in Cramon Papers, no. 34. For Wilhelm's fear of Nazi reprisals against his family's property: Robert H. Bruce Lockhart, *Comes the Reckoning*, p. 38; Ilsemann, 2:235. Jonas, *Crown Prince William*, p. 182, refers to an agreement (not recorded elsewhere), signed in the late summer of 1933 between Wilhelm's friend *Geheimrat* Berg and Göring, that provided for annual payments to the Kaiser, the crown prince, and the prince's brothers in return for their promise not to criticize Hitler's regime.

35. Ilsemann, 2:250–51. By 1936 the Kaiser was described by a guest at Doorn as "very anti-Nazi." Kenneth Young, *Diaries*, p. 347.

36. For the prince's support of the regime: Gutsche and Petzold, "Verhältnis der Hohenzollern zum Faschismus," pp. 934–35; Jonas, *Crown Prince William*, chap. 8. On Auwi's support: Schneider, *Verhüllter Tag*, p. 107; Ilsemann, 2:266, 277, 280; Viktoria Luise, *Tochter des Kaisers*, pp. 270–72. On Princess Viktoria Luise, see Kenneth Young, *Diaries*, p. 348.

37. Sweetman, "Unforgotten Crowns," p. 438. Robert Bruce Lockhart rather enigmatically described her in 1935 as "not very pro-Hitler." Kenneth Young, *Diaries*, p. 322.

38. Ilsemann, 2:280.

39. Hermine to Buchner (7 Nov. 1933), Buchner Papers, no. 114; same to Schwertfeger (4 Jan. 1934), Schwertfeger Papers, no. 443; same to Haller (31 Jan. 1934), Haller Papers, no. 20; Jonas, *Crown Prince William*, pp. 189–90.

40. Hermine to Mackensen (3 Feb. 1934), Mackensen Papers, no. 40.

41. Hermine to Schwertfeger (22 May 1935), Schwertfeger Papers, no. 443; also same to Bigelow (18 Apr. 1935), Bigelow Papers, no. 34a, which describes Hitler as "smart" (*klug*).

42. Ilsemann, 2:247, 268.

43. Ibid., 2:285.

44. Ibid., 2:252–53, 260–61, 275, 282. The gigantic swindles of Serge Stavisky led to scandalous revelations that brought down the government.

45. Ibid., 2:252, 265, 306, 334.

46. Ibid., 2:264–66, 270.

47. On the army, see ibid., 2:300, 306; on Mackensen, see ibid., 2:278, 290, 308.

48. Ibid., 2:313–14; Gutsche, *Kaiser im Exil*, p. 190.

49. Ibid., 2:279, also 285.

50. Ilsemann diary (8 Apr. 1937), ibid., 2:296; also ibid., 2:304–7, 323; Sweetman, "Unforgotten Crowns," p. 493. Hermine's last positive word about Hitler before 1939 came in a letter to Mackensen (12 Apr. 1937), in which she expressed the hope that the Führer might find the right way to guide Germany with a strong hand. Mackensen papers, no. 40. Once the war began, she reverted to greeting friends with "*Heil Hitler!*" Gutsche, *Kaiser im Exil*, p. 210.

51. Ilsemann, 2:283–85; other Nazi-inflicted indignities are in ibid., 2:267, 308, 319.

52. Ibid., 2:273–74.

53. Ibid., 2:274.

54. For his coldness to Friedrich von Berg, one of his oldest and most intimate advisers, see ibid., 2:281, also 295.

55. Letter (21 Jan. 1936), Rijksarchief Papers, no. 7; Kenneth Young, *Diaries*, p. 74.

56. The letters are in Rijksarchief Papers, no. 7, and RA, Geo V CC 45, no. 1199, no. 1210.

57. Ilsemann, 2:302, 325.

58. Wilhelm to Lady Jellicoe (n.d. [ca. 20 Nov. 1935, the date of the admiral's death, and 6 Jan. 1936]), Jellicoe Papers.

59. Ilsemann, 2:161, 190; Sherrill, *Bismarck and Mussolini*, pp. 113–14; Robert H. Bruce Lockhart, *Retreat from Glory*, p. 326; Wilhelm to Viereck (27 Apr. 1924), Viereck Papers.

60. On the uprising, see Lochner, *Always the Unexpected*, pp. 254–55; Victor Emmanuel in Ilsemann, 2:287–89.

61. Ilsemann, 2:304, 317, 321.

62. Ibid., 2:301.

63. Ibid., 2:311, 313. For the Kaiser's approval of Hitler's occupation of the Rheinland in March 1936, see ibid., 2:286, 288.

64. Letter (1 Oct. 1938), RA, Geo V CC 46, no. 270.

65. Letter (12 Dec. 1938), ibid., V O 2578, no. 96.

66. Ilsemann, 2:320; Hermine's delight is in Gutsche, *Kaiser im Exil*, p. 194.

67. Lochner, *Always the Unexpected*, p. 256.

68. Jonas, *Crown Prince William*, p. 224; Ilsemann, 2:327.

69. Ilsemann, 2:322, 334.

70. Ibid., 2:327, 332.

71. RA, Geo V CC 45, no. 1199.

72. Wilhelm to Cramon (9 Oct. 1939), Cramon Papers, no. 20; Hermine to Buchner (5 Oct. 1939), Buchner Papers, no. 114.

73. Notes by Dommes (25 Sept. 1939), HA, Rep. 192, no. 17.

74. Wilhelm to Fräulein Marianne Geibel (28 July 1940), Rijksarchief Papers, no. 263.

75. Same to Niemann (24 Dec. 1940), HA, Rep. 192, no. 16.

76. Wilhelm to Bigelow (14 Sept. 1940), Rijksarchief Papers, no. 39.

77. Ilsemann, 2:325–26; also Gutsche, *Kaiser im Exil*, p. 199.

78. Hermine to her cousin, Princess Solms (6 June 1940), KE, no. 240.

79. Wilhelm to Bigelow (14 Sept. 1940), Bigelow Papers, no. 34a. See also Wilhelm's adjutant, Count Moltke, to his wife (n.d. [ca. 15 May 1940]), KE, no. 240; undated report by Dommes to the Reuss *Hofkammer* in Gera describing the events of 10–15 May 1940, ibid.; Ilsemann, 2:341.

80. Adjutant Count Moltke to his wife (n.d. [ca. 15 May 1940]), and Adjutant General Dommes to Reuss *Hofkammer*, KE, no. 240; also Ilsemann, 2:342–43.

81. Wilhelm's telegram (17 June 1940) and Hitler's reply (25 June 1940), HA, Rep. 192, no. 17.

82. Taylor, *Goebbels Diaries* (4 Feb., 1 Oct. 1940), pp. 112, 126.

83. For his fear of early death: Szögyényi to Kálnoky (2 Feb. 1895), HHStA, no. 146(V); same to Goluchowski (16 Jan. 1900), ibid., no. 153(B); Tirpitz, *Erinnerungen*, p. 468; for his fear of disease: Eppstein, *Bismarcks Entlassung*, pp. 65–67; Topham, *Memories*, 282–85; Zedlitz-Trützschler, p. 109; Princess Friedrich Leopold of Prussia, *Behind the Scenes*, p. 112; Wetterlé, *Behind the Scenes*, p. 157.

84. For his notions about cancer: Szögyényi to Goluchowski (18 Jan. 1904), HHStA, no. 160(V); Paget, *Tower*, 2:409; Davis, *The Kaiser*, p. 198; Eulenburg Papers, no. 80, p. 15.

85. Hermine's secretary Wunderlich to Buchner (19 Jan. 1932), Buchner Papers, no. 112; Ilsemann, 2:179, 188, 196.

86. Louis Ferdinand, *Kaiserenkel*, p. 347; Viktoria Luise, *Tochter des Kaisers*, p. 295. There were also funeral directions dated 26 Oct. 1919; see HA, Rep. 192, no. 19.

87. Ilsemann diary (29 June 1933), Ilsemann, 2:226.

88. Wilhelm to Professor Hans Naumann, Bonn (12 Mar. 1941), Rijksarchief Papers, no. 269; notes (28 May 1941) by illegible hand, Mackensen Papers, no. 267. The 1938 episode is described in Ilsemann, 2:302–4.

89. Accounts of the Kaiser's death: the crown prince's notes (17 June 1941), HA, Rep. 192, no. 18; Dr. Ortenburg, the attending physician, in Rijksarchief Papers, no. 128; Dommes notes (29 June 1941), Schwertfeger Papers, no. 443; Dommes's diary (2–4 June 1941), Dommes Papers, no. 3/9, and his notes (June 1941) in Mackensen Papers, no. 267; Ilsemann, 2:346–49.

90. Crown prince's notes (17 June 1941), HA, Rep. 192, no. 18.

91. Taylor, *Goebbels Diaries*, p. 391.

92. Louis Ferdinand, *Kaiserenkel*, pp. 348–49; Sweetman, "Unforgotten Crowns," p. 654.

93. "Der Tod des Kaisers und die Reise des Generalfeldmarschall von Mackensen zur Beisetzung 8–10.6.41," Schwertfeger Papers, no. 443.

94. Notes by Wilhelm (25 May 1937), HA, Rep. 192, no. 19.

95. Lascelles to Grey (24 Jan. 1907), FO 371/260.

Bibliography

MANUSCRIPT SOURCES

The manuscript sources listed below have been used in this volume. The dates given indicate the materials consulted, not the full run of the various collections. After the name of the collection is its location, for which the following abbreviations are used:

BA   Bundesarchiv, Koblenz
BA-MA   Bundesarchiv-Militärarchiv, Freiburg i.B.
GS   Geheimes Staatsarchiv Preussischer Kulturbesitz, Berlin-Dahlem
HHStA   Haus-, Hof- und Staatsarchiv, Vienna
PRO   Public Record Office, London and Kew Gardens
RA   The Royal Archives, Windsor Castle, Berks

In addition, the following abbreviations have been used in describing the collections.

(B)   Berichte
FO   Foreign Office, London
GFO   German Foreign Office, Berlin
HA   Haus Archiv, Berlin
KE   Kleine Erwerbungen
(V)   Varia

Bauer Papers, BA. Colonel Hermann Bauer, General Staff officer.
         No. 16   Diary and correspondence with the crown prince (1916).
         No. 18   Correspondence with Hindenburg (1918), Hindenburg to Wilhelm (1918).
Below Papers, BA-MA. General Otto von Below, army commander in World War I.
         No. 2   Correspondence with Hans von Below (1920–33).
         No. 35   Collapse in 1918.
Beseler Papers, BA-MA. General Hans von Beseler.
         Nos. 53–55   Correspondence with his wife (1915–17); Count Bodgan von Hutten-Czapski to Wilhelm (1916).
Bigelow Papers, New York Public Library, Manuscript Division. Poultney Bigelow, a childhood friend of the Kaiser's, resumed his friendship in the postwar years and had many contacts with members of the Hohenzollern family.

Nos. 34, 34a   Correspondence with Wilhelm II and other
Hohenzollerns (1927–41)
Bismarck Papers, BA. Microfilm copy of papers of Count Herbert von Bismarck,
the chancellor's son and Wilhelm's friend in the 1880s.
No. FC 2958   Correspondence with Bernhard von Bülow (1888).
No. FC 3018   Undated memoir entitled *Tagebuch*.
Boyd Carpenter Papers, British Library, London. William Boyd Carpenter, Angli-
can bishop of Ripon and a prolific writer on Jesus, was a friend to the Kaiser
and his mother.
Add MS 46721   Correspondence with Wilhelm (1909).
Add MS 46741–42   Diary (1900–1901).
Add MS 47751–52   Diary (1910).
Buchner Papers, BA. Max Buchner, a Bavarian historian, was a friend of Her-
mine's, Wilhelm's second wife.
Nos. 112–115, 122   Correspondence with Hermine (1928–39).
Bülow Papers, BA. Bernhard von Bülow (1899, count; 1905, prince), was a diplo-
mat and intimate of the Kaiser's and became chancellor in 1900.
No. 30   Monarchy and Wilhelm II (1897).
Nos. 33–34   *Daily Telegraph* Crisis (1908–9).
No. 35   Press clippings (1909).
No. 39   Mission to Rome (1915).
No. 60   Correspondence with Albert Ballin (1914).
No. 74   Correspondence with Count August zu Eulenburg
(1902).
No. 76   Correspondence with Count Philipp zu Eulenburg
(1896–97).
No. 90   Correspondence with Friedrich von Holstein (1895–
97).
No. 92   Correspondence with Holstein and Alfred von
Kiderlen-Wächter (1895–97).
No. 98   Correspondence with Prince Karl von Lichnowsky
(1910).
No. 99   Correspondence with Karl von Lindenau (1897).
No. 106   Correspondence with Count Anton Monts (1896).
No. 109   Correspondence with Kaiserin Augusta Victoria
(1899).
No. 112   Correspondence with Wilhelm II (1898–1908).
No. 113   Correspondence with the crown prince of Prussia
(1924).
No. 117   Correspondence with Friedrich Rosen (1921).
No. 126   Correspondence with Alfred Tirpitz (1919).
No. 150   Correspondence with Wilhelm II (1908).
No. 153   Notes and numbered slips of paper (1895–1908).
No. 154   Correspondence with Wilhelm II (1899).
Capelle Papers, BA-MA. Admiral Eduard von Capelle was Tirpitz's successor in
1916 as state secretary of the Imperial Naval Office.
Nos. 1, 5   Miscellaneous correspondence (1915–26).

Cramon Papers, BA. General August von Cramon, adjutant in the 1920s and 1930s.

No. 22   Miscellaneous correspondence (1925–33).

No. 31   Hentsch Mission (1925).

No. 34   Correspondence with Wilhelm II and others (1927–34).

No. 46   Memorandum by Cramon for Hindenburg (1933).

Deines Papers, BA-MA. Adolf von Deines served as tutor to Wilhelm's older sons.

Nos. 13, 14   Diary letters to Deines's father (1895–98).

Dommes Papers, BA-MA. General Wilhelm von Dommes was for many years an adjutant and had particularly close relations with the Kaiser.

Nos. 3/3, 9   Diary (1920, 1938–41).

No. 15   "Aufzeichnungen" by Prince Oskar of Prussia (27 Aug. 1946).

No. 17   Wilhelm II's notes on the Jewish question (n.d.).

No. 18   Material on 9 Nov. 1918.

No. 21   Extradition of Wilhelm II (1918–20).

No. 23   Hermine's finances (1935).

Einem Papers, BA-MA. General Karl von Einem was a leading military figure from the 1890s and a devoted monarchist.

No. 30   Private papers, including a letter from Wilhelm (1933).

Eulenburg Papers, BA. Count (1900, prince) Philipp zu Eulenburg was for many years Wilhelm's closest friend. In disgrace after accusations of homosexuality, he assembled from his papers a number of accounts of his career, a considerable portion of which has been published in John C. G. Röhl, *Philipp Eulenburgs Politische Korrespondenz*, 3 vols. (Boppard, 1976–83).

Nos. 1–59   "Familiengeschichte" (1886–1902). This is an immense file, consisting of copies of correspondence and other materials together with Eulenburg's comments added in later years.

No. 73   Typescript "Ich Selbst" (1900).

No. 74   Typescript "Die Nordlandsreise, 1903," divided into part 1 ("Geselliger Verkehr") and part 2 ("Zur Psyche und Politik Kaiser Wilhelms II").

Nos. 75–76   Typescript "Aufzeichnungen des Fürsten Philipp zu Eulenburg-Hertefeld" (ca. 1910).

No. 80   Typescript "Kaiser Wilhelm II" (1908).

No. 81   Typescript "Hineinregende Persönlichkeiten" (1911), divided into two parts, both entitled "Drei Freunde."

No. 84   Typescript "Kaiser Wilhelm II und Gräfin Mathilde Stubenberg. Die Geschichte einer Intrigue im Hause Eulenburg-Liebenberg, 1902–1904."

FO Papers, PRO.

No. 64   Correspondence with the legation in Berlin (1888–1914), cited by volume number.

No. 371   Correspondence with the legation in Berlin (1909–14), cited by volume number.

No. 800 Vols. 128–30 are the private papers of Lord Lansdowne, the foreign secretary from 1902 to 1905 (1901–5); vols. 9–13 are the private papers of Sir Frank Lascelles, ambassador in Berlin from 1896 to 1908 (1900–1906); vols. 61–62 are the papers of Sir Edward Grey, foreign secretary from 1905 to 1916 (1906–13); vols. 907, 1370–650 (1910–13) are correspondence with British diplomats in Germany.

Francke Papers, BA. Ernst Francke was a journalist with wide connections.

Nos. 6–7 Correspondence with Albert Ballin (1908–18).

Franz Ferdinand Papers, HHStA. Archduke Franz Ferdinand, assassinated at Sarajevo in 1914, was the heir-apparent to the Habsburg throne and a friend and correspondent of Wilhelm II's. A part of the correspondence has been printed in Robert A. Kann, "Emperor William II and Archduke Francis Ferdinand in Their Correspondence," *American Historical Review* 57 (Jan. 1952): 323–51.

No. X/11 Wilhelm II's correspondence with Franz Ferdinand (1889–1914).

Fürstenberg Papers, Fürstliche Fürstenbergsches Archiv, Donaueschingen. Prince Max Egon von Fürstenberg was a close friend and frequent companion of the Kaiser's. Three files contain correspondence: "Wilhelm II. c. 1908–1918"; "Briefe von I.I.M.M. Kaiser Wilhelm II. von 1909–1940"; and "Briefe vom Gefolge S. Majestät" (1913). There are in addition miscellaneous envelopes containing correspondence by Wilhelm and members of his entourage (1905–9).

GFO Papers, National Archives, Washington, D.C. These records are contained in microfilm series T-149 and are cited by reel and frame numbers. Most of the material is from the diplomatic file "England 81/1 *geheim* (1903–8)."

Glücksburg Papers, Schlossarchiv, Glücksburg, Holstein. These are the papers of the house of Schleswig-Holstein-Sonderburg-Augustenburg.

Nos. 22, 38, 39 Correspondence, in series 23A, by the Kaiserin with her sister Princess Caroline Mathilde of Schleswig-Holstein-Sonderburg-Glücksburg (1901–20) and a letter by Prince Eitel Friedrich to Wilhelm (1920).

No. 36-B/1 Notes by Princess Caroline Mathilde of a conversation with Wilhelm (19 Nov. 1911).

No. 36-B/2 A memo, dated 30 July 1919, by Prince Max of Baden, "Der 9. November 1918," and another by Count Friedrich von der Schulenburg-Tressow, dated 7 Dec. 1918, both contained in a pamphlet *Der 9. November 1918. Material zur Begutachtung der Vorgänge des 9. November 1918* (Linzgau-Bole, n.d.) (ca. 1919).

Gossler Papers, BA-MA. Conrad von Gossler was a military officer.

Nos. 7, 19 Correspondence with Bernhard, duke of Saxe-Meiningen, brother-in-law of the Kaiser (1918–22).

Groener Papers, BA-MA. Wilhelm Groener served as quartermaster general under Hindenburg in October–November 1918.

No. 63 Miscellaneous papers (1918).

No. 75 Microfilm copy of address by Groener before the *Mittwochsgesellschaft* (1 Nov. 1933).

No. 162 Political affairs (1919).

Haeften Papers, BA-MA. Colonel Hans von Haeften, Ludendorff's assistant.

No. 1 Memoirs (1914).

Nos. 4, 6 Memoirs (1918).

Hahnke Papers, BA-MA. Wilhelm von Hahnke, son of the Kaiser's longtime adjutant, was a friend of the crown prince's.

No. 10 Correspondence with the crown prince (1922).

Haller Papers, BA. Johannes Haller was a noted historian.

No. 4 Excerpts from Dora von Beseler's diary (1917).

No. 13 Undated memoir by Ferdinand Kyhnzlmann de Beauchamps, "Zwei Fürsten: Philipp Eulenburg und Bülow."

No. 20 Correspondence with Hermine (1930–31).

Harden Papers, BA. Maximilian Harden, journalist and editor of *Die Zukunft*.

No. 75 Correspondence with Count Anton Monts (1909).

Hardinge Papers, University Library, Cambridge, England. Sir Charles Hardinge (1910, Baron Hardinge of Penshurst), was a prominent diplomat and intimate of King Edward VII's.

Nos. 8–15 Correspondence (1906–9).

No. 93 Correspondence (1914).

HA Papers, GS. This is the remnant of the Hohenzollern family archive in Berlin that survived the Second World War. Relevant documents are found in Rep[ositur] 53, 53a, and 192.

Rep. 53 No. 2 Wilhelm to Gen. Baron Moritz von Lyncker (1922).

Rep. 53 No. 24 Correspondence with Prof. Dörpfeld (1921).

Rep. 53 No. 168 Correspondence with Adm. von Levetzow (1932–33).

Rep. 53 No. 180 Count Schlitz zu Görtz to Wilhelm (1903).

Rep. 53 No. 190 *Daily Telegraph* crisis (1908).

Rep. 53 No. 342 Undated typescript by Col. Nicolai, General Staff officer, "Kaiser Wilhelm II.: Persönliche Erinnerungen während des 1. Weltkrieges."

Rep. 53 No. 352 Wilhelm to Prof. Bluher (1929).

Rep. 53 No. 399 Marriage settlement with Hermine (1923).

Rep. 53a No. 20 Wilhelm's letters to his aunt, Grand Duchess Louise of Baden (1909–18).

Rep. 53a Nos. 27, 29 Papers of Adjutant-General Gustav von Kessel (1908–15).

Rep. 53a No. 33 Wilhelm's notes (1927).

Rep. 53a No. 58 Martin von Rücker-Jenisch to Wilhelm (1908).

Rep. 53a No. 62 Notes by Baron von Maltzahn-Gultz on Hindenburg's role in 9 Nov. 1918 (1922).

Rep. 53a No. 63 Correspondence by Eulenburg with Wilhelm, Bülow, and others (1900) and a memoir by Eulenburg, "Liebensberger Jagd 1900."

Rep. 53a No. 77 A letter by the Kaiserin to her children (Dec. 1918).

Rep. 53a No. 176   Wilhelm to the crown prince (1932).
Rep. 53a No. 190   Letters by Mary Montagu to Wilhelm II (1908).
Rep. 53a No. 435   Printed memoir by Count Detlev von Moltke, *Die
                    Letzten Tage Seiner Majestät des Kaisers und Königs
                    im Grossen Hauptquartier* (Berlin, 1921).
Rep. 94 No. 975   Typescript "Kaiser Wilhelm II. Persönliche
                    Erinnerungen von Oberst Nicolai" (undated).
Rep. 192 No. 13   Nazi-Hohenzollern relations (1933–38).
Rep. 192 No. 16   Wilhelm's correspondence with Dommes and others
                    (1940).
Rep. 192 No. 17   Wilhelm II–Hitler correspondence (1940), Dommes
                    notes (1939).
Rep. 192 No. 18   The crown prince's account of his father's death (1941).
Rep. 192 No. 19   Wilhelm's will, burial instructions, and estate
                    inventory (1919–41).
Rep. 192 No. 20   Wilhelm's correspondence with Countess Brockdorff
                    (1922–23) and his notes (1934) on Dora von Beseler's
                    translation of J. Daniel Chamier, *Fabulous Monster*
                    (London, 1934).
Rep. 192 No. 22   Papers of Adj.-Gen Gustav von Plessen (1916–18).
Hertling Papers, BA. Count Georg von Hertling, Bavarian statesman, served as
    minister-president of Prussia and imperial chancellor from Oct. 1917 to Oct.
    1918.
        No. 23   Correspondence with his wife (1917–18).
        Nos. 40–41 Typescript "Aus der Reichskanzlei," vol. 2 (1918).
Heye Papers, BA-MA. General Wilhelm Heye, officer at headquarters.
        Nos. 4, 6   Typescript "Lebenserinnerungen" (1918).
HHStA. These are the reports of the Austrian ambassadors and staff in Berlin to
    Vienna, filed as Preussen III (1900–18). The documents are cited by volume,
    which are further identified as *Berichte* (B) or *Varia* (V).
Hintze Papers, BA-MA. Paul von Hintze was a naval officer, diplomat, and state
    secretary of the Foreign Office (1918).
        No. 13   Militärberollmächtigter (1908).
        No. 42   Papers as state secretary (1918).
        No. 56   Manuscript in Hintze's hand entitled "Vertraulich"
                    (1918).
        No. 63   4th Untersuchungsausschuss (1922).
        No. 65   Notes by Hintze on Alfred Niemann's *Revolution von
                    Oben, Umsturz von Unten* (Berlin, 1927) (ca. 1928).
        No. 105   Imperial Court (1914).
Hoffmann Papers, BA-MA. Colonel Max Hoffmann, General Staff officer.
        No. 2   Correspondence with his wife (1915).
Chlodwig Hohenlohe Papers, BA. Prince Chlodwig zu Hohenlohe-Schillingsfürst
    served as chancellor from 1894 to 1900.
        No. 1673   Correspondence with the Kaiserin Augusta Victoria
                    (1896).
Holstein Papers, National Archives, Washington, D.C. Friedrich von Holstein, a

close friend of Chancellor Bülow's, was the leading official in the Foreign Office until his resignation in 1906. The papers, partially printed in Norman Rich and M. H. Fisher, *The Holstein Papers*, 4 vols. (Cambridge, Eng., 1955–63), are filed under T-120 and cited by reel and frame number.

Hopman Papers, BA-MA. Admiral Albert Hopman, naval officer attached to headquarters, 1914–15.

Nos. 9–12 Diary (1912–14).

KE, BA. These are for the most part small collections, some of them of considerable value.

No. 240 Miscellaneous papers of Princess Hermine and Adj. Gen. von Dommes (1940); letter by Adj. Count Moltke to his wife (1940).

No. 283/49 Papers of Chancellor Michaelis (1917–26).

No. 317/2 "Manuskript über den 1sten Weltkrieg" by Count Siegfried von Roedern (n.d.).

No. 330 Papers of Paul Persius, Prussian judge (1894).

No. 331/1 Correspondence between Wilhelm II and Bethmann Hollweg (1911).

No. 331/2 Typescript by Friedrich von Berg-Markienen "Aufzeichnungen" (1920).

No. 341/1, 2, 4, 6 Miscellaneous papers, diaries, and correspondence of Rudolf von Valentini (1904–18).

No. 342/3 Undated memoir by Bethmann Hollweg on Tirpitz's *Erinnerungen*.

No. 381 Memoir by Baron Lothar von Spitzemberg, *Kabinettsrat* to Kaiserin Augusta Victoria (1918).

No. 382 Manuscript "Mein Lebensbuch" by Paul von Breitenbach, Prussian minister of Railroads (n.d.).

No. 517/5 Diary of Wolfgang von Oettingen, friend of Bethmann Hollweg (1911–16).

No. 576/1 Manuscript "Lebenserinnerungen" by Count Friedrich Wilhelm von Limburg-Stirum, Conservative member of the Prussian legislature and of the Reichstag (n.d.).

No. 578/1 Papers of Professor Wilhelm Dörpfeld (1920–30).

No. 591/11–13 Papers of Baron Kurt von Lersner, a diplomat (1917–18).

No. 659 Papers of Georg Wagner, Posen journalist, including a memoir (1916) by Prince Lichowsky, former ambassador in London, and one (1914) by Johannes Mühlon, an official of the Krupp firm.

No. 708/1 Manuscript entitled "Lebenserinnerungen" by Countess Antonie zu Eulenburg-Prassen (n.d.).

No. 809 Two sermons by the Kaiser (1925).

No. 814 Undated Manuscript entitled "Erinnerungen aus meinem Leben" by Adolf von Oechelhaeuser, a friend of Wilhelm's from his university days.

Jellicoe Papers, British Library.

    Add MS 49037   Correspondence between Wilhelm and Florence, Countess Jellicoe (1936).

Kiderlen Papers, Sterling Library, Yale University, New Haven, Connecticut. Alfred von Kiderlen-Wächter, German diplomat, served as state secretary of the Foreign Office from 1910 to 1912. This is a very ill-assorted collection covering the period from 1892 to 1912, filed with the Colonel Robert M. House Papers. All materials cited are from Box 4/004, followed by document number.

Kurowsky Papers, BA. Papers of Friedrich von Kurowsky, Prussian bureaucrat.

    No. 6   Correspondence regarding Wilhelm's finances (1926–29).

Loebell Papers, BA. Friedrich Wilhelm von Loebell served as chief of the Reichskanzlei from 1904 until 1909 and was a close associate of Chancellor Bülow's.

    No. 5   Correspondence with Bethmann Hollweg (1910–17).

    Nos. 6–7   Correspondence with Bülow (1909–12).

    Nos. 26–27   Undated manuscript "Lebenserinnerungen."

Mackensen Papers, BA-MA. Field Marshal August von Mackensen was one of the Kaiser's closest military friends.

    No. 39   Notes of Dr. Vogel's talk with Wilhelm (1918).

    No. 40   Correspondence with Wilhelm and the crown prince (1919–21).

    No. 41   Correspondence with Hermine (1934–37).

    No. 42   Correspondence with the crown prince (1921).

    No. 256   Correspondence by Wilhelm II (1925).

    No. 263   Correspondence and a sermon by Wilhelm II (1930).

    No. 267   Wilhelm's death (1941).

Georg Michaelis Papers, BA. Michaelis served as chancellor from July until late October 1917.

    Nos. 48–49   Correspondence with Wilhelm (1917–26).

Wilhelm Michaelis Papers, BA-MA. Michaelis was a naval officer on the Admiralty Staff.

    No. 4   Manuscript entitled "Erinnerungen" (1910–12).

Montagu-Stuart-Wortley Papers, Bodleian Library, Oxford. Colonel the Honorable Edward Montagu-Stuart-Wortley was an English officer acquainted with the Kaiser. The papers, filed as MS Eng. hist. d.256, consist of letters between the two men (1907–8).

Müller Papers, BA-MA. Admiral Georg von Müller, chief of the Naval Cabinet (1908–18), was frequently with the Kaiser and kept a most informative diary, parts of which have been published — with important omissions — in Walter Görlitz, ed., *Der Kaiser . . . : Aufzeichnungen des Chefs des Marinekabinetts Admiral Georg v. Müller über die Ära Wilhelms II.* (Göttingen, 1965), and *Regierte der Kaiser? Kriegstagebücher, Aufzeichnungen und Briefe des Chefs der Marine-Kabinetts Admiral Georg Alexander von Müller 1914–1918* (Göttingen, 1959).

    Nos. 3–7   Diary (1905–18).

Münster Papers, Gräfliches Münstersches Familien- und Gutsarchiv, Derneburg, Hanover. Papers of Prince Georg Münster von Derneburg, German diplomat.

    No. 9   Hohenlohe to Münster (1896).

Mutius Papers, BA. Max von Mutius, an adjutant of the Kaiser's.

      No. 2   Manuscript entitled "Lebenserinnerungen, 1865–1918."

PRO. T 1/12319, folder 18615. British Treasury file on Wilhelm II's finances (1919).

RA. All materials are cited by the folder or document number.

Add MS U/32	Copies of Queen Victoria's letters to Wilhelm's mother (1899).
Geo V AA 31, 32	Correspondence of Princess Alexandra, duchess of York, with her husband (1880–1900).
Geo V AA 43	Correspondence between Wilhelm and King George V (1911).
Geo V CC 22	Letter by the princess of Wales to the Grand Duchess Augusta of Mecklenburg-Strelitz (1901).
Geo V CC 45–46	Correspondence between Wilhelm and Queen Mary (1938–39).
Geo V M 450	Memo by Arthur Davidson (1912).
Geo V M 688a	Memo by Sir Schomberg McDonnell on Wilhelm II (ca. 1914).
Geo V M 1515	Memoir "The Last Days at Spa," written by General Groener (1921).
Geo V O 320a	Letter by Arthur Davidson to Lord Stamfordham (1912).
Geo V O 1177	Memo by H. N. Andersen of meeting with Wilhelm II (1915).
Geo V O 2578	Correspondence by Wilhelm and Hermine with Colonel Wallscourt H.-H. Waters, former military attaché in Berlin (1928–38).
Geo V O 2580	Miscellaneous correspondence (1911).
Geo V P 452	Letter by Mansfeldt Findlay, minister to Norway, to Lord Stamfordham (1913).
Geo V Q 724	Letter by Lord Esher to Sir Arthur Bigge (1909).
Geo V Q 1549	Wilhelm II to King George V (31 Jul. 1914).
I 59–62	Miscellaneous correspondence, including letters between Queen Victoria and Wilhelm II (1894–1901).

Queen Victoria's Journal (1896–99)

T 10	Correspondence between Wilhelm and the Prince of Wales (1900).
Vic Add MSS U 38	Letter by Edward VII to Admiral Fisher (1908).
W 44	Letter by Wilhelm to Edward VII (1904).
W 53	Letter of Edward VII to Lord Knollys (1908).
W 54, 55	Correspondence of Sir Charles Hardinge (1908–9).
X 37	Correspondence between Wilhelm and King Edward VII (1901–6).
Z 43	Correspondence by the Empress Frederick to Queen Victoria (1888).
Z 500	Correspondence between Wilhelm and Queen Victoria (1897).

Reichskanzlei Papers, BA. File R 43F, cited by microfiche number.

No. 806/6   Correspondence by Hertling and others (1916–17).
No. 810   Correspondence by Wilhelm and Bülow (1908).
No. 951/1, 952   Kriegsmarine (1911–12).
No. 1466   Caprivi memo (1892).

Reichsmarineamt (RMA) Papers, BA-MA. The following files from RMA 2 were consulted:

No. 118   Correspondence by Wilhelm II, Bülow, and others (1908).
No. 123   Letters by Admiral Victor Montagu to Wilhelm (1907–8).
Nos. 951/1, 952   Correspondence by Bethmann Hollweg (1911–12).
No. 1756   Reports on military-political matters (1914).
No. 1764   Correspondence of Albert Ballin with Wilhelm (1912).
No. 1940   Kiel Week (1914).
No. 2009   Prize rights at sea (1907).

Rijksarchief Papers, Rijksarchief, Utrecht. These are the Kaiser's files taken from Doorn in 1945. There is a comprehensive guide in D. T. Coen, *Inventaria van het Archief van Ex-Keiser Wilhelm II tidjenszijn Verblift in Nederland, 1918–1941* (Utrecht, 1977).

Nos. 6–8   Correspondence by Wilhelm (1928–39).
Nos. 39, 40   Correspondence by Wilhelm with Bigelow and Professor Dörpfeld (1934–40).
No. 128   Wilhelm's death (1941).
No. 151, 52   Kaiserin Augusta Victoria's funeral (1921).
Nos. 161–64   Wilhelm's funeral (1941).
Nos. 240, 241   Correspondence with Wilhelm (1922–26).
No. 242   Correspondence by Wilhelm (1925) and a typescript by George S. Viereck, "The Kaiser and the Fourteen Points" (1925).
No. 248   Wilhelm's notes (1929).
No. 249   Correspondence with General W. H.-H. Waters (1928–32).
No. 251   Miscellaneous household correspondence (1928–32).
No. 253   Fleet policy (1926).
No. 263   Correspondence by Wilhelm with clerical figures and others on religious subjects (1926–40).
No. 266   Correspondence by Wilhelm with Alfred Jeremias and others (ca. 1930).
No. 267   Wilhelm's correspondence on religious matters (1930–32).
No. 268   Wilhelm's notes on Harnack (1929) and correspondence with Jeremias.
No. 269   Letter by Wilhelm to Professor Hans Naumann, Bonn (1941).
No. 273   Correspondence with Max Buchner (1930).

Nos. 275–76   Correspondence with Leo Frobenius and Countess
                Salm (1930–38).
Nos. 277, 287   History of the *Doorner Arbeits-Gemeinschaft* (1937).
No. 288   Correspondence and drafts of archaeological paper by
                Wilhelm (1931).
No. 296   Speech by Wilhelm to *Doorner Arbeits-Gemeinschaft*
                (1937).
No. 301   Typescript "Erinnerungen an Korfu" (1924).
No. 366   Guestbook (1930–38).
No. 392   Guestbook (1913–33).
No. 422   Purchase of Doorn (1919).
No. 437   Inventory of goods taken from Germany to Doorn
                (1919–21).
No. 440   Inventory of contents of Doorn (1941).
No. 572   Wilhelm's bank books.
Nos. 646–51   Bolshevism. These are typescripts of excerpts of
                newspaper articles with comments by Wilhelm (1923–
                25).

Salisbury Papers, Hatfield House, Hertfordshire. Papers of Robert Arthur Talbot
Gascoyne-Cecil, third marquess of Salisbury, prime minister 1885–86, 1886–
92, 1895–1902.
Series A, vols. 46, 62,
    120–22   Correspondence (1889–1900).
    Class E   Correspondence with Sir Frank Lascelles (1899).
Schiemann Papers, GS. Theodor Schiemann was a prominent journalist and
friend of the Kaiser's.
No. 85   Correspondence with Wilhelm (1907–20).
Schiffer Papers, BA. Eugen Schiffer was a liberal and a member of both the Prus-
sian legislature and the Reichstag.
Nos. 2–5   Manuscript entitled "Memoiren" (1914–16).
Schulenburg-Tressow Papers, BA-MA. Colonel Count Friedrich von der
Schulenburg-Tressow was a friend of both Wilhelm II's and the crown prince's.
No. 1   Manuscript "Erlebnisse" (1920–21), dealing with
                relations with the Hohenzollerns from 1904 to 1918.
Schwertfeger Papers, BA. Bernhard Schwertfeger was a prominent journalist and
editor.
No. 206   Materials by and concerning Rudolf von Valentini
                (1904–25); Wilhelm's notes on Locarno (1925).
No. 443   Letters from Hermine (1934–35).
No. 545   Correspondence with General Scheüch and other
                military figures (1922–27).
Seeckt Papers, BA-MA. General Hans von Seeckt, head of the Reichswehr, 1920–
26.
No. 69   Correspondence with Friedrich von Berg concerning
                Wilhelm's extradition (1919).

Selasen-Selasinsky Papers, BA-MA. Eberhard Selasen von Selasinsky was an army officer and a good friend of the crown prince's.

No. 1   Correspondence with the crown prince (1921–33).
No. 7   Correspondence with Baron von Loën (1923).
No. 10   Correspondence with the crown prince (1932).

Senden Papers, BA-MA. Admiral Baron Gustav von Senden und Bibran served as chief of the naval cabinet from 1889 to 1906.

No. 11   Correspondence and notes (1895).

Solf Papers, BA. Wilhelm Solf served as state secretary of the Foreign Office (Oct.–Nov. 1918).

Nos. 56, 58   Papers as state secretary (1918).

Tambach Papers, Naval Historical Branch, Ministry of Defense, Lillie Rd., S.W.6, London. These are microfilms of the records of the *Marinekabinett*, discovered in 1945 at Schloss Tambach in Bavaria, from series GFO 26 or 31. They are cited by numerical series, reel number, and (where available) frame numbers. Also contained in this depository is a printed copy of Wilhelm II's speech (8 Feb. 1895) to the *Kriegs-Akademie*, filed in PG/50658.

Tappen Papers, BA-MA. General Gerhard Tappen, head of the operations division of the General Staff.

No. 1   Diary (1915).
Nos. 6, 7   Correspondence with the *Reichsarchiv* (1920).

Thimme Papers, BA. Friedrich Thimme, a historian, collected extensive materials for a history of Wilhelm II's reign, but the account was never written.

No. 4   Correspondence with Bethmann Hollweg (1919).
No. 9   Correspondence with Gottlieb von Jagow (1921).
No. 14   Correspondence with Admiral Georg von Müller (1923).
No. 16   Undated manuscript entitled "Aus den Erinnerungen des verstorbenen Staathalters von Dallwitz."
No. 17   Correspondence (1930) and printed article "Bethmann Hollweg" by Gerhard von Mutius (ca. 1929).
No. 18   Correspondence with Max von Mutius (1933).
No. 26   Excerpts from Rudolf von Valentini's diary (1908–18).
No. 28   Undated memoirs by Paul von Breitenbach.
No. 61   Correspondence with General Erich von Falkenhayn and other military figures (1915–17).

Tirpitz Papers, BA-MA. Admiral Alfred Tirpitz (von, 1900) was head of the Imperial Naval Office from 1897 to 1916.

No. 4   Fleet law (1897).
No. 8   Top secret correspondence (1909).
Nos. 20–27a   Development of the navy (1901–12).
No. 54   Negotiations with England (1908–9).
No. 100   Private papers regarding the war (1914).
No. 169   Correspondence with Admiral Adolf von Trotha (1915–17).
No. 172   Correspondence with Admiral Albert Hopman (1926).

No. 177   Correspondence with Houston Stewart Chamberlain (1926).

No. 198   Correspondence with Admiral Gustav Bachmann (1925).

No. 200   Correspondence with Admiral Wilhelm Büchsel (1899).

No. 203   Correspondence with Count August zu Eulenburg (1916–18).

No. 205   Correspondence with Admiral Henning von Holtzendorff (1916).

No. 207   Correspondence with Admiral Georg von Müller (1905–15).

Treutler Papers, in the possession of Baroness Anne-Katrin von Ledebur, Schwenningdorf/Westphal. Karl Georg von Treutler was a diplomat and a friend of the Kaiser's. A considerable portion of his papers have been published in Karl-Heinz Janssen, ed., *Die Graue Exzellenz: Zwischen Staatsräson und Vassallentreue. Aus den Papieren des kaiserlichen Gesandten Karl Georg von Treutler* (Frankfurt, 1971). Cited by folder.

Tweedmouth Papers, Bodleian Library, Oxford. Lord Tweedmouth was First Lord of the Admiralty (1905–8). His papers, filed as MS Eng. Hist. c.264, deal with the so-called Tweedmouth letter affair (1908).

Viereck Papers, Houghton Library, Harvard University, Cambridge, Mass. George Sylvester Viereck was a journalist and a friend of the Kaiser's. The papers, filed as MS Ger 49, consist of letters written by Viereck to Wilhelm and one by the Kaiser to Viereck (1923–29).

Widenmann Papers, BA-MA. Wilhelm Widenmann was naval attaché in London from 1906 to 1912.

No. 1   Manuscript entitled "Erinnerungen und Erlebnisse mit Geschlichten Personen" (1934–35), dealing with the period 1907–16, which extends Widenmann's published memoir, *Marine-Attaché an der Kaiserlich-Deutschen Botschaft in London, 1907–1912*. (Göttingen, 1952).

Wild von Hohenborn Papers, BA-MA. General Adolf Wild von Hohenborn was a childhood friend of the Kaiser's.

No. 2   Manuscript entitled "Aufzeichnungen . . ." (1915–16).

No. 3   Correspondence with his wife (1915).

No. 7   Correspondence with Tirpitz (1916).

Wolff Papers, BA. Theodor Wolff was a prominent Berlin journalist.

No. 6   Correspondence with Bülow (1923–25).

Zorn Papers, BA. Philipp Zorn was tutor to four of Wilhelm's sons (1901–9).

No. 1   Undated manuscript entitled "Lebenserinnerungen."

PRINTED SOURCES

Albertini, Luigi. *The Origins of the War of 1914.* 3 vols. London, 1952–57.

Alter, Junius (pseudonym for Franz Sontag), ed. *Ein Armeeführer Erlebt den*

Weltkrieg: Persönliche Aufzeichnungen des Generalobersten v. Einem. Leipzig, 1938.

Anderson, Eugene N. *The First Moroccan Crisis, 1904–1906.* Chicago, 1930.

Arnhold, Eduard. *Ein Gedenkbuch.* Berlin, n.d.

Asquith, Herbert H. *The Genesis of the War.* New York, 1923.

Athlone, Countess Alice of. *For My Grandchildren: Some Reminiscences.* London, 1966.

Austria-Hungary, Foreign Office. *Die Österreich-Ungarischen Dokumente zum Kriegsausbruch. Diplomatische Aktenstücke zur Vorgeschichte des Krieges 1914.* 3 vols. Berlin, 1923.

Ayme, Franz. *Kaiser Wilhelm II. und seine Erziehung. Aus den Erinnerungen seines Französischen Lehrers.* Leipzig, 1898.

Bach, August, ed. *Die Gesandtschaftsberichte zum Kriegsausbruch. Berichte und Telegramme der Badischen, Sächsischen und Württembergischen Gesandtschaften in Berlin aus dem Juli und August 1914.* Berlin, 1937.

Bachem, Karl. *Vorgeschichte, Geschichte und Politik der Deutschen Zentrumspartei.* 9 vols. Cologne, 1927–32.

Baden, Prince Max von. *Erinnerungen und Dokumente.* Berlin, 1927.

Baernreither, Joseph M. *Fragments of a Political Diary.* London, 1930.

Bakker, Angelique. *Huis Doorn.* Zwolle, 1993.

Baldwin, Simeon. "The Proposed Trial of the Former Kaiser." *Yale Law Journal* 29 (1919): 75–82.

Balfour, Michael. *The Kaiser and His Times.* London, 1964.

Bariatinsky, Anatole Princess. *My Russian Life.* London, 1923.

Bartning, Otto. "Zur Baugeschichte des Letzten Jahrzehnts." *Der Kunstwart* 20 (Sept. 1907): 607–11.

Battersea, Baroness Constance. *Reminiscences.* London, 1922.

Bauer, Oberst. *Der Grosse Krieg in Feld und Heimat. Erinnerungen und Betrachtungen.* Tübingen, 1922.

Baumgart, Winfried. *Deutsche Ostpolitik 1918. Von Brest-Litovsk bis zum Ende des Ersten Weltkrieges.* Vienna, 1966.

Bell, G. K. A. *Randall Davidson. Archbishop of Canterbury.* London, 1952.

Benoist, Charles. "Guillaume II en Hollande." *Revue des Deux Mondes* 19 (Jan. 1924): 386–403.

Benson, E. F. *The Kaiser and His English Relations.* London, 1936.

Bentinck, Lady Norah. *The Ex-Kaiser in Exile.* New York, n.d.

Berghahn, Volker R. *Der Tirpitz-Plan. Genesis und Verfall einer Innenpolitischen Krisenstrategie unter Wilhelm II.* Düsseldorf, 1971.

Bernhardi, Friedrich von. *Denkwürdigkeiten aus meinem Leben. Nach Gleichzeitigen Aufzeichnungen und im Lichte der Erinnerungen.* Berlin, 1927.

Bernstein, Herman, ed. *The Willy-Nicky Correspondence, Being the Secret Telegrams Exchanged between the Kaiser and the Tsar.* New York, 1918.

Bethmann Hollweg, Theobald von. *Betrachtungen zum Weltkriege.* 2 vols. Berlin, 1919–21.

Beyens, Baron Napoléon. *Deux Années à Berlin, 1912–1914.* 2 vols. Paris, 1931.

———. *Germany before the War.* London, 1916.

Bigelow, Poultney. *The German Emperor and His Eastern Neighbors.* New York, 1892.

——. *Prussian Memories, 1864–1914.* New York, 1915.

——. *Seventy Summers.* 2 vols. New York, 1925.

Bing, Edward J., ed. *The Secret Letters of Tsar Nicholas and Empress Marie, Being the Confidental Correspondence between Nicholas, Last of the Tsars, and His Mother, Dowager Empress Maria Feodorovna.* London, 1937.

Bismarck-Schönhausen, Otto Prince von. *Gedanken und Erinnerungen.* Vol. 15 in H. von Petersdorff et al., eds., *Bismarck. Die Gesammelten Werke.* 15 vols. Berlin, 1923–33.

Bittner, Ludwig, and Hans Uebersberger, eds. *Österreich-Ungarns Aussenpolitik von der Bosnischen Krise bis zum Kriegsausbruch 1914.* 9 vols. Vienna, 1931.

"Björkö. L'Essai Allemand pour Rompre l'Alliance Franco-Russe et l'Entente Cordiale (Octobre 1904–November 1905) d'après les Documents Russes." *Le Monde Slave* 6 (Jun. 1927): 437–61, 7 (Jul. 192): 94–120.

Blücher von Wahlstatt, Evelyn Princess. *An English Wife in Berlin: A Private Memoir of Events, Politics, and Daily Life in Germany throughout the War and the Social Revolution of 1918.* New York, n.d.

Blücher von Wahlstatt, Gebhard Prince. *Memoirs of Prince Blücher.* London, 1932.

Blunt, Wilfrid Scawen. *My Diaries, Being a Personal Narrative of Events, 1888–1914.* 2 vols. London, 1919–20.

Bode, Wilhelm. *Fünfzig Jahre Museumarbeit von Wilhelm von Bode.* Bielefeld, 1922.

——. *Mein Leben.* 2 vols. Berlin, 1930.

Bodenhausen-Degener, Dora Freifrau von, ed. *Eberhard von Bodenhausen: Ein Leben für Kunst und Wirtschaft.* Düsseldorf, 1955.

Boelcke, Willi, ed. *Krupp und die Hohenzollern. Aus der Korrespondenz der Familie Krupp 1850–1916.* Berlin, 1956.

Bonn, Ferdinand. *Mein Künsterleben: Was ich mit dem Kaiser Erlebte und Andere Erinnerungen.* Munich, 1920.

Bonn, Moritz J. *Wandering Scholar.* New York, 1948.

Brabant, Artur, ed. *Generaloberst Max Freiherr von Hausen, ein Deutscher Soldat. Nach seinen Tagebüchern, Aufzeichnungen und Briefen.* Dresden, 1926.

Brauer, Arthur von. *Im Dienste Bismarcks. Persönliche Erinnerungen.* Berlin, 1936.

Brauer, Arthur von, Erich Marks, and Karl Alexander von Müller, eds. *Erinnerungen an Bismarck. Aufzeichnungen von Mitarbeitern und Freunden des Fürsten....* Stuttgart, 1915.

Braun, Baron Magnus von. *Von Ostpreussen bis Texas: Erlebnisse und Zeitgeschichtliche Betrachtungen eines Ostdeutschen.* Stollhamm, 1955.

——. *Weg durch 4. Zeitepochen....* Limburg/Lahn, 1964.

Brecht, Arnold. *Aus Nächster Nähe. Lebenserinnerungen, 1884–1927.* Stuttgart, 1966.

Brett, Maurice V., ed. *Journals and Letters of Reginald Viscount Esher.* 4 vols. London, 1934–38.

Breysig, Kurt. *Aus meinen Tagen und Träumen. Memoiren, Aufzeichnungen, Briefe, Gespräche.* Berlin, 1962.

Brocke, Bernhard von. "Hochschul und Wissenschaftspolitik in Preussen und im Deutschen Kaiserreich 1882–1907: das 'System Althoff.' " In Peter Baumgart, ed., *Bildungspolitik in Preussen zur Zeit des Kaiserreichs,* pp. 9–118. Stuttgart, 1980.

Buchanan, Meriel. *Diplomacy and Foreign Courts.* London, n.d.

Buckle, George E., ed. *The Letters of Queen Victoria,* 3d ser. 3 vols. London, 1930.

Bülow, Bernhard Prince von. *Denkwürdigkeiten.* 4 vols. Berlin, 1930–31.

———. *Deutsche Politik.* Berlin, 1916.

Bülow, Kurt Ernst von. *Preussischer Militärismus zur Zeit Wilhelms II. Aus meiner Dienstzeit im Heer.* Schweidnitz, 1930.

Bülow, Paula von. *Aus Verklungenen Zeiten. Lebenserinnerungen 1833–1920.* Leipzig, 1925.

Bunsen, Marie von. *Die Welt in der Ich Lebte. Erinnerungen aus Glücklichen Jahren 1860–1912.* Leipzig, 1929.

———. *Lost Courts of Europe: The World I Used to Know, 1860–1912.* London, 1930.

———. *Zeitgenossen die ich Erlebte 1900–1930.* Leipzig, 1932.

Burchardt, Lothar. *Wissenschaftspolitik im Wilhelminischen Deutschland.* Göttingen, 1975.

Busch, Moritz. *Bismarck: Some Secret Pages of His History.* 3 vols. London, 1898.

Bussmann, Walter, ed. *Staatssekretär Graf Herbert von Bismarck. Aus seiner Politischen Privatkorrespondenz.* Göttingen, 1964.

Butler, Nicholas Murray. *Across the Busy Years: Recollections and Reflections.* 2 vols. New York, 1939–40.

Cahén, Fritz Max. *Der Weg nach Versailles: Erinnerungen 1912–1919....* Boppard/Rhein, 1963.

Caillaux, Joseph. *Agadir: Ma Politique Extérieure.* Paris, 1919.

Cecil, Lady Gwendolen. *Life of Robert Marquis of Salisbury.* 4 vols. London, 1921–32.

Cecil, Lamar. *Albert Ballin: Business and Politics in Imperial Germany, 1888–1918.* Princeton, 1967.

———. "Coal for the Fleet That Had to Die." *American Historical Review* 69 (Jul. 1964): 990–1005.

———. "The Creation of Nobles in Prussia, 1871–1918." *American Historical Review* 75 (Feb. 1970): 757–95.

———. *The German Diplomatic Service, 1871–1914.* Princeton, 1976.

———. "History as Family Chronicle: Kaiser Wilhelm II and the Dynastic Roots of the Anglo-German Antagonism." In John C. G. Röhl and Nicolaus Sombart, eds., *Kaiser Wilhelm II, New Interpretations: The Corfu Papers,* pp. 91–119. Cambridge, Eng., 1982.

———. "Jew and Junker in Imperial Berlin." In Leo Baeck Institute, *Year Book XX,* pp. 47–58. London, 1975.

———. *Wilhelm II: Prince and Emperor, 1859–1900.* Chapel Hill, 1989.

———. "William II and His Russian 'Colleagues.' " In Carole Fink et al., eds., *German Nationalism and the European Response 1890–1945*, pp. 94–134. Norman, Okla., 1985.

———. "Wilhelm II. und die Juden." In Werner E. Mosse, ed., *Juden im Wilhelminischen Deutschland, 1890–1914*, pp. 313–47. Tübingen, 1976.

Cecilie, Crown Princess of Prussia. *Erinnerungen an den Deutschen Kronprinzen.* Bieberach an der Riss, 1952.

Chamberlain, Anna Horst. *Meine Erinnerungen an Houston Stewart Chamberlain.* Munich, 1923.

Chamberlain, Austen. *Down the Years.* London, 1935.

———. *Politics from Inside: An Epistolary Chronicle, 1906–1914.* London, 1936.

Chamberlain, Houston Stewart. *Briefe, 1882–1924, und Briefwechsel mit Kaiser Wilhelm II.* 2 vols. Munich, 1928.

———. "Kaiser Wilhelm II." *Jugend. Münchner Illustrierte Wochenschrift für Künst und Leben* 1 (1900): 370–72.

Chilston, Viscount Erich Akers-Douglas. *W. H. Smith.* London, 1965.

Churchill, Randolph. *Winston S. Churchill.* 23 vols. Boston, 1966–88.

Churchill, Winston. *The World Crisis.* 4 vols. New York, 1923–29.

Clark, Alan, ed. *"A Good Innings": The Private Papers of Viscount Lee of Fareham.* London, 1974.

Clarke, R. Floyd. "The Allied Demand on Holland for the Kaiser." *American Law Review* 55 (1921): 558–84.

Cleinow, Georg. "Diplomaten-Erziehung: Eine Erinnerungen zum Bismarcks Geburtstag." *Die Grenzboten* 72 (1913): 72–79.

Chlumecky, Leopold von. *Erzherzog Franz Ferdinands Wirken und Wollen.* Berlin, 1929.

Cole, Terence F. *"The Daily Telegraph* Affair and Its Aftermath: The Kaiser, Bülow, and the Reichstag, 1908–1909." In John C. G. Röhl and Nicolaus Sombart, eds., *Kaiser Wilhelm II, New Interpretations: The Corfu Papers*, pp. 249–68. Cambridge, Eng., 1982.

———. "Kaiser versus Chancellor: The Crisis of Bülow's Chancellorship in 1905–6." In Richard J. Evans, ed., *Society and Politics in Wilhelmine Germany*, pp. 40–70. London, 1978.

Conrad von Hötzendorf, Count Franz. *Aus meiner Dienstzeit.* 7 vols. Vienna, 1921–25.

Corey, Lewis. *The House of Morgan: A Social Biography of the Masters of Money.* New York, 1930.

Craig, Gordon A. *The Politics of the Prussian Army, 1640–1945.* New York, 1956.

Cramon, A. von. *Unser Österreich-Ungarischer Bundesgenosse im Weltkriege: Erinnerungen aus meiner Vierjährigen Tätigkeit als Bevollmächtigter Deutscher General beim K. u. K. Armeeoberkommando.* Berlin, 1920.

Crothers, George D. *The German Elections of 1907.* New York, 1941.

Czernin von und zu Chudenitz, Count Ottokar. *Im Weltkriege.* Berlin, 1919.

Davis, Arthur N. *The Kaiser as I Know Him.* New York, 1918.

Deichmann, Baroness. *Impressions and Memories.* N.p., 1926.

Deimling, Berthold von. *Aus den Alten in die Neue Zeit. Lebenserinnerungen.* Berlin, 1930.

Deist, Wilhelm, ed. *Flottenpolitik und Flottenpropaganda. Das Nachrichten-bureau des Reichsmarineamtes 1897–1914.* Stuttgart, 1976.
———. *Militär und Innenpolitik im Weltkrieg 1914–1918.* 2 vols. Düsseldorf, 1970.
Delbrück, Clemens von. *Die Wirtschaftliche Mobilmachung in Deutschland 1914.* Munich, 1924.
Del Mar, Norman. *Richard Strauss: A Critical Commentary on His Life and Works.* 3 vols. New York, 1962–72.
Deshmukh, Marion F. "Max Liebermann: Observations on the Politics of Painting in Imperial Germany, 1870–1914." *German Studies Review* 53 (May 1980): 172–206.
Deuerlein, Ernst, ed. *Briefwechsel Hertling-Lerchenfeld 1912–1917: Dienstliche Privatkorrespondenz.* . . . 2 vols. Boppard/Rhein, 1973.
Dickie, J. F. *In the Kaiser's Capital.* New York, 1910.
Dietrich, Otto. *12 Jahre mit Hitler.* Munich, 1955.
Doede, Werner. *Die Berliner Secession.* Berlin, 1977.
Doerries, Reinhard R. *Imperial Challenge: Ambassador Count Bernstorff and German-American Relations, 1908–1914.* Chapel Hill, 1989.
Dorpalen, Andreas. "Empress Auguste Victoria and the Fall of the German Monarchy." *American Historical Review* 58 (Oct. 1952): 17–38.
———. *Hindenburg and the Weimar Republic.* Princeton, 1964.
Dove, Alfred, ed. *Gustav Freytag und Heinrich von Treitschke im Briefwechsel.* London, 1900.
Dryander, Ernst von. *Erinnerungen aus meinem Leben.* Bielefeld, 1922.
Dülffer, Jost, ed. *Regeln gegen den Krieg? Die Haager Friedenskonferenzen von 1899 und 1907 in der Internationalen Politik.* Berlin, 1981.
———. *Theobald von Bethmann Hollweg: Betrachtungen zum Weltkriege.* Essen, n.d. [ca. 1989].
Dungern, Baron Otto von. *Unter Kaiser und Kanzlern: Erinnerungen.* Coburg, 1953.
Durieux, Tilla. *Meine Ersten Neunzig Jahre.* Berlin, 1971.
Ebart, Paul von. *Am Herzogshofe und im Dienste der Kunst. Blätter der Erinnerungen.* Berlin, 1928.
Ebel, Gerhard, ed. *Botschafter Graf Paul von Hatzfeldt. Nachgelassene Papiere 1838–1901.* 2 vols. Boppard/Rhein, 1976.
Eckardstein, Baron Hermann von. *Die Entlassung des Fürsten Bülows.* Berlin, 1931.
———. *Lebenserinnerungen u. Politische Denkwürdigkeiten.* 3 vols. Leipzig, 1919–21.
———. *Persönliche Erinnerungen an König Eduard aus der Einkreisungszeit.* Dresden, 1927.
Egan, Maurice. *Ten Years near the German Frontier: A Retrospect and a Warning.* New York, 1919.
Eggeling, Bernhard von. *Die Russische Mobilmachung und der Kriegsausbruch: Beiträage zur Schuldfrage am Weltkriege.* Oldenburg i.O., 1919.
Einem, Karl von. *Erinnerungen eines Soldaten 1853–1933.* Leipzig, 1933.
Eisenhardt-Rothe, Ernst von. *Im Bann der Persönlichkeit.* Berlin, 1931.

Elkind, Louis, ed. *The German Emperor's Speeches, Being a Selection from the Speeches, Edicts, Letters, and Telegrams of the Emperor William II.* London, 1904.

Epkenhans, Michael. *Die Wilhelminische Flottenrüstung 1908–1914. Weltmachtstreben, Industrieller Fortschritt, Soziale Integration.* Munich, 1991.

Eppstein, Baron Georg von, ed. *Fürst Bismarcks Entlassung: Nach den Hintergelassenen . . . Aufzeichnungen des Staatsekretärs des Innern, Staatsministers Dr. Karl Heinrich von Boetticher und des Chefs der Reichskanzlei unter dem Fürsten Bismarck Dr. Franz Johannes von Rottenburg.* Berlin, 1920.

Erbach-Schönberg, Marie Princess zu. *Erklugenes und Verklugenes.* Darmstadt, 1923.

Erdmann, Karl Dietrich, ed. *Kurt Riezler. Tagebücher, Aufsätze, Dokumente.* Göttingen, 1972.

Ernst, Johann, ed. *Reden des Kaisers.* Munich, 1966.

Ernst Heinrich, Duke of Saxony. *Mein Lebensweg vom Königsschloss zum Bauernhof.* Munich, 1968.

Ernst Ludwig, Grand Duke of Hesse. *Erinnertes. Aufzeichnungen. . . .* Darmstadt, 1983.

Erzberger, Matthias. *Erlebnisse im Weltkriege.* Stuttgart, 1920.

Eulalia, Enfanta of Spain. *Memoirs of HRH the Infanta Eulalia.* London, 1936.

Eulenburg-Hertefeld, Philipp Prince zu. *Das Ende König Ludwigs II. und Andere Erlebnisse.* Leipzig, 1924.

——. *Erlebnisse an Deutschen und Fremden Höfen.* Leipzig, 1934.

——. *Mit dem Kaiser als Staatsmann und Freund auf Nordlandsreisen.* 2 vols. Dresden, 1931.

Falkenhayn, Erich von. *Die Oberste Kriegsleitung 1914–1916.* Berlin, 1920.

Faramond, Viscount Gontram Marie Auguste de. *Souvenirs d'un Attaché Naval en Allemagne et en Austriche 1910–1914.* Paris, 1932.

Fechter, Paul. *An der Wende der Zeit. Menschen und Begegnungen.* Gütersloh, 1949.

Feder, Ernst, ed. *Bismarcks Grosses Spiel. Die Geheimer Tagebücher Ludwig Bambergers.* Frankfurt/Main, 1933.

——. *Heute Sprach Ich Mit . . . Tagebücher eines Berliner Publizisten, 1926–32.* Stuttgart, 1971.

Fehrenbach, Elisabeth. *Wandlungen des Deutschen Kaisergedankens 1871–1918.* Munich, 1969.

Field, Goeffrey G. *Evangelist of Race: The Germanic Vision of Houston Stewart Chamberlain.* New York, 1981.

Fink, Carole, Isabel V. Hull, and MacGregor Knox. *German Nationalism and the European Response, 1890–1945.* Norman, Okla., 1985.

Fischer, Fritz. *Griff nach der Weltmacht. Die Kriegszielpolitik des Kaiserlichen Deutschland 1914/18.* Düsseldorf, 1961.

——. *Krieg der Illusionen. Die Deutsche Politik von 1911 bis 1914.* Düsseldorf, 1969.

Fisher, John. *Memories and Records.* 2 vols. New York, 1920.

Fitzroy, Sir Almeric. *Memoirs*. 2 vols. London, n.d.

Flotow, Hans. "Bülows Römische Mission." *Süddeutsche Monatshefte* 28 (Mar. 1931): 399–404.

Foulke, William Dudley. *A Hoosier Autobiography*. New York, 1922.

France, Ministry of Foreign Affairs. *Documents Diplomatiques Français 1871–1914*. 40 vols. Paris, 1929–59.

Francke, Kuno, ed. *The German Classics of the Nineteenth and Twentieth Centuries*. 16 vols. New York, 1914.

Freytag, Gustav. *Briefe an seine Gattin*. Berlin, 1912.

Freytag-Loringhoven, Baron Hugo von. *Menschen und Dinge wie ich sie in meinem Leben Sah*. Berlin, 1923.

Friedländer, Max J. *Reminiscences and Reflections*. Greenwich, Conn., 1969.

Friedrich, Julius. *Wer Spielte Falsch? Hitler, Hindenburg, der Kronprinz, Hugenburg, Schleicher. Ein Tatsachenbericht aus Deutschlands Jüngster Vergangenheit nach Authentischem Material*. Hamburg, n.d.

Friedrich Leopold of Prussia, Princess. *Behind the Scenes at the Prussian Court*. London, 1939.

Fromm, Bella. *Blood and Banquets: A Berlin Social Diary*. Garden City, N.Y., 1944.

Fuchs, Walther Peter, ed. *Großherzog Friedrich I. von Baden und die Reichspolitik 1871–1907*. 4 vols. Stuttgart, 1968–80.

Fugger, Nora Princess. *Im Glanz der Kaiserzeit*. Zurich, 1932.

Fürstenberg, Hans. *Carl Fürstenberg. Die Lebensgeschichte eines Deutschen Bankiers*. Wiesbaden, n.d. [1961].

———, ed. *Carl-Fürstenberg-Anekdoten: Ein Unterschied Muss Sein*. Düsseldorf, 1978.

Gallwitz, M[ax] von. *Erleben im Westen 1916–1918*. Berlin, 1932.

———. *Meine Führertätigkeit im Weltkrieg 1914/1916. Belgien-Osten-Balkan*. Berlin, 1929.

Gatzke, Hans W. *Germany's Drive to the West (Drang nach Westen): A Study of Germany's Western War Aims during the First World War*. Baltimore, 1950.

Gauss, Christian, ed. *The German Emperor as Shown in His Public Utterances*. New York, 1915.

Gerard, James W. *Face to Face with Kaiserism*. New York, 1918.

———. *My First Eighty-Three Years in America*. Garden City, N.Y., 1951.

———. *My Four Years in Germany*. New York, 1917.

Gerlach, Hellmuth. *Erinnerungen eines Junkers*. Berlin, n.d.

Germany, Nationalversammlung. *Die Ursachen des Deutschen Zusammenbruchs im Jahre 1918*. 4th ser. *Das Werk des Untersuchungsausschusses*. 12 vols. Berlin, 1925–29.

Germany, Reichstag. *Stenographische Berichte über die Verhandlungen des Reichstages*. 308 vols. Berlin, 1873–1918.

Glaise-Horstenau, Edmund von. *Franz Josephs Weggefährte. Das Leben des Generalstabschefs Grafen Beck. . . .* Zurich, n.d.

Gleichen, Lord Edward. *A Guardsman's Memoirs*. London, 1932.

Glum, Friedrich. *Zwischen Wissenschaft, Wirtschaft und Politik. Erlebtes und Erdachtes in Vier Reichen*. Bonn, 1964.

Goetz, Walter, ed. *Briefe Wilhelms II. an den Zaren, 1894–1914.* Berlin, n.d.

Göhler, Georg. "Das Kaiserliche Volks-Liederbuch." *Der Kunstwart* 20 (1907): 70–72.

Goltz, Baron Colmar von der. *Denkwürdigkeiten.* Berlin, 1929.

Gooch, George P., and H. W. Temperley, eds. *British Documents on the Origins of the War, 1898–1914.* 11 vols. London, 1925–38.

Görlitz, Walter, ed. *Der Kaiser . . . Aufzeichnungen des Chefs des Marine-kabinetts Admiral Georg Alexander v. Müller über die Ära Wilhelms II.* Berlin, 1965.

———. *Regierte der Kaiser? Kriegstagebücher, Aufzeichnungen und Briefe des Chefs des Marine-Kabinetts Admiral Georg Alexander von Müller 1914–1918.* Göttingen, 1959.

Granier, Gerhard. *Magnus von Levetzow. Seeoffizier, Monarchist und Wegbereiter Hitlers. Lebensweg und Ausgewählte Dokumente.* Boppard/Rhein, 1982.

Grenville, J. A. S. *Lord Salisbury and Foreign Policy at the Close of the Nineteenth Century.* London, 1964.

Groener, Wilhelm. *Lebenserinnerungen. Jugend-Generalstab-Weltkrieg.* Göttingen, 1957.

Groener-Geyer, Dorothea. *General Groener. Soldat und Staatsmann.* Frankfurt/Main, 1954.

Gschliesser, Oswald. "Das Wissenschaftliche Oeuvre des Ehemaligen Kaisers Wilhelm II." *Archiv für Kulturgeschichte* 54 (1972): 385–92.

Gurlitt, Cornelius. "Der Platz der Republik und der Wallotbau." *Wasmuths Monatshefte für Baukunst und Städtbau* 14 (1930): 340–47.

Güssfeldt, Paul. *Kaiser Wilhelms II. Reisen nach Norwegen in den Jahren 1889 und 1890.* Berlin, 1890.

Gutsche, Willibald. *Ein Kaiser im Exil: Der Letzte Deutsche Kaiser Wilhelm II. in Holland. Eine Kritische Biographie.* Marburg, 1991.

———. *Wilhelm II. der Letzte Kaiser des Deutschen Reiches. Eine Biographie.* Berlin, 1991.

Gutsche, Willibald, and Joachim Petzold. "Das Verhältnis der Hohenzollern zum Faschismus." *Zeitschrift für Geschichtswissenschaft* 29 (1981): 917–39.

Gwynn, Stephen, ed. *The Letters and Friendships of Sir Cecil Spring Rice: A Record.* 2 vols. Boston, 1929.

Haldane, Viscount Richard B. *An Autobiography.* Garden City, N.Y., 1929.

Haller, Johannes, ed. *Aus dem Leben des Fürsten Philipp zu Eulenburg-Hertefeld.* Berlin, 1924.

———. *Aus 50 Jahren. Erinnerungen, Tagebücher und Briefe aus dem Nachlass des Fürsten Philipp zu Eulenburg-Hertefeld.* Berlin, 1923.

Hammann, Otto. "Aufzeichnungen." *Archiv für Politik und Geschichte* 4 (1925): 541–53.

———. *Bilder aus der Letzten Kaiserzeit.* Berlin, 1921.

———. *Um den Kaiser. Erinnerungen aus den Jahren 1906–1909.* Berlin, 1919.

———. *Zur Vorgeschichte des Weltkrieges. Erinnerungen aus den Jahren 1897–1906.* Berlin, 1919.

Hantsch, Hugo. *Leopold Graf Berchtold. Grandseigneur und Staatsmann.* 2 vols. Graz, 1963.

Hardinge of Penshurst, Baron Charles Hardinge. *Old Diplomacy: The Reminiscences of Lord Hardinge of Penshurst.* London, 1947.

Hassell, Ulrich von. *Tirpitz. Sein Leben und Wirken mit Berücksichtigung seiner Beziehungen zu Albrecht von Stosch.* Stuttgart, 1920.

Haussmann, Conrad. *Schlaglichter. Reichstagsbriefe und Aufzeichnungen.* Frankfurt/Main, 1924.

Hecker, Gerhard. *Walther Rathenau und sein Verhältnis zu Militär und Krieg.* Boppard/Rhein, 1983.

Hegermann-Lindencrone, Lillie de. *The Sunny Side of Diplomatic Life.* London, 1914.

Heinig, Kurt. *Hohenzollern. Wilhelm II. und sein Haus. Der Kampf um den Kronbesitz.* Berlin, 1921.

Helfferich, Karl. *Der Weltkrieg.* 3 vols. Karlsruhe, 1925.

Hellige, Hans Dieter, ed. *Walther Rathenau Maximilian Harden. Briefwechsel 1897–1920.* Munich, 1982.

Hermine, Princess. *An Empress in Exile: My Days in Doorn.* New York, 1928.

———. "In Unsrem Heim." In Paul Lindenburg, *Wir Denken Seiner. Zur 75. Geburtstag des Kaisers*, pp. 1–5. Berlin, 1924.

Hertling, Count Georg von. *Erinnerungen aus meinem Leben.* 2 vols. Munich, 1919–20.

Hertling, Count Karl von. *Ein Jahr in der Reichskanzlei. Erinnerungen an die Kanzlerschaft meines Vaters.* Freiburg i.B., 1919.

Herwig, Holger. *"Luxury Fleet": The Imperial German Navy, 1888–1918.* London, 1980.

Herzfeld, Hans, ed. *Johannes von Miquel. Sein Anteil am Ausbau des Deutschen Reiches bis zur Jahrhundertwende.* 2 vols. Detmold, 1938.

Hill, David Jayne. *Impressions of the Kaiser.* New York, 1918.

Hill, Leonidas E., ed. *Die Weizsäcker-Papiere, 1900–1932.* N.p., n.d.

Hiller von Gaertringen, Baron Friedrich von. *Fürst Bülows Denkwürdigkeiten. Untersuchungen zu ihrer Entstellungsgeschichte und ihrer Kritik.* Tübingen, 1956.

Hiltebrandt, Philipp. *Erinnerungen an den Fürsten Bülow.* Bonn, 1930.

Hindenburg, Herbert von. *Am Rande Zweier Jahrhunderte. Momentbilder aus einem Diplomatenleben.* Berlin, 1938.

Hindenburg, Paul von. *Aus meinem Leben.* Leipzig, 1920.

Hinzpeter, Georg. *Kaiser Wilhelm II. Eine Skizze nach der Natur Gezeichnet.* Bielefeld, 1888.

Hoffmann, Max. *Der Krieg der Versäumten Gelegenheiten.* Munich, 1923.

———. *Die Aufzeichnungen des General Max Hoffmann.* 2 vols. Berlin, 1928.

Hohenlohe, Alexander Prince von. *Aus meinem Leben.* Frankfurt/Main, 1925.

Hohenlohe-Schillingsfürst, Chlodwig Prince zu. *Denkwürdigkeiten.* 2 vols. Stuttgart, 1907.

———. *Denkwürdigkeiten der Reichskanzlerzeit.* Stuttgart, 1931.

Hopman, Albert. *Das Kriegstagebuch eines Deutschen Seeoffiziers.* Berlin, 1925.

Hötzsch, Otto, ed. *Fürst Bülows Reden. Nebst Urkundlichen Beiträgen zu seiner Politik.* 3 vols. Berlin, 1909.

Hough, Richard A. *Louis and Victoria: The First Mountbattens.* London, 1974.

House, Edward M., and Charles Seymour. *What Really Happened at Paris: The Story of the Peace Conference, 1918–1919, by American Delegates.* New York, 1921.

Howard, Christopher H. D., ed. *The Diary of Edward Goschen, 1900–1914.* London, 1980.

Howard, Ethel. *Potsdam Princess.* New York, n.d. [1915].

Howe, M. A. De Wolfe. *George von Lengerke Meyer: His Life and Public Services.* New York, 1920.

Hubatsch, Walther, ed. *Hindenburg und der Staat. Aus der Papieren des Generalfeldmarschalls und Reichspräsidenten von 1878 bis 1934.* Göttingen, 1966.

Hull, Isabel V. *The Entourage of Kaiser Wilhelm II, 1888–1918.* Cambridge, Eng., 1982.

———. "Kaiser Wilhelm II and the Liebenberg Circle." In John C. G. Röhl and Nicolaus Sombart, eds., *Kaiser Wilhelm II, New Interpretations: The Corfu Papers,* pp. 193–220. Cambridge, Eng., 1982.

Huret, Jules. *En Allemagne. Berlin.* Paris, 1909.

Hutten-Czapski, Count Bogdan von. *Sechzig Jahre Politik und Gesellschaft.* 2 vols. Berlin, 1936.

Ilsemann, Sigurd von. *Der Kaiser in Holland. Aufzeichnungen.* 2 vols. Munich, 1967–68.

Iswolsky, Alexander. *Au Service de la Russie. Correspondence Diplomatique 1906–1911.* 2 vols. Paris, 1937–39.

Jäckh, Ernst, ed. *Kiderlen-Wächter, der Staatsmann und Mensch: Briefwechsel und Nachlass.* 2 vols. Berlin, 1924.

Jagemann, Eugen von. *Fünfundsiebzig Jahre des Erlebens und Erfahrens (1849–1924).* Heidelberg, 1925.

Janssen, Karl-Heinz. *Der Kanzler und der General. Die Führungskrise um Bethmann Hollweg und Falkenhayn (1914–1916).* Göttingen, 1967.

———. *Macht und Verblendung. Kriegszielpolitik der Deutschen Bundesstaaten 1914/18.* Göttingen, 1963.

———, ed. *Die Graue Exzellenz. Zwischen Staatsräson und Vasallentreue. Aus den Papieren des Kaiserlichen Gesandten Karl Georg von Treutler.* Frankfurt/Main, 1971.

Jarausch, Konrad H. *The Enigmatic Chancellor: Bethmann Hollweg and the Hubris of Imperial Germany.* New Haven, 1973.

Johnson, Robert Underwood. *Remembered Yesterdays.* Boston, 1923.

Johnston, Harry. *Alexander Johnston: The Life and Letters of Sir Harry Johnston.* New York, 1929.

Jonas, Klaus W. *The Life of Crown Prince William.* London, 1961.

Jonescu, Take. *Some Personal Impressions.* London, 1919.

Justi, Ludwig. *Die Nationalgalerie und die Moderne Kunst. Rückblicke und Ausblick.* Leipzig, 1918.

Kardorff, Siegrfied von. *Wilhelm von Kardorff. Ein Nationaler Parlamentarier im Zeitalter Bismarcks und Wilhelms II. 1828–1907.* Berlin, 1936.

Karow, Leonhard. *Neun Jahre in Marokkanischen Diensten.* Berlin, 1909.

Kaulisch, Baldur. *Alfred von Tirpitz und die Imperialistische Deutsche Flottenrüstung. Eine Politische Biographie.* Berlin, 1982.

Keen, Edith. *Seven Years at the Prussian Court*. New York, 1917.

Keim, August. *Erlebtes und Erstrebtes. Lebenserinnerungen*. Hanover, 1925.

Keller, Countess Mathilde von. *Vierzig Jahre im Dienst der Kaiserin. Ein Kultur-bild aus den Jahren 1881–1921*. Leipzig, 1935.

Kennedy, Paul M. *The Rise of the Anglo-German Antagonism, 1860–1914*. London, 1980.

Kessler, Count Harry. *Gesichter und Zeiten. Erinnerungen*. Berlin, 1962 [1935].

——. *Tagebücher 1918–1937*. Frankfurt/Main, 1961.

Kessler, Johannes. *Ich Schwöre mir Ewige Jugend*. Munich, 1935.

Kiaulehn, Walther. *Berlin. Schicksal einer Weltstadt*. Munich, 1968.

Kielmansegg, Count Erich von. *Kaiserhaus, Staatsmänner und Politiker. Auf-zeichnungen des K.u.K. Staathalters Erich Graf Kielmansegg*. Vienna, 1966.

Kinsky, Countess Elisabeth von, ed. *Hans Wilczek Erzählt seinen Enkeln. Erin-nerungen aus seinem Leben*. Graz, 1933.

Kitchen, Martin. *The German Officer Corps, 1890–1914*. Oxford, 1968.

Kleinmichel, Countess Marie. *Memories of a Shipwrecked World*. New York, 1923.

Kluck, Alexander von. *Wanderjahre-Kriege-Gestalten*. Berlin, 1928.

Knodt, Manfred. *Ernst Ludwig Grossherzog von Hessen und bei Rhein. Sein Leben und seine Zeit*. Darmstadt, 1978.

Koenigswald, Harald von, ed. *Sigurd von Ilsemann. Der Kaiser in Holland. Aufzeichhnungen des Letzten Flügeladjutanten Kaiser Wilhelms II*. 2 vols. Munich, 1967–68.

Kohut, Thomas A. "Kaiser Wilhelm II and His Parents: An Inquiry into the Psychological Roots of German Policy towards England before the First World War." In John C. G. Röhl and Nicolaus Sombart, eds., *Kaiser Wilhelm II, New Interpretations: The Corfu Papers*, pp. 63–89. Cambridge, Eng., 1982.

Korostowetz, Wladimir von. *Graf Witte, der Steuermann in der Not*. Berlin, 1929.

Kospoth, Count C. A. *Wie ich zu meinem Kaiser Stand. Persönliche Erinnerungen an Kaiser Wilhelm II*. Breslau, 1924.

Koss, Stephen E. *Lord Haldane: Scapegoat for Liberalism*. New York, 1969.

Kraft, Heinz. *Staatsräson und Kriegsführung im Kaiserlichen Deutschland 1914–1916. Der Gegensatz zwischen dem Generalstabschef von Falkenhayn und dem Oberbefehlshaber Ost im Rahmen des Bundniskrieges der Mittelmächte*. Göttingen, 1980.

Krause, Ernst. *Richard Strauss: The Man and His Work*. London, 1964 [1955].

Kühlmann, Richard von. *Erinnerungen*. Heidelberg, 1948.

Kürenberg, Joachim von [Hans von Reichel]. *War Alles Falsch? Das Leben Kaiser Wilhelms II*. Bonn, 1951.

Laforgue, Jules. *Berlin. La Cour et la Ville*. Paris, 1922.

Lambi, Ivo N. *The Navy and German Power Politics, 1862–1914*. Boston, 1984.

Lambsdorff, Count Gustav von. *Die Militärbevollmächtigten Kaiser Wilhelms II. am Zarenhofe 1904–1914*. Berlin, 1937

Lange, Helene. *Lebenserinnerungen*, Berlin, 1925.

Larsen, Mogens T. "Orientalism and the Ancient Near East." *Culture and History* 2 (1987): 96–115.

Lee, Arthur G., ed. *The Empress Writes to Sophie, Her Daughter, Crown Princess and Later Queen of the Hellenes: Letters, 1889–1901.* London, n.d. [1955].

Lee, S. *King Edward VII: A Biography.* 2 vols. London, 1925–27.

Lee of Fareham, Viscount. *'A Good Innings': The Private Papers of Viscount Lee of Fareham.* London, 1974.

Lenman, Robin. "Politics and Culture: The State and the Avant-Garde in Munich, 1886–1914." In Richard J. Evans, ed., *Society and Politics in Wilhelmine Germany*, pp. 90–111. New York, 1976.

Lepsius, Johannes, Albrecht Mendelssohn-Bartholdy, and Friedrich Thimme, eds. *Die Grosse Politik der Europäischen Kabinette, 1871–1914.* 40 vols. Berlin, 1922–27.

Lerchenfeld-Koefering, Count Hugo. *Erinnerungen und Denkwürdigkeiten.* Berlin, 1935.

———. *Kaiser Wilhelm II. als Persönlichkeit und Herrscher.* Kallmünz, 1985.

Lerman, Katharine F. *The Chancellor as Courtier: Bernhard von Bülow and the Governance of Germany, 1900–1909.* Cambridge, Eng., 1990.

———. "The Decisive Relationship: Kaiser Wilhelm II and Chancellor Bernhard von Bülow, 1900–1905." In John C. G. Röhl and Nicolaus Sombart, eds., *Kaiser Wilhelm II, New Interpretations: The Corfu Papers*, pp. 221–48. Cambridge, Eng., 1982.

Leslie, Shane. *Long Shadows.* London, 1966.

Liebert, E[duard] von. *Aus einem Bewegten Leben. Erinnerungen.* Munich, 1925.

Lister, Roma. *Reminiscences, Social and Political.* London, n.d.

Litzmann, Berthold, *Ernst von Wildenbruch.* 2 vols. Berlin, 1913–16.

Lochner, Louis. *Always the Unexpected.* New York, 1956.

Lockhart, J. G. *Charles Lindley, Viscount Halifax.* 2 vols. London, 1936.

———. *Cosmo Gordon Lang.* London, 1949.

Lockhart, Sir Robert H. Bruce. *Charles Lindley, Viscount Halifax.* 2 vols. London, 1936.

———. *Comes the Reckoning.* London, 1947.

———. *Retreat from Glory.* London, 1934.

Lossberg, Fritz von. *Meine Tätigkeit im Weltkriege 1914–1918.* Berlin, 1939.

Louise, Duchess of Coburg. *Throne die ich Stürzen Sah.* Zurich, 1927.

Louise, Princess of Belgium. *My Own Affairs.* New York, 1921.

Louise, Princess of Tuscany. *My Own Story.* New York, 1911.

Louis Ferdinand, Prince of Prussia. *Als Kaiserenkel durch die Welt.* Berlin, 1952.

Lucius von Ballhausen, Baron Robert. *Bismarck-Erinnerungen.* Stuttgart, 1920.

Luckner, Count Felix von. *Out of an Old Sea Chest.* London, 1958.

Ludendorff, Erich. *Ludendorff's Own Story, August 1914–November 1918: The Great War. . . .* 2 vols. New York, 1919.

Ludwig Ferdinand of Bavaria, Princess. *Through Four Revolutions, 1862–1933.* London, 1933.

Makela, Maria. *The Munich Secession: Art and Artists in Turn-of-the-Century Munich.* Princeton, 1990.

Mannix, Daniel P. *The Old Navy.* New York, 1983.

Marder, Arthur J., ed. *Fear God and Dreadnought: The Correspondence of Admiral of the Fleet Lord Fisher of Kilverstone.* 3 vols. Cambridge, Mass., 1952–59.

Marie, Queen of Rumania. *The Story of My Life.* 2 vols. London, 1934.

Marie Louise, Princess. *My Memories of Six Reigns.* London, 1956.

Marks, Sally. "My Name Is Ozymandias: The Kaiser in Exile." *Central European History* 16 (Jun. 1983): 122–70.

Marschall, Birgit. *Reisen und Regieren. Die Nordlandsfahrten Kaiser Wilhelms II.* Heidelberg, 1991.

Marwitz, Georg von der. *Weltkriegsbriefe.* Berlin, 1940.

McClelland, Charles E. *State, Society, and the University in Germany, 1700– 1914.* Cambridge, Eng., 1980.

Meisner, Heinrich O., ed. *Denkwürdigkeiten des General-Feldmarschalls Alfred Grafen von Waldersee.* 3 vols. Stuttgart, 1923–25.

——. "Gespräche und Briefe Holsteins." *Preussischer Jahrbücher* 227 (1932): 1–11.

Meister, Lelia von. *Gathered Yesterdays.* London, 1963.

Melgunoff, S., ed. *Das Tagebuch des Letzten Zaren von 1890 bis zum Fall. Nach den Unveröffentlichten Russischen Handschriften.* Berlin, 1923.

Menken, Edward. *The Trial of the Kaiser.* Chicago, 1918.

Meyer, Klaus. *Theodor Schiemann als Politischer Publizist.* Frankfurt/Main, 1956.

Michaelis, Georg. *Für Staat und Volk. Eine Lebensgeschichte.* Berlin, 1922.

Milner, Viscountess Violet Georgina Maxse. *My Picture Gallery, 1886–1901.* London, 1951.

Möckl, Karl. *Die Prinzregentenzeit. Gesellschaft und Politik während der Ära der Prinzregenten Luitpold in Bayern.* Munich, 1972.

Mohl, Ottomar von. *Fünfzig Jahre Reichsdienst. Lebenserinnerungen.* Leipzig, 1921.

Moltke, Countess Eliza von, ed. *Hellmuth von Moltke. Erinnerungen Briefe Dokumente 1877–1916. Ein Bild vom Kriegsausbruch, Erster Kriegsführung und Persönlichkeit des Ersten Militärischen Führers des Krieges.* Stuttgart, 1922.

Monger, George, L. *The End of Isolation Britain, Germany, and Japan, 1900– 1902.* London, 1963.

Montgelas, Count Max von, and Walther Schücking, eds. *Outbreak of the World War: German Documents Collected by Karl Kautsky.* New York, 1924.

Monts, Count Anton. *Erinnerungen und Gedanken des Botschafters Anton Graf Monts.* Berlin, 1932.

[Morel, Madame]. *From an Eastern Embassy: Memories of London, Berlin, and the East.* Philadelphia, 1920.

Morison, Elting E. *The Letters of Theodore Roosevelt.* 8 vols. Cambridge, Mass., 1951–54.

Morsey, Rudolf, and Erich Matthias, eds. *Quellen zur Geschichte des Parlamentarismus und der Politischen Parteien.* Vol. 1, *Der Interfraktionelle Ausschuss.* Düsseldorf, 1959. Vol. 2, *Die Regierung des prinzen Max von Baden.* Düsseldorf, 1962.

Mosse, Werner E. *The German-Jewish Economic Elite, 1820–1935: A Socio-Cultural Profile.* Oxford, 1989.

——. "Wilhelm II and the *Kaiserjuden*: A Problematical Encounter." In Jehuda

Reinharz and Walter Schalzberg, eds., *The Jewish Response to German Culture: From the Enlightenment to the Second World War*, pp. 164–94. Hanover, 1985.

Mossolov, A. A. *At the Court of the Last Tsar*. London, 1935.

Mühleisen, Horst. *Kurt Freiherr v. Lersner: Diplomat im Umbruch der Zeiten 1918–1920, Eine Biographie*. Göttingen, 1988.

Münz, Sigmund. *Fürst Bülow der Staatsmann und Mensch. Aufzeichnungen, Erinnerungen und Erwägungen*. Berlin, 1930.

———. *King Edward VII at Marinebad: Political and Social Life at the Bohemian Spas*. London, 1934.

Naso, Eckard von. *Ich Liebe das Leben. Erinnerungen aus Fünf Jahrzehnten*. Hamburg, 1953.

Naumann, Viktor. *Dokumente und Argumente*. Berlin, 1928.

———. *Profile*. Munich, 1925.

Nekludov, A. "Autour de l'Entrevue de Bjoerkoe." *Revue des Deux Mondes* 88 (1918): 127–44.

Newton, Baron Thomas Legh. *Lord Lansdowne: A Biography*. London, 1929.

Nicolai, Walter. *Nachrichtendienst. Presse und Volksstimmung im Weltkrieg*. Berlin, 1920.

Nicolson, Harold. *King George the Fifth: His Life and Reign*. London, 1952.

Niemann, Alfred. *Kaiser und Revolution, Die Entscheidenden Ereignisse im Grossen Hauptquartier*. Berlin, 1922.

———. *Revolution von Oben Umsturz von Unten. Entwicklung und Verlauf der Staatsumwälzung in Deutschland 1914–1918*. Berlin, 1927.

———. *Wanderungen mit Kaiser Wilhelm II*. Leipzig, 1924.

Nikitsch-Boulles, Paul. *Vor dem Sturm. Erinnerungen an Erzherzog Thronfolger Franz Ferdinand*. Berlin, 1925.

Nostitz, Herbert von. *Bismarcks Unbotmässiger Botschafter Fürst Münster von Derneburg*. Göttingen, 1968.

Nostitz-Rieneck, Georg, ed. *Briefe Kaiser Franz Josephs an Kaiserin Elisabeth 1859–1898*. 2 vols. Vienna, 1966.

Obkircher, Walther, ed. *Erich von Gündell. Aus seinen Tagebüchern*. Hamburg, 1939.

Oldenburg-Januschau, Elard von. *Erinnerungen*. Leipzig, 1936.

Olfers, Marie von. *Briefe und Tagebücher*. 2 vols. Berlin, 1928.

Osborn, Max. *Der Bunte Spiegel. Erinnerungen aus dem Kunst-, Kultur- und Geistesleben der Jahre 1890–1933*. New York, 1945.

Pachnicke, Hermann. *Führende Männer im Alten und im Neuen Reich*. Berlin, 1930.

Paget, Lady Walpurga. *Embassies of Other Days and Further Recollections*. 2 vols. London, 1923.

———. *In My Tower*. London, 1924.

Paléologue, Maurice. *Three Critical Years (1904–05–06)*. New York, 1957.

Pallat, Ludwig. *Richard Schöne, Generaldirektor der Königlichen Museen zu Berlin. Ein Beitrag zur Geschichte der Preussischen Kunstverwaltung 1872–1905*. Berlin, 1959.

Panofsky, Walter. "L'Apothéose du Festival." In *Richard Wagner* (Collection Génies et Réalités), pp. 251–69. Paris, 1962.

Paret, Peter. *The Berlin Secession: Modernism and Its Enemies in Imperial Germany.* Cambridge, Mass., 1980.

——. "The Tschudi Affair." *Journal of Modern History* 53, no. 4 (Dec. 1981): 589–618.

Pastor, Baron Ludwig von. *Tagebücher, Briefe, Erinnerungen 1854–1928.* Heidelberg, 1950.

Payer, Friedrich. *Von Bethmann Hollweg bis Ebert. Erinnerungen und Bilder.* Frankfurt/Main, 1923.

Peignot, Étienne. "Le Châtiment Légal et Possible de Guillaume II." *La Revue* 6 (1919): 282–87.

Persius, L. *Menschen und Schiffe in der Kaiserlichen Flotte.* Berlin, 1925.

Pfefferkorn, Rudolf. *Die Berliner Secession.* Berlin, 1972.

Pless, Princess Daisy. *Better Left Unsaid.* New York, 1931.

——. *Daisy, Princess of Pless, by Herself.* London, 1929.

Pogge von Strandmann, Hartmut, ed. *Walther Rathenau Tagebuch 1907–22.* Düsseldorf, 1967.

Pohl, Hugo von. *Aus Aufzeichnungen und Briefe während der Kriegszeit.* Berlin, 1920.

Ponsonby, Sir Frederick, ed. *Letters of the Empress Frederick.* New York, 1928.

——. *Recollections of Three Reigns.* New York, 1952.

Pope-Hennessy, James. *Queen Mary, 1867–1953.* New York, 1960.

Pückler, Count Karl von. *Aus meinem Diplomatenleben.* Schweidnitz, 1934.

Radziwill, Princess Marie. *Lettres de la Princesse Radziwill au Général de Robilant 1889–1914. Une Grande Dame d'avant Guerre.* 4 vols. Bologna, 1933–34.

Raeder, Erich. *Mein Leben.* 2 vols. Tübingen, 1956–57.

Raschdau, Ludwig. "Bülow und Holstein." *Süddeutsche Monatshefte* 28 (Mar. 1931): 389–90.

——. *In Weimar als Preussischer Gesandter. Ein Buch der Erinnerungen an Deutsche Fürstenhöfe 1894–1897.* Berlin, 1939.

——. *Unter Bismarck und Caprivi. Erinnerungen eines Deutschen Diplomaten aus den Jahren 1885–1894.* Berlin, 1939.

——. "Zum Kapitel Holstein." *Deutsche Rundschau* 51 (1924): 237–47.

Rattigan, Frank. *Diversions of a Diplomat.* London, 1924.

Raulff, Heiner. *Zwischen Machtpolitik und Imperialismus. Die Deutsche Frankreichpolitik 1904/06.* Düsseldorf, 1976.

Réal, Jean. "La Lettre à l'Amiral Hollmann." *Études Germaniques* 6 (1951): 303–12.

Redlich, Josef. *Schicksalsjahre Österreichs 1908–1919. Das Politische Tagebuch Josef Redlichs.* 2 vols. Graz, 1953–54.

Redwitz, Baroness Marie von. *Hofchronik 1888–1921.* Munich, 1924.

Regele, Oskar. *Feldmarschall Conrad. Auftrag und Erfüllung 1906–1918.* Vienna, 1955.

Reid, Michaela. *Ask Sir James: Sir James Reid, Personal Physician to Queen Victoria and Physician-in-Ordinary to Three Monarchs.* New York, 1987.

Reischach, Count Hugo von. *Unter Drei Kaisern.* Volksausgabe. Berlin, 1925.

Repington, Charles à Court. *Vestigia: Reminiscences of Peace and War.* Boston, 1919.

Reynoso, Marquis Francisco de. *50 Jahre Dipolmat in der Grossen Welt. Erinnerungen.* Dresden, 1935.

Rheinbaben, Baron Werner von. *Kaiser Kanzler Präsidenten. Erinnerungen.* Mainz, 1968.

Rich, Norman. *Friedrich von Holstein: Politics and Diplomacy in the Era of Bismarck and Wilhelm II.* 2 vols. Cambridge, Eng., 1965.

Rich, Norman, and M. H. Fisher, eds. *The Holstein Papers.* 4 vols. Cambridge, Eng., 1955–63.

Roddie, Stewart. *Peace Patrol.* New York, 1933.

Rogge, Helmuth, ed. *Friedrich von Holstein. Lebensbekenntnis in Briefen an eine Frau.* Berlin, 1932.

——. *Holstein und Harden. Politisch-Publizistisches Zusammenspiel zweier Aussenseiter des Wilhelminischen Reichs.* Munich, 1959.

——. *Holstein und Hohenlohe. Neue Beiträge zu Friedrich von Holsteins Tätigkeit als Mitarbeiter Bismarcks und als Ratgeber Hohenlohes....* Stuttgart, 1957.

Röhl, John C. G. "An der Schwelle zum Weltkrieg: Eine Dokumentation über den 'Kriegsrat' vom 8. Dezember 1912." *Militärgeschichtliche Mitteilungen* 1 (1977): 77–134.

——. *Germany without Bismarck: The Crisis of Government in the Second Reich, 1890–1900.* Berkeley, 1967.

——. *Kaiser, Hof und Staat. Wilhelm II. und die Deutsche Politik.* Munich, 1987.

——. *Wilhelm II. Die Jugend des Kaisers 1859–1888.* Munich, 1993.

——, ed. *Der Ort Kaiser Wilhelms II. in der Deutschen Geschichte.* Munich, 1991.

——. *Philipp Eulenburgs Politische Korrespondenz.* 3 vols. Boppard am Rheim, 1976–83.

Röhl, John C. G., and Nicolaus Sombart, eds. *Kaiser Wilhelm II, New Interpretations: The Corfu Papers.* Cambridge, Eng., 1982.

Roloff, Ernst M. *In Zwei Welten. Aus den Erinnerungen und Wanderungen eines Deutschen Schulmannes und Lexikographers.* Berlin, 1920.

Rose, Kenneth. *King George V.* London, 1983.

Rosebrock, Heinrich. *Kaiser Wilhelm II. und die Frauenfrage.* Berlin, 1910.

Rosen, Friedrich. *Aus einem Diplomatischen Wanderleben.* 4 vols. in 3. Berlin, 1931–59.

Rosen, Baron [Roman]. *Forty Years of Diplomacy.* 2 vols. New York, 1922.

Rosner, Karl, ed. *Erinnerungen des Kronprinzen Wilhelm. Aus den Aufzeichnungen, Dokumenten, Tagebüchern und Gesprächen.* Stuttgart, 1922.

Rupprecht, Crown Prince of Bavaria. *Mein Kriegstagebuch.* 3 vols. Berlin, 1929.

Russell, Hon. A. V. F. V. "Reminiscences of the German Court." *Fighting Forces* 1, no. 1 (March 1924): 58–71.

Salburg, Countess Edith. *Erinnerungen einer Respektlosen. Ein Lebensbuch.* 3 vols. Leipzig, 1927–28.

Sauerbruch, Ferdinand. *Das War mein Leben.* Munich, 1951.

Sazonov, Sergei. *Fateful Years, 1909–1916: The Reminiscences of Serge Sazonov.* London, 1928.

Scheer, Reinhard. *Deutschlands Hochseeflotte im Weltkrieg. Persönliche Erinnerungen.* Berlin, 1919.

Scheffler, Karl. *Berlin. Wandlungen einer Stadt.* Berlin, 1931.

———. *Die Fetten und die Mageren Jahre. Ein Arbeits- und Lebensbericht.* Leipzig, 1948.

Scheidemann, Philipp. *The Making of New Germany.* 2 vols. New York, 1929.

———. *Memoirs of a Social Democrat.* 2 vols. London, 1929.

Schelking, Eugene de. *Recollections of a Russian Diplomat: The Suicide of the Monarchies (Wilhelm II and Nicholas II).* New York, 1918.

Schierbrand, Wolf von, ed. *The Kaiser's Speeches: Forming a Character Portrait of Emperor William II.* New York, 1903.

Schiffer, Eugen. *Ein Leben für den Liberalismus.* Berlin, 1951.

Schlözer, Leopold von. *Aus der Jugendzeit.* Dresden, 1938.

Schmidt-Bückeburg, R. *Das Militärkabinett der Preussischen Könige und Deutschen Kaiser.* Berlin, 1933.

Schmidt-Ott, Friedrich. *Erlebtes und Erstrebtes 1860–1950.* Wiesbaden, 1952.

Schnee, Heinrich. *Als Letzter Gouverneur in Deutsch-Ostafrika. Erinnerungen.* Heidelberg, 1964.

Schneider, Reinhold. *Verhüllter Tag.* Cologne, 1934.

Schneller, Ludwig. *Königs-Erinnerungen.* Leipzig, 1926.

Schoen, Baron Wilhelm von. "Die Tangerfahrt des Kaisers im Jahre 1905." *Süddeutsche Monatshefte* 28 (Mar. 1931): 393–95.

———. *Erlebtes. Beiträge zur Politischen Geschichte der Neuesten Zeit.* Stuttgart, 1921.

Schoenaich, Baron Paul von. *Mein Damaskus. Erlebnisse und Bekenntnisse.* Berlin, 1926.

Schoenbaum, David. *Zabern 1913. Consensus Politics in Imperial Germany.* London, 1982.

Schönburg-Waldenburg, Heinrich Prince von. *Erinnerungen aus Kaiserlicher Zeit.* Leipzig, 1929.

Schott, Walther. *Ein Künstler-Leben und Gesellschaftliche Erinnerungen.* Dresden, 1930.

Schramm, Percy Ernst. "Notizen über einen Besuch in Doorn (1930)." In Konrad Repgen and Stephan Skalweit, eds., *Spiegel der Geschichte. Festgabe für Max Braubach zum 10. April 1964,* pp. 942–50. Munich, 1964.

Schulthess' Europäischer Geschichtskalender. 82 vols. Munich, 1860–1941.

Schwabach, Paul H. von. *Aus meinen Akten.* Berlin, 1927.

Schwabe, Klaus. *Woodrow Wilson, Revolutionary Germany, and Peacemaking, 1918–1919: Missionary Diplomacy and the Realities of Power.* Chapel Hill, 1985.

Schwering, Count Axel von (pseud.). *The Berlin Court under William II.* London, 1915.

Schwertfeger, Bernhard, ed. *Kaiser und Kabinettschef: Nach Eigenen Aufzeichnungen und dem Briefwechsel des Wirklichen Geheimen Rats Rudolf von Valentini.* Oldenburg i.O., 1931.

Seeckt, Hans von. *Aus meinem Leben 1866–1917.* Leipzig, 1938.

Seidel, Paul. *Der Kaiser und die Kunst.* Berlin, 1907.

Shaw, Stanley. *William of Germany*. New York, 1913.

Sherrill, Charles H. *Bismarck and Mussolini*. Boston, 1931.

Siebert, Benno von, ed. *Graf Benckendorff Diplomatischer Schriftwechsel*. 3 vols. Berlin, 1928.

Silverman, Albert T. "Kidnapping the Kaiser." *American History Illustrated* 14 (January 1980): 36–43.

Simon, Christian. "Kaiser Wilhelm II. und die Deutsche Wissenschaft." In John C. G. Röhl, ed., *Der Ort Kaiser Wilhelms II. in der Deutschen Geschichte*, pp. 91–110. Munich, 1991.

Smith, Truman. *Berlin Alert: The Memoirs and Reports of Truman Smith*. Stanford, 1984.

Sommer, Dudley. *Haldane of Cloan: His Life and Times, 1856–1928*. London, 1960.

Sonntag, Josef. *Begegnungen mit Bülow und Anderen*. Berlin, 1935.

Sosnosky, Theodor von. *Franz Ferdinand, der Erzherzog-Thronfolger. Ein Lebensbild*. Munich, 1929.

Ssuworin, A[leksei]. S. *Das Geheimtagebuch*. Berlin, 1925.

Stanislavsky, Konstantin. *My Life in Art*. Boston, 1924.

Stein, August. *Es War Alles Ganz Anders. Aus der Werkstätte eines Politischen Journalisten*. Frankfurt/Main, 1926.

Stein, Hermann von. *Erlebnisse und Betrachtungen aus der Zeit des Weltkrieges*. Leipzig, 1919.

Steinberg, Jonathan. *Yesterday's Deterrent: Tirpitz and the Birth of the German Battle Fleet*. London, 1965.

Steinitz, Eduard von. *Erinnerungen an Franz Joseph I., Kaiser von Österreich, Apostolischer König von Ungarn*. Berlin, 1931.

Stephanie, Princess of Belgium. *I Was to Be Empress*. London, 1937.

Stöwer, Willy. *Zur See mit Pinsel und Palette. Erinnerungen. . . .* Brunswick, 1929.

Stürgkh, Count Joseph von. *Politische und Militärische Erinnerungen*. Leipzig, 1922.

Swaine, Leopold. *Camp and Chancery in a Soldier's Life*. London, 1926.

Sweetmann, Jack. "The Unforgotten Crowns: The German Monarchist Movements, 1918–1945." Ph.D. diss., Emory University, 1973.

Taube, Baron Otto von, ed. *Das Buch der Keyserlinge. An der Grenze Zweier Welten. Lebenserinnerungen aus einem Geschlecht*. Berlin, 1937.

Taylor, Robert R. *Hohenzollern Berlin: Construction and Reconstruction*. Port Credit, Ont., 1985.

Taylor, Telford. *The Goebbels Diaries, 1939–1945*. New York, 1983.

Thaer, Albrecht von. *Generalstabsdienst an der Front und in der O.H.L. Aus Briefen und Tagebuchaufzeichnungen 1915–1919*. Göttingen, 1958.

Thimme, Friedrich, ed. *Front wider Bülow. Staatsmänner, Diplomaten und Forscher zu seinen Denkwürdigkeiten*. Munich, 1931.

Tirpitz, Alfred von. *Erinnerungen*. Leipzig, 1919.

——. *Politische Dokumente*. 2 vols. Stuttgart, 1924–26.

Topham, Anne. *Chronicles of the Prussian Court*. London, 1926.

——. *Memories of the Fatherland*. New York, 1916.

Townley, Lady Susan. *"Indiscretions."* New York, 1922.

Trefz, Friedrich. "Fürst Bülows Denkwürdigkeiten." *Süddeutsche Monatshefte* 28 (Mar. 1931): 377–89.

Tresckow, Hans von. *Von Fürsten und Anderen Sterblichen. Erinnerungen eines Kriminalkommissars.* Berlin, 1922.

Treuberg, Countess Hetta. *Zwischen Politik und Diplomatie. Memoiren.* Strassburg, 1921.

Trevor Roper, H. R. *Hitler's Secret Conversations, 1941–1944.* New York, 1972 [1953].

Trotha, Adolf von. *Grossadmiral von Tirpitz. Flottenbau und Reichsgedanke.* Breslau, 1933.

Trotha, Friedrich von. *Fritz von Holstein als Mensch und Politiker.* Berlin, 1931.

Tschirschky, Fritz Günther von. *Erinnerungen eines Hochverräters.* Stuttgart, 1972.

Tuchman, Barbara. *The Proud Tower: A Portrait of the World before the War, 1890–1914.* New York, 1962.

Vasili, Paul (pseud.). *La Société de Berlin.* Paris, 1884.

Velde, Henry van de. *Geschichte meines Lebens.* Munich, 1962.

Victoria, Princess of Prussia. *My Memories.* London, 1929.

Vierhaus, Rudolf, ed. *Das Tagebuch der Baronin Spitzemberg geb. Freiin von Varnbüler. Aufzeichnungen aus der Hofgesellschaft des Hohenzollernreiches.* Göttingen, 1960.

Vietsch, Eberhard von. *Bethmann Hollweg. Staatsmann zwischen Macht und Ethos.* Boppard/Rhein, 1969.

———. *Gegen die Unvernunft. Der Briefwechsel zwischen Paul Graf Wolff Metternich und Wilhelm Solf 1915–1918 mit Zwei Briefen Albert Ballins.* Bremen, 1964.

Viktoria Luise, Duchess of Brunswick-Lüneburg. *Ein Leben als Tochter des Kaisers.* Göttingen, 1965.

———. *Im Glanz der Krone.* Göttingen, 1967.

Vogel, Barbara. *Deutsche Russlandpolitik. Das Scheitern der Deutschen Weltpolitik unter Bülow 1900–1906.* Düsseldorf, 1973.

Vorres, Ian. *The Last Granduchess: Her Imperial Highness Granduchess Olga Alexandrovich, 1882–1960.* New York, 1964.

Wagemann, Anna. *Prinzessin Feodora. Erinnerungen an den Augustenburger und den Preussischen Hof....* Berlin, 1932.

Wahlendorf, Willy Ritter Liebermann von. *Erinnerungen eines Deutschen Juden 1863–1936.* Munich, 1968.

Walworth, Arthur. *Wilson and His Peacemakers: American Diplomacy at the Paris Peace Conference.* New York, 1986.

Waters, Wallscourt H.-H. *Potsdam and Doorn.* London, 1935.

———. *"Private and Personal": Further Experiences of a Military Attaché.* London, 1928.

———. *"Secret and Confidential": The Experiences of a Military Attaché.* London, 1926.

Weber, Marianne. *Max Weber. Ein Lebensbild.* Heidelberg, 1950.

Wedel, Count Carl von. *Zwischen Kaiser und Kanzler. Aufzeichnungen des General-adjutanten Grafen Carl von Weden aus den Jahren 1890–1894.* . . . Leipzig, 1943.

Wegerer, Alfred von. "Björkoe." *Die Kriegsschuldfrage* 2 (Nov. 1924): 453–501.

Wentzcke, Paul, ed. *Im Neuen Reich 1871–1890. Politische Briefe aus dem Nachlass Liberaler Parteiführer.* 2 vols. Osnabrück, 1967 [1926].

Wermuth, Adolf. *Ein Beamtenleben. Erinnerungen.* Berlin, 1922.

Wertheimer, Eduard von. "Ein Kaiser- und Königlicher Militärattaché über das Politische Leben in Berlin 1880–1895." *Preussischer Jahrbücher* 201 (1925): 264–82.

Westarp, Count Kuno von. *Das Ende der Monarchie am 9. November 1918.* Berlin, 1952.

———. "Die Konservative Partei und das Eude des Bülow blocks." In *Süddeutsche Monatshefte* 28, no. 6 (Mar. 1931).

———. *Konservative Politik im Letzten Jahrzehnt des Kaiserreiches.* 2 vols. Berlin, 1935.

Wetterlé, Emile. *Behind the Scenes in the Reichstag: Sixteen Years of Parliamentary Life in Germany.* New York, n.d. [1918].

Wheeler-Bennett, Sir John. *Hindenburg, the Wooden Titan.* London, 1967.

———. *Knaves, Fools, and Heroes: In Europe between the Wars.* London, 1974.

White, Andrew Dickson. *Autobiography.* 2 vols. New York, 1905.

Whitman, Sidney. *German Memories.* New York and London, 1912.

Widenmann, Wilhelm. *Marine-Attaché an der Kaiserlich-Deutschen Botschaft in London 1907–1912.* Göttingen, 1952.

Wilamowitz-Moellendorff, Countess Fanny von. *Erinnerungen und Begegnungen.* Berlin, 1936.

Wilamowitz-Moellendorff, Ulrich von. *Erinnerungen 1848–1914.* Leipzig, 1928.

Wilhelm II, German Emperor and King of Prussia. *Aus Meinem Leben 1859–1888.* Berlin, 1927.

———. *Comparative Historical Tables from 1878 to the Outbreak of War.* Leipzig, 1921.

———. *Ereignisse und Gestalten aus den Jahren, 1878–1918.* Leipzig, 1922.

———. *Erinnerungen an Korfu.* Berlin, 1924.

———. "The Sex of Nations." *Century Magazine* 116 (1928): 129–39.

Wilhelm II. und Hermine: Geschichte und Kritik von Doorn. Berlin, 1929.

Wilke, Adolf von. *Alt-Berliner Erinnerungen.* Berlin, 1930.

Williamson, John G. *Karl Helfferich, 1872–1924: Economist, Financier, Politician.* Princeton, 1971.

Williamson, Samuel R., Jr. *Austria-Hungary and the Origins of the First World War.* New York, 1991.

Wilson, John. *CB: A Life of Sir Henry Campbell-Bannerman.* London, 1973.

Winterfeldt-Menkin, Joachim von. *Jahreszeiten des Lebens. Das Buch meiner Erinnerungen.* Berlin, 1942.

With, Christopher. "The Emperor, the National Gallery, and Max Slevogt." *Zeitschrift des Deutschen Vereins für Künstwissenschaft* 30 (1976): 86–94.

Witt, Peter-Christian. *Die Finanzpolitik des Deutschen Reiches von 1903–1913.* Lübeck, 1970.

Wrisberg, Ernst von. *Erinnerungen an die Kriegsjahre im Königlich-Preussischen Kriegsministerium.* 3 vols. Leipzig, 1921–22.

Young, Harry F. *Prince Lichnowsky and the Great War.* Athens, Ga., 1977.

Young, Kenneth. *Arthur James Balfour: The Happy Life of the Politician, Prime Minister, Statesman, and Philosopher, 1848–1930.* London, 1963.

———, ed. *The Diaries of Sir Robert Bruce Lockhart: Volume One, 1915–1938.* New York, 1973.

Youssoupoff, Felix Prince. *Lost Splendour.* London, 1953.

Zahn-Harnack, Agnes von. *Adolf von Harnack.* Berlin, 1951.

Zechlin, Egmont. *Die Deutsche Politik und die Juden im Ersten Weltkrieg.* Göttingen, 1969.

Zedlitz-Trützschler, Count Robert. *Zwölf Jahre am Deutschen Kaiserhof: Aufzeichnungen.* Berlin, 1924.

Zelinsky, Hartmut. "Kaiser Wilhelm II., die Werk-Idee Richard Wagners und der 'Weltkampf.' " In John C. G. Röhl, ed., *Der Ort Kaiser Wilhelms II. in der Deutschen Geschichte*, pp. 197–356. Munich, 1991.

Ziekursch, Johannes. *Politische Geschichte des Neuen Deutschen Kaiserreiches.* 3 vols. Frankfurt/Main, 1925–30.

Zimmermann, Arthur. "Bülow and Holstein—die Daily Telegraph Affäre— Bülow und Bethmnan Hollweg." *Süddeutsche Monatshefte* 28 (Mar. 1931): 390–93.

Zmarzlik, Hans-Günter. *Bethmann Hollweg als Reichskanzler 1909–1914.* Düsseldorf, 1957.

Zobeltitz, Fedor von. *Chronik der Gesellschaft unter dem Letzten Kaiserreich.* 2 vols. Hamburg, 1922.

———. *Ich Hab so Gern Gelebt. Lebenserinnerungen.* Berlin, 1934.

Zorn, Philipp. *Aus einem Deutschen Universitätsleben.* Bonn, 1927.

Zwehl, H. von. *Erich von Falkenhayn, General der Infanterie.* Berlin, 1926.

Index